INTERNATIONAL MANAGEMENT

McGraw-Hill Series in Management

Fred Luthans, *Consulting Editor*

INTERNATIONAL MANAGEMENT

THIRD EDITION

Richard M. Hodgetts
Florida International University

Fred Luthans
University of Nebraska

The McGraw-Hill Companies, Inc.

New York   St. Louis   San Francisco   Auckland   Bogotá   Caracas
Lisbon   London   Madrid   Mexico City   Milan   Montreal
New Delhi   San Juan   Singapore   Sydney   Tokyo   Toronto

McGraw-Hill

*A Division of The **McGraw·Hill** Companies*

International Management

This book is printed on acid-free paper.

1 2 3 4 5 6 7 8 9 0 DOW DOW 9 0 9 8 7 6

ISBN 0-07-029226-4

This book was set in Palatino by Graphic World, Inc.
The editors were Adam Knepper and Valerie Raymond;
the production supervisor was Louise Karam.
Project supervision was done by Hockett Editorial Service.
The cover was designed by Karen K. Quigley.
R.R. Donnelley & Sons Company was printer and binder.

Cover photo:
Joshua Sheldon/Photonica

Library of Congress Cataloging-in-Publication Data

Hodgetts, Richard M.
    International management / Richard M. Hodgetts, Fred Luthans.—
  3rd ed.
      p.   cm.—(McGraw-Hill series in management)
    Includes bibliographical references and indexes.
    ISBN 0-07-029226-4
    1. International business enterprises—Management.
  2. International business enterprises—Management—Case studies.
  I. Luthans, Fred.   II. Title.   III. Series.
  HD62.4.H63   1997
  658'.049—dc20   96-9314

International Edition

When ordering this title, use ISBN 0-07-114314-9.

RICHARD M. HODGETTS is a professor at Florida International University in the Department of Management and International Business. He is a Fellow of the Academy of Management and in recent years has been extremely involved in international activity. He has lectured in Chile, Denmark, Jamaica, Kuwait, Mexico, Peru, Trinidad, and Venezuela, and he has worked with, among others, Exxon International, the government of Kuwait, the Revenue Department of Mexico, and Carrier Corporation's Latin American operations. He is the author of numerous texts, many of which have been translated and are used in countries around the world. Some of his latest articles include "North American Management," which appeared in the *International Encyclopedia of Business and Management;* "Management in America," which appeared in *International Cross-Cultural Perspectives;* and "The Challenge Facing MNCs: Overcoming the Quality/Cost Technology Paradox and Becoming Learning Organizations," which appeared in the *Pan Pacific Proceedings;* all these articles were co-authored with Fred Luthans. In addition, he is author of the "Business" section of the latest edition of Microsoft's Encarta Encyclopedia. He also is on the editorial boards of *Organizational Dynamics, Journal of Business Research,* and *Journal of Economics and Business.* Currently, he serves as a member of the World-Class Committee of the National Research Council, studying the development and application of metrics to Army Research, Development, and Engineering Centers.

FRED LUTHANS is the George Holmes Distinguished Professor of Management at the University of Nebraska-Lincoln. He has been a visiting scholar at a number of colleges and universities and has lectured in most European and Pacific Rim countries. He has taught entire international management courses as a visiting faculty member at the Universities of Hawaii, Macau, Chemnitz in the former East Germany, and Tirane in Albania. A past president of the Academy of Management, he has been active in the management field for over 30 years. Currently, he is consulting editor of the McGraw-Hill Management Series, editor of *Organizational Dynamics,* and the author of numerous books. His book *Organizational Behavior* is now in its eighth edition. He is one of a very few management scholars who is a Fellow of the Academy of Management, the Decision Sciences Institute, and the Pan Pacific Business Association, and he has been a member of the Executive Committee for the Pan Pacific Conference since its beginning 13 years ago. This committee helps to organize the annual meeting held in Pacific Rim countries. He has been involved with some of the premier empirical studies on motivation and behavioral management techniques and the analysis of managerial activities in Russia; these articles have been published in the *Academy of Management Journal, Journal of International Business Studies,* and *Journal of Organizational Behavior Management.* Since the very beginning of the transition to a market economy after the fall of communism in Eastern Europe, he continues to be actively involved in management education programs sponsored by the U.S. Agency for International Development in Albania (about a dozen trips) and Macedonia (twice), and U.S. Information Agency programs involving the Central Asian countries of Kazakhstan, Kyrgyzstan, and Tajikstan. Professor Luthans's most recent international research involves the use of meta-analytic techniques to cluster countries for cross-cultural, comparative management.

Dedicated to
Henry H. Albers
Scholar, Mentor, and Friend

ix

PART FIVE International Management Horizons

PART SIX International Management Cases

PART FOUR Organizational Behavior and Human Resources Management

PART FIVE # International Management Horizons

◗ PART SIX International Management Cases

Welcome to the world of international management. This third edition reflects this dynamically changing field, and almost unheard of in textbook revisions, it contains four brand new and three substantially new chapters. In addition, there are many new sections, boxed inserts, research results, examples, tables, references, and, now placed at the end of the text, 16 longer discussion, strategy-type cases (14 of which are new). In other words, about one-half of this third edition did not appear in the second when it came out just 3 years ago. This type of change is exactly what is happening in the real world of international management.

Along with information technology, international management is the major challenge facing organizations entering the new millennium. All countries and companies now are part of the supercompetitive global marketplace, which is sometimes referred to as the "4 Any's" environment—anybody, anywhere, anytime, anyway. Such an environment points to one incontestable fact: Students of management must be more knowledgeable about the international dimensions of management than at any time in the past. Although much of this book and most of the examples are from the perspective of the United States, because most of the student readers will be Americans, it is recognized that a global perspective is needed and becoming more of a reality. This is why a conscious effort is made to include as many different parts of the world as possible in the text discussion and cases.

Internationalism is one of the four major areas of development that is targeted for attention by the AACSB (American Assembly of Collegiate Schools of Business) during the 1990s. (Ethics, entrepreneurship, and business communications are the other three.) As a result of this stimulation as well as the demands of students, faculty members, administrators, practitioners, and the general public, most business colleges and departments now have an international course in their curriculum. Traditionally, this has been an international *business* course, but now, international *management* is being offered. This text is aimed at the course that students who are majoring in international business or general management would take, or as a required course to meet the intent of the AACSB guidelines for internationalizing the business school curriculum. It primarily is aimed at the business student, although majors in other areas, such as international relations, government, political science, and curricula lending itself to international focuses and, of course, practicing managers, also should find this book to be useful. It is intended that most students using *International Management,* third edition, normally will already have had principles of management and maybe (but not necessarily) a course in international business or some preliminary introduction to the world of international commerce/economics. However, *International Management,* third edition, is written so that it can stand alone without any prerequisite.

The strengths of the successful previous editions are retained (conceptual framework, research-base, up-to-date topical coverage, real-world examples, and lively reading style). Because the field is rapidly expanding, however, and the cultural context is changing so much and given more weight, we have designed this new edition accordingly. Relatively more attention is given to the important environmental foundation (Part One) and cultural context (Part Two) for international management. These first two parts have the four completely new chapters and two of the three substantially new chapters. Also, in response to our users and reviewers, we now focus more on the strategy and management functions in one part (Part Three) and organizational behavior and human resources management in another (Part Four). Also, we have given a great deal more attention to ethics and women in management throughout the world (Part Five).

Here is a brief summary of some of the major additions and changes:

1. Chapter 1, "Worldwide Developments," was in the second edition, but because things have changed so much, this chapter was rewritten from scratch. We give fairly comprehensive, up-to-date coverage for most regions of the world.

2. Chapter 2, "The Environment for International Management," is brand new and gives added depth of coverage to the opening chapter. Specifically, the political (especially China as well as Central and Eastern Europe), legal (regulatory), economic, and technical parts of today's environment facing MNCs are given detailed attention.

3. The third chapter, "Global Competitiveness: Anybody, Anywhere, Anytime, Anyway," is unique to international texts, and we feel it is a strong feature of the new edition. This chapter's coverage moves from total quality to learning to world-class organizations. We feel we are practicing what we preach with our text, and this chapter reflects what really is happening in the international arena.

4. The first two chapters in the second part, on cultural context, are greatly expanded by significant new work on cultural dimensions (based on about 15,000 managers from 28 countries) by Dutch researcher (via Wharton School of Business) Fons Trompenaars. Hofstede's well-known cultural dimensions still are included (although cut back some), but because this research is getting quite dated, we feel that Trompenaars' work on cultural dimensions adds considerable value and updates the cultural context relevant to today's international management.

5. Chapter 6, "Managing Organization Cultures and Diversity," is brand new to this edition. This chapter recognizes the more micro-oriented role that organizational culture and diverse teams play in international management. Interesting emerging research on the impact that national cultures have on organizational participants in foreign assignments and the impact that multiculturalism and diversity have on team performance in today's MNCs are included.

6. The heart of the previous edition, containing five chapters (7–11) on strategy and functions and five chapters (12–16) on organizational behavior and human resources management remain fairly intact in this new edition. Considerable effort was made to keep these topics completely up to date, and each chapter has some new sections, tables and figures, and many new examples, research findings, and references.

7. Chapter 17, on ethics/social responsibility, has been revised extensively. Particular attention now is given to women in management around the world.

8. Finally, new to this edition are the end-of-book cases. With the exception of the classic "Road to Hell," all were written specifically for this text and carefully edited by the text authors. These cases are designed for high-interest discussion and strategic analysis. Unlike the shorter end-of-chapter cases on a specific country ("In the International Spotlight") and cases covering specific topics in the preceding chapter ("You Be the International Consultant"), which can be read and discussed in class, these new, longer, end-of-book cases normally would be read outside of class and then discussed in depth. Along with the boxed application examples within each chapter and other pedagogical features at the end of each chapter (e.g., Key Terms, Review and Discussion Questions, and Practical International Management Assignment), the new, longer cases provide the complete package for relating text material to the real world of international management.

To help instructors teach international management, this text is accompanied by a combined Instructor's Resource Manual and Test Bank.

We would like to acknowledge those who have helped to make this book a reality. Special thanks go to our growing number of friends throughout the world who have given us many ideas and inspired us to think internationally. Closer to home, we would like to give special recognition to two international management scholars who have had a direct influence on both of us. First is Henry H. Albers, former Chair of the Management Department at the University of Nebraska and former Dean at the University of Petroleum and Minerals, Saudi Arabia, to whom we have dedicated this book. He had a significant influence on our early careers and stimulated us to research and write in the field of management but, most importantly, to think internationally. More recently, we would like to acknowledge the influence of Sang M. Lee, currently Chair of the Management Department at Nebraska and President of the Pan Pacific Business Association. He is a true "Global-Academic," and we appreciate his stimulation, advice, and support. Also, we would like to thank Phyllis Jacobsen, Katherine Gulland, and Cathy Watson for their word-processing skills and hard work on various stages of the manuscript.

In addition, we would like to acknowledge the help that we received from reviewers on all three editions: Yohannan T. Abraham, Southwest Missouri State University; Kibok Baik, James Madison University; R.B. Barton, Murray State University; Mauritz Blonder, Hofstra University; Charles M. Byles, Virginia Commonwealth University; Helen Deresky, SUNY Plattsburgh; David M. Flynn, Hofstra University; Robert T. Green, University of Texas at Austin; Jean M. Hanebury, Salisbury State University; Robert Kuhne, Hofstra University; Robert C. Maddox, University of Tennessee; Ray Montagno, Ball State University; Yongsun Paik, Loyola Marymount University; Richard David Ramsey, Southeastern Louisiana University; Mansour Sharif-Zadeh, California State Polytechnic University, Pomona; Jane H. Standford, Texas A & I University; Randall Stross, San Jose State University; George Sutija, Florida International University; David Turnipseed, Georgia Southern College; Katheryn H. Ward, Chicago State University; and Marion M. White, James Madison University.

Last, but by no means least, we greatly appreciate the love and support provided by our families—Sally, Steven, and Jennifer; and Kay, Kristin, Todd, Brett, Kyle, Dina, Paige, and Kourtney.

Richard M. Hodgetts
Fred Luthans

INTRODUCTORY ENVIRONMENTAL FOUNDATION AND PERSPECTIVE FOR INTERNATIONAL MANAGEMENT

WORLDWIDE DEVELOPMENTS

OBJECTIVES OF THE CHAPTER

The global economy has arrived. In the United States, a dramatically increasing number of firms are going international, and a growing percentage of overall revenue is coming from overseas markets. The same is true throughout Europe, Asia, and the rest of the world. As a result, *international management,* the process of applying management concepts and techniques in a multinational environment, is rapidly gaining importance.

Although there has been considerable historical evolution, the overriding focus of this opening chapter is to examine the worldwide economic and managerial developments of the last few years. These developments both create and influence the opportunities, challenges, and problems that managers in the international arena will face during the years ahead. The specific objectives of this chapter are:

1. **REVIEW** current trends in international investment and trade.
2. **EXAMINE** the present economic status in the major regions of the global community.
3. **ANALYZE** some of the major developments and issues in the various regions of the world.

3

INTRODUCTION

The world of international management is changing rapidly, and one primary reason is because increased foreign investment and trade are bringing managers from one country into ongoing contact with those in others. For example, Motorola has been investing heavily in China over the last 5 years and is finding this to be one of the fastest growing markets for its paging products. At the same time, Motorola is helping to develop a cadre of Chinese managers to run these operations. Because China currently does not have a large pool of experienced managers to draw from, Motorola is bringing personnel from its Singapore operations to help start things in China and to train and develop local managers. As a result, senior-level personnel from the company's headquarters in Schaumberg, Illinois, as well as from its paging operations in Boynton Beach, Florida, continually interact with both the Chinese and Singaporean managers in China.

Motorola is not alone in this new transnational environment. Increasingly, firms are finding that they must develop international management expertise. Managers from today's multinational firms must learn to work effectively with those from many different countries. Multinational corporations or *MNCs* can be defined as firms having operations in more than one country, international sales, and a nationality mix of managers and owners. For example, MNCs such as Ford Motor have operations in Mexico, Latin America, Europe, and Asia, as do General Motors, Volkswagen, and Toyota. International computer, electronics, and consumer-goods firms also fit the definition of MNCs. Examples include IBM, General Electric, Coca-Cola, Unilever, and PepsiCo. In fact, some MNCs depend on the international market for well over 25 percent of their total revenue. Figure 1-1 shows some of these. At the top of the list is Nestlé, which generates 98 percent of its sales outside of Switzerland. Exxon gets 80 percent of its revenue from the international market, as does Unilever. Even Chrysler, at the bottom of the list, earns one-sixth of its gross income outside the U.S. market, which for a firm with over $50 billion in annual sales is a significant amount.[1] Just several years ago, Chrysler sold virtually no automobiles overseas.

The data in Figure 1-1 point out two important findings. First, MNCs now must rely heavily on the international market for sales growth. Second, as the breadth and scope of their operations increase, other firms will need to address the impact of this development. Competitors will have to respond by going international and fighting harder for their local market share; suppliers and vendors will have to offer higher quality and competitive prices if they hope to get and hold business with these multinationals. The result has been an increasing internationalization of business.

INCREASING INTERNATIONALIZATION

International business is not a new phenomenon; however, the volume of international trade has increased dramatically over the last decade. Today, every nation and an increasing number of companies buy and sell goods in the international marketplace. A number of developments in regions around the world have helped to fuel this activity.

FIGURE 1-1

FOREIGN SALES AS A PERCENTAGE OF TOTAL SALES (1993)

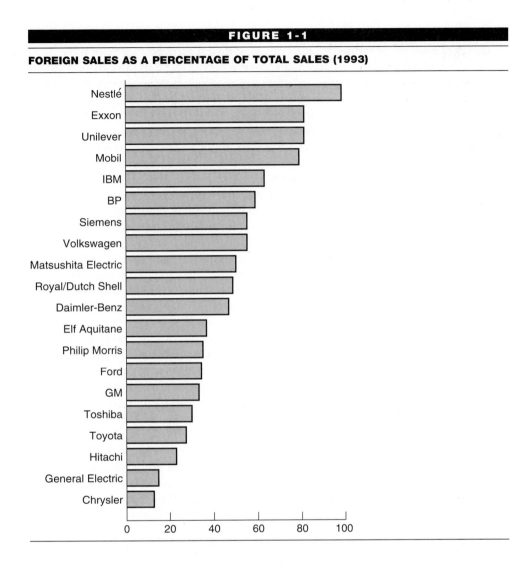

Regional Developments Impacting Internationalization

Although the status and issues facing major regions of the global economy are given detailed attention in the last part of this chapter, several important developments have had a direct impact on internationalization and should be noted. Some of the most important have been:

1. The United States, Canada, and Mexico have signed the ***North American Free Trade Agreement (NAFTA),*** which eventually will remove all barriers to trade between these countries and create a huge North American market. This market eventually will be expanded to include Latin American countries as well. Chile will probably join NAFTA in the near future, and others, such as Argentina and Brazil, are likely to follow. The result may be a giant "American Market" that would parallel similar developments in Europe and Asia.

2. The European Union (EU) is now well on its way to creating a unified market that best may be described as the United States of Europe. Not only have most trade barriers between the members been eliminated, some progress also has been made in overcoming the only remaining major barrier: a unified currency. Additionally, the 12 members of the Common Market (Belgium, France, Germany, Holland, Italy, and Luxembourg were the original six, and they were joined by Britain, Denmark, Greece, Ireland, Portugal, and Spain) most recently have added Austria, Finland, and Sweden. Only Switzerland and Norway in Western Europe have opted to stay out of the EU. The current 15 member countries have a combined gross domestic product above that of either the United States or Japan.[2] Of even more importance is that the EU is better integrated as a single market than either NAFTA or the allied Asian countries. Additionally, other nations such as Turkey have applied for membership. In the near future, the former communist bloc countries of Central and Eastern Europe undoubtedly also will become part of the EU. For example, Poland and Hungary already have applied, and the Czech Republic, Albania, Romania, Slovakia, Lithuania, Latvia, Estonia, and Bulgaria are in the process of applying. Once East and West join together, the result will be a giant economic market that no major MNC can afford to ignore.

3. The most recent changes of the General Agreement on Tariffs and Trade (GATT) are stimulating increased world trade. Under the new agreement, tariffs will be reduced worldwide by 38 percent, and in some cases eliminated completely. The percentage of products entering the United States duty free will rise from the current 10 percent to 40 percent, and for industrialized countries worldwide, the percentage will rise from 20 to 44. Under the new agreement, GATT itself has been replaced by the *World Trade Organization (WTO)*, which came into existence on January 1, 1995.[3] The newly created WTO will have more power to enforce rulings on trade disputes and create a more efficient system for monitoring trade policies. Perhaps most important, however, is that two-thirds of former GATT members have agreed to join the WTO. World economic powers such as the EU, United States, Canada, and Japan are now part of the WTO. Collectively, those who have joined so far account for two-thirds of world trade.[4]

4. Although Japan has had some economic problems in the 1990s, it continues to be the major economic force in the Pacific Rim. Japan recently has invested relatively more in its own backyard of Asia than in any other part of the world. Japanese MNCs want to take advantage of the underdeveloped and rapidly growing Asian markets. At the same time, China is proving to be a major economic force (most experts forecast that China eventually will be the biggest economy in the world), and the Four Tigers (Hong Kong, Taiwan, South Korea, and Singapore) have arrived as developed economic powers. Also poised and ready to join as full-fledged members of the global economy are the fast-growing, export-driven Southeast Asian countries of Malaysia, Thailand, Indonesia, and most recently, Vietnam. As in other parts of the world, an economic bloc called ASEAN (Association of Southeast Asian Nations) made up of Indonesia, Malaysia, the Philippines, Singapore, and Thailand, promotes exports to other countries. These developments in Asia are helping to create a major market and very strong, competitive players in the world economy.

5. Both Central and Eastern Europe, Russia, and the other republics of the former Soviet Union currently are making the transition to market economies. Although some (the Czech Republic, Slovenia, Poland, and Hungary) are making much faster progress than others (the Balkan countries, Russia, and especially the other republics of the former Soviet Union), all are becoming a target for MNCs looking for expansion opportunities. For example, after the fall of the Berlin Wall in 1989, Coca-Cola quickly began to sever its relations with most of the state-run bottling companies in the former communist bloc countries. The soft-drink giant began investing heavily to import its own manufacturing, distribution, and marketing techniques. To date, Coca-Cola has pumped more than $1.5 billion into Eastern Europe—and this investment is beginning to pay off. Its business in Central and Eastern Europe has been expanding at twice the rate of its other foreign operations. For example, in Romania, which Coca-Cola entered in 1992, Coke is the dominant soft drink, outselling competitor Pepsi, which has been there for years, by a ratio of 2:1.[5]

6. Economic activity in Latin America continues to increase. Despite the political and economic setbacks recently suffered by Mexico, economic growth and export volume remain strong in Argentina, Chile, Venezuela, and Mexico. Additionally, while outside MNCs continually target this geographic area, there also is a great deal of cross-broder investments between Latin American countries, as Table 1-1 shows. A number of regional trade agreements are helping in this cross-border process, including Mercosur, a common market created by Argentina, Brazil, Paraguay, and Uruguay, scheduled to be fully operational in 1996, and the Andean Common Market, a subregional free trade compact that is designed to promote economic and social integration and co-operation between Bolivia, Colombia, Ecuador, Peru, and Venezuela.[6]

7. There also is recent economic progress among less developed nations. A good example is India, which for years has had a love–hate relationship with multinational businesses. The Indian government has been known for its slow-moving bureaucracy and this has been a major stumbling block in attracting foreign capital. Over the last few years, however, there has been a dramatic turnaround in government policy, and between 1991 and 1995, foreign direct investment rose from $200 million to over $1 billion. A large number of multinationals recently have been attracted to India. For example, India is now closing deals worth $5 billion for eight privately financed power plants and has approved projects for well-known MNCs such as Coca-Cola, Daimler Benz, Ford Motor, General Electric, Kellogg, and Wrigley. Much of this spurt has resulted from the current Indian government's willingness to reduce the bureaucratic red tape that accompanies the necessary approvals to move forward with investments.[7]

These are specific, geographic examples of emerging internationalism. Equally important to this new climate of globalization, however, are the recent developments in both international investment and trade.

International Investment and Trade

Approximately 80 percent of all international investments come from developed countries. The United States, for example, has invested over $400 billion abroad, and foreign investments in the United States is approximately $450 billion. Most

TABLE 1-1

EXAMPLES OF RECENT CROSS-BORDER INVESTMENTS IN LATIN AMERICA

Investor (country)	Business	Target country	Amount (in millions)
Endesa, Chilgener, Chilectra (Chile)	Electric power and distribution	Argentina	$856
Cemex (Mexico)	Cement	Venezuela	$300
Banamex-Accival (Mexico)	Banks	Argentina	$190
Usiminas, Cvrd (Brazil); Aceros del Pacifico (Chile)	Steel	Argentina	$152
Embotelladora Andina (Chile)	Soft drinks	Brazil	$120
Perez Companc (Argentina)	Oil production	Venezuela	$103
CMP (Chile with U.S. partner)	Paper products	Argentina, Uruguay	$100
Femsa (Mexico)	Soft drinks	Argentina	$100
10 Pension Management Firms (Chile)	Pension funds	Argentina, Peru, Colombia	$91
Brahma (Brazil)	Beer and malt	Venezuela, Argentina	$90

U.S. investment goes to Canada, Latin America, and Europe, and a much smaller relative amount goes to Asia. Recently, however, Asia has become more attractive to U.S.-based MNCs because of its rapid economic growth and emerging market potential. China alone has 1.2 billion people, and more and more of them are becoming consumers of MNC products and services.

European MNCs have been targeting Eastern Europe in recent years as well as Asia. In the mean time, the Japanese have been reducing their investment in the U.S. market and shifting attention to their Asian neighbors. Figure 1-2 shows a breakdown of where MNCs are investing and their priorities for the mid-1990s. As shown, Asia will continue to be a primary target area, although among U.S. MNCs, Latin America also seems to be a priority. In particular, U.S. MNCs are interested in Mexico and Brazil.[8]

Besides international investment, trade has increased substantially over the last decade as well. For example, in 1983, the United States exported slightly over $200 billion of goods and services and imported $269 billion of goods and services. Ten years later, exports were in the range of $450 billion annually, and imports were over $550 billion. In other words, during this 10-year period, the United States more than doubled its trade with the rest of the world.

The EU countries, mainly because of within-EU trading, had even more dramatic activity. In 1983, they exported almost $600 billion of goods and services while importing just over $625 billion of goods and services. Ten years later, their exports were $1457 billion, and imports were $1524 billion.

Japan's increased trade has been even more spectacular. In 1983, Japanese exports and imports were $147 and $126 billion, respectively. Ten years later, exports had risen to $340 billion, and imports stood at $233 billion.[9]

What is particularly interesting about these data is that the *percentage* of world trade that is accounted for by the three major trading blocs, typically referred to as the "triad" (the United States, the EU, and Japan), has remained fairly consistent. Between 1983 and 1992, the triad's share of world exports rose from 56.5 percent to 59.1 percent. During this same period, its share of world imports dropped

FIGURE 1-2

ERNEST & YOUNG REPORT (1994) ON WHERE MULTINATIONALS ARE INVESTING *(A)* AND THEIR PRIORITIES FOR THE MID-1990S *(B)*.

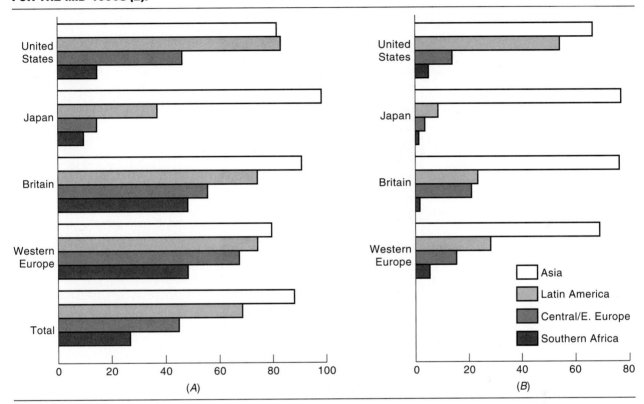

slightly, from 59.4 percent to 56.4 percent. Simply stated, the triad accounts for most of the world's international trade.

Trade barriers continue to fall (as discussed earlier with the new GATT agreement and creation of the WTO), so the amount of trade undoubtedly will continue to rise. Moreover, recent statistics show that most developed countries now export a growing share of their output. Figure 1-3 provides some data related to this finding. Except in the case of Japan, exports as a percentage of gross domestic product (GDP) have been rising over the last 35 years. One reason why Japan's percentage has not increased is that, in contrast to those of other nations, its GDP has increased significantly, thus holding down the exports/GDP percentage. Countries such as Italy and Spain have seen their exports double as a percentage of GDP between 1960 and 1994, and the same is true for the United States, whose percentage rose from 5.2 in 1960 to 10.5 in 1994.

During the rest of this decade, exports are projected to rise, although the trade flows are likely to change. For example, the percentage of exports that the United States sells to Japan, public perception to the contrary, has begun to shrink. U.S. sales to Japan are increasing in absolute terms, but exports to Japan are at a lower rate than to other countries. U.S. MNCs are finding more lucrative markets—and the same is true for Japan. Both are turning their attention to Asia,

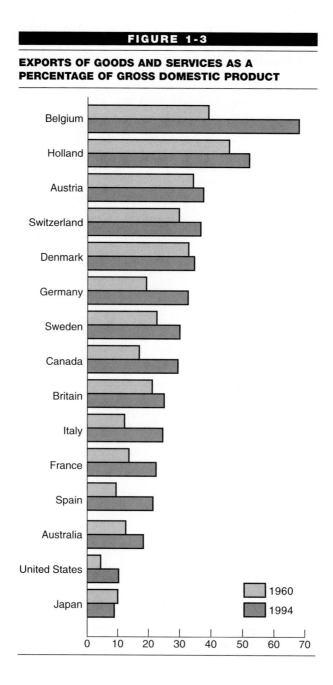

FIGURE 1-3

EXPORTS OF GOODS AND SERVICES AS A PERCENTAGE OF GROSS DOMESTIC PRODUCT

where economic growth is faster than in the West. Additionally, as nations become more economically interdependent and national currencies better adjusted to reflect both strengths and weaknesses, trade flow will adjust accordingly.

For example, in 1994 and 1995, the Japanese yen rose significantly against the U.S. dollar. From 115 yen per dollar, Japanese currency strengthened to 84 yen per dollar and as of April, 1996, stood at 105 yen per dollar. The result has been a rapid rise in the price of Japanese goods entering the U.S. market, thus helping to slow

U.S. import purchases. The auto market was hit particularly hard by the strong yen. Japanese firms found their share of the American car market beginning to slide, and much of this decline resulted from the approximate $2500 price differential between U.S.-produced cars and those imported from Japan.[10] Responding to this problem, Japanese auto firms have shifted production to the United States, and they are developing cost-cutting techniques in their home-based plants. As other automakers respond to these developments, the result likely will be an even more competitive auto market that generates still greater worldwide sales.

Finally, it is important to note that foreign investment and trade do not rely exclusively on MNCs exporting or setting up operations locally. In some cases, it is far easier to buy a domestic firm. Beer companies, for example, are finding that customers like local products, so rather than trying to sell them an imported beer, the MNC will invest in or buy a local brewery. Moreover, the name of the local company may remain the same, so that many local residents are unaware that the firm has changed hands. To illustrate this point, answer the following questions about well-known products sold in the United States, then check your answers at the end of the chapter:

1. *Where is the parent company of Braun household appliances (electric shavers, coffee markers, etc.) located?*
   a. *Switzerland*   **b.** *Germany*   **c.** *the United States*   **d.** *Japan*

2. *The BIC pen company is:*
   a. *Japanese*   **b.** *British*   **c.** *American*   **d.** *French*

3. *The company that owns Häagen-Dazs ice cream is in:*
   a. *Germany*   **b.** *Great Britain*   **c.** *Sweden*   **d.** *Japan*

4. *RCA television sets are produced by a company based in:*
   a. *France*   **b.** *the United States*   **c.** *Malaysia*   **d.** *Taiwan*

5. *The firm that owns Green Giant vegetables is:*
   a. *American*   **b.** *Canadian*   **c.** *British*   **d.** *Italian*

6. *The owners of Godiva chocolate are:*
   a. *American*   **b.** *Swiss*   **c.** *Dutch*   **d.** *Swedish*

7. *The company that produces Vaseline is:*
   a. *French*   **b.** *Anglo-Dutch*   **c.** *German*   **d.** *American*

8. *Wrangler jeans are made by a company that is:*
   a. *Japanese*   **b.** *Taiwanese*   **c.** *British*   **d.** *American*

9. *The company that owns Holiday Inn is headquartered in:*
   a. *Saudi Arabia*   **b.** *France*   **c.** *the United States*   **d.** *Britain*

10. *Tropicana orange juice is owned by a company that is headquartered in:*
    a. *Mexico*   **b.** *Canada*   **c.** *the United States*   **d.** *Japan*

This quiz helps to illustrate how transnational today's MNCs have become. This trend is not restricted to firms in North America, Europe, or Japan. An emerging global community is becoming increasingly interdependent economically. Although there may be a true, totally integrated global market in the near future, at present regionalization, as represented by North America, Europe, Asia (the so-called triad or "Golden Triangle"), and the less developed countries, is most descriptive of the world economy.

THE ECONOMIC STATUS AND ISSUES OF THE MAJOR REGIONS

International investment and trade are more likely to occur between nations in close geographic proximity; for example, in North America, Mexico and Canada are two of the United States' largest trading partners. However, there also is a growing trend toward expanding these horizons and doing business with nations thousands of miles away. For example, Japan is the second-largest trading partner of the United States, and China does more business with the United States than with most other nations. The following sections examine trends that are occurring in each major region of the world and the impact of these developments on international management.

North America

As noted earlier, North America constitutes one of the three largest trading blocs in the world. The combined purchasing power of the United States, Canada, and Mexico is close to $7 trillion. In 1989, the United States and Canada signed a free trade agreement, and in 1994, Mexico officially joined, thereby creating the North American Free Trade Agreement (NAFTA). A number of economic developments will occur because of this agreement, and all are designed to remove trade barriers and promote commerce between these three countries. Some of the more important include: (1) the eventual elimination of tariffs as well as import and export quotas; (2) the opening of government procurement markets to companies in the other two nations; (3) an increase in the opportunity to make investments in each others' country; (4) an increase in the ease of travel between countries; and (5) the eventual removal of restrictions on agricultural products, auto parts, and energy goods.[11]

The NAFTA provisions will take place over time. For example, in the case of Mexico, the most recent country to join, quotas on Mexican products in the textile and apparel sectors will be phased out, and customs duties on all textile and apparel products will be completely eliminated by the year 2004. At the same time, investment in Mexico will be easier for Canadian and U.S. businesses. In the automotive sector, Mexico will allow 49 percent ownership of auto and truck companies by 1997, 51 percent by 2001, and 100 percent by 2004. Steps such as these will go far toward creating a unified trading bloc.[12] Even though there will be more integration both globally and regionally, effective international management still requires knowledge of individual countries.

United States U.S. MNCs have holdings throughout the world. In Europe, General Motors and Ford command dominant market positions, and they are finally beginning to make inroads in Japan as well. U.S. MNCs also do extremely well in the European computer market and are becoming a major force in this industry throughout the Pacific Rim. Telecommunications is another high-tech area where the United States has been garnering international market share. U.S. firms compete with each other in the international arena as well. For example, AT&T now finds itself getting international competition from the U.S. "Baby Bells" (the regional firms that used to be part of AT&T). These firms are becoming more interested in expanding their market coverage and meeting the growing worldwide demand for higher-quality telephone services.[13]

U.S. consumer-goods companies also are finding overseas markets to be very attractive. For example, Coca-Cola has opened a soft-drink plant and distribution operation in Moscow and, as stated earlier, is vigorously targeting Eastern Europe. Toys "R" Us has expanded in Germany and Japan, and it is gaining market share in both locales. U.S. airline companies, such as Delta, United, and American, also are vigorously expanding into Europe and anxiously waiting to take advantage of the fact that local government price-setting in this industry is scheduled to end in the near future.[14]

At the same time, foreign MNCs are finding the United States to be a lucrative market for expansion. BMW is setting up operations in South Carolina, and Mercedes has announced plans to sell a lower-priced car ($20,000 range) designed to help it gain U.S. market share. Additionally, the United States has again become an attractive target for acquisitions. In 1994, the United States replaced China as the country in which the greatest annual foreign direct investment was made. Examples of outside investment in the United States include SmithKline Beecham PLC of Britain, which paid almost $3 billion to acquire the over-the-counter drug business of Sterling Winthrop, Inc., an Eastman Kodak unit.[15] Hoechst AG of Germany paid over $7 billion for Marion Merrell Dow, Inc., a Dow Chemical subsidiary.[16] France Telecom and Deutsche Telecom combined to pay over $4 billion for a 20-percent stake in the Sprint Corporation.[17]

Even though Japanese firms are going to Asia more than in the past, they now are turning to the United States to find suppliers who can help increase the quality of their products while keeping down costs. Ricoh, for example, is purchasing customized microcontrollers from Motorola that allow a digital office copier to double as a high-quality printer or fax machine. Toyota, Isuzu, and Suzuki all are buying antilock brake systems from General Motors. IBM is selling mainframes to Mitsubishi Electric, and Sun Microsystems Inc. is selling workstations to a dozen Japanese firms. Understanding these developments in the United States contributes to the field of international management.[18]

Canada Canada is the United States' largest trading partner, a position it has held for many years. The United States also has more direct foreign investment in Canada than in any other country, including Great Britain or Japan. This helps to explain why most of the largest foreign-owned companies in Canada are totally, or heavily, U.S.-owned. Table 1-2 shows the 20 largest of these firms, along with their respective ownership.

The legal and business environment in Canada is similar to that in the United States, and this similarity helps to promote trade between the two countries. Geography, language, and culture also help, as does NAFTA, which will help Canadian firms become more competitive worldwide. They will have to be able to go head-to-head with their U.S. and Mexican competitors as trade barriers are removed. This should result in greater efficiency and market prowess on the part of the Canadian firms, which must compete successfully or go out of business.

In recent years, Canadian firms have begun investing heavily in the United States. For example, Canadian Pacific has purchased the Delaware & Hudson Railway, and Bombardier, Inc., has bought the Learjet Corporation of Wichita, Kansas. Meanwhile, Bronfman, Inc., best known for its Canadian whiskeys, has a major investment in Scott Paper and most recently sold its large stake in Du Pont for $1.4 billion (less than market value) to buy 80 percent of MCA from

TABLE 1-2

THE LARGEST FOREIGN-OWNED COMPANIES IN CANADA BY SIZE

Rank	Firm	Industry	Ownership (percentage)
1	General Motors Canada	Auto	U.S. (100)
2	Ford Motor of Canada	Auto	U.S. (94)
3	Chrysler Canada Ltd.	Auto	U.S. (100)
4	Imperial Oil Ltd.	Oil	U.S. (70)
5	IBM Canada	Information technology	U.S. (100)
6	Shell Canada	Oil	Netherlands (78)
7	Canada Safeway	Food	U.S. (100)
8	Sears Canada	Retail	U.S. (61)
9	Amoco Canada Petroleum	Oil	U.S. (100)
10	Total Petroleum Ltd.	Oil	France (52)
11	Mitsui & Company	Import/export	Japan (100)
12	Great Atlantic & Pacific Company	Food	U.S. (100)
13	Maple Leaf Foods	Food	Great Britain (56)
14	Honda Canada Inc.	Auto	Japan (100)
15	United Westburne Inc.	Wholesale	France (69)
16	F.W. Woolworth Co.	Retail	U.S. (100)
17	Mobil Oil Canada	Oil	U.S. (85)
18	Consumer's Gas	Gas	Great Britain (85)
19	Cargill	Grains	U.S. (100)
20	Procter & Gamble	Consumer products	U.S. (100)

Matsushita.[19] Canadian firms also do business in many other countries, including Mexico, Great Britain, Germany, and Japan, where they find ready markets for Canada's vast natural resources, including lumber, natural gas, crude petroleum, and agriproducts.

At the same time, Canada is becoming a target for increased international investment, especially by firms from the United States. American, Delta, and Northwest airlines all have expanded their Canadian routes. Chrysler, Ford, and General Motors (as seen in Table 1-2) all have plants in Canada, and so do other major U.S. MNCs, including IBM, Kodak, and Xerox. Again, a major reason for this outside investment is to tap Canada's vast natural resources, which offer a potential bonanza to enterprising firms. Another reason is the growing population and increasing purchasing power of the country. Still another is the chance to take advantage of the opportunities provided under the NAFTA provisions.

Mexico   By the early 1990s, Mexico had recovered from its economic problems of the previous decade and become the strongest economy in Latin America. In 1994, Mexico became part of NAFTA, and it appeared to be on the verge of becoming the major economic power in Central and South America. The country's economic optimism proved to be short-lived, however. By late 1994, the value of the peso collapsed, and the economy took a nosedive. By early 1995, the United States, the

International Monetary Fund, and the Bank for International Settlements were teaming up to create a $50 billion assistance package.[20] At the same time, the government of Mexico was instituting a number of important economic changes, which included cutting the federal budget (thus holding down the country's spiraling deficit), instituting wage and price controls to limit growing inflation, and privatizing more state-held businesses to raise money and stimulate economic growth.[21] These moves have helped slow Mexico's economic slide, but a number of major problems still face this country, including inflation (consumer prices rose 40 percent during the first 3 months of 1995) and a declining GDP, which fell from 2 percent in 1994 to the minus range in 1995.[22]

Despite this setback, Mexico has a foundation of economic strength to draw from, and it is trying to ride out the storm. In particular, the focus now is turning to exports. Because the value of the peso collapsed by over 50 percent, Mexican goods suddenly became cheaper on the world market.[23] If Mexico can continue to exploit this export opportunity, this can help the country to right its economic ship.

Until these recent problems, there had been considerable foreign direct investment in Mexico, much of it brought on by the then-overvalued peso, which made it attractive to sell products there. These investing foreign firms now are having to cut back their operations, but their very presence can still help to generate economic activity for Mexico's recovery. This is particularly true of those companies that invested in the Mexican infrastructure. A good example is Bell Atlantic, which has purchased a 42 percent stake in the Mexican cellular company Iusacell.[24] Such investments are critical to Mexico's turnaround, because a successful export strategy requires a strong infrastructure, of which a good communications system is paramount.

Mexico also has built a very strong *maquiladora industry.* Long before NAFTA, this was an arrangement by the Mexican government that permitted foreign manufacturers to send materials to their Mexican-based plants, process or assemble the products, and then ship them back out of Mexico with only the value added being taxed. Ford Motor, for example, took advantage of this opportunity and annually exports over 250,000 engines from its Chihuahua plant to the United States. General Motors assembles 3 million car radios a year in its Matamoros plant for shipment north. Hundreds of other large firms have followed suit, taking advantage of the low-cost, but quality conscious, Mexican work force.[25]

U.S. labor unions argue that this arrangement has cost many jobs in the United States, but the U.S. Department of Labor reports that *maquiladora* operations actually support over 1 million jobs by helping U.S. firms maintain their international competitiveness. For example, Packard Electric has noted that without *maquiladora* operations, it would have closed its Warren, Ohio, plant and moved everything to Southeast Asia. The argument that the close economic relationship with Mexico is mutually rewarding, such as in the U.S. auto industry, has been summarized by one analyst as follows:

> In a larger sense, both countries have a lot to gain from the continued development of the Mexican industry. The U.S. wants a prosperous, stable Mexico, and the automobile industry is a magnificent engine for raising unskilled workers into the middle class. It creates not only better-paying jobs but also a class of skilled workers and managers, and demand for roads, services, gas stations, drive-ins, repairs. Perhaps, most important, it creates mobility and enables people to look about for the best job, the best price, the best

place to live. Yes, growth of the Mexican industry will cost U.S. autoworkers jobs, but these jobs may be doomed anyway. As David Hendrickson, manager of GM's Deltronics in Matamoros, puts it: "I'd rather see a job go to Mexico than to Taiwan."[26]

Although the *maquiladora* arrangement will be phased out over time because of NAFTA, its presence provides an important foundation and lessons for free trade in the future.

At the same time that U.S. firms are going to Mexico, Mexican businesses, stimulated by NAFTA, are expanding their links into the American market. For example, Cifra, Mexico's largest retailer, has two joint ventures (JVs) with Wal-Mart, the largest retailer in the United States. One of these JVs is to build wholesale discount stores in Mexico, but the other provides Cifra's Mexican suppliers with access to Wal-Mart outlets in the north. In another example, Cementos Mexicanos (Cemex, for short) has expanded into the U.S. southwest by purchasing cement companies. Interestingly, Cemex has become the largest cement maker in North America.

Mexico's economic future is more closely tied to the United States than to any other country. The merchandise trade balance went from a $1.3 billion surplus for the United States in 1994 to a record $15.4 billion deficit in 1995. Exports of U.S. goods to Mexico fell 9 percent, and imports from Mexico rose 25 percent.

Even with this favorable trade balance, Mexico is not depending just on the United States for its economic future. Mexico currently is increasing exports to Canada and to countries outside North America. In particular, Mexico is turning more and more to South American countries, where trade pacts recently have been signed. Although this economic activity is still small compared with their big neighbor to the north, Mexico is increasingly becoming a major player in the global economy.

South America

In the 1980s and early 1990s, many countries in South America had difficult economic problems. The major countries of Argentina, Brazil, Chile, and Venezuela accumulated heavy foreign debt obligations, and along with the other countries in the region they were devastated by severe inflation. For example, both Argentina's and Brazil's inflation rates ran up to four digits in the late 1980s and into the 1990s.

More recently, most South American countries have undertaken the necessary economic reforms, such as reducing their debt, and are on the rebound. For example, in 1989 Argentina's consumer prices rose by 5000 percent; in 1990, they rose by another 1,500 percent. From 1991 to 1994, however, under the administration of Carlos Menem, inflation in Argentina dropped sharply, and the gross domestic product rose by over 5 percent annually.[27] With his re-election in 1995, it appears that efforts to woo international investors will continue, and there should be sustainable economic growth.[28]

Brazil has had similar success. From 1992 to 1995, the country's GDP rose by 5 percent annually, and inflation, which was running as high as 50 percent in some months, had dropped to 3 percent by mid-1995. Most important, like Argentina, Brazil has been attracting outside investors. Examples include Compaq Computer, which has opened a new factory capable of producing 400,000 personal computers annually. Anheuser-Busch is spending $105 million to build a brewery to market Budweiser to Brazilians, and General Electric has signed a contract to study constructing $9 billion worth of coal-fired power electricity plants in the southern part of the country. At the same time, many other well-known companies are setting up operations in Brazil, including Arby's, J.C. Penney, Kentucky Fried Chicken, McDonald's, and Wal-Mart.[29] All of this international business activity is causing a sharp increase in both imports and exports. For example, 10 years ago, Brazil and the United States did approximately $10 billion in trade, with over $6 billion of this being imports from Brazil; by 1995, the two nations were doing almost twice as much trade ($20 billion), with the United States holding a very slight export advantage.[30]

Recently, Chile has been the economic success story in South America. Annual average growth of GDP from 1989 to 1994 averaged 6 percent, which is higher than that for any other country in South America except Argentina. In addition, Chile's export volume during this 6-year period increased by 80 percent, more than double that of Brazil, Venezuela, or Mexico.[31] At the same time, the amount of foreign direct investment has been increasing, and the nation is being targeted by multinationals that believe Chile will eventually enter NAFTA. If the long-run objective is to have a free trade zone throughout the Western Hemisphere, then Chile is in an enviable position.[32]

Another major development in South America is the growth of intercountry trade, spurred on by the progress toward free market policies.[33] For example, beginning in 1995, 90 percent of trade among Mercosur members was duty free. Also, members of the Andean Pact formed a customs union by adopting common external tariffs and eliminating most duties between the members. Currently, negotiations are underway for merging Mercosur and the Andean Pact into a South American Free Trade Association.[34] Because of such developments, intercountry trade is increasing sharply. Among Mercosur countries, trade rose from $3.5 billion to $10 billion annually between 1990 and 1994, and total trade among South American countries has risen from $7 billion in 1983 to $21 billion in 1994.

At the same time, South American countries are increasingly looking to do business with the United States. In fact, a recent survey of businesspeople from Argentina, Brazil, Chile, Colombia, and Venezuela found that the U.S. market, on average, was more important for them than any other. Some of these countries, however, also are looking outside of the Americas for growth opportunities. Mercosur has begun talks with the EU to create free trade between the two blocs, and Chile has joined the Asia-Pacific Economic Cooperation group. These developments help to illustrate the economic dynamism of South America and explain why so many multinationals are interested in doing business within this part of the world.

Europe

Although often overshadowed because of Asia's spectacular growth, major economic developments also have occurred in Europe over the past decade. One interesting development has been the privatization of traditionally nationalized industries (see the accompanying box, "Privatization in Great Britain"). Another has been the emergence of the EU as an operational economic union, and yet another the close economic linkages established between the EU and other European nonmember countries, especially the newly emerging Central and Eastern European

Privatization in Great Britain

Many people think that privatization is a strategy confined to former communist governments that now are moving toward free enterprise. In fact, a number of Western countries have been selling off their state-owned properties, and they are finding that this economic strategy can be extremely profitable. Great Britain is an excellent example.

By the late 1970s, the British government had nationalized a sizable number of industries, including steel, coal, electricity generation, trucking, and railways. The government also owned most of the telecommunications industry, as well as aircraft, shipbuilding, car manufacture, silicon-chip production, and North Sea oil holdings. The borrowings and losses of these operations were running 3 billion pounds annually. A number of reasons can be cited for these results, including high cost, low productivity, poor labor relations, inefficient use of resources, and unsatisfactory customer service. It was at this time the government embarked on a new strategy: Sell these industries and businesses to private buyers, and let them operate the companies based on market economics principles.

By the early 1990s, many of the national firms had been privatized, and the results were astounding. In virtually all cases, the operations were profitable, and productivity, labor relations, and customer service had improved. For example, at British Airways and British Gas, productivity per employee was up 20 percent. At Associated British Ports, there were virtually no labor disputes, in sharp contrast to the major disruptions of earlier years. At British Telecom, the call failure rate (a quality service measure) had declined from 4 percent to one-half of 1 percent, and the long waiting list for telephone installation, so common before privatization, had all but disappeared. Moreover, while under government ownership, the company reported that three-quarters of its public telephones were operational (a statistic vigorously denied as overinflated by most members of the general public). In contrast, today, with many more public telephones in existence, 96 percent of them work.

The 15-year transition of Great Britain from government-owned enterprises to privatization has greatly improved the nation's economic performance. No wonder so many other countries, both in the EU and outside, are currently following a similar strategy. As one ex-government minister who was part of Britain's privatization effort put it, "The worldwide collapse of state socialism has created a new inevitability—the rise of free economic institutions."

Of course, this is not to say that all privatization efforts have dramatically increased productivity, and not everyone agrees that all state-owned businesses should be sold. For example, recent research shows that only 16 percent of the British population believe the railway system should be privatized, while 64 percent oppose such action. Nevertheless, the question facing nations—"is no longer whether to introduce or expand the practice of capitalism but only how to do it." For many, privatization will be an important part of how to accomplish the transition to a market economy.

countries. Including the former communist bloc, by the year 2000, Greater Europe will be a trading area of about 550 million, mostly middle-class consumers in at least 25 countries.

The EU   The ultimate objective of the EU is to eliminate all trade barriers among member countries (like between the states in the United States). This economic community eventually will have common custom duties as well as unified industrial and commercial policies regarding countries outside the union. Another goal also is to have a single currency and a regional central bank, although this will still take years to accomplish.[35]

Such developments will allow companies based in EU nations that are able to manufacture high-quality, low-cost goods to ship them anywhere within the EU without paying duties or being subjected to quotas. This helps to explain why many North American and Pacific Rim firms have established operations in Europe; however, all these outside firms are finding their success tempered by the necessity to address local needs. This need for local differentiation in Europe has been explained by a marketing expert as follows:

> The fact is that dissimilarities exist in the way products are viewed within countries in the [EU]. The Renault 11, for example, may be a good economy car in the U.K., but in Spain it is still perceived as a luxury item. These ways of thinking, desires, needs, and consumer habits are not going to change considerably, and this cannot be ignored in a positioning strategy. Toothpaste and oral care are another example of products which cannot be marketed in the same way across Europe. In Spain and Greece, toothpaste is regarded as cosmetic, so their commercials look glamorous, like soft drink ads. In the U.K. and in Holland toothpaste is seen as a therapeutic product and its consumption is three times as high as in Spain and Greece.[36]

As a result of differing local tastes, EU-based firms follow the strategy adage, "plan globally, act locally." Although this strategy also applies to other parts of the world and will be covered in subsequent chapters, it must be given special consideration if unity in Europe is to become a reality. For example, EU appliance makers will add a self-cleaning option to those ovens for the French market, but leave this option out of units for the German market, where food generally is cooked at lower temperatures. Another interesting strategy is to draw heavily on a network of factories in the EU that can produce both components and finished goods. For example, the Philips television factory in Brugge, Belgium, uses tubes that are supplied from a factory in Germany, transistors that come from France, plastics that are produced in Italy, and electronic components that come from another factory in Belgium.[37]

The most common way that foreign MNCs have gained a foothold in the EU is by using two strategy approaches: acquisitions and alliances. There are situations when each approach is particularly effective. For example, a study reported in the *Harvard Business Review* analyzed 49 strategic acquisitions or alliances and uncovered five important findings:

1. Acquisitions tend to work well when trying to expand one's core business or enlarge an existing geographic market area; alliances are more effective for entering related businesses or moving into new geographic markets.
2. Alliances between strong and weak companies seldom work out well, because they fail to provide the missing skills that are needed for growth and typically result in mediocre performance.
3. The hallmark of successful alliances is the ability to evolve beyond initial expectations and objectives.
4. Alliances with an even split of financial ownership are more likely to succeed than those in which one partner holds a majority interest.
5. More than 75 percent of the alliances studied that terminated ended with an acquisition by one of the parents.[38]

There are many examples of successful strategic alliances in the EU. Northern Telecom has teamed with Daimler-Benz Aerospace to compete for the German telephone market, and the BellSouth Company has formed a partnership with Thyssen, the German Steel Company, to compete in this same market.[39] Britain's General Electric Company and Cie Générale d'Electricité of France have formed a 50-50 alliance to create GEC Alsthom, the EU's largest manufacturer of generating equipment and other power systems. Ford and Volkswagen have an alliance in Portugal to develop a minivan.[40] Still another example is Motorola's recent purchase of 10 percent of Machines Bull, the French government-owned computer company.[41]

Co-operative research and development (R&D) programs also are becoming increasingly common as firms team up to share expenses. Siemens and Philips have used this approach to develop computer chips, and IBM has a number of agreements with European firms for developing advanced computer technology. EU-based firms also are able to obtain financial assistance through the *European Research Cooperation Agency (Eureka,* for short), which funds projects in the fields of energy, medical technology, biotechnology, communications, information technology, transportation, new materials, robotics, production automation, lasers, and the environment.[42] The objective of Eureka is to make Europe more productive and competitive in the world market. In the years ahead, the EU will continue to be a major focal point for international investment; U.S. firms in particular have been buying businesses in the EU, joining in strategic alliances with EU firms, and exporting into the European market.

The challenge for the future of the EU is to absorb their Eastern neighbors, the former communist bloc countries. This could result in a giant, single European market. In fact, a unified Europe could become the largest economic market in the world.[43] Such a development is not lost on U.S. firms, which are working to gain a stronger foothold in Eastern European countries as well as the existing EU. In recent years, the U.S. government has been very active in helping to stimulate and develop the market economies of Central and Eastern Europe to enhance U.S. economic growth as well as world peace.

Central and Eastern Europe   In December 1989, the Berlin Wall came down, and about 2 years later, on December 8, 1991, the Soviet Union ceased to exist. Each of the individual republics that made up the U.S.S.R. in turn declared its independence. The Russian Republic has the most population, territory, and influence, but others, such as Ukraine, also are highly industrialized and potentially can be important in the global economy. Many of the ideas that had been promoted by former Soviet president Mikhail Gorbachev, including *glasnost* (openness) and *perestroika* (economic and political restructuring) have sputtered but still are continuing slowly in Russia. A brief overview of the historical developments in Russia is shown in Table 1-3. Of most importance to the study of international management are the Russian economic reforms, the dismantling of Russian price controls (allowing supply and demand to determine prices), and privatization (converting the old communist-style public enterprises to private ownership).

Clearly, Russia still has tremendous problems. In fact, in the 1990s, once-mighty Russia's economy was not as strong as those of its once-dominated neighbors, the Czech Republic, Hungary, and Poland. Even with rapid economic progress, closing the gap with their Western European neighbors will take many years.

One of the ways that Russia is attempting to get its economy going is by removing many administered prices and subsidies and letting free market forces take over. The problem with this strategy is that it results in very high inflation (demand is much greater than supply). Hyperinflation is very hard on the people, and for political expediency, this slows down price reforms. For example, the ultranationalist Liberal Democratic party gained considerable support a few years ago. This party is determined to slow the economic changes in Russia, which may mean even more economic problems in the long run.

TABLE 1-3		

THE THREE ERAS OF THE SOVIET UNION

Traditional Russian society (pre-1917)	Red executive managers (1917–1987)	Market-oriented (1987–present)
Centralization of authority and responsibility	Centralized leadership	Sharing of power with numerous stakeholders in state enterprises
Collective action	Communist domination	
Dual ethical standards (honesty in personal relationships, deception in business relationships)	Party service	Responsibility for private enterprise success
	Rise of collective enterprises	
	Dual ethical standards (honesty in personal conduct with employees, dishonesty in business dealings)	Effective delegation of responsibility to employees
Feelings ranging from helplessness (only a religious savior will deliver people from their plight) to bravado (belief in one's ability to outsmart others)		Use of informal influence to obtain favors
	Use of informal influence to obtain favors	Bipolar extremes of cynicism in problem-solving
	Feelings of helplessness due to producing inferior products and bravado in operating some of the world's largest organizations	Use of overpromising to both clients and business partners
		A high degree of achievement motivation regarding quality service and products but social contempt for success

Source: Adapted from Sheila Puffer, "Understanding the Bear: A Portrait of Russian Business Leaders," *Academy of Management Executive,* February, 1994, pp. 41–61. Used with permission.

On the positive side, many efforts are underway to help stimulate the Russian economy. Russia has been given membership in the International Monetary Fund (IMF), which has pledged $1 billion in development loans with more to come to help make the transition to a free market economy. In addition, the Group of Seven (the United States, Germany, France, England, Canada, Japan, and Italy) has pledged billions for humanitarian and other types of assistance. So, while the Russian economy likely will have a number of years of painfully slow economic recovery and many current problems, most economic experts predict that if the Russians can hold things together politically, things should get better in the long run.[44]

Besides freeing up prices, the other major development that is needed for Russia to transform into a market economy is privatization. Russian enterprises no longer are fully subsidized, and they no longer can automatically sell all their output to the state. Enterprises are increasingly becoming more self-sustaining and are operating in more of a market-based environment.[45] Privatization is taking a number of different forms, including turning a large number (25 to 35 percent) of state-run businesses over to the workers and managers, letting them set up a board of directors and run the operation. In addition, an increasing number of public enterprises are being allowed to issue stock, and both employees and outside investors can purchase ownership. Shareholders not only get equity but also a vote in how the company will be run.

Although these economic reforms are being implemented slowly, there are significant problems in Russia associated with growing crime of all kinds as well as political uncertainty. Many foreign investors feel that the risk is too high. Russia is such a large market, however, and has so much potential for the future, many

MNCs feel they must get involved. For example, IBM is providing 40,000 personal computers for Russian schools. Daimler-Benz of Germany has a contract for a $140 million plant to build buses. The Carroll Group of Britain is constructing a $250 million hotel-trade center. Alcatel, the giant French telecommunications company, has a $2.8 billion contract to supply advanced digital telephone equipment switches. McDonald's opened a restaurant in Moscow several years ago and now plans to open 20 additional restaurants throughout the country and construct an office building in downtown Moscow. United Technologies is installing the first-ever data communications switching center to handle fax and electronic mail. Overall, however, Russia has a long way to go in becoming like its Western neighbors. The *Economist* Intelligence Unit (EIU) recently reported that Russia was one of the least successful countries in Central and Eastern Europe in making the transition to a market economy, and it also was ranked as one of the most politically risky countries in the world.[46]

Former communist countries that have become most visible in the international arena include the Czech Republic, Hungary, and Poland.[47] All three initially were battered by inflation, unemployment, and slow economic growth during their transition efforts. Now, however, all three are making significant progress, and they have been successful in attracting Western capital. The EIU recently reported that the Czech Republic in particular has made a successful transition. For example, more than one-half the Czech labor force now works in the private sector. In addition, inflation is under control, unemployment is low, and GDP has shown strong growth. Much of this success has resulted from outside investors, including: (1) Volkswagen taking a $6.6 billion stake in the Skoda Auto Works; (2) Japan's Fravalex purchasing the glass manufacturer Sklo-Union Teplice for $1 billion; (3) Linde of Germany investing $106 million in Technoplyn, a natural gas company; (4) US West and Bell Atlantic entering into an $80 million telecommunications joint venture with the Czech government to produce telephone switches; (5) Swedish furniture maker Ikea investing $60 million in a furniture production plant in Trnava; and (6) Siemens of Germany investing $35 million for an interest in Electromagnetica, a medical equipment company, and $15 million in Tesla Karin, a telecommunications firm. There also is a movement toward teaching Western-style business courses, as well as the MBA program, recently established jointly under the auspices of the Czech Technical Institute and America's Rochester Institute of Technology.

In Hungary, state-owned hotels have been privatized, and Western firms, attracted by the low cost of highly skilled, professional labor, have been entering into joint ventures with local companies. MNCs also have been making direct investments, as in the case of General Electric's purchase of Tungsram, the giant Hungarian electric company. Another example is Britain's Telfos Holdings, which paid $19 million for 51 percent of Ganz, a Hungarian locomotive and rolling stock manufacturer. Still others include Suzuki's investment of $110 million in a partnership arrangement to produce cars with local manufacturer Autokonzern, Ford Motor's construction of a new $80 million car component plant, and Italy's Ilwa $25 million purchase of the Salgotarjau Iron Works.

Poland had a head start on the other former communist bloc countries. General political elections were held in June 1989, and the first noncommunist government was established, well before the fall of the Berlin Wall. In 1990, the Communist Polish United Workers Party dissolved, and Lech Walesa was elected President. Earlier than its neighbors, Poland instituted radical economic reforms (characterized as the so-called "shock therapy"). In 1991, Walesa began his presidency, but most recently, former communists (now called "socialists") have been elected and now control the Polish government. Although the relatively swift transition to a market economy has been very difficult for the Polish people, with very high inflation initially, continuing unemployment, and the decline of public services, Poland's economy has done relatively well. However, political instability and risk, large external debts, a still-deteriorating infrastructure, and only modest education levels may bode poorly for the future.

Despite these problems, the international business climate in Poland remains optimistic. Western businesses continue to bring in capital and technology, and they are looking for opportunities to help rebuild the Polish economy. For example, Pilkington, the internationally known British glass manufacturer, has invested in HSO Sandomierz, a local firm in the same industry. Asea Brown Boveri (ABB), the giant Swiss conglomerate, purchased Zamech, a turbine manufacturer. At the same time, the Polish economy is being spurred forward by the rapid growth of new, small, private businesses. There now are over 500,000 entrepreneurially driven firms in Poland, accounting for over one-third of GDP and most of the economic growth in recent years.

Although Russia, the Czech Republic, Hungary, and Poland are the largest and receive the most media coverage, the other former communist countries also are struggling to right their economic ships. A small but particularly interesting example is Albania. Ruled ruthlessly by the Stalinist dictator Enver Hoxha for over four decades following World War II, Albania was the last, but most devastated, Eastern European country to abandon communism and institute radical economic reforms.[48] At the beginning of the decade, Albania started from zero. Industrial output initially fell over 60 percent, and inflation reached 40 percent monthly. Today, Albania remains the poorest country in Europe, but progress is being made. In the last few years, the Albanian economy has been growing almost 10 percent per year, the highest in all of Europe. A National Privatization Agency has been created and legislation enacted relating to private property, joint stock companies, and individual rights. Agriculture and housing have been privatized, and most small shops and services have been bought by their former operators. The key for Albania and the other Eastern European countries, however, is to rebuild the collapsed infrastructure and get factories and other value-added, job-producing firms up and running. Foreign investment must be forthcoming for these countries to join the global economy. A key challenge for Albania and the other "have-not" Eastern European countries will be to make themselves less risky and more attractive for international business.

Asia

During the years ahead, Asia promises to continue being one of the fastest-growing regions in the world.[49] Because there are far too many nations to allow for comprehensive coverage here, the following provides insights into the current economic status and international management challenges of selected Asian countries.

Japan   Japan's international economic success during the last 25 years is without precedent. The country's presence is felt everywhere. For many years now, Japan has had a positive trade balance, and even as it began to feel the pressures of

INTERNATIONAL MANAGEMENT IN ACTION

Separating Myths from Reality

One objective of multicultural research is to learn more about the customs, cultures, and work habits of people in other countries. After all, a business can hardly expect to capture an overseas market without knowledge of the types of goods and services the people there want to buy. Equally important is the need to know the management styles that will be effective in running a foreign operation. Sometimes this information can be quite surprising. For example, recent analysis of Japanese management styles and techniques reveals that much of what Americans "know" about the Japanese may not always be true. Here are some examples that provide food for thought about Japanese management:

1. Many people believe that the Japanese are hardworking by nature. However, recent research shows that there is little difference in productivity among workers in Japanese plants throughout the world. Moreover, many of the differences that do exist are a result of factors such as subcontracting, vendors, and labor regulation. In addition, research among workers at Japanese municipal offices and the national railways shows that many of these workers are not industrious at all.

2. Most Japanese do not have lifelong employment. In fact, only about 30 percent do, and these work for the large corporations. The rest of the work force can be let go whenever the firm wants. In addition, because of compulsory retirement, workers must leave their jobs be-

tween the ages of 55 and 60. If they do not have a good retirement program or have not saved enough for their later years, they may have to get another job at a greatly reduced salary.

3. Many Japanese managers are not participative managers; they are autocratic. A recent study found that almost half of all Japanese executives indicated that they autocratically set annual goals for their division; in contrast, only 32 percent of U.S. managers follow this practice.

4. Young Japanese college graduates entering the work force express a desire to stay with their firm for a lifetime and say they are willing to work hard to get ahead. After only a few years on the job, however, these attitudes change, and only about one-third feel this way. In short, company loyalty among many Japanese may not be as high as commonly believed.

5. Most Japanese do not work long hours because they enjoy work. The most common reason is that their family needs the money for living expenses. A second common reason is that the boss works long hours, and the staff are afraid to leave the office until the manager does. As a result, many employees end up staying at the office until late in the evening.

These examples show the importance of studying international management and learning via systematic analysis and firsthand information how managers in other countries really do behave toward their employees and their work. Such analysis is critical in separating international management myths from reality.

economic problems in recent years, most economists continue to forecast Japanese trade surpluses in the future. Analysts ascribe Japan's phenomenal success to a number of factors. Some areas that have received a lot of attention are the Japanese cultural values supporting a strong work ethic, the motivational effects of guaranteed lifetime employment, and the overall commitment that Japanese workers have to their organizations. However, as seen in "International Management in Action: Separating Myths from Reality," at least some of these assumptions about the Japanese work force may be more myth than reality.

Some of the success of the Japanese economy can be attributed to the *Ministry of International Trade and Industry (MITI)*. This is a governmental agency that identifies and ranks national commercial pursuits and guides the distribution of of national resources to meet these goals. In recent years, MITI has given primary attention to the so-called "ABCD" industries: automation, biotechnology, computers, and data processing.

Another major reason for Japanese success is the use of *keiretsus*. This Japanese term stands for the large, vertically integrated corporations whose holdings provide much of the assistance needed in providing goods and services to end users. Being able to draw from the resources of the other parts of the keiretsu, a

Japanese MNC often can get things done more quickly and profitably than its international competitors.

Over the last decade, Japanese multinationals have invested billions of dollars abroad. In both the United States and the EU, Japanese auto firms have built new assembly plants. Japanese MNCs have made controversial acquisitions as well, including such well-known U.S. landmarks as Rockefeller Center, the Pebble Beach golf course, and Columbia Pictures. Beginning in the 1990s, however, there was a marked slowdown in overseas investment, and Japan's international holdings declined. This decline was mostly attributable to the slowing of the Japanese economy; however, poor management decisions also played an important role. For example, in the case of Rockefeller Center, Mitsubishi found that it was unable to generate sufficient revenue to pay the huge interest on its mortgage. As a result, it recently sought protection under American bankruptcy laws, causing a furor among the investors who held the mortgage and demanded the company dip into its corporate coffers and make the payments.[50] Despite such recent setbacks, Japan remains a formidable international competitor and is well poised in all three major economic regions: the Pacific Rim, North America, and Europe.

Japan also has been the target of foreign investment. Automakers such as BMW and Mercedes annually dominate foreign auto sales in the Japanese market. Meanwhile, Ford has been improving its sales in Japan each year, and General Motors now is creating a sales network that will allow the company greater access to the Japanese market. IBM, Coca-Cola, Dow, McDonald's, and Toys "R" Us also do extremely well in Japan, collectively accounting for annual sales of over $100 billion. Moreover, the future likely will see even greater progress as the U.S. government continues its efforts to force Japan into opening its markets to American firms.[51] Other MNCs, particularly those from the EU and newly industrialized Pacific Rim countries, are targeting the Japanese market as well. Given that Japan relies heavily on exporting to sustain its economic growth, the years ahead should prove to be interesting as international managers from around the world begin their counterattack on the formidable Japan, Inc.

China   During the 1980s, China's average annual real economic growth was about 10 percent. From 1990 to 1995 its GDP has maintained this spectacular rate of growth. Additionally, since 1990 GDP per capita on a purchasing-power basis has risen to over $2000, this means that with China's 1.2 billion people, the overall economy is approximately the same size as Germany's.[52] In addition, China's exports are increasing rapidly. Between 1980 and 1994, when world exports doubled, China's exports increased by 400 percent.[53] In recent years, trade with the United States has been so strong that as of 1995 China had a $35 billion surplus.[54]

After the setback from its bloody crackdown on protesters in Beijing's Tiananmen Square in June 1989, China is definitely back on track as an emerging economic power in Asia. At current growth rates, China is projected to be the biggest economy in the world. One pragmatic reason for China's growth is its low wage rates, which make it extremely attractive to manufacturers looking to control their production costs. As these wages begin to rise, however, as they have throughout Asia, then the Chinese will be challenged to increase the productivity of their workers and leverage technology to sustain economic growth and compete internationally. Southeast China already is a modern hub of economic activity, and many companies, especially those in nearby Hong Kong, use China as a major manufacturing source. In fact, southeast China has become such an industrial powerhouse that some observers predict this area of China alone will soon enjoy a GDP that is larger than that of every other nation except Japan and the United States.

Many multinationals are making investments in China to tap this country's resources. U.S. energy firm Wig-Merrill signed a $2 billion deal to build power plants. Motorola has put $120 million into facilities to produce semiconductors and mobile phones. General Motors has a $100 million investment in a truck assembly plant, and Procter & Gamble has invested $10 million in a joint-venture factor to produce laundry and person-care products. Although the current communist government still requires local partners, this has not deterred MNCs from targeting China as a major market for the years ahead.

At the same time, however, China remains a major political risk for investors, and it has many problems to overcome. For example, product pirating is still common, and while the government has promised to prosecute companies that engage in this illegal and unethical practice, very little is done about it.[55] In fact, many Chinese admire counterfeiting and believe it should be allowed.[56] Inflation is another problem. In recent years, consumer prices have risen at an annual rate of 30 percent,[57] and local banks often charge interest rates of up to 40 percent.[58] Perhaps more disconcerting for outside firms is that contractual agreements often prove to be worthless. For example, McDonald's received a long-run lease on property in Beijing and built a large restaurant there; since then the government has told the company that it must move because the entire area was to be razed and turned into a huge office and retail complex. This is not an isolated incident. Outside chemical producers have found themselves facing $10,000-per-product "registration fees," and U.S. law firms operating in Shanghai recently were forced to close until the government granted them new licenses. German and Japanese banks have found that collecting loans from the government can be extremely difficult as well. In addition, some securities firms have learned that Chinese clients sometimes refuse to pay for trades that turn out to be losers, and there is no government protection for such actions.[59] Simply put, China remains a complicated and high-risk venture. Even so, effective MNCs know that China is and will be a major world market and that they must have a presence there.

The Arrived Four Tigers   In addition to Japan and China, there are four other widely recognized economic powerhouses in Asia. Note that the traditionally used term "newly industrialized countries" (NICs) is not used, because they are not really new anymore. South Korea, Hong Kong, Singapore, and Taiwan have arrived as major economic powers and probably now should be referred to more accurately as the "Four Tigers." The GDP of all four has grown rapidly in recent years, and each is export driven. They have been particularly effective in developing overseas markets for their goods.

In South Korea, the major conglomerates, traditionally called *chaebols,* include such internationally known firms as Samsung, Daewoo, Hyundai, and the LG Group. Many key managers in these huge firms have attended universities in the West, where in addition to their academic programs, they learned the culture, customs, and language. Now they are able to use this information to help formulate successful international strategies for their firms. Even though South Korea still faces some internal political problems as well as the uncertainty and risk of future unification with communist North Korea, the *chaebols* are doing increasingly well in the global marketplace.[60] For example, Samsung recently became the number one computer chip maker in the world.

Bordering southeast China, Hong Kong has been the headquarters for some of the most successful multinational operations in Asia. Hong Kong suffered in the aftermath of the Tiananmen Square incident because of the specter of the Chinese takeover of Hong Kong in 1997. Although it has bounced back and is relying heavily on southeast China for manufacturing, there is still uncertainty about the future; however, the former British colony continues to play a strong international role in the Pacific Rim.

Singapore is another major success story. It has seen rapid economic growth in recent years, largely because of exports. A major problem Singapore now faces is how to continue expanding its economic base in the face of increasing international competition. To date, however, Singapore has emerged as the leader and financial center of newly emerging Southeast Asia. In 1995, the World Economic Forum using a variety of criteria named Singapore the second most competitive nation in the world.[61] (The United States was first, Hong Kong third, and Japan fourth).

The fourth Tiger, Taiwan, has been moving from a labor-intensive economy to one that is dominated by more technologically sophisticated industries, including banking, electricity generation, petroleum refining, and computers. Today, Taiwan has become a major economic power in the Pacific Rim. Although China still considers Taiwan to be a breakaway province and conducted high-powered war games dangerously close to Taiwan's borders in March of 1996, Taiwan's government continues to work out its relationship with the mainland to become an even bigger force in the future.

Each of the Four Tigers has been the target of foreign MNCs. For example, IBM and Hewlett-Packard, determined to build their local shares of the computer market, have invested in laboratories and factories within these countries. Motorola has followed the same strategy in enlarging its telecommunications market. Other major MNCs in "Tiger Country" range from the Japanese (Matsushita, Nissan, and Sharp) to the Europeans (Volkswagen, Philips, and Nestlé). As a result, the amount of trade and investment occurring between the Four Tigers and the rest of the world continues to expand.

Other Southeast Asian Countries   Besides the Four Tigers, other emerging countries of Southeast Asia also should be recognized. Although not yet having the economic prowess of the Four Tigers, Thailand, Malaysia, Indonesia (sometimes called the "Baby Tigers"), and now Vietnam[62] are fast becoming economic powerhouses along the lines of the Four Tigers. All have a relatively large population base, inexpensive labor, natural resources, and except for Thailand, political stability. As Japan and the Four Tigers have begun to level off and mature, these export-driven Southeast Asian countries have become very attractive to outside investors. MNCs from Japan, the Four Tigers, North America, and the EU all want to have a presence in these rapidly expanding countries.

Less Developed Countries

In contrast to the fully developed countries of North America, Europe, and Asia are the less developed countries (LDCs) around the world. An LDC typically is characterized by two or more of the following: low GDP, slow (or negative) GDP growth per capita, high unemployment, high international debt, a large population, and a work force that is either unskilled or semiskilled. In some cases, such as in the Middle East, there also is considerable government intervention in economic affairs. In recent years, some of these LDCs have shown improvement, but they still have a long way to go to fully compete in the world marketplace. Although complete coverage of all LDCs is beyond the scope of this chapter, the following focuses on representative LDCs and regions.

India With a population of almost 900 million and growing, India has traditionally had more than its share of economic problems. Per-capita GDP remains very low (about a dollar per day), but there is still a large middle- and upper-class market for goods and services. Although India's economic growth does not compare with that of countries in Southeast Asia, there has been a steady 4 to 5 percent growth in recent years. The current government is vigorously attempting to attract investors and further stimulate economic growth.

For a number of reasons, India is attractive to multinationals, and especially to U.S. and British firms. Many Indian people speak English and are well educated. Also, the Indian government is providing funds for economic development. For example, India intends to spend $30 billion by the year 2000 to expand its telecommunication systems and increase the number of phone lines fivefold, a market that AT&T is vigorously pursuing. Many frustrations remain in doing business in India (see "In the International Spotlight" at the end of this chapter), but there is little question that the country will receive increased attention in the years ahead. Recent foreign direct investments in India include $1.1 billion by Enron, which is engaged in offshore oil and gas exploration; $400 million by Mission Energy, which is building a power plant; and $100 million by US West Inc. to provide a pilot project for the nation's first privately operated telecommunications service.[63]

Middle East and Central Asia Israel, the Arab countries, Iran, Turkey, and the Central Asian countries of the former Soviet Union are considered by the World Bank to be LDCs. Because of their wealth in oil, however, some people would consider these countries to be economically successful.[64] In recent years, Israel has been the target of terrorists. It has also been hard hit by inflation, and although the GDP per capita is well over $6000, there are balance-of-payment problems. Despite the tragedies and economic problems, the Israelis continue to be active in the international arena, and students of international management should have a working knowledge of the country's customs, culture, and management practices.

The same is true for Arab nations, which rely almost exclusively on oil production. The price of oil, which reached almost $40 per barrel by the late 1970s, fell below $15 a barrel in the mid-1980s as the Organization of Petroleum Exporting Countries (OPEC) had trouble holding together its cartel. During the Persian Gulf war, the price of oil again rose to almost $40 a barrel, but by 1995, it had fallen to a little less than one-half this amount.

Because most industrial nations, rely, at least to some degree, on imported oil, an understanding of this part of the world is important to the study of international management. So, too, is the fact that Arab countries have invested billions of dollars in U.S. property and businesses, and many people around the world, including Americans, work for Arab employers. For example, the bankrupt United Press International was purchased by the Middle East Broadcasting Centre, a London-based MNC owned by the Saudis.

Africa   Even though they have considerable natural resources, African nations for the most part are very poor and undeveloped, and international trade is not a major source of income. Although African countries do business with developed countries, it is on a limited scale. One major problem of doing business in the African continent is the overwhelming diversity of about 700 million people divided into 3000 tribes that speak 1000 languages and dialects.

In recent years, Africa, especially sub-Saharan Africa, has had tremendous problems. In addition to tragic tribal wars such as those in Rwanda and Somalia, there has been the spread of terrible diseases such as AIDS and Ebola, which recently broke out in Zaire.[65] Other severe problems include poverty, starvation, illiteracy, corruption, social breakdown, vanishing resources, overcrowded cities, drought, and homeless refugees. There is still hope in the future for Africa despite this bleak situation, however, because African countries remain virtually untapped and because of continuing efforts to stimulate economic growth. Examples of what can be done include Togo, which has sold off many of its state-owned operations and leased a steel-rolling mill to a U.S. investor, and Guinea, which has sold off some of its state-owned enterprises and cut its civil service force by 30 percent. A special case is South Africa, where apartheid, the former white government's policies of racial segregation and oppression, has finally been dismantled. Long-jailed black leader Nelson Mandela is now president. These significant developments have led to an increasing number of the world's MNCs returning to South Africa; however, there continue to be both social and political unrest, which despite Mandela's best efforts signal difficult times for the years ahead.

SUMMARY OF KEY POINTS

1. International trade and investment have increased dramatically over the last decade. Major multinational corporations (MNCs) have holdings throughout the world, from North America to Europe to the Pacific Rim to Africa. Some of these holdings are a result of direct investment; others are partnership arrangements with local firms. Small firms also are finding that they must seek out international markets to survive in the future. There definitely is a trend toward the internationalization of all business.

2. International economic activity is most pronounced in the triad of North America, Europe, and the Pacific Rim. In North America, the United States, Canada, and Mexico have signed a North American Free Trade Agreement (NAFTA) that eventually will turn the region into one giant market. In South America, there is an increasing amount of intercountry trade, sparked by Mercosur and the Andean Pact nations. Additionally, Chile has been projected to join NAFTA, and other South American countries may in the future follow suit. In Europe, the 15 countries of the European Union (EU) form a major economic power, and the former communist countries to the east are seeking membership in the EU. The Central European countries of the Czech Republic, Poland, and Hungary already are becoming trading partners, and if Russia and the other Eastern European countries make progress in their transformation efforts, then Greater Europe will be an even more formidable market in the future. Asia is another major regional power, as shown not only by Japan but also the high-growth economies of China and the Four Tigers (Singapore, South Korea, Hong Kong, and Taiwan). Other areas of the world,

including India, the Middle East and Central Asia, and Africa also hold economic promise.

KEY TERMS

international management
MNC
North American Free Trade Agreement (NAFTA)
World Trade Organization (WTO)
maquiladora industry

European Research Cooperation Agency (Eureka)
Ministry of International Trade and Industry (MITI)
keiretsus
chaebols

REVIEW AND DISCUSSION QUESTIONS

1. How is NAFTA likely to have an impact on the economies of North America? What importance would such a development have for international managers in Europe and the Pacific Rim?
2. How has the formation of the EU created new opportunities for member countries and for countries affiliated with the EU? Of what importance are these opportunities to international managers in other geographic regions such as North America or the Pacific Rim?
3. Why are Russia and Eastern Europe of interest to international managers? Identify and describe some reasons for such interest.
4. Many MNCs have secured a foothold in the Pacific Rim, and many more are looking to develop business relations there. Why does this region of the world hold such interest for international management? Identify and describe some reasons for such interest.
5. Why would MNCs be interested in South America, India, the Middle East and Central Asia, Africa, or the LDCs of the world? Would MNCs be better off focusing their efforts on more industrialized regions? Explain.

PRACTICAL INTERNATIONAL MANAGEMENT ASSIGNMENT

Go to the library and gather data on your home country's investments in overseas nations for the last 5 years. Note how much is invested in each major geographic area. Then, do the same for direct investments in your nation by other countries, such as Japan, South Korea, Canada, Great Britain, and Germany. Based on your data, what conclusions can you draw about international investment trends in recent years? Of what value would this information be to the study of international management?

ANSWERS TO THE IN-CHAPTER QUIZ

1. **c.** Gillette, a U.S.-based MNC, owns the Braun company.
2. **d.** Bic SA is a French company.
3. **b.** The British MNC Grand Metropolitan PLC owns Häagen-Dazs.
4. **a.** Thomson SA of France produces RCA televisions.
5. **c.** Britain's Grand Metropolitan PLC owns Green Giant.
6. **a.** Godiva chocolate is owned by Campbell Soup, an American firm.
7. **b.** Vaseline is manufactured by the Anglo-Dutch MNC Unilever PLC.
8. **d.** Wrangler jeans are made by the VF Corporation based in the United States.
9. **d.** Holiday Inn is owned by Britain's Bass PLC.
10. **b.** Tropicana orange juice is owned by the Canadian MNC Seagram Co. Ltd.

In the International Spotlight

India

Because beef is taboo to Hindus, who make up the vast majority of the Indian population, chicken burgers are the hottest item on McDonald's menu, and Wimpy's advertises its hamburgers as 100 percent lamb.

India is located in southern Asia, with the Bay of Bengal on the east and the Arabian Sea on the west. One-sixth of the world's population (approximately 900 million people) lives within the country's 1.27 million square miles. Over 80 percent of the population are Hindus, and the official language is Hindi, although many people also speak English. Because the literacy rate is less than 40 percent, radio and television are the most influential media. The country operates as a democratic republic, and for the most part, one party has dominated the government since independence in 1947. At that time, India was born of the partition of the former British Indian empire into the new countries of India and Pakistan. This division has been a source of many problems through the years. Many millions of Indians still live at the lowest level of subsistence, and the per-capita income is about a dollar a day ($350 a year).

In the past, doing business in India has been quite difficult. For example, it took PepsiCo 3 years just to set up a soft-drink concentrate factory, and Gillette, the U.S. razor blade company, had to wait 8 years for its application to enter the market to be accepted. Additionally, many MNCs have complained that there are too many barriers to effective operations. In the mid-1970s, the country changed its rules and required that foreign partners hold no more than 40 percent ownership in any business. As a result, both Coca-Cola and IBM left India.

More recently, the government has been relaxing its bureaucratic rules, particularly those relating to foreign investments. From 1981 to 1991, total foreign direct investment in India increased by $250 million, and between 1991 and 1993, it jumped by an additional $2.5 billion! Most of this new investment has come from the United States and nonresident Indians. One reason for this change in the nation's policies toward business is that the government realizes many MNCs are making a critical choice: India or China? Any monies not invested in India may be lost to China forever. Additionally, it can be seen that foreign investments are having a very positive effect on the Indian economy. After the first big year of new investments (1991), India's annual GDP jumped to over 4 percent and remained there through 1994, the most recent year for which statistics are available.

The relaxation of rules definitely has encouraged more foreign investment. Coca-Cola was able to get permission for a 100-percent-owned unit in India in 8 weeks, and Motorola received clearance in 2 days to add a new product line—and did all of this via fax. Other companies that have reported rapid progress include Daimler-Benz, Enron, Procter & Gamble, and Whirlpool. At the same time, however, not everything is roses. Enron is finding that while it received permission in record time to build a power plant, there are a great many political roadblocks that still must be overcome in pushing the project through to completion.

Nevertheless, the Indian government's new approach is helping a great deal. In addition, there are other attractions that entice MNCs to India. These include: (1) a large number of highly educated people; (2) widespread use of English, long accepted as the international language of business; and (3) low wages and salaries, which often are 10 to 30 percent of those in the world's economic superpowers.

1. What is the climate for doing business in India? Is it supportive of foreign investment?
2. How important is a highly educated human resource pool for MNCs wanting to invest in India? Is it more important for some businesses than for others?
3. Given the low per-capita income of the country, why would you still argue for India to be an excellent place to do business in the coming years?

You Be the International Management Consultant

Here Comes the Competition

The Wadson Company is a management research firm headquartered in New Jersey. The company was recently hired by a large conglomerate with a wide range of products, ranging from toys to electronics and financial services. This conglomerate wants Wadson to help identify an acquisition target. The conglomerate is willing to spend up to $2.5 billion to buy a major company anywhere in the world.

One of the things the research firm did was to identify the amount of foreign direct investment in the United States by overseas companies. The research group also compiled a list of major acquisitions by non-U.S. companies. It gathered these data to show the conglomerate the types of industries and companies that are currently attractive to international buyers. "If we know what outside firms are buying," the head of the research firm noted, "this can help us identify similar overseas businesses that may also have strong growth potential. In this way, we will not confine our list of recommendations to U.S. firms only." In terms of direct foreign investment by industry, the researchers found that the greatest investment was being made in manufacturing (almost $100 billion). Then, in descending order, came wholesale trade, petroleum, real estate, and insurance.

On the basis of this information, the conglomerate has decided to purchase a European firm. "The best acquisitions in the United States have already been picked," the president told the board of directors. "However, I'm convinced that there are highly profitable enterprises in Europe that are ripe for the taking. I'd particularly like to focus my attention on France and Germany." The board gave the president its full support, and the research firm will begin focusing on potential European targets within the next 30 days.

1. Is Europe likely to be a good area for direct investment during the years ahead?
2. Why is so much foreign money being invested in U.S. manufacturing? Based on your conclusions, what advice would be in order for the conglomerate?
3. If the conglomerate currently does not do business in Europe, what types of problems is it likely to face?

CHAPTER 1 ENDNOTES

1. *Fortune*, May 15, 1995, p. F57.
2. *Economist*, January 7, 1995, p. 88.
3. "No End of Woe at the WTO?" *Economist*, February 4, 1995, p. 59; "The WTO: A Rocky Start," *Economist*, March 25, 1995, pp. 82–83.
4. "Viewpoint," *Economist*, March 25, 1995, p. 66.
5. Nathaniel C. Nash, "Coke's Great Romanian Adventure." *New York Times*, February 26, 1995, Section 3, pp. 1, 10.
6. Alan M. Rugman and Richard M. Hodgetts, *International Business* (New York: McGraw-Hill, 1995), p. 532.
7. Sharon Moshavi et al., "India Shakes Off Its Shackles," *BusinessWeek*, January 30, 1995, pp. 48–49; Rahul Jacob, "India Gets Moving," *Fortune*, September 5, 1994, pp. 100–104.
8. "Emerging-Market Indicators," *Economist*, November 26, 1994, p. 120.
9. These data have been adapted from the International Monetary Fund, *Direction of Trade Statistics Yearbook 1990 and 1993*, pp. 2–7.
10. Angelo B. Henderson, "Surging Yen Hurts U.S. Sales of Japanese Cars," *Wall Street Journal*, May 3, 1995, pp. A3, A5.
11. Rugman and Hodgetts, *International Business*, p. 527.
12. See, for example, Douglas Harbrecht et al., "What Has NAFTA Wrought? Plenty of Trade," *BusinessWeek*, November 21, 1994, pp. 48–50.
13. Andrew Kupfer, "Ma Bell and the Seven Babies Go Global," *Fortune*, November 4, 1994, pp. 118–128.
14. Stewart Toy, Mark Maremont, and John Rossant, "The Carnival Is Over," *BusinessWeek*, December 9, 1991, pp. 1, 6.
15. Fred R. Bleakley, "Foreign Investment in U.S. Surged in 1994," *Wall Street Journal*, March 15, 1995, p. A2.
16. Milt Freudenheim, "Hoechst to Pay $7.1 Billion for Dow Unit," *New York Times*, May 5, 1995, pp. C21, C5.
17. Bleakeley, "Foreign Investment."
18. Larry Holyoke, William Spindle, and Neil Gross, "Doing the Unthinkable," *Business Week*, January 10, 1994, pp. 52–53.
19. Stratford Sherman, "Bronfman's Buying Binge Isn't Finished." *Fortune*, May 1, 1995, p. 77.
20. "Putting Mexico Together Again," *Economist*, February 4, 1995, pp. 65–67.
21. Geri Smith et al., "Mexico: Can It Cope?" *BusinessWeek*, January 16, 1995, pp. 42–46.
22. "What Goes Down May Not Come Up," *Economist*, March 18, 1995, p. 41.
23. Craig Torres and Paul R. Carroll, "Mexico's Mantra for Salvation? Export, Export, Export," *Wall Street Journal*, March 17, 1995, p. A6.
24. Ibid.
25. Martha Peak, "Maquiladoras: Where Quality Is a Way of Life," *Management Review*, March 1993, pp. 19–23.
26. Jerry Flint, "We Do What Mexicans Do," *Forbes*, September 2, 1991, p. 80.
27. Jonathan Friedland, "Argentine Election Isn't Likely to Change Anti-Inflation Course Charted by Menem," *Wall Street Journal*, May 2, 1995, p. A15.
28. Jonathan Friedland, "Menem Leads Argentine Election As Voters Back Economic Reform," *Wall Street Journal*, May 15, 1995, p. A18.
29. James Brooke, "U.S. Investors Stampede Into Brazil," *New York Times*, April 17, 1995, p. C10.
30. Ibid.
31. "Latin American Growth," *Economist*, February 18, 1995, p. 110.
32. Helene Cooper and Jose de Cordoba, "Chile Is Invited to Join NAFTA as U.S. Pledges Free-Trade Zone for Americans," *Wall Street Journal*, December 12, 1994, p. A23.
33. Mark Moffett, Paul B. Carroll, and Jonathan Friedland, "As the Crunch Eases, Latin Economies Stay for Free-Market Path," *Wall Street Journal*, May 12, 1995, pp. A1, A7.
34. James Brooke, "South America's Big Trade Strides," *New York Times*, December 10, 1994, pp. 17, 27.
35. "The Case for a Single Currency," *Economist*, March 4, 1995, pp. 58–59.
36. Gianluigi Guido, "Implementing a Pan European Marketing Strategy," *Long-Range Planning*, October 1991, p. 30.
37. For still another example, see Richard G. Holder, "Reynolds Wraps up Its Manufacturing Strategies for a Global Marketplace," *Journal of European Business*, September/October 1991, pp. 37–41.
38. Joe Bleeke and David Ernst, "The Way to Win in Cross-Border Alliances," *Harvard Business Review*, November-December 1991, pp. 127–128.
39. Nathaniel C. Nash, "Germany's Telephone Pie Is Just Too Big To Pass Up," *New York Times*, January 30, 1995, pp. C1–C2.
40. Jeremy Main, "Making Global Alliances Work," *Fortune*, December 17, 1990, pp. 121–126.
41. Douglas Lavin, "Motorola, NEC to Buy Stakes in Bull from French State at Bargain Prices," *Wall Street Journal*, April 14, 1995, p. B3; Douglas Lavin, "Bull Appears to Be Getting Back Into Ring," *Wall Street Journal*, April 18, 1995, p. A17.
42. Rugman and Hodgetts, *International Business*, p. 470.
43. Sara Hammes, "Europe's Growing Market," *Fortune*, December 2, 1995, pp. 144–145.

44. Also see Neela Banerjee, "Russia Taking Privatization to the Bank," *Wall Street Journal,* April 20, 1995, p. A8.

45. Fred Luthans, Richard R. Patrick, and Brett C. Luthans, "Doing Business in Central and Eastern Europe: Political, Economic, and Cultural Diversity," *Business Horizons,* September–October 1995, pp. 9–16.

46. "Transition Economics," *Economist,* March 25, 1995, p. 116.

47. See Tina Rosenberg, *The Haunted Land* (New York: Random House, 1995).

48. Fred Luthans and Sang Lee, "There Are Lessons to Be Learned as Albania Undergoes a Paradigm Shift," *International Journal of Organizational Analysis,* January 1994, p. 12.

49. See Pete Engardio and Joyce Barnathan, "Marching Toward Free Trade in Asia?" *BusinessWeek,* November 12, 1994, pp. 52–54.

50. Stephanie Strom, "Japanese Majority Owner Forces Bankruptcy of Rockefeller Center," *New York Times,* May 12, 1995, pp. A1, C4; Mitchell Pacelle and Steven Lipin, "Japanese Firm Turns to Laws on Bankruptcy," *Wall Street Journal,* May 15, 1995, p. A4.

51. See Helene Cooper, "U.S., Japanese Auto Talks Face New Venue," *Wall Street Journal,* May 5, 1995, p. A3; Sheryl WuDunn, "American Insurers Seek More Business in Japan," *New York Times,* February 11, 1995, p. 17.

52. "For Richer, For Poorer," *Economist,* March 18, 1995, p. 9.

53. "Quick, Quick, Slow," *Economist,* March 18, 1995, p. 17.

54. "Rethinking China," *BusinessWeek,* March 4, 1996, p. 57.

55. Seth Faison, "Razors, Soap, Cornflakes: Pirating in China Balloons," *New York Times,* February 17, 1995, pp. A1, C2; Seth Faison, "Fighting Piracy and Frustration in China," *New York Times,* May 17, 1995, pp. C1, C8.

56. Louis Kraar, "The Risks Are Rising in China," *Fortune,* March 6, 1995, pp. 179–180.

57. *Economist,* March 18, 1995, p. 6.

58. *Economist,* March 18, 1995, p. 15.

59. Craig R. Smith and Marcus W. Brauchli, "To Invest Successfully in China, Foreigners Find Patience Crucial" *Wall Street Journal,* February 23, 1995, p. 1.

60. Also see Laxmi Nakarmi, "A Flying Leap Toward the 21st Century?" *BusinessWeek,* March 20, 1995, pp. 78–80.

61. "U.S. Tops List for 2nd Year," *Omaha World Herald,* August 7, 1995, p. 17.

62. Mary Ann Von Glinow and Linda Clarke, "Vietnam: Tiger or Kitten," *Academy of Management Executive,* November 1995, pp. 35–47. "Vietnam Beats China at its Own Game," *Economist,* November 5, 1994, pp. 31–32; and Joyce Barnathan, Alex McKinnon, and Doug Harbrecht, "Destination, Vietnam," *BusinessWeek,* February 14, 1994, pp. 26–27.

63. Sharon Moshavi et al., "India Shakes Off Its Shackles," *BusinessWeek,* January 30, 1995, pp. 48–49.

64. Also see "Saudi Arabia's Future: The Cracks in the Kingdom" *Economist,* March 18, 1995, pp. 21–23.

65. Geoffrey Cowley et al., "Outbreak of Fear," *Newsweek,* May 22, 1995, pp. 48–55.

THE ENVIRONMENT FOR INTERNATIONAL MANAGEMENT

OBJECTIVES OF THE CHAPTER

The environment that international managers face is changing rapidly. The past is proving to be a poor indicator of what will happen in the future. Changes are not only more common now but also more significant than ever before, and these dramatic forces of change are creating new challenges. Although there are many dimensions in this new environment, those most relevant to international management include the political, legal and regulatory, economic, and technological. The previous chapter covered some of the political and especially economic developments around the world, but this chapter gives added depth to these two very important environmental dimensions.

The overriding objective of this chapter is to examine the relevant environment for today's international management. Particular attention is given to how the political, legal and regulatory, economic, and technological environments have changed in recent years. Some major trends in each that will help dictate the world in which international managers will compete also are presented. The specific objectives of this chapter are:

1. **EXAMINE** some of the major changes that are currently taking place in the political environment of China, Europe, Russia, and Central and Eastern Europe.
2. **PRESENT** an overview of the legal and regulatory environment in which MNCs operate worldwide.
3. **DISCUSS** some of the major changes that are taking place in the economies of both developed and developing countries.
4. **REVIEW** key technological developments as well as their impact on MNCs now and in the future.

POLITICAL ENVIRONMENT

The domestic and international political environment has a major impact on MNCs. As government policies change, MNCs must adjust their strategies and practices to accommodate the new perspectives and actual requirements. Moreover, in a growing number of geographic regions and countries, governments appear to be less stable; therefore, these areas carry more risk than they have in the past. The assessment of political risk will be given specific attention in Chapter 7, but the following examines political developments in selected areas and countries that are particularly relevant to today's international management.

China

As discussed in Chapter 1, China is such an emerging economic power that it cannot be ignored by international business. The Chinese political environment, however, is very complex and risky. Aside from being one of the few remaining communist countries, a major concern is what will happen after long-time leader Deng Xiaoping finally dies. As Deng's health continues to deteriorate, a power struggle is underway as various factions jockey for control. At the same time, the Chinese political structure is dominated by often-corrupt Communist Party officials, and although privatization continues, nearly one-half the economy still consists of inefficient, state-run firms.[1] This problem will be helped by further privatization efforts and legal bankruptcy procedures, but the government currently has no real safety net for displaced workers. The current government seems merely to be trying to keep a lid on things and delaying the inevitable outcome: high inflation and massive unemployment.

At the same time, the Chinese people are facing what is being called the "four fears." The first is the average Chinese consumer's fear of being robbed by inflation, and the second is the workers' fear of growing underemployment. The third is the anger of farmers, whose land is being encroached on by industrialization and who prefer to sell their output to local entities and black markets rather than Beijing's state purchasers. The fourth is the general fear and disgust of the pervasive corruption that exists throughout the political system.[2]

Despite this bad news, several developments currently reshaping China also may prove to be effective in helping the country become a major economic power.[3] For example, the first group of students after the Cultural Revolution to gain entry to universities based on competitive exams rather than political connections now are coming into influential positions. Commonly referred to as the "Class of '77," many of these graduates have risen largely on merit rather than political or family ties, and they represent some of the country's brightest minds. This new generation has built extensive personal networks based on friendships during the Cultural Revolution, and they are more open to Western ideas and less bound by communist ideology than the older leaders. Here is how one close observer describes them:

> They are by no means a monolithic group. Highly independent, they hold varying opinions on such issues as political and economic reforms. But most want a China that is more open to the outside world, tolerates greater debate, is driven by the private sector, and is run by modern institutions and the rule of law. While a more liberal China is a long-term goal, some support a government run by pragmatic technocrats. Above all,

members of the Class of '77 believe they are the most qualified to lead China, by virtue of their experience with rural poverty and Western society. With Deng Xiaoping near death and doddering Communist Party career men fading from the scene, members of the Class of '77 are preparing to take the reins.[4]

If the Class of '77 end up in charge, the political environment in China will be markedly different than if cronyism and corruption continues and the old-line communists continue running the country.

Europe

Far away from Chinese politics, the political situation in Europe also continues to change. One reason is that leaders in major countries, as well as the EU itself, are finding it difficult to firmly establish a foothold of power.[5] As a result, international managers must remain alert as to how political changes may impact their business. For example, in France, the 12-year reign of the Socialists under François Mitterand ended in mid-1995. Mitterand has been replaced by Jacques Chirac, a more conservative Gaullist, and this likely heralds a host of political changes impacting on doing business in France.

The same kind of changes are occurring in the other major European countries. In Germany, Helmut Kohl was re-elected in late 1994 but soon was having troubles. Three months into his new term, he was forced to consider forming a coalition with the opposition Social Democrats, who already controlled the upper house of Parliament. In Italy, Prime Minister Lamberto Dini took office in January 1995 and immediately ran into resistance from other political parties, which insisted on early elections in return for their not voting "no confidence" in his government. At the same time, political jitters led to the transfer of assets out of the country, and both the lira and Italian stock exchange lost value.[6] As of 1996, the British government is still under the leadership of John Major. Given the economic and social problems that Britain has had in recent years, however, this may change. The winds of political change can alter very quickly.

That the nations of Europe, with the exception of Norway and Switzerland, now are part of the EU only adds to the complexity of the political environment. MNCs cannot avoid political risks even when doing business with individual countries because of what the EU may dictate. It is important to realize that the fate of the EU members is interdependent, and what happens to one often influences the others. A good example is provided by France and Germany. Today, Franco-German relations are the cornerstone of a united Europe.[7] The two are tied closely together in a number of ways. For example, the Bank of France has linked French monetary policy to the deutsche mark. Also, each is the other's major trading partner; each has a vested interest in the other doing well. MNCs doing business in either country find that they must focus on developments in both nations, as well as in the EU at large. Simply put, Europe is no longer a series of fragmented countries; it is a giant, interwoven region in which international management must be aware of what is happening politically both in the immediate area of operations as well as throughout the continent.[8]

Russia

Russia presents the most extreme example of how the political environment impacts on international management. For the last 5 years, Boris Yeltsin has governed Russia by barely holding together a number of broad-based coalitions.[9] His power has been steadily deteriorating, however, and the war in Chechnya has badly hurt his standing both at home and in the world community.[10] Additionally, the future stability of Russia's political situation is in further doubt, because newly proposed election laws potentially could disbar presidential candidates, hamper the growth of political parties, and even cause the annulment of elections.[11] In short, it is difficult to determine political trends in Russia, because rules that will govern the voting process are still being hammered out. For example, there is a strong likelihood that for a candidate to be elected, at least 50 percent of the eligible voters must cast ballots. Given that in the general election of 1993 only 54 percent of the Russian electorate voted, this is a very large percentage, especially as public apathy about politics has increased greatly since then.

Another major piece in the Russian political puzzle is being created by the several psychologic and social forces that currently dominate the public's thinking. One such psychologic development is a sense of near-despair that grips many Russians. There is a feeling among many people that things are totally out of control and that the government does not care. A second development is the battle for power between generations. For example, the major economic reformers have a much younger average age than the core of advisors to Boris Yeltsin. In addition, the Russians who are least willing to accept either economic or political changes are older still. This older group resents watching younger people take charge of reforms that are making life very difficult for them. Still another psychologic problem is that most older Russians grew up believing their country was a superpower, the equal of the United States. Now they see that Russia has lost its world leadership and is sliding into an economic abyss, and they feel embarrassed and humiliated. On top of all this is that every period of radical reform in Russia has been followed by further problems. Yeltsin was supposed to be taking the country on the road to democracy and economic recovery, but then he got bogged down in the war over Chechnya. Such developments leave the Russian people confused and angry.

Presently in Russia, a number of political groups are emerging, and each has views that are radically different from the others. For example, a group called *Pymat* ("Memory" in Russian) is a leading exponent for a return to tsarism and submission to the authority of the Russian Orthodox church. There also are a group of reactionary neocommunists who refuse to cooperate with the main Communist Party, because they regard the latter as a bunch of compromisers. This radical group supports the overthrow of the present government and restoration of the Soviet Union—by violence if necessary. Most of their supporters are old and poor, and most informed observers believe this group will fade before long. Yet another radical group is the Russian National Unity party, which is an extremely conservative group with a neofascist philosophy. This party consists of army officers, former KGB members, and those who argue that Russia has no friends in the outside world and can cleanse itself "of disgrace only by blood."[12]

Still another group consists of nationalists who are neither ex-communists nor religio-tsarist enthusiasts. Its best-known member is radical Vladimir Zhirinovsky, who among other things has suggested the conquest of Alaska, free vodka, and shooting criminals on sight.[13] Radical reformers such as Yegor Gaidar in the party called "Russia's Choice" still have a presence, but they currently are losing ground. In the latest general election in December 1995, the communists received the largest number of votes. Russia continues to be in a state of political turmoil and high risk (the *Economist* Intelligence Unit recently ranked them right behind Iraq as the riskiest country in the world).

Central and Eastern Europe

Besides Russia, the political situation in the rest of Central and Eastern Europe is also in a state of flux and resulting risk for the full transition to a market economy. For example, the political situation in Poland seems to be reflective of that throughout Central and Eastern Europe (CEE): communists out, free marketers in, ex-communists (now called socialists) back in.[14] The champion of democracy, Lech Walesa, was defeated in the most recent presidential election by a former communist with an upbeat leadership style who has promised to continue reforms. With the exception of the Czech Republic and Albania, at the beginning of 1996, all the former communist countries have basically followed what has happened in Poland. For example, in Bulgaria, ex-communist Zhan Videnov's Socialist party won control in 1994; the Socialist party in Hungary under Prime Minister Gyula Horn (who was Foreign Minister in the communist government that fell in 1990) holds a large majority in parliament; Romanian President Ion Iliescu was a minister in the deposed communist regime of executed Nicolae Ceausescu; and in Slovakia, both Premier Vladimir Meciar and President Michal Kovac are ex-communists.

The euphoria of 1989 and 1990, in which most people with their new-found freedom in Central and Eastern Europe hoped that democratic leaders who were untainted by communism would emerge, has proven to be wishful thinking. There are a number of reasons for this. Those with responsible positions in government and business had to hold communist-party cards to get their jobs, but they were really not, at least ideologically, pure communists. Many of the ruling elite also were at least somewhat associated with the communists. If a country were to exclude all former card-carrying or real communists from government positions, there would be no one with experience, and some talented people would not be given a chance.[15] This is a dilemma that is yet to be resolved. At present, however, the ex-communists/socialists seem to have, although at a slower pace, free market objectives for their economies: (1) remove enterprises from state ownership as quickly as possible; (2) sell these firms for as much money as possible; and (3) spread the ownership widely throughout the society.[16]

At the same time, different approaches are being used by these countries. The Czechs have privatized very quickly, gambling that private owners can reorganize and manage firms more effectively than the state. The Poles and Hungarians have preferred to organize first and sell later. Also, in the Czech Republic, the government allows citizens to bid for shares in newly privatized firms; in Poland, the government is trying to develop a systematic method for selling state firms to small shareholders by creating stock funds that will sell these shares. In Hungary, the government has temporarily suspended the sale of state businesses and seems to be rethinking its entire strategy. The Hungarian government likely will continue privatizing, however, because it needs the funds to balance the budget. Overall, these political developments in Central and Eastern Europe, as well as in others parts of the world, must be monitored closely and assessed by MNCs expecting to do international business effectively.

LEGAL AND REGULATORY ENVIRONMENT

One reason that today's international environment is so confusing and challenging for MNCs is because there are so many different laws and regulations. There are four foundations on which laws are based around the world. Briefly summarized, these are:

1. *Islamic Law.* This is law derived from interpretation of the *Qur'an* and the teachings of the Prophet Mohammed. It is found in most Islamic countries in the Middle East and Central Asia.
2. *Socialist law.* This law comes from the Marxist socialist system and continues to influence regulations in former communist countries, especially those from the former Soviet Union, as well as present-day China, North Korea, and Cuba.
3. *Common law.* This comes from English law, and it is the foundation of legislation in the United States, Canada, England, Australia, New Zealand, and others.
4. *Civil or code law.* This law is derived from Roman law and is found in the non-Islamic and nonsocialist countries.[17]

With these broad foundations serving as points of departure, the following sections discuss basic principles and examples of the international legal environment facing MNCs today.

Basic Principles of International Law

When compared with domestic law, international law is less coherent, because its sources embody not only the laws of individual countries concerned with any dispute but also treaties (universal, multilateral, or bilateral) and conventions (such as the Geneva Convention on Human Rights or the Vienna Convention of Diplomatic Security). In addition, international law contains unwritten understandings that arise from repeated interactions among nations. Conforming to all the different rules and regulations can create a major problem for MNCs. Fortunately, much of what they need to know can be subsumed under several broad and related principles that govern the conduct of international law.[18]

Sovereignty and Sovereign Immunity   The *principle of sovereignty* holds that governments have the right to rule themselves as they see fit. In turn, this implies that one country's court system cannot be used to rectify injustices or impose penalties on another unless that country agrees. So, while U.S. laws require equality in the workplace for all employees, U.S. citizens who take a job in Japan cannot sue their Japanese employer under the provisions of U.S. law for failure to provide equal opportunity for them.

International Jurisdiction   International law provides for three types of jurisdictional principles. The first is the *nationality principle,* which holds that every country has jurisdiction (authority or power) over its citizens no matter where they are located. Therefore, a U.S. manager who violates the American Foreign Corrupt Practices Act while traveling abroad can be found guilty in the United States. The second is the *territoriality principle,* which holds that every nation has the right of jurisdiction within its legal territory. Therefore, a German firm that sells a defective product in England can be sued under English law even though the company is headquartered outside of England. The third is the *protective principle,* which holds that every country has jurisdiction over behavior that adversely affects its national security, even if that conduct occurred outside the country. Therefore, a French firm that sells secret U.S. government blueprints for a satellite system can be subjected to U.S. laws.

Doctrine of Comity   The *doctrine of comity* holds that there must be mutual respect for the laws, institutions, and government of other countries in the matter of jurisdiction over their own citizens. Although this doctrine is not part of international law, it is part of international custom and tradition.

Act of State Doctrine   Under the *act of state doctrine,* all acts of other governments are considered to be valid by U.S. courts, even if such acts are inappropriate in the United States. As a result, for example, foreign governments have the right to set limits on the repatriation of MNC profits and to forbid companies from sending more than this amount out of the host country.

Treatment and Rights of Aliens   Countries have the legal right to refuse admission of foreign citizens and to impose special restrictions on their conduct, right of travel, where they can stay, and what business they may conduct. Nations also can deport aliens. For example, the United States has the right to limit the travel of Iranian or Chinese scientists coming into this country to attend a scientific convention and can insist they remain within 5 miles of the hotel.

Forum for Hearing and Settling Disputes   This is a principle of U.S. justice as it applies to international law. At their discretion, U.S. courts can dismiss cases brought before them by foreigners; however, they are bound to examine issues such as where the plaintiffs are located, where the evidence must be gathered, and where property to be used in restitution is located. One of the best examples of this principle is the Union Carbide pesticide plant disaster in Bhopal, India. Over 2000 people were killed and thousands left permanently injured when a toxic gas enveloped 40 square kilometers around the plant. The New York Court of Appeals sent the case back to India for resolution.

Examples of Legal and Regulatory Issues

The principles described earlier help to form the international legal and regulatory framework within which MNCs must operate. The following examines some examples of specific laws and situations that can have a direct impact on international business.

Foreign Corrupt Practices Act   During the special prosecutor's investigation of the Watergate scandal in the early 1970s, a number of questionable payments made by U.S. corporations to public officials abroad were uncovered. These bribes became the focal point of investigations by the U.S. Internal Revenue Service, Securities and Exchange Commission (SEC), and Justice Department. This concern over bribes in the international arena eventually culminated in the 1977 passage of the *Foreign Corrupt Practices Act (FCPA),* which makes it illegal to influence foreign officials through personal payment or political contributions. The objectives of the FCPA were to stop U.S. MNCs from initiating or perpetuating corruption in foreign governments and to upgrade the image of both the United States and its businesses abroad.[19]

Critics of the FCPA fear the loss of sales to foreign competitors, especially in those countries where bribery is an accepted way of doing business. Nevertheless, the U.S. government pushed ahead and attempted to enforce the act. Some of the countries that were named in early bribery cases under the law included Algeria, Kuwait, Saudi Arabia, and Turkey. The U.S. State Department tried to convince the SEC and Justice Department not to reveal countries or foreign officials who were involved in its investigations for fear of creating internal political problems for U.S. allies. Although this political sensitivity was justified, for the most part, several interesting developments occurred: (1) MNCs found that they could live within the guidelines set down by the FCPA; and (2) many foreign governments actually applauded these investigations under the FCPA, because it helped them to crack down on corruption in their own country.

One analysis has reported that since passage of the FCPA, U.S. exports to "bribe prone" countries actually has increased.[20] Investigations reveal that once bribes were removed as a key competitive tool, more MNCs were willing to do business in that country. This proved to be true even in the Middle East, where many U.S. MNCs always assumed that bribes were required to ensure contracts. Data show this no longer is true. Additionally, one informed observer of the current state of affairs notes:

> Multinational managers should be wary of believing the comforting writers . . . who assured them that bribing in developing countries was an accepted cultural norm. . . . The fact is that revolutionary new social orders *are* changing the patterns of centuries. Revolutionary forces swept away the Pahlavi dynasty in Iran and the Marcos regime in the Philippines. In the Middle East alone, numerous heads of state are scrambling to somehow deal with issues of corruption before revolutionary movements affect them. If multinational managers wish to remain cynical in the face of these evolving social changes, they may; but, in the meantime, they should be careful whom they bribe.[21]

Bureaucratization   Very restrictive foreign bureaucracies are one of the biggest problems facing MNCs. This is particularly true when bureaucratic government controls are inefficient and not corrected. A good example is Japan, whose political parties feel more beholden to their local interests than to those in the rest of the country.[22] As a result, it is extremely difficult to reorganize the Japanese bureaucracy and streamline the ways things are done, because so many politicians are more interested in the well-being of their own districts than in the long-run well-being of the nation as a whole.[23] In turn, parochial actions create problems for MNCs trying to do business there. By one count, more than 11,000 rules regulate business operations in Japan, and these are estimated to cost Japanese industry and consumers from $75 to $100 billion a year.[24] For example, it costs $1888 to ship a standard, 20-foot container from Tokyo to Osaka, but only $1444 to ship that same container all the way to Europe. MNCs operating in Japan must learn to accept the high cost of doing business there.

Another example of bureaucratic problems in Japan is the powerful Ministry of Finance (MOF). While other industrial powers largely have opened their economies to the realities of global finance and trade, the Japanese MOF has kept a tight grip on the financial sector. It has artificially pumped up stock prices and allowed banks and companies to continue operations when these institutions should have been restructured and forced to become more financially sound. These questionable actions created a false sense of security for Japanese firms, many of which now are unprepared to face the harsh realities of the international market place.

One good example of the economic realities now facing Japan is the rising value of the yen, which increased so sharply during 1994 and 1995 that small domestic Japanese firms now find their international markets drying up. Buyers cannot afford Japanese products that now cost 20 to 30 percent more than they did just a few years ago. Large Japanese businesses are not faring much better either. The 200 major Japanese companies in 1995 had average pretax earnings of a mere 5.1 percent.[25] There are two widely recognized reasons for this poor showing. One is the loss of earning power from international sales. For example, the United States is Japan's largest overseas market, and as the value of the U.S. dollar declines, so does the value of profits earned in this market. A second is the decrease of the Japanese domestic market share, lost to U.S. companies that are exploiting the weak dollar. For example, Chrysler recently announced plans to cut the price of its Jeep Cherokee by 10 percent in the Japanese market, and U.S. computer manufacturers Apple, Compaq, and IBM have collectively doubled their market share to around 30 percent of Japan's $9 billion PC market.

In addition to those doing international business, small businesses in Japan are being hit hard by government bureaucratic policies. As prices fall for imported goods such as beef, vegetables, and luxury items, Japanese firms that stock only domestic items find they cannot compete. Wholesale distributors and retailers in particular are facing strong competition. To make matters even worse, the government now is facing increased pressure from other countries to open its market to external competition or face retaliatory action. The accompanying boxed story "America Goes to the Mat" provides further examples.

Clearly, the Japanese government bureaucracy is creating major obstacles for outside MNCs doing business in Japan as well as Japanese firms themselves. The days when foreign governments would accept huge trade imbalances with Japan as a matter of course are now over. Without trade reciprocity, Japan will continue to find its strong yen and closed markets to be a big problem.

Privatization   Another example of the changing international regulatory environment is the current move toward privatization by an increasing number of countries. The German government, for example, has decided to speed up deregulation of the $66 billion telecommunications market. This has opened a host of opportunities for MNCs looking to create joint ventures with local German firms. Britain's Cable & Wireless PLC, for instance, is teaming up with Veba, a German energy company. This group already has its own fiber optic network, which it now is seeking to offer to third parties, such as corporate network operators, at rates as much as 67 percent lower than that being quoted by the state telephone company.[26] At the same time, Thyssen, the German steelmaker, has teamed with the U.S. Bell South Corporation to fight for a share of this giant communications market, and Viag, an energy utility, has 4000 kilometers of a fiber optic network and hopes to wire the cities of Munich and Nürnberg.

America Goes to the Mat

For a number of years, the United States has demanded that Japan open its markets and provide the same access that Japanese MNCs are accorded. One of the strategies used by the U.S. government has been to negotiate purchasing targets. For example, in the case of automobiles, the Japanese government accommodated requests from the Bush administration and agreed to buy a specific amount of U.S.-made auto parts. This strategy now seems to be a thing of the past, however. Japanese negotiators believe it was a mistake to accede to President Bush's request and say they will hold fast in future negotiations.

For their part, the current U.S. administration is pushing hard to level the playing field for trading with Japan. In 1995, the United States threatened to impose a major import tax on luxury Japanese cars coming into America. Some observers noted, however, that the U.S. government immediately tempered its hard line with a willingness to set an early date for talks with the Japanese about the trade impasse. The administration countered that this concession was quite minor and used simply to meet a condition set forth by the World Trade Organization (WTO). According to WTO rules, in the absence of a mutual agreement on a date to meet, the parties are required to get together before new sanctions are instituted. This does not mean that there will be a settlement, however, only that the two parties will discuss their differences.

One major roadblock to an early resolution of U.S. demands is that EU countries want to be included in these negotiations. They argue that any arrangement between the United States and Japan will result in their being denied market access. After all, if the Japanese agree to buy $6 billion of U.S.-made auto parts, this is market share that cannot be captured by EU MNCs. The EU wants Japan to open its markets to all countries and let each compete on the level playing field.

How far will Japan go in giving concessions? How determined is the United States to wrestle additional agreements from the Japanese? These questions are yet unanswered. One thing is certain, however: Japan is a major world market, and its citizens have enormous purchasing power. Therefore, all nations will continue efforts to break down trade walls and get into the lucrative Japanese market. For example, General Motors recently announced plans to sell its Saturn line in Japan through a network of stand-alone dealerships. The cost of distributing and retailing vehicles in Japan is extremely high, but GM feels that the strong market there is worth the risk. Additionally, GM has been selling Saturns in Taiwan and believes this experience will be invaluable in the Japanese market.

The steps being taken by the U.S. government and some of the major MNCs, such as GM, are important in opening up the Japanese market. Much needs to be done, however, and the U.S. government believes that success in this area will require it to "go to the mat" with Japan. The outcome promises to be not only interesting, but vital to the success of world trade.

The emergence of greater competition could result in a chain reaction that accelerates the opening of markets throughout the EU. In particular, France, Italy, and Spain likely will feel pressure to speed up their own planned privatization efforts. In response to these latest developments in Germany, Deutsche Telekom, the state-owned phone company, feels that it must eliminate up to 50,000 jobs by the end of the decade to become more cost-efficient.[27]

ECONOMIC ENVIRONMENT

The economic environment for international management is undergoing even more rapid change than the political and legal environments. As seen in the accompanying "International Management in Action," the increasing number of firms that are beginning to enter and expand their overseas operations has impacted the world economy dramatically. Simply stated, the future will not be a mere reflection of the past, and the following discussion helps to bring the emerging global economy into focus.

INTERNATIONAL MANAGEMENT IN ACTION

A Global Expansion

The global market is helping an increasing number of firms to expand. By carefully modifying their offerings to meet the varied needs of the world's customers, these new entrants into the global economy are discovering a largely untapped demand. In the past, the best-known example of MNC activity was the auto industry, where manufacturers sold in markets from Maine to Malaysia and from Texas to Timbuktu. Now firms in other industries are beginning to jump on the international bandwagon, and an excellent example is the retail industry.

The biggest U.S. retailer, Wal-Mart, has just begun to expand into Mexico and Hong Kong, and it also has its eye on China. In contrast to its U.S. operations, however, Wal-Mart is finding that in Asia, a smaller selection of products is more profitable, because customers are more interested in price than multiple buying options. This experience of Wal-Mart in Asia is in stark contrast with the situation faced by another giant retailer, Toys "R" Us, which has opened stores in Europe. Surprisingly, Toys "R" Us has found that its wide selection is a favorite drawing card for customers who are less concerned about price than the choices they are given.

U.S. retailers are not the only ones going international. Marks & Spencer, Britain's largest retailer for more than a century, has over 150 small stores selling private-brand merchandise worldwide. Its six Hong Kong outlets are the most profitable, although other units (including those in France, where the company sells a diverse product line ranging from white bread to English clothes) also are doing very well.

Some innovative retailers are getting into international markets as well. The British Airport Authority (BAA) now sells merchandise in-flight, to generate increased revenues. The BAA has reduced the markups that it charges to its airport mall retailers. The result has been a sharp increase in purchases, earning even greater revenues for the BAA. In fact, this idea of tapping the buying power of travelers has sparked additional expansion plans from companies such as W.H. Smith, Britain's largest bookstore firm. This company is setting up bookstores in U.S. airports, which provides it easy access to customers and severely reduces the competition these units would face if they tried entering the mainstream market. W.H. Smith currently does over $500 million of business in the U.S. market.

How attractive will the international market be in the future? This, of course, will depend on a number of factors, including economic growth, government regulation, and competition. Today, however, firms in all industries throughout the world realize that they cannot maintain strong growth if they do not enter the international market and appeal to the world's customers. So, for the foreseeable future, all firms, large and small, in every industry, throughout the world are planning to continue their global expansion. They really do not have a choice if they expect to prosper, or even survive, in the long run.

Economic Superpowers

As noted in Chapter 1, the triad countries of the United States, Europe, and Japan constitute a major percentage of all international investment and trade. A brief look at the 25 largest MNCs shown in Table 2-1 indicates that all are triad-based. Moreover, while there has been some change in the composition of this group (Japanese MNCs have improved their position in recent years), the superpower nations and their MNCs remain the same.

Additionally, the impact of the triad on international business extends well beyond the foreign direct investment (FDI) and trade that occur among these three groups. Triad members also recently have become major sources of investment for other countries. The United Nations Centre on Transnational Cooperation (UNCTC) reports that triad members accounted for over 40 percent of the FDI in 25 of the 37 developing countries this organization was studying.[28] Typically, recipients of these funds are part of an *FDI cluster*, which is a group of countries usually in the same geographic region as the triad member and having some form of economic relationship. For example, the United States tends to be a dominant investor in Latin America, Eastern Europe is a favorite investment target for EU countries, and Japan has major investments in the Pacific Rim. Figure 2-1 looks at some of these FDI clusters.

TABLE 2-1

THE 25 LARGEST MULTINATIONAL CORPORATIONS

1994	Sales ($ millions)	Profits ($ millions)	Employees (number)
1. Mitsubishi (Japan)	175,835.6	218.7	36,000
2. Mitsui (Japan)	171,490.5	263.8	80,000
3. Itochu (Japan)	167,824.7	81.6	7,345
4. Sumitomo (Japan)	162,475.9	73.2	22,000
5. General Motors (U.S.)	154,951.2	4,900.6	692,800
6. Marubeni (Japan)	150,187.4	104.4	9,911
7. Ford Motor (U.S.)	128,439.0	5,308.0	337,778
8. Exxon (U.S.)	101,459.0	5,100.0	86,000
9. Nissho Iwai (Japan)	100,875.5	52.7	17,008
10. Royal Dutch/Shell Group (Brit./Neth.)	94,881.3	6,235.6	106,000
11. Toyota Motor (Japan)	88,158.6	1,184.6	110,534
12. Wal-Mart Stores (U.S.)	83,412.4	2,681.0	600,000
13. Hitachi (Japan)	76,430.9	1,146.7	331,673
14. Nippon Life Insurance (Japan)	75,350.4	2,682.1	90,132
15. AT&T (U.S.)	75,094.0	4,676.0	304,500
16. Nippon Telegraph & Telephone (Japan)	70,843.6	767.9	194,700
17. Matsushita Electrical Industrial (Japan)	69,946.7	911.0	265,397
18. Tomen (Japan)	69,901.5	10.2	3,192
19. General Electric (U.S.)	64,687.0	4,726.0	221,000
20. Daimler-Benz (Germany)	64,168.6	649.9	330,551
21. IBM (U.S.)	64,052.0	3,021.0	243,039
22. Mobil (U.S.)	59,621.0	1,079.0	58,500
23. Nissan Motor (Japan)	58,731.8	(1,671.7)	145,582
24. Nichimen (Japan)	56,202.6	39.7	2,591
25. Kanematsu (Japan)	55,856.1	(153.0)	8,431

Source: Reported in Fortune, August 7, 1995, p. F-1.

Because of its close links to trade, financial flows, and technology transfer, FDI is becoming increasingly important in economic development. Not all developing countries have been equally successful in attracting triad investment, however. Much of these funds have been used by multinationals to build regional networks, often starting near their home base and then working outward. This helps to explain why 61 percent of all FDI in Mexico comes from U.S. firms and 52 percent in South Korea from Japanese firms. At present, more than one-half of all investment moving into developing countries is concentrated in Brazil, China, Hong Kong, Mexico, and Singapore, and one major reason is their relation to the triad members.

It is important to realize that investment policies appear to be helping create and promote regional economic clusters. For example, a civic activist group in Seattle, Washington, advocates a Pacific Northwest economy called "Cascadia,"

FIGURE 2-1

FOREIGN DIRECT INVESTMENT (FDI) CLUSTERS

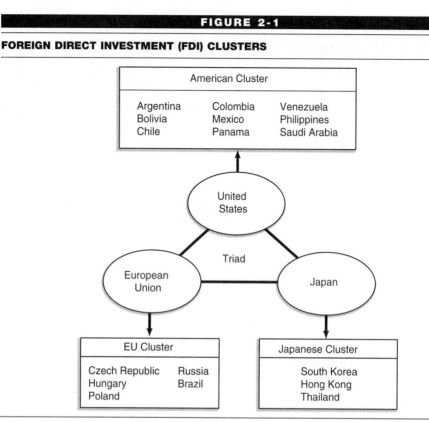

Source: Adapted from information found in the *Economist*, August 24, 1991, p. 57.

which includes Washington, Oregon, British Columbia, and Alberta.[29] Therefore, in the future, international managers within triad countries may well turn their attention to investing in geographic regions rather than specific countries. This also may stimulate investment opportunities for an increasing number of less developed countries.

After Communism

The collapse of communism had tremendous implications for the balance of political power in the world, but it also is having a major impact on international management through the economic fallout. Of particular importance is the rate of progress at which these countries are transforming to market economies. This road has been a difficult one. By the end of the 1980s, all the Soviet-bloc economies were bankrupt except for the former Czechoslovakia.[30] The communist economies had failed so totally that when given the chance, these countries opted to abandon their old systems totally rather than to patch them together into some form of "central planning coupled with capitalism." From the beginning, the main argument was whether to employ "shock therapy," with its immediate radical reforms, or some form of gradualism, which would bring about the needed changes in a slower, more moderately paced way that was easier in the short run on people.

While the means were controversial, no one argued about the desired end results: a fully functioning market economy. Trade had to be liberalized, prices decontrolled, banking and financial institutions constructed, and state-owned assets privatized. Inflation had to be controlled as the prices were freed, and unemployment had to be dealt with as the old, inefficient state enterprises were downsized or closed. The radical reformers saw all of this as interlinked, and they believed that there might be short-run hardships but a quick recovery and prosperity for all. The gradualists wanted to go slower, stagger the reforms, and believed this would have a less severe impact on the people.

In the short run, both approaches resulted in economic problems, but shock therapy had a more immediate severe impact. Trade collapsed, prices soared, unemployment increased, and public services as well as the standard of living fell dramatically. Those countries that stayed with shock therapy, however, recovered fastest and best. Poland, for example, which was the first country to adopt shock therapy, had the fastest recovery. Other fast-reforming economies, such as the Czech Republic, Slovenia, and the Baltic states of Estonia, Latvia, and Lithuania, also had the foundations of a market economy early on in the transformation. By 1995, inflation and unemployment were under reasonable control in these countries, and they have begun to shift trade toward the West and are looking to join the EU. A closer look at the status of Central and Eastern Europe as of 1996 is important to international management.

The Czechs are generally regarded as the model economic reformers among ex-communist nations. They have low inflation, and as shown in Table 2-2, their privatization program is almost complete. One reason for their success is that pre-World War II Czechoslovakia was close to a mainstream European country, and the Czech communists who ruled after the war turned out to be better managers than those in neighboring countries. Today, at least economically, the Czech Republic is fortunate to be closely linked geographically and culturally to Western Europe.

Poland was the first former communist country to show positive economic growth in 1992, and it has been slowly improving ever since. By 1995, inflation was running at an annual rate of 35 percent, and the country still had a way to go on privatizing some of its large public enterprises (see Table 2-2). Compared with 1990, however, when the nation was in the throes of hyperinflation, the turnaround has been impressive. Additionally, a new private sector of entrepreneurial companies have been created since the fall of communism and currently helps to account for 25 percent of the nation's manufacturing output[31] and over one-third of GDP.

The Baltic states began their reforms as recently as 1991. Progress here has been good, because they largely have embraced radical programs. The Baltic countries have slashed their budget deficits; introduced stable, convertible currencies, and beat down inflation. What has been particularly helpful is that these three nations are small and manageable, which has allowed them to sidestep many problems that have confronted the larger former communist countries.

While still one of the most successful of the former communist countries, Hungary offers a mixed picture. The Hungarians had many of the same advantages as the Czechs carrying over from the old days, and they started economic reforms very early. Thus, they attracted a great deal of foreign investment. They never really implemented radical reforms, however, and by 1995, Hungary had begun to

TABLE 2-2

PROGRESS TOWARD FREE MARKETS BY EX-COMMUNIST NATIONS

| | Private sector share of GDP, 1994, % | Score: 4 = market economy, 1 = little progress | | | | | |
| | | Privatization | | Restructuring of companies | Prices, competition | Trade, foreign exchange | Banks |
		Large	Small				
Albania	50	1	3	2	3	4	2
Armenia	40	1	3	1	3	2	1
Azerbaijan	20	1	1	1	3	1	1
Belarus	15	2	2	2	2	1	1
Bulgaria	40	2	2	2	3	4	2
Croatia	40	3	4	2	3	4	3
Czech Republic	65	4	4	3	3	4	3
Estonia	55	3	4	3	3	4	3
Georgia	20	1	2	1	2	1	1
Hungary	55	3	4	3	3	4	3
Kazakhstan	20	2	2	1	2	2	1
Kyrgizstan	30	3	4	2	3	3	2
Latvia	55	2	3	2	3	4	3
Lithuania	50	3	4	2	3	4	2
Macedonia	35	2	4	2	3	4	2
Moldova	20	2	2	2	3	2	2
Poland	55	3	4	3	3	4	3
Romania	35	2	3	2	3	4	2
Russia	50	3	3	2	3	3	2
Slovakia	55	3	4	3	3	4	3
Slovenia	30	2	4	3	3	4	3
Tajikistan	15	2	2	1	3	1	1
Turkmenistan	15	1	1	1	2	1	1
Ukraine	30	1	2	1	2	1	1
Uzbekistan	20	2	3	1	3	2	1

Source: European Bank for Reconstruction and Development.

retreat even further from needed reforms. In the process, the country's budget deficit has begun to increase sharply, its balance of payments is reaching precarious levels, and the economy is not judged to be as strong as that of the Czechs or the Poles.

Besides the Czech Republic, Poland, Hungary, and the Baltic States, other countries, such as Slovenia, and Slovakia, are making good progress in their transformations. A good example of a country that has bottomed out and is now on the road to recovery, but with many remaining major problems, is Albania.[32] Completely isolated from the outside world for about 45 years by the Stalinist dictator Enver Hoxha, Albania was completely devastated both economically and spiritually when the first democratic government was elected in March 1992. Unlike other former communist countries, the Albanian people were so happy to be rid of their very oppressive past that they welcomed radical change. Prices were freed and both agriculture and housing completely privatized, but their infrastructure (e.g., electricity, water, roads, health care, transportation, communication) completely collapsed. Although as Chapter 1 pointed out, Albania has had the highest economic growth rate in all of Europe in recent years, this small country continues struggling to rebuild the infrastructure that is needed to support yet-to-be-built factories, attract foreign capital, and provide a minimum standard of living for its people. Even though the right steps are being taken, this poor Balkan country has tremendous difficulties ahead, because in many ways, they are starting from less than zero.

The other Balkan countries of Bulgaria and Romania as well as the former Soviet republics started off better than Albania as far as their past economic foundation and infrastructure, but they have delayed needed reforms and made little progress. The Balkan countries were too dependent on trade with the former Yugoslavia or Soviet Union, both of which are now in shambles. Also, countries such as Romania are having difficulty rising from the ashes of communism because many who held important positions during the totalitarian past remain in power and are not making the necessary economic reforms.

The least amount of reform has occurred in the larger former Soviet republics, such as Belarus and Ukraine, and the Central Asian republics, such as Kazakhstan and Kyrgyzstan. These republics have opted for gradualism and been slow to implement needed economic reforms. They still subsidize farms and factories, and they are running up huge deficits. Also, they have largely depended on ex-communists for political leadership, which has slowed their economic progress as well. On the positive side, these republics have bottomed out, appear to be changing their approach, and are realizing that the procrastination after ridding themselves of communism is not proving to be effective. For example, oil-rich Kazakhstan now is pushing for faster reform; and Uzbekistan is trying to reach an agreement with the International Monetary Fund regarding economic changes that must be made to qualify for assistance.

These changes in Central and Eastern Europe as well as Central Asia indicate that an increased number of people now are accepting not just the possibility but also the desirability of creating free market economies. A recent report summed up the success in Central Europe this way:

> The success of Central Europe has made its mark. Lenin is being proved wrong for a second time, in effect, and even more rudely: countries escaping from communism have shown that they can indeed change the economic structure of their societies in as little as three years. What is more, they have done so with little outside help. History and living memory have played an important part. So too has the presence of capable and committed leaders able to marshall public support. But most decisive of all has surely been a simple recognition of the superiority of capitalism as an economic system. That has been the real economic revolution across this other Europe. With luck, it will produce rather better results than the previous one did.[33]

The Rise of Developing Economies

As noted earlier, huge MNCs from the large, developed triad nations currently account for most world trade. The next 25 years, however, should see major shifts

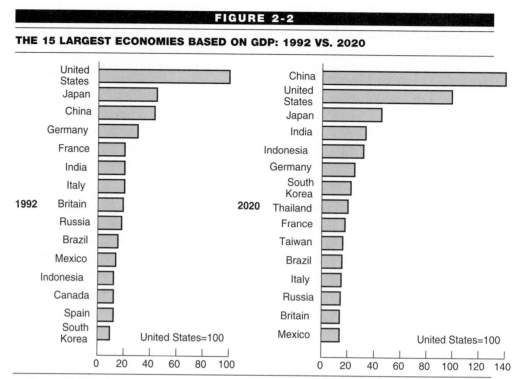

FIGURE 2-2

THE 15 LARGEST ECONOMIES BASED ON GDP: 1992 VS. 2020

Source: World Bank.

in economic strength. In particular, countries such as China, India, Indonesia, and Thailand will gain significant economic power. Figure 2-2 contrasts the 15 largest economies in 1992 and 2020.

High Growth Rates   One reason for these changes is that according to the World Bank, growth of real GDP over the next 20 years will be around 2.7 percent annually for the wealthy, developed countries but 4.8 percent for developing countries. This is a substantial gap, and it already is materializing. As a recent economic report noted:

> The rich industrial economies' dominance over the world economy is already smaller than is generally recognized. If output is measured on the basis of purchasing-power parities, then the developing countries and former Soviet bloc already account for 44% of world output. At current growth rates, the industrial economies will account for less than half of world output by the end of the decade. And if developed and developing countries continue to grow at the pace forecast by the World Bank for this next decade, by 2020 the rich world's share of global output could shrink to less than two-fifths.[34]

The largest gains are projected for countries in east Asia, south Asia, and Latin America. One reason is that developing countries continue to account for an increasing percentage of manufactured-goods exports. In 1955, these nations provided 5 percent of this output; today they provide almost two-thirds.

Economic Linkages   Another interesting development is the close economic linkage that now exists between developing and developed countries. In the past, wealthy nations provided large markets for the products of developing nations. Today, however, the tables are turning; the big and wealthy depend more and more on developing countries' markets for their goods and services. For example, since the beginning of the 1990s, U.S. exports to developing nations have been growing at an annual rate of 12 percent, while U.S. exports to developed countries have been increasing at a mere 2 percent annually. Moreover, some economists predict that over the next decade, U.S. exports to giant markets such as China and India could grow by 15 percent annually.[35]

At the same time, developing countries are finding the triad nations to be major markets for their goods. During the 1980s, the major North American nations doubled the percentage of manufactured imports they received from developing countries, and they are not alone. The EU and Japan also increasingly rely on manufactured imports from developing nations. The new economic world order that is emerging in the last decade of this century is one in which interdependency is much more common than ever before. So far, these economic linkages are proving to be a boon for both the developed and developing groups of nations. Some of the major reasons for this include:

1. Rising productivity in developing countries will cut the cost of rich countries' imports, thus giving consumers a boost in real income. For example, about 30 percent of all clothes purchased in the United States come from developing countries, and over the last decade, average prices of clothing in America have fallen by more than 20 percent in real terms.

2. Increased competition from nontriad world producers will stimulate more efficient use of resources in rich economies, and productivity in the developed countries will be spurred on by this competition. At the same time, developed countries will work harder to maintain the existing markets for their goods and services. This increased activity will cause greater investment in both human- and technology-based capital, helping to speed worldwide economic growth.

3. As larger international markets develop, producers will be able to exploit economies of scale by spreading their fixed costs more widely. This will be true not only for production costs but also for areas such as training and research and development. In turn, this should bring about higher returns from innovation and further speed economic progress.

4. As economic conditions in developing countries improve, "savers" in first-world countries will be attracted to invest there. These fast-growing, emerging economies will offer higher returns than the mature, slower-growing industrial economies. In fact, this shift in investment dollars from developed to developing countries already is happening to some degree, as illustrated in Figure 2-3.

TECHNOLOGICAL ENVIRONMENT

The technological environment is moving at lightning speed. Computers, telephones, televisions, and wireless forms of communication now are merging into telecommunications both to create multimedia products and to allow individuals anywhere in the world to communicate with each other. Some specific ways in

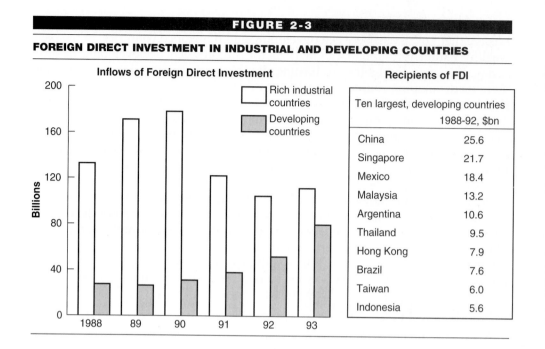

FIGURE 2-3

FOREIGN DIRECT INVESTMENT IN INDUSTRIAL AND DEVELOPING COUNTRIES

Inflows of Foreign Direct Investment

Recipients of FDI

Ten largest, developing countries 1988-92, $bn	
China	25.6
Singapore	21.7
Mexico	18.4
Malaysia	13.2
Argentina	10.6
Thailand	9.5
Hong Kong	7.9
Brazil	7.6
Taiwan	6.0
Indonesia	5.6

which this emerging technology will affect international management in the next decade include:

1. Rapid advances in biotechnology that are built on the precise manipulation of organisms, which will revolutionize the fields of agriculture, medicine, and industry.
2. The emergence of nanotechnology, in which nanomachines will possess the ability to remake the whole physical universe.
3. Satellites that will play a role in learning. For example, Motorola, with its Iridium system, will place 77 tiny satellites into low orbit, thus making it possible for millions of people, even in remote or sparsely populated regions like Siberia, the Chinese desert, and the African interior, to send and receive voice, data, and digitized images through hand-held telephones.
4. Automatic translation telephones, which will allow people to communicate naturally in their own language with anyone in the world who has access to a telephone.
5. Artificial intelligence and embedded learning technology, which will allow thinking that formerly was felt to be only the domain of humans to occur in machines.
6. Silicon chips containing up to 100 million transistors, allowing computing power that now rests only in the hands of supercomputer users to be available on every desktop.
7. Supercomputers that are capable of 1 trillion calculations per second, which will allow advances such as simulations of the human body for testing new drugs and computers that respond easily to spoken commands.[36]

Although all these technological wonders will affect international management, more specific technologies also will have an even more direct impact. The following discussion highlights some specific dimensions of the technological environment currently facing international management.

E-Cash

As the Internet becomes increasingly common in international commerce, the way in which financial transactions are conducted will change significantly. Customers already can use their computers to travel through electronic shops, view products, and read descriptions of merchandise. Not yet common, however, is use of their keyboard to pay by credit card, transmitting the necessary information by modem. This currently is frowned on because of security. It is still too easy for hackers to gain access to such credit card information and use it to make purchases of their own. The day is fast approaching, however, when electronic cash (e-cash) will be common. When this happens, there will be a convergence of money, commerce, and personal computers. Here is a brief description of how e-cash might work:

> To see how e-cash might evolve on the Internet, start with the rudimentary transaction scheme run by Mr. Stein's First Virtual Holdings. Both buyer and seller must have accounts at the "bank." In the case of the buyer, this amounts to an authority for First Virtual to make charges against his credit card. When the buyer, having investigated the seller's wares on the Internet and found something that he likes, makes a purchase, he gives his account number to the seller, who ships the product. Each day or each week the merchant sends his list of who-bought-what to First Virtual, which sends e-mail messages to buyers asking them to confirm the transactions. Once a buyer confirms, his (conventional) credit card is charged and the money is transferred to the seller's account. If the buyer withholds confirmation, First Virtual withholds settlement.[37]

This scenario already occurs in a number of not-as-sophisticated forms. A good example is prepaid smart cards, which are being used mostly in Europe for telephone calls and public transportation. An individual can purchase one of these cards and use it in lieu of cash. This idea will blend into the Internet, allowing individuals to buy and sell merchandise and transfer funds electronically. The result will be global digital cash, which will open up worldwide markets and allow buying and selling on a 24-hour basis.[38]

This technological development also will have a major impact on financial institutions. After all, who will need the local corner ATM when they can tap into their funds through the Internet? Similarly, companies will not have to wait for their money from buyers, thus eliminating (or at least substantially reducing) bad debts while increasing their working capital. Therefore, if Wal-Mart shipped $12 million of merchandise to Cifra, its Mexican partner, with payment due on delivery, the typical 7- to 10-day waiting period between payment and collection of international transactions would, for all intents and purposes, be eliminated.

Of course, e-cash will create many problems, and it will take some time for these to be resolved. For example, if Cifra pays for its merchandise in Mexican pesos, there must be some system for converting these pesos into U.S. dollars. At present, such transactions are handled through regulated foreign exchange markets. In the near future, these transactions likely will be denominated in a single, conventional currency and exchanged at conventional market rates. It is equally likely, however, that the entire system of transactions eventually will become seamless and require no processing through foreign exchange markets. One expert explained it this way:

> Ideally, the ultimate e-cash will be a currency without a country (or a currency of all countries), infinitely exchangeable without the expense and inconvenience of conversion between local denominations. It may constitute itself as a wholly new currency with its own denomination—the "cyber dollar," perhaps. Or, it may continue to fix itself by reference to a traditional currency, in which case the American dollar would seem to be the likeliest possibility. Either way, it is hard to imagine that the existence of an international, easy-to-use, cheap-to-process, hard-to-tax electronic money will not then force freer convertibility on traditional currencies.[39]

Telecommunications

The most obvious dimension of the technological environment facing international management today is telecommunications. To begin with, it no longer is necessary to hardwire a city to provide residents with telephone service. This can be done wirelessly, thus allowing people to use cellular phones, beepers, and other telecommunications services. As a result, growth in the wireless technology business worldwide has been rapid, and the future promises even more. Figure 2-4 illustrates the number of telephone lines in Asia for 1993 and the increase that is expected by the year 2000. This region of the world is not alone. In South America, customers once waited years to get a telephone installed. Now, thanks to cellular phones, a form of technologic leapfrogging is occurring, in which the populace is moving from a situation where phones were unavailable to one where cellular is available throughout the country, including rural areas, because the infrastructure needed to support this development can be installed both quickly and easily.[40]

One reason for this rapid increase in telecommunications services is many countries believe that without an efficient telephone system, their economic growth may stall. Additionally, governments are accepting the belief that the only way to attract foreign investment and know-how in telecommunications is to give up control to private industry. As a result, while most telecommunications operators in the Asia-Pacific region were state-run in 1990, approximately 30 percent were in private hands by 1995. Singapore Telecommunications, Pakistan Telecom, Thailand's Telecom Asia, and Globe Telecom in the Philippines all have been privatized, and MNCs have helped in this process by providing investment funds. Today, NYNEX holds a stake in Telecom Asia; US West owns 20 percent of Binariang, which is building a digital cell-phone system in Malaysia; Bell Atlantic and Ameritech each own 25 percent of Telecom New Zealand; and Bell South has an ownership position in Australia's Optus. At the same time, Australia's Telestra is moving into Vietnam; Japan's NTT is investing in Thailand, and Korea Telecommunications is in the Philippines and Indonesia.[41]

Many governments are reluctant to allow so much private and foreign ownership of such a vital industry; however, they also are aware that foreign investors will go elsewhere if the deal is not satisfactory. The Hong Kong office of Salomon Brothers, a U.S. investment bank, estimates that to meet the expanding demand for telephone service in Asia, companies will need to increase the number of telephone lines by 17 percent annually. This will require raising $90 billion in capital, most of which will have to come from overseas. MNCs are unwilling to put up

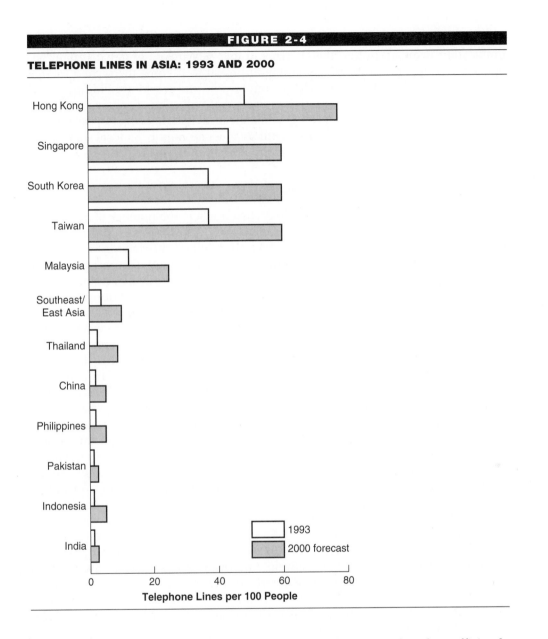

FIGURE 2-4

TELEPHONE LINES IN ASIA: 1993 AND 2000

this much money unless they are assured of operating control and a sufficiently high return on their investment.

A good example occurred in China, where in 1994 the government announced that foreign investors who were interested in building and operating power plants would have their annual rate of return (ROI) capped at 12 percent. Investors immediately began looking for more lucrative opportunities in other power-hungry Asian nations, and now China has increased the ROI cap to continue attracting deals. China presently is facing a similar backlash from telecommunications firms as well, which are only allowed to provide advice and to supply and manufacture telecommunication equipment for the Chinese market and are banned from the potentially more lucrative business of owning and/or operating these services.

Unlike China, however, other developing countries are eager to attract telecommunication firms and offer liberal terms. Cable & Wireless of Great Britain has opened an office in Hanoi after winning approval to become the second foreign operator in Vietnam. In India, MNCs from around the world are bidding to become part of a joint venture with Indian firms that will compete against state monopolies in 21 regions. In Hong Kong, while the local telephone monopoly will not lose its grip on international services until 2006, its monopoly on local services recently ended, and private groups are competing to provide service.

The Employment Fallout from Technology

In international management, technology also impacts the number of employees who are needed to carry out operations effectively. As MNCs use advanced technology to help them communicate, produce, and deliver their goods and services internationally, they face a new challenge: how technology will affect the nature and number of their employees. Some informed observers note that technology already has eliminated much, and in the future will eliminate even more of the work now being done by middle management and white-collar staff. In this century, machines have replaced millions of manual laborers, but those who worked with their minds were able to thrive and survive. During the past two decades in particular, blue-collar, smoke-stack industries such as steel and autos have been downsized by technology, and the result has been a permanent restructuring of the number of employees needed to run factories efficiently. In the 1990s, the same thing is happening in the white-collar service industries (insurance, banks, and even government).

Some experts predict that in the future technology will be so all-pervasive that it has the potential to largely displace employees in all industries, from those doing low-skilled jobs to those holding positions traditionally reserved for human thinking. For example, voice recognition is helping to replace telephone operators; the demand for postal workers has been reduced severely by address-reading devices; and cash-dispensing machines can do 10 times more transactions in a day than bank tellers, so the number of tellers can be reduced, or even eliminated entirely, in the future. Also, expert (sometimes called "smart") systems can eliminate human thinking completely. For example, American Express has an expert system that performs the credit analysis formerly done by college-graduate financial analysts. In the medical field, expert systems can diagnose some illnesses as well as doctors, and robots capable of performing hip replacements are under development.

Emerging information technology also makes work more portable. This is especially true for work that can be easily contracted with overseas locations. For example, low-paid workers in India and Asian countries now are being given subcontracted work such as labor-intensive software development and data-entry jobs in preparing tax returns. A restructuring of the nature of work and of employment is resulting from such information technology; Figure 2-5 provides some specific, projected winners and losers in the work force of the future.

The new technological environment has both positives and negatives for MNCs and societies as a whole. On the positive side, the cost of doing business worldwide should go down thanks to the opportunities that technology offers in substituting lower-cost machines for higher-priced labor. Productivity should go

FIGURE 2-5

WINNERS AND LOSERS IN SELECTED OCCUPATIONS (PERCENTAGE CHANGE FORECASTS FOR 1992–2005)

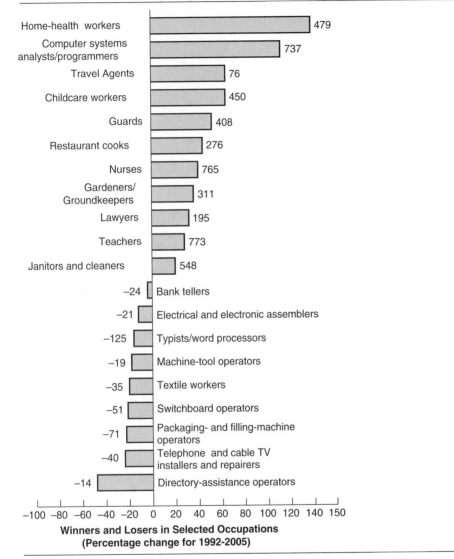

**Winners and Losers in Selected Occupations
(Percentage change for 1992-2005)**

Source: U.S. Bureau of Labor Statistics.

up, and prices should go down. On the negative side, many employees will find either their jobs eliminated or their wages and salaries reduced because they have been replaced by machines and their skills are no longer in high demand. In the computer and information technology industry itself, the negative has been offset by the positive. For example, over the last decade, employment in the U.S. computer-software industry has tripled, and the Bureau of Labor Statistics forecasts even more rapid growth in the next decade. Additionally, even though Japan and the United States are the two countries most affected by technological

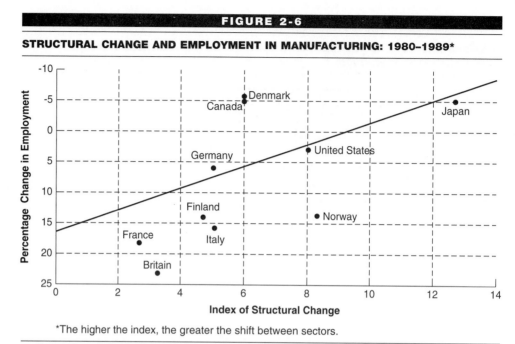

FIGURE 2-6

STRUCTURAL CHANGE AND EMPLOYMENT IN MANUFACTURING: 1980–1989*

*The higher the index, the greater the shift between sectors.

Source: Organization for Economic Cooperation and Development.

displacement of workers, both nations still lead the world in creating new jobs and shifting their traditional industrial structure toward a high-tech, knowledge-based economy. Figure 2-6 illustrates this development.

The precise impact that the advanced technological environment will have on international management over the next decade is difficult to forecast. One thing is certain, however, there is no turning back the technological clock. MNCs and nations alike must evaluate the impact of these changes carefully and realize that their economic performance is closely tied to keeping up, or ahead, of advancing technology.

SUMMARY OF KEY POINTS

1. Today's political environment presents a myriad of challenges for MNCs. China is going through a transition as the old guard passes from the scene. The political situation in Europe also continues to change. Russia is facing economic problems and social upheaval, and the rest of Central and Eastern Europe has had varying degrees of success with their new-found freedom and continue to struggle with their past.

2. The current legal and regulatory environment is both complex and confusing. There are many different laws and regulations to which MNCs doing business internationally must conform, and each nation is unique. Also, MNCs must abide by the laws of their own country. For example, U.S. MNCs must obey the rules set down by the Foreign Corrupt Practices Act. MNCs doing business in Japan face a wide range of bureaucratic rules and regulations that often are both time-wasting and inefficient, and MNCs in Europe have to adapt to the ever-changing guidelines accompanying the respective government's privatization programs.

3. The world economic environment also is characterized by a number of dramatic developments. The major MNCs in traditional markets continue to dominate the international

scene; however, the opening of markets and expansion of the economies in China and Southeast Asia as well as the fall of communism and emergence of market economies in Central and Eastern Europe have created new opportunities for established MNCs and new entrepreneurial firms. In addition, developing countries are garnering a larger share of world trade, and developed countries are finding that they need to rely on these developing countries as a source of imports as well as an export market.

4. The technological environment is changing quickly and is having a major impact on international business. This will continue in the future. For example, money transfers and exchange are changing dramatically. Also, areas such as telecommunications offer developing countries new opportunities to leapfrog into the twenty-first century. New markets are being created for high-tech MNCs that are eager to provide telecommunications service. Technological developments also impact on both the nature and the structure of employment, shifting the industrial structure toward a more high-tech, knowledge-based economy. MNCs who understand and take advantage of this high-tech environment should prosper, but they also must keep up, or ahead, to survive the highly competitive years ahead.

KEY TERMS

Islamic law	territoriality principle
Socialist law	protective principle
Common law	doctrine of comity
Civil or code law	act of state doctrine
principle of sovereignty	Foreign Corrupt Practices Act (FCPA)
nationality principle	FDI cluster

REVIEW AND DISCUSSION QUESTIONS

1. In what way does the new political environment around the world create challenges for MNCs? Would these challenges be less for those operating in the EU than for those in Russia or China? Why, or why not?
2. How do the following legal principles impact on MNC operations: the principle of sovereignty, the nationality principle, the territoriality principle, the protective principle, and principle of comity?
3. How could the national and local government bureaucracy in Japan impede the operations of a U.S. MNC doing business there? What are some Japanese laws or regulations that would reduce the MNC's effectiveness?
4. If an MNC were determined to set up operations in Central and Eastern Europe, which country would you recommend? On what basis would you make this recommendation?
5. Today, developed countries rely more and more on developing countries, and vice versa. This symbiotic relationship is proving to be helpful to both. What is meant by these statements? Do you agree or disagree? Explain.
6. Why are developing countries interested in privatizing their telecommunications industries? What opportunities does this privatization have for telecommunication MNCs?

PRACTICAL INTERNATIONAL MANAGEMENT ASSIGNMENT

Pick a country in a developing area of the world, and gather data related to this nation's political, legal, economic, and technological environments. Based on this information, what conclusions can you draw regarding the attractiveness of this nation for MNCs to do business there? Are there any specific types of MNCs that would find this country to be particularly attractive to enter?

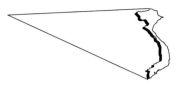

Vietnamese people often have to remind Americans that Vietnam is a country, not a war.

In the International Spotlight

Vietnam

Located in Southeast Asia, the Socialist Republic of Vietnam is bordered to the north by the People's Republic of China, to the west by Laos and Cambodia, and to the east and south by the South China Sea. The country is a mere 127,000 square miles but has a population of almost 72 million. The language is Vietnamese and the principal religion Buddhism, although there are a number of small minorities, including Confucian, Christian (mainly Catholic), Caodist, Daoist, and Hoa Hao. In recent years, the country's economy has been improving dramatically, but average per-capita income still is in the hundreds of dollars as the peasants still remain very poor.

One of the reasons that Vietnam has lagged behind its fast-developing neighbors in Southeast Asia, such as Thailand, Malaysia, and Indonesia, is its isolation from the industrial west, and the United States in particular, because of the Vietnam war. From the mid-1970s, the country had close relations with the U.S.S.R., but the collapse of communism there forced the still-communist Vietnamese government to work on establishing stronger economic ties with other countries. The nation recently has worked out many of its problems with China, and today, the Chinese have become a useful economic ally. Vietnam would most like to establish a vigorous trade relationship with the United States, however. Efforts toward this end

began over a decade ago, but because of lack of information concerning the many U.S. soldiers still unaccounted for after the war, it was not until 1993 that the United States permitted U.S. companies to take part in ventures in Vietnam that were financed by international aid agencies. Then, in 1994, the U.S. trade embargo was lifted, and a growing number of American firms began doing business in Vietnam.

Caterpillar began supplying equipment for a $2 billion highway project. Mobil teamed with three Japanese partners to begin drilling offshore. Exxon, Amoco, Conoco, Unocal, and Arco negotiated production-sharing contracts with Petro Vietnam. General Electric opened a trade office and developed plans to use electric products throughout the country. AT&T began working to provide long-distance service both in and out of the country. Coca-Cola began bottling operations. Within the first 12 months, 70 U.S. companies obtained licenses to do business in Vietnam. Mobil and Occidental Petroleum are actively exploring for offshore oil, and U.S. consumer products from Pepsi to Motorola are big sellers. Convenience stores carry Heinz ketchup and Kraft salad dressing, and Baskin-Robbins has opened an ice-cream parlor in Ho Chi Minh City. If relations between the two countries continue on their present course, more and more opportunities will open up for U.S. MNCs.

1. In what way does the political environment in Vietnam pose both an opportunity and a threat for American MNCs seeking to do business there?
2. Why are U.S. multinationals so interested in going into Vietnam? How much economic potential does the country offer? Conversely, how much economic benefit can Vietnam derive from a business relationship with U.S. MNCs?
3. Would there be any opportunities in Vietnam for high-tech American firms? Why or why not?

You Be the International Management Consultant

A Chinese Venture

The Darby Company is a medium-size communications technology company headquartered on the west coast of the United States. Among other things, Darby holds a patent on a portable telephone that can operate effectively within a 5-mile radius. The phone does not contain state-of-the-art technology, but it can be produced extremely cheaply. As a result, the Chinese government has expressed interest in manufacturing and selling this phone throughout their country.

Preliminary discussions with the Chinese government reveal that some major terms of the agreement that it would like include: (1) Darby will enter into a joint venture with a local Chinese firm to manufacture the phones to Darby's specifications; (2) these phones would be sold throughout China at a 100 percent markup, and Darby will receive 10 percent of the profits; (3) Darby will invest $35 million in building the manufacturing facility, and these costs will be recovered over a 5-year period; and (4) the government in Beijing will guarantee that at least 100,000 phones are sold every year, or it will purchase the difference.

The Darby management is not sure whether this is a good deal. In particular, Darby executives have heard all sorts of horror stories regarding agreements that the Chinese government has made and then broken. The company also is concerned that once its technology is understood, the Chinese will walk away from the agreement and start making these phones on their own. Because the technology is not state-of-the-art, the real benefit is in the low production costs, and this knowledge is more difficult to protect.

For its part, the Chinese government has promised to sign a written contract with Darby, and it has agreed that any disputes regarding enforcement of this contract can be brought, by either side, to the World Court at the Hague for resolution. Should this course of action be taken, each side would be responsible for its own legal fees, but the Chinese have promised to accept the decision of the court as binding.

Darby has 30 days to decide whether to sign the contract with the Chinese. After this time, the Chinese intend to pursue negotiations with a large telecommunications firm in Europe and try cutting a deal with them. Darby is more attractive to the Chinese, however, because of the low cost of producing its telephone. In any event, the Chinese are determined to begin mass producing cellular phones in their country. "Our future is tied to high-tech communication," the Chinese Minister of Finance recently told Darby's president. "That is why we are so anxious to do business with your company; you have quality phones at low cost." Darby management is flattered by these kind words but still not sure if this is the type of business deal in which it wants to get involved.

1. How important is the political environment in China for the Darby Company? Explain.
2. If a disagreement arises between the two joint-venture partners and the government of China reneges on its promises, how well protected is Darby's position? Explain.
3. Are the economic and technological environments in China favorable for Darby? Why, or why not?

CHAPTER 2 ENDNOTES

1. Joyce Barnathan et al., "Will Power Struggle Spell Paralysis?" *BusinessWeek*, February 6, 1995, pp. 52–54.
2. William Safire, "China's 'Four Fears,'" *New York Times*, May 22, 1995, p. A11.
3. Seth Faison, "Fighting Piracy and Frustration in China," *New York Times*, May 17, 1995, pp. C1, C8.
4. Pete Engardio, Dexter Roberts, and Bruce Einhorn, "China's New Elite," *BusinessWeek*, June 5, 1995, pp. 48–49.
5. "Europe's Diminished Leaders," *Economist*, January 21, 1995, pp. 51–53.
6. John Rossant, "Political Pandemonium Could Fracture Italy's Economy," *BusinessWeek*, January 9, 1995, p. 51.
7. Craig R. Whitney, "Chirac Assures Kohl on Europe's Monetary Policy," *New York Times*, May 22, 1995, p. A3.
8. Also see Craig R. Whitney, "French Annoyance at the U.S. Comes in Several Courses," *New York Times*, June 4, 1995, p. E6.
9. "The Wrong Man for Russia," *Economist*, January 7, 1995, pp. 13–14.
10. See "The Chechen Trap," *Economist*, January 7, 1995, pp. 39–40; Peter Galuszka and Geoff Winestock, "Who's Puling the Strings at the Kremlin?" *BusinessWeek*, January 16, 1995, p. 59.
11. "Democracy's Secret Enemies," *Economist*, March 4, 1995, p. 54.
12. "The Rise of the New Right," *Economist*, January 28, 1995, p. 23.
13. "Bazaar Politics," *Economist*, September 9, 1995, pp. 55–56.
14. "Walesa's Return," *Economist*, March 18, 1995, p. 54.
15. "A Phoenix Phenomenon," *Economist*, February 25, 1995, pp. 52–53.
16. "Tired Of Capitalism? So Soon?" *Economist*, January 21, 1995, p. 61.
17. Abbass F. Alkhafaji, *Competitive Global Management: Principles and Strategies* (Delray Beach, FL: St. Lucie Press, 1995), p. 382.
18. More details on these principles can be found in Anant K. Sundaram and J. Stewart Black, *The International Business Environment: Text and Cases* (Englewood Cliffs, NJ: Prentice-Hall, 1995), pp. 120–122.
19. Kate Gillespie, "Middle East Response to the U.S. Foreign Corrupt Practices Act," *California Management Review*, Summer 1987, p. 9.
20. John Graham, "Foreign Corruption Practices Act: A Manager's Guide," *California Management Review*, Summer 1987, p. 9.
21. Gillespie, "Middle East Response," p. 28.
22. Also see Nicholas D. Kristof, "Dutchman Strikes Chord in a Less Confident Japan," *New York Times*, June 4, 1995, p. Y40.
23. "The Next Target in Japan," *Economist*," February 18, 1995, pp. 29–30.
24. Robert Neff, "Why Japanese Deregulation Won't Much Help America," *BusinessWeek*, April 3, 1995, p. 72.
25. Brian Bremner, "Fraying Nerves in Tokyo," *BusinessWeek*, April 24, 1995, p. 50.
26. Gail Edmondson et al., "Bonn's Telecom Bombshell," *BusinessWeek*, February 13, 1995, pp. 54–55.
27. Ibid., p. 55.
28. "Foreign Investment and the Triad," *Economist*, August 24, 1991, p. 57.
29. Rosabeth Moss Kanter, *World Class* (New York: Simon & Schuster, 1995), p. 22.
30. "Counter-Revolution." *Economist*, December 3, 1994, p. 23.
31. Ibid., p. 24.
32. See Fred Luthans and Sang M. Lee, "There Are Lessons to Be Learned as Albania Undergoes a Paradigm Shift," *The International Journal of Organizational Analysis*, January 1994, pp. 5–17.
33. "War of the Worlds," *Economist*, October 1, 1994, p. 4.
34. Ibid., p. 13.
35. Michael J. Marquardt and Dean W. Engel, *Global Human Resource Management* (Englewood Cliffs, NJ: Prentice-Hall, 1993), p. 296.

36. "So Much for the Cashless Society," *Economist,* November 26, 1994, pp. 21–22.

37. See Kelley Holland and Amy Cortese, "The Future of Money," *BusinessWeek,* June 12, 1995, pp. 66–78.

38. Ibid., p. 23.

39. See "In Peru, A Cellular Revolution," *Miami Herald,* May 22, 1995, p. 6A.

40. "Private Numbers," *Economist,* February 4, 1995, p. 60.

41. Ibid.

GLOBAL COMPETITIVENESS: ANYBODY, ANYWHERE, ANYTIME, ANYWAY

OBJECTIVES OF THE CHAPTER

As MNCs continue to expand their operations and begin to do business in every part of the globe, the competitive pressures will mount. In the type of environment outlined in Chapter 2, all MNCs must become increasingly competitive, if only to protect their home turf. They must be able to compete with anybody, anywhere, anytime, and anyway (the "Four Any's"). Being third or fourth in an industry or the world market in this competitive environment is not sufficient in the long run. Organizations must strive to be the best: a world-class organization (WCO).

The overriding objective of this chapter is to examine how MNCs are trying to become WCOs. First, attention is given to the issues of quality and how total quality management (TQM) is trying to develop the highest-quality goods and services anywhere. Next, the discussion shifts beyond total quality management to learning organizations and their major characteristics. Finally, the characteristics of WCOs and some specific, real-world examples of how some MNCs are becoming WCOs are considered. These MNCs are able to compete with anybody, anywhere, anytime, anyway. The specific objectives of this chapter are:

1. **DESCRIBE** the importance of quality in helping multinational organizations in Four Any's competitiveness.

2. **IDENTIFY** and **DISCUSS** the characteristics of total quality management (TQM).

3. **DEFINE** learning organizations and their key characteristics.

4. **DESCRIBE** the major pillars of world-class organizations (WCOs) and how these pillars are critical in Four Any's competitiveness.

THE TOTAL QUALITY ISSUE

Total quality has emerged as a—if not the—major issue for MNCs in the 1990s. One major reason is because in the international marketplace customers do not care who provides the goods and services they want; they simply want their expectations to be met or exceeded. This is why auto consumers across the world now pay little attention to where the company is headquartered. International consumers are more concerned that the autos perform well, have few (if any) mechanical defects, last a long time, and are competitively priced, than whether the firm is Japanese, Korean, U.S. or German based. The same is true for many other products, from cameras and televisions to computers and video laser disks. To meet or exceed customer expectations, at minimum the MNC must give attention to total quality. A technology paradox is inherent in this total quality emphasis, however, and of course, innovation takes on new importance.

The Technology Paradox Facing MNCs

A *paradox* is a statement that appears to be contradictory but is not. For example, when Motorola began developing a worldwide strategy for its cellular telephones and pagers, it faced the "quality versus cost" dilemma. If the firm increased the quality of its products to unprecedented levels, would their price not become prohibitive? For years, engineers contended that it would, and they explained this idea in terms of a "bath tub" diagram, an example of which is provided in Figure 3-1. As the number of failures is reduced, the cost of achieving these quality levels goes up dramatically. As a result, the company at first attempted to balance quality and cost by producing products that offered "sufficient" quality and fairly low price.

By the early 1980s, however, Motorola began to challenge this thinking by asking: How much will it cost to increase quality to ever-higher levels? In particular, the MNC decided to reduce the number of errors to as low a level as possible and compute the cost of producing these quality products. In doing so, Motorola engineers began measuring quality in terms of defective parts per million. This answer can be expressed in terms of sigma, and the higher the sigma, the lower the number of defects per million parts. Here are four examples:

Sigma	Errors per million
3	66,810.0
4	6,210.0
5	233.0
6	3.4

Now Motorola began to examine the costs associated with these various levels of sigma. As the error rate fell, so did the cost of producing the product. Figure 3-2 shows this graphically. Clearly, what this amazingly showed was that quality and cost are inversely related! In other words, MNCs that produce quality products can do so at a lower cost per unit than for products with higher error rates. The reason that so many MNCs did not see this relationship earlier is that they were blind-sided by the old quality/cost paradox.

FIGURE 3-1

THE QUALITY/COST CURVE AS INITIALLY PERCEIVED

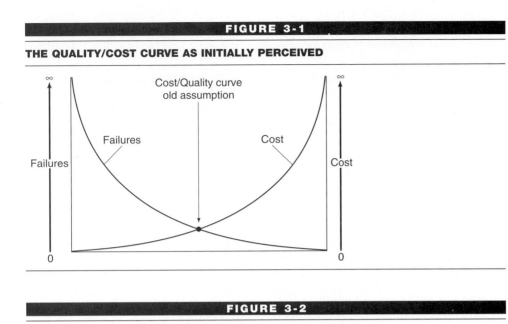

FIGURE 3-2

QUALITY/COST CURVE AS DETERMINED THROUGH RESEARCH

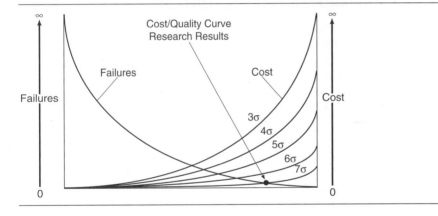

Technology also presents MNCs with a paradox, but this one is far more significant. For many years, multinational firms believed that new technology could be exploited best by getting to the market first and charging premium prices. Now, however, they are learning that perhaps the best way to exploit their advantage is to lower prices as quickly as possible. The lower price helps them to grow international market share and substantially increase their revenues and profits. In fact, in many cases, MNCs now are even giving away their technology or selling it at a very low price, because the follow-on market is where the most profits are generated. For example, the Japanese MNC Toshiba will not earn back the investment poured into its digital-movie player through sales of this piece of equipment; however, it likely will more than recover its money by selling spinoff products, such as high-capacity audio players, storage devices for laptop computers, and other products that use related technology.[1] Similarly, Teleport Communications Group Inc. will install a dozen optical fibers with 1 million times more capacity than a customer needs, at no extra charge, because this MNC realizes optical fibers are so inexpensive that it makes sense to install enough capacity to last a lifetime. Sooner or later, the customer will begin using this added capacity.

The Toshiba and Teleport examples illustrate the *technology paradox:* high-tech MNCs can thrive at the very moment their prices are falling the fastest. As George Fisher, past CEO of Motorola and now head of Eastman Kodak, puts it, "The only thing that matters is if the exponential growth of your market is faster than the exponential decline of your prices."[2] Today, successful MNCs are less interested in developing a single product than they are in creating a technology allowing them to develop a series of interrelated products that provide them with entry into an increasing number of markets around the world. Informed observers explain this new development as follows:

> Successful strategists soak out costs, cut prices, and then wait for business to roll in. Step 1 is a price decline—say, in DRAM chips. At first it causes chaos, as in the early 1980s, when American producers fled the DRAM market amid cries of Japanese dumping. In Step 2, the market finds a new use for the cheap resource. Case in point: Windows software, which is ubiquitous and gobbles megabytes of DRAMs. Unit prices of the chips may fall, but gross revenue soars—a point that is lost on those who once again predict doom for commodity chipmakers. The next wave of chip demand will come from the likes of computers that obey spoken commands and communicate in 3-D images. After that? Believable virtual reality and intelligent artificial intelligence.[3]

Successful MNCs understand the impact of the technology paradox, and they are prepared to pursue international market share by competing anytime and anywhere through creating total quality products. These products' "technology architecture" allows for the development or integration of many other products. For example, personal computer makers know their success would be greatly limited if all they did was sell these machines; however, by combining other value-added features, such as software, trouble shooting, and training, they can add to their initial package and keep their product from becoming a generic offering sold strictly on price. Additionally, in the case of firms such as Dell Computer, these machines can be tailor-made to meet the expectations of international customers. This strategy, commonly referred to as *mass customization,* helps to maintain product uniqueness and prevents the machine from being viewed as a generic offering. A major part of the success equation remains the MNC's ability to develop and maintain its innovative capacity.

The Innovation Challenge Facing MNCs

Michael Porter has emphasized that the key to successful multinational efforts in global competitive battles is the ability to innovate continually.[4] This has been especially true for the most successful MNCs. For example, 3M generates 30 percent of its annual revenues from products that were brought to market in the last 4 years, and the number of patents issued to the MNC annually continues to increase. In 1990, it received 350,000 patents; by 1994, this had risen to over 500,000.[5] At the same time, 3M has managed to accelerate the product cycle by reducing cost and waste and bringing their products to fruition in record time. One way in which this is accomplished is through vast databases that allow employees bureaucracy-free access to company experts in each of its diverse technologies; in this way, one good idea is more likely to team up with another. The company also brings in outside experts, and it encourages scientists to present innovations to their peers, thus increasing the opportunities for cross-fertilization. Despite this drive for innovation, 3M also never loses sight of its customers, and this is noted in one report as follows:

> At the same time, 3M's inventors are getting closer to its customers, whose needs and preferences have sometimes taken second place to the firm's obsessive quest for innovation. Now customer preferences are constantly reassessed at each stage of a new product's development. Marketing folk have been moved closer to scientists: R&D staff are now more closely involved in overall product strategy. "Cross-functional" teams abound. To squeeze every last product out of each innovation, says Mr. Coyne [head of R&D], the company must empower every employee. "Managers must set goals, then get out of the way."[6]

The approaches of other successful MNCs in developing total quality products often are quite similar. One such approach to stimulate innovation involves having a vision. The MNC will develop an idea of how the market will look in the future, then create products or services based on this vision. For example, Canon of Japan envisioned a world in which photocopiers were small, cheap, and ubiquitous, then used this vision to drive its developmental and production strategies. Harley-Davidson has its senior-level executives spend time in the field with bikers, visiting rallies, and discussing with customers what they like about their bikes and what changes they would like to see. Epson, which is world famous for its small printers, has its young engineers spend 6 months as salespeople, and then 6 months in the service department, so they can learn directly what the customer wants and expects.

Another approach commonly used by MNCs in their relentless effort to develop innovative products is the effective use of **benchmarking.** This is the process of identifying what leading-edge competitors are doing, then using information to produce improved products or services. Among the best MNCs, benchmarking often entails competing against oneself and producing products that outmode those the MNC sells currently. A good example is Raychem, a U.S. firm that for years has focused on supplying technology-intensive products to customers throughout the industrial world.

> One of its best-selling products was a system for sealing splices in telephone cables. The product generated over $125 million annually and the customers were happy with it. However, Raychem introduced a new splice-closure technology that tremendously improved performance. Today the firm is converting customers to the new technology and has stopped manufacturing the old product. As a result, competitors who were working on developing a product to compete with Raychem's original product have found that they must start all over again.[7]

Still another innovative approach is **product proliferation,** which involves the creation of a wide array of products that the competition cannot copy quickly enough. Additionally, as the firm begins offering different versions of a product, the customer often becomes confused and is not sure which is the best buy. As a result, the company offering the large number of products often succeeds, because it gains market share at the expense of its competitors, which offer far fewer products. Moreover, this process of creating new versions of current products is ongoing; for example, Canon started planning its second-generation personal copier before the first had even come off the assembly line.[8]

Quality Pays Off for MNCs

Besides recognizing the technology paradox and creating a climate of innovation, quality goods and services simply pay off. The following sections examine some specific examples of the importance of quality.

Auto Manufacturing   Auto firms that produce quality products appeal to customers throughout the world, and quality products can lead to increased market share and profits. In the United States, the Big Three Automakers (General Motors, Ford, and Chrysler) all increased quality in the 1990s, and this helped them to hold off imports, especially from Japan, in world markets. According to the J.D. Power ratings, well-known for their independent research on auto quality, General Motors had 0.99 defects per car; Ford 1.14 defects, and Chrysler 1.37 defects in 1995. These numbers represented improvements in quality over the 1980s, but they still were not as good as those of their Japanese competitors.[9] For instance, Chrysler's defect rate was nearly twice that of Honda and Toyota.[10] The Honda Prelude had just 0.48 defects per car, and the Toyota Lexus LS 400 luxury sedan had a mere 0.51 defects per car.

It will be difficult for American manufacturers to meet these outstanding quality levels, but they must try in this competitive market. One strategy has been to start from scratch and do it right, as in the case of Saturn, which has done well. Another has been to replace old car lines with new ones. GM emphasized the completely redesigned Chevrolet Lumina and Chevrolet Cavalier, both of which had far fewer defects than the previous versions they replaced, and this helped to drive up GM's average overall quality.

Aircraft Manufacturing   Another example that quality pays is Boeing, the giant commercial aircraft manufacturer. Boeing has been known for its quality aircraft, and this is paying off in international sales. The MNC recently announced a combined order from five Asian airlines including Cathay Pacific Airlines, Japan Air Lines, Korean Airlines, All Nippon Airways, and Thai International Airways, for more than 30 of the company's 777 stretch jet. These orders officially launched production of the firm's new 368-passenger plane, the 777-300X, which is a larger-capacity variant of Boeing's two-engine 777 airliner. In addition to these 30 orders, Boeing also received orders from Eva Airways and China Airways of Taiwan, United Parcel Service, Lauda Air, Eurobelgian, Air Europa, and Saudia, the Saudi Arabian state-run carrier.

At the same time, other high-quality airplane builders from others parts of the world are becoming more competitive with Boeing. Airbus Industrie of Europe, the second-largest aircraft manufacturer, recently announced that it had landed orders for 20 A-319s from Lufthansa and 10 more from Air Canada; the total value of this deal was $1.1 billion. U.S.-based McDonnell Douglas, the world's third-largest aircraft maker, announced orders for 33 MD-90s and MD-11s from Saudia (29 of the firm's passenger airliners, and 4 of its big freighters). In all of these cases, orders were based on proven track records that showed the MNC was able to deliver a high-quality, cost-effective product.[11]

Asian Services   Still another good example of how quality pays off is Asia's infant service industry, which now is preparing for international competition. When

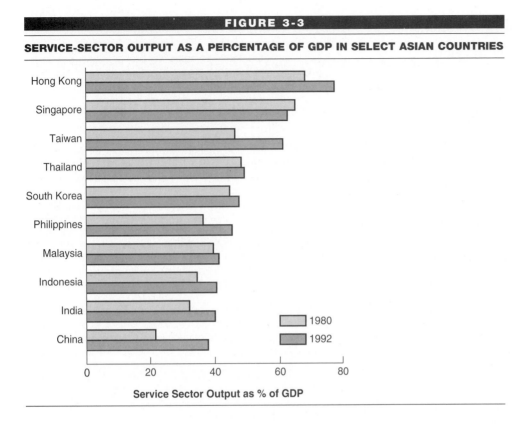

FIGURE 3-3

SERVICE-SECTOR OUTPUT AS A PERCENTAGE OF GDP IN SELECT ASIAN COUNTRIES

Service Sector Output as % of GDP

most people think of Asia, they picture countries that produce competitive manufactured products; however, these countries also are becoming very competitive in the services area. For example, the national airlines of Malaysia, Singapore, and Thailand regularly top the quality-service rankings in polls of international businesspeople. So, too, do Asian hotel groups such as the Shangri-La and Mandarin Oriental chains. Now an increasing number of Asian governments and businesses hope to build on such successes and create a service sector that is just as competitive as their manufacturing sector.

In particular, as Asian countries have become wealthier, they have devoted an increasing portion of their economies to services (see Figure 3-3), while manufacturing jobs have moved to their poorer neighbors. In the case of Hong Kong, there were 1.5 million manufacturing workers in the Kowloon area in 1980, by 1995, however, this number had declined to around 600,000. Today, Hong Kong is a city devoted to service industries such as finance, marketing, and design; and other Asian economies, such as Singapore and even Thailand, are following a similar route.

The government of Thailand is trying to make Bangkok the financial and transport hub for Indochina, and Singapore now is marketing itself as a headquarters for firms operating as far away as India and China. Singapore also is competing aggressively with Hong Kong to become a regional base for the satellite broadcasters who are zooming into the region. Even China is trying to follow this route, emphasizing the service sector of the economy and not allowing itself to become

INTERNATIONAL MANAGEMENT IN ACTION

Where's the Quality Service in Deutschland?

Service productivity is on the rise in a number of countries, most notably the United States and Asia, and one of the major issues this raises deals with the loss of employment. For example, many who are employed in the traditionally labor-intensive service sector now are being let go in the name of efficiency and increased service productivity. Will this downsizing become a worldwide development, resulting in massive unemployment? This is unlikely, but one thing is certain: Among those countries where service productivity does not increase, there likely will be an influx of outside competition. A good example is Germany (Deutschland).

Conventional wisdom holds that the Germans are industrious, efficient, and hard-working people. This does not always seem to carry over into their service sector, however. Consider the case of Deutsche Telekom (DT), the nation's phone monopoly. Everyone in the country seems to have their own story about poor telephone service. One favorite is the woman who waited 23 years to get a phone in old East Germany and, after unification, is now in her second year of waiting for one from DT. This contrasts sharply with the United States, where most people can get a new line installed in a few days at most, and they pay much lower rates than those charged by the German phone company.

While DT is a very visable example, it is by no means the only firm that has poor service in Germany. Many German retail establishments also provide notoriously bad service: customers who walk in near closing time often are greeted by rude stares from the clerks. Some restaurants still refuse to take credit cards as well.

Even so, the phone company still probably deserves the vocal criticism. Here are some of the facts. In terms of productivity, NTT of Japan has 42.4 employees per 10,000 phone lines, and the U.S. Baby Bells average 43.2 per 10,000. Deutsche Telekom has 62.6 employees per 10,000 phones lines, a number higher than that in any other major EU power. For example, over 20 years ago, France launched a massive digitalization effort and significantly increased its productivity. British Telecom PLC, the former phone monopoly, also began modernizing and has cut its work force by almost 50 percent since 1988.

What can German customers do about this? One step that many German businesses are taking is to find alternative sources. The giant German chemical firm BASF AG has switched to British Telecom for all of its international service, and it saves between 15 and 60 percent on each call. On the other hand, individual customers have no alternative but to use the German service. This undoubtedly helps to explain why the average German makes only 600 calls a year, compared with the average U.S. citizen who makes over three times this number.

The good news for Germans is that the telephone monopoly is coming to an end and DT is undertaking a massive TQM effort. Also, as new competitors enter the market, quality of service undoubtedly will increase sharply. The bad news is that these new entrants likely will pick the most lucrative market niches and ignore the rest. This means that large German businesses, which spend thousands of dollars on telephone calls, will be targeted; the average customer will be far down the list.

At least in the short run, German customers may still be asking, "Where's the quality service?" In the long run, however, DT's quality efforts should begin to pay off.

a mere Mecca for low-tech, labor-intensive factories scattered around the countryside.

Because of such activity throughout Asia, the total trade in services of the 10 largest Asian economies increased almost 300 percent in the last 10 years. Much of this was accounted for by small firms, and many Asian governments have been slow to open up their service industries to foreign competition. This is slowly beginning to change, however, because governments realize that if they are going to have other industries such as manufacturing compete worldwide, they must withstand international competition for their service industry as well. As a result, Thailand has granted a number of banking licenses to foreign firms, the Philippine government has concluded that it cannot revamp its domestic telephone system without outside help and allowed a number of foreign firms into this marketplace, and India has opened cellular and basic telephone service to foreign investors.

These developments all point to the fact that if countries close themselves to outside competition, they will be unable to compete worldwide. This is because

FIGURE 3-4

NEW PARADIGM ORGANIZATIONS

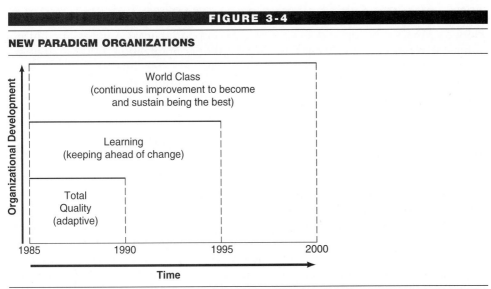

Source: Fred Luthans, Richard Hodgetts, and Sang M. Lee, "New Paradigm Organizations: From Total Quality to Learning to World-Class," *Organizational Dynamics*, Winter 1994, p. 10. Used with permission of the publisher, © 1994. American Management Association, New York. All rights reserved.

they become isolated and fail to develop state-of-the-art goods and services. By opening their markets to the outside world, Asian nations are able to attract MNCs that place a premium on knowledge, technology, and capital. Additionally, while these MNCs are anxious to sell things such as environmental services, computer software, and health care, these outputs also help Asian nations to develop low-tech services industries, such as retailing. One recent report notes that:

> In retailing, for example, the ties made by Goldlion, a firm based in Hong Kong, are as hot in China as those produced by any Paris fashion house. Five Hong Kong firms—Lane Crawford, a department store; two supermarket chains, Dairy Farm and A.S. Watson; and two clothing chains, Esprit Asia and Giordano—have with varying degrees of success opened stores in others parts of the region. Giordana has stressed customer service. The firm encourages its staff to be friendly (in Hong Kong they even smile), and it accepts returns, something almost unheard of in Asia retailing. Esprit Asia's chairman, Michael Ying, originally worked as a supply scout for Esprit's San Francisco headquarters before acquiring marketing rights for the brand in Asia.[12]

Service is becoming as important as manufacturing as economies grow around the world. If this does not happen, both developed and developing countries eventually will find their growth being severely limited. "International Management in Action: Where's the Quality Service in Deutschland?" examines the traditionally ignored, but now recognized, importance of customer service in Germany.

What are MNCs doing to develop and sustain a competitive edge? They employ a number of strategies that best can be summarized in terms of three stages or paradigm shifts through which organizations must progress to compete in today's Four Any's environment. Figure 3-4 illustrates these: from total quality, adaptive organizations to anticipative learning organizations to being simply the best, world-class organizations (WCOs).

TOTAL QUALITY AND LEARNING ORGANIZATIONS

How do MNCs develop and sustain world competitiveness? A necessary, but not sufficient, requirement is becoming a total quality organization. In these dramatically changing times, it also is necessary to go one step further and become a learning organization. The following discussion examines the overall nature and specifics of both total quality and learning organizations.

Total Quality MNCs

By the early 1980s, the quality of many Japanese products (e.g., autos and electronics) began to increase sharply, and as a result Japanese MNCs began to gain significant worldwide market share. In response to this Japanese competitiveness, U.S. MNCs in particular began to examine their own operating procedures and to identify perspectives, approaches, and techniques that could help them to become more competitive. Becoming a total quality organization involved a number of important operating changes. Some of the most significant included vision formulation, empowerment, and benchmarking.

Vision Formulation   To be able to compete with anybody, anywhere, anytime, anyway, U.S. MNCs started by defining their vision of quality. What did the term mean to them? What core values were needed to support a total quality organization? What direction would the program take to implement total quality? While answering these types of questions, MNCs carefully began to formulate their vision of quality. Here are examples of vision statements from Xerox and Motorola, two American multinationals that have successfully moved to total quality organizations:[13]

Xerox
Xerox is a quality company. Quality is the basic business principle for Xerox. Quality means providing external and internal customers with innovative products and services that fully satisfy their requirements. Quality improvement is the job of every Xerox employee.

Motorola
Dedication to quality is a way of life at our company, so much so that it goes far beyond rhetorical slogans. Our ongoing program of continued improvement reaches out for change, refinement and even revolution in our pursuit of quality excellence. It is the objective of Motorola, Inc., to produce and provide products and services of the highest quality. In its activities, Motorola will pursue goals aimed at the achievement of quality excellence. These results will be derived from the dedicated efforts of each employee in conjunction with supportive participation from management at all levels of the corporation.

The purpose of such vision statements is to provide direction for the organization's total quality efforts.

Empowerment   Total quality organizations empower their people. *Empowerment* can be defined as the process of giving employees the resources, information, and authority needed to carry out their jobs effectively. Empowerment helps total quality organizations to flatten their structures, decentralize authority to the lowest possible levels, and allow employees who interact directly with customers to have the necessary information and make the decisions needed to deliver quality service that meets or exceeds customer expectations.[14]

Motorola again provides a good example of empowerment. This MNC has created empowered teams that have helped to flatten the structure as well as get things done both faster and less expensively. In fact, empowerment recently has resulted in reductions of inventory, processing time, and overtime hours, while increasing the volume handled, improving customer service, and helping to create greater profits. Some of the steps that Motorola used in achieving these results include: (1) setting clear goals for all employees; (2) using state-of-the-art business systems and process technology; (3) redesigning jobs, classifications, and compensation; (4) carefully selecting people for all jobs; (5) training employees in all the major skills required for their work (Motorola spends about $100 million and requires a minimum of 40 hours of training per employee per year)[15]; (6) allowing work teams to schedule assignments; (7) using group problem-solving approaches, including functional, cross-functional, and ad hoc teams; and (8) ensuring timely and complete feedback on results.[16]

A major prerequisite for empowerment is that people are trained to handle the situation. Empowered teams at Motorola are trained extensively on both hard-side (technical, engineering) and soft-side (interpersonal relations, customer service) skills. As a result, team members learn how to handle their own situations, leading to greater productivity and quality. They create production schedules and job assignments, set up equipment and conduct routine maintenance, develop and manage budgets, and train new employees.

Benchmarking   Benchmarking is the process of comparing a company's current performance with that of organizations that are judged to be the "best in class." In this way, total quality MNCs find out where they are doing extremely well and where the competition has a lead on them. They focus on the gaps and begin studying and developing action plans to close them. In the case of Motorola, the success of its benchmarking effort is evident from its six sigma program. By driving down the defect rate to under 3.4 errors per million, the company has emerged as a world-class manufacturer.

IBM Rochester, who won the coveted Baldrige Award (the U.S. quality award) is another example. The AS/400 minicomputer proved to be one of the MNC's most successful product launches ever, thanks to effective benchmarking. IBM Rochester did this by examining the design and production processes of best practices within other divisions of IBM and other firms throughout the world. They gained valuable information regarding defect-prevention processes, effective use of service representatives, just-in-time inventory, and hardware-process documentation.

Areas discussed in the preceding sections—vision formulation, empowerment, and benchmarking—are characteristics of total quality MNCs. Important as it is, it recently has become evident in today's highly competitive world environment that total quality is just the cost of entry. MNCs now also must continue to learn and get progressively better; they must anticipate change and learn how to learn. In others words, MNCs today and in the future must become learning organizations.

MNCs as Learning Organizations

Increasingly common are MNCs that achieve quality and excellence but then slip back either because they were too slow in keeping up with needed changes or did not anticipate changes.[17] These MNCs typically are referred to as *adaptive organizations,* which are characterized by reaction to required changes but a failure to anticipate and stay on or ahead of the cutting edge. Those MNCs such as Motorola or Sony that do succeed in keeping ahead are learning organizations.

A *learning organization* is able to transform itself by anticipating change and discovering new ways of creating products and services; it has learned how to learn. Kodak is a good example. Under George Fisher, the former head of Motorola, this MNC is changing direction and engaging in large-scale experimentation with new technologies that move across the boundaries of traditional silver-based film and into the area of electronic photography, now possible by high-resolution imaging. Importantly, Kodak also is focusing on digital technology, which it anticipates will be the wave of the future.

Another example of an MNC that is a learning organization is Gruppo GFT, the world's largest manufacturer of designer clothing. Unlike its competitors, who tend to view the world market in terms of standardized apparel with universal appeal, GFT focuses on designing products in response to a host of local differences in key markets. This MNC learned the needs of those markets and anticipated appropriately—redefining the way it did business in the process. In other words, GFT learned how to learn; and they anticipated the needed changes.

Three common characteristics of learning organizations are openness, creativity, and personal efficacy.[18] The following discussion examines each of these, and Table 3–1 provides additional comparisons between MNCs that are traditional adaptive and generative learning organizations.[19]

Openness   Learning organizations not only are prepared to accept new trends, they encourage and anticipate changes. Rather than fight change, they learn how to accommodate, create, and profit from it. Although the chapters in Part II on the cultural context will point out the need to understand and apply concepts such as openness differently across cultures, MNCs that are learning organizations will in general try to suspend their need to control all aspects of operations as well as the people who run the place and interact with customers. Their managers empower associates, flatten the structure, and allow flexibility on everything; they examine their core values and try to identify how these must change for the MNC to grow and prosper.

Whirlpool is a good example. Several years ago, this MNC analyzed its markets and structure, and it concluded that the U.S. market no longer would be the largest, nor would it provide enough business for them to grow and prosper. They found that growth would come from untapped markets, such as in Central and Eastern Europe, Mexico, and Asia. Here is how the company reacted to this future world market:

> Today, Whirlpool has oriented itself to a new vision: growing a transnational company and creating value for stakeholders. To translate vision into action, the company has indicated that all its senior managers will have global experience by the year 2000. In addition, it created a joint venture with N.V. Philips to capture the European market and started joint ventures in India and Mexico. To build shared cross-cultural values, in June of 1990 Whirlpool staged a worldwide leadership conference in Montreux, Switzerland.

TABLE 3-1		

CHARACTERISTICS OF TRADITIONAL ADAPTIVE AND GENERATIVE LEARNING ORGANIZATIONS

Characteristics	Adaptive	Generative
Strategic		
Core competence	Better sameness	Meaningful difference
Source of strength	Stability	Change
Output	Market share	Market creation
Organizational perspective	Compartmentalization (SBU)	Systemic
Developmental dynamic	Change	Transformation
Structural		
Structure	Bureaucratic	Network
Control systems	Formal rules	Values, self-control
Power bases	Hierarchic position	Knowledge
Integrating mechanisms	Hierarchy	Teams
Networks	Disconnected	Strong
Communications flow	Hierarchic	Lateral
Human resource practices		
Performance appraisal system	Rewards stability	Flexibility
Reward basis	Short-term financial	Long-term financial and human resource development
Focus of rewards	Distribution of scarcity	Determination of synergy
Status symbols	Rank and title	Making a difference
Mobility patterns	Within division or function	Across divisions or functions
Mentoring	Not rewarded	Integral part of performance appraisal process
Culture	Market	Clan
Managers' behaviors		
Perspective	Controlling	Openness
Problem-solving orientation	Narrow	Systemic thinking
Response style	Conforming	Creative
Personal Control	Blame and acceptance	Efficacious
Commitment	Ethnocentric	Empathetic

Source: Michael E. McGill, John W. Slocum, Jr., and David Lei, "Management Practices in Learning Organizations," *Organizational Dynamics,* Summer 1992, p. 14. Used with permission of the publisher, © 1992. American Management Association, New York. All rights reserved.

One-hundred forty managers got to know each other and understand each others' cultural backgrounds. To achieve a "one company" culture, it established fifteen cross-national-functional teams to establish and implement specific plans of action.[20]

Creativity   Of all the requisite skills and abilities for learning, creativity is the most widely and readily acknowledged, and two of the most important aspects of creativity are critical to effective learning: personal flexibility, and a willingness to take risks. MNCs that are learning organizations nurture and promote both of these dimensions.

In the case of flexibility, MNCs such as Emerson, General Electric, and RCA missed the boat in their analysis of changes in the radio market. They believed that sales would follow a natural growth curve, eventually reach maturity and

INTERNATIONAL MANAGEMENT IN ACTION

Bit Players Bite the Dust

Keeping up with the competition can be difficult, especially for small MNCs that lack the resources and flexibility to change quickly. Small Japanese exporters that in recent years have found their competitiveness being slowly eroded provide a good example.

For many of these small MNCs the downhill slide began when the Japanese yen started rising against the U.S. dollar. As exports to the United States and other countries that were tied to the dollar became more expensive for buyers, Japanese MNCs, large and small, quickly realized they needed to control costs. Many of Japan's small manufacturing firms are suppliers to large MNCs such as Toyota, Nissan, and Sony, and they soon found these giant MNCs beginning to demand that products be produced at a lower price.

In the last decade, thousands of small Japanese enterprises have been driven out of business. One primary reason is that these small companies borrowed large sums of money during the early 1990s to upgrade their equipment and remain state-of-the-art for their big domestic customers. This strategy appeared to be very effective, because it meant these firms would be able to design, develop, and manufacture all sorts of output, from specialized machine parts to high-tech components. However, this

strategy was premised on the companies continuing to garner orders from their giant customers. As the yen's value increased sharply and the large Japanese MNCs saw that the only way to protect their overseas markets was by remaining price competitive, these giant customers began demanding that their suppliers cut prices or lose their business—and this is exactly what happened to many of them. As an example, one small firm that made lenses and other camera parts found that when it could no longer drive down prices, the orders stopped coming. At its peak, this company made 5000 lenses a month, but this eventually dropped to under 2000 and the firm had trouble surviving. In the case of run-of-the-mill parts, many Japanese MNCs found they could easily replace their domestic producers by outsourcing to cheaper, offshore resources. As a result, Ricoh, the big Japanese office-equipment MNC, now imports 10 percent of its parts from China and other low-cost world locations, in contrast to the 2 percent the MNC used to purchase just a few years ago.

Those small Japanese manufacturers that have survived and prospered have market niches where more sophisticated parts and components are needed and face very limited competition. In these markets, the small firms are not bit players. They are mainstream competitors, and this makes all the difference for their present survival. However, they also must anticipate future changes and learn how to learn. In other words, they must become learning organizations.

decline. In contrast, learning organizations such as Sony were highly flexible and saw a variety of different, alternative possibilities for the radio. Sony believed that it could alter the product life cycle through creative innovation; the result was the Sony Walkman, which changed how, where, and when people listened to radios. MNCs lacking the flexibility to anticipate and make such changes end up losing out. Examples are provided in the accompanying "International Management in Action: Bit Players Bite The Dust."

In the case of risk-taking, many MNCs are losing out because they remain overly conservative. Japanese automakers conducted marketing research in the United States and found no support from U.S. customers for minivans. As a result, they decided not to enter this market. Chrysler also conducted marketing research and received the same results, but this MNC was convinced there was a market for these vehicles and decided to take the risk. This decision proved to be one of the most profitable in Chrysler's history, helping the firm to attain record annual profits.

Personal Efficacy A psychologic characteristic of confidence, *personal efficacy* is defined as the belief that one both can and should learn to influence significantly the world in which one lives. Learning organizations promote such personal efficacy by teaching their associates self-awareness and active problem-solving.

Self-awareness is fostered by a clear organizational vision that gives direction regarding critical choices and provides feedback about results. In particular, associates are taught to actively seek information about the impact of their behavior on others, and on issues that are important to others, as a means of maximizing their own effectiveness. In other words, "information seeking" is turning out to be an important characteristic of effective employees in learning organizations. At Whirlpool, for example, the assessment of managerial talent is multiple and conducted on a worldwide basis. They conduct what are termed "360 (degrees) evaluations," which include self-assessments as well as assessments from peers, subordinates, direct supervisors, and managers a level above one's own supervisor. These 360 assessments are not performance reviews per se. Instead, they focus on people's potential and capability, and they help individuals to understand themselves better. Most often, only the target individual, not his or her boss, receives the feedback.

Proactive problem-solving is used to teach managers how to anticipate and deal with issues before they become serious. Managers also learn how to prevent these problems from recurring. For example, IBM used to rely on customer feedback to help identify service problems. The MNC eventually discovered, however, that most customers who are dissatisfied with service do not fill out questionnaire surveys—they simply stop doing business with the firm. Now, IBM handles customer problems proactively by contacting customers who have stopped doing business with them and finding out what went wrong and how they can win back this customer.

WORLD-CLASS ORGANIZATIONS

Today, the very best MNCs are going beyond even the learning organization and have become what can be called "world-class organizations." *World-class organizations (WCOs)* are enterprises that are able to compete with anybody, anywhere, anytime, anyway. In most cases, WCOs have operations throughout the globe. Motorola and Sony, discussed so far as total quality and learning organizations, are also WCOs, but so are MNCs such as Hewlett-Packard, Kodak, Honda, and Xerox. In a few cases, WCOs may focus heavily on only one geographic locale and have only limited worldwide operations; examples here include the Ritz-Carlton Hotel chain, Wainwright Industries, and Wal-Mart. In either case, WCOs are able to compete effectively against all comers, whether foreign or domestic.

To become a WCO, an organization must excel in a number of dimensions that in both an additive and synergistic way, create a new level of competitive excellence that goes beyond the total quality and learning organizations. Figure 3-5 illustrates some major pillars forming the basis of WCOs.

Customer-Based Focus

WCOs are customer-driven. They have identified their internal and external customers and have determined how to serve them effectively. In doing so, WCOs tend to have flat structures, so that everyone can be closer to the customer. Additionally, WCOs go beyond just satisfying their customers; they work very hard to delight their customers and have a bond with them. In the process, they also create new demands for their goods and services. A good example again is Sony's

---

FIGURE 3-5

SOME MAJOR PILLARS OF WORLD-CLASS ORGANIZATIONS

WORLD CLASS ORGANIZATIONS

| Customer-based focus | Continuous improvement | Fluid, flexible or "virtual organizations" | Creative HRM | Egalitarian climate | Technological support |

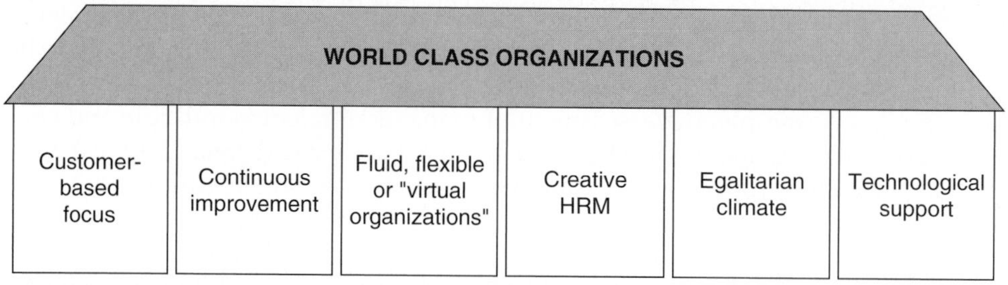

Source: Fred Luthans, Richard M. Hodgetts, and Sang M. Lee, "New Paradigm Organizations: From Total Quality to Learning to World-Class," *Organizational Dynamics*, Winter 1994, p. 15. Used with permission of the publisher, © 1994. American Management Association, New York. All rights reserved.

Walkman. The buyers were impressed not only with the innovativeness of the product but also, with the CD version, and how much value they were receiving.

Another example is Wal-Mart, which has dominated the U.S. retail market and now is beginning to make in-roads in Mexico and China, among other international markets. Focusing heavily on the customer, this firm has helped to break the old retailing model in which manufacturers would "push" their goods to retail stores and the latter in turn would push them onto customers. Wal-Mart, relying heavily on its ability to identify customer needs and negotiate competitive prices from suppliers, has created a "pull" system, in which customers buy things they need and thus pull the goods from the store. This strategy is not unique to Wal-Mart. Successful retailers in others parts of the world such as Metro International of Germany, Ito-Yokado of Japan, and Carrefour of France also employ customer-driven, market-pull strategies.

Continuous Improvement

A second distinctive characteristic of WCOs is their commitment to continuous improvement (CI). In contrast to their competitors, WCOs can improve faster, more efficiently, and more effectively. A good example is Ford Motor, which found that it took weeks to process vendor receipts because so many people had to approve the payment. By carefully studying this process, Ford was able to reduce sharply the number of individuals who needed to sign off on payments—and cut the processing time by 90 percent.

Motorola is another example of a WCO that continually has driven down its production costs and reduced the time needed to both plan and manufacture products by carefully flowcharting the process and then eliminating or combining steps. This MNC also has used CI to reduce the time needed to process an order. In the past, it took almost 11 days for order processing, because nothing was done until all the paperwork was received—and then the orders were handled in sequential order. Therefore, if a delay occurred in one step, the order went no farther until that roadblock was removed. This world class MNC now has revamped its entire approach to processing orders, set up an approval system that in most cases automatically accepts all credit requests of $5000 or less, and computerized all order entries. As a result, the average time for processing orders has been reduced to 2.7 days.[21]

Use of Flexible or Virtual Organizations

Another characteristics of WCOs is their use of flexible or virtual organizations. A *virtual organization* is one that is able to conduct business as if it were a very large enterprise with major facilities while in fact it is much smaller, made up of core business competencies with the rest outsourced. How is this possible? One major way is through outsourcing or, when taken into the international arena, global sourcing.

Global sourcing is the use of worldwide suppliers, regardless of where they are located geographically, who are best able to provide the needed output.[22] For example, Japanese automakers today rely increasingly on U.S. suppliers for their cars. Similarly, U.S. laptop computer firms rely on Japanese sources to provide screen technology. Where possible, however, MNCs prefer home-based suppliers because of the benefit this provides them in maintaining their worldwide competitive advantage. Michael Porter explains it this way:

> Perhaps the most important benefit of home-based suppliers . . . is the *process of innovation and upgrading.* Competitive advantage emerges from close working relationships between world-class suppliers and the industry. Suppliers help firms perceive new methods and opportunities to apply new technology. Firms gain quick access to information, to new ideas and insights, and to supplier innovations. They have the opportunity to influence suppliers' technical efforts, as well as to serve as test sites for development work. The exchange of R&D and joint problem solving lead to faster and more efficient solutions. Suppliers also tend to be a conduit for transmitting information and innovations from firm to firm. Through this process, the pace of innovation within the entire national industry is accelerated. All these benefits are enhanced if suppliers are located in proximity to firms, shortening the communication lines.[23]

This also helps to explain why suppliers often locate near their major customers. When Ford Motor decides to set up new facilities in Europe, its U.S.-based suppliers will locate nearby so that they can continue to work closely with the giant automaker. This strategy helps Ford to become, essentially, a virtual organization, because it does not have to produce these supplies in-house but derives the same benefits as if it did. During the remainder of this decade, an increasing number of MNCs will rely on global sourcing to provide materials and products that once were produced in-house. As a result, these companies can act like larger enterprises when in fact they are smaller and depend on outsourcing or global sourcing to take care of many of their needs.

Creative Human Resource Management

Human resources generally are acknowledged to be the most important asset for any organization. This has become especially true in recent times, when knowledge-based organizations are replacing traditional asset-based MNCs. WCOs know they must compete based on what their human resources are capable of doing rather than on mere physical assets, such as buildings, machinery, and equipment. WCOs have state-of-the-art, creative approaches to managing their human resources, and they effectively stimulate and have a supportive climate for employee creativity. More specifically, their human resource management (HRM) programs are designed to help their people share ownership of problems and solutions, achieve a strong commitment and involvement by top management, communicate consistent goals and objectives to all levels and functions in the organization, and help develop an effective use of recognition and reward programs.

There are many examples of creative HRM practices. One is the use of empowered teams with the authority to make all decisions in their own work area. For example, at the world-famous Ritz-Carlton Hotels, employees can spend up to $1000 on customer service–related matters. Another example is the creation of suggestion systems that generate new, useful ideas for better serving clients. Wainwright Industries, a small but world-class U.S. manufacturer, has a suggestion system so effective that it annually generates 55 suggestions per employee, which is sharply higher than the 12 generated by typical Japanese MNCs and the 0.3 by the typical U.S. firm.[24]

Still another example of world-class HRM involves the effective use of training programs. For instance, last year's world leader in the microchip business was Samsung, the largest *chaebol* (conglomerate) in South Korea. Besides electronics, this emerging WCO is involved in computers, software development, automotive parts, chemicals, aerospace, construction, textiles, department stores, and telecommunications. A major reason for its success is commitment to training. Here is a description of Samsung's recently launched, year-long training program for promising middle managers:

> The training program involves overseas travel to increase the managers' global perspective and cultural knowledge. The cost for each trainee exceeds $80,000 and Samsung has selected more than 1,000 managers for such training. This so-called "goof around and learn" program has become a necessary step for future promotion. This type of financial commitment to management training has dramatically enhanced the already outstanding corporate culture of Samsung.[25]

Another important aspect of WCO HRM strategy is effective recognition and monetary reward systems. In particular, WCOs ensure that rewards are positive, given openly, and highly publicized. At the Ritz-Carlton chain, any employee can send a "First Class" card—a 3" × 5" card designed with the company logo—to express his or her appreciation to anyone else in the organization for a job well done. The company also uses "Lightning Strikes"—monetary rewards granted by a member of the Executive Committee to any employee for outstanding service. In addition, individuals who submit the best ideas for improvement are listed on a bulletin board and given a dinner for two, and those who generate the greatest number of useful ideas are honored at quarterly receptions.

Egalitarian Climate

WCOs create an egalitarian climate in which all stakeholders—employees, customers, owners, suppliers, and the community—are treated with dignity and respect. This is done in a number of ways. At Wal-Mart, everyone is referred to as an "associate," there are no subordinates or employees. Another common approach is the way in which customers are treated. At the Ritz-Carlton chain, when a guest asks for directions to a particular locale in the hotel, the associate will stop whatever he or she is doing and become a personal escort to that location.

Another sign of an egalitarian approach is the way in which WCOs treat their suppliers. In the past, companies would negotiate with vendors and pit one against the other to get the lowest possible price. Under an egalitarian approach, this strategy is abandoned in favor of a team approach, in which the supplier is regarded as an integral part of the in-house team. For example, at IBM, suppliers

---

FIGURE 3-6

COST REDUCTION APPROACHES: THE UNITED STATES VERSUS JAPAN

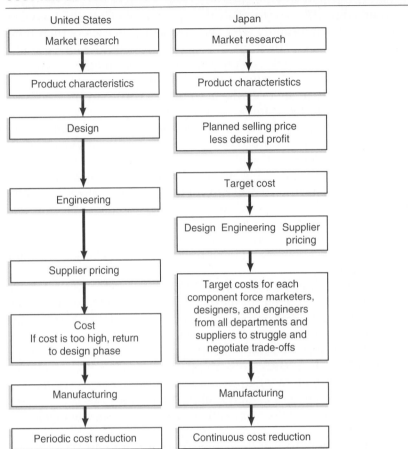

Source: Adapted from Ford S. Worthy, "Japan's Smart Secret Weapon," *Fortune*, August 12, 1995, p. 73.

participate in new product design, learn the company's needs, and work with the firm to provide materials and parts at the highest quality levels and most competitive prices. In the process, suppliers learn their customer's culture and how the organization operates. Suppliers then are in a better position to integrate their own approach with that of their partner company. Japanese WCOs such as Sony and Mitsubishi take this idea a step further, getting suppliers involved in helping cost the product and continually working together to drive down expenses. Figure 3-6 provides an example.

Technological Support

Most of the creative, innovative, and effective approaches of WCOs are supported by advanced, cutting-edge technological support. Examples of such technology include computer-aided design and computer-aided manufacturing (CAD/CAM), telecommunications networks, expert or "smart" systems, distributed information systems, multimedia systems, and executive or management information systems. One good example is found in the retailing industry, where competition is fierce and profit margins are typically low.

Information technology (IT) is critical to the operations of retailing WCOs. Thanks to IT, retailers can tell instantly what they are selling in each of their hundreds of stores, how much money they are making on each sale, and increasingly, who their customers are. Additionally, an effective IT system can help a company to minimize its inventory but still reduce the likelihood of stockouts. Wal-Mart uses such a just-in-time (JIT) inventory system to reduce costs and increase revenue-producing sales space in their stores.

Computers also have helped world-class retailers to exercise closer control over their international units and thus transform themselves into truly global firms. Again, the best example is Wal-Mart, which has been the leader in blending IT with operations. More recently, other big retailers have followed suit. Tesco, the giant British supermarket chain, has used IT to cut the amount of stock in its distribution chain to a mere 2 weeks' supply.[26] Tesco is using automated picking and sorting systems to break down deliveries into smaller units and believes that within 5 years, it will be operating with only 1 week's supply. Like Wal-Mart, Tesco also is using computer modeling derived from electronic point-of-sale data to predict future demand.

Another example is The Limited, a world-class fashion chain based in Columbus, Ohio. This WCO has set up an electronic data interchange (EDI) with clothes makers based in Hong Kong. Using computer-aided design (CAD) and air freight, the firm has been able to cut the lag between order and delivery to 5 weeks instead of the 9 months that has been standard for department stores. The system also allows The Limited to adjust the sizes, colors, and patterns of its collections in response to actual sales rather than relying purely on its buyers' hunches or market research. Marks and Spencer, one of Britain's top retailers, also uses EDI to keep track of its suppliers, compare their prices, and search for new suppliers that offer better quality or cost.

Thanks to inexpensive yet powerful PC-based computer systems, WCO retailers now can identify small suppliers that offer special niche products. For example, a small, local cheese producer now can supply a single Tesco supermarket in York, England. Five years ago, it would not have been economically feasible to identify such a small supplier and negotiate a contract; Tesco would have opted for a larger supplier who could provide a wider range of products to a greater number of stores. Because of effective technological support, WCOs are able to increase their market coverage while simultaneously reducing price and improving customer service.

In the years ahead, all MNCs will begin to recognize and attempt to adopt the types of WCO characteristics discussed in this chapter. If MNCs do not become world class, they may not survive in the long run. If they take on the characteristics of WCOs, however, they increasingly should be able to compete with anybody, anywhere, anytime, anyway.

SUMMARY OF KEY POINTS

1. Quality is having a major impact on international operations. One reason is because it transcends national boundaries and allows firms to compete in a borderless world. Another is because paradoxically, as technology increases, costs tend to be driven down,

and only the most effective MNCs succeed. This is leading MNCs to become increasingly more competitive in terms of both products and services.

2. One way in which successful MNCs are going beyond total quality to sustain, and even increase, their world competitiveness is through learning. In particular, the very best MNCs are moving from total quality to learning organizations, and then on to world-class organizations (WCOs).

3. Total quality organizations are characterized by vision formulation, empowerment, and benchmarking. These help the MNC to develop a strong quality focus and compete effectively; however, they no longer are enough. Total quality has become just the cost of entry into today's highly competitive world economy. Now, MNCs not only must adapt, they must anticipate and even create change. They must transform themselves into learning organizations. Three of the major characteristics of learning organizations are openness, creativity, and personal efficacy.

4. World-class organizations (WCOs) are able to compete with anybody, anywhere, anytime, anyway. There are several major pillars that form the basis for WCOs: customer-based focus, continuous improvement, flexible or virtual organizations, creative human resource management practices, an egalitarian climate, and technological support. Today, more and more firms are adopting the characteristics of WCOs, because they realize this is the only way of ensuring that they can compete, and in the long-run even survive, in today's Four Any's environment.

KEY TERMS

paradox

technology paradox

mass customization

benchmarking

product proliferation

empowerment

adaptive organizations

learning organizations

personal efficacy

world-class organizations (WCOs)

virtual organizations

global sourcing

REVIEW AND DISCUSSION QUESTIONS

1. What is the relationship between quality and cost? Why is this relationship important to MNCs that want to develop products for the international market?

2. Why would an understanding of the technology paradox be valuable to high-tech MNCs? What practical value would it offer these firms regarding how to price and market their products?

3. Why would MNCs be interested in developing a total quality organization? In doing so, what are some things that a firm would need to do? Identify and explain each.

4. How do learning organizations differ from traditional adaptive organizations? Why would MNCs be interested in developing the characteristics of learning organizations? What value would it have for stakeholders? In your answer, be sure to identify and incorporate the three characteristics of learning organizations.

5. As MNCs try to become world-class organizations, what are some of the steps that they should take? In your answer, be sure to identify and incorporate the six pillars.

PRACTICAL INTERNATIONAL MANAGEMENT ASSIGNMENT

Construct a table that compares total quality, learning, and world-class organizations. What changes occur as an MNC moves from one to the next? Based on your analysis, what conclusions can you draw regarding MNCs in the 21st century? How will they differ from those of the 1990s?

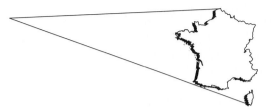

France

In a Paris hotel elevator, a little sign in English read: Please leave your values at the front desk.

The French Republic is situated in Western Europe. It is bounded on the north by the English Channel; to the east by Belgium, Luxembourg, Germany, Switzerland, and Italy; to the south by the Mediterranean Sea and Spain; and to the west by the Atlantic Ocean. The island of Corsica is part of metropolitan France, while four overseas departments, two overseas *collectivites territoriales,* and four overseas territories also form an integral part of the Republic. The principal language is French, which has numerous regional dialects; small minorities speak Breton and Basque. There were approximately 57 million residents in France during the latest census.

France is one of the most economically powerful countries in Europe, and it is one of the G-7 nations. According to United Nations estimates, the country currently has a GDP of over $1 trillion and a per-capita GDP of about $23,000. During recent years, the GDP has continued to grow at an annual rate of 3.0 to 3.5 percent.

Mining, manufacturing, construction, and power provide around 30 percent of French GDP, and industrial production in this decade grew at a 3.3 to 3.5 percent annual rate. Manufacturing in particular accounts for a sizable portion of economic activity, and the country is a net exporter. In 1994, France had a trade surplus of over $17 billion, and the nation typically has a favorable balance of trade with the United States. Its major trading partner is Germany, however, which buys 18 percent of all France's exports and accounts for about 19 percent of French imports. Most of the rest of the country's import and export activity occurs between other EU nations.

Because of France's recent steady economic growth, the country has been the target of much MNC activity. The purchasing power of an average French family is far higher than that in many other EU nations, including Spain, Portugal, Greece, and Finland. Additionally, MNCs from around the world doing business in Germany have found that the French economy is so interrelated that France becomes a second market. France also is a target for new expansion, as in the case of the big German auto firm Mercedes-Benz, which has decided to build its new factory in France because of its faith in the workers' productivity and work ethic.

On the negative side, the near future likely will see more difficult times for this country. French GDP has not grown as fast as that in Germany, and the gap continues to widen. At the same time, government spending as a percentage of GDP remains higher than that of Germany or the United States. Additionally, the unemployment rate in France is higher than that in other economic powers, and in fact, by mid-1995, it was twice that of the United States.

To get the French economy moving, President Jacques Chirac, the first conservative president in 14 years, has promised to give tax breaks, speed up privatization, and institute pension reform. Recently there have been demonstrations against these reforms and many French businesspeople still complain that the government has too much control and prevents them from making needed changes to ensure the efficiency of their operations. For example, when Perrier, the world-famous French bottling MNC, wanted to cut 600 jobs to boost efficiency, the government turned down its request. When Michelin, the tire maker, tried to increase productivity by running its plants 24 hours a day, the government delayed a long time before giving the MNC permission to run one of its five plants continuously. The other four must still close on weekends, conforming to the current rules requiring French businesses to operate only 5 days a week. These bureaucratic rules have a negative effect on productivity and could begin to weaken France's competitive position in the world economy.

1. Why would MNCs be interested in doing business in France?
2. How would French customers be likely to measure quality in products such as cars? Computers? Televisions? What would they be looking for?
3. Why would MNCs need to have a total quality commitment if they hoped to succeed in the French market.
4. Would successful MNCs in France need to be learning organizations? Why, or why not?
5. If a WCO were successful in France, might it also do well throughout the EU? Why or why not?

You Be the International Management Consultant

It's a Price and Quality Issue

A German high-tech firm has just achieved a major breakthrough in cellular technology that likely will drive down the cost of such phones. The company estimates that it can manufacture a phone for less than $4 that will retail for approximately $15, and these units will have higher quality and more features than any others on the market. The company intends to have a prototype completed within 60 days and is planning a worldwide launch within 4 months.

The initial market will be Germany and then the European Union; however, the company also intends to begin selling these phones in the United States and Japan within 6 months. At present, the firm is focusing on three key areas. First are the distribution channels that will be needed to successfully market the product in Europe, North America, and Japan. Second is continuing research and development (R&D) efforts to increase the quality of the product even further. Third are the manufacturing processes that will be used to build the units, because the company wants to continue driving down the cost. To senior-level management, these three areas constitute the major opportunities and threats for the firm. The head of R&D put it this way:

When we first release this product, there will be a wave of initial demand that will sustain us through the first 90 days. However, we will not be able to rest on this initial success. We must continue improving our technology. Ideally, we would like to come out with a new version of the phone within 6 months, and we have to continue this improvement for the indefinite future. At the same time, we must work to drive down our costs, so that it becomes less and less expensive for people to purchase our product. If we don't do this, the competition will be able to reverse engineer our product and soon have a similar offering on the market that will be just as good as ours, but at a lower price. To achieve these goals, we must be flexible and prepared to change and rethink everything we are doing. We are in a fast-moving industry, and if we cannot keep up, we are going to fall behind and not even survive. This new product should thrust us into the lead, but the real challenge will be sustainability and, hopefully, growth.

The head of manufacturing agreed with this statement but also believes that the firm can meet the challenge. "We have been carefully designing the production processes that will be needed to produce this product," he recently told the board of directors, "and if we continue to improvise and modify our manufacturing approaches, we will be able to drive down costs by 40 percent within 12 months while maintaining a sigma level of close to six." The board members agree that if this can be done, the company likely will do very well indeed. As one board member put it, "It's all a matter of controlling price and quality."

1. How would the technology paradox help to shape the strategy of this German firm?
2. In what way would a total quality approach be valuable to this firm? Explain.
3. Why would the company need to become a learning organization if it hopes to dominate the cellular phone market?
4. If the firm wanted to become a WCO, what are some steps it would need to take? Identify and describe four of the most important.

CHAPTER 3 ENDNOTES

1. Neil Gross and Peter Coy, "The Technology Paradox," *Business Week*, March 6, 1995, p. 77.
2. Ibid.
3. Ibid., p. 78.
4. Michael E. Porter, *Competitive Advantages of Nations* (New York: Free Press, 1990).
5. "The Mass Production of Ideas, and Other Impossibilities," *Economist*, March 18, 1995, p. 72.
6. Ibid.
7. Cited in Alan M. Rugman and Richard M. Hodgetts, *International Business* (New York: McGraw-Hill, 1995), p. 13.
8. "Producer Power," *Economist*, March 4, 1995, p. 70.
9. Neal Templin, "GM Overtakes Ford as No. 1 in Quality Among Domestic Car Firms, Study Says," *Wall Street Journal*, May 25, 1995, p. A4.
10. Also see "Saturn Rated No. 1 in J.D. Power Survey," *Miami Herald*, June 16, 1995, p. 3C.
11. Jeff Cole, "In Jets, The U.S. Makes, the World Takes," *Wall Street Journal*, June 13, 1995, p. A14.
12. "Asia, At Your Service," *Economist*, February 11, 1995, p. 54.
13. Richard M. Hodgetts, *Blueprints for Continuous Improvement* (New York: American Management Association, 1993), p. 25.
14. See H. James Harrington, *Total Quality Improvement: The Next Generation in Performance Improvement* (New York: McGraw-Hill, 1995), p. 294.
15. See James Champy, *Reengineering Management: The Mandate for New Leadership* (New York: Harper Business, 1995).
16. Hodgetts, *Blueprints for Continuous Improvement*, p. 91.
17. Peter M. Senge, *The Fifth Dimension* (New York: Doubleday, 1990).
18. Michael E. McGill, John W. Slocum, Jr., and David Lei, "Management Practices in Learning Organizations," *Organizational Dynamics*, Summer 1992, pp. 10–16.
19. For additional insights see Fred Luthans, Michael Rubach, and Paul Marsnik, "Going Beyond Total Quality: The Characteristics, Techniques and Measures of Learning Organizations," *International Journal of Organizational Analysis*, January 1995, pp. 24–44.
20. Ibid., p. 11.
21. Hodgetts, *Blueprints for Continuous Improvement*, p. 78.
22. Rugman and Hodgetts, *International Business*, p. 270.
23. Michael E. Porter, *Competitive Advantage of Nations*, p. 103.
24. Richard M. Hodgetts, *Implementing TQM in Small- and Medium-Sized Organizations* (New York: American Management Association, 1996), Chapter 7.
25. Fred Luthans, Richard M. Hodgetts, and Sang Lee, "New Paradigm Organizations: From Total Quality to Learning to World-Class," *Organizational Dynamics*, Winter 1994, p. 17.
26. "Stores of Value," *Economist*, March 4, 1995, p. 6.

PART TWO

THE CULTURAL CONTEXT FOR INTERNATIONAL MANAGEMENT

THE MEANINGS AND DIMENSIONS OF CULTURE

OBJECTIVES OF THE CHAPTER

A major challenge of doing business internationally is to adapt effectively to different cultures. Such adaptation requires an understanding of cultural diversity, perceptions, stereotypes, and values. In recent years, a great deal of research has been conducted on cultural dimensions and attitudes, and the findings have proved useful in providing integrative profiles of international cultures.

This chapter examines the meaning of culture as it applies to international management, reviews some of the value differences and similarities of various national groups, studies important dimensions of culture and their impact on behavior, and finally, examines attitudinal dimensions and country clusters. The specific objectives of this chapter are:

1. **DEFINE** the term "culture," and discuss some of the comparative ways of differentiating cultures.
2. **DESCRIBE** the concept of cultural values, and relate some of the international differences, similarities, and changes occurring in terms of both work and managerial values.
3. **IDENTIFY** the major dimensions of culture relevant to work settings, and discuss their effect on behavior in an international environment.
4. **DISCUSS** the value of country cluster analysis and relational orientations in developing effective international management practices.

NATURE OF CULTURE

Culture is acquired knowledge that people use to interpret experience and generate social behavior.[1] This knowledge forms values, creates attitudes, and influences behavior. Most scholars of culture would agree on the following characteristics of culture:

1. *Learned.* Culture is not inherited or biologically based; it is acquired by learning and experience.
2. *Shared.* People as members of a group, organization, or society share culture; it is not specific to single individuals.
3. *Transgenerational.* Culture is cumulative, passed down from one generation to the next.
4. *Symbolic.* Culture is based on the human capacity to symbolize or use one thing to represent another.
5. *Patterned.* Culture has structure and is integrated; a change in one part will bring changes in another.
6. *Adaptive.* Culture is based on the human capacity to change or adapt, as opposed to the more genetically driven adaptive process of animals.[2]

Because different cultures exist in the world, an understanding of the impact of culture on behavior is critical to the study of international management.[3] If international managers do not know something about the cultures of the countries they deal with, the results can be quite disastrous.[4] For example, a partner in one of New York's leading private banking firms tells the following story:

> I traveled nine thousand miles to meet a client and arrived with my foot in my mouth. Determined to do things right, I'd memorized the names of the key men I was to see in Singapore. No easy job, inasmuch as the names all came in threes. So, of course, I couldn't resist showing off that I'd done my homework. I began by addressing top man Lo Win Hao with plenty of well-placed Mr. Hao's—sprinkled the rest of my remarks with a Mr. Chee this and a Mr. Woon that. Great show. Until a note was passed to me from one man I'd met before, in New York. Bad news. 'Too friendly too soon, Mr. Long,' it said. Where diffidence is next to godliness, there I was, calling a room of VIPs, in effect, Mr. Ed and Mr. Charlie. I'd remembered everybody's name—but forgot that in Chinese the surname comes *first* and the given name *last*.[5]

Cultural Diversity

There are many ways of examining cultural differences and their impact on international management.[6] Culture can affect technology transfer, managerial attitudes, managerial ideology,[7] and even business–government relations.[8] Perhaps most important, culture affects how people think and behave.[9] Table 4-1, for example, compares the most important cultural values of the United States, Japan, and Arab countries. A close look at this table shows a great deal of difference between these three cultures. Culture affects a host of business-related activities, even including the common handshake. Here are some contrasting examples:

Culture	Type of handshake
United States	Firm
Asian	Gentle (shaking hands is unfamiliar and uncomfortable for some; the exception is the Korean, who usually has a firm handshake)

British	Soft
French	Light and quick (not offered to superiors); repeated on arrival and departure
German	Brusk and firm; repeated on arrival and departure
Latin American	Moderate grasp; repeated frequently
Middle Eastern	Gentle; repeated frequently[10]

In overall terms, the cultural impact on international management is reflected by these basic beliefs and behaviors. Here are some specific examples where the culture of a society can directly affect management approaches:

- *Centralized vs. decentralized decision making.* In some societies, all important organizational decisions are made by top managers. In others, these decisions are diffused throughout the enterprise, and middle- and lower-level managers actively participate in, and make, key decisions.
- *Safety vs. risk.* In some societies, organizational decision makers are risk-aversive and have great difficulty with conditions of uncertainty. In others, risk-taking is encouraged, and decision making under uncertainty is common.
- *Individual vs. group rewards.* In some countries, personnel who do outstanding work are given individual rewards in the form of bonuses and commissions. In others, cultural norms require group rewards, and individual rewards are frowned on.
- *Informal vs. formal procedures.* In some societies, much is accomplished through informal means. In others, formal procedures are set forth and followed rigidly.
- *High vs. low organizational loyalty.* In some societies, people identify very strongly with their organization or employer. In others, people identify with their occupational group, such as engineer or mechanic.
- *Co-operation vs. competition.* Some societies encourage co-operation between their people. Others encourage competition between their people.

TABLE 4-1		
PRIORITIES OF CULTURAL VALUES: UNITED STATES, JAPAN, AND ARAB COUNTRIES		
United States	**Japan**	**Arab countries**
1. Freedom	1. Belonging	1. Family security
2. Independence	2. Group harmony	2. Family harmony
3. Self-reliance	3. Collectiveness	3. Parental guidance
4. Equality	4. Age/seniority	4. Age
5. Individualism	5. Group consensus	5. Authority
6. Competition	6. Cooperation	6. Compromise
7. Efficiency	7. Quality	7. Devotion
8. Time	8. Patience	8. Patience
9. Directness	9. Indirectness	9. Indirectness
10. Openness	10. Go-between	10. Hospitality

Note: "1" represents the most important cultural value, "10" the least.
Source: Adapted from information found in F. Elashmawi and Philip R. Harris, *Multicultural Management* (Houston; Gulf Publishing, 1993), p. 63.

Business Customs in Japan

When doing business in Japan, foreign businesspeople should follow certain customs if they wish to be as effective as possible. Experts have put together the following guidelines:

1. Always try to arrange for a formal introduction to any person or company with whom you want to do business. These introductions should come from someone whose position is at least as high as that of the person whom you want to meet or from someone who has done a favor for this person. Let the host pick the subjects to discuss. One topic to be avoided is World War II.

2. If in doubt, bring a translator along with you. For example, the head of Osaka's $7 billion international airport project tells the story of a U.S. construction company president who became indignant when he discovered that the Japanese project head could not speak English. By the same token, you should not bring along your lawyer, because this implies a lack of trust.

3. Try for a thorough personalization of all business relationships. The Japanese trust those with whom they socialize and come to know more than they do those who simply are looking to do business. Accept after-hours invitations. However, a rollicking night out on the town will not necessarily lead to signing the contract to your advantage the next morning.

4. Do not deliver bad news in front of others, and if possible, have your second-in-command handle this chore. Never cause Japanese managers to lose face by putting them in a position of having to admit failure or say they do not know something that they should know professionally.

5. How business is done often is as important as the results. Concern for tradition, for example, is sometimes more important than concern for profit. Do not appeal solely to logic, because in Japan, emotional considerations often are more important than facts.

6. The Japanese often express themselves in a vague and ambiguous manner, in contrast to the specific language typically used in the United States. A Japanese who is too specific runs the risk of being viewed as rudely displaying superior knowledge. The Japanese avoid independent or individual action, and they prefer to make decisions based on group discussions and past precedent. The Japanese do not say no in public, which is why foreign businesspeople often take away the wrong impression.

- *Short-term vs. long-term horizons.* Some nations focus most heavily on short-term horizons, such as short-range goals of profit and efficiency. Others are more interested in long-range goals, such as market share and technologic development.
- *Stability vs. innovation.* The culture of some countries encourages stability and resistance to change. The culture of others puts high value on innovation and change.[11]

These cultural differences influence the way that international management should be conducted. The accompanying sidebar, "Business Customs in Japan," provides some examples in a country where many international managers are unfamiliar with day-to-day business protocol.

Values in Culture

A major dimension in the study of culture is values. *Values* are basic convictions that people have regarding what is right and wrong, good and bad, important or unimportant. These values are learned from the culture in which the individual is reared, and they help to direct the person's behavior.[12] Differences in cultural values often result in varying management practices.[13] Table 4-2 provides an exam-

TABLE 4-2

U.S. VALUES AND POSSIBLE ALTERNATIVES

U.S. cultural values	Alternative values	Examples of management function affected
Individuals can influence the future (when there is a will there is a way).	Life follows a preordained course, and human action is determined by the will of God.	Planning and scheduling.
Individuals should be realistic in their aspirations.	Ideals are to be pursued regardless of what is "reasonable."	Goal-setting and career development.
We must work hard to accomplish our objectives (Puritan ethic).	Hard work is not the only prerequisite for success. Wisdom, luck, and time also are required.	Motivation and reward system.
A primary obligation of an employee is to the organization.	Individual employees have a primary obligation to their family and friends.	Loyalty, commitment, and motivation.
Employees can be removed if they do not perform well.	The removal of an employee from a position involves a great loss of prestige and will rarely be done.	Promotion.
Company information should be available to anyone who needs it within the organization.	Withholding information to gain or maintain power is acceptable.	Organization, communication and managerial style.
Competition stimulates high performance.	Competition leads to unbalances and disharmony.	Career development and marketing.
What works is important.	Symbols and the process are more important than the end point.	Communication, planning, and quality control.

Source: Adapted from information found in Philip R. Harris and Robert T. Moran, *Managing Cultural Differences* (Houston: Gulf Publishing, 1991), pp. 79–80.

ple. Note that U.S. values can result in one set of business responses, and alternative values can bring about different responses.

Value Differences and Similarities across Cultures   Personal values have been the focus of numerous intercultural studies. In general, the findings show both differences and similarities between the work values and managerial values of different cultural groups. For example, one study found differences in work values between Western-oriented and tribal-oriented black employees in South Africa.[14] The Western-oriented group accepted most of the tenets of the Protestant work ethic, but the tribal-oriented group did not. The results were explained in terms of the differences of the cultural backgrounds of the two groups.

Differences in work values also have been found to reflect culture and industrialization. Researchers gave a personal-values questionnaire (PVQ) to over 2000 managers in five countries: Australia ($n = 281$), India ($n = 485$), Japan ($n = 301$), South Korea ($n = 161$), and the United States ($n = 833$).[15] The PVQ consisted of 66 concepts related to business goals, personal goals, ideas associated with people and groups of people, and ideas about general topics. Ideologic and philosophic concepts were included to represent major value systems of all groups. The results showed some significant differences between the managers in each group. U.S. managers placed high value on the tactful acquisition of influence and regard for others. Japanese managers placed high value on deference to superiors, on company commitment, and on the cautious use of aggressiveness and control. Korean managers placed high value on personal forcefulness and aggressiveness and low value on recognition of others. Indian managers put high value on the nonaggressive pursuit of objectives. Australian managers placed major importance on values reflecting a low-keyed approach to management and a high concern for others.[16] In short, value systems across national boundaries often are different.

At the same time, value similarities exist between cultures.[17] In fact, research shows that managers from different countries often have similar personal values that relate to success. England and Lee examined the managerial values of a diverse sample of U.S. ($n = 878$), Japanese ($n = 312$), Australian ($n = 301$), and Indian managers ($n = 500$). They found that:

1. There is a reasonably strong relationship between the level of success achieved by managers and their personal values.
2. It is evident that value patterns predict managerial success and could be used in selection and placement decisions.
3. Although there are country differences in the relationships between values and success, findings across the four countries are quite similar.
4. The general pattern indicates that more successful managers appear to favor pragmatic, dynamic, achievement-oriented values, while less successful managers prefer more static and passive values. More successful managers favor an achievement orientation and prefer an active role in interaction with other individuals who are instrumental to achieving the managers' organizational goals. Less successful managers have values associated with a static and protected environment in which they take relatively passive roles.[18]

"International Management in Action: Common Personal Values" discusses these findings in more depth.

Values in Transition   Do values change over time? England found that personal value systems are relatively stable and do not change rapidly.[19] However, changes are taking place in managerial values as a result of both culture and technology. A good example is the Japanese. Reichel and Flynn examined the effects of the U.S. environment on the cultural values of Japanese managers working for Japanese firms in the United States. In particular, they focused attention on such key organizational values as lifetime employment, formal authority, group orientation, seniority, and paternalism. Here is what they found:

1. Lifetime employment is widely accepted in Japanese culture, but the stateside Japanese managers did not believe that unconditional tenure in one organization was of major importance. They did believe, however, that job security was important.
2. Formal authority, obedience, and conformance to hierarchic position are very important in Japan, but the stateside managers did not perceive obedience and conformity to be very important and rejected the idea that one should not question a superior. However, they did support the concept of formal authority.
3. Group orientation, co-operation, conformity, and compromise are important organizational values in Japan. The stateside managers supported these values but also believed it was important to be an individual, thus maintaining a balance between a group and a personal orientation.
4. In Japan, organizational personnel often are rewarded based on seniority, not merit. Support for this value was directly influenced by the length of time the

INTERNATIONAL MANAGEMENT IN ACTION

Common Personal Values

One of the most interesting findings about successful managers around the world is that while they come from different cultures, many have similar personal values. Of course, there are large differences in values within each national group. For example, some managers are very pragmatic and judge ideas in terms of whether they will work; others are highly ethical-moral and view ideas in terms of right or wrong; still others have a "feeling" orientation and judge ideas in terms of whether they are pleasant. Some managers have a very small set of values; others have a large set. Some have values that are related heavily to organization life; others include a wide range of personal values; others have highly group-oriented values. There are many different value patterns; however, overall value profiles have been found within successful managers in each group. Here are some of the most significant:

U.S. managers
- Highly pragmatic
- High achievement and competence orientation
- Emphasis on profit maximization, organizational efficiency, and high productivity

Japanese managers
- Highly pragmatic
- Strong emphasis on size and growth
- High value on competence and achievement

Korean managers
- Highly pragmatic
- Highly individualistic
- Strong achievement and competence orientation

Australian managers
- High moral orientation
- High humanistic orientation
- Low value on achievement, success, competition, and risk

Indian managers
- High moral orientation
- Highly individualistic
- Strong focus on organization compliance and competence

The findings listed here show important similarities and differences. Most of the profiles are similar in nature; however, note that successful Indian and Australian managers have values that are distinctly different. In short, although values of successful managers within countries often are similar, there are intercountry differences. This is why the successful managerial value systems of one country often are not ideal in another country.

Japanese managers had been in the United States. The longer they had been there, the lower their support for this value.

5. Paternalism, often measured by a manager's involvement in both personal and off-the-job problems of subordinates, is very important in Japan. Stateside Japanese managers disagreed, and this resistance was positively associated with the number of years they had been in the United States.[20]

Other researchers have found supporting evidence that Japanese values are changing—and not just among managers outside the country. One study examined value systems among three groups of managers in Japan: (1) a group of Japanese managers who had graduated from the Japanese Institute for International Studies and Training at least 10 years previously; (2) a group of Japanese management trainees who currently were enrolled in the institute; and (3) a group of U.S. M.B.A. students who were taking M.B.A. courses at the institute.[21] The results showed that the Japanese managers were greatly concerned with job security, whereas the U.S. M.B.A. students valued achievement. The Japanese managers put great importance on group success; the U.S. M.B.A. students highly valued personal success. Although there were some exceptions, the two groups had contrasting values. The profiles of the Japanese students, meanwhile, fell between these two extremes. Two-thirds of responses were in this middle range. The researchers therefore concluded that "the data seem to indicate a significant difference in values between Japanese respondents who have already attained responsible managerial positions in their organization and the Japanese management trainees, who have held lower positions and been employed less long with their present company or government agency."[22]

CULTURAL DIMENSIONS

Some researchers have attempted to provide a composite picture of culture by examining its subparts, or dimensions. In particular, Dutch researcher Geert Hofstede found there are four dimensions of culture that help to explain how and why people from various cultures behave as they do.[23] His initial data were gathered from two questionnaire surveys with over 116,000 respondents from over 70 different countries around the world—making it the largest organizationally based study ever conducted.[24] The individuals in these studies all worked in the local subsidiaries of IBM. As a result, Hofstede's research has been criticized because of its focus on just one company; however, he has recently countered this criticism. Hofstede is well aware of

> the amazement of some people about how employees of a very specific corporation like IBM can serve as a sample for discovering something about the culture of their countries at large. "We know IBMers," they say, "they are very special people, always in a white shirt and tie, and not at all representative of our country." The people who say this are quite right. IBMers do not form representative samples from national populations. . . . However, samples for cross-national comparison need not be representative, as long as they are functionally equivalent. IBM employees are a narrow sample, but very well matched. Employees of multinational companies in general and of IBM in particular form attractive sources of information for comparing national traits, because they are so similar in respects other than nationality: their employers . . . , their kind of work, and—for matched occupations—their level of education. The only thing that can account for systematic and consistent differences between national groups *within* such a homogenous multinational population is nationality itself—the national environment in which people were brought up *before* they joined this employer. Comparing IBM subsidiaries therefore shows national culture differences with unusual clarity.[25]

Hofstede's massive study continues to be a focal point for additional research. The four now-well-known dimensions that Hofstede examined were: (1) power distance, (2) uncertainty avoidance, (3) individualism, and (4) masculinity.

Power Distance

Power distance is "the extent to which less powerful members of institutions and organizations accept that power is distributed unequally."[26] Countries in which people blindly obey the orders of their superiors have high power distance. In many societies, lower-level employees tend to follow orders as a matter of procedure. In societies with high power distance, however, strict obedience is found even at the upper levels; examples include Mexico, South Korea, and India. For example, a senior Indian executive with a Ph.D. from a prestigious U.S. university related the following story:

> What is most important for me and my department is not what I do or achieve for the company, but whether the [owner's] favor is bestowed on me. . . . This I have achieved by saying "yes" to everything [the owner] says or does. . . . To contradict him is to look for another job. . . . I left my freedom of thought in Boston.[27]

The effect of this dimension can be measured in a number of ways. For example, organizations in low power-distance countries generally will be decentralized and have flatter organization structures. These organizations also will have a smaller proportion of supervisory personnel, and the lower strata of the work force often will consist of highly qualified people. By contrast, organizations in high power-distance countries will tend to be centralized and have tall organization structures. Organizations in high power-distance countries will have a large proportion of supervisory personnel, and the people at the lower levels of the structure often will have low job qualifications. This latter structure encourages and promotes inequality between people at different levels.[28]

Uncertainty Avoidance

Uncertainty avoidance is "the extent to which people feel threatened by ambiguous situations, and have created beliefs and institutions that try to avoid these."[29] Countries populated with people who do not like uncertainty tend to have a high need for security and a strong belief in experts and their knowledge: examples include Germany, Japan, and Spain. Cultures with low uncertainty avoidance have people who are more willing to accept that risks are associated with the unknown, that life must go on in spite of this. Examples here include Denmark and Great Britain.

The effect of this dimension can be measured in a number of ways. Countries with high uncertainty-avoidance cultures have a great deal of structuring of organizational activities, more written rules, less risk-taking by managers, lower labor turnover, and less ambitious employees.

Low uncertainty-avoidance societies have organization settings with less structuring of activities, fewer written rules, more risk-taking by managers, higher labor turnover, and more ambitious employees. The organization encourages personnel to use their own initiative and assume responsibility for their actions.

Individualism

Individualism is the tendency of people to look after themselves and their immediate family only.[30] Hofstede measured this cultural difference on a bipolar continuum, with individualism on one end and collectivism on the other. *Collectivism* is the tendency of people to belong to groups or collectives and to look after each other in exchange for loyalty.[31]

Similar to those of the other cultural dimensions, the effects of individualism and collectivism can be measured in a number of different ways. Hofstede has found that wealthy countries have higher individualism scores and poorer countries higher collectivism scores (see Table 4-3 for the country abbreviations used in Figure 4-1 and subsequent figures). Note that in Figure 4-1, the United States, Canada, Australia, Denmark, and Sweden, among others, have high individualism and high GDP. Conversely, Guam, Pakistan, and a number of South American countries have low individualism (high collectivism) and low GDP. Countries with high individualism also tend to have greater support for the Protestant work ethic, greater individual initiative, and promotions based on market value. Countries with low individualism tend to have less support for the Protestant work ethic, less individual initiative, and promotions based on seniority.

TABLE 4-3

COUNTRIES AND REGIONS USED IN HOFSTEDE'S RESEARCH

ARA	Arab countries (Egypt, Lebanon, Libya, Kuwait, Iraq, Saudi Arabia, U.A.E.)	JPN	Japan
		KOR	South Korea
ARG	Argentina	MAL	Malaysia
AUL	Australia	MEX	Mexico
AUT	Austria	NET	Netherlands
BEL	Belgium	NOR	Norway
BRA	Brazil	NZL	New Zealand
CAN	Canada	PAK	Pakistan
CHL	Chile	PAN	Panama
COL	Colombia	PER	Peru
COS	Costa Rica	PHI	Philippines
DEN	Denmark	POR	Portugal
EAF	East Africa (Kenya, Ethiopia, Zambia)	SAF	South Africa
EQA	Equador	SAL	Salvador
FIN	Finland	SIN	Singapore
FRA	France	SPA	Spain
GBR	Great Britain	SWE	Sweden
GER	Germany	SWI	Switzerland
GRE	Greece	TAI	Taiwan
GUA	Guatemala	THA	Thailand
HOK	Hong Kong	TUR	Turkey
IDO	Indonesia	URU	Uruguay
IND	India	USA	United States
IRA	Iran	VEN	Venezuela
IRE	Ireland	WAF	West Africa (Nigeria, Ghana, Sierra Leone)
ISR	Israel		
ITA	Italy	YUG	Former Yugoslavia
JAM	Jamaica		

Source: Adapted from Geert Hofstede, *Cultures and Organizations: Software of the Mind* (London: McGraw-Hill U.K., Ltd., 1991), p. 55. Used with permission.

Masculinity

Masculinity is defined by Hofstede as "a situation in which the dominant values in society are success, money, and things."[32] Hofstede measured this dimension on a continuum ranging from masculinity to femininity. Contrary to some stereotypes and connotations, *femininity* is the term used by Hofstede to describe "a situation in which the dominant values in society are caring for others and the quality of life."[33] Countries with a high masculinity index, such as Japan, place great importance on earnings, recognition, advancement, and challenge. Individuals are encouraged to be independent decision makers, and achievement is defined in terms of recognition and wealth. The workplace often is characterized by high job stress, and many managers believe that their employees dislike work and must be kept under some degree of control.

Countries with a low masculinity index (Hofstede's femininity dimension), such as Norway, tend to place great importance on co-operation, a friendly

---

FIGURE 4-1

INDIVIDUALISM INDEX VS. PER CAPITA GNP

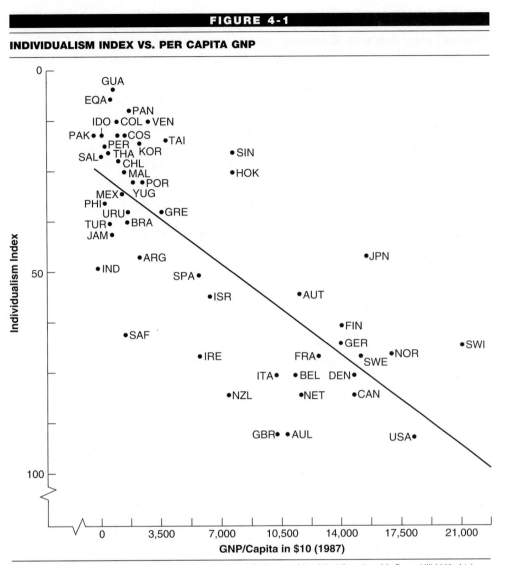

Source: Geert Hofstede, *Cultures and Organizations: Software of the Mind* (London: McGraw-Hill U.K., Ltd., 1991), p. 75. Used with permission.

atmosphere, and employment security. Individuals are encouraged to be group decision makers, and achievement is defined in terms of human contacts and the living environment. The workplace tends to be characterized by low stress, and managers give their employees more credit for being responsible and allow them more freedom.

Cultures with a high masculinity index tend to favor large-scale enterprises, and economic growth is seen as more important than conservation of the environment. The school system is geared toward encouraging high performance. Young men expect to have careers, and those who do not often view themselves as failures. Fewer women hold higher-level jobs, and these individuals often find it necessary to be assertive. There is high job stress in the workplace, and industrial conflict is common.

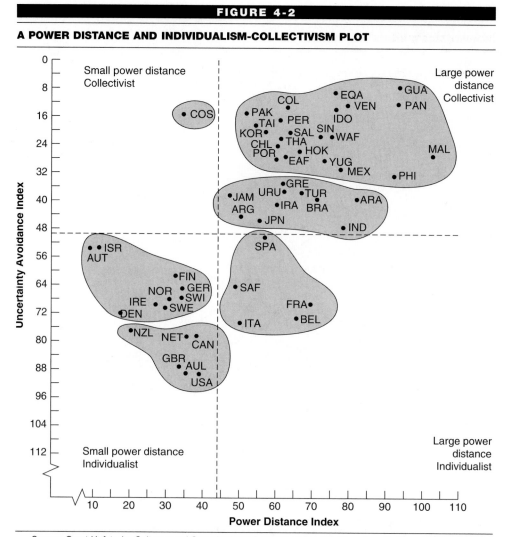

FIGURE 4-2

A POWER DISTANCE AND INDIVIDUALISM-COLLECTIVISM PLOT

Source: Geert Hofstede, *Cultures and Organizations: Software of the Mind* (London: McGraw-Hill U.K., Ltd., 1991), p. 54. Used with permission.

Cultures with a low masculinity index (high femininity) tend to favor small-scale enterprises, and they place great importance on conservation of the environment. The school system is designed to teach social adaptation. Some young men and women want careers; others do not. Many women hold higher-level jobs, and they do not find it necessary to be assertive. Less job stress is found in the workplace, and there is not much industrial conflict.

Integrating the Dimensions

A description of the four dimensions of culture is useful in helping to explain the differences between various countries, and Hofstede's research has extended beyond this focus and showed how countries can be described in terms of pairs of dimensions. Figure 4-2, which incorporates power distance and individualism, provides an example.

FIGURE 4-3

A POWER DISTANCE AND UNCERTAINTY AVOIDANCE PLOT

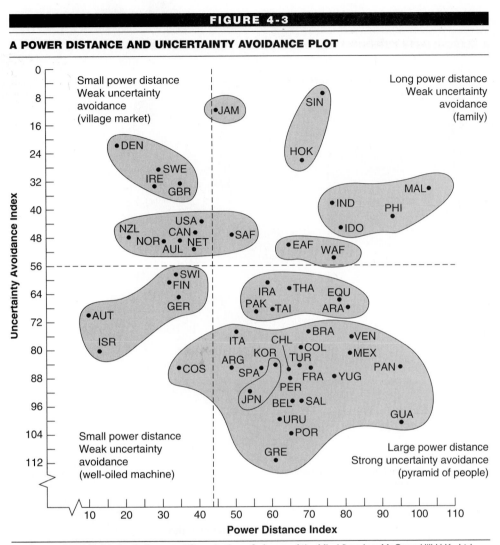

Source: Geert Hofstede, *Cultures and Organizations: Software of the Mind* (London: McGraw-Hill U.K., Ltd., 1991), p. 141. Used with permission.

In Figure 4-2, the United States is located in the lower left-hand quadrant. Americans have very high individualism and relatively low power distance. They prefer to do things for themselves and are not upset when others have more power than they do. In fact, Americans are taught to believe that everyone is equal, so they are not overly impressed by individuals with important titles or jobs. Australians, Canadians, British, Dutch, and New Zealanders have the same basic values. Conversely, many of the underdeveloped or newly industrialized countries, such as Colombia, Hong Kong, Portugal, and Singapore, are characterized by large power distance and low individualism. These nations tend to be collectivist in their approach.

Figure 4-3 plots the uncertainty avoidance index for the 53 countries against the power-distance index. Once again, there are clusters of countries. Many of the Anglo nations tend to be in the upper left-hand quadrant, which is characterized by

FIGURE 4-4

A MASCULINITY-FEMININITY AND UNCERTAINTY AVOIDANCE PLOT

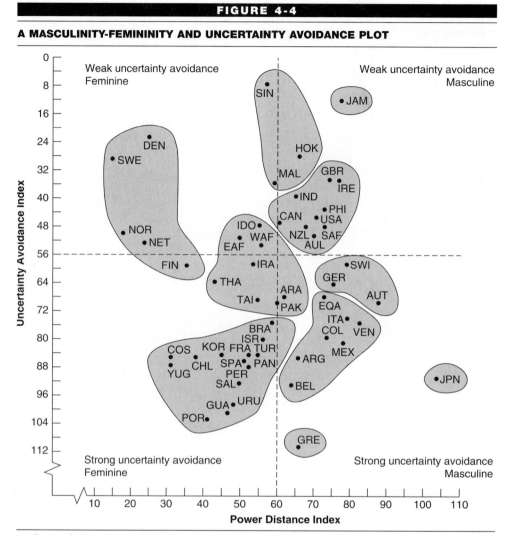

Source: Geert Hofstede, *Cultures and Organizations: Software of the Mind* (London: McGraw-Hill U.K., Ltd., 1991), p. 123. Used with permission.

small power distance and weak uncertainty avoidance (they do not try to avoid uncertainty). These countries tend to be moderately unconcerned with power distance, and they are able to accept conditions of uncertainty. In contrast, many Latin countries (both in Europe and the Western hemisphere), Mediterranean countries, and Asian nations (e.g., Japan and Korea) are characterized by high power distance and strong uncertainty avoidance. Most other Asian countries are characterized by large power distance and weak uncertainty avoidance.

Figure 4-4 plots the position of 53 countries in terms of uncertainty avoidance and masculinity-femininity. The most masculine country is Japan, followed by the Germanic countries (Austria, Switzerland, Germany) and Latin countries (Venezuela, Mexico, Italy). Many countries in the Anglo cluster, including Ireland, Australia, Great Britain, and the United States, have moderate degrees of masculinity. So do some of the former colonies of Anglo nations, including India and the Philippines. The Northern European cluster (Denmark, Sweden, Norway, the Netherlands) has low masculinity, indicating that these countries place high value on factors such as quality of working life, preservation of the environment, and the importance of relationships with people over money.

The integration of these cultural factors into two-dimensional plots helps to illustrate the complexity of understanding culture's effect on behavior. A number of dimensions are at work, and sometimes, they do not all move in the anticipated direction. For example, at first glance, a nation with high power distance would appear to be low in individualism, and vice versa, and Hofstede found exactly that (see Figure 4-2). However, low uncertainty avoidance does not always go hand-in-hand with high masculinity, even though those who are willing to live with uncertainty will want rewards such as money and power and accord low value to the quality of work life and caring for others (see Figure 4-4). Simply put, empiric evidence on the impact of cultural dimensions may differ from commonly held beliefs or stereotypes. Research-based data are needed to determine the full impact of differing cultures. However, some interesting attempts have been made to classify countries into uniform clusters on variables such as attitudes and deal with cultures on a more structured basis. These efforts are described in the next section.

ATTITUDINAL DIMENSIONS OF CULTURE

For over a decade, researchers have attempted to cluster countries into similar cultural groupings for the purpose of studying similarities and differences. Such research also helps us to learn the reasons for cultural differences and how they can be transcended. Much of the initial research in this area examined similarities among countries based on employee work values and attitudes.

Work Value and Attitude Similarities

Drawing on his extensive data, Hofstede was able to use the four cultural dimensions discussed in the last section to compile a series of country clusters, as shown in Figures 4-2, 4-3, and 4-4. His work was only preliminary, but it served as a point of departure for other multicultural research, which revealed many similarities in both work values and attitudes among certain countries. For example, early research by Ronen and Kraut reported that "countries could be clustered into more or less homogeneous groups based on intercorrelations of standard scores obtained for each country from scales measuring leadership, role descriptions, and motivation."[34] These researchers then attempted to cluster the countries by use of the mathematic technique of nonparametric multivariate analysis, known as *smallest space analysis (SSA).* Simply put, this approach maps the relationships of various cultural dimensions among the countries by showing the distance between each. By looking at the resulting two-dimensional map, one can see those countries that are similar to each other and those that are not.

Drawing on the work of many earlier researchers[35] as well as that of 4000 technical employees in 15 countries, Ronen and Kraut were able to construct SSA maps of various countries, including the United States, France, India, Sweden, and Japan. These maps showed five country clusters: (1) Anglo-American (United States, United Kingdom, Australia); (2) Nordic (Norway, Finland, Denmark);

(3) South American (Venezuela, Mexico, Chile); (4) Latin European (France and Belgium); and (5) Central European (Germany, Austria, and Switzerland). Commenting on the overall value of their research, Ronen and Kraut concluded:

> An important aspect of this study is the potential for practical application by multinational organizations. For example, knowledge of relative similarities among countries can guide the smooth placement of international assignees, the establishment of compatible regional units, and predict the ease of implementing various policies and practices across national boundaries.[36]

Since Ronen and Kraut, additional multicultural studies have been conducted, and the number of countries and clusters has increased. These country clusters are particularly important in providing an overall picture of international cultures.

Country Clusters

To date, perhaps the most integrative analysis of all available findings has been provided by Ronen and Shenkar.[37] After conducting a thorough review of the literature, they found that eight major cluster studies had been conducted over the previous 15 years. These studies examined variables in four categories: (1) the importance of work goals; (2) need deficiency, fulfillment, and job satisfaction; (3) managerial and organizational variables; and (4) work role and interpersonal orientation. Each of the eight country cluster studies had produced different results. Some had focused only on one part of the world, such as the Far East or Arabia; others had been more international in focus but arrived at different cluster groupings. Based on careful analysis of these research efforts, Ronen and Shenkar identified eight country clusters and four countries that are independent and do not fit into any of the clusters (see Figure 4-5).

Each country in Figure 4-5 that has been placed in a cluster is culturally similar to the others in that cluster. In addition, the closer a country is to the center of the overall circle, the greater its per-capital gross national product (GNP). Those countries with similar GNPs will not necessarily have intercluster similarity, but to the extent that GNP influences values and culture, these countries will have converging cultural values.

Not everyone agrees with the synthesis presented in Figure 4-5. Some researchers place India and Israel in the Anglo culture because of the strong Anglo ties of these countries. Others combine the Nordic and Germanic clusters into one. Still others believe that some of the Latin European countries, such as Italy, Portugal, and Spain, are culturally much closer to those of the South American culture and cluster them there. Nevertheless, Figure 4-5 does provide a useful model and point of departure for examining international culture. The concept of country clusters is useful to those studying multinational management as well. Ronen and Shenkar note:

> As multinational companies increase their direct investment overseas, especially in less developed and consequently less studied areas, they will require more information concerning their local employees in order to implement effective types of interactions between the organization and the host country. The knowledge acquired thus far can help one to understand better the work values and attitudes of employees throughout the world. American theories work very well for Western nations. Are they equally applicable in non-Western countries? Clearly, more cluster research is called for, including research in countries from all parts of the globe.[38]

FIGURE 4-5

A SYNTHESIS OF COUNTRY CLUSTERS

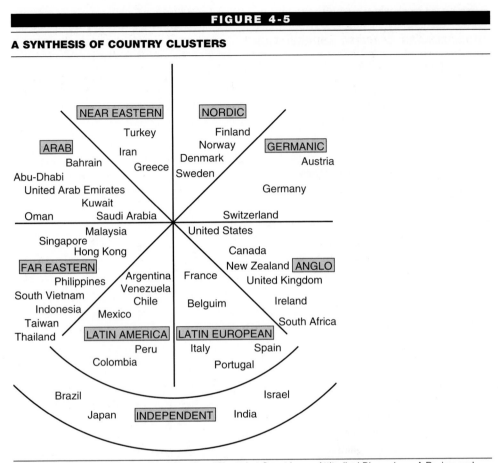

Source: Simcha Ronen and Oded Shenkar, "Clustering Countries on Attitudinal Dimensions: A Review and Synthesis," *Academy of Management Journal*, September, 1985, p. 449. Used with permission.

Empiric evidence shows that international managers share a common international culture, so there may well be much more convergence than previously has been believed.[39] There also may be much more recent adaptation to the local culture by national firms than many outside observers realize. In short, although recognizing cultural diversity still is vital, convergence and flexibility in the international arena are gaining momentum.[40]

TROMPENAARS' CULTURAL DIMENSIONS

Both the Hofstede cultural dimensions and the Ronen and Shenkar country clusters are widely recognized and accepted in the study of international management. A more recent description of how cultures differ, by another Dutch researcher, Fons Trompenaars, is receiving increasing attention as well. Trompenaars' research was conducted over a 10-year period and published in 1994.[41] He administered research questionnaires to over 15,000 managers from 28 countries and received usable responses from at least 500 in each nation; the 23 countries in his research are presented in Table 4-4. Building heavily on value orientations and

TABLE 4-4	
TROMPENAARS' COUNTRY ABBREVIATIONS	
Abbreviation	**Country**
ARG	Argentina
AUS	Austria
BEL	Belgium
BRZ	Brazil
CHI	China
CIS	Former Soviet Union
CZH	Former Czechoslovakia
FRA	France
GER	Germany (excluding former East Germany)
HK	Hong Kong
IDO	Indonesia
ITA	Italy
JPN	Japan
MEX	Mexico
NL	Netherlands
SIN	Singapore
SPA	Spain
SWE	Sweden
SWI	Switzerland
THA	Thailand
UK	United Kingdom
USA	United States
VEN	Venezuela

the relational orientations of well-known sociologist Talcott Parsons,[42] Trompenaars derived five relationship orientations that address the ways in which people deal with each other; these can be considered to be cultural dimensions that are analogous to Hofstede's dimensions. Trompenaars also looked at attitudes toward both time and the environment, and the result of his research is a wealth of information helping to explain how cultures differ and offering practical ways in which MNCs can do business in various countries. The following discussion examines each of the five relationship orientations as well as attitudes toward time and the environment.[43]

Universalism vs. Particularism

Universalism is the belief that ideas and practices can be applied everywhere without modification. *Particularism* is the belief that circumstances dictate how ideas and practices should be applied. In cultures with high universalism, the focus is more on formal rules than on relationships, business contracts are adhered to very closely, and people believe that "a deal is a deal." In cultures with high

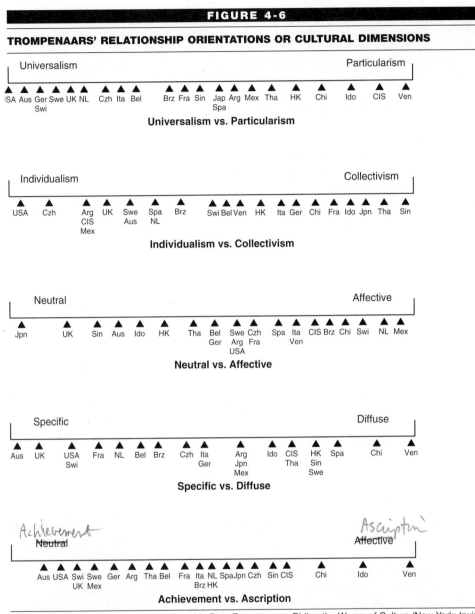

FIGURE 4-6

TROMPENAARS' RELATIONSHIP ORIENTATIONS OR CULTURAL DIMENSIONS

Universalism ... Particularism

Universalism vs. Particularism

Individualism ... Collectivism

Individualism vs. Collectivism

Neutral ... Affective

Neutral vs. Affective

Specific ... Diffuse

Specific vs. Diffuse

Neutral ... Affective

Achievement vs. Ascription

Source: Adapted from information found in Fons Trompenaars, *Riding the Waves of Culture* (New York: Irwin, 1994).

particularism, the focus is more on relationships and trust than on formal rules. In a particularist culture, legal contracts often are modified, and as people get to know each other better, they often change the way in which deals are executed. Trompenaars found that in countries such as the United States, Australia, Germany, Sweden, and the United Kingdom, there was high universalism, while countries such as Venezuela, the former Soviet Union, Indonesia, and China were high on particularism. Figure 4-6 shows the continuum.

Based on these findings, Trompenaars recommends that when individuals from particularist cultures do business in a universalist culture, they should be prepared for rational, professional arguments and a "let's get down to business" attitude. Conversely, when individuals from universalist cultures do business in a particularist environment, they should be prepared for personal meandering or irrelevancies that seem to go nowhere and should not regard personal, get-to-know-you attitudes as mere small talk.

Individualism vs. Collectivism

Individualism and collectivism are key dimensions in Hofstede's earlier research. Although Trompenaars derived these two relationships differently than Hofstede, they still have the same basic meaning. Individualism refers to people regarding themselves as individuals, while collectivism refers to people regarding themselves as part of a group. As shown in Figure 4-6, the United States, Czechoslovakia, Argentina, the former Soviet Union, and Mexico have high individualism. These findings of Trompenaars are particularly interesting, because they differ somewhat from those of Hofstede, as reported in Figure 4-2. Although the definitions are not exactly the same, the fact that there are differences (e.g., Mexico and Argentina are collectivist in Hofstede's findings but individualistic in Trompenaars' research) points out that cultural values may be changing (i.e., Hofstede's findings may be dated). For example, with Mexico now part of NAFTA and the global economy, this country may have moved from dominant collectivist cultural values to more individualist values. Trompenaars also found that the former communist countries of Czechoslovakia and the Soviet Union now appear to be quite individualistic, which of course is contrary to assumptions and conventional wisdom about the former communist bloc. In other words, Trompenaars points out the complex, dynamic nature of culture and the danger of overgeneralization.

Applied to international management guidelines, negotiations in cultures with high individualism typically are made on the spot by a representative, people ideally achieve things alone, and they assume a great deal of personal responsibility. In cultures with high collectivism, decisions typically are referred to committees, people ideally achieve things in groups, and they jointly assume responsibility.

Trompenaars recommends that when people from cultures with high individualism deal with those from collectivist cultures, they should have patience for the time taken to consent and to consult, and they should aim to build lasting relationships. When people from cultures with high collectivism deal with those from individualist cultures, they should be prepared to make quick decisions and commit their organization to these decisions. Also, collectivists dealing with individualists should realize that the reason they are dealing with only one negotiator (as opposed to a group) is that this person is respected by his or her organization and has its authority and esteem.

Neutral vs. Affective

A *neutral culture* is one in which emotions are held in check. As seen in Figure 4-6, both Japan and the United Kingdom are high neutral cultures. People in these countries try not to show their feelings; they act stoically and maintain their composure. An *affective culture* is one in which emotions are openly and naturally expressed. People in affective cultures often smile a great deal, talk loudly when they are excited, and greet each other with a great deal of enthusiasm. Mexico, the Netherlands, and Switzerland are examples of high affective cultures.

Trompenaars recommends that when individuals from affective cultures do business in neutral cultures, they should put as much as they can on paper and submit it to the other side. They should realize that lack of emotion does not mean disinterest or boredom, but rather that people from neutral cultures do not like to show their hand. Conversely, when those from neutral cultures do business in affective cultures, they should not be put off stride when the other side creates scenes or grows animated and boisterous, and they should try to respond warmly to the affections of the other group.

Specific vs. Diffuse

A *specific culture* is one in which individuals have a large public space they readily let others enter and share and a small private space they guard closely and share with only close friends and associates. A *diffuse culture* is one in which both public and private space are similar in size and individuals guard their public space carefully, because entry into public space affords entry into private space as well. As shown in Figure 4-6, Austria, the United Kingdom, the United States, and Switzerland all are specific cultures, while Venezuela, China, and Spain are diffuse cultures. In specific cultures, people often are invited into a person's open, public space; individuals in these cultures often are open and extroverted; and there is a strong separation of work and private life. In diffuse cultures, people are not quickly invited into a person's open, public space, because once they are in, there is easy entry into the private space as well. Individuals in these cultures often appear to be indirect and introverted, and work and private life often are closely linked.

An example of these specific and diffuse cultural dimensions is provided by the United States and Germany. A U.S. professor, such as Robert Smith, Ph.D., generally would be called Dr. Smith by students when at his U.S. university. When shopping, however, he might be referred to by the store clerk as Bob, and he might even ask the clerk's advice regarding some of his intended purchases. When bowling, Bob might just be one of the guys, even to a team member who happens to be a graduate student in his department. The reason for these changes in status is that, with the specific U.S. cultural values, people have large public spaces and often conduct themselves differently depending on their public role. At the same time, however, Bob has private space that is off-limits to the students who must call him Doctor in class. In high diffuse cultures, on the other hand, a person's public and private life often are similar. Therefore, in Germany, Herr Professor Doktor Hans Schmidt would be referred to this way at the university, local market, and bowling alley—and even his wife might address him formally in public. A great deal of formality is maintained, often giving the impression that Germans are stuffy or aloof.

Trompenaars recommends that when those from specific cultures do business in diffuse cultures, they should respect a person's title, age, and background connections, and they should not get impatient when people are being indirect or circuitous. Conversely, when individuals from diffuse cultures do business in specific cultures, they should try to get to the point and be efficient, learn to structure meetings with the judicious use of agendas, and not use their titles or acknowledge achievements or skills that are irrelevant to the issues being discussed.

Achievement vs. Ascription

An *achievement culture* is one in which people are accorded status based on how well they perform their functions. An *ascription culture* is one in which status is attributed based on who or what a person is. Achievement cultures give high status to high achievers, such as the company's number one salesperson or the medical researcher who has found a cure for a rare form of bone cancer. Ascription cultures accord status based on age, gender, or social connections. For example, in an ascription culture, a person who has been with the company for 40 years may be listened to carefully because of the respect that others have for the individual's age and longevity with the firm, and an individual who has friends in high places may be afforded status because of whom she knows. As shown in Figure 4-6, Austria, the United States, Switzerland, and the United Kingdom are achievement cultures, while Venezuela, Indonesia, and China are ascription cultures.

Trompenaars recommends that when individuals from achievement cultures do business in ascription cultures, they should make sure that their group has older, senior, and formal position-holders who can impress the other side, and they should respect the status and influence of their counterparts in the other group. Conversely, he recommends that when individuals from ascription cultures do business in achievement cultures, they should make sure that their group has sufficient data, technical advisers, and knowledgeable people to convince the other that they are proficient, and they should respect the knowledge and information of their counterparts on the other team.

Time

Aside from the five relationship orientations, another major cultural difference is the way in which people deal with the concept of time. Trompenaars has identified two different approaches: sequential, and synchronous. In cultures where sequential approaches are prevalent, people tend to do only one activity at a time, keep appointments strictly, and show a strong preference for following plans as they are laid out and not deviating from them. In cultures where synchronous approaches are common, people tend to do more than one activity at a time, appointments are approximate and may be changed at a moment's notice, and schedules generally are subordinate to relationships. People in synchronous-time cultures often will stop what they are doing to meet and greet individuals coming into their office.

A good contrast is provided by the United States, Mexico, and France. In the United States, people tend to be guided by sequential-time orientation and thus set a schedule and stick to it. Mexicans operate under more of a synchronous-time orientation and thus tend to be much more flexible, often building slack into their schedules to allow for interruptions. The French are similar to the Mexicans and, when making plans, often determine the objectives they want to accomplish but leave open the timing and other factors that are beyond their control; this way, they can adjust and modify their approach as they go along. As Trompenaars noted, "For the French and Mexicans, what was important was **that** they get to the end, **not** the particular path or sequence by which that end was reached."[44]

Another interesting time-related contrast is the degree to which cultures are past- or present-oriented as opposed to future-oriented. In countries such as the United States, Italy, and Germany, the future is more important than the past or the present. In countries such as Venezuela, Indonesia, and Spain, the present is most important. In France and Belgium, all three time periods are of approximately equal importance. Because different emphases are given to different time periods, adjusting to these cultural differences can create challenges.

Trompenaars recommends that when doing business with future-oriented cultures, effective international managers should emphasize the opportunities and limitless scope that any agreement can have, agree to specific deadlines for getting things done, and be aware of the core competence or continuity that the other party intends to carry with it into the future. When doing business with past- or present-oriented cultures, he recommends that managers emphasize the history and tradition of the culture, find out whether internal relationships will sanction the types of changes that need to be made, and agree to future meetings in principle but fix no deadlines for completion.

The Environment

Trompenaars also examined the ways in which people deal with their environment. Specific attention should be given to whether they believe in controlling outcomes (inner-directed) or letting things take their own course (outer-directed). One of the things he asked managers to do was choose between the following statements:

1. What happens to me is my own doing.
2. Sometimes I feel that I do not have enough control over the directions my life is taking.

Managers who believe in controlling their own environment would opt for the first choice; those who believe that they are controlled by their environment and cannot do much about it would opt for the second. Here is an example by country of the sample respondents who believe that what happens to them is their own doing[45]:

United States	89%
Switzerland	84%
Australia	81%
Belgium	76%
Indonesia	73%
Hong Kong	69%
Greece	63%
Singapore	58%
Japan	56%
China	35%

TABLE 4-5

CULTURAL GROUPS BASED ON TROMPENAARS' RESEARCH

Relationship	Anglo cluster	
	United States	United Kingdom
Individualism	X	X
Collectivism		
Specific relationship	X	X
Diffuse relationship		
Universalism	X	X
Particularism		
Neutral relationship		X
Affective relationship	X	
Achievement	X	X
Ascription		

Relationship	Asian cluster				
	Japan	China	Indonesia	Hong Kong	Singapore
Individualism					
Collectivism	X	X	X	X	X
Specific relationship					
Diffuse relationship	X	X	X	X	X
Universalism					
Particularism	X	X	X	X	X
Neutral relationships					
Affective relationships	X	X	X	X	X
Achievement					
Ascription	X	X	X	X	X

Relationship	Latin American cluster			
	Argentina	Mexico	Venezuela	Brazil
Individualism	X	X		X
Collectivism			X	
Specific relationship				X
Diffuse relationship	X	X	X	
Universalism				X
Particularism	X	X	X	
Neutral relationships	X	X	X	
Affective relationships				X
Achievement	X	X		
Ascription			X	X

Relationship	Latin European cluster			
	France	Belgium	Spain	Italy
Individualism			X	
Collectivism	X	X		X
Specific relationship	X	X		
Diffuse relationship			X	X
Universalism	X	X		X
Particularism			X	

TABLE 4-5 (Continued)

Relationship	Latin European cluster (Continued)			
	France	Belgium	Spain	Italy
Neutral relationships			X	
Affective relationships	X	X		X
Achievement			X	
Ascription	X	X		X

Relationship	Germanic cluster			
	Austria	Germany	Switzerland	Czechoslovakia
Individualism	X			
Collectivism		X	X	X
Specific relationship	X		X	X
Diffuse relationship		X		
Universalism	X	X	X	X
Particularism				
Neutral relationships	X			X
Affective relationships		X	X	
Achievement	X	X		X
Ascription			X	

Source: Adapted from information in Fons Trompenaars, *Riding the Waves of Culture* (New York: Irwin, 1994).

In the United States, managers feel strongly that they are masters of their own fate. This helps to account for their dominant attitude (sometimes bordering on aggressiveness) toward the environment and discomfort when things seem to get out of control. Many Asian cultures do not share these views. They believe that things move in waves or natural shifts and one must "go with the flow," so a flexible attitude, characterized by a willingness to compromise and maintain harmony with nature, is important.

Trompenaars recommends that when dealing with those from cultures that believe in dominating the environment, it is important to play hard ball, test the resilience of the opponent, win some objectives, and always lose from time to time. When dealing with those from cultures that believe in letting things take their natural course, it is important to be persistent and polite, maintain good relationships with the other party, and try to win together and lose apart.

Cultural Patterns or Clusters

Like Hofstede's and the earlier work of Ronen and Shenkar, Trompenaars' research lends itself to cultural patterns or clusters. Table 4-5 relates his findings to the five relational orientations, categorized into the same types of clusters that Ronen and Shenkar used (see Figure 4-5). There is a great deal of similarity between the Trompenaars and the Ronen and Shenkar clusters. Both the United States and United Kingdom profiles are the same, except for the neutral (U.K.) and affective (U.S.) dimension. So are those in most of the Asian countries, including Japan, which was left out of the Ronen and Shenkar clusters and labeled an independent.

Brazil, which also was left out of the Ronen and Shenkar clusters, continues to be sufficiently different from other members of the Latin American group in the Trompenaars-derived Table 4.5. In other words, Brazil still appears to be independent. Additionally, while France and Belgium, in the Latin European Trompenaars group, have identical profiles, Spain is significantly different from both them as well as from Italy. This shows that earlier cluster groups, such as that of Ronen and Shenkar, may need to be revised in light of more recent data.

Overall, Table 4-5 shows that a case can be made for cultural similarities between clusters of countries. With only small differences, Trompenaars' research helps to support, and more important, to extend, the work of Hofstede as well as Ronen and Shenkar. Such research provides a useful point of departure for recognizing cultural differences, and it provides guidelines for doing business effectively around the world.

SUMMARY OF KEY POINTS

1. Culture is acquired knowledge that people use to interpret experience and generate social behavior. Culture also has the characteristics of being learned, shared, transgenerational, symbolic, patterned, and adaptive. There are many dimensions of cultural diversity, including centralized vs. decentralized decision making, safety vs. risk, individual vs. group rewards, informal vs. formal procedures, high vs. low organizational loyalty, co-operation vs. competition, short-term vs. long-term horizons, and stability vs. innovation.

2. Values are basic convictions that people have regarding what is right and wrong, good and bad, important and unimportant. Research shows that there are both differences and similarities between the work values and managerial values of different cultural groups. Work values often reflect culture and industrialization, and managerial values are highly related to success. Research shows that values tend to change over time and often reflect age and experience.

3. Hofstede has identified and researched four major dimensions of culture: power distance, uncertainty avoidance, individualism, and masculinity. Each will affect a country's political and social system. The integration of these factors into two-dimensional figures can illustrate the complexity of culture's effect on behavior.

4. In recent years, researchers have attempted to cluster countries into similar cultural groupings to study similarities and differences. Through use of smallest space analysis, they have constructed two-dimensional maps that illustrate the similarities in work values and attitudes between countries. These syntheses, one of which is provided in Figure 4-5, help us to understand intercultural similarities.

5. Recent research by Trompenaars has examined five relationship orientations: universalism-particularism, individualism-collectivism, affective-neutral, specific-diffuse, and achievement-ascription. Trompenaars also looked at attitudes toward time and the environment. The result is a wealth of information helping to explain how cultures differ as well as practical ways in which MNCs can do business effectively in these environments. In particular, his findings update those of Hofstede while at the same time help to support the previous work by both Hofstede and Ronen and Shenkar on clustering countries.

KEY TERMS

culture

values

power distance

uncertainty avoidance

individualism

collectivism

masculinity

femininity

smallest space analysis (SSA)

universalism

particularism

neutral culture

affective culture

specific culture

diffuse culture

achievement culture

ascription culture

REVIEW AND DISCUSSION QUESTIONS

1. What is meant by the term "culture"? In what way can measuring attitudes about the following help to differentiate between cultures: centralized or decentralized decision making, safety or risk, individual or group rewards, high or low organizational loyalty, co-operation or competition? Use these attitudes to compare the United States, Germany, and Japan. Based on your comparisons, what conclusions can you draw regarding the impact of culture on behavior?

2. What is meant by the term "value"? Are cultural values the same worldwide, or are there marked differences? Are these values changing over time, or are they fairly constant? How does your answer relate to the role of values in a culture?

3. What are the four dimensions of culture studied by Geert Hofstede? Identify and describe each. What is the cultural profile of the United States? Of Asian countries? Of Latin American countries? Of Latin European countries? Based on your comparisons of these four profiles, what conclusions can you draw regarding cultural challenges facing individuals in one group when they interact with individuals in one of the other groups?

4. Of what value is Figure 4-5 to the study of international management? Offer at least three advantages or benefits of the figure.

5. As people engage in more international travel and become more familiar with other countries, will cultural differences decline as a roadblock to international understanding, or will they continue to be a major barrier? Defend your answer.

6. What are the characteristics of each of the following pairs of cultural characteristics derived from Trompenaars' research: universalism vs. particularism, neutral vs. affective, specific vs. diffuse, achievement vs. ascription? Compare and contrast each pair.

7. In what way is time a cultural factor? In what way is the need to control the environment a cultural factor? Give an example for each.

PRACTICAL INTERNATIONAL MANAGEMENT ASSIGNMENT

Interview three foreign students from different countries, preferably one from Europe, one from Asia, and one from a developing country elsewhere in the world, who attend your school. Ask each to describe the three biggest cultural problems that Americans face when communicating and interacting with people from his or her country. Based on your interviews, what conclusions can you draw? Compare your answers with those of your classmates. What overall conclusion can you draw about the impact of culture on behavior?

In Taiwan, blinking the eyes at someone is considered to be impolite.

In the International Spotlight

Taiwan

Taiwan (long called "Formosa" by Westerners) is an island located 100 miles off the southeast coast of the China mainland. The island is only 13,900 square miles, but its population is approximately 21 million, one of the highest population densities in the world. In 1949, the government of the Republic of China (ROC) moved to Taiwan after establishment of the communist government on the mainland. China still considers Taiwan to be a break-away province. Taiwan has been controlled by the Nationalists through the years, but Lee Teng-hui was chosen in the first democratic election on March 23, 1996. The literacy rate is 90 percent, and many people speak English. Taiwan is known as one of the four Tigers of Asia (along with South Korea, Singapore, and Hong Kong). The gross national product is approximately $225 billion, and per-capita income is around $15,000. This is relatively low by U.S., Japanese, and Western European standards, but much higher than that in mainland China. This so-called "Other China" has moved its export-oriented economy into high gear: a good example is the computer industry, which is growing by leaps and bounds.

A few years ago, many people would have scoffed at a consumer who was buying computer equipment made in Taiwan. The country's computer equipment, in the eyes of the world, consisted of rip-offs or copycat machines clearly inferior to the name brands. However, Taiwan's computer industry now has a very different reputation. In recent years, Sun Microsystems, Microsoft, and Intel, to name but three computer firms, have gone to Taiwan and cut deals to have hardware built there; Sun Microsystems, for example, has entered into a deal with the Taiwanese to build versions of SPARCstation, Sun's newest product. Aware that this development could greatly affect their own ability to produce chips for PC clones, Microsoft and Intel immediately started their own search for Taiwanese suppliers. All three MNCs have come to realize not only that Taiwan manufacturers are less expensive but also have highly developed technology and likely will be a major source of PCs during the years ahead.

In 1987, Taiwan shipped 2 million personal computers. By the early 1990s, this number was up to 3 million and still is growing today. In fact, Taiwan has now leapfrogged South Korea in the production of PCs and entered into a series of private-label contracts with U.S. importers. Not only were Taiwanese firms able to offer state-of-the-art technology, but because they could obtain more of their components locally, they offered lower prices than even the Japanese.

Taiwan does not intend to rest on its laurels. As one knowledgeable observer has noted, "Ultimately, Taiwan's PC makers will have to shift to more sophisticated machines. They'll also have to time the move right—before the market takes off, but not way before." Many international experts believe that because of its previous successes, Taiwan will be able to meet this new challenge.

1. What are some current issues facing Taiwan? What is the climate for doing business in Taiwan today?

2. In terms of cultural dimensions, is Taiwan much different from the United States? (Use Figure 4-5 in your answer.) Why, or why not?

3. In what way might culture be a stumbling block for firms seeking to set up businesses in Taiwan?

4. How are the three firms in this case managing to sidestep or overcome the cultural barriers?

You Be the International Management Consultant

A Jumping-Off Place

A successful, medium-sized U.S. manufacturing firm in Ohio has decided to open a plant near Madrid, Spain. The company was attracted to this location for three reasons. First, the firm's current licensing agreement with a German firm is scheduled to come to an end within 6 months, and the U.S. manufacturer feels that it can do a better job of building and selling heavy machinery in the EU than the German firm. Second, the U.S. manufacturer has invested almost $300 million in R&D over the last 3 years. The result is a host of new patents and other technological breakthroughs that now make this company a worldwide leader in the production of specialized heavy equipment. Third, labor costs in Spain are lower than in most other EU countries, and the company feels that this will prove extremely helpful in its efforts to capture market share in Greater Europe.

Because this is the manufacturer's first direct venture into the EU, it has decided to take on a Spanish partner. The latter will provide much of the on-site support, such as local contracts, personnel hiring, legal assistance, and governmental negotiations. In turn, the U.S. manufacturer will provide the capital for renovating the manufacturing plant, the R&D technology, and the technical training.

If the venture works out as planned, the partners will expand operations into Italy and use this location as a jumping-off point for tapping the Central and Eastern European markets. Additionally, because the cultures of Spain and Italy are similar, the U.S. manufacturer feels that staying within the Latin European cultural cluster can be synergistic. Plans for later in the decade call for establishing operations in northern France, which will serve as a jumping-off point for both Northern Europe and other major EU countries, such as Germany, the Netherlands, and Belgium. However, the company first wants to establish a foothold in Spain and get this operation working successfully, then it will look into expansion plans.

1. In what way will the culture of Spain be different from that of the United States? In answering this question, refer to Figures 4-2, 4-3, 4-4, and 4-5.
2. If the company expands operations into Italy, will its experience in Spain be valuable, or will the culture be so different that the manufacturer will have to begin anew in determining how to address cultural challenges and opportunities? Explain.
3. If the firm expands into France, will its previous experiences in Spain and Italy be valuable in helping the company address cultural challenges? Be complete in your answer.

CHAPTER 4 ENDNOTES

1. Also see Richard Mead, *International Management* (Cambridge, MA: Blackwell Publishing, 1994), pp. 6–14.
2. Fred Luthans, *Organizational Behavior,* 7th ed. (New York: McGraw-Hill, 1995), pp. 534–535; J. P. Spradley, *The Ethnographic Interview* (New York: Holt, 1979).
3. Gary Bonvillian and William A. Nowlin, "Cultural Awareness: An Essential Element of Doing Business Abroad," *Business Horizons,* November-December 1994, pp. 44–54.
4. Srilata Zaheer, "Overcoming the Liability of Foreignness," *Academy of Management Journal,* June 1995, pp. 341–363.
5. Roger E. Axtell (ed.), *Do's and Taboos around the World,* 2nd ed. (New York: Wiley, 1990), p. 3.
6. Nancy J. Adler, "Cross-Cultural Management: Issues to Be Faced," *International Studies of Management & Organization,* Spring-Summer 1983, pp. 7–45; Nancy J. Adler, "A Typology of Management Studies Involving Culture," *Journal of International Business Studies,* Fall 1983, pp. 29–47.
7. R. Miyajima, "Organization Ideology of Japanese Managers," *Management International Review,* vol. 26, no. 1, 1986, pp. 73–76.
8. Pat Choate and Juyne Linger, *The High-Flex Society* (New York: Alfred K. Knopf, 1986), p. 65; Pat Choate and Juyne Linger, "Tailored Trade: Dealing with the World as It Is," *Harvard Business Review,* January-February 1988, p. 90.
9. "Teaching Asia to Stay Asia," *Economist,* October 8, 1994, p. 39.
10. Lillian H. Chaney and Jeanette S. Martin, *Intercultural Business Communication* (Englewood Cliffs, NJ: Prentice-Hall, 1995), p. 115.
11. For more on this topic, see Paul D. Reynolds, "Organizational Culture as Related to Industry, Position, and Performance: A Preliminary Report," *Journal of Management Studies,* May 1986, pp. 333–345.
12. Barry Z. Posner and William H. Schmidt, "Values of American Managers: Then and Now," *HR Focus,* March 1992, p. 13.
13. Philip R. Harris and Robert T. Moran, *Managing Cultural Differences* (Houston: Gulf Publishing, 1991), pp. 78–81.
14. Christopher Orpen, "The Work Values of Western and Tribal Black Employees," *Journal of Cross-Cultural Psychology,* March 1978, pp. 99–111.
15. William Whitely and George W. England, "Variability in Common Dimensions of Managerial Values due to Value Orientation and Country Differences," *Personnel Psychology,* Spring 1980, pp. 77–89.

16. Ibid., p. 87.
17. See David G. Myers, *Social Psychology,* 3rd ed. (New York: McGraw-Hill, 1990), pp. 171–172.
18. George W. England and Raymond Lee, "The Relationship between Managerial Values and Managerial Success in the United States, Japan, India, and Australia," *Journal of Applied Psychology,* August 1974, pp. 418–419.
19. George W. England, "Managers and Their Value Systems: A Five-Country Comparative Study," *Columbia Journal of World Business,* Summer 1978, p. 39.
20. A. Reichel and D. M. Flynn, "Values in Transition: An Empirical Study of Japanese Managers in the U.S.," *Management International Review,* vol. 23, no. 4, 1984, pp. 69–70.
21. Hermann F. Schwind and Richard B. Peterson, "Shifting Personal Values in the Japanese Management System," *International Studies of Management & Organization,* Summer 1985, pp. 60–74.
22. Ibid., p. 72.
23. Geert Hofstede, *Culture's Consequences: International Differences in Work-Related Values* (Beverly Hills: Sage Publications, 1980).
24. Derek S. Pugh and David J. Hickson, *Writers on Organizations,* 4th ed. (Newbury Park, CA: Sage Publications, 1989), p. 92.
25. Geert Hofstede, *Cultures and Organizations: Software of the Mind* (London: McGraw-Hill U.K., Ltd., 1991), pp. 251–252.
26. Geert Hofstede and Michael Bond, "The Need for Synergy among Cross-Cultural Studies," *Journal of Cross-Cultural Psychology,* December 1984, p. 419.
27. A. R. Negandhi and S. B. Prasad, *Comparative Management* (New York: Appleton-Century-Crofts, 1971), p. 128.
28. For additional insights, see Mark F. Peterson et al., "Role Conflict, Ambiguity, and Overload: A 21-Nation Study," *Academy of Management Journal,* June 1995, pp. 429–452.
29. Hofstede, *Culture's Consequences.*
30. Ibid.
31. Ibid.
32. Ibid., pp. 419–420.
33. Ibid., p. 420.
34. Simcha Ronen and Allen I. Kraut, "Similarities among Countries Based on Employee Work Values and Attitudes," *Columbia Journal of World Business,* Summer 1977, p. 90.
35. Mason Haire, Edward E. Ghiselli, and Lyman W. Porter, *Managerial Thinking: An International Study* (New York: John Wiley & Sons, 1966); D. Sirota and J.

M. Greenwood, "Understand Your Overseas Work Force," *Harvard Business Review,* January-February 1971, pp. 53–60.

36. Ronen and Kraut, "Similarities among Countries," p. 95.

37. Simcha Ronen and Oded Shenkar, "Clustering Countries on Attitudinal Dimensions: A Review and Synthesis," *Academy of Management Journal,* September 1985, pp. 435–454.

38. Ibid., p. 452.

39. James E. Everett, Bruce W. Stening, and Peter A. Longton, "Some Evidence for an International Managerial Culture," *Journal of Management Studies,* April 1982, pp. 153–162.

40. Dexter Dunphy, "Convergence/Divergence: A Temporal Review of the Japanese Enterprise and Its Management," *Academy of Management Review,* July 1987, pp. 445–459.

41. Fons Trompenaars, *Riding the Waves of Culture* (New York: Irwin, 1994), p. 10.

42. Talcott Parsons, *The Social System* (New York: Free Press, 1951).

43. Also see Lisa Hoecklin, *Managing Cultural Differences* (Workingham, England: Addison-Wesley Publishing, 1995).

44. Trompenaars, *Riding the Waves of Culture,* p. 131.

45. Ibid., p. 140.

MANAGING ACROSS CULTURES

OBJECTIVES OF THE CHAPTER

Traditionally, both scholars and practitioners have assumed the universality of management. There was a tendency to take those management concepts and techniques that worked at home into other countries and cultures. It is now clear, both from practice[1] and cross-cultural research,[2] that this universality assumption of management, at least across cultures, does not hold up. Although there is a tendency in a borderless economy and with global integration strategies of MNCs to promote a universalist approach, there is enough evidence from cross-cultural researchers such as Nancy Adler and others to conclude that the universalist assumption that may have held for U.S. organizations and employees is not generally true in other cultures.[3]

The overriding purpose of this chapter is to examine how MNCs can and should manage across cultures. This chapter puts into practice the previous Chapter 4 on the meaning and dimensions of culture and serves as a foundation and point of departure for subsequent Chapters 7 and 8 on strategic management. The first part addresses the traditional tendency to attempt to replicate successful home country operations overseas without addressing cultural differences. Next, attention is given to cross-cultural challenges, focusing on how differences can impact on multinational management strategies. Finally, the cultures in specific countries and geographic regions are examined. The specific objectives of this chapter are:

1. **EXAMINE** the impact of globalization and national responsiveness on international strategic management.
2. **DISCUSS** cross-cultural differences and similarities.
3. **REVIEW** cultural differences in select countries and regions, and note some of the important strategic guidelines for doing business in each.

THE STRATEGY FOR MANAGING ACROSS CULTURES

Awareness of cultural similarities and differences is becoming increasingly important to the successful strategies of MNCs as they become more transnational. A good example is Asea Brown Boveri (ABB), the giant multinational conglomerate formed by the merger of Swedish, German, and Swiss firms. Although headquartered in Zurich, Switzerland, it has operations throughout the world.[4] Over the past decade, this MNC has bought or taken minority positions in 60 firms, including U.S. companies such as Combustion Engineering, well-known for its manufacture of power generation and process automation equipment, and Westinghouse's transmission and distribution operations. In addition to making locomotives in Sweden, this MNC has a diverse product line, including robots, electric power equipment, thermonuclear reaction equipment, and hospital instruments. Because of its global business, ABB is forced to balance a concern for globalization with a need to address local or regional needs. The head of ABB puts it this way:

> The vast majority of our businesses . . . fall somewhere between the superlocal and the superglobal. These are the businesses in which building a multidomestic organization offers powerful advantages. You want to be able to optimize a business globally—to specialize in the production of components, to drive economies of scale as far as you can, to rotate managers and technologists around the world to share expertise and solve problems. But you also want to have deep local roots everywhere you operate—build products in the countries where you sell them, recruiting the best local talent from the universities, working with the local government to increase exports. If you build such an organization, you create a business advantage that's damn difficult to copy.[5]

How does ABB accomplish this feat? Obviously, the MNC must develop state-of-the-art quality products and services; however, it also needs to learn about the differing cultural contexts of the far-flung operations and unique needs of its customers. For example, ABB recently won a $420 million contract to build locomotives for moving freight through the Alps. Part of this success resulted from realizing the deep concern that the Swiss have for the environment. Realizing this cultural value resulted in the company's designing trains that would be strong enough to get the job done but not pollute the environment. Recently, ABB also won a contract to manufacture locomotives for India. The Indian government needed credit to pay for these imports, and the two countries most willing to grant such credit were Germany and Italy. Because ABB has operations in both of these nations and is building locomotive components there, it was able to persuade the German and Italian governments to give India the credit that it needed. In short, ABB has learned to balance a concern for selling its products worldwide with a need to address local concerns. As the chairman of ABB recently noted, "We can't have people abdicating their nationalities, saying 'I am no longer German, I am international.' The world doesn't work like that. If you are selling products and services in Germany, you better be German!"[6]

The ABB example helps to illustrate one of the major problems facing MNCs as they attempt to manage across cultures: a natural tendency to do things abroad the way they are done at home. This commonly is referred to in strategic international management as the "globalization vs. national responsiveness conflict." As used here, *globalization* is the production and distribution of products and services of a homogeneous type and quality on a worldwide basis.[7] To a growing

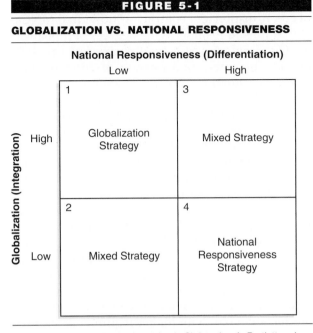

FIGURE 5-1

GLOBALIZATION VS. NATIONAL RESPONSIVENESS

Source: Adapted from information in Christopher A. Bartlett and Sumantra Ghoshal, *Managing across Borders: The Transnational Solution* (Boston: Harvard Business School Press, 1989).

extent, the customers of MNCs have homogenized tastes, and this has helped to spread international consumerism. For example, throughout North America, the EU and Japan, there has been a growing acceptance of standardized consumer electronic goods, automobiles, computers, calculators, and similar products. This goal of efficient economic performance through a universal globalization strategy, however, has left MNCs open to the charge that they are overlooking the need to address national responsiveness. *National responsiveness* is the need to understand the different consumer tastes in segmented regional markets[8] and respond to different national standards and regulations imposed by autonomous governments and agencies.[9]

Globalization vs. National Responsiveness Matrix

The issue of globalization vs. national responsiveness can be analyzed conceptually via a two-dimensional matrix.[10] Figure 5-1 provides an example.[11]

The vertical axis in the figure measures the need for economic integration, frequently referred to as globalization. Movement up the axis results in a greater degree of economic integration. Globalization generates economies of scale (takes advantage of large size) as a firm moves into worldwide markets selling a single product or service. These economies are captured through centralizing specific activities in the value-added chain. They also occur by reaping the benefits of increased coordination and control of geographically dispersed activities.

The horizontal axis measures the need for multinationals to respond to national responsiveness or differentiation. This suggests that MNCs must address local tastes and government regulations. The result may be a geographic dispersion of activities or a decentralization of co-ordination and control for individual MNCs.

Figure 5-1 depicts four basic situations in relation to the degrees of globalization vs. national responsiveness. Quadrants 1 and 4 are the simplest cases. In quadrant 1, the need for integration is high and for awareness of differentiation low. In terms of economies of scale, this situation leads to competitive strategies based on price competition. In this quadrant 1–type of environment, mergers and acquisitions often occur. The opposite situation is represented by quadrant 4, where the need for differentiation is high but the concern for integration low. In this case, niche companies adapt products to satisfy the high demands of differentiation and ignore economies of scale because integration is not very important.

Quadrants 2 and 3 reflect more complex environmental situations. Quadrant 2 incorporates those cases in which both the need for integration and awareness of differentiation are low. Both the potential to obtain economies of scale and the benefits of being sensitive to differentiation are of little value. Typical strategies in quadrant 2 are characterized by increased international standardization of products and services. This situation can lead to lower needs for centralized quality control and centralized strategic decision making, while simultaneously eliminating requirements to adapt activities to individual countries.

In quadrant 3, the needs for integration and differentiation are high. There is a strong need for integration in production along with higher requirements for regional differentiation in marketing. Quadrant 3 is the most challenging quadrant and one where successful MNCs seek to operate. The problem for many MNCs, however, is the cultural challenges associated with "localizing" a global focus.

Meeting the Challenge

Recent research reveals that far from addressing regional differentiation issues, many MNCs are committed to a *globalization imperative,* which is a belief that one worldwide approach to doing business is the key to both efficiency and effectiveness. One study, involving extensive examination of 115 medium and large MNCs and 103 affiliated subsidiaries in the United States, Canada, France, Germany, Japan, and the United Kingdom, found an overwhelming preponderance to use the same strategies abroad as at home.[12]

Despite these tendencies to use home strategies, effective MNCs are continuing their efforts to address local needs. A number of factors are helping to facilitate this need to develop unique strategies for different cultures, including:

1. The diversity of worldwide industry standards such as those in broadcasting, where television sets must be manufactured on a country-by-country basis.
2. A continual demand by local customers for differentiated products, as in the case of consumer goods that must meet local tastes.
3. The importance of being an insider, as in the case of customers who prefer to "buy local."
4. The difficulty of managing global organizations, as in the case of some local subsidiaries that want more decentralization and others that want less.
5. The need to allow subsidiaries to use their own abilities and talents and not be restrained by headquarters, as in the case of local units that know how to customize products for their market and generate high returns on investment with limited production output.

By responding to the cultural needs of local operations and customers, MNCs find that regional strategies can be used effectively in capturing and maintaining worldwide market niches. One of the best examples is Thomson Consumer Electronics, which has factories in four European countries: France, Germany, Spain, and the United Kingdom. Each factory assembles specific types of television sets for the European market. The German plant, for example, makes high-feature, large TV sets; the Spanish plant focuses on low-cost, small-screen sets. At the same time, Thomson has operations in North America, where it makes TV sets under the RCA and GE nameplates, drawing on suppliers and subassemblers, mostly in Mexico, to produce units for the regional market. Another example is Warner-Lambert, which has manufacturing facilities in Belgium, France, Germany, Italy, Ireland, Spain, and the United Kingdom. Each plant is specialized and produces a small number of products for the entire European market; in this way, each can focus on tailoring products for the unique demands of the various markets.

The globalization vs. national responsiveness challenge is even more acute when marketing cosmetics and other products that vary greatly in consumer use. For example, marketers sell toothpaste as a cosmetic product in Spain and Greece but as a cavity-fighter in the Netherlands and United States. Soap manufacturers market their product as a cosmetic item in Spain but as a functional commodity in Germany. Moreover, the way in which the marketing message is delivered also is important. For example:

- Germans want advertising that is factual and rational; they fear being manipulated by "the hidden persuader." The typical German spot features the standard family of two parents, two children, and grandmother.
- The French avoid reasoning or logic. Their advertising is predominantly emotional, dramatic, and symbolic. Spots are viewed as cultural events—art for the sake of money—and are reviewed as if they were literature or films.
- The British value laughter above all else. The typical broad, self-deprecating British commercial amuses by mocking both the advertiser and consumer.[13]

In some cases, both the product and the marketing message are similar worldwide. This is particularly true for high-end products, where the lifestyles and expectations of the market niche are similar regardless of the country. Heineken beer, Hennessey brandy, Porsche cars, and the *Financial Times* all appeal to consumer niches that are fairly homogeneous, regardless of geographic locale. The same is true at the lower end of the market for goods that are impulse purchases, novel products, or fast foods, such as Coca-Cola's soft drinks, McDonald's restaurants, Levi's jeans, pop music, and ice-cream bars. In most cases, however, it is necessary to modify products as well as the marketing approach for the regional or local market. One analysis noted that the more marketers understand about the way in which a particular culture tends to view emotion, enjoyment, friendship, humor, rules, status, and other culturally based behaviors, the more control they have over creating marketing messages that will be interpreted in the desired way.[14]

Figure 5-2 provides an example of the role that culture should play in advertising by recapping the five relationship orientations identified through Trompenaars' research (see Chapter 4). Figure 5-2 shows how value can be added to the marketing approach by carefully tailoring the advertising message to the particular culture. For example, advertising in the United States should target individual achievement, be expressive and direct, and appeal to U.S. values of success

FIGURE 5-2

TROMPENAARS' CULTURAL DIMENSIONS AND ADVERTISING: ADJUSTING THE MESSAGE FOR LOCAL MEANING

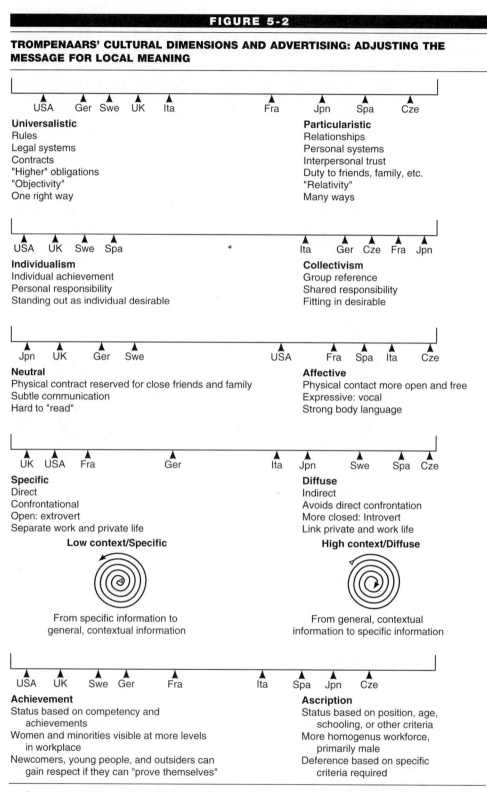

USA   Ger Swe UK   Ita   Fra   Jpn   Spa   Cze

Universalistic
Rules
Legal systems
Contracts
"Higher" obligations
"Objectivity"
One right way

Particularistic
Relationships
Personal systems
Interpersonal trust
Duty to friends, family, etc.
"Relativity"
Many ways

USA   UK   Swe   Spa   Ita   Ger Cze Fra   Jpn

Individualism
Individual achievement
Personal responsibility
Standing out as individual desirable

Collectivism
Group reference
Shared responsibility
Fitting in desirable

Jpn   UK   Ger   Swe   USA   Fra   Spa   Ita   Cze

Neutral
Physical contract reserved for close friends and family
Subtle communication
Hard to "read"

Affective
Physical contact more open and free
Expressive: vocal
Strong body language

UK   USA   Fra   Ger   Ita   Jpn   Swe   Spa   Cze

Specific
Direct
Confrontational
Open: extrovert
Separate work and private life

Diffuse
Indirect
Avoids direct confrontation
More closed: Introvert
Link private and work life

Low context/Specific

From specific information to
general, contextual information

High context/Diffuse

From general, contextual
information to specific information

USA   UK   Swe Ger   Fra   Ita   Spa Jpn   Cze

Achievement
Status based on competency and
  achievements
Women and minorities visible at more levels
  in workplace
Newcomers, young people, and outsiders can
  gain respect if they can "prove themselves"

Ascription
Status based on position, age,
  schooling, or other criteria
More homogenus workforce,
  primarily male
Deference based on specific
  criteria required

Source: Lisa Hoecklin, *Managing Cultural Differences* (Workingham, England: Addison-Wesley, 1995), p. 107, which is drawn from information found in Fons Trompenaars, *Riding the Waves of Culture* (New York: Irwin, 1994).

INTERNATIONAL MANAGEMENT IN ACTION

Ten Key Factors for MNC Success

Why are some international firms successful while others are not? Some of the main reasons are that successful multinational firms take a worldwide view of operations, support their overseas activities, pay close attention to political winds, and use local nationals whenever possible. These are the overall findings of a report that looked into the development of customized executive education programs. Specifically, there are 10 factors or guidelines that successful global firms seem to employ. Successful global competitors:

1. See themselves as multinational enterprises and are led by a management team that is comfortable in the world arena.
2. Develop integrated and innovative strategies that make it difficult and costly for other firms to compete.
3. Aggressively and effectively implement their worldwide strategy and back it with large investments.
4. Understand that technologic innovation no longer is confined to the United States and develop systems for tapping technologic innovation abroad.
5. Operate as if the world is one large market rather than a series of individual, small markets.
6. Have organization structures that are designed to handle their unique problems and challenges and thus provide them the greatest efficiency.
7. Develop a system that keeps them informed about political changes around the world and the implications of these changes on the firm.
8. Have management teams that are international in composition and thus better able to respond to the various demands of their respective markets.
9. Allow their outside directors to play an active role in the operation of the enterprise.
10. Are well managed and tend to follow such important guidelines as sticking close to the customer, having lean organization structures, and encouraging autonomy and entrepreneurial activity among the personnel.

through personal hard work. On the other hand, the focus in China and other Asian countries should be much more indirect and subtle, emphasizing group references, shared responsibility, and interpersonal trust.

The need to adjust global strategies for regional markets presents three major challenges for most MNCs.[15] First, the MNC must stay abreast of local market conditions and sidestep the temptation to assume that all markets are basically the same. Second, the MNC must know the strengths and weaknesses of its subsidiaries so that it can provide these units with the assistance needed in addressing local demands. Third, the multinational must give the subsidiary more autonomy so that it can respond to changes in local demands. "International Management in Action: Ten Key Factors for MNC Success" provides additional insights into the ways that successful MNCs address these challenges.

CROSS-CULTURAL DIFFERENCES AND SIMILARITIES

As shown in Chapter 4, culture can be similiar or quite different across countries. The challenge for MNCs is to recognize and effectively manage these similarities and differences. For instance, the way in which MNCs manage their home businesses often should be different from the way they manage their overseas operations. After recognizing the danger for MNCs to drift toward parochialism and simplification because of cultural differences, the discussion shifts to some examples of both cultural similarities and differences and how to effectively manage across cultures by a contingency approach.

Parochialism and Simplification

Parochialism is the tendency to view the world through one's own eyes and perspectives. This can be a difficult problem for many international managers, who often come from advanced economies and believe that their state-of-the-art knowledge is more than adequate to handle the challenges of doing business in lesser-developed countries. In addition, many of these managers have had a parochial point of view fostered by their education. Commenting on the parochialism of U.S. managers, Adler has pointed out the role that the academic community plays in this process. She notes:

> The vast majority of management schools are in the United States; the majority of management professors and researchers are American trained; and the majority of management research focuses on U.S. companies. Out of over 11,000 articles published in 24 management journals between 1971 and 1980, approximately 80 percent were found to be studies of the United States conducted by Americans. Fewer than 5 percent of the articles describing the behavior of people in organizations included the concept of culture. Fewer than 1 percent focused on people from two or more cultures working together, a crucial area for international business. The publishing of cross-cultural management articles has increased only slightly during the 1980s. The manager about to negotiate a major contract with a foreign national (a citizen of another country), the executive about to become a director of operations in another country, and the newly promoted vice president for international sales, all receive little guidance from the available management literature.[16]

Simplification is the process of exhibiting the same orientation toward different cultural groups. For example, the way in which a U.S. manager interacts with a British manager is the same way in which he or she behaves when doing business with an Asian executive. Moreover, this orientation reflects one's basic culture. Table 5-1 provides an example, showing several widely agreed-on, basic cultural orientations and the range of variations for each. Asterisks indicate the dominant U.S. orientation. Quite obviously, U.S. cultural values are not the same as those of managers from other cultures; as a result, a U.S. manager's attempt to simplify things results in erroneous behavior.

Understanding the culture in which they do business can make international managers more effective. Unfortunately, when placed in a culture with which they are unfamiliar, most international managers are not culturally knowledgeable, so they often misinterpret what is happening. This is particularly true when the environment is markedly different from the one in which they live. Consider, for example, the difference between the cultures in Japan and the United States. Japan has what could be called a high-context culture, which possesses characteristics such as:

1. Relationships between people are relatively long-lasting, and individuals feel deep personal involvement with each other.
2. Communication often is implicit, and individuals are taught from an early age to interpret these messages accurately.
3. People in authority are personally responsible for the actions of their subordinates, and this places a premium on loyalty to both superiors and subordinates.
4. Agreements tend to be spoken rather than written.
5. Insiders and outsiders are easily distinguishable, and outsiders typically do not gain entrance to the inner group.

These Japanese cultural characteristics are markedly different from those of low context cultures such as the United States, which possess the following characteristics:

TABLE 5-1	

SIX BASIC CULTURAL VARIATIONS

Orientations	Range of variations
What is the nature of people?	Good (changeable/unchangeable) A mixture of good and evil* Evil (changeable/unchangeable)
What is the person's relationship to nature?	Dominant* In harmony with nature Subjugation
What is the person's relationship to other people?	Lineal (hierarchic) Collateral (collectivist) Individualist*
What is the modality of human activity?	Doing* Being and becoming Being
What is the temporal focus of human activity?	Future* Present Past
What is the conception of space?	Private* Mixed Public

Note: *indicates the dominant U.S. orientation.
Source: Adapted from information found in Florence Rockwood Kluckhohn and Fred L. Stodtbeck, *Variations in Value Orientations* (New York: Peterson Publishing, 1961).

1. Relationships between individuals are relatively short in duration, and in general, deep personal involvement with others is not valued greatly.
2. Messages are explicit, and individuals are taught from a very early age to say exactly what they mean.
3. Authority is diffused throughout the bureaucratic system, and personal responsibility is hard to pin down.
4. Agreements tend to be in writing rather than spoken.
5. Insiders and outsiders are not readily distinguished, and the latter are encouraged to join the inner circle.[17]

These differences help to explain why Japanese managers in the United States often have trouble managing local operations, and vice versa. At the same time, it is important to realize that while there are cultural differences, there also are similarities. Therefore, in managing across cultures, not everything is totally different. Some approaches that work at home also work well in other cultural settings.

Similarities across Cultures

When internationalization began to take off in the 1970s, many companies quickly admitted that it would not be possible to do business in the same way in every corner of the globe. There was a secret hope, however, that many of the procedures and strategies that worked so well at home could be adopted overseas without modification. This has proved to be a false hope. At the same time, some similarities across cultures have been uncovered by researchers. For example, the co-author of this text (Luthans) and his associates studied through direct observation a sample of managers ($n = 66$) in the largest textile factory in Russia to determine their activities.[18] Similar to U.S. managers studied earlier, Russian managers carried out traditional management, communication, human resources, and networking activities. The study also found that again similar to U.S. managers, the relative attention given to the networking activity increased the Russian managers' opportunities for promotion, and communication activity was a significant predictor of effective performance in both Russia and the United States.[19]

Besides the similarities of managerial activities, another study at the same Russian factory tested whether organizational behavior modification (O.B. Mod.) interventions that led to performance improvements in U.S. organizations would hold true in Russia.[20] As with the applications of O.B. Mod. in the United States, Russian supervisors were trained to administer contingently social rewards (attention and praise) and positive feedback when they observed workers engaging in behaviors that contributed to the production of quality fabric. In addition, Russian supervisors were taught to give corrective feedback for behaviors that reduced product quality. The researchers found that this O.B. Mod. approach, which had worked so well in the United States, also produced positive results in the Russian factory, and they concluded that "the class of interventions associated with organizational behavior modification are likely to be useful in meeting the challenges faced by Russian workers and managers is given initial support by the results of this study."[21]

In another cross-cultural study, this time using a large Korean sample (1,192 employees in 27 large Korean firms), Luthans and colleagues analyzed whether demographic and situational factors identified in the U.S.-based literature had the same antecedent influence on the commitment of Korean employees.[22] As in U.S. studies, Korean employees' position in the hierarchy, tenure in their current position, and age all related to organizational commitment. Other similarities with U.S. firms included: (1) as organizational size increased, commitment declined; (2) as structure became more employee-focused, commitment increased; and (3) the more positive the perceptions of organizational climate, the greater the employee commitment. The following conclusion was drawn:

> This study provides beginning evidence that popular constructs in the U.S. management and organizational behavior literature should not be automatically dismissed as culture bound. Whereas some organizational behavior concepts and techniques do indeed seem to be culture specific . . . a growing body of literature is demonstrating the ability to cross-culturally validate other concepts and techniques, such as behavior management. . . . This study contributed to this cross-cultural evidence for the antecedents to organizational commitment. The antecedents for Korean employees' organizational commitment was found to be similar to their American counterparts.[23]

Many Differences across Cultures

Despite similarities between cultures in some studies, far more differences than similarities have been found. In particular, MNCs are discovering that they must carefully investigate and understand the culture of where they intend to do business and modify their approaches appropriately. One good example is human resources management (HRM). Here are some representative examples:

| | TABLE 5-2 | | | |

CULTURAL CLUSTERS IN THE PACIFIC RIM, EU, AND UNITED STATES

	Power distance	Individualism	Masculinity	Uncertainty avoidance
Pacific Rim				
Hong Kong, Malaysia, Philippines, Singapore	+	−	+	−
Japan	+	−	+	+
South Korea, Taiwan	+	−	−	+
EU and United States				
France, Spain	+	+	−	+
Italy, Belgium	+	+	+	+
Portugal	+	−	−	+
Greece	+	−	+	+
Denmark, Netherlands	−	+	+	−
Germany	−	+	+	+
Great Britain, Ireland, United States	−	+	+	−

Note: + indicates high or strong; − indicates low or weak.
Source: Based on research by Hofstede and put together in Richard M. Hodgetts and Fred Luthans, "U.S. Multinationals' Compensation Strategies for Local Management: Cross-Cultural Implications," *Compensation & Benefits Review*, March-April 1993, p. 47. Used with permission of the publisher, © 1993. American Management Association, New York. All rights reserved.

1. The concept of an hourly wage does not exist in Mexico. Labor law requires that employees receive full pay 365 days a year.
2. In Austria and Brazil, employees with 1 year of service are automatically given 30 days of paid vacation.
3. Some jurisdictions in Canada have legislated pay equity—known in the United States as comparable worth—between male- and female-intensive jobs.
4. In Japan, compensation levels are determined using the objective factors of age, length of service, and educational background rather than skill, ability, and performance. Performance does not count until after an employee reaches age 45.
5. In the United Kingdom, employees are allowed up to 40 weeks of maternity leave, and employers must provide a government-mandated amount of pay for 18 of those weeks.
6. In 87% of large Swedish companies, the head of human resources is on the board of directors.[24]

These HRM practices certainly are quite different from those in the United States, and U.S. MNCs need to modify their approaches when they go into these countries if they hope to be successful. Compensation plans in particular provide an interesting area of contrast across different cultures.

Drawing on the work of Hofstede (see Chapter 4), it is possible to link cultural clusters and compensation strategies. Table 5-2 shows a host of different cultural groupings, including some in Asia, the EU, and Anglo countries. Each cluster

TABLE 5-3	

PROBLEMS WITH EMPLOYEE STOCK PLANS IN SELECT COUNTRIES

Country	Reasons for lack of success
Belgium	Problematic. Some stock plans conflict with a government-imposed wage freeze.
Brazil	Impossible. Foreign-exchange controls prohibit out-of-country stock investment; phantom stock plans are a headache.
Britain	Easy. But sometimes labor unions can get in the way.
Eastern Europe	Forget it. Even if you get government permission, chances are you talked to the wrong bureaucrat.
Germany	Can I get that in deutsche marks? U.S. plans suffer when the dollar is weak.
Israel	Difficult. Exchange controls forced National Semiconductor to a third-party system, but the plan has only scant participation.
Luxembourg	Tax haven. Great place to set up a trust to administer stock plans.
Mexico	May regret it. Labor laws can force a one-time stock grant into an annual event.
Netherlands	No thanks. Employees may like the stock options, but they will not appreciate a hefty tax bill upfront.
Philippines	Time-consuming. Requires government approval and lots of worker education.

Source: Adapted from information found in Tara Parker-Pope, "Culture Clash," *Wall Street Journal,* April 12, 1995, p. R7.

requires a different approach to formulating an effective compensation strategy, and after analyzing each such cluster, we suggest that:

1. In Pacific Rim countries, incentive plans should be group-based. In high masculinity cultures (Japan, Hong Kong, Malaysia, the Philippines, Singapore), high salaries should be paid to senior-level managers.
2. In EU nations such as France, Spain, Italy, and Belgium, compensation strategies should be similar. In the latter two nations, however, significantly higher salaries should be paid to local senior-level managers because of the high masculinity index. In Portugal and Greece, both of which have a low individualism index, profit-sharing plans would be more effective than individual incentive plans, while in Denmark, the Netherlands, and Germany, personal-incentive plans would be highly useful because of the high individualism in these cultures.
3. In Great Britain, Ireland, and the United States, managers value their individualism and are motivated by the opportunity for earnings, recognitions, advancement, and challenge. Compensation plans should reflect these needs.[25]

Additionally, some MNCs have found that compensation plans which are very attractive to their local work force have no value for members of their international work force. For example, when the Gillette Company decided to offer stock to its 33,000 employees worldwide, the firm discovered that its plan was not global in terms of worker interest.[26] Other companies have had similar experiences. Some of the reasons are provided in Table 5-3; others include low employee disposable income and a feeling that stocks are risky investments. Simply put, workers in other cultures often do not have the same view of compensation plans as U.S. workers do. This is why many MNCs now are developing their own

FIGURE 5-3

A PARTIALLY-COMPLETED CONTINGENCY MATRIX FOR INTERNATIONAL HUMAN RESOURCES MANAGEMENT

	Japan	Germany	Mexico	China
Recruitment & Selection	• Prepare for long process • Ensure that your firm is "here to stay" • Develop trusting relationship with recruit	• Obtain skilled labor from government subsidized apprenticeship program	• Use expatriates sparingly • Recruit Mexican Nationals at U.S. colleges	• Recent public policy shifts encourage use of sophisticated selection procedures
Training	• Make substantial investment in training • Use general training & cross-training • Training as everyone's responsibility	• Recognize & utilize apprenticeship programs • Be aware of government regulations on training	• Use bilingual trainers	• Careful observations of existing training programs • Utilize team training
Compensation	• Use recognition and praise as motivator • Avoid pay for performance	• Note high labor costs for manufacturing	• Consider all aspects of labor cost	• Use technical training as reward • Recognize egalitarian values • Use "more work more pay" with caution
Labor Relations	• Treat unions as partners • Allow time for negotiations	• Be prepared for high wages & short work week • Expect high productivity from unionized workers	• Understand changing Mexican labor law • Prepare for increasing unionization of labor	• Tap large pool of labor cities • Lax labor laws may become more stringent
Job Design	• Include participation • Incorporate group goal setting • Use autonomous work teams • Use uniform, formal approaches • Encourage co-worker input • Empower teams to make decision	• Utilize works councils to enhance worker participation	• Approach participation cautiously	• Determine employee's motives before implementing participation

Source: Fred Luthans, Paul A. Marsnik, and Kyle W. Luthans, "A Contingency Matrix Approach to IHRM," *Human Resource Management Journal,* © 1997. Reprinted with permission of John Wiley & Sons, Inc.

contingency-based compensation strategies that are geared toward meeting the needs of the local workers.

Figure 5-3 shows how specific HRM areas can be analyzed contingently on a country-by-country basis. Take, for example, the information on Japan. When contrasted with U.S. approaches, a significant number of differences are found. Recruitment and selection in Japanese firms often are designed to help identify those individuals who will do the best job over the long run. In the United States, people often are hired based on what they can do for the firm in the short run, because many of them eventually will quit or be downsized. Similarly, the Japanese use a great deal of cross-training, while the Americans tend to favor specialized training. The Japanese use group performance appraisal and reward people as a group; at least traditionally, Americans use manager–subordinate performance appraisal and reward people as individuals. In Japan, unions are regarded as partners; in the United States, both management and unions view each other in a much more adversarial way. Only in the area of job design, where the Japanese use a great deal of participative management and autonomous work teams, are the Americans beginning to employ a similar approach. The same types of differences can be seen in the matrix of Figure 5-3 between the United States, Germany, Mexico and China.

These differences should not be interpreted to mean that one set of HRM practices are superior to another. In fact, recent research from Japan and Europe shows these firms often have a higher incidence of personnel-related problems than U.S. companies. For example, one study found that Japanese MNCs ($n = 34$) and European MNCs ($n = 23$) had more problems than U.S. MNCs ($n = 24$) in areas such as: (1) home-country personnel who possessed sufficient international management skills; (2) home-country personnel who wanted to work abroad; (3) difficulty in attracting high-caliber local nationals; and (4) high turnover of local employees. Additionally, when compared with Japanese MNCs, U.S. multinationals had less friction and better communication between their home-country expatriates and local employees, and there were fewer complaints by local employees regarding their ability to advance in the company.[27]

Figure 5-3 clearly indicates the importance of MNCs using a contingency approach to HRM across cultures. Not only are there different HRM practices in different cultures, there also are different practices within the same cultures. For instance, one study involving 249 U.S. affiliates of foreign-based MNCs found that in general, affiliate HRM practices closely follow local practices when dealing with the rank-and-file but even more closely approximate parent-company practices when dealing with upper-level management.[28] In other words, this study found that a hybrid approach to HRM was being used by these MNCs.

Aside from the different approaches used in different countries, it is becoming clear that common assumptions and conventional wisdom about HRM practices in certain countries no longer are valid. For example, for many years, it has been assumed that Japanese employees do not leave their jobs for work with other firms. They are loyal to their first employer, and it would be virtually impossible for MNCs operating in Japan to recruit talent from Japanese firms. Recent evidence, however, reveals that job-hopping among Japanese employees is increasingly common. One report concluded:

> While American workers, both the laid-off and the survivors, grapple with cutbacks, one in three Japanese workers willingly walks away from his job within the first 10 years of his career, according to the Japanese Institute of Labor, a private research organization. And many more are thinking about it. More than half of salaried Japanese workers say they would switch jobs or start their own business if a favorable opportunity arose, according to a survey by the Recruit Research Corporation.[29]

These findings clearly illustrate one important point: managing across cultures requires careful understanding of the local environment, because common assumptions and stereotypes may not be valid. Cultural differences must be addressed, and this is why cross-cultural research will continue to be critical in helping firms learn how to manage across cultures.[30]

Managing in Hong Kong

Managing across cultures has long been recognized as a potential problem for multinationals. To help expatriates who are posted overseas deal with a new culture, many MNCs offer special training and coaching. Often, however, little is done to change expatriates' basic cultural values or specific managerial behaviors. Simply put, this traditional approach could be called the *practical school of management thought*, which holds that effective managerial behavior is universal and a good manager in the United States also will be effective in Hong Kong or any other location around the world. In recent years, it generally has been recognized that such an approach no longer is sufficient, and there is growing support for what is called the *cross-cultural school of management thought*, which holds that effective managerial behavior is a function of the specific culture. As Black and Porter point out in a recent article, successful managerial action in Los Angeles may not be effective in Hong Kong.

Black and Porter investigated the validity of these two schools of thought by surveying U.S. managers working in Hong Kong, U.S. managers working in the United States, and Hong Kong managers working in Hong Kong. Their findings revealed some interesting differences. The U.S. managers in Hong Kong exhibited managerial behaviors similar to those of their counterparts

back in the United States; however, Hong Kong managers had managerial behaviors different from either group of U.S. managers. Commenting on these results, the researchers noted:

> This study . . . points to some important practical implications. It suggests that American firms and the practical school of thought may be mistaken in the assumption that a good manager in Los Angeles will necessarily do fine in Hong Kong or some other foreign country. It may be that because firms do not include in their selection criteria individual characteristics such as cognitive flexibility, cultural flexibility, degree of ethnocentricity, etc., they end up sending a number of individuals on international assignments who have a tendency to keep the same set of managerial behaviors they used in the U.S. and not adjust or adapt to the local norms and practices. Including the measurement of these characteristics in the selection process, as well as providing cross-cultural training before departure, may be a means of obtaining more effective adaptation of managerial behaviors and more effective performance in overseas assignments.

Certainly the study shows that simplistic assumptions about culture are erroneous and that what works in one country will not necessarily produce the desired results in another. If MNCs are going to manage effectively throughout the world, they are going to have to give more attention to training their people about intercultural differences.

CULTURAL DIFFERENCES IN SELECTED COUNTRIES AND REGIONS

Chapter 4 introduced the concept of country clusters, which is the idea that certain regions of the world have similar cultures. For example, the way that Americans do business in the United States is very similar to the way that British do business in England. Even in this Anglo culture, however, there are pronounced differences, and in other clusters, such as in Asia, these differences become even more pronounced. The accompanying box, "Managing in Hong Kong," depicts such differences. Chapter 1 examined some important worldwide developments, and the following sections focus on cultural highlights and differences in selected countries and regions that provide the necessary understanding and perspective for effective management across cultures.

Doing Business in China

The People's Republic of China (PRC or China, for short) has had a long tradition of isolation. In 1979, Deng Xiaoping opened his country to the world. Although his bloody 1989 put-down of protestors in Tiananmen Square was a definite setback for progress, China is rapidly trying to close the gap between itself and economically advanced nations and to establish itself as an economic power in the Pacific Rim. As noted in Chapter 1, southeast China in particular has become a hotbed of business activity. Presently, China is actively encouraging trade with the West, and it is a major trading partner of the United States. Despite this progress, many U.S. and European multinationals find that doing business in the PRC can be a long, grueling process that often results in failure. One primary reason is that Western-based MNCs do not understand the role and impact of Chinese culture.

Experienced travelers report that the primary criterion for doing business in China is technical competence. For example, in the case of MNCs selling machinery, the Chinese want to know exactly how the machine works, what its capabilities are, and how repairs and maintenance must be handled. Sellers must be prepared to answer these questions in precise detail. This is why successful multinationals send only seasoned engineers and technical people to the PRC. They know that the questions to be answered will require both knowledge and experience, and young, fresh-out-of-school engineers will not be able to answer them.

A major cultural difference between the PRC and many Western countries is the issue of time. The Chinese tend to be punctual, so it is important that those who do business with them arrive on time. During meetings, such as those held when negotiating a contract, the Chinese may ask many questions and nod their assent at the answers. This nodding usually means that they understand or are being polite; it seldom means that they like what they are hearing and want to enter into a contract. For this reason, when dealing with the Chinese, one must keep in mind that patience is critically important. The Chinese will make a decision in their own good time, and it is common for outside businesspeople to make several trips to China before a deal is finally concluded. Moreover, not only are there numerous meetings, sometimes these are unilaterally canceled at the last minute and rescheduled. This often tries the patience of outsiders and is inconvenient in terms of rearranging travel plans and other problems.

In China, it is important to be a good listener. This may mean having to listen to the same stories about the great progress that has been made by the PRC over the past decade. The Chinese are very proud of their recent accomplishments and want to share these feelings with outsiders.

When dealing with the Chinese, one must realize they are a collective society in which people pride themselves on being members of a group. This is in sharp contrast to the situation in the United States and other Western countries, where individualism is highly prized. For this reason, one must never single out a Chinese and praise him or her for a particular quality, such as intelligence or kindness, because this may well embarrass the individual in the face of his or her peers. It is equally important to avoid using self-centered conversation, such as excessive use of the word "I," because it appears that the speaker is trying to single him- or herself out for special consideration.

The Chinese also are much less animated than Westerners. They avoid open displays of affection, do not slap each other on the back, and are more reticent, retiring, and reserved than North or South Americans. They do not appreciate loud, boisterous behavior, and when speaking to each other, they maintain a greater physical distance than is typical in the West.

Cultural highlights that affect doing business in China can be summarized and put into some specific guidelines as follows:

1. The Chinese place a great deal of emphasis on trust and mutual connections, and they are true to their word.
2. Business meetings typically start with pleasantries such as tea and general conversation about the guest's trip to the country, local accommodations, and family. In most cases, the host already has been briefed on the background of the visitor.
3. When a meeting is ready to begin, the Chinese host will give the appropriate indication. Similarly, when the meeting is over, the host will indicate that it is time for the guest to leave.
4. Once the Chinese decide who and what is best, they tend to stick with these decisions. Therefore, they may be slow in formulating a plan of action, but once they get started, they make fairly good progress.
5. In negotiations, reciprocity is important. If the Chinese give concessions, they expect some in return. Additionally, it is common to find them slowing down negotiations to take advantage of Westerners desiring to conclude arrangements as quickly as possible. The objective of this tactic is to extract further concessions. Another common ploy used by the Chinese is to pressure the other party during final arrangements by suggesting that this counterpart has broken the spirit of friendship in which the business relationship originally was established. Again, through this ploy, the Chinese are trying to gain additional concessions.
6. Because negotiating can involve a loss of face, it is common to find Chinese carrying out the whole process through intermediaries. This allows them to convey their ideas without fear of embarrassment.[31]

Doing Business in India

Foreign trade is critical to India's economy. In recent years, the country has been particularly interested in promoting exports and creating import substitutions. The government plays an important role in this process, and approval for investment is selective and typically granted only on a case-by-case basis.[32] In addition, although most Indian businesspeople speak English, many of their values and beliefs are markedly different from those in the West. Thus, understanding Indian culture is critical to doing business in India.

Shaking hands with male business associates is almost always an acceptable practice. U.S. businesspeople in India are considered equals, however, and the universal method of greeting an equal is to press one's palms together in front of the chest and say *namaste*, which means "greetings to you." Therefore, if a handshake appears to be improper, it always is safe to use *namaste*.

Western food typically is available in all good hotels. Most Indians do not drink alcoholic beverages, however, and many are vegetarians or eat chicken but not beef. Therefore, when foreign businesspeople entertain in India, the menu often is quite different from that back home. Moreover, when a local businessperson invites an expatriate for dinner at home, it is not necessary to bring a gift, although it is acceptable to do so. The host's wife and children usually will provide help from the kitchen to ensure that the guest is well treated, but they will not be at the table. If they are, it is common to wait until everyone has been seated and the host begins to eat or asks everyone to begin. During the meal, the host will ask the guest to have more food. This is done to ensure that the person does not go away hungry; however, once one has eaten enough, it is acceptable to politely refuse more food.

For Western businesspeople in India, shirt, trousers, tie, and suit are proper attire. In the southern part of India, where the climate is very hot, a light suit is preferable. In the north during the winter, a light sweater and jacket are a good choice. Indian businesspeople, on the other hand, often will wear local dress. In many cases, this includes a *dhoti,* which is a single piece of white cloth (about 5 yards long and 3 feet wide) which is passed around the waist up to half its length, then the other half is drawn between the legs and tucked at the waist. Long shirts are worn on the upper part of the body. In some locales, such as Punjab, Sikhs will wear turbans, and well-to-do Hindus sometimes will wear long coats like the Rajahs. This coat, known as a *sherwani,* is the dress recognized by the government for official and ceremonial wear. Foreign businesspeople are not expected to dress like locals, and in fact, many Indian businesspeople will dress like Europeans. Therefore, it is unnecessary to adopt local dress codes.

When doing business in India, one will find a number of other customs useful to know. Some of the most useful include:

1. It is important to be on time for meetings.
2. Personal questions should not be asked unless the other individual is a friend or close associate.
3. Titles are important, so people who are doctors or professors should be addressed accordingly.
4. Public displays of affection are considered to be inappropriate, so one should refrain from backslapping or touching others.
5. Beckoning is done with the palm turned down, while pointing often is done with the chin.
6. When eating or accepting things, use the right hand, because the left is considered to be unclean.
7. The *namaste* gesture can be used to greet people; it also is used to convey other messages, including a signal that one has had enough food.
8. Bargaining for goods and services is common; this contrasts with Western traditions, where bargaining might be considered rude or abrasive.[33]

Finally, it is important to remember that Indians are very tolerant of outsiders and understand that many are unfamiliar with local customs and procedures. Therefore, there is no need to make a phony attempt to conform to Indian cultural traditions. Making an effort to be polite and courteous is sufficient.

Doing Business in France

Many in the United States believe that it is more difficult to get along with the French than with other Europeans. This feeling probably reflects the French culture, which is markedly different from that in the United States. In France, one's social class is very important, and these classes include the aristocracy, the upper bourgeoisie, the upper-middle bourgeoisie, the middle, the lower-middle, and the lower. Social interactions are affected by class stereotypes, and during their lifetime, most French people do not encounter much change in social status. Unlike an American, who through hard work and success can move from the lowest economic strata to the highest, a successful French person might, at best, climb one or two rungs of the social ladder. Additionally, the French are very status conscious, and they like to provide signs of this status, such as a knowledge of literature and the arts; a well-designed, tastefully decorated house; and a high level of education.

The French also tend to be friendly, humorous, and sardonic (sarcastic), in contrast to Americans, for example, who seldom are sardonic. The French may admire or be fascinated with people who disagree with them; in contrast, Americans are more attracted to those who agree with them. As a result, the French are accustomed to conflict and during negotiations accept that some positions are irreconcilable and must be accepted as such. Americans, on the other hand, believe that conflicts can be resolved and that if both parties make an extra effort and have a spirit of compromise, there will be no irreconcilable differences. Moreover, the French often determine a person's trustworthiness based on their firsthand evaluation of the individual's character. This is in marked contrast to Americans, who tend to evaluate a person's trustworthiness based on past achievements and other people's evaluations of this person.

In the workplace, many French people are not motivated by competition or the desire to emulate fellow workers. They often are accused of not having as intense a work ethic as, for example, Americans or Asians. Many French workers frown on overtime, and statistics show that on average, they have the longest vacations in the world (4 to 5 weeks annually). On the other hand, few would argue that they work extremely hard in their regularly scheduled time and have a reputation for high productivity. Part of this reputation results from the French tradition of craftsmanship. Part of it also is accounted for by a large percentage of the work force being employed in small, independent businesses, where there is widespread respect for a job well done.

Most French organizations tend to be highly centralized and have rigid structures. As a result, it usually takes longer to carry out decisions. Because this arrangement is quite different from the more decentralized organizations in the United States, both middle- and lower-level U.S. expatriate managers who work in French subsidiaries often find bureaucratic red tape a source of considerable frustration. There also are marked differences at the upper levels of management. In French companies, top managers have far more authority than their U.S. counterparts, and they are less accountable for their actions. While top-level U.S. executives must continually defend their decisions to the CEO or board of directors, French executives are challenged only if the company has poor performance. As a result, those who have studied French management find them to take a more autocratic approach.[34]

In countries such as the United States, a great deal of motivation is derived from professional accomplishment. Americans realize there is limited job and social security in their country, so it is up to them to work hard and ensure their future. The French do not have the same view. While they admire Americans' industriousness and devotion to work, they believe that quality of life is what really matters. As a result, they attach a great deal of importance to leisure time, and many are unwilling to sacrifice the enjoyment of life for a dedication to work.

The values and beliefs discussed here help to explain why French culture is so different from that in other countries. Some of the sharp contrasts with the United States, for example, provide insights regarding the difficulties of doing business in France. Additional cultural characteristics, such as the following, also help to explain the difficulties that outsiders may encounter in France:

1. When shaking hands with a French person, use a quick shake with some pressure in the grip. A firm, pumping handshake, which is so common in the United States, is considered to be uncultured.
2. It is extremely important to be on time for meetings and social occasions. Being "fashionably late" is frowned on.
3. During a meal, it is acceptable to engage in pleasant conversation, but personal questions and the subject of money are never brought up.
4. Great importance is placed on neatness and taste. Therefore, visiting businesspeople should try very hard to be cultured and sophisticated.[35]

Doing Business in Arab Countries

The media attention given during the Gulf war pointed out that Arab cultures are distinctly different from Anglo cultures. Americans often find it extremely hard to do business in Arab countries, and a number of Arab cultural characteristics can be cited for this difficulty.

One is the Arabian view of time. In the United States, it is common to use the cliche "time is money." In Arab countries, a favorite expression is *Bukra insha Allah,* which means "tomorrow if God wills," an expression that explains the Arabs' fatalistic approach to time. Arabs believe that Allah controls time, in contrast to Westerners, who believe that they control their own time. As a result, if Arabs commit themselves to a date in the future and fail to show up, there is no guilt or concern on their part, because they have no control over time in the first place.

An accompanying cultural belief is that destiny depends more on the will of a supreme being than on the behavior of individuals. A higher power dictates the outcome of important events, so individual action is of little consequence. This thinking affects not only Arabs' aspirations but also their motivation. Also of importance is that the status of Arabs largely is determined by family position and social contact and connections, not necessarily by their own accomplishments. This view helps to explain why some Middle Easterners take great satisfaction in appearing to be helpless. In fact, helplessness can be used as a source of power, for in this area of the world, the strong are resented and the weak compensated. Here is an example:

> In one Arab country, several public administrators of equal rank would take turns meeting in each other's offices for their weekly conferences, and the host would serve as chairman. After several months, one of these men had a mild heart attack. Upon his recovery, it was decided to hold the meetings only in his office, in order not to inconvenience him. From then on, the man who had the heart attack became the permanent chairman of the conference. This individual appeared more helpless than the others, and his helplessness enabled him to increase his power.[36]

This approach is quite different from that in the United States, where the strong tend to be compensated and rewarded. If a person were ill, such as in this example, the individual would be relieved of this responsibility until he or she had regained full health. In the interim, the rest of the group would go on without the sick person, and he or she may have lost power.

Another important cultural contrast between Arabs and Americans is that of emotion and logic. Arabs often act based on emotion; in contrast, those in an

Anglo culture are taught to act on logic. Many Arabs live in unstable environments where things change constantly, so they do not develop trusting relationships with others. Americans, on the other hand, live in a much more predictable environment and develop trusting relationships with others.

Arabs also make wide use of elaborate and ritualized forms of greetings and leave-takings. A businessperson may wait far past the assigned meeting time before being admitted to an Arab's office. Once there, the individual may find a host of others present; this situation is unlike the typical one-on-one meetings that are so common in the United States. Moreover, during the meeting, there may be continuous interruptions, visitors may arrive and begin talking to the host, and messengers may come in and go out on a regular basis. The businessperson is expected to take all this activity as perfectly normal and remain composed and ready to continue discussions as soon as the host is prepared to do so.

Business meetings typically conclude with an offer of coffee or tea. This is a sign that the meeting is over and that future meetings, if there are to be any, should now be arranged.

Unlike the case in many other countries, titles are not in general use on the Arabian Peninsula, except in the case of royal families, ministers, and high-level military officers. Additionally, initial meetings typically are used to get to know the other party. Business-related discussions may not occur until the third or fourth meeting. Also, in contrast to the common perception among many Western businesspeople who have never been to an Arab country, it is not necessary to bring the other party a gift. If this is done, however, it should be a modest gift. A good example is a novelty or souvenir item from the visitor's home country.

Arabs attach a great deal of importance to status and rank. When meeting with them, one should pay deference to the senior person first. It also is important never to criticize or berate anyone publicly. This causes the individual to lose face, and the same is true for the person who makes these comments. Mutual respect is required at all times.

Other useful guidelines for doing business in Arab cultures include:

1. It is important never to display feelings of superiority, because this makes the other party feel inferior. No matter how well someone does something, the individual should let the action speak for itself and not brag or put on a show of self-importance.

2. One should not take credit for joint efforts. A great deal of what is accomplished is a result of group work, and to indicate that one accomplished something alone is a mistake.

3. Much of what gets done is a result of going through administrative channels in the country. It often is difficult to sidestep a lot of this red tape, and efforts to do so can be regarded as disrespect for legal and governmental institutions.

4. Connections are extremely important in conducting business. Well-connected businesspeople can get things done much faster than their counterparts who do not know the ins and outs of the system.

5. Patience is critical to the success of business transactions. This time consideration should be built into all negotiations, thus preventing one from giving away too much in an effort to reach a quick settlement.

6. Important decisions usually are made in person, not by correspondence or telephone. This is why an MNC's personal presence often is a prerequisite for

success in the Arab world. Additionally, while there may be many people who provide input on the final decision, the ultimate power rests with the person at the top, and this individual will rely heavily on personal impressions, trust, and rapport.[37]

SUMMARY OF KEY POINTS

1. One major problem facing MNCs is that they attempt to manage across cultures just the way they do in their home country. Globalization is given greater attention than national responsiveness or sovereignty; however, in recent years, under strategic international management, this globalization imperative has begun to be de-emphasized and the need for local focus has gained in importance. A number of factors help to account for this new strategy: (1) the need to address diverse worldwide standards; (2) the importance of differentiating products for local markets; (3) the need to become an insider rather than relying solely on export policies; and (4) the need to give subsidiaries more authority to respond to local conditions.

2. One major challenge when dealing with cross-cultural problems is that of overcoming parochialism and simplification. Parochialism is the tendency to view the world through one's own eyes and perspectives. Simplification is the process of exhibiting the same orientation toward different cultural groups. Another problem is that of doing things the same way in foreign markets as they are done in domestic markets. Research shows that in some cases, this approach can be effective; however, effective cross-cultural management more commonly requires approaches different than those used at home. One area where this is particularly evident is human resource management. Recruitment, selection, training, and compensation often are carried out in different ways in different countries, and what works in the United States may have limited value in other countries and geographic regions.

3. Doing business in various parts of the world requires the recognition and understanding of cultural differences. Some of these differences revolve around the importance the society assigns to time, status, control of decision making, personal accomplishment, and work itself. These types of cultural differences help to explain why effective managers in China often are quite different from those in France, and why a successful style in the United States will not be ideal in Arab countries.

KEY TERMS

globalization
national responsiveness
globalization imperative
parochialism
simplification

practical school of management thought
cross-cultural school of management thought

REVIEW AND DISCUSSION QUESTIONS

1. Define "globalization" as used in strategic international management. In what way might globalization be a problem for a successful national organization that is intent on going international? In your answer, provide an example of the problem.

2. Some international management experts contend that globalization and national responsiveness are diametrically opposed forces, and that to accommodate one, a multinational must relax its efforts in the other. In what way is this an accurate statement? In what way is it incomplete or inaccurate?

3. In what way are parochialism and simplification barriers to effective cross-cultural management? In each case, give an example.
4. Many MNCs would like to do business overseas in the same way that they do business domestically. Do research findings show that any approaches that work well in the United States also work well in other cultures? If so, identify and describe two.
5. In most cases, local managerial approaches must be modified when doing business overseas. What are three specific examples that support this statement? Be complete in your answer.
6. What are some categories of cultural differences that help make one country or region of the world different from another? In each case, describe the value or norm and explain how it would result in different behavior in two or more countries. If you like, use the countries discussed in this chapter as your point of reference.

PRACTICAL INTERNATIONAL MANAGEMENT ASSIGNMENT

In a 2- or 3-page paper, compare and contrast some of the major cultural dimensions that MNC managers must know about doing business in China, India, France, and Arab countries. Drawing on your analysis, what are some common behaviors or practices across all four countries? Are these extremely important, or are they minor behaviors or practices? Based on your answer, what conclusions can you draw about managing in these cultures?

Mexico

In Mexico, the 2- or 3-hour midday siesta is the most common time for business appointments.

Located directly south of the United States, Mexico covers an area of 756,000 square miles. It is the third-largest country in Latin America and the thirteenth-largest in the world. The 1993 census placed the population at 91.2 million, and this number is increasing at a rate of approximately 2.3 percent annually because of a traditionally high birth rate and a sharply reduced death rate. Today, Mexico is one of the "youngest" countries in the world. Approximately 55 percent of the population is under the age of 20, while a mere 4 percent is 60 years of age or older.

During the 1980s, Mexico encountered severe economic crises. From 1982 to 1988, the economy was basically stagnant, the average annual growth of GDP was less than 0.1 percent, and for most of this period, inflation was above 60 percent a year. Beginning in 1988, however, the economy started to improve. By 1991, inflation was under 20 percent, and the federal deficit, which was 16 percent of GDP in 1988, had shrunk to 1.3 percent. During this same period, GDP rose from less than 1 percent annually to over 4 percent.

A number of factors have helped to account for this economic turnaround. One was the 1988 election of president Carlos Salinas, a Harvard-educated economist and minister of planning in the previous administration. A second was the change in economic policy designed to radically improve the country. Some of the key aspects of this policy

included: (1) privatization of publicly owned businesses; (2) debt reduction and fiscal constraints; (3) movement toward development of a North American Free Trade Agreement with the United States and Canada; (4) steps toward elimination of corruption in government; (5) a broadening of the tax base and reduction of tax rates; (6) a strengthening of the manufacturing sector; and (7) encouragement of foreign direct investment.

These changes obviously were very positive for the Mexican economy. NAFTA became a reality, and foreign investment flooded into the country during the early 1990s. Then, the bottom dropped out. The economy grew too fast, there was political unrest, and there were some widely publicized assasinations and peasant uprisings. As a result, the value of the peso sharply declined in late 1994 and early 1995. The economy took a nosedive, inflation escalated, and foreign investment began to leave. At this point, the Mexican government, with help from the United States, made some needed reforms, and the economy began to recover from this severe setback.

Mexico has made itself attractive for foreign investment. In particular, foreign investors like the fact that they now can hold 100 percent ownership in many firms without having to get government approval. Included in this list are cement, computers, electronics, most manufacturing, pharmaceuticals, and tourism, among others. The only restrictions on new majority-owned foreign investment projects in areas not reserved to the state or to Mexican nationals are: (1) the investment not exceed $100 million; (2) the funding be external; (3) investments in industrial facilities be located outside the country's three largest metropolitan areas (Mexico City, Guadalajara, and Monterrey); (4) the investment create permanent jobs and establish job training and personnel development programs; and (5) the project use adequate technologies and comply with basic environmental requirements. If the project does not meet with these requirements, the investors must file an application with the National Commission on Foreign Investment, which has 45 business days to rule on the application or it is automatically approved.

Before and after the collapse of the peso, there has been considerable foreign investment in Mexico. The largest investor by far is the United States, which accounts for over 60 percent of all outside investment. The largest investments are in the manufacturing and industrial sector (around 60 percent of the total) and services (around 30 percent).

One major benefit of locating in Mexico is a highly skilled labor force that can be hired at fairly low wages when compared with those paid elsewhere. Additionally, manufacturing firms that have located there report high productivity growth rates and quality performance. A study by the Massachusetts Institute of Technology on auto assembly plants in Canada, the United States, and Mexico reported that Mexican plants performed well. Another by J. D. Power and Associates noted that Ford Motor's Hermisillo plant was the best in North America. Computer and electronics firms also are finding Mexico to be an excellent choice for new expansion plants.

1. Why would multinationals be interested in setting up operations in Mexico? Give two reasons.
2. In what way would national responsiveness be a strategic issue that these firms would have to face?
3. Would cultural differences be a major stumbling block for U.S. firms doing business in Mexico? For European firms? For Japanese firms? Explain your answer.
4. Why might MNCs be interested in studying the organizational culture in Mexican firms before deciding whether to locate there? Explain your logic.

You Be the International Management Consultant

Beijing, Here We Come!

A large toy company located in Canada is considering a business arrangement with the government of China. Although company representatives have not yet visited the PRC, the president of the firm recently met with Chinese representatives in Ottawa and discussed the business proposition. The Canadian CEO learned that the Chinese government would be quite happy to study the proposal, and the company's plan would be given a final decision within 90 days of receipt. The toy company now is putting together a detailed proposal and scheduling an on-site visit.

The Canadian firm would like to have the Chinese manufacture a wide variety of toys for sale in Asia as well as in Europe and North America. Production of these toys requires a large amount of labor time, and because China is reputed to have one of the largest and least expensive work forces in the world, the company believes that it can maximize profit by having the work done there. For the past 5 years, the company has had its toys produced in Taiwan. Costs there have been escalating recently, however, and because 45 percent of the production expense goes for labor, the company is convinced that it will soon be priced out of the market if it does not find another source.

The company president and three officers plan on going to Beijing next month to talk with government officials. They would like to sign a 5-year agreement with a price that will not increase by more than 2 percent annually. Production operations then will be turned over to the Chinese, who will have a free hand in manufacturing the goods.

The contract with the Taiwanese firm runs out in 90 days. The company already has contacted this firm, and the latter understands that its Canadian partner plans to terminate the arrangement. One major problem for the Canadian company, however, is that if it cannot find another supplier soon, it will have to go back to the Taiwanese firm for at least 2 more years. The contract stipulates that the agreement can be extended for another 24 months if the Canadian firm makes such a request; however, this must be done within 30 days of expiration of the contract. This is not an alternative that appeals to the Canadians, but they feel they will have to take it if they cannot reach an agreement with the Chinese.

1. What is the likelihood that the Canadians will be able to reach an agreement with the Chinese and not have to go back to their Taiwanese supplier? Explain.
2. Are the Canadians making a strategically wise decision in letting the Chinese handle all the manufacturing, or should they insist on getting more actively involved in the production process? Defend your answer.
3. What specific cultural suggestions would you make to the Canadians regarding how to do business with the Chinese?

CHAPTER 5 ENDNOTES

1. Myron Magnet, "The Truth about the American Worker," *Fortune*, May 4, 1992, pp. 48–65.
2. See, for example, Geert Hofstede, *Cultures and Organizations: Software of the Mind* (London: McGraw-Hill U.K., Ltd., 1991); Jeremiah J. Sullivan and Richard B. Peterson, "A Test of Theories Underlying the Japanese Lifetime Employment System," *Journal of International Business Studies*, First Quarter 1991, pp. 79–97.
3. Nancy J. Adler, *International Dimensions of Organizational Behavior*, 2nd ed. (Boston: Kent, 1991).
4. For more on this topic, see Paul Klebnikov, "The Powerhouse," *Forbes*, September 2, 1991, pp. 46–49.
5. William Taylor, "The Logic of Global Business: An Interview with ABB's Percy Barnevik," *Harvard Business Review*, March-April 1991, p. 92.
6. Ibid., p. 94.
7. Herbert G. Ramrath, "Globalization Isn't for Whiners," *Wall Street Journal*, April 6, 1992, p. A18.
8. Andrew Tanzer, "Hot Wings Take Off," *Forbes*, January 18, 1993, p. 74.
9. See, for example, Keith Bradsher, "New Policy Forming on Asian Trade," *The New York Times*, March 11, 1993, pp. C1, C6.
10. Also see Philip M. Rosenzweig and Jitendra V. Singh, "Organizational Environments and the Multinational Enterprise," *Academy of Management Review*, June 1991, pp. 340–361.
11. This model and discussion of it has been adapted from Christopher A. Bartlett and Sumantra Ghoshal, *Managing across Borders: The Transnational Solution* (Boston: Harvard Business School Press, 1989).
12. For a more detailed analysis, see Allen J. Morrison, David A. Ricks, and Kendall Roth, "Globalization versus Regionalization: Which Way for the Multinational?" *Organizational Dynamics*, Winter 1991, pp. 17–28.
13. Lisa Hoecklin, *Managing Cultural Differences* (Workingham, England: Addison-Wesley, 1995), pp. 98–99.
14. Ibid., p. 97.
15. Mary Sullivan Taylor, "American Managers in Japanese Subsidiaries: How Cultural Differences Are Affecting the Work Place," *Human Resource Planning*, vol. 14, no. 1, 1992, pp. 43–49.
16. Nancy J. Adler, *International Dimensions of Organizational Behavior*, p. 13.
17. Adapted from Richard Mead, *International Management* (Cambridge, MA: Blackwell, 1994), pp. 57–59.
18. Fred Luthans, Richard M. Hodgetts, and Stuart A. Rosenkrantz, *Real Managers* (Cambridge, MA: Ballinger Publishing, 1988).
19. Fred Luthans, Dianne H. B. Welsh, and Stuart A. Rosenkrantz, "What Do Russian Managers Really Do? An Observational Study with Comparisons to U.S. Managers," *Journal of International Business Studies*, Fourth Quarter 1993, pp. 741–761.
20. Diane H. B. Welsh, Fred Luthans, and Steven M. Sommer, "Organizational Behavior Modification Goes to Russia: Replicating an Experimental Analysis Across Cultures and Tasks," *Journal of Organizational Behavior Management*, vol. 13, no. 2, 1993, pp. 15–35; Diane H. B. Welsh, Fred Luthans, and Steven M. Sommer, "Managing Russian Factory Workers: The Impact of U.S.-Based Behavioral and Participative Techniques," *Academy of Management Journal*, February 1993, pp. 58–79.
21. Welsh, Luthans, and Sommer, "Organizational Behavior Modification," p. 31.
22. Steven M. Sommer, Seung-Hyun Bae, and Fred Luthans, "The Structure-Climate Relationship in Korean Organizations," *Asia Pacific Journal of Management*, vol. 12, no. 2, 1995, pp. 23–36. Also see: Steven Sommer, Seung-Hyun Bae, and Fred Luthans, "Organizational Commitment Across Cultures," *Human Relations, vol. 49* (in press).
23. Sommer, Bae, and Luthans, "The Structure-Climate Relationship."
24. Shari Caudron, "Lessons for HR Overseas," *Personnel Journal*, February 1995, p. 92.
25. Richard M. Hodgetts and Fred Luthans, "U.S. Multinationals' Compensation Strategies for Local Management: Cross-Cultural Implications," *Compensation & Benefits Review*, March-April 1993, pp. 42–48.
26. Tara Parker-Pope, "Culture Clash," *Wall Street Journal*, April 12, 1995, p. R7.
27. Rochelle Kopp, "International Human Resource Policies and Practices in Japanese, European, and United States Multinationals," *Human Resource Management*, Winter 1994, p. 590.
28. Philip M. Rosenzweig and Nitin Nohria, "Influences on Human Resource Management Practices in Multinational Corporations," *Journal of International Business Studies*, Second Quarter 1994, pp. 229–251.
29. Miki Tanikawa, "In Japan, Some Shun Lifetime Jobs to Chase Dreams," *New York Times*, June 25, 1995, p. F11.
30. Also see Richard W. Wright, "Trends in International Business Research: Twenty-Five Years Later," *Journal of International Business Studies*, Fourth Quarter 1994, pp. 687–701; Schon Beechler and John Zhuang Yang, "The Transfer of Japanese-Style Management to American Subsidiaries: Contingencies, Constraints,

and Competencies," *Journal of International Business Studies*, Third Quarter 1994, pp. 467–491.

31. For more on this topic, see Philip R. Harris and Robert T. Moran, *Managing Cultural Differences*, 3rd ed. (Houston: Gulf Publishing, 1991), pp. 410–411.

32. John F. Burns, "Indian Politics Derail A Big Power Supply," *New York Times*, July 5, 1995, pp. C1, C4.

33. Adapted from Harris and Moran, *Managing Cultural Differences*, p. 447.

34. Jean-Louis Barsoux and Peter Lawrence, "The Making of a French Manager," *Harvard Business Review*, July-August 1991, pp. 58–67.

35. Adapted from Harris and Moran, *Managing Cultural Differences*, p. 471.

36. Changiz Pezeshkpur, "Challenges to Management in the Arab World," *Business Horizons*, August 1978, p. 50.

37. Adapted from Harris and Moran, *Managing Cultural Differences*, p. 503.

MANAGING ORGANIZATIONAL CULTURES AND DIVERSITY

OBJECTIVES OF THE CHAPTER

The previous two chapters focused on national cultures. The overriding objective of this chapter is to examine more micro-oriented organizational cultures and to discuss ways in which MNCs can resolve the often inherent conflicts between national and organizational cultures. Many times, the cultural values and resulting behaviors that are common in a particular country are not the same as those needed for a successful MNC; therefore, MNCs must learn to deal with this challenge. Although the field of international management has long recognized the impact of national cultures, only recently has attention been given to the importance of managing organizational cultures and diversity. This chapter first examines common organizational cultures that exist in MNCs, then presents and analyzes ways in which multiculturalism and diversity are being addressed by the best, world-class multinationals. The specific objectives of this chapter are:

1. **DEFINE** exactly what is meant by "organizational culture," and discuss the interaction between national and MNC culture.
2. **IDENTIFY** the four most common categories of organizational culture that have been found through research, and discuss the characteristics of each.
3. **PROVIDE** an overview of the nature and degree of multiculturalism and diversity in today's MNCs.
4. **DISCUSS** common guidelines and principles that are used in building multicultural effectiveness at the team and the organizational levels.

THE NATURE OF ORGANIZATIONAL CULTURE

The chapters in Part I provided the background on the external environment, and the chapters so far in this part have been concerned with the external culture. Regardless of this environment or cultural context impacting on the MNC, when individuals join an MNC, they not only bring their national culture, which greatly affects their learned beliefs, attitudes, values, and behaviors, with them, but at the same time, they enter into an organizational culture. Employees of MNCs are expected to "fit in." For example, at PepsiCo, personnel are expected to be cheerful, positive, enthusiastic, and have committed optimism; at Ford, they are expected to show self-confidence, assertiveness, and machismo.[1] Regardless of the external environment or their national culture, managers and employees must understand and follow their organization's culture to be successful.[2] After first defining organizational culture, the interaction between national and organizational culture is analyzed.

Definition and Characteristics

Organizational culture has been defined in several different ways. Widely recognized organizational cultural theorist Edgar Schein defines it as a

> pattern of basic assumptions—invented, discovered, or developed by a given group as it learns to cope with its problems of external adaptation and internal integration—that has worked well enough to be considered valuable and, therefore, to be taught to new members as the correct way to perceive, think, and feel in relation to those problems.[3]

Regardless of how the term is defined, a number of important characteristics are associated with an organization's culture. These have been summarized as:

1. Observed behavioral regularities, as typified by common language, terminology, and rituals;
2. Norms, as reflected by things such as the amount of work to be done and the degree of cooperation between management and employees;
3. Dominant values that the organization advocates and expects participants to share, such as high product and service quality, low absenteeism, and high efficiency;
4. A philosophy that is set forth in the MNC's beliefs regarding how employees and customers should be treated;
5. Rules that dictate the do's and don'ts of employee behavior relating to areas such as productivity, customer relations, and intergroup cooperation; and
6. Organizational climate, or the overall atmosphere of the enterprise as reflected by the way that participants interact with each other, conduct themselves with customers, and feel about the way they are treated by higher-level management.[4]

These characteristics are not intended to be all-inclusive, but they do help to illustrate the nature of organizational culture. The major problem is that sometimes, an MNC's organizational culture in one country's facility differs sharply from those in other countries. For example, managers who do well in England may be ineffective in Germany, despite the fact that they work for the same MNC. In addition, the cultures of the English and German subsidiaries may differ sharply from those of the home U.S. location. Effectively dealing with this multiculturalism within the various locations of an MNC is a major challenge for international management.

Interaction between National and Organizational Cultures

There is a widely held belief that organizational culture tends to moderate or erase the impact of national culture. The logic of such conventional wisdom is that if a U.S. MNC set up operations in France, it would not be long before the French employees began to "think like Americans." In fact, evidence is accumulating that just the opposite may be true. Hofstede's research found that the national cultural values of employees have a significant impact on their organizational performance, and that the cultural values employees bring to the workplace with them are not easily changed by the organization. So, for example, while some French employees would have a higher power distance than Swedes and some a lower power distance, chances are "that if a company hired locals in Paris, they would, on the whole, be less likely to challenge hierarchical power than would the same number of locals hired in Stockholm."[5]

Andre Laurent's research supports Hofstede's conclusions.[6] He found that cultural differences actually are more pronounced among foreign employees working within the same multinational organization than among personnel working for firms in their native lands. Nancy Adler summarized these research findings as follows:

> When they work for a multinational corporation, it appears that Germans become more German, Americans become more American, Swedes become more Swedish, and so on. Surprised by these results, Laurent replicated the research in two other multinational corporations, each with subsidiaries in the same nine Western European countries and the United States. Similar to the first company, corporate culture did not reduce or eliminate national differences in the second and third corporations. Far from reducing national differences, organization culture maintains and enhances them.[7]

There often are substantial differences between the organizational cultures of different subsidiaries, and of course, this can cause co-ordination problems. Once again, Hofstede provided the early database of a set of proprietary cultural-analysis techniques and programs known as DOCSA (*D*iagnosing *O*rganizational *C*ulture for *S*trategic *A*pplication). This approach has identified the dimensions of organizational culture summarized in Table 6-1. It was found that when cultural comparisons were made between different subsidiaries of an MNC, different cultures often existed in each one. Such cultural differences within an MNC could reduce the ability of units to work well together; an example is provided in Figure 6-1, which shows the cultural dimensions of a California-based MNC and its European subsidiary as perceived by the Europeans. A close comparison of these perceptions reveals some startling differences.

The Europeans viewed the culture in the U.S. facilities as only slightly activities-oriented (see Table 6-1 for a description of these dimensions), but they saw their own European operations much more heavily activities-oriented. The U.S. operation was viewed as moderately people-oriented, but their own relationships were viewed as very job-oriented. The Americans were seen as having a slight identification with their own organization, while the Europeans had a much stronger identification. The Americans were perceived as being very open in their communications; the Europeans saw themselves as moderately closed. The Americans were viewed as preferring very loose control, while the Europeans felt they preferred somewhat tight control. The Americans were seen as somewhat conventional in their conduct, while the Europeans saw themselves as somewhat pragmatic. If these perceptions are accurate, then it obviously would be necessary for both

TABLE 6-1

DIMENSIONS OF CORPORATE CULTURE

Motivation

Activities	Outputs
To be consistent and precise. To strive for accuracy and attention to detail. To refine and perfect. Get it right.	To be pioneers. To pursue clear aims and objectives. To innovate and progress. Go for it.

Relationship

Job	Person
To put the demands of the job before the needs of the individual.	To put the needs of the individual before the needs of the job.

Identity

Corporate	Professional
To identify with and uphold the expectations of the employing organizations.	To pursue the aims and ideals of each professional practice.

Communication

Open	Closed
To stimulate and encourage a full and free exchange of information and opinion.	To monitor and control the exchange and accessibility of information and opinion.

Control

Tight	Loose
To comply with clear and definite systems and procedures.	To work flexibly and adaptively according to the needs of the situation.

Conduct

Conventional	Pragmatic
To put the expertise and standards of the employing organization first. To do what we know is right.	To put the demands and expectations of customers first. To do what they ask.

Source: Reported in Lisa Hoecklin, *Managing Cultural Differences: Strategies for Competitive Advantage* (Workingham, England: Addison-Wesley, 1995), p. 146.

groups to discuss their cultural differences and carefully co-ordinate their activities to work well together.

This analysis is relevant to multinational alliances. It shows that even though an alliance may exist, the partners will bring different organizational cultures with them. Lessem and Neubauer, who have portrayed Europe as offering four distinct ways of dealing with multiculturalism (based on the United Kingdom, French, German, and Italian characteristics), provide an example, and Table 6-2 briefly describes each of these sets of cultural characteristics. A close examination of the differences highlights how difficult it can be to do business with two or more of these groups, because each perceives things differently from the others. Another example is the way in which negotiations occur between groups; here are some contrasts between French and Spanish negotiators[8]:

FIGURE 6-1

EUROPEANS' PERCEPTION OF THE CULTURAL DIMENSIONS OF U.S. OPERATIONS (A) AND EUROPEAN OPERATIONS (B) OF THE SAME MNC

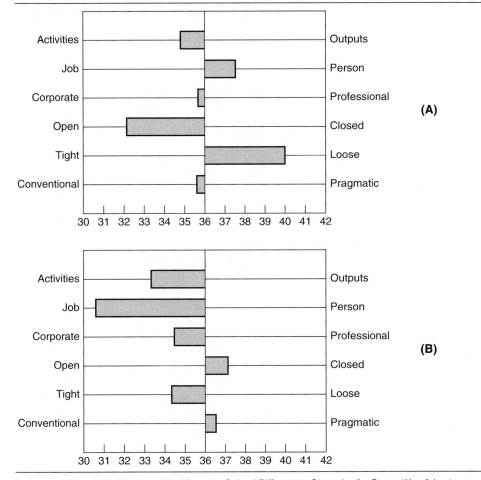

Source: Reported in Lisa Hoecklin, *Managing Cultural Differences: Strategies for Competitive Advantage* (Workingham, England: Addison-Wesley, 1995), pp. 147–148.

French	Spanish
Look for a meeting of minds.	Look for a meeting of people.
Intellectual competence is very important.	Social competence is very important.
Persuasion through carefully prepared and skilled rhetoric is employed.	Persuasion through emotional appeal is employed.
Strong emphasis is given to a logical presentation of one's position coupled with well-reasoned, detailed solutions.	Socialization always precedes negotiations, which are characterized by an exchange of grand ideas and general principles.
A contract is viewed as a well-reasoned transaction.	A contract is viewed as a long-lasting relationship.
Trust emerges slowly and is based on the evaluation of perceived status and intellect.	Trust is developed on the basis of frequent and warm interpersonal contact and transaction.

TABLE 6-2

EUROPEAN MANAGEMENT CHARACTERISTICS

	CHARACTERISTIC			
DIMENSION	**Western (United Kingdom)**	**Northern (France)**	**Eastern (Germany)**	**Southern (Italy)**
Corporate	Commercial	Administrative	Industrial	Familial
Management attributes				
Behavior	Experiential	Professional	Developmental	Convivial
Attitude	Sensation	Thought	Intuition	Feeling
Institutional models				
Function	Salesmanship	Control	Production	Personnel
Structure	Transaction	Hierarchy	System	Network
Societal ideas				
Economics	Free market	Dirigiste	Social market	Communal
Philosophy	Pragmatic	Rational	Holistic	Humanistic
Cultural images				
Art	Theatre	Architecture	Music	Dance
Culture	(Anglo-Saxon)	(Gallic)	(Germanic)	(Latin)

Source: Reported in Lisa Hoecklin, *Managing Cultural Differences: Strategies for Competitive Advantage* (Workingham, England: Addison-Wesley, 1995), p. 149.

Such comparisons also help to explain why it can be difficult for an MNC to break into foreign markets where there is only local competition. The accompanying sidebar, "The Big Gamble," provides an illustration. When dealing with these challenges, MNCs must work hard to understand the varying nature of the organizational cultures in their worldwide network and to both moderate and adapt their operations in a way that accommodates these individual units. A large part of this process calls for carefully understanding the nature of the various organizational cultures, and the next section examines the different types in detail.

ORGANIZATIONAL CULTURES IN MNCs

Organizational cultures of MNCs are shaped by a number of factors, including the cultural preferences of the leaders and employees. In the international arena, some MNCs have subsidiaries that, except for the company logo and reporting procedures, would not be easily recognizable as belonging to the same multinational.[9] In particular, there are three aspects of organizational functioning that seem to be especially important in determining MNC organizational culture: (1) the general relationship between the employees and their organization; (2) the hierarchical system of authority that defines the roles of managers and subordinates; and (3) the general views that employees hold about the MNC's purpose, destiny, goals, and their places in them.[10] When examining these dimensions of organizational culture, Trompenaars has suggested the use of two continua. One distinguishes between equity and hierarchy; the other examines orientation to the person and the task. Along these continua, which are shown in Figure 6-2, he identifies and describes four different types of organizational cultures: family, Eiffel Tower, guided missile, and incubator.

INTERNATIONAL MANAGEMENT IN ACTION

The Big Gamble

One of the biggest challenges facing U.S. multinationals is breaking into foreign markets that have been closed for years. Not only are customers in these markets unaccustomed to purchasing from outsiders, they have come to rely on domestically produced products and often take pride in "buying local." A good example of this challenge is Ford Motor, which is trying very hard to break into the Japanese market.

At present, there are fewer than 150 Ford dealerships in all of Japan, and most of them sell very few cars. Ford believes it is in the process of turning this around, however. The big automaking MNC recently signed an agreement with the Katsumata Group, the company's largest privately held auto dealer in Japan. Since the early 1960s, Katsumata has been selling Toyotas, and the president of Katsumata had to persuade Toyota that sales of the Ford line would not detract from Toyota sales, which average 75,000 autos annually. Toyota agreed, but it refused to allow the dealership to cross-train salespeople so that they could sell both types of cars. Katsumata therefore has had to assemble a sales team from scratch and comply with a host of Japanese government regulations that slowed its progress. On the positive side, however, Katsumata believes that these early efforts are important steps in changing the Japanese consumers' preference for buying local. Katsumata also is trying to change its organizational culture and make its personnel realize that the future of car sales in Japan will include a wide array of foreign offerings.

At present, the going is slow. Katsumata today sells fewer than 500 Fords annually. However, Katsumata believes that as it gains a reputation as a seller of foreign cars, customers will be drawn into its showrooms when they want to look at a car manufactured overseas. Katsumata has joined forces with Ford to help in this effort.

One way that Ford has helped is its ability to sharply reduce the cost of its cars. Ten years ago, a base Mustang coupe sold for $49,000 in Japan; today, it carries a price sticker of around $27,000. In addition, Ford is adding on a number of safety features that Japanese buyers like (e.g., dual air bags and antilock brakes). The company also is producing more right-hand-drive models. All these changes are good, but Ford must go even further in its efforts to penetrate the tough Japanese market. For example, Ford wants all its showrooms to be uniform Ford blue to promote the corporate identity, but Katsumata feels the showrooms should be designed in any way that promotes sales. As the president of the group recently remarked, "Toyota wants just one thing: a sign." Additionally, there must be a closer linkage between the two partners so that replacement orders are filled more quickly and greater attention is given to researching the market, not simply doing things the way that they are done in the United States.

Simply put, the organizational cultures of Katsumata and Ford must change if Ford hopes to penetrate the Japanese market in a big way. Given the size and growth potential of this market, however, Ford likely will make whatever changes are needed. The challenge will be to make these changes as soon as possible and thus maintain the jump that Ford has on its main rivals, Chrysler and General Motors; otherwise, this strategy could turn into a bigger gamble than Ford would like.

In practice, of course, organizational cultures do not fit neatly into any of these four, but the groupings can be useful in helping to examine the bases of how individuals relate to each other, think, learn, change, are motivated, and resolve conflict. The following discussion examines each of these cultural types.

Family Culture

Family culture is characterized by a strong emphasis on the hierarchy and orientation to the person. The result is a family-type environment that is power-oriented and headed by a leader who is regarded as a caring parent and one who knows what is best for the personnel. Trompenaars has found that this organizational culture is common in countries such as Turkey, Pakistan, Venezuela, China, Hong Kong, and Singapore.

In this culture, personnel not only respect the individuals who are in charge but look to them for both guidance and approval as well. In turn, management assumes a paternal relationship regarding their personnel, looks after them, and

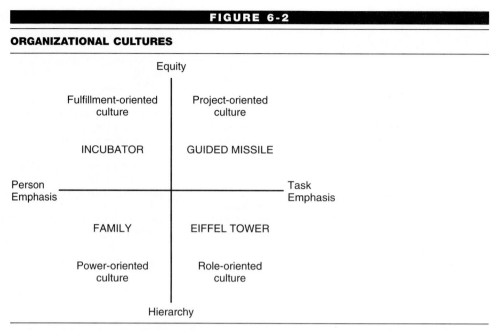

FIGURE 6-2

ORGANIZATIONAL CULTURES

Source: Adapted from Fons Trompenaars, *Riding the Waves of Culture: Understanding Diversity in Global Business* (Burr Ridge, IL: Irwin, 1994), p. 154.

tries to ensure that they are treated well and have continued employment. These cultures also are characterized by traditions, customs, and associations that bind together the personnel and make it difficult for outsiders to become members.

When it works well, the family culture can catalyze and multiply the energies of the personnel and appeal to their deepest feelings and aspirations. When it works poorly, members of the organization end up supporting a leader who is ineffective and drains their energies and loyalties.

This type of culture is foreign to most in the United States, who believe in valuing people based on their abilities and achievements, not on their age or position in the hierarchy. As a result, many managers in U.S.-based MNCs fail to understand why senior-level managers in overseas subsidiaries might appoint a relative to a high-level, sensitive position even though that individual might not appear to be the best qualified for the job. They fail to realize that family ties are so strong that the appointed relative would never do anything to embarrass or let down the family member who made the appointment. Here is an example:

> A Dutch delegation was shocked and surprised when the Brazilian owner of a large manufacturing company introduced his relatively junior accountant as the key coordinator of a $15 million joint venture. The Dutch were puzzled as to why a recently qualified accountant had been given such weighty responsibilities, including the receipt of their own money. The Brazilians pointed out that the young man was the best possible choice among 1,200 employees since he was the nephew of the owner. Who could be more trustworthy than that? Instead of complaining, the Dutch should consider themselves lucky that he was available.[11]

Other characteristics of family culture include the emphasis given to intuitive rather than rational knowledge. More concern is given to the development of people rather than their deployment or use. Personal knowledge of others is more important than empiric knowledge about them. Conversations are more important than research questionnaires, and subjective data are superior to objective data. In addition, people in family cultures tend to be motivated more by praise and appreciation than by money. They tend to socialize risk by spreading it among the members, and they resist motivation programs that threaten family bonds. These cultural values suggest that human-resource approaches such as pay-for-performance plans may be ineffective in this type of culture.

Eiffel Tower Culture

Eiffel Tower culture is characterized by a strong emphasis on the hierarchy and orientation to the task. Under this organizational culture, jobs are well defined, employees know what they are supposed to do, and everything is co-ordinated from the top. As a result, this culture is steep, narrow at the top, and broad at the base, thus the term "Eiffel Tower," which is constructed in this manner.

Unlike family culture, where the leader is revered and considered to be the source of all power, the person holding the top position in the Eiffel Tower culture could be replaced at any time, and this would have no effect on the work that organization members are doing or on the organization's reasons for existence. In this culture, relationships are specific, and status remains with the job. Therefore, if the boss of an Eiffel Tower subsidiary were playing golf with a subordinate, the subordinate would not feel any pressure to let the boss win. In addition, these managers seldom create off-the-job relationships with their people, because they believe this could affect their rational judgment. In fact, this culture operates very much like a formal hierarchy—impersonal and efficient.

> Each role at each level of the hierarchy is described, rated for its difficulty, complexity, and responsibility, and has a salary attached to it. There then follows a search for a person to fill it. In considering applicants for the role, the personnel department will treat everyone equally and neutrally, match the person's skills and aptitudes with the job requirements, and award the job to the best fit between role and person. The same procedure is followed in evaluations and promotions.[12]

Eiffel Tower cultures most commonly are found in North American and Northwest European countries. Examples include Canada, Denmark, France, Norway, and the United Kingdom. The way that people in this culture learn and change differs sharply from that in the family culture. Learning involves the accumulation of skills necessary to fit a role, and organizations will use qualifications in deciding how to schedule, deploy, and reshuffle personnel to meet their needs. The organization also will employ such rational procedures as assessment centers, appraisal systems, training and development programs, and job rotation in managing its human resources. All these procedures help to ensure that a formal hierarchic or bureaucracy-like approach works well. When changes need to be made, however, the Eiffel Tower culture often is ill-equipped to handle things. Manuals must be rewritten, procedures changed, job descriptions altered, promotions reconsidered, and qualifications reassessed.

This same, methodic approach is used in motivating and rewarding people and in resolving conflict. Carefully designed rules and policies are relied on, and things are done "by the book." Conflicts are viewed as irrational and offenses against efficiency; criticisms and complaints are handled through channels. The organizational participants carry out these tasks by viewing them as obligations to their jobs, not as responsibilities to specific individuals. Because the Eiffel Tower culture does not rely on values that are similar to those in most U.S. MNCs, U.S. expatriate managers often have difficulty initiating change in these cultures. As Trompenaars notes:

> An American manager responsible for initiating change in a German company described to me the difficulties he had in making progress, although the German managers had discussed the new strategy in depth and made significant contributions to its formulation. Through informal channels, he had eventually discovered that his mistake was not having formalized the changes to structure or job descriptions. In the absence of a new organization chart, this Eiffel Tower company was unable to change.[13]

Guided Missile Culture

Guided missile culture is characterized by a strong emphasis on equality in the work place and orientation to the task. This organizational culture is oriented to work, which typically is undertaken by teams or project groups. Unlike the Eiffel Tower culture, where job assignments are fixed and limited, personnel in the guided missile culture do whatever it takes to get the job done. This culture derived its name from high-tech organizations such as the National Aeronautics and Space Administration (NASA), which pioneered the use of project groups working on space probes that resembled guided missiles. In these large project teams, more than a hundred different types of engineers often were responsible for building, say, a lunar landing module. The team member whose contribution would be crucial at any given time in the project typically could not be known in advance. Therefore, all types of engineers had to work in close harmony and cooperate with everyone on the team.

To be successful, the best form of synthesis must be used in the course of working on the project. For example, in a guided missile project, formal hierarchical considerations are given low priority, and individual expertise is of greatest importance. Additionally, everyone in the team is equal (or at least potentially equal), because their relative contributions to the project are not yet known. All teams treat each other with respect, because they may need the other for assistance. This egalitarian and task-driven organizational culture fits well with the national cultures of the United States and United Kingdom, which helps to explain why high-tech MNCs commonly locate their operations in these countries.

Guided missile organizational cultures generally are made up of professionals who are formed into cross-disciplinary teams. Moreover, the objectives of project teams are time bound; once objectives are accomplished, the team members move to other groups. An interesting situation sometimes develops in MNCs where an operation with a guided missile culture is combined (superimposed) with another unit having a more traditional, Eiffel Tower culture into what is called a "matrix structure." Of course, given the nature of both organizations, there can be a culture clash, because the bureaucratic design of the Eiffel Tower arrangement contrasts sharply with the flexible, changing design of the guided missile group.

The way in which members of a guided missile organizational culture learn and change differs sharply from that of either family or Eiffel Tower cultures. The missile structure could be called "cybernetic," meaning that the focus is on a particular objective and there is direct feedback to measure progress. Additionally, changes typically are corrective and conservative, because the overall goal remains constant. Learning involves finding out how to get along with people; playing the role of an active, contributing team member; being practical rather than theoretic; and focusing on problem-solving. Moreover, in these missile cultures, performance appraisal often is carried out by peers and subordinates rather than just the boss. When bosses, peers, and subordinates all have an input into the evaluation, this is called "360-degree feedback," which is becoming increasingly popular in these organizations.

Unlike the family and Eiffel Tower cultures, change in the guided missile culture comes quickly. Goals are accomplished, and teams are reconfigured and assigned new objectives. People move from group to group, and loyalties to one's profession and project often are greater than those to the organization per se.

Trompenaars found that the motivation of those in guided missile cultures tends to be more intrinsic than just concern for money and benefits. Team members become enthusiastic about, and identify with, the struggle toward attaining their goal. For example, a project team that is designing and building a new computer for the Asian market may be highly motivated to create a machine that is at the leading edge of technology, user friendly, and will sweep the market. Everything else is secondary to this overriding objective. Thus, both intragroup and intergroup conflicts are minimized and petty problems between team members set aside; everyone is so committed to the project's main goal that they do not have time for petty disagreements. As Trompenaars notes:

> This culture tends to be individualistic since it allows for a wide variety of differently specialized persons to work with each other on a temporary basis. The scenery of faces keeps changing. Only the pursuit of chosen lines of personal development is constant. The team is a vehicle for the shared enthusiasm of its members, but is itself disposable and will be discarded when the project ends. Members are garrulous, idiosyncratic, and intelligent, but their mutuality is a means, not an end. It is a way of enjoying the journey. They do not need to know each other intimately, and may avoid doing so. Management by objectives is the language spoken, and people are paid for performance.[14]

Incubator Culture

Incubator culture is the fourth major type of organizational culture that Trompenaars identified, and it is characterized by a strong emphasis on equality and personal orientation. This culture is based heavily on the existential idea that organizations per se are secondary to the fulfillment of the individuals within them. This culture is based on the premise that the role of organizations is to serve as incubators for the self-expression and self-fulfillment of their members; as a result, this culture often has little formal structure. Participants in an incubator culture are there primarily to perform roles such as confirming, criticizing, developing, finding resources for, and/or helping to complete the development of an innovative product or service. These cultures often are found among start-up firms in Silicon Valley, California, or Silicon Glen, Scotland. These incubator-type organizations typically are entrepreneurial and often founded and made up by a creative team who left larger, Eiffel-Tower-type employers. They want to be part of an organization where their creative talents will not be stifled.

TABLE 6-3

SUMMARY CHARACTERISTICS OF THE FOUR CORPORATE CULTURES

Characteristic	CORPORATE CULTURE			
	Family	**Eiffel Tower**	**Guided missile**	**Incubator**
Relationships between employees	Diffuse relationships to organic whole to which one is bonded	Specific role in mechanical system of required interaction	Specific tasks in cybernetic system targeted on shared objectives	Diffuse, spontaneous relationships growing out of shared creative process
Attitude toward authority	Status is ascribed to parent figures who are close and powerful	Status is ascribed to superior roles that are distant yet powerful	Status is achieved by project group members who contribute to targeted goal	Status is achieved by individuals exemplifying creativity and growth
Ways of thinking and learning	Intuitive, holistic, lateral and error-correcting	Logical, analytical, vertical, and rationally efficient	Problem centered, professional, practical, cross-disciplinary	Process oriented, creative, ad hoc, inspirational
Attitudes toward people	Family members	Human resources	Specialists and experts	Co-creators
Ways of changing	"Father" changes course	Change rules and procedures	Shift aim as target moves	Improvise and attune
Ways of motivating and rewarding	Intrinsic satisfaction in being loved and respected	Promotion to greater position, larger role	Pay or credit for performance and problems solved	Participation in the process of creating new realities
	Management by subjectives	Management by job description	Management by objectives	Management by enthusiasm
Criticism and conflict resolution	Turn other cheek, save other's face, do not lose power game	Criticism is accusation of irrationalism unless there are procedures to arbitrate conflicts	Constructive task-related only, then admit error and correct fast	Improve creative idea, not negate it

Source: Adapted from Fons Trompenaars, *Riding the Waves of Culture: Understanding Diversity in Global Business* (Burr Ridge, IL: Irwin, 1994), p. 176.

Incubator cultures often create environments where participants thrive in an intense, emotional commitment to the nature of the work. For example, the group may be in the process of gene splitting that could lead to radical medical breakthroughs and extend life. Often, personnel in such cultures are overworked, and the enterprise typically is underfunded. As breakthroughs occur and the company gains stability, however, it starts moving down the road toward commercialization and profit. In turn, this engenders the need to hire more people and develop formalized procedures for ensuring the smooth flow of operations. In this process of growth and maturity, the unique characteristics of the incubator culture begin to wane and disappear, and the culture is replaced by one of the other types (family, Eiffel Tower, or guided missile).

As noted, change in the incubator culture often is fast and spontaneous. All participants are working toward the same objective. Because there may not yet be a customer who is using the final output, however, the problem itself often is open to redefinition, and the solution typically is generic in that it is aimed at a universe of applications. Meanwhile, motivation of the personnel remains highly intrinsic and intense, and it is common to find them working 70 hours a week—and loving it. The participants are more concerned with the unfolding creative process than

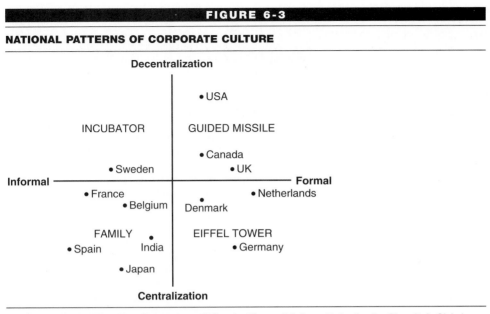

FIGURE 6-3

NATIONAL PATTERNS OF CORPORATE CULTURE

Source: Adapted from Fons Trompenaars, *Riding the Waves of Culture: Understanding Diversity in Global Business* (Burr Ridge, IL: Irwin, 1994), p. 178.

they are in gathering power or ensuring personal monetary gain. In sharp contrast to the family culture, leadership in this incubator culture is achieved, not gained by position.

Organizational Cultures and Country Preferences

Trompenaars intends for the four organizational cultures described earlier to be "pure" types. Table 6-3 provides a brief summary. In practice, however, these types most often are mixed or overlaid on each other. If one organizational culture dominates, it will be through the influence of the national culture. Recent evidence from the Centre for International Business Studies has been particularly helpful in showing the relationship between organizational and national cultures. The Centre devised a questionnaire that asked respondents to choose between four possible descriptions of their organization. The four were geared to the power-priority of the family, the role-dominance of the Eiffel Tower, the task-orientation of the guided missile, or the person-orientation of the incubator. Their database included 3000 respondents from 12 countries, and the results are presented in Figure 6-3. As shown, respondents in the United States on average described their organizational cultures as guided missile, Germans as Eiffel Tower, Japanese as family, and Swedes as incubator.

This analysis would suggest that MNCs who have operations in a number of different countries should adjust their local organizational cultures to fit that country's culture. At the same time, however, these subsidiaries must be able to co-ordinate their local operations with other organizational groups in the MNC so that all units operate in harmony and unity of purpose. A good example is provided by the accompanying "International Management in Action: Matsushita Goes Global."

INTERNATIONAL MANAGEMENT IN ACTION

Matsushita Goes Global

In recent years, a growing number of multinationals have begun to expand their operations, realizing that if they do not increase their worldwide presence now, they likely will be left behind in the near future. In turn, this has created a number of different challenges for these MNCs, including making a fit between their home organizational culture and those at local levels in the different countries where the MNC operates. Matsushita provides an excellent example in how they have handled this challenge with their macro/micro approach. This huge, Japanese MNC has developed a number of guidelines that it uses in setting up and operating its more than 150 industrial units. At the same time, the company complements these macro guidelines with on-site micro techniques that help to create the most appropriate organizational culture in the subsidiary.

At the macro level, Matsushita employs six overall guidelines that are followed in all locales. They include: (1) be a good corporate citizen in every country, among other things, by respecting cultures, customs, and languages; (2) give overseas operations the best manufacturing technology the company has available; (3) keep the expatriate head count down, and groom local management to take over; (4) let operating plants set their own rules, fine-tuning manufacturing processes to match the skills of the workers; (5) create local research and development to tailor products to markets; and (6) encourage competition between overseas outposts and with plants back home.

Working within these macro guidelines, Matsushita then allows each local unit to create its own culture. The Malaysian operations are a good example. Since 1987, Mat-sushita has set up 13 new subsidiaries in Malaysia, and employment there has more than quadrupled, to approximately 25,000 people. Only 230 of these employees, however, are Japanese. From these Malaysian operations, Matsushita currently produces 1.3 million televisions and 1.8 million air conditioners annually, and 90 percent of these units are shipped overseas. To produce this output, local plants reflect Malaysia's cultural mosaic of Muslim Malays, ethnic Chinese, and Indians. To accommodate this diversity, Matsushita cafeterias offer Malaysian, Chinese, and Indian food, and to accommodate Muslim religious customs, Matsushita provides special prayer rooms at each plant and allows two prayer sessions per shift.

How well does this Malaysian work force perform for the Japanese MNC? In the past, the Malaysian plants' slogan was "Let's catch up with Japan." Today, however, these plants frequently outperform their Japanese counterparts in both quality and efficiency. The comparison with Japan no longer is used. Additionally, Matsushita has found that the Malaysian culture is very flexible, and the locals are able to work well with almost any employer. Commenting on Malaysia's multiculturalism, Matsushita's managing director notes, "They are used to accommodating other cultures, and so they think of us Japanese as just another culture. That makes it much easier for us to manage them than some other nationalities."

Today, Matsushita faces a number of important challenges, including remaining profitable in a slow-growth, high-cost Japanese economy. Fortunately, this MNC is doing extremely well overseas, which is buying it time to get its house in order back home. A great amount of this success results from the MNC's ability to nurture and manage overseas organizational cultures (such as in Malaysia) that are both diverse and highly productive.

MANAGING MULTICULTURALISM AND DIVERSITY

As the "International Management in Action" box on Matsushita indicates, success in the international arena often is greatly determined by an MNC's ability to manage both multiculturalism and diversity. Both domestically and internationally, organizations find themselves leading work forces that have a variety of cultures (and subcultures) and consist of a largely diverse population of women, men, young and old people, blacks, whites, Latins, Asians, Arabs, Indians, and many others.

Phases of Multicultural Development

The effect of multiculturalism and diversity will vary depending on the stage of the firm in its international evolution. Table 6-4 depicts the characteristics of the major phases in this evolution. For example, Adler has noted that international cultural diversity has minimal impact on domestic organizations, although domestic multiculturalism has a highly significant impact. As firms begin exporting to foreign

TABLE 6-4

THE EVOLUTION OF INTERNATIONAL CORPORATIONS

Characteristics/ activities	Phase I (domestic corporations)	Phase II (international corporations)	Phase III (multinational corporations)	Phase IV (global corporations)
Primary orientation	Product/service	Market	Price	Strategy
Competitive strategy	Domestic	Multidomestic	Multinational	Global
Importance of world business	Marginal	Important	Extremely important	Dominant
Product/service	New, unique	More standardized	Completely standardized (commodity)	Mass-customized
	Product engineering emphasized	Process engineering emphasized	Engineering not emphasized	Product and process engineering
Technology	Proprietary	Shared	Widely shared	Instantly and extensively shared
R&D/sales	High	Decreasing	Very low	Very high
Profit margin	High	Decreasing	Very low	High, yet immediately decreasing
Competitors	None	Few	Many	Significant (few or many)
Market	Small, domestic	Large, multidomestic	Larger, multinational	Largest, global
Production location	Domestic	Domestic and primary markets	Multinational, least cost	Imports and exports
Exports	None	Growing, high potential	Large, saturated	Imports and exports
Structure	Functional divisions	Functional with international division	Multinational lines of business	Global alliances, hetarchy
	Centralized	Decentralized	Centralized	Coordinated, decentralized
Primary orientation	Product/service	Market	Price	Strategy
Strategy	Domestic	Multidomestic	Multinational	Global
Perspective	Ethnocentric	Polycentric/ regiocentric	Multinational	Global/multicentric
Cultural sensitivity	Marginally important	Very important	Somewhat important	Critically important
With whom	No one	Clients	Employees	Employees and clients
Level	No one	Workers and clients	Managers	Executives
Strategic assumption	"One way"/ "one best way"	"Many good ways," equifinality	"One least-cost way"	"Many good ways," simultaneously

Source: Nancy J. Adler, *International Dimensions of Organizational Behavior,* 2nd ed. (Boston: PWS-Kent Publishing, 1991), pp. 7–8.

clients, however, and become what she calls "international organizations" (Phase II in Table 6-4), they must adapt their approach and products to those of the local market. For these international firms, the impact of multiculturalism is highly significant. As companies become what she calls "multinational firms" (Phase III), they often find that price tends to dominate all other considerations, and the direct impact of culture may lessen slightly. For those who continue this international evolution, however, and become full-blown "global companies" (Phase IV), the impact of culture again becomes extremely important. Notes Adler:

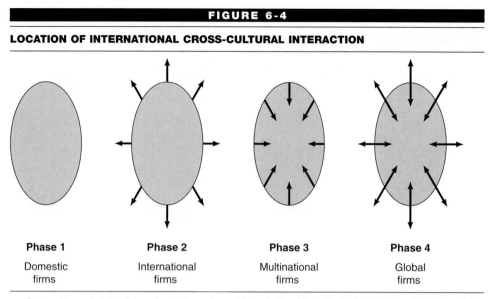

FIGURE 6-4

LOCATION OF INTERNATIONAL CROSS-CULTURAL INTERACTION

Phase 1	Phase 2	Phase 3	Phase 4
Domestic firms	International firms	Multinational firms	Global firms

Source: Nancy J. Adler, *International Dimensions of Organizational Behavior,* 2nd ed. (Boston: PWS-Kent Publishing, 1991), p. 123.

Global firms need an understanding of cultural dynamics to plan their strategy, to locate production facilities and suppliers worldwide, to design and market culturally appropriate products and services, as well as to manage cross-cultural interaction throughout the organization—from senior executive committees to the shop floor. As more firms today move from domestic, international, and multinational organizations to operating as truly global organizations and alliances, the importance of cultural diversity increases markedly. What once was "nice to understand" becomes imperative for survival, let alone success.[15]

As shown in Figure 6-4, international culture diversity traditionally affects neither the domestic firm's organizational culture nor its relationship with its customers or clients. These firms work domestically, and only domestic multiculturalism has a direct impact on their dynamics as well as their relationship to the external environment.

Among international firms, which focus on exporting and producing abroad, cultural diversity has a strong impact on their external relationships with potential buyers and foreign employees. In particular, these firms rely heavily on expatriate managers to help manage operations; as a result, the diversity focus is from the inside out. This is the reverse of what happens in multinational firms, where there is less emphasis on managing cultural differences outside the firm and more on managing cultural diversity within the company. This is because multinational firms hire personnel from all over the world. Adler notes that these multinational firms need to develop cross-cultural management skills up the levels of the hierarchy. As shown in Figure 6-4, this results in a diversity focus that is primarily internal.

Global firms need both an internal and an external diversity focus (again see Figure 6-4). To be effective, everyone in the global organization needs to develop cross-cultural skills that allow them to work effectively with internal personnel as well as external customers, clients, and suppliers.

TABLE 6-5			

U.S. CIVILIAN LABOR FORCE: 1990–2005

	Percentage		
Group	Labor force, 1990	Entrants, 1990–2005	Labor force, 2005
Share			
Total	100.0	100.0	100.0
Male	54.7	50.5	52.6
Female	45.3	49.5	47.4
White non-Hispanic	78.5	65.3	73.0
Male	43.1	32.2	38.2
Female	35.4	33.1	34.8
African-American	10.7	13.0	11.6
Male	5.3	6.2	5.7
Female	5.4	6.8	5.9
Hispanic	7.7	15.7	11.2
Male	4.6	9.1	6.6
Female	3.1	6.6	4.6
Asian and other	3.1	6.0	4.3
Male	1.7	3.0	2.2
Female	1.4	3.0	2.1

Source: "Outlook 1990–2005," Bureau of Labor Statistics, U.S. Department of Labor, May 1992.

Types of Multiculturalism

For the international management arena, there are several ways of examining multiculturalism and diversity. One is to focus on the domestic multicultural and diverse work force that operates in the MNC's home country. In addition to domestic multiculturalism, there is the diverse work force in other geographic locales, and increasingly common are the mix of domestic and overseas personnel found in today's MNCs. The following discussion examines both domestic and group multiculturalism and the potential problems and strengths.

Domestic Multiculturalism   It is not necessary for today's organizations to do business in another country to encounter people with diverse cultural backgrounds. Culturally distinct populations can be found within organizations almost everywhere in the world. In Singapore, for example, there are four distinct cultural and linguistic groups: Chinese, Eurasian, Indian, and Malay. In Switzerland, there are four distinct ethnic communities: French, German, Italian, and Romansch. In Belgium, there are two linguistic groups: French and Flemish. In the United States, millions of first-generation immigrants have brought both their language and their culture. In Los Angeles, for example, there are more Samoans than on the island of Samoa, more Israelis than in any other city outside Israel, and more first- and second-generation Mexicans than in any other city except Mexico City. In Miami, over one-half the population is Latin, and most residents speak Spanish fluently. More Puerto Ricans live in New York City than in Puerto Rico.

In short, there is considerable multicultural diversity domestically in organizations throughout the world, and this trend will continue. As shown in Table 6-5, the U.S. civilian labor force of the next decade will change in ethnic composition.

In particular, there will be a significantly lower percentage of white males in the work force and a growing percentage of women, African-Americans, Hispanics, and Asians.

Group Multiculturalism   There are a number of ways that diverse groups can be categorized. Four of the most common include:

1. *Homogeneous groups,* which are characterized by members who share similar backgrounds and generally perceive, interpret, and evaluate events in similar ways. An example would be a group of male German bankers who are forecasting the economic outlook for a foreign investment.
2. *Token groups,* in which all members but one have the same background. An example would be a group of Japanese retailers and a British attorney who are looking into the benefits and shortcomings of setting up operations in Bermuda.
3. *Bicultural groups,* which have two or more members of a group represent each of two distinct cultures. An example would be a group of four Mexicans and four Canadians who have formed a team to investigate the possibility of investing in Russia.
4. *Multicultural groups,* in which there are individuals from three or more different ethnic backgrounds. An example is a group of three American, three German, three Uruguayan, and three Chinese managers who are looking into mining operations in Chile.

As the diversity of a group increases, the likelihood of all members perceiving things in the same way decreases sharply. Attitudes, perceptions, and communication in general may be a problem. On the other hand, there also are significant advantages associated with the effective use of multicultural, diverse groups. The following sections examine both of these.

Potential Problems Associated with Diversity

Overall, diversity may cause a lack of cohesion that results in the unit's inability to take concerted action, be productive, and create a work environment that is conducive to both efficiency and effectiveness. These potential problems are rooted in people's attitudes.

An example of an attitudinal problem in a diverse group may be the mistrust of others. For example, many U.S. managers who work for Japanese operations in the United States complain that Japanese managers often huddle together and discuss matters in their native language. The U.S. managers wonder aloud why the Japanese do not speak English. What are they talking about that they do not want anyone else to hear? In fact, the Japanese often find it easier to communicate among themselves in their native language, and because no Americans are present, the Japanese managers ask why they should speak English. If there is no reason for anyone else to be privy to our conversation, why should we not opt for our own language? Nevertheless, such practices do tend to promote an attitude of mistrust.

Another potential problem may be perceptual. Unfortunately, when culturally diverse groups come together, they often bring preconceived stereotypes with them. In initial meetings, for example, engineers from economically advanced countries often are perceived as more knowledgeable than those from less advanced countries. In turn, this can result in status-related problems, because some of the group initially are regarded as more competent than others and likely are accorded status on this basis. As the diverse group works together, erroneous perceptions often are corrected, but this takes time. In one diverse group consisting of engineers from a major Japanese firm and a world-class U.S. firm, a Japanese engineer was assigned a technical task because of his stereotyped technical educational background. The group soon realized that this particular Japanese engineer was not capable of doing this job, however, because for the last 4 years, he had been responsible for co-ordinating routine quality and no longer was on the technologic cutting edge. His engineering degree from the University of Tokyo had resulted in the other members perceiving him as technically competent and able to carry out the task; this perception proved to be incorrect.

Still another potential problem with diverse groups is inaccurate communication, which could occur for a number of reasons. One is misunderstandings caused by words used by a speaker that are not clear to other members. For example, in a diverse group in which one of the authors was working, a British manager told her U.S. colleagues, "I will fax you this report in a fortnight." When the author asked the Americans when they would be getting the report, most of them believed it would be arriving in 4 days. They did not know that the common British word "fortnight" (14 nights) means 2 weeks.

Another contribution to miscommunication may be the way in which situations are interpreted. Many Japanese nod their heads when others talk, but this does not mean that they agree with what is being said. They merely are being polite and attentive. In many societies, it is impolite to say no, and if the listener believes that the other person wants a positive answer, the listener will say yes even though this is incorrect. As a result, many U.S. managers find out that promises made by individuals from other cultures cannot be taken at face value—and in many instances, the other individual assumes that the American realizes this!

Diversity also may lead to communication problems because of the different uses of time. For example, many Japanese will not agree to a course of action on-the-spot. They will not act until they have discussed the matter with their own people, because they do not feel empowered to act alone. Many Latin managers refuse to be held to a strict timetable, because they do not have the same time-urgency that U.S. managers do. Here is another example, as described by a European manager:

> In attempting to plan a new project, a three-person team composed of managers from Britain, France, and Switzerland failed to reach agreement. To the others, the British representative appeared unable to accept any systematic approach; he wanted to discuss all potential problems before making a decision. The French and Swiss representatives agreed to examine everything before making a decision, but then disagreed on the sequence and scheduling of operations. The Swiss, being more pessimistic in their planning, allocated more time for each suboperation than did the French. As a result, although everybody agreed on its validity, we never started the project. If the project had been discussed by three Frenchmen, three Swiss, or three Britons, a decision, good or bad, would have been made. The project would not have been stalled for lack of agreement.[16]

Advantages of Diversity

While there are some potential problems to overcome when using culturally diverse groups in today's MNCs, there also are a host of benefits to be gained. In particular, there is growing evidence that culturally diverse groups can enhance creativity, lead to better decisions, and result in more effective and productive performance.[17]

One main benefit of diversity is the generation of more and better ideas. Because group members come from a host of different cultures, they often are able to create a greater number of unique (and thus creative) solutions and recommendations. For example, a U.S. MNC recently was preparing to launch a new software package aimed at the mass consumer market. The company hoped to capitalize on the upcoming Christmas season with a strong advertising campaign in each of its international markets. A meeting of the sales managers from these markets in Spain, the Middle East, and Japan helped the company to revise and better target its marketing effort. The Spanish manager suggested that the company focus its campaign around the coming of the Magi (January 6) and not Christmas (December 25), because in Latin cultures, gifts typically are exchanged on the date that the Magi brought their gifts. The Middle East manager pointed out that most of his customers were not Christians, so a Christmas campaign would not have much meaning in this area. Instead, he suggested the company focus its sales campaign around the value of the software and how it could be useful to customers and not worry about getting the product shipped by early December. The Japanese manager concurred with his Middle East colleague, but additionally suggested that some of the colors being proposed for the sales brochure be changed to better fit with Japanese culture. Thanks to these ideas, the sales campaign proved to be one of the most effective in the company's history.

A second major benefit is that culturally diverse groups can prevent *groupthink*, which is social conformity and pressures on individual members of a group to conform and reach consensus.[18] When this occurs, group participants believe that their ideas and actions are correct and that those who disagree with them are either uninformed or deliberately trying to sabotage their efforts. Multicultural diverse groups often are able to avoid this problem, because the members do not think similarly or feel pressure to conform. As a result, they typically question each other, offer opinions and suggestions that are contrary to those held by others, and must be persuaded to change their minds. Therefore, unanimity is achieved only through a careful process of deliberation. Unlike homogeneous groups, where everyone can be "of one mind," diverse groups may be slower in reaching a general consensus; however, the decision may be more effective.

Building Multicultural Team Effectiveness

Multiculturally diverse teams have a great deal of potential to be either very effective or very ineffective. As shown in Figure 6-5, Kovach reports that if cross-cultural groups are led properly, they can indeed be highly effective; unfortunately, she also found that if they are not managed properly, they can be highly ineffective. In other words, diverse groups are more powerful than single-culture groups. They can hurt the organization, but if managed effectively, they can be the best. The following sections provide the conditions and guidelines for managing diverse groups in today's organizations effectively.

Understanding the Conditions for Effectiveness   Multicultural teams are most effective when they face tasks requiring innovativeness. They are far less effective when they are assigned to routine tasks. As Adler explained:

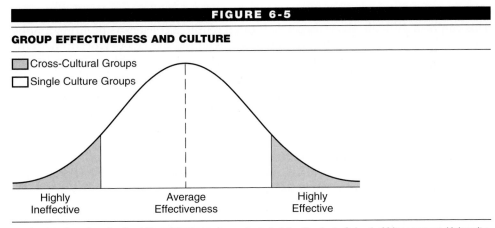

FIGURE 6-5

GROUP EFFECTIVENESS AND CULTURE

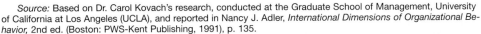

Source: Based on Dr. Carol Kovach's research, conducted at the Graduate School of Management, University of California at Los Angeles (UCLA), and reported in Nancy J. Adler, *International Dimensions of Organizational Behavior,* 2nd ed. (Boston: PWS-Kent Publishing, 1991), p. 135.

Cultural diversity provides the biggest asset for teams with difficult, discretionary tasks requiring innovation. Diversity becomes less helpful when employees are working on simple tasks involving repetitive or routine procedures. Therefore, diversity generally becomes more valuable during the planning and development of projects (the "work" stage) and less helpful during their implementation (the "action" stage). The more senior the team members, the more likely they are to be working on projects that can benefit from diversity. Diversity is therefore extremely valuable to senior executive teams, both within and across countries.[19]

In achieving the greatest amount of effectiveness from diverse teams, activities must be determined by the stage of team development (e.g., entry, working, and action). For example, in the entry stage, the focus should be on building trust and developing team cohesion. This can be a difficult task for diverse teams, whose members are accustomed to working in different ways. For example, Americans, Germans, and Swiss typically spend little time getting to know each other; they find out the nature of the task and set about pursuing it on their own without first building trust and cohesion. This contrasts sharply with individuals from Latin America, Southern Europe, and the Middle East, where a great deal of initial time is spent getting to know each other. This contrast between task-oriented and relationship-oriented members of a diverse team may cause difficulty in creating cohesion. To counteract this problem, it is common in the entry stage of development to find experienced multicultural managers focusing attention on the team members' equivalent professional qualifications and status. Once this professional similarity and respect are established, the group can begin forming itself into a cohesive team.

In the work stage of development, attention may be directed more toward describing and analyzing the problem or task that has been assigned. This stage often is fairly easy for managers of multicultural teams, because they can draw on the diversity of the members in generating ideas. As noted earlier, diverse groups tend to be most effective when dealing with situations that require innovative approaches.

In the action stage, the focus shifts to decision making and implementation. This can be a difficult phase, because it often requires consensus building among the members. In achieving this objective, experienced managers work to help the diverse group recognize and facilitate the creation of ideas with which everyone can agree. In doing so, it is common to find strong emphasis on problem-solving techniques such as the nominal group technique (NGT), where the group members individually make contributions before group interaction and consensus is reached.[20]

Using the Proper Guidelines Besides some overall conditions, a number of specific guidelines for effectively managing culturally diverse groups have been identified. Here are some of the most useful:

1. Team members must be selected for their task-related abilities and not solely based on ethnicity. If the task is routine, homogeneous membership often is preferable; if the task is innovative, multicultural membership typically is best.
2. Team members must recognize and be prepared to deal with their differences. The goal is to facilitate a better understanding of cross-cultural differences and generate a higher level of performance and rapport. In doing so, members need to become aware of their own stereotypes, as well as those of the others, and use this information to better understand the real differences that exist between them. This can then serve as a basis for determining how each individual member can contribute to the overall effectiveness of the team.
3. Because members of diverse teams tend to have more difficulty agreeing on their purpose and task than members of homogeneous groups, the team leader must help the group to identify and define its overall goal. This goal is most useful when it requires members to co-operate and develop mutual respect in carrying out their tasks.
4. Members must have equal power so that everyone can participate in the process; cultural dominance always is counterproductive. As a result, managers of culturally diverse teams distribute power according to each person's ability to contribute to the task, not according to ethnicity.
5. It is important that all members have mutual respect for each other. This often is accomplished by managers choosing members of equal ability, making prior accomplishments and task-related skills known to the group, and minimizing early judgments based on ethnic stereotypes.
6. Because teams often have difficulty determining what is a good or a bad idea or decision, managers must give teams positive feedback on their process and output. This feedback helps the members to see themselves as a team, and it teaches them to value and celebrate their diversity, recognize contributions made by the individual members, and trust the collective judgment of the group.

These guidelines can be useful in helping leaders to manage culturally diverse teams effectively. World-class organizations use such an approach, and one good example is NUMMI (New United Motor Manufacturing), a joint venture between General Motors and Toyota that transformed an out-of-date GM plant in Fremont, California, into a world-class organization. This joint-venture partnership, formed over 10 years ago, continues to be a success story of how a culturally diverse work force can produce state-of-the-art automobiles. The successful approach to culturally diverse work teams at NUMMI was built around four principles:

1. Both management and labor recognized that their futures were interdependent, thus committing them to a mutual vision.
2. Employees felt secure and trusted assurances that they would be treated fairly, thus enabling them to become contributors.
3. The production system formed interdependent relationships throughout the plant, thus helping to create a healthy work environment.
4. The production system was managed to transform the stress and conflict of everyday life into trust and mutual respect.[21]

In achieving success at NUMMI, Toyota sent trainers from Japan to work with its U.S. counterparts and teach the production system that would be used throughout the plant. During this period, both groups searched for points of agreement, establishing valuable relationships in the process. In addition, the Japanese taught the Americans some useful techniques for increasing productivity, including how to focus on streamlining operations, reduce waste, and learn how to blame mistakes on the situation or themselves (not on team members).

In overcoming multicultural differences at NUMMI, several changes were introduced, including: (1) reserved dining rooms were eliminated, and all managers now eat in a communal cafeteria; (2) all reserved parking spaces were eliminated; and (3) GM's 80 job classifications were collapsed into only 3 to equalize work and rewards and ensure fairness.[22] Commenting on the overall success of the joint venture, it was noted that

> Toyota managers resisted temptations to forge ahead with a pure version of the system. Both the Japanese and Americans learned as they went. By adopting a "go slow" attitude, the Japanese and Americans remained open to points of resistance as they arose and navigated around them. By tolerating ambiguity and by searching for consensus, Toyota managers established the beginnings of mutual respect and trust with the American workers and managers.[23]

NUMMI is only one example of the many successful multicultural work forces producing world-class goods and services.[24] In each case, however, effective multinationals rely on the types of guidelines that have been highlighted in this discussion.[25]

SUMMARY OF KEY POINTS

1. Organizational culture is a pattern of basic assumptions that are developed by a group as it learns to cope with its problems of external adaptation and internal integration and that are taught to new members as the correct way to perceive, think, and feel in relation to these problems. Some important characteristics of organizational culture include observed behavioral regularities, norms, dominant values, philosophy, rules, and organizational climate.
2. Organizational cultures are shaped by a number of factors. These include the general relationship between employees and their organization, the hierarchic system of authority that defines the roles of managers and subordinates, and the general views that employees hold about the organization's purpose, destiny, goals, and their place in them. When examining these differences, Trompenaars has suggested the use of two continua: equity/hierarchy, and person/task orientation, resulting in four basic types of organizational cultures: family, Eiffel Tower, guided missile, and incubator.
3. The family culture is characterized by a strong emphasis on hierarchic authority and orientation to the person. The Eiffel Tower culture is characterized by a strong emphasis

on hierarchy and orientation to the task. The guided missile culture is characterized by a strong emphasis on equality in the workplace and orientation to the task. The incubator culture is characterized by a strong emphasis on equality and orientation to the person.

4. Success in the international arena often is heavily determined by a company's ability to manage multiculturalism and diversity. There are four phases through which firms progress in their international evolution: (1) domestic corporation; (2) international corporation; (3) multinational corporation; and (4) global corporation.

5. There are a number of ways to examine multiculturalism and diversity. One is by looking at the domestic multicultural and diverse work force that operates in the MNC's home country. Another is by examining the variety of diverse groups that exist in MNCs, including homogeneous groups, token groups, bicultural groups, and multicultural groups. Several potential problems as well as advantages are associated with multicultural, diverse teams.

6. A number of guidelines have proven to be particularly effective in managing culturally diverse groups. These include careful selection of the members, identification of the group's goals, establishment of equal power and mutual respect among the participants, and delivering positive feedback on performance. A good example of how these guidelines have been used is the NUMMI joint venture created by General Motors and Toyota.

KEY TERMS

organizational culture

family culture

Eiffel Tower culture

guided missile culture

incubator culture

homogeneous group

token group

bicultural group

multinational group

groupthink

REVIEW AND DISCUSSION QUESTIONS

1. Some researchers have found that when Germans work for a U.S. MNC, they become even more German, and when Americans work for a German MNC, they become even more American. Why would this knowledge be important to these MNCs?

2. When comparing the negotiating styles and strategies of French versus Spanish negotiators, a number of sharp contrasts are evident. What are three of these, and what could MNCs do to improve their position when negotiating with either group?

3. In which of the four types of organizational cultures—family, Eiffel Tower, guided missile, incubator—would most people in the United States feel comfortable? In which would most Japanese feel comfortable? Based on your answers, what conclusions could you draw regarding the importance of understanding organizational culture for international management?

4. Most MNCs need not enter foreign markets to face the challenge of dealing with multiculturalism. Do you agree or disagree with this statement? Explain your answer.

5. What are some potential problems that must be overcome when using multicultural, diverse teams in today's organizations? What are some recognized advantages? Identify and discuss two of each.

6. A number of guidelines can be valuable in helping MNCs to make diverse teams more effective. What are five of these? Additionally, what underlying principles guided NUMMI in its effective use of multicultural teams? Were the principles used by NUMMI similar to the general guidelines identified in this chapter, or were they significantly different? Explain your answer.

PRACTICAL INTERNATIONAL MANAGEMENT ASSIGNMENT

Review recent issues of popular business magazines and newspapers such as *Business Week*, the *Economist, Forbes, Fortune,* and the *Wall Street Journal* and identify a joint venture that is now being created by MNCs from different countries. Identify the type of organizational culture that is likely to exist in each partner. Compare and contrast these organizational cultures. Based on your analysis, what conclusions can you draw regarding the potential problems and strengths that organizational culture might create for this joint venture?

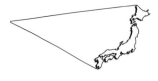

Japan

In Japan, pay is considered to be a reward for patience and sacrifice, not performance.

Japan is located in eastern Asia, and it comprises a curved chain of more than 3000 islands. Four of these—Hokkaido, Honshu, Shikoku, and Kyushi—account for 98 percent of the country's land area. The population of Japan was approximately 126 million in the mid-1990s, with over 8 million people living in the nation's capital, Tokyo. According to the World Bank, Japan's gross national product (GNP) during this time, approximately, was a very high $32,000 per capita. At the same time, the country was in the throes of an economic recession, and growth had slowed considerably from that of the 1980s when an average annual increase of 6 percent in GNP was common. International economists, however, believe that these last few years have merely been a lull in what has been the most rapid economic growth of any nation in the history of the twentieth century. Most forecasts indicate that by the end of this century, Japan's economy should be stronger than ever.

This optimistic outlook is shared by two multinationals, one from the United States and the other from Germany. These two MNCs recently joined forces with a large Japanese MNC to create a new retailing chain throughout Japan. The joint venture will limit its merchandise selection to clothing and toys, which are two product areas where Japanese prices are relatively higher than those paid by consumers in other countries. The U.S. and German partners will design the clothing and toys, but they will be produced in Japan by local labor and sold there. The U.S. and German partners will con-

tribute most of the capital needed for the venture, and they also will help to design the production and distribution system as well as the retail-store layout. The Japanese partner will be responsible for choosing the type of merchandise to be produced, manage and/or co-ordinate (for subcontractors) the production facilities, and handle the marketing.

To provide a managerial presence in Japan, the two foreign partners will share a new headquarters building with their local partner. Located approximately 60 miles outside of Tokyo, this building will house the senior-level management from all three MNCs as well as key finance, production, and marketing personnel. The plan is to have strategy and major decisions made at this headquarters, then disseminated to the production facilities and retail stores. The joint venture hopes to have 6 stores operating within 24 months, and 20 more within 5 years.

1. What type of organizational culture is each of the three partners likely to have? (Use Figure 6-3 as a guide in answering this question.)
2. Which of the organizational cultures will be most different from that of the other two? Explain.
3. What types of problems might the culturally diverse top-management team at headquarters create for the joint venture? Give some specific examples. How could these problems be overcome?
4. In terms of organizational culture, what is your estimate of success for this joint venture?

You Be the International Management Consultant

A Good Faith Effort Is Needed

Excelsior Manufacturing is a medium-sized firm located in the northeast part of the United States. Excelsior has long been known as a high-quality, world-class producer of precision tools. Recently, however, this MNC has been slowly losing market share in Europe, because many EU companies are turning to other European firms to save on taxes and transportation costs. Realizing that it needed a European partner if it hoped to recapture this lost ground, Excelsior began looking to buy a firm that could provide it a strong foothold in this market. After a brief search, the MNC made contact with Quality Instrumentation, a Madrid-based firm that was founded 5 years ago and has been growing at 25 percent annually. Excelsior currently is discussing a buyout with Quality Instrumentation, and the Spanish firm appears to be interested in the arrangement as it will provide them with increased technology, a quality reputation, and more funding for European expansion.

Next week, owners of the two companies are scheduled to meet in Madrid to discuss purchase price and potential plans for integrating their overall operations. The biggest sticking point appears to be a concern for meshing the organizational cultures and the work values and habits of the two enterprises. Each is afraid that the other's way of doing business might impede overall progress and lead to wasted productivity and lost profit. To deal with this issue, the president of Excelsior has asked his management team to draft a plan that could serve as a guide in determining how both groups could co-ordinate their efforts.

On a personal level, the head of Excelsior believes that it will be important for the Spanish management team to understand that if the Spaniards sell the business, they must be prepared to let U.S. managers have final decision-making power on major issues, such as research and development efforts, expansion plans, and customer segmentation. At the same time, the Americans are concerned that their potential European partners will feel they are being told what to do and resist these efforts. "We're going to have to make them understand that we must work as a unified team," the president explained to his planning committee, "and create a culture that will support this idea. We may not know a lot about working with Spaniards and they may not understand a great deal about how Americans do things, but I believe that we can resolve these differences if we put forth a good faith effort."

1. What do you think some of the main organizational culture differences between the two companies would be?
2. Why might the cultural diversity in the Spanish firm not be as great as that in the U.S. firm, and what potential problems could this create?
3. What would you recommend be done to effectively merge the two organizational cultures and ensure they operate harmoniously? Offer some specific recommendations.

CHAPTER 6 ENDNOTES

1. Lisa Hoecklin, *Managing Cultural Differences* (Workingham, England: Addison-Wesley, 1995), p. 146.
2. See D. Preston, "Management Development Structures and Organizational Culture," *Personnel Review,* vol. 22, no. 1, 1993, pp. 18–30.
3. Edgar Schein, *Organizational Culture and Leadership* (San Francisco: Jossey Bass, 1985), p. 9.
4. Fred Luthans, *Organizational Behavior,* 7th ed. (New York: McGraw-Hill, 1995), pp. 497–498.
5. Hoecklin, *Managing Cultural Differences,* p. 145.
6. Andre Laurent, "The Cultural Diversity of Western Conceptions of Management," *International Studies of Management and Organization,* Spring-Summer 1983, pp. 75–96.
7. Nancy J. Adler, *International Dimensions of Organizational Behavior,* 2nd ed. (Boston: PWS-Kent Publishing, 1991), pp. 58–59.
8. Hoecklin, *Managing Cultural Differences,* p. 151.
9. Carla Rapoport and Justin Martin, "Retailers Go Global," *Fortune,* February 20, 1995, pp. 102–108.
10. See Maddy Janssens, Jeanne M. Brett, and Frank J. Smith, "Confirmatory Cross-Cultural Research: Testing the Viability of a Corporation-Wide Safety Policy," *Academy of Management Journal,* June 1995, pp. 364–382.
11. Fons Trompenaars, *Riding the Waves of Culture: Understanding Diversity in Global Business* (Burr Ridge, IL: Irwin, 1994), p. 156.
12. Ibid., p. 164.
13. Ibid., p. 167.
14. Ibid., p. 172.
15. Adler, *International Dimensions of Organizational Behavior,* p. 121.
16. Ibid., p. 132.
17. For a summary of these and other benefits, see Baily W. Jackson, Frank LaFasto, Henry G. Schultz, and Don Kelly, "Diversity," *Human Resource Management,* Spring/Summer, 1992, pp. 22–24.
18. Irving L. Janis, *Victims of Groupthink* (Boston: Houghton Mifflin, 1972). Also see Richard M. Hodgetts, *Human Relations at Work,* 6th ed. (Fort Worth, TX: Dryden Press, 1996), p. 118; Fred Luthans, *Organizational Behavior,* pp. 259–260.
19. Adler, *International Dimensions of Organizational Behavior,* p. 137.
20. See Andre L. Delbecq, Andrew H. Van deVen, and David H. Gustafson, *Group Techniques for Program Planning* (Glenview, IL: Scott, Foresman, 1975).
21. Wellford W. Wilms, Alan J. Hardcastle, and Deone M. Zell, "Cultural Transformation at NUMMI," *Sloan Management Review,* Fall 1994, p. 103.
22. Ibid., p. 105.
23. Ibid., p. 111.
24. For additional insights into other work systems, see Joel Cutcher-Gershenfeld *et al.,* "Japanese Team-Based Work Systems in North America," *California Management Review,* Fall 1994, pp. 42–64.
25. Peter B. Smith, Mark F. Peterson, and Jyuji Mismumi, "Event Management and Work Team Effectiveness in Japan, Britain and the USA," *Journal of Occupational and Organizational Psychology,* vol. 67, 1994, pp. 33–43.

PART THREE

INTERNATIONAL MANAGEMENT: STRATEGY AND FUNCTIONS

MANAGING POLITICAL RISK AND NEGOTIATIONS

OBJECTIVES OF THE CHAPTER

Firms go international to become more competitive and profitable. Unfortunately, many risks accompany this internationalization. One of the biggest involves the political situation of the countries in which the MNC does business, and MNCs must be able to assess political risk and conduct skillful negotiations. An overview of the political environment in selected areas of the world has already been provided, but this chapter specifically examines what political risk is all about and how MNCs try to manage this risk. One major way is through effective evaluation and risk reduction. This process extends from risk identification and quantification to the formulation of appropriate responses, such as integration and protective and defensive techniques. This chapter also examines how negotiations are managed and actually carried out, and it reviews some of the common tactics that are used. The specific objectives of this chapter are:

1. **EXAMINE** how MNCs evaluate political risk.
2. **PRESENT** some common methods used for managing and reducing political risk.
3. **DISCUSS** how the negotiation process works, and how cultural differences can affect this process.
4. **DESCRIBE** some common negotiation tactics.

THE NATURE AND ANALYSIS OF POLITICAL RISK

Applied to international management, *political risk* is the likelihood that an MNC's foreign investment will be constrained by a host government's policies. Such risk is of particular concern to companies entering Third World countries or doing business with governments that, at least until now, have not encouraged direct foreign investment (where outside countries own the means of production). For example, the newly emerged countries in Eastern Europe are highly unstable and therefore quite risky for MNCs doing business there. The same can be said for countries such as China,[1] Mexico,[2] Saudi Arabia, and the Balkan nations.[3]

Some U.S. companies are being forced to renegotiate their contracts in Russia and accept less favorable terms.[4] U.S., Japanese, and European banks now find they must write off some of their loans to Third World countries and restructure the remaining debt, because these governments no longer are willing to make payments on the current loan portfolio. In other cases, multinationals have found that a rapid turn of events has left them with large losses. For example, the Chinese massacre in Tiananmen Square in 1989 resulted in many MNCs' pulling their people out of the country and closing their offices both there and in Hong Kong, which reverts to the PRC in 1997. The Iraqi invasion of Kuwait resulted in the destruction of MNC assets in that country. The lesson from these events is clear: Political climate can change quickly, and safe investments can become high-risk investments overnight.

Some specific reasons why MNCs fear political risk include expropriation or nationalization of property or resources, inconvertibility of currency, war damage, civil-strife damage, breach of contract for political reasons, limits on remittance, government interference with terms of a contract, discriminatory taxation, and loss of copyright protection.[5] Figure 7-1 reports the relative levels of loss from these types of causes; as shown, foreign investors recently have suffered losses in a wide number of countries and geographic regions. This is why it is so important that MNCs carefully assess political risk.

Macro and Micro Analysis of Political Risk

Firms evaluate political risk in a number of ways. One is through *macro political risk analysis,* which reviews major political decisions that are likely to affect all enterprises in the country. Recent elections in France, for example, gave the conservatives new power and certainly will influence political risk in that country. Political swings to the left can create even more problems. For example, when Michael Manley was prime minister of Jamaica a number of years ago, the country took a decided swing to the left, and U.S. investment dropped to a trickle. Manley's subsequent election defeat resulted in a government that was much more capitalistic in orientation. With Manley's return to power in the late 1980s, however, foreign firms maintained their presence in Jamaica, because Manley had moved sharply to the middle of the political continuum. Because favorable policies have remained in effect after his departure from government in the early 1990s, the political risk in Jamaica has remained low. In contrast, the Philippines continues to present a fairly high political risk area, despite the removal of the Marcos government. The Aquino government was unable to create a stable political environment for investment, and the new government that took office in 1992 is just starting to reverse this trend.

FIGURE 7-1

LOSSES TO FOREIGN INVESTORS BECAUSE OF SOCIOPOLITICAL CAUSES: 1987–1992

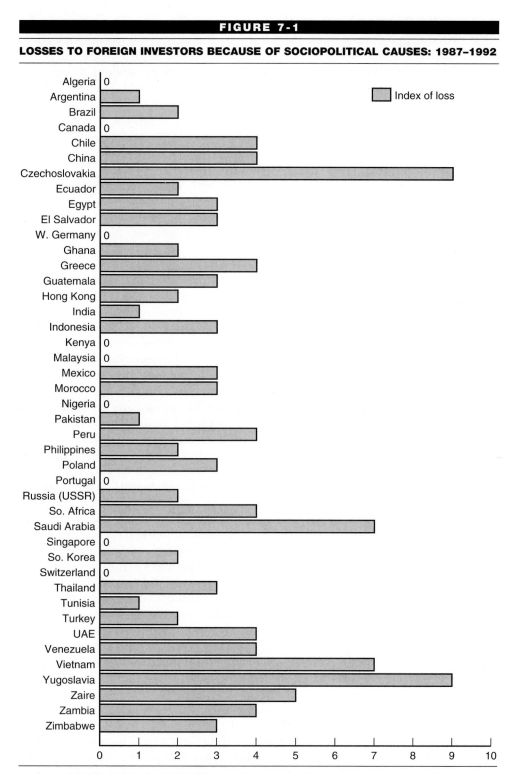

Source: Llewellyn D. Howell and Brad Chaddick, "Model of Political Risk for Foreign Investment and Trade: An Assessment of Three Approaches," *Columbia Journal of World Business,* Fall 1994, p. 75. © 1994, *Columbia Journal of World Business.* Reprinted with permission.

Another example of a macro consideration of political risk is an analysis of what would happen to a company's investment if opposition government leaders were to take control. Many U.S. companies in Iran failed to forecast the fall of the Shah and rise of Khomeini. As a result, they lost their investment. Because of this Iranian experience and the situation in Iraq under militant dictator Saddam Hussein, however, many multinationals now are very reluctant to invest very heavily in most Middle Eastern countries. In the early 1990s, the government of Iran appeared to be interested in attracting foreign investment, but there is still a great deal of concern that this region is too politically explosive. Eastern Europe appears to be a better bet, as seen by the millions of dollars that MNCs have poured into countries such as Hungary and Poland. This geographic region also is regarded as politically risky, however, as shown in the Bosnian conflict, the breakup of Czechoslovakia, and the political instability in Poland.[6] As a result, many multinationals have been tempering their expansion plans in Eastern Europe.

Whereas macro analysis looks at the whole country, *micro political risk analysis* is directed toward government policies and actions that influence selected sectors of the economy or specific foreign businesses in the country. These policies often take the form of industry regulation, taxes on specific types of business activity, and local content laws. The essence of these actions is that some businesses are treated differently from others. A good recent example was the Clinton administration's threat to implement trade sanctions against Japanese luxury cars in the United States. Faced with the loss of a major market, Japanese negotiators eventually agreed that their country's automakers would buy more U.S. parts, that their government would take steps to open its market for repair parts and encourage domestic auto dealers to sell more U.S. cars, and that Toyota, Honda, and Mitsubishi all would build more facilities in the United States.[7] These terms should help to reduce the U.S. trade imbalance with Japan. This latest round of negotiations likely will not be the last, however, as the United States continues to seek greater access to the Japanese auto market.[8] One reason is because the Europeans have been quite successful in negotiating a managed trade agreement with the Japanese, and the United States would like to do the same. For example, while Japanese firms dominate almost 30 percent of the U.S. market, their share of the European market is a mere 11 percent, and the Europeans have negotiated successfully for large quotas of European-made parts in Japanese cars built in Europe.[9]

Another example of micro political risk is provided by countries in South America that face an indebtedness crisis and have introduced a variety of policies to promote exports and discourage imports. MNCs that feel they cannot abide by these policies will stay out; however, some that are looking for a location from which to produce and export goods will view these same government policies as very attractive. Table 7-1 lists criteria that MNCs could use to evaluate the degree of political risk.

Analyzing the Expropriation Risk

Expropriation is the seizure of businesses with little, if any, compensation to the owners. Such seizures of foreign enterprises by developing countries were quite common in the old days. In addition, some takeovers were caused by *indigenization laws,* which required that nationals hold a majority interest in the operation.

TABLE 7-1

A GUIDE TO EVALUATION OF POLITICAL RISK

External factors affecting subject country
Prospects for foreign conflict
Relations with border countries
Regional instabilities
Alliances with major and regional powers
Sources of key raw materials
Major foreign markets
Policy toward United States
U.S. policy toward country

Internal groupings (points of power):
Government in power:
  Key agencies and officials
  Legislative entrenched bureaucracies
  Policies—economic, financial, social, labor, etc.
  Pending legislation
  Attitude toward private sector
  Power networks

Political parties (in and out of power):
  Policies
  Leading and emerging personalities
  Internal power struggles
  Sector and area strengths
  Future prospects for retaining or gaining power

Other important groups:
  Unions and labor movements
  Military, special groups within military
  Families
  Business and financial communities
  Intelligentsia
  Students
  Religious groups
  Media
  Regional and local governments
  Social and environmental activists
  Cultural, linguistic, and ethnic groups
  Separatist movements
  Foreign communities
  Potential competitors and customers

Internal factors
Power struggles amongst elites
Ethnic confrontations
Regional struggles
Economic factors affecting stability (consumer inflation, price and wage controls, unemployment, supply shortages, taxation, etc.)
Anti-establishment movements

Factors affecting a specific project
(Custom-designed for each project)

Note: Information in the table is an abridged version of Probe's Political Agenda Worksheet, which may serve as a guide for corporate executives initiating their own political evaluations. Probe International is located in Stamford, Conn.
  Source: Benjamin Weinger, "What Executives Should Know about Political Risk," *Management Review*, January 1992, p. 20.

In the main, expropriation is more likely to occur in non-Western governments that are poor, relatively unstable, and suspicious of foreign multinationals.

Some firms are more vulnerable to expropriation than others. Those at greatest risk often are in extractive, agricultural, or infrastructural industries such as utilities and transportation because of the importance of these industries to the country. In addition, large firms often are more likely targets than small firms, because more is to be gained by expropriating from large firms.

MNCs can take a wide variety of strategies to minimize their chances of expropriation. They can bring in local partners. They can limit the use of high technology so that if the firm is expropriated, the country cannot duplicate the technology. They also can acquire an affiliate that depends on the parent company for key areas of the operation, such as financing, research, and technology transfer, so that no practical value exists in seizing the affiliate.

The Role of Operational Profitability in Risk Analysis

Although expropriation is a major consideration, most MNCs are more directly concerned with operational profitability.[10] Will they be able to make the desired return on investment?[11] A number of government regulations can have

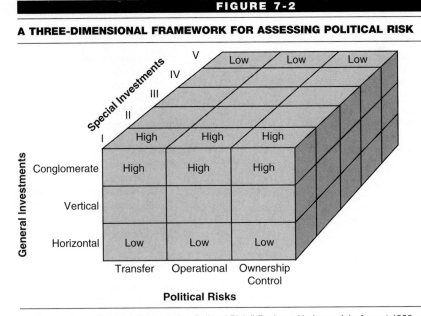

FIGURE 7-2

A THREE-DIMENSIONAL FRAMEWORK FOR ASSESSING POLITICAL RISK

Source: David A. Schmidt, "Analyzing Political Risk," *Business Horizons,* July-August 1986, p. 50. Copyright 1986 by the Foundation for the School of Business at Indiana University. Used with permission.

a negative impact on their profitability.[12] Requiring MNCs to use domestic suppliers instead of bringing in components or raw materials from other company-owned facilities or purchasing them more cheaply in the world market is one such regulation. Another is a restriction on the amount of profit that can be taken out of the country. A third is the wages and salaries that must be paid to the employees. Despite these difficulties, MNCs have become very interested in designing models and frameworks for helping them to better understand and manage their political risk.

MANAGING POLITICAL RISK

For well over two decades, businesses have been looking for ways to manage their political risk.[13] Quite often, the process begins with a detailed analysis of the various risks with which the MNC will be confronted, including development of a comprehensive framework that identifies the various risks and then assigns a quantitative risk or rating factor to them.

Developing a Comprehensive Framework

A comprehensive framework for managing political risk should consider all political risks and identify those that are most important. Schmidt has offered a three-dimensional framework that combines political risks, general investments, and special investments.[14] Figure 7-2 illustrates this framework, and the following sections examine each dimension in detail.

Sometimes It's All Politics

One of the biggest problems in doing business internationally is that yesterday's agreement with a government may be cancelled or delayed by today's politicians who disagree with that earlier decision. Enron, the Houston-based U.S. energy consortium, recently discovered this when its power project in Dabhol, India, became the focal point of political interest. India's economic nationalists began accelerating a campaign to scrap a high-profile, U.S.-backed power project despite warnings of potential damage to the confidence of foreign investors in the country. These politicians wanted to abandon the $28 billion deal as well as all other power projects in the country that had been approved under the government's "fast track" provisions. The contract for the two-stage, 2000+ megawatt plant was signed before the current politicians came to power in Maharashtra, the state where Dabhol is located.

What effect would this latest political move have on foreign investment in India? A number of foreign investors indicated that if the Enron project were cancelled, they would review their investment plans for the country. A recent survey of international energy companies by the East-West Center in Hawaii found that of 13 Asian economies, India's investment climate ranked fifth from the bottom for power-sector investment. This seemed to have little effect on the politicians, who proceeded to cancel the project. Members of the political opposition, who supported the project, called it a mere political ploy designed to appeal to voters in the upcoming elections, and they urged foreign investors to sit tight and ride out the political storm. Many of these investors appeared to be apprehensive about taking such advice, and Enron announced plans for taking the case to international arbitration to reclaim the $300 million they have invested in the project—as well as $300 million in damages.

The political climate in India is not unique. Russia also offers its share of jitters to investors. In particular, many joint ventures that were created during the Gorbachev era now are having problems. A good example is Moscow's Radisson-Slavjanskaya Hotel venture, in which American Business Centers of Irvine, California, owns a 40 percent stake. American Business Centers manages several floors of offices in the hotel, and now that the venture is making money, it appears that the Irvine firm's Russian partners and the Radisson hotel people are trying to oust them. The president of American Business Centers claims that his partners feel they do not need him any longer.

The dilemma faced by American Business Centers is becoming increasingly common in Russia. For example, the Seattle-based firm Radio Page entered into a joint venture with Moscow Public Telephone Network and another Russian company in 1992 to offer paging services. Together, they built a system of telephone pagers in the Moscow region. Radio Page held a 51 percent stake. When annual revenues hit $5 million and the venture was on the verge of making $1 million, however, the agreement began to unravel. The Russian partners demanded control of the operation and even threatened to pull the critical radio frequencies if they did not get their way.

There is little that foreign joint-venture firms doing business in high-risk countries can do except try to negotiate with their partners. For instance, the political situation in Russia is so unstable that support from one government ministry may be offset by opposition from another, or worse yet, the individuals supporting the foreign firm may be ousted from their jobs tomorrow. Economic considerations tend to be the main reason why firms seek international partners, but sometimes, it seems that everything boils down to politics and the risks associated with dealing in this political environment.

Political Risks   Political risks can be broken down into three basic categories: transfer risks, operational risks, and ownership-control risks. *Transfer risks* stem from government policies that limit the transfer of capital, payments, production, people, and technology in or out of the country. Examples include tariffs on exports and imports as well as restrictions on exports, dividend remittance, and capital repatriation. *Operational risks* result from government policies and procedures that directly constrain the management and performance of local operations. Examples include price controls, financing restrictions, export commitments, taxes, and local-sourcing requirements. *Ownership-control risks* are brought about by government policies or actions that inhibit ownership or control of local operations. Examples include foreign ownership limitations, pressure for local participation, confiscation, expropriation, and abrogation of proprietary rights. For a more detailed example, see "International Management in Action: Sometimes It's All Politics."

General Nature of Investment The general nature of investment examines whether the company is making a conglomerate, vertical, or horizontal investment (see Figure 7-2). In a *conglomerate investment,* the goods or services produced are not similar to those produced at home. These types of investments usually are rated as high risk, because foreign governments see them as providing fewer benefits to the country and greater benefits to the MNC than other investments. *Vertical investments* include the production of raw materials or intermediate goods that are to be processed into final products. These investments run the risk of being taken over by the government because they are export-oriented, and governments like a business that helps it to generate foreign capital. *Horizontal investments* involve the production of goods or services that are the same as those produced at home. These investments typically are made with an eye toward satisfying the host country's market demands. As a result, they are not very likely to be takeover targets.

Special Nature of Investment The special nature of foreign direct investment relates to the sector of economic activity, technological sophistication, and pattern of ownership. There are three sectors of economic activity: (1) the primary sector, which consists of agriculture, forestry, and mineral exploration and extraction; (2) the industrial sector, consisting of manufacturing operations; and (3) the service sector, which includes transportation, finance, insurance, and related industries. Technological sophistication consists of science-based industry and non-science-based industry; the difference between the two is that science-based industry requires the continuous introduction of new products and/or processes. Patterns of ownership relate to whether the business is wholly or partially owned.

The special nature of foreign direct investments can be categorized as one of five types (see Figure 7-2). Type I is the highest-risk venture; type V is the lowest-risk venture. This risk factor is assigned based on sector, technology, and ownership. Primary sector industries usually have the highest risk factor, service sector industries have the next highest, and industrial sector industries have the lowest. Firms with technology that is not available to the government should the firm be taken over have lower risk than those with technology that is easily acquired. Wholly owned subsidiaries have higher risk than partially owned subsidiaries.

Using a framework similar to that provided in Figure 7-2 helps MNCs to manage their political risks. A way to complement this framework approach is to give specific risk ratings to various criteria.

Quantifying the Variables in Managing Political Risk

Some MNCs attempt to manage political risk through a quantification process that identifies important factors and then compares the results from different geographic locales. This comparison allows them, for example, to identify how risky a venture is in Argentina versus Russia.

Factors that typically are quantified reflect the political and economic environment, domestic economic conditions, and external economic conditions. Each factor is given a minimum and maximum score, and the person(s) responsible for making the evaluation will determine the score for each. When this process is complete, a total risk evaluation number is computed by simply adding the individual scores. Table 7-2 provides an example of a quantitative list of political risk criteria.

TABLE 7-2

CRITERIA FOR QUANTIFYING POLITICAL RISK

Major area	Criteria	Scores	
		Minimum	**Maximum**
Political and economic environment	1. Stability of the political system	3	14
	2. Imminent internal conflicts	0	14
	3. Threats to stability emanating from the outside world	0	12
	4. Degree of control of the economic system	5	9
	5. Reliability of the country as a trading partner	4	12
	6. Constitutional guarantees	2	12
	7. Effectiveness of public administration	3	12
	8. Labor relations and social peace	3	15
Domestic economic conditions	9. Size of population	4	8
	10. Per capita income	2	10
	11. Economic growth during previous 5 years	2	7
	12. Prospective growth during next 3 years	3	10
	13. Inflation during previous 2 years	2	10
	14. Accessibility of domestic capital market to foreigners	3	7
	15. Availability of high-quality local labor	2	8
	16. Possibility of giving employment to foreign nationals	2	8
	17. Availability of energy resources	2	14
	18. Legal requirements concerning environmental protection	4	8
	19. Traffic system and communication	2	14
External economic relations	20. Restrictions imposed on imports	2	10
	21. Restrictions imposed on exports	2	10
	22. Restrictions imposed on foreign investments in the country	3	9
	23. Freedom to set up or engage in partnerships	3	9
	24. Legal protection for brands and products	3	9
	25. Restrictions imposed on monetary transfers	2	8
	26. Revaluations against the DM during previous 5 years	2	7
	27. Development of the balance of payments	2	9
	28. Drain on foreign funds through oil and other energy imports	3	14
	29. International financial standing	3	8
	30. Restrictions imposed on the exchange of local money into foreign currencies	2	8

Source: Adapted from E. Dichtl and H. G. Koglmayr, "Country Risk Ratings," *Management International Review,* vol. 26, no. 4, 1986, p. 6. Used with permission.

Formulating Appropriate Responses

Once political risk has been analyzed by either the framework or quantitative approach, or both, the MNC then will attempt to manage the risk further by minimizing or limiting it through carefully formulated responses. Two such common approaches are the use of relative bargaining power and the use of integrative as well as protective and defensive techniques.

Relative Bargaining Power   The theory behind relative bargaining power is quite simple. The firm works to maintain a stronger bargaining power position than that of the host country. A good example is when the firm has proprietary technology that will be unavailable to the host country if the operation is expropriated or the firm is forced to abide by government decisions that are

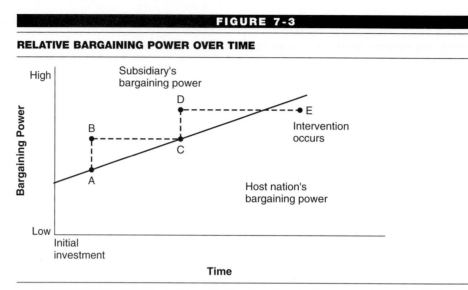

FIGURE 7-3

RELATIVE BARGAINING POWER OVER TIME

Source: Adapted from Thomas A. Pointer, "Political Risk: Managing Government Intervention," in Paul W. Beamish, J. Peter Killing, Donald J. LeCraw, and Harold Crookell, *International Management: Text and Cases* (Homewood, IL: Irwin, 1991), p. 125.

unacceptable to it. Over time, of course, this technology may become common, and the firm will lose its bargaining power. To prevent this from happening, however, the firm will work to develop new technology that again establishes the balance of power in its favor. As long as the host country stands to lose more than it will gain by taking action against the company, the firm has successfully minimized its political risk by establishing an effective bargaining position. Figure 7-3 provides an example. As long as the MNC's bargaining power remains at or above the diagonal line, the government will not intervene. At point E in the figure, however, this power declines, and the host country will begin to intervene.[15]

Integrative as well as Protective and Defensive Techniques Another way that MNCs attempt to protect themselves from expropriation and/or minimize government interference in their operations is to use integration and the implementation of protective and defensive techniques. *Integrative techniques* are designed to help the overseas operation become part of the host country's infrastructure. The objective is to be perceived as "less foreign" and thus unlikely to be the target of government action. Some of the most integrative techniques include: (1) developing good relations with the host government and other local political groups; (2) producing as much of the product locally as possible with the use of in-country suppliers and subcontractors, thus making it a "domestic" product[16]; (3) creating joint ventures[17] and hiring local people to manage and run the operation; (4) doing as much local research and development as possible; and (5) developing effective labor-management relations.

 Protective and defensive techniques are designed to discourage the host government from interfering in operations. In contrast to the integrative techniques, these actually encourage nonintegration of the enterprise in the local environment. Examples include: (1) doing as little local manufacturing as possible and conducting all research and development outside the country; (2) limiting

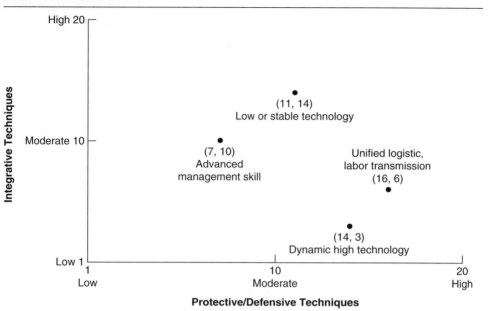

FIGURE 7-4

USE OF INTEGRATIVE AND PROTECTIVE AND DEFENSIVE TECHNIQUES BY FIRMS IN SELECT INDUSTRIES

Source: Adapted from Ann Gregory, "Firm Characteristic and Political Risk Reduction in Overseas Ventures," *National Academy of Management Proceedings*, 1982, p. 77. Used with permission.

the responsibility of local personnel and hiring only those who are vital to the operation; (3) raising capital from local banks and the host government as well as outside sources; and (4) diversifying production of the product among a number of countries.[18]

When should a company use integrative techniques? Under what conditions should it employ protective and defensive techniques? Gregory has suggested that this choice will be heavily influenced by characteristics such as the firm's technology, management skills, and logistics and labor transmission.[19] In all, four basic types of firms can be described using these characteristics.

The first type consists of dynamic, high-technology firms that have unique knowledge that the host country would like. Computer companies are a good example. As seen in Figure 7-4, these firms do not rely very much on integrative techniques. They attempt to keep their distance from the host country and rely heavily on protective and defensive strategies.

The second type consists of firms with low or stable technology. These companies make products that require little innovation or use relatively unsophisticated technology. Steel firms are an example. As seen in Figure 7-4, these firms typically use both high integration and high protective and defensive strategies, although they generally rely more on integration than the defensive approach.

The third type consists of firms whose managers need to be highly skilled. For example, food production firms require advanced marketing and management skills to be competitive. These companies typically use a balanced approach of integration and protective and defensive techniques, but they are less concerned with either than low or stable technology firms are.

The fourth type consists of companies characterized by highly labor-intensive products, high value in relation to weight and/or volume, and the need for a strong global marketing system for selling the product. Sewing machine companies are an example. Firms in this category tend to rely more heavily on protective and defensive measures than any of the other three groups and to employ only moderate concern for integrative techniques (again, see Figure 7-4.)

The strategic response that a firm takes in managing its political risk will be influenced by a variety of factors besides the firm's technology, management skills, logistics, and labor transmission. Others include the nature of the industry, local conditions in the host country, and philosophy of the management. Whatever variables are considered, however, firms are going to use a combination of integrative and protective and defensive techniques.

MANAGING INTERNATIONAL NEGOTIATIONS

Closely related to managing political risk, but deserving special attention, is managing negotiations. *Negotiation* is the process of bargaining with one or more parties to arrive at a solution that is acceptable to all. Negotiation often follows assessing political risk and can be used as an approach to conflict management. If the risk is worth it, then the MNC must negotiate with the host country to secure the best possible arrangements. The MNC and the host country will discuss the investment the MNC is prepared to make in return for certain guarantees and/or concessions. The initial range of topics typically includes critical areas such as hiring practices, direct financial investment, taxes, and ownership control. Negotiation also is used in creating joint ventures with local firms and in getting the operation off the ground. After the firm is operating, additional areas of negotiation often include expansion of facilities, use of more local managers, additional imports or exports of materials and finished goods, and recapture of profits.

On a more macro level of international trade are the negotiations conducted between countries. The current balance-of-trade problems between the United States and Japan are one example. The massive debt problems of Third World countries and the opening of trade doors with Eastern European countries are other current examples.[20]

The Negotiation Process

There are several basic steps that can be used in managing the negotiation process.[21] Regardless of the issues or personalities of the parties involved, this process typically begins with planning.

Planning Planning starts with the negotiators' identifying those objectives they would like to attain. Then, they explore the possible options for reaching these objectives. Research shows that the greater the number of options, the greater the chances for successful negotiations.[22] While this appears to be an obvious statement, research also reveals that many negotiators do not alter their strategy when negotiating across cultures.[23] Next, consideration is given to areas of common ground between the parties. Other major areas include: (1) the setting of limits on single-point objectives, such as deciding to pay no more than $10 million for the factory and $3 million for the land; (2) dividing issues into short- and long-term considerations and deciding how to handle each; and (3) determining the sequence in which to discuss the various issues.[24]

Interpersonal Relationship Building   The second phase of the negotiation process involves getting to know the people on the other side. This "feeling out" period is characterized by the desire to identify those who are reasonable and those who are not. In contrast to negotiators in many other countries, those in the United States often give little attention to this phase; they want to get down to business immediately, which often is an ineffective approach. Adler notes:

> Effective negotiators must view luncheon, dinner, reception, ceremony, and tour invitations as times for interpersonal relationship building, and therefore as key to the negotiating process. When American negotiators, often frustrated by the seemingly endless formalities, ceremonies, and "small talk," ask how long they must wait before beginning to "do business," the answer is simple: wait until your opponents bring up business (and they will). Realize that the work of conducting a successful negotiation has already begun, even if business has yet to be mentioned.[25]

Exchanging Task-Related Information   In this part of the negotiation process, each group sets forth its position on the critical issues. These positions often will change later in the negotiations. At this point, the participants are trying to find out what the other party wants to attain and what it is willing to give up.

Persuasion   This step of negotiations is considered by many to be the most important. No side wants to give away more than it has to, but each knows that without giving some concessions, it is unlikely to reach a final agreement. The success of the persuasion step often depends on: (1) how well the parties understand each other's position; (2) the ability of each to identify areas of similarity and differences; (3) the ability to create new options; and (4) the willingness to work toward a solution that allows all parties to walk away feeling they have achieved their objectives.

Agreement   The final phase of negotiations is the granting of concessions and hammering out a final agreement. Sometimes, this phase is carried out piecemeal, and concessions and agreements are made on issues one at a time. This is the way those from the United States like to negotiate. As each issue is resolved, it is removed from the bargaining table and interest focused on the next. Asians and Russians, on the other hand, tend to negotiate a final agreement on everything, and few concessions are given until the end.[26] Simply put, to negotiate effectively in the international arena, it is necessary to understand how cultural differences between the parties affect the process.[27]

Cultural Differences Affecting Negotiations

In negotiating effectively, it is important to have a sound understanding of the other side's culture. This includes consideration of areas such as communication patterns, time orientation, and social behaviors. A number of useful steps can help in this process.[28] One negotiation expert recommends the following:

1. Do not identify the counterpart's home culture too quickly. Common cues (e.g., name, physical appearance, language, accent, location) may be unreliable. The counterpart probably belongs to more than one culture.
2. Beware of the Western bias toward "doing." In Arab, Asian, and Latin groups, ways of being (e.g., comportment, smell), feeling, thinking, and talking can shape relationships more powerfully than doing.
3. Try to counteract the tendency to formulate simple, consistent, stable images. Not many cultures are simple, consistent, or stable.
4. Do not assume that all aspects of the culture are equally significant. In Japan, consulting all relevant parties to a decision is more important than presenting a gift.
5. Recognize that norms for interactions involving outsiders may differ from those for interactions between compatriots.
6. Do not overestimate your familiarity with your counterpart's culture. An American studying Japanese wrote New Year's wishes to Japanese contacts in basic Japanese characters, but omitted one character. As a result, the message became "Dead man, congratulations."[29]

U.S. negotiators have a style that often differs from that of negotiators in many other countries. Americans believe it is important to be factual and objective. In addition, they often make early concessions to show the other party that they are flexible and reasonable. Moreover, U.S. negotiators typically have authority to bind their party to an agreement, so if the right deal is struck, the matter can be resolved quickly. This is why deadlines are so important to Americans. They have come to do business, and they want to get things resolved immediately.

A comparative example would be the Arabs, who in contrast to Americans, with their logical approach, tend to use an emotional appeal in their negotiation style. They analyze things subjectively and treat deadlines as only general guidelines for wrapping up negotiations. They tend to open negotiations with an extreme initial position. However, the Arabs believe strongly in making concessions, do so throughout the bargaining process, and almost always reciprocate an opponent's concessions. They also seek to build a long-term relationship with their bargaining partners. For these reasons, Americans typically find it easier to negotiate with Arabs than with representatives from many other regions of the world.[30]

Before beginning any negotiations, negotiators should review the negotiating style of the other parties. (Table 7-3 provides some insights regarding negotiation styles of the Americans, Japanese, Arabs, and Mexicans.) This review should help to answer certain questions: What can we expect the other side to say and do? How are they likely to respond to certain offers? When should the most important matters be introduced? How quickly should concessions be made, and what type of reciprocity should be expected? These types of questions help effectively prepare the negotiators. In addition, the team will work on formulating negotiation tactics. The accompanying sidebar, "Negotiating with the Japanese," demonstrates such tactics, and the following discussion gets into some of the specifics.[31]

Negotiation Tactics

A number of specific tactics are used in international negotiating. The following discussion examines some of the most common.[32]

TABLE 7-3			

NEGOTIATION STYLES FROM A CROSS-CULTURAL PERSPECTIVE

Element	United States	Japanese	Arabians	Mexicans
Group composition	Marketing oriented	Function oriented	Committee of specialists	Friendship oriented
Number involved	2–3	4–7	4–6	2–3
Space orientation	Confrontational; competitive	Display harmonious relationship	Status	Close, friendly
Establishing rapport	Short period; direct to task	Longer period; until harmony	Long period; until trusted	Longer period; discuss family
Exchange of information	Documented; step-by-step; multimedia	Extensive; concentrate on receiving side	Less emphasis on technology, more on relationship	Less emphasis on technology, more on relationship
Persuasion tools	Time pressure; loss of saving/making money	Maintain relationship references; intergroup connections	Go-between; hospitality	Emphasis on family and on social concerns; goodwill measured in generations
Use of language	Open, direct, sense of urgency	Indirect, appreciative, cooperative	Flattery, emotional, religious	Respectful, gracious
First offer	Fair ±5 to 10%	±10 to 20%	±20 to 50%	Fair
Second offer	Add to package; sweeten the deal	−5%	−10%	Add an incentive
Final offer package	Total package	Makes no further concessions	−25%	Total
Decision-making process	Top management team	Collective	Team makes recommendation	Senior manager and secretary
Decision maker	Top management team	Middle line with team consensus	Senior manager	Senior manager
Risk taking	Calculated personal responsibility	Low group responsibility	Religion based	Personally responsible

Source: Lillian H. Chaney and Jeanette S. Martin, *Intercultural Business Communication* © 1995, pp. 183–184. Reprinted by permission of Prentice Hall, Inc. Englewood Cliffs, New Jersey.

Location Where should negotiations take place? If the matter is very important, most businesses will choose a neutral site. For example, U.S. firms negotiating with companies from the Far East will meet in Hawaii. South American companies negotiating with European firms will meet halfway, in New York City. A number of benefits derive from using a neutral site. One is that each party has limited access to its home office for receiving a great deal of negotiating information and advice and thus gaining an advantage on the other. A second is that the cost of staying at the site often is quite high, so both sides have an incentive to conclude their negotiations as quickly as possible. (Of course, if one side enjoys the facilities and would like to stay as long as possible, the negotiations could drag on.) A third is that most negotiators do not like to return home with nothing to show for their efforts, so they are motivated to reach some type of agreement.

Time Limits Time limits are an important negotiation tactic when one party is under a time constraint. This is particularly true when this party has agreed to

Negotiating with the Japanese

Some people believe that the most effective way of getting the Japanese to open up their markets to the United States is to use a form of strong-arm tactics, such as putting the country on a list of those to be targeted for retaliatory action. Others believe that this approach will not be effective, because the interests of the United States and Japan are intertwined and we would be hurting ourselves as much as them. Regardless of which group is right, one thing is certain: U.S. MNCs must learn how to negotiate more effectively with the Japanese. What can they do? Researchers have found that besides patience and a little table pounding, a number of important steps warrant consideration.

First, business firms need to prepare for their negotiations by learning more about Japanese culture and the "right" ways to conduct discussions. Those companies with experience in these matters report that the two best ways of doing this are to read books on Japanese business practices and social customs and to hire experts to train the negotiators. Other steps that are helpful include putting the team through simulated negotiations and hiring Japanese to assist in the negotiations.

Second, U.S. MNCs must learn patience and sincerity. Negotiations are a two-way street that require the

mutual co-operation and efforts of both parties. The U.S. negotiators must understand that many times, Japanese negotiators do not have full authority to make on-the-spot decisions. Authority must be given by someone at the home office, and this failure to act quickly should not be interpreted as a lack of sincerity on the part of the Japanese negotiators.

Third, the MNC must have a unique good or service. So many things are offered for sale in Japan that unless the company has something that is truly different, persuading the other party to buy it is difficult.

Fourth, technical expertise often is viewed as a very important contribution, and this often helps to win concessions with the Japanese. The Japanese know that the Americans, for example, still dominate the world when it comes to certain types of technology and that Japan is unable to compete effectively in these areas. When such technical expertise is evident, it is very influential in persuading the Japanese to do business with the company.

These four criteria are critical to effective negotiations with the Japanese. MNCs that use them report more successful experiences than those who do not.

meet at the home site of the other party. For example, U.S. negotiators who go to London to discuss a joint venture with a British firm often will have a scheduled return flight. Once their hosts find out how long these individuals intend to stay, the British can plan their strategy accordingly. The "real" negotiations are unlikely to begin until close to the time that the Americans must leave. The British know that their guests will be anxious to strike some type of deal before returning home, so the Americans are at a disadvantage.

Time limits can be used tactically even if the negotiators meet at a neutral site. For example, most Americans like to be home with their families for Thanksgiving, Christmas, and the New Year holiday. Negotiations held right before these dates put Americans at a disadvantage, because the other party knows when the Americans would like to leave.

Buyer–Seller Relations   How should buyers and sellers act? As noted earlier, Americans believe in being objective and trading favors. When the negotiations are over, Americans walk away with what they have received from the other party, and they expect the other party to do the same. This is not the way negotiators in many other countries think, however.

The Japanese, for example, believe that the buyers should get most of what they want. On the other hand, they also believe that the seller should be taken care of through reciprocal favors. The buyer must ensure that the seller has not been "picked clean." For example, when many Japanese firms first started doing business with large U.S. firms, they were unaware of U.S. negotiating tactics. As a result, the Japanese thought the Americans were taking advantage of them, whereas the Americans believed they were driving a good, hard bargain.

The Brazilians are quite different from both the Americans and Japanese. Researchers have found that Brazilians do better when they are more deceptive and self-interested and their opponents more open and honest than they are.[33] Brazilians also tend to make fewer promises and commitments than their opponents, and they are much more prone to say no. However, Brazilians are more likely to make initial concessions. Overall, Brazilians are more like Americans than Japanese in that they try to maximize their advantage, but they are unlike Americans in that they do not feel obligated to be open and forthright in their approach. Whether they are buyer or seller, they want to come out on top.

Bargaining Behaviors

Closely related to the discussion of negotiation tactics are the different types of bargaining behaviors, including both verbal and nonverbal behaviors. Verbal behaviors are an important part of the negotiating process, because they can improve the final outcome. Research shows that the profits of the negotiators increase when they make high initial offers, ask a lot of questions, and do not make many verbal commitments until the end of the negotiating process. In short, verbal behaviors are critical to the success of negotiations.

Use of Extreme Behaviors   Some negotiators begin by making extreme offers or requests. The Chinese and Arabs are examples. Some negotiators, however, begin with an initial position that is close to the one they are seeking. The Americans and Swedes are examples here.

Is one approach any more effective than the other? Research shows that extreme positions tend to produce better results. Some of the reasons relate to the fact that an extreme bargaining position: (1) shows the other party that the bargainer will not be exploited; (2) extends the negotiation and gives the bargainer a better opportunity to gain information on the opponent; (3) allows more room for concessions; (4) modifies the opponents' beliefs about the bargainer's preferences; (5) shows the opponent that the bargainer is willing to play the game according to the usual norms; and (6) lets the bargainer gain more than would probably be possible if a less extreme initial position had been taken.[34]

Although the use of extreme position bargaining is considered to be "un-American," many U.S. firms have used it successfully against foreign competitors. When Peter Ueberroth managed the Olympic Games in the United States in 1984, he turned a profit of well over $100 million—and that was without the participation of Soviet bloc countries, which would have further increased the market potential of the games. In past Olympiads, sponsoring countries have lost hundreds of millions of dollars. How did Ueberroth do it? One way was by using extreme position bargaining. For example, the Olympic Committee felt that the Japanese should pay $10 million for the right to televise the games in that country, so when the Japanese offered $6 million for the rights, the Olympic Committee countered with $90 million. Eventually, the two sides agreed on $18.5 million. Through the effective use of extreme position bargaining, Ueberroth got the Japanese to pay over three times their original offer, an amount well in excess of the committee's budget.

TABLE 7-4

CROSS-CULTURAL DIFFERENCES IN VERBAL BEHAVIOR OF JAPANESE, U.S., AND BRAZILIAN NEGOTIATORS

Behavior and definition	Number of times tactic was used in a half-hour bargaining session		
	Japanese	United States	Brazilian
Promise. A statement in which the source indicated an intention to provide the target with a reinforcing consequence which source anticipates target will evaluate as pleasant, positive, or rewarding.	7	8	3
Threat. Same as promise, except that the reinforcing consequences are thought to be noxious, unpleasant, or punishing.	4	4	2
Recommendation. A statement in which the source predicts that a pleasant environmental consequence will occur to the target. Its occurrence is not under the source's control.	7	4	5
Warning. Same as recommendation except that the consequences are thought to be unpleasant.	2	1	1
Reward. A statement by the source that is thought to create pleasant consequences for the target.	1	2	2
Punishment. Same as reward, except that the consequences are thought to be unpleasant.	1	3	3
Positive normative appeal. A statement in which the source indicates that the target's past, present, or future behavior was or will be in conformity with social norms.	1	1	0
Negative normative appeal. Same as positive normative appeal, except that the target's behavior is in violation of social norms.	3	1	1
Commitment. A statement by the source to the effect that its future bids will not go below or above a certain level.	15	13	8
Self-disclosure. A statement in which the source reveals information about itself.	34	36	39
Question. A statement in which the source asks the target to reveal information about itself.	20	20	22
Command. A statement in which the source suggests that the target perform a certain behavior.	8	6	14
First offer. The profit level associated with each participant's first offer.	61.5	57.3	75.2
Initial concession. The difference in profit between the first and second offer.	6.5	7.1	9.4
Number of no's. Number of times the word "no" was used by bargainers per half-hour.	5.7	9.0	83.4

Source: Adapted from John L. Graham, "The Influence of Culture on the Process of Business Negotiations in an Exploratory Study," *Journal of International Business Studies,* Spring 1983, pp. 84, 88. Used with permission.

TABLE 7-5

CROSS-CULTURAL DIFFERENCES IN NONVERBAL BEHAVIOR OF JAPANESE, U.S., AND BRAZILIAN NEGOTIATORS

	Number of times tactic was used in a half-hour bargaining session		
Behavior and definition	Japanese	United States	Brazilian
Silent period. The number of conversational gaps of 10 seconds or more per 30 minutes.	5.5	3.5	0
Facial gazing. The number of minutes negotiators spend looking at their opponent's face per randomly selected 10-minute period.	1.3 minutes	3.3 minutes	5.2 minutes
Touching. Incidents of bargainers' touching one another per half-hour (not including handshakes).	0	0	4.7
Conversational overlaps. The number of times (per 10 minutes) that both parties to the negotiation would talk at the same time.	12.6	10.3	28.6

Source: Adapted from John L. Graham, "The Influence of Culture on the Process of Business Negotiations in an Exploratory Study," *Journal of International Business Studies*, Spring 1983, p. 84. Used with permission.

Promises, Threats, and Other Behaviors   Another approach to bargaining is the use of promises, threats, rewards, self-disclosures, and other behaviors that are designed to influence the other party. These behaviors often are greatly influenced by the culture. Graham conducted research using Japanese, U.S., and Brazilian businesspeople and found that they employed a variety of different behaviors during a buyer–seller negotiation simulation.[35] Table 7-4 presents the results.

The table shows that Americans and Japanese make greater use of promises than Brazilians. The Japanese also rely heavily on recommendations and commitment. The Brazilians use a discussion of rewards, commands, and self-disclosure more than Americans and Japanese. The Brazilians also say no a great deal more and make first offers that have higher-level profits than those of the others. Americans tend to operate between these two groups, although they do make less use of commands than either of their opponents and make first offers that have lower profit levels than their opponents.

Nonverbal Behaviors   Nonverbal behaviors also are very common during negotiations. These behaviors refer to what people do rather than what they say. Nonverbal behaviors sometimes are called the "silent language." Typical examples include silent periods, facial gazing, touching, and conversational overlaps. As seen in Table 7-5, the Japanese tend to use silent periods much more often than either Americans or Brazilians during negotiations. In fact, in this study, the latter did not use them at all. The Brazilians did, however, make frequent use of other nonverbal behaviors. They employed facial gazing almost four times more often than the Japanese, and almost twice as often as the Americans. In addition, although the latter two groups did not touch their opponents, the Brazilians made wide use of this nonverbal tactic. They also relied heavily on conversational overlaps, employing them more than twice as often as the Japanese and almost three times as often as Americans. Quite obviously, the Brazilians rely very heavily on nonverbal behaviors in their negotiating.

TABLE 7-6

CULTURE-SPECIFIC CHARACTERISTICS NEEDED BY INTERNATIONAL MANAGERS FOR EFFECTIVE NEGOTIATIONS

U.S. managers	Preparation and planning skill
	Ability to think under pressure
	Judgment and intelligence
	Verbal expressiveness
	Product knowledge
	Ability to perceive and exploit power
	Integrity
Japanese managers	Dedication to job
	Ability to perceive and exploit power
	Ability to win respect and confidence
	Integrity
	Listening skill
	Broad perspective
	Verbal expressiveness
Chinese managers (Taiwan)	Persistence and determination
	Ability to win respect and confidence
	Preparation and planning skill
	Product knowledge
	Interesting
	Judgment and intelligence
Brazilian managers	Preparation and planning skill
	Ability to think under pressure
	Judgment and intelligence
	Verbal expressiveness
	Product knowledge
	Ability to perceive and exploit power
	Competitiveness

Source: Adapted from Nancy J. Adler, *International Dimensions of Organizational Behavior,* 2nd ed. (Boston: PWS-Kent Publishing, 1991), p. 187, and from material provided by Professor John Graham, School of Business Administration, University of Southern California, 1983.

The important thing to remember is that in international negotiations, people use a wide variety of tactics, and the other side must be prepared to counter or find a way of dealing with them. The response will depend on the situation. Managers from different cultures will give different answers. Table 7-6 provides some examples of the types of characteristics needed in effective negotiators. To the extent that international managers have these characteristics, their success as negotiators should increase.

SUMMARY OF KEY POINTS

1. Political risk is the likelihood that the foreign investment of a business will be constrained by a host government's policies. In dealing with this risk, companies conduct both macro and micro political risk analyses. Specific consideration is given to expropriation and operational profitability risk.
2. MNCs attempt to manage their political risk in two basic ways. One is by developing a comprehensive framework for identifying and describing these risks. This includes consideration of political, operational, and ownership-control risks. A second is by quantifying the variables that help constitute the risk.

3. Two common risk formulation strategies are the use of relative bargaining power and of integrative as well as protective and defensive techniques. Figure 7-4 illustrates how firms in various industries use a combination of the integrative and the protective and defensive techniques in developing an overall response strategy.
4. Negotiation is the process of bargaining with one or more parties to arrive at a solution that is acceptable to all. This process involves five basic steps: planning, interpersonal relationship building, exchanging task-related information, persuasion, and agreement. The way in which the process is carried out often will vary because of cultural differences.
5. There are a wide variety of tactics used in international negotiating. These include location, time limits, buyer–seller relations, verbal behaviors, and nonverbal behaviors.

KEY TERMS

political risk

macro political risk analysis

micro political risk analysis

expropriation

indigenization laws

transfer risks

operational risks

ownership-control risks

conglomerate investment

vertical investments

horizontal investments

integrative techniques

protective and defensive techniques

negotiation

REVIEW AND DISCUSSION QUESTIONS

1. What types of political risk would a company entering Russia face? Identify and describe three. What types of political risk would a company entering France face? Identify and describe three. How are these risks similar? How are they different?
2. Most firms attempt to quantify their political risk, although they do not assign specific weights to the respective criteria. Why is this approach so popular? Would the companies be better off assigning weights to each of the risks being assumed? Defend your answer.
3. If a high-tech firm wanted to set up operations in Iran, what steps might it take to ensure that the subsidiary would not be expropriated? Identify and describe three strategies that would be particularly helpful.
4. If a company new to the international arena was negotiating an agreement with a potential partner in an overseas country, what basic steps should it be prepared to implement? Identify and describe them.
5. Wilsten, Inc., has been approached by a Japanese firm that wants exclusive production and selling rights for one of Wilsten's new, high-tech products. What does Wilsten need to know about Japanese bargaining behaviors to strike the best possible deal with this company? Identify and describe five.

PRACTICAL INTERNATIONAL MANAGEMENT ASSIGNMENT

Choose a critical business negotiating issue that currently is relevant for a U.S. MNC. Possible choices might include negotiations with an EU firm to establish a joint venture or with a Third World country to set up operations in that locale. Based on your choice of country, identify the negotiating tactics likely to be used by the other side and the response strategies that you would recommend if you were part of the negotiation team. Use the material in this chapter, the references cited, and additional library research to help you in this effort.

In the International Spotlight

Peru

A Peruvian's raised eyebrow means "money" or "pay me."

Peru is located on the west coast of South America. It is the third-largest nation on the continent (only Brazil and Argentina have more area), and it covers almost 500,000 square miles (about 14 percent of the size of the United States). The land has enormous contrasts, with a desert (drier than the Sahara), the towering snow-capped Andes Mountains, sparkling grass-covered plateaus, and thick rain forests. Peru has approximately 23 million people, of which about 20 percent live in Lima, the capital. More Indians (one-half the population) live in Peru than any other country in the Western Hemisphere. The ancestors of Peru's Indians are the famous Incas, who built a great empire. The rest of the population is mixed, and a small percentage is white. The economy depends heavily on agriculture, fishing, mining, and services. GNP is around $22 billion, and per-capita income is about $1000. At present, the economy is in poor shape. Much of this has been the result of poor economic planning and decision making by the government. High inflation and a gigantic foreign debt continue to plague the country.

Although the poor economic conditions make Peru an unattractive investment target for multinationals, a large New York bank currently is considering making a $25 million loan to the owner of a Peruvian fishing fleet. The owner wants to refurbish the fleet and add one new ship.

During the 1970s, the Peruvian government nationalized a number of industries and factories and began running them for the profit of the state. In most cases, these state-run ventures became disasters. In the late 1970s, the fishing fleet owner was given back his ships and allowed to operate his business as before. Since then, he has managed to remain profitable, but the biggest problem is that his ships are getting old and he needs an influx of capital to make repairs and add new technology. As he explained it to the New York banker: "Fishing is no longer just an art. There is a great deal of science involved. And to keep costs low and be competitive on the world market, you have to have the latest equipment for both locating as well as catching and then loading and unloading the fish."

Having reviewed the fleet owner's operation, the large multinational bank believes that the loan is justified. The financial institution is concerned, however, that the Peruvian government might step in during the next couple of years and again take over the business. If this were to happen, it might take an additional decade for the loan to be repaid. If the government were to allow the fleet owner to operate the fleet the way he has over the last decade, the loan could be repaid within 7 years.

Right now, the bank is deciding the specific terms of the agreement. Once these have been worked out, either a loan officer will fly down to Lima and close the deal or the owner will be asked to come to New York for the signing. Whichever approach is used, the bank realizes that final adjustments in the agreement will have to be made on the spot. Therefore, if the bank sends a representative to Lima, the individual will have to have the authority to commit the bank to specific terms. These final matters should be worked out within the next 10 days.

1. What are some current issues facing Peru? What is the climate for doing business in Peru today?

2. What type of political risks does this fishing company need to evaluate? Identify and describe them.

3. What types of integrative and protective and defensive techniques can the bank use?

4. Would the bank be better off negotiating the loan in New York or in Lima? Why?

You Be the International Management Consultant

Going to Gdansk

When Poland made the necessary reforms to move toward a market economy, Andrzej Jaworski from Chicago, Illinois, began thinking this might be an excellent place to set up an overseas operation. Andrzej and his two brothers own a firm that produces specialized computer chips. The company has a series of patents that provide legal protection and allow it to dominate a small but growing segment of the computer market. Their sales estimates reached $147 million within 3 years, but they believe that this could rise to $200 million if they were to expand internationally. They have thought about setting up a plant in Belgium so that they could take advantage of the European market growth. They would prefer Poland, however, because their parents grew up there before leaving for the United States in 1948. "We feel that we know the Poles because we have grown up in a Polish household here in the midwest," Andrzej explained to his banker. "We would like to see if the government would allow us to set up a small plant in Gdansk, train the necessary workers, and then export our product into the European Community."

One of the primary reasons that Andrzej believes that the Polish government would be agreeable to the plan is that not only is Poland trying to move more toward a market economy, but the country has foreign debt, inflation, and outmoded technology. A state-of-the-art plant could help to reduce unemployment and provide an inflow of needed capital. However, the banker is concerned that because of the political risks and uncertainty in Eastern Europe in general and Poland in particular, the company may either lose its investment through government expropriation or find itself unable to get profits out of the country. Given that the company will have to invest approximately $20 million, the venture could seriously endanger the company's financial status.

Andrzej understands these risks but believes that with the help of an international management consultant, he can identify and minimize the problems. "I'm determined to push ahead," he told the banker, "and if there is a good chance of making this project a success, I'm going to Gdansk."

1. What are some of the political risks that Andrzej's firm will face if he decides to go ahead with this venture? Identify and describe two or three.
2. Using Figure 7-2, what strategy would you recommend that the firm use? Why?
3. In his negotiations with the government, what suggestions or guidelines would you offer to Andrzej? Identify and describe two or three.

CHAPTER 7 ENDNOTES

1. Louis Kraar, "The Risks Are Rising in China," *Fortune*, March 6, 1995, pp. 179–180; "The Risk in Asia," *Economist*, January 28, 1995, p. 13.
2. "The Mexico Syndrome, and How to Steer Clear of It," *Economist*, March 18, 1995, pp. 73–75; "Brinkmanship," *Economist*, January 28, 1995, pp. 68–69; and "Tobasco Sauce," *Economist*, January 28, 1995, p. 15.
3. For a list of country-risk ratings, see "Country Risk," *Economist*, March 4, 1995, p. 106.
4. Also see Peter Galuszka et al., "The Great Game Comes to Baku," *BusinessWeek*, July 17, 1995, pp. 48–52.
5. Llewellyn D. Howell and Brad Chaddick, "Model of Political Risk for Foreign Investment and Trade: An Assessment of Three Approaches," *Columbia Journal of World Business*, Fall 1994, p. 73.
6. See, for example, "Can Peacekeeping Survive?" *Economist*, February 11, 1995, pp. 37–38; "Calling Dr. Kissinger," *Economist*, January 14, 1995, pp. 23–24.
7. David E. Sanger, "U.S. Settles Trade Dispute, Averting Billions in Tariffs on Japanese Luxury Autos," *New York Times*, June 29, 1995, pp. A1, C4.
8. For more, see Angelo B. Henderson and Gabriella Stern, "Producers of Luxury Autos Still Face a Tough Market," *Wall Street Journal*, June 29, 1995, p. A6; "U.S. Auto Parts Industry Is Winner in Trade Accord," *Wall Street Journal*, June 29, 1995, p. A6; and Helene Cooper and Valerie Reitman, "Averting a Trade War, U.S. and Japan Reach Agreement on Autos," *Wall Street Journal*, June 29, 1995, pp. A1, A6.
9. John Taglilabue, "For Japan Auto Makers, It's Tougher in Europe," *New York Times*, June 28, 1995, p. C4.
10. Joel Millman, "Club Medellin," *Forbes*, January 4, 1993, pp. 44–45.
11. Phyllis Berman, "Contrarian Investing 101," *Forbes*, January 4, 1993, pp. 68–69.
12. Damon Darlin, "Protecting Whom?" *Forbes*, March 29, 1993, p. 42.
13. See, for example, Weijian Shan, "Environmental Risks and Joint Venture Sharing Arrangement," *Journal of International Business Studies*, Fourth Quarter 1991, pp. 555–578; June N. P. Francis, "When in Rome? The Effects of Cultural Adaptation of Intercultural Business Negotiations," *Journal of International Business Studies*, Third Quarter 1991, pp. 403–428; James N. Gardner, "Charming the Eurocrats: How to Lobby Effectively in the EC," *Journal of European Business*, January-February 1991, pp. 13–18; and James and Lynda Gardner, "Euro-Lobbying by Foreign Interests: New Trends and Strategies," *Journal of European Business*, November/December 1991, pp. 50–54.
14. David A. Schmidt, "Analyzing Political Risk," *Business Horizons*, July-August 1986, pp. 43–50.
15. For more, see Thomas A. Pointer, "Political Risk: Managing Government Intervention," in Paul W. Beamish, J. Peter Killing, Donald J. LeCraw, and Harold Crookell (eds.), *International Management: Text and Cases* (Homewood, IL: Irwin, 1991), pp. 119–133.
16. See Doron P. Levin, "Domestic Label Sought for a Mazda," *New York Times*, February 7, 1992, p. C16.
17. Jordan D. Lewis, "How to Build Successful Strategic Alliances," *Journal of Business Strategy*, November/December 1991, pp. 18–29; Bernard M. Wolf, "The Role of Strategic Alliances in the European Automotive Industry," Research Program Working Paper No. 52, August 1991, Ontario Center for International Business.
18. Mark L. Fagan, "A Guide to Global Sourcing," *Journal of Business Strategy*, March/April 1991, pp. 21–25.
19. Ann Gregory, "Firm Characteristics and Political Risk Reduction in Overseas Ventures," *National Academy of Management Proceedings*, 1982, pp. 73–77.
20. For more, see Richard Mead, *International Management: Cross-Cultural Dimensions* (Cambridge, MA: Blackwell Publishing, 1994), Chapter 10; Gary Bonvillian and William A. Nowlin, "Cultural Awareness: An Essential Element of Doing Business Abroad," *Business Horizons*, November-December 1994, pp. 44–50.
21. See, for example, Peter D. Miller, "Getting Ready for Japan: What *Not* to Do," *Journal of Business Strategy*, January/February 1991, pp. 32–35; Brian Mark Hawrysh, "Cultural Approaches to Negotiations: Understanding the Japanese," *International Marketing Review*, vol. 7, no. 2, 1990, pp. 28–42.
22. Nancy J. Adler, *International Dimensions of Organizational Behavior*, 2nd ed. (Boston: PWS-Kent Publishing, 1991), p. 195.
23. David K. Tse, June Francis, and Jan Walls, "Cultural Differences in Conducting Intra- and Inter-Cultural Negotiations: A Sino-Canadian Comparison," *Journal of International Business Studies*, Third Quarter 1994, pp. 537–555.
24. Also see Lillian H. Chaney and Jeanette S. Martin, *International Business Communication* (Englewood Cliffs, NJ: Prentice-Hall, 1995), pp. 203–204.
25. Adler, *Organizational Behavior*, p. 197.
26. Peter J. Pettibone, "Negotiating a Business Venture in the Soviet Union," *Journal of Business Strategy*,

January/February 1991, pp. 18–23; Peter J. Pettibone, "Negotiating a Joint Venture in the Soviet Union: How to Protect Your Interests," *Journal of Business Strategy,* November/December 1990, pp. 5–12.

27. For more, see Kathleen Kelly Reardon and Robert E. Spekman, "Starting Out Right: Negotiation Lessons for Domestic and Cultural Business Alliances," *Business Horizons,* December 1994, pp. 71–79.

28. Stephen E. Weiss, "Negotiating with 'Romans'—Part 1," *Sloan Management Review,* Winter 1994, pp. 51–61.

29. Stephen E. Weiss, "Negotiating with 'Romans'—Part 2," *Sloan Management Review,* Spring 1994, p. 89.

30. For more, see Nancy J. Adler, John L. Graham, and Theodore Schwarz Gehrke, "Business Negotiations in Canada, Mexico, and the United States," *Journal of Business Research,* vol. 15, 1987, pp. 411–429; John L. Graham, Dong Ki Kim, Chi-Yuan Lin, and Michael Robinson, "Buyer-Seller Negotiations around the Pacific Rim: Differences in Fundamental Exchange Processes," *Journal of Consumer Research,* June 1988, pp. 48–54.

31. For an interesting comparison of negotiating tactics in the Far East, see Rosalie L. Tung, "Handshakes across the Sea: Cross-Cultural Negotiating for Business Success," *Organizational Dynamics,* Winter 1991, pp. 30–40.

32. For additional insights, see Jane W. Gibson and Richard M. Hodgetts, *Managerial Communication,* 2nd ed. (New York: Harper & Row, 1990), chapter 12.

33. John L. Graham, "Brazilian, Japanese, and American Business Negotiations," *Journal of International Business Studies,* Spring/Summer 1983, pp. 47–61; John L. Graham, "The Influence of Culture on the Process of Business Negotiations in an Exploratory Study," *Journal of International Business Studies,* Spring 1983, pp. 81–96.

34. For more, see Adler, *Organizational Behavior,* pp. 204–209.

35. Graham, "Influence on Culture," pp. 84, 88.

CHAPTER 8

STRATEGIC PLANNING

OBJECTIVES OF THE CHAPTER

All major MNCs employ strategic planning. The strategic plan results from a careful analysis of both the external and internal environments. For example, in developing its plan, an MNC identifies the market environment for its goods and services, then evaluates its ability to capture this market. The success of this strategic planning largely depends on accurate forecasting of the external environment and a realistic appraisal of internal company strengths and weaknesses. In recent years, MNCs have relied on their strategic plans to help refocus their efforts by abandoning old domestic markets and entering new global markets. This strategic global planning process has been critical in their drive to gain market share, increase profitability, and in some cases, even survive.

Chapter 5 addressed overall strategic management across cultures. This chapter focuses on strategic planning in the international context, and the basic steps by which a strategic plan is formulated and implemented are examined. The specific objectives of this chapter are:

1. **DISCUSS** the meaning, needs, benefits, approaches, and predispositions of the strategic planning process for today's MNCs.
2. **IDENTIFY** the basic steps in strategic planning, including environmental scanning, internal resource analysis of the MNC's strengths and weaknesses, and goal formulation.
3. **DESCRIBE** how an MNC implements the strategic plan, such as how it chooses a site for overseas operations.
4. **EXPLAIN** how an MNC implements an ownership and/or entry strategy.
5. **REVIEW** the three major functions of marketing, production, and finance that are used in implementing a strategic plan.

INTERNATIONAL STRATEGIC PLANNING

Strategic planning is the process of determining an organization's basic mission and long-term objectives, then implementing a plan of action for accomplishing this mission and attaining these objectives. As a company goes international, this process takes on new dimensions. Ford Motor is a good example. Under the leadership of Alexander Trotman, its chairman, this company is determined to replace General Motors as the number one automaker in the world.[1] The timing may be ideal, given that Ford's two major rivals, General Motors and Toyota, appear to be having problems of their own. General Motors is struggling through a long-term restructuring that may be focusing more on profit than on market growth, and Toyota is being handicapped by the strong Japanese yen, which has gained in value by more than 50 percent in recent years.

Since the beginning of the decade, Ford's share of the U.S. auto market has increased from around 23 percent to approximately 27 percent, while GM's has fallen from 35 percent to around 32 percent. At the same time, Toyota's share has remained about the same. Part of Ford's success results from the fact that by the mid-1990s, 5 of the top 10 best-selling vehicles in the United States were being produced by Ford, and research shows that market share tends to drive profitability. Therefore, as market share rises, Ford's return on investment should follow. The strategic plans of GM and Toyota, however, are geared to enhancing their own profitability. In the case of GM, for example, the company has given up market share in areas where profit has been low and maintained market share in high-profit areas. This has led some industry analysts to ask whether Ford is trying to buy market share at the price of profitability. Ford has responded by noting that its current strategy calls for both increased market share and profitability. In particular, Ford aims to freeze all costs at 1995 levels for the next 4 years by pressing suppliers to cut their costs by 5 percent annually. If Ford can do this, its international strategic plan may well produce both market growth and profitability.

The Growing Need for Strategic Planning

One of the primary reasons that MNCs need strategic planning is to keep track of their increasingly diversified operations. This need is particularly obvious when one considers the amount of direct foreign investment that has occurred in recent years (see Chapter 1).[2] There is a need to co-ordinate and integrate diverse operations with a unified and agreed-on focus.[3]

A good example is Navix Corporation, the shipping company that recently moved its vessel-management operation to Singapore to hunt for bargains on docking and supplies. Through staffing cuts and other savings, profits now are rising on lower sales, and the firm is able to operate more efficiently than ever. A good portion of this success has resulted from the firm's well-formulated strategic plan.[4]

Another example is Hugo Boss, the giant German apparel maker. This firm's new strategic plan calls for a reduction in labor costs by seeking suppliers worldwide that can provide the same output at lower prices. In particular, the company is looking for production sites in North America that will help the firm to increase its presence here as well as reduce the cost of bringing products to this market. The carefully crafted strategic plan will attempt to ensure the success of these expansion efforts.[5]

A third example of the growing need for strategic planning is NEC, the giant Japanese electronics firm that recently purchased nearly 20 percent of Packard Bell Electronics. This acquisition provided a crucial financial infusion for Packard Bell, which by 1995 held 12.7 percent of the PC market and thanks to its success in selling PCs through mass merchants such as Sears and Wal-Mart, was the industry leader. The strategy of the new NEC/Packard Bell strategic alliance will include the joint purchase, as well as co-operative development and manufacturing, of computer parts and use of each other's marketing channels. The two firms were brought together by Groupe Bull, the French computer company that holds 19.9 percent of Packard Bell and stands to gain substantially from this new arrangement. One reason is because collectively, Packard Bell and NEC now have nearly the largest worldwide share of the PC market. A strategic plan that helps these firms to capitalize on their strengths likely will make them a formidable opponent during this time of rapid growth in the worldwide personal computer market.[6]

The German electronics giant Siemens, which recently announced that it will invest 2 billion marks in a new microchip factory in northeastern England, is a further example. This move is part of a massive expansion of Siemens' semiconductor-manufacturing capacity worldwide, including Austria, China, France, Indonesia, Malaysia, and Singapore, as well as Germany itself. The new British factory is scheduled to begin production later in the decade and will manufacture chips for mobile telephones and radios as well as multimedia markets. This expansion decision is important to Siemens to offset the strength of the German mark, which is affecting the company's exports, as well as the high cost of German labor, which is greater than that in any other EU country.[7]

Still another example is the giant Korean firm LG Electronics (formerly Lucky Goldstar), which has purchased a controlling stake in Zenith Electronics. The purpose of this acquisition was to gain important television technology that would have taken years to develop internally. This strategy is becoming increasingly popular, especially among Korean MNCs, which long have focused on their home market and now feel that in addition to technology, they need brand-name recognition and international marketing skills, all of which can be obtained through acquisitions. This strategy also helps to explain why Samsung Electronics purchased a large share of AST Research (computers) and why Hyundai Electronics bought NCR's microelectronics division (integrated circuits) and made a major investment in Maxtor (disk drives).[8] Strategic planning is critically important in dealing successfully with these types of issues.

Benefits of Strategic Planning

Now that the needs for strategic planning have been explored, what are some of the benefits? Many MNCs are convinced that strategic planning is critical to their success, and these efforts are being conducted both at the home office and in the subsidiaries. For example, one study found that 70 percent of the 56 U.S. MNC subsidiaries in Asia and Latin America had comprehensive 5- to 10-year plans.[9] Others found that U.S., European, and Japanese subsidiaries in Brazil were heavily planning-driven[10] and that Australian manufacturing companies use planning systems that are very similar to those of U.S. manufacturing firms.[11]

Do these strategic planning efforts really pay off? To date, the evidence is mixed. Certainly, that the strategic plan helps an MNC to co-ordinate and monitor its far-flung operations must be viewed as a benefit. Similarly, that the plan helps an MNC to deal with political risk problems (see Chapter 7), competition, and currency instability cannot be downplayed.

Despite some obvious benefits, there is no definitive evidence that strategic planning in the international arena always results in higher profitability. Most studies that report favorable results were conducted at least a decade ago.[12] More recent evidence tempers these findings with contingency-based recommendations. For example, one study found that when decisions were made mainly at the home office and close co-ordination between the subsidiary and home office was required, return on investment was negatively affected.[13] Simply put, the home office ends up interfering with the subsidiary, and profitability suffers.

A more recent study found that planning intensity (the degree to which a firm carries out strategic planning) is an important variable in determining performance.[14] Drawing on results from 22 German MNCs representing 71 percent of that country's multinational enterprises, one study found that companies with only a few foreign affiliates performed best with medium planning intensity. Those firms with high planning intensity tended to exaggerate the emphasis, and profitability suffered. Companies that earned a high percentage of their total sales in overseas markets, however, did best with a high-intensity planning process and poorly with a low-intensity process. Therefore, although strategic planning usually seems to pay off, as with most other aspects of international management, the specifics of the situation will dictate the success of the process.[15]

Approaches to Formulating and Implementing Strategy

Four common approaches to strategic planning are: (1) focusing on the economic imperative; (2) focusing on the political imperative; (3) addressing the quality imperative; and (4) implementing an administrative co-ordination strategy.[16]

Economic Imperative MNCs that focus on the *economic imperative* employ a worldwide strategy based on cost leadership, differentiation, and segmentation. These companies typically sell products for which a large portion of value is added in the upstream activities of the industry's value chain. By the time the product is ready to be sold, much of its value has already been created through research and development and manufacturing. Some of the industries in this group include automobiles, chemicals, heavy electrical systems, motorcycles, and steel.[17] Because the product is basically homogeneous and requires no alteration to fit the needs of the specific country, management uses a worldwide strategy that is consistent on a country-to-country basis.

The strategy also is used when the product is regarded as a generic good and therefore does not have to be sold based on name brand or support service. A good example is the European PC market. Until the early 1990s, this market was dominated by such well-known companies as IBM, Apple, and Compaq. However, more recently in Europe, clone manufacturers have begun to gain market share.[18] This is because the most influential reasons for buying a PC have changed. A few years ago, the main reasons were brand name, service, and support. Today, price has emerged as a major input into the purchasing decision. Customers now

INTERNATIONAL MANAGEMENT IN ACTION

Point/Counterpoint

A good example of the political imperative in action is the recent Kodak/Fuji dispute. Kodak has accused Fuji of blocking its growth in the Japanese market. Fuji has responded by arguing that Kodak has long held a monopoly-type position in the United States. This debate began when Kodak complained to the U.S. government and asked for help in further opening the door to the Japanese market. Kodak's argument included the following points:

1. Unlike the United States, film manufacturers in Japan do not sell directly to retailers or photofinishers but to distributors, and Fuji has close ties with the four dominant distributors. Fuji holds an equity position in two of them and gives all four both rebates and cash payments.
2. Fuji controls 430 Japanese wholesale photofinishing labs through ownership, loans, rebates, and other forms of operational support. Additionally, the Japanese government has helped to establish the system to impede Kodak.
3. Kodak has invested $750 million in Japan and garnered less than 10 percent of the market.
4. Fuji uses profits from the Japanese market to subsidize the dumping of its products in other countries, thus effectively reducing Kodak's worldwide market share.
5. The Japanese government has not vigorously enforced antimonopoly legislation, and this has helped Fuji to establish distribution dominance.

These charges are answered by Fuji, which contends that Kodak uses many tactics that prevent Fuji from gaining U.S. market share. These include:

1. Kodak gives U.S. retailers rebates and upfront payments that effectively exclude competitors. For example, Kodak offered Genovese Drug Stores of Glen Cove, NY, $40,000 plus rebates if the company would carry no branded film but Kodak, use only Kodak paper and processing chemicals, and give Kodak 80 percent of the chain's shelf-space allotment for film.
2. Kodak holds 70 percent of the U.S. wholesale photofinishing market through ownership and by giving discounts, advertising dollars, and other investments to land exclusive accounts.
3. Fuji has invested $2 billion in the United States and holds less than 11 percent of the market.
4. Kodak's worldwide operating profit margin over the last two decades is 13 percent, close to Fuji's 15.5 percent.
5. The U.S. government has not vigorously enforced consent decrees that were created to limit Kodak's U.S. marketing practices and ensure that it did not gain an unfair advantage over competitors.

Will the U.S. government prevail in its efforts to help Kodak? Will Fuji be able to make further gains in the U.S. market? What role will political intervention play? These questions are yet to be answered. In the meantime, the two firms continue to compete—and co-operate. Together, they currently are developing a so-called "smart film," which is a new system that offers small cameras and film that can record information to improve the quality of processing. Whatever the outcome of their market-share argument, this strategic co-operative effort likely will continue.

---

are much more computer literate, and they realize that many PCs offer identical quality performance. Therefore, it does not pay to purchase a high-priced name brand when a lower-priced clone will do the same things. As a result, the economic imperative dominates the strategic plans of computer manufacturers.

Political Imperative   MNCs using the *political imperative* approach to strategic planning are country-responsive; their approach is designed to protect local market niches. "International Management in Action: Point/Counterpoint" demonstrates this political imperative. The products sold by MNCs often have a large portion of their value added in the downstream activities of the value chain. Industries such as insurance and consumer packaged goods are examples—the success of the product or service generally depends heavily on marketing, sales, and service. Typically, these industries use a country-centered strategy.

MNCs that use a political imperative develop strategies targeted for the local market. A good example is Bandag, Inc., which is well known for its tire retreading business. In the past several years, the company has revamped its European strategy and introduced a greater level of customer service. European companies, unaccustomed to having tire retread service provided at their place of business, have responded enthusiastically. Bandag franchisees use specially designed trucks that allow them to remove the worn tires on customer vehicles and replace them with retreads on the spot. This lets the customers keep their trucks on the road during the day, then have them serviced after hours by Bandag. The strategy has worked so well that Bandag's share of the European market has shot from 5 percent to 20 percent.[19]

Quality Imperative   In recent years, there has been a quality revolution among both domestic companies and MNCs. This *quality imperative* is taking two interdependent paths: (1) a change in attitudes and a raising of expectations for service quality; and (2) the implementation of management practices that are designed to make quality improvement an ongoing process.[20] Commonly called "total quality management," or simply TQM, the approach takes a wide number of forms, including cross-training personnel to do the jobs of all members in their work group, process re-engineering designed to help identify and eliminate redundant tasks and wasteful effort, and reward systems designed to reinforce quality performance.[21]

TQM covers the full gamut, from strategy formulation to implementation, and briefly can be summarized as follows:

1. Quality is operationalized by meeting or exceeding customer expectations. Customers include not only the buyer or external user of the product or service, but also the support personnel both inside and outside the organization who are associated with the good or service.
2. The quality strategy is formulated at the top management level and is diffused throughout the organization. From top executives to hourly employees, everyone operates under a TQM strategy of delivering quality products and/or services to internal and external customers.
3. The techniques range from traditional inspection and statistical quality control to cutting-edge human resource management techniques, such as self-managing teams.[22]

Many MNCs make quality a major part of their overall strategy, because they have learned that this is the way to increase market share and profitability. For example, while the U.S. automakers have dramatically increased their overall quality in recent years to close the gap with Japanese auto quality, Japanese firms continue to have fewer safety recalls. On the other hand, many U.S. firms are world-class competitors thanks to their total quality imperative. For example, Stanley Works, which is known for its tools, was being hammered by Asian competition in the early 1980s before incorporating a quality imperative into its strategic plan. Today, the firm's scrap rate is 20 percent of what it was 6 years ago, products are developed and improved for the world market based on the recommendations of engineers in each local area, and both profits and revenues have more than doubled in the last decade.[23] Another example is Monroe Auto Equipment, which has increased its productivity by 26 percent and profits by 70 percent in the last several years. Monroe's quality is so high that Toyota buys shock absorbers from the firm for assembly in its Toyoda City, Japan, plant. Moreover, a recent quality control check by Toyota of 60,000 shocks shipped to it by Monroe found a zero defect rate. Simply put, the quality imperative is becoming an integral part of strategic planning in international management.

Administrative Co-ordination An *administrative co-ordination* approach to formulation and implementation is one in which the MNC makes strategic decisions based on the merits of the individual situation rather than using a predetermined economic or political strategy. This approach is the most flexible. As Doz explains:

> Instead of taking a stable proactive stance vis-à-vis the environment and relying on the chosen strategy to provide a framework within which to deal with sources of uncertainties and to make specific decisions as the need arises, companies using administrative coordination absorb uncertainties and try to resolve conflicts internally each time new uncertainties question prior allocations of strategic resources. In short, strategy becomes unclear, shifting with the perceived importance of changes in the economic or political environment, and it may become dissolved into a set of incremental decisions with a pattern which may make sense only [later on].[24]

Many large MNCs combine the economic, political, quality, and administrative approaches to strategic planning. For example, IBM relies on the economic imperative when it has strong market power (especially in Third World countries), the political and quality imperatives when the market requires a calculated response (European countries), and an administrative co-ordination strategy when rapid, flexible decision making is needed to close the sale. Of the four, however, the first three approaches are much more common because of the firm's desire to co-ordinate its strategy both regionally and globally.

Strategic Predispositions

In addition to the economic, political, quality, and administrative approaches, most MNCs also have a strategic predisposition toward doing things in a particular way. This orientation or predisposition helps to determine the specific steps the MNC will follow. Four distinct predispositions have been identified: ethnocentric, polycentric, regiocentric, and geocentric.

A company with an *ethnocentric predisposition* allows the values and interests of the parent company to guide the strategic decisions. Firms with a *polycentric predisposition* make strategic decisions tailored to suit the cultures of the countries where the MNC operates. A *regiocentric predisposition* causes a firm to try to blend its own interests with those of its subsidiaries on a regional basis. A company with a *geocentric predisposition* tries to integrate a global systems approach to decision making.[25] Table 8-1 provides details of each of these orientations.

If an MNC relies on one of these profiles over an extended time, the approach may become institutionalized and greatly influence strategic planning. By the same token, a predisposition toward any of these profiles can provide problems for a firm if it is out of step with the economic or political environment. For example, a firm with an ethnocentric predisposition may find it difficult to implement a geocentric strategy, because it is unaccustomed to using global integration. Commonly, successful MNCs use a mix of these predispositions based on the demands of the current environment.

TABLE 8-1

ORIENTATION OF AN MNC UNDER DIFFERENT PROFILES

	Orientation of the firm			
	Ethnocentric	**Polycentric**	**Regiocentric**	**Geocentric**
Mission	Profitability (viability)	Public acceptance (legitimacy)	Both profitability and public acceptance (viability and legitimacy)	Same as regiocentric
Governance	Top-down	Bottom-up (each subsidiary decides on local objectives)	Mutually negotiated between region and its subsidiaries	Mutually negotiated at all levels of the corporation
Strategy	Global integration	National responsiveness	Regional integration and national responsiveness	Global integration and national responsiveness
Structure	Hierarchical product divisions	Hierarchical area divisions, with autonomous national units	Product and regional organization tied through a matrix	A network of organizations (including some stakeholders and competitor organizations)
Culture	Home country	Host country	Regional	Global
Technology	Mass production	Batch production	Flexible manufacturing	Flexible manufacturing
Marketing	Product development determined primarily by the needs of home country customers	Local product development based on local needs	Standardize within region, but not across regions	Global product, with local variations
Finance	Repatriation of profits to home country	Retention of profits in host country	Redistribution within region	Redistribution globally
Personnel practices	People of home country developed for key positions everywhere in the world	People of local nationality developed for key positions in their own country	Regional people developed for key positions anywhere in the region	Best people everywhere in the world developed for key positions everywhere in the world

Source: Adapted from Balaji S. Chakravarthy and Howard V. Perlmutter, "Strategic Planning for a Global Business," *Columbia Journal of World Business,* Summer 1985, pp. 5–6. Copyright 1985, Columbia Journal of World Business. Used with permission.

THE BASIC STEPS IN FORMULATING STRATEGY

The needs, benefits, approaches, and predispositions of strategic planning serve as a point of departure for the basic steps in formulating strategy. In international management, strategic planning can be broken into the following steps: (1) scanning the external environment for opportunities and threats; (2) conducting an internal resource analysis of company strengths and weaknesses; and (3) formulating goals in light of the external scanning and internal analysis. These steps are graphically summarized in Figure 8-1. The following sections discuss each step in detail.[26]

Environmental Scanning

Environmental scanning provides management with accurate forecasts of trends that relate to external changes in geographic areas where the firm is currently do-

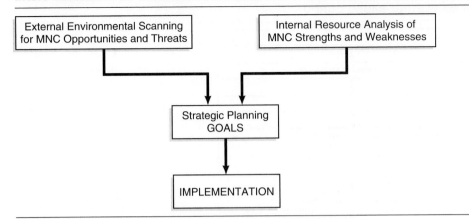

FIGURE 8-1

BASIC ELEMENTS OF STRATEGIC PLANNING FOR INTERNATIONAL MANAGEMENT

TABLE 8-2

INDICATORS OF ECONOMIC DEVELOPMENT IN EMERGING MARKETS

Country	GDP per capita[a]	Percentage of rural population in 1992	Percent of total employment, 1990–1992			Telephones per 1000 population[b]
			Agriculture	Industry	Services	
China	2100	72	73	14	13	11
Indonesia	2960	70	56	14	30	6
Poland	4880	37	27	37	36	86
Brazil	5250	23	25	25	47	63
Hungary	5730	34	15	31	54	96
Thailand	5900	77	67	11	22	24
Argentina	6080	13	13	34	53	96
Russia	6220	26	20	46	34	149
Mexico	7420	26	23	29	48	66
Malaysia	8050	55	26	28	46	89

Note: [a]In 1992 U.S. dollars. [b]As of 1990.
Source: Human Development Report of the World Development Report, 1995.

ing business and/or considering setting up operations. These changes relate to the economy, competition, political stability, technology, and demographic consumer data. Table 8-2 provides the types of data that would be used in evaluating emerging markets, and Figure 8-2 details the steps that a marketing-based MNC might take in conducting an environmental scan of an international market.[27]

Typically, the MNC will begin by conducting a forecast of macroeconomic performance dealing with factors such as markets for specific products, per-capita income of the population, and availability of labor and raw materials.[28] A second

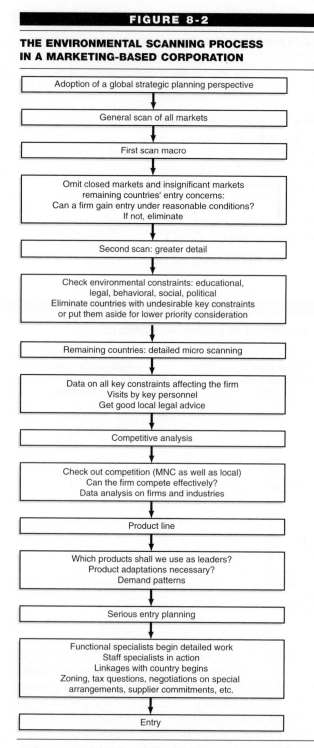

FIGURE 8-2

**THE ENVIRONMENTAL SCANNING PROCESS
IN A MARKETING-BASED CORPORATION**

Adoption of a global strategic planning perspective

General scan of all markets

First scan macro

Omit closed markets and insignificant markets
remaining countries' entry concerns:
Can a firm gain entry under reasonable conditions?
If not, eliminate

Second scan: greater detail

Check environmental constraints: educational,
legal, behavioral, social, political
Eliminate countries with undesirable key constraints
or put them aside for lower priority consideration

Remaining countries: detailed micro scanning

Data on all key constraints affecting the firm
Visits by key personnel
Get good local legal advice

Competitive analysis

Check out competition (MNC as well as local)
Can the firm compete effectively?
Data analysis on firms and industries

Product line

Which products shall we use as leaders?
Product adaptations necessary?
Demand patterns

Serious entry planning

Functional specialists begin detailed work
Staff specialists in action
Linkages with country begins
Zoning, tax questions, negotiations on special
arrangements, supplier commitments, etc.

Entry

Source: John Garland and Richard N. Farmer, *International Dimensions of Business Policy and Strategy* (Boston: Kent Publishing, 1986), p. 43. Copyright 1986 by Wadsworth, Inc. Reprinted by permission of PWS-Kent Publishing Company, a Division of Wadsworth, Inc.

common forecast will predict monetary exchange rates, exchange controls, balance of payments, and inflation rates. A third is the forecast of the company's potential market share in a particular geographic area as well as that of the competitors. Other considerations include political stability, government pressure, nationalism, and related areas of political risk. These assessments are extremely important in determining the profit potential of the region, which always is a major consideration when deciding where to set up international operations.

Mercedes is a good example of how this environmental scanning process is done.[29] This German firm recently was chosen by China to build minivans, and this is the last major vehicle project that China will approve until the year 2000. What makes Mercedes' success so impressive is that initially, the company was not a leading contender for the contract. Chrysler had the lead in this bid to make vans as well as gas and diesel engines in China. Chrysler badly wanted this contract, because it would provide an important entry into the growing Chinese market. By mid-1994, Chrysler had agreed to invest over $1 billion to build vans, engines, and transmissions. At this point, however, negotiations turned sour. Chinese negotiators changed their tactics and introduced a host of new demands, including: (1) the right to export Chrysler vans and components without paying a license fee; (2) insistence that Chrysler invest the $1 billion up front rather than in phases, as was previously agreed; and (3) deletion of intellectual property protections from the contract, thus allowing the Chinese to copy Chrysler components freely. Chrysler refused to give such concessions, and the Chinese began looking at other bids, including one from Mercedes that gave them much of what they wanted. Mercedes has agreed to eventually base all of its van production in China, set up technology centers, develop a components industry, and let the Chinese export 12,000 units annually. At the same time, Mercedes' parent company, Daimler Benz, has pledged to put China "on the map" in industries ranging from passenger aircraft to high-speed trains. By carefully scanning the environment and making the necessary concessions, Mercedes has placed itself in an ideal position to gain a significant share of the rapidly expanding Chinese auto market.

Many other firms also have profited from astute environmental scanning. For example, recently Alcatel Alsthom of France made a series of clever acquisitions and alliances and now is the worlds's largest telephone equipment company. This has put Alcatel in an ideal position to garner market share in the rapidly growing telecommunications market.[30] U.S. MNCs Ford and General Motors have been positioning themselves carefully in Europe and, thanks to their environmental scanning, now are two of the major automakers there.[31] IBM also has begun to fight for market share in Europe and has formed a subsidiary to buy clones made in Asia and sell them in the European market. IBM also is reselling laptop computers made by Bull's Zenith Data Systems subsidiary to remain competitive in the portable computer market niche.[32] Even Japanese MNCs are getting into the act. For example, Matsushita is looking for new markets to improve its position, which has been dimmed by product quality problems and strong competition.[33]

Sometimes, companies will take the result of their environmental scanning and construct an evaluation matrix. Table 8-3 illustrates a matrix that was constructed for strategic analysis of the economic potential of Eastern European countries. As shown, Eastern Europe was divided into three groups based on a number of evaluative criteria. Similar matrixes can be constructed for many other areas of strategic analysis for MNCs, such as market entry or location sites.

TABLE 8-3			
AN EVALUATION MATRIX FOR EASTERN EUROPE			
Country	Economic potential	Receptiveness to foreign investment	Speed of reform
Most Promising			
Czech Republic	B+	B	C−
Hungary	B	A	A
Promising			
Poland	C+	A	A
Least Promising			
Bulgaria	C	B	C−
Romania	D+	C−	F

Source: Reported in David Pitt-Watson and Scott Frazer, "Eastern Europe: Commercial Opportunity or Illusion?" *Long Range Planning,* vol. 24, no. 5, 1991, p. 19. Used with permission.

Internal Resource Analysis

When formulating strategy, some firms wait until they have completed their environmental scanning before conducting an internal resource analysis. Others perform these two steps simultaneously. Internal resource analysis helps the firm to evaluate its current managerial, technical, material, and financial strengths and weaknesses. This assessment then is used by the MNC to determine its ability to take advantage of international market opportunities. The primary thrust of this analysis is to match external opportunities (gained through the environmental scan) with internal abilities (gained through the internal resource analysis).

An internal analysis identifies the key factors for success that will dictate how well the firm is likely to do. A *key factor for success (KFS)* is a factor that is necessary for a firm to compete effectively in a market niche. For example, a KFS for an international airline is price. An airline that discounts its prices will gain market share vis-à-vis those that do not. A second KFS for the airline is safety, and a third is quality service in terms of on-time departures and arrivals, convenient schedules, and friendly, helpful personnel. In the automobile industry, quality of products has emerged as the number-one KFS in world markets. Japanese firms have been able to invade the U.S. auto market successfully, because they have been able to prove that the quality of their cars is better than the average domestically built U.S. car. Toyota and Honda have had such a quality edge over the competition in recent years in the eyes of U.S. car buyers. A second KFS is styling. The Ford Taurus has been very successful in recent years because customers like its looks, and Ford has gained market share both domestically and in Europe.

The key question for the management of an MNC is: Do we have the people and resources that can help us to develop and sustain the necessary KFSs, or can we acquire them? If the answer is yes, the recommendation would be to proceed. If the answer is no, management would begin looking at other markets where it has, or can develop, the necessary KFSs.

Sometimes, however, this KFS analysis is much more difficult to perform than would initially appear. For example, both Sony and Matsushita recently have bought Hollywood studios and failed to capitalize on their investments. In 1989,

Sony purchased Columbia Pictures, put over $6 billion into the venture, and in 1994 alone took a $2.7 billion write-down on its investment. Matsushita paid $6.1 billion for MCA in 1990, and by 1995, its losses were so great that the company was anxiously looking for a buyer. In both cases, analysts believe the investments failed because the firms did not have the necessary internal resources. One analysis put it this way:

> Although their multinational delegation was bold, the way it was done was defeatist, not visionary, since Matsushita left MCA's previous managers in place, and Sony hired two American film producers with no real managerial experience to run Columbia. Both firms showed they hadn't a clue how to run a studio. By giving the studios so much freedom, the firms in effect guaranteed they would not be run in the parents' interest.[34]

Another example of the need to develop and sustain KFSs comes from Japanese exporters, who have long relied on domestic suppliers to provide critical parts and components. As the value of the yen increased during the mid-1990s, there was an increased need for these suppliers to cut their costs and thus ensure their MNC customers remained competitive in the international market. Today, these suppliers are under a mandate: cut costs or lose business to suppliers from other countries who can provide resources within the necessary cost and quality specifications.[35]

Goal Setting for Strategy Formulation

In a sense, general goals concerning the philosophy of "going international" or growth actually precede the first two steps of environmental scanning and internal resource analysis. As used here, however, the more specific goals for the strategic plan come out of external scanning and internal analysis. MNCs pursue a variety of such goals; Table 8-4 provides a list of the most common ones. These goals typically serve as an umbrella beneath which the subsidiaries and other international groups operate.

Profitability and marketing goals almost always dominate the strategic plans of today's MNCs. Profitability, as shown in Table 8-4, is so important because MNCs generally need higher profitability from their overseas operations than they do from their domestic operations. The reason is quite simple: setting up overseas operations involves greater risk and effort. In addition, a firm that has done well domestically with a product or service usually has done so because the competition is minimal or ineffective. Firms with this advantage often find additional lucrative opportunities outside their borders. Moreover, the more successful a firm is domestically, the more difficult it is to increase market share without strong competitive response. International markets, however, offer an ideal alternative to the desire for increased growth and profitability.

Another reason that profitability and marketing top the list is that these tend to be more environmentally responsive, whereas production, finance, and personnel functions tend to be more internally controlled. Thus, for strategic planning, profitability and marketing goals are given higher importance and warrant closer attention.

Once the strategic goals are set, the MNC will develop specific operational goals and controls, usually through a two-way process at the subsidiary or

TABLE 8-4

AREAS FOR FORMULATION OF MNC GOALS

Profitability

Level of profits

Return on assets, investment, equity, sales

Yearly profit growth

Yearly earnings per share growth

Marketing

Total sales volume

Market share—worldwide, region, country

Growth in sales volume

Growth in market share

Integration of country markets for marketing efficiency and effectiveness

Production

Ratio of foreign to domestic production volume

Economics of scale via international production integration

Quality and cost control

Introduction of cost-efficient production methods

Finance

Financing of foreign affiliates—retained earnings or local borrowing

Taxation—minimizing tax burden globally

Optimum capital structure

Foreign exchange management—minimizing losses from foreign fluctuations

Personnel/Human Resources

Development of managers with global orientation

Management development of host-country nationals

Source: Adapted from information found in Arvind V. Phatak, *International Dimensions of Management,* 2nd ed. (Boston: PWS-Kent Publishing, 1989), p. 72.

affiliate level (organization is covered in Chapter 9). Home office management will set certain parameters, and the overseas group will operate within these guidelines. For example, the MNC headquarters may require periodic financial reports, restrict on-site decisions to matters involving less than $20,000, and require that all client contracts be cleared through the home office. These guidelines are designed to ensure that the overseas group's activities support the goals in the strategic plan and that all units operate in a co-ordinated effort.[36]

STRATEGY IMPLEMENTATION

Once formulated, the strategic plan next must be implemented. *Strategy implementation* provides goods and services in accord with a plan of action. Quite often, this plan will have an overall philosophy or series of guidelines that direct the process. In the case of Japanese electronic-manufacturing firms entering the U.S. market, Chang has found a common approach:

> To reduce the risk of failure, these firms are entering their core businesses and those in which they have stronger competitive advantages over local firms first. The learning from early entry enables firms to launch further entry into areas in which they have the next strongest competitive advantages. As learning accumulates, firms may overcome the disadvantages intrinsic to foreignness. Although primary learning takes place within firms through learning by doing, they may also learn from other firms through the transfer or diffusion of experience. This process is not automatic, however, and it may be enhanced by membership in a corporate network: in firms associated with either horizontal or vertical business groups were more likely to initiate entries than independent firms. By learning from their own sequential entry experience as well as from other firms in corporated networks, firms build capabilities in foreign entry.[37]

International management must consider three general areas in strategy implementation. First, the MNC must decide where to locate operations. Second, the MNC must carry out entry and ownership strategies. Finally, management must implement functional strategies in areas such as marketing, production, and finance.

Location Considerations for Implementation

In choosing a location, today's MNC has two primary considerations: the country, and the specific locale within the chosen country. Quite often, the first choice is easier than the second, because there are many more alternatives from which to choose a specific locale.

The Country   Traditionally, MNCs have invested in industrialized countries. For example, in the 1980s and 1990s, most foreign investment by U.S. MNCs has been in Europe and Canada. The small percentage that has gone into less-developed countries is heavily concentrated in extractive (e.g., mining) rather than manufacturing activities.

MNCs invest in industrialized countries primarily because these advanced nations offer the largest markets for goods and services. In addition, the established country or geographic locale may have legal restrictions related to imports, encouraging a local presence.[38] Japanese firms, for example, in complying with their voluntary export quotas of cars to the United States as well as responding to dissatisfaction in Washington regarding the large trade imbalance with the United States, have established U.S.-based assembly plants. In Europe, because of EU regulations for outsiders, most U.S. and Japanese MNCs have operations in at least one European country, thus ensuring access to the European community at large. In fact, the huge U.S. MNC ITT now operates in each of the original 12 EU countries.

Another consideration in choosing a country is the amount of government control. Traditionally, MNCs from around the world refused to do business in Eastern European countries with central planning economies. The recent relaxing of the trade rules and move toward free market economies in the republics of the former Soviet Union and the other Eastern European nations, however, have encouraged MNCs to rethink their positions; more and more are making moves into this largely untapped part of the global market.[39] The same seems to be true in India as well, where the federal government now is considering private bids to build and operate 20-million telephone lines by the turn of the century.[40] Only 1 percent of India's population currently have telephones, so the market potential is huge. At the same time, the political climate is volatile, and MNCs must carefully weigh the risks of investing there.[41]

MNCs tend to avoid entering or expanding operations in countries where there is political turmoil or spillover effects caused by retaliation from other nations. For example, companies that did business in South Africa during the height of apartheid policies found retaliatory action from other African nations as well as politically active consumer groups in their own country.

Still another consideration in selecting a country is restrictions on foreign investment. Traditionally, countries such as China and India have required that control of the operation be in the hands of local partners.[42] MNCs that are reluctant to accept such conditions will not establish operations there.

In addition to these considerations, MNCs will examine the specific benefits offered by host countries, including low tax rates, rent-free land and buildings, low-interest or no-interest loans, subsidized energy and transportation rates, and a well-developed infrastructure that provides many of the services found back home (good roads, communication systems, schools, entertainment, and housing). These benefits will be weighed against any disincentives or performance requirements that must be met by the MNC, such as job-creation quotas, export minimums for generating foreign currency, limits on local market growth, labor regulations, wage and price controls, restrictions on profit repatriation, and controls on the transfer of technology.

Commenting on the overall effect of these potential gains and losses, Garland and Farmer noted:

> These incentives and disincentives often make operations abroad less amenable to integration on a global basis; essentially they may alter a company's strategy for the region. They affect, for example, a firm's make-or-buy decision, intracorporate transfer policies (e.g., between subsidiaries or between headquarters and the subsidiaries), both horizontal and vertical sourcing arrangements, and so on. In effect, they weaken the MNC's mandate for global efficiency by encouraging the firm to suboptimize.[43]

Local Issues   Once the MNC has decided the country in which to locate, the firm must choose the specific locale. A number of factors influence this choice. Common considerations include access to markets, proximity to competitors, availability of transportation and electric power, and desirability of the location for employees coming in from the outside.[44]

One study found that in selecting U.S. sites, both German and Japanese firms place more importance on accessibility and desirability and less importance on financial considerations.[45] However, financial matters remain important: Many countries attempt to lure MNCs to specific locales by offering special financial packages.

Another common consideration is the nature of the work force. MNCs prefer to locate near sources of available labor that can be readily trained to do the work. A complementary consideration that often is unspoken is the presence and strength of organized labor (Chapter 16 covers this topic in detail). Japanese firms in particular tend to avoid heavily unionized areas.

Still another consideration is the cost of doing business. Manufacturers often set up operations in rural areas, commonly called "green field locations," which are much less expensive and do not have the problems of urban areas. Conversely, banks often choose metropolitan areas, because they feel they must have a presence in the business district.

Some MNCs opt for locales where the cost of running a small enterprise is significantly lower than that of running a large one. In this way, they spread their risk, setting up many small locations throughout the world rather than one or two large ones. Manufacturing firms are a good example. Some production firms feel that the economies of scale associated with a large-scale plant are more than offset by potential problems that can result should economic or political difficulties develop in the country. These firms' strategy is to spread the risk by opting for a series of small plants throughout a wide geographic region.

Ownership and Entry Considerations for Implementation

There are a number of common forms of ownership in international operations. These extend from fully owned subsidiaries to joint ventures to franchising and licensing agreements to basic export and import operations. Depending on the situation, any one of these can be a very effective way to implement an MNCs' strategy.

Fully Owned Subsidiary   *A fully owned subsidiary* is an overseas operation that is totally owned and controlled by an MNC. The subsidiary is a part of the organization's formal structure, and its formation involves the direct investment of both capital and company personnel. Many such subsidiaries are created by the MNC, but in some cases, these subsidiaries are purchased from other firms. An example of the latter is the acquisition of International Harvester's agricultural equipment group by J. I. Case. This purchase both reinforced and expanded Cases's product line, tripled its number of dealers around the world, and put it in an excellent position to compete with the industry leader, John Deere.

The primary reasons for this form of ownership are the desire of the MNC for total control and the belief that managerial efficiency will be better without outside partners. Host countries, however, often feel that the MNC is trying to gain economic control by setting up local operations but refusing to take in local partners. Some countries are concerned that the MNC will drive out local enterprises. In dealing with these concerns, many Third World countries prohibit fully owned subsidiaries. A second drawback is that home country unions sometimes oppose the creation of foreign subsidiaries, which they see as an attempt to "export jobs," particularly when the MNC exports goods to another country and then decides to set up manufacturing operations there. A good example is the decision by U.S. automakers to transfer assembly line work for U.S. factories to newly established plants in Mexico.[46] Today, many MNCs opt for a joint venture rather than a fully owned subsidiary.

Joint Venture   As it relates to international operations, a *joint venture* is an agreement in which two or more partners own and control an overseas business. This business typically is located in the home country of one of the partners.

There are two types of joint ventures. The least common is the *nonequity venture,* which is characterized by one group's merely providing a service for another.

The group providing the service typically is more active than the other. Examples include a consulting firm that is hired to provide analysis and evaluation and then make its recommendations to the other party, an engineering or construction firm that contracts to design or build a dam or series of apartment complexes in an undeveloped area of a partner's country, or a mining firm that has an agreement to extract a natural resource in the other party's country.

The more common arrangement is the *equity joint venture,* which involves a financial investment by the MNC in a business enterprise with a local partner. Many variations of this arrangement adjust the degree of control that each of the parties will have and the amount of money, technological expertise,[47] and managerial expertise each will contribute.

Most foreign firms are more interested in the amount of control they will have over the venture than in their share of the profits.[48] Many local partners feel the same way, and this can result in problems. Nevertheless, joint ventures have become very popular in recent years because of the benefits they offer to both parties. Figure 8-3 summarizes these benefits. As shown, the technological innovation and convergence of the joint venture both affects and is affected by ownership, location, and internalization advantages. These advantages also affect and are affected by globalization. Perhaps the major advantage is sharing investments and risks. For example, a firm with little cash but a great deal of international experience can team up with a company that has cash but lacks such experience.

Partners in joint ventures can complement each other and thus reduce the risks associated with their undertaking. A good example is European truck manufacturing and auto component industries. Firms in both groups have found that the high cost of developing and building their products can be offset through joint ventures. In particular, some partners to these ventures have contributed financial assistance while others provide the distribution networks needed to move the product through channels. Another example is the recent decision by Japanese semiconductor firms to consider banding together and jointly developing new chip production methods. The chip makers also have invited U.S. firms to join them in creating 12-inch wafer technology, but it appears likely that the Americans will form their own joint-venture group.[49]

Although much negotiation may be necessary before a joint-venture agreement is hammered out, the final result must be one that both sides can accept. Many successful examples of such agreements have emerged in recent years. One of the most complex was the General Motors–Toyota agreement, which involved scores of groups and thousands of individuals. Other more recent examples include General Motors' venture with the Polish government to build Opels in that country,[50] L. L. Bean's decision to sell clothing and equipment under a joint-venture agreement with two Japanese companies in Tokyo,[51] and Occidental Petroleum's joint venture in a northern China coal mining project.[52]

Joint ventures are proving to be particularly popular as a means for doing business in emerging market economies. For example, in the early 1990s, foreigners had signed more than 3000 joint-venture agreements in Eastern Europe and the former republics of the Soviet Union, and interest remains high today.[53] Careful analysis must be undertaken to ensure that the market for the desired goods and services is sufficiently large, however, that all parties understand their responsibilities, and that all parties agree regarding the overall operation of the venture. If these problems can be resolved, the venture stands a good chance of success.[54] The

FIGURE 8-3

THE BENEFITS OF JOINT VENTURES

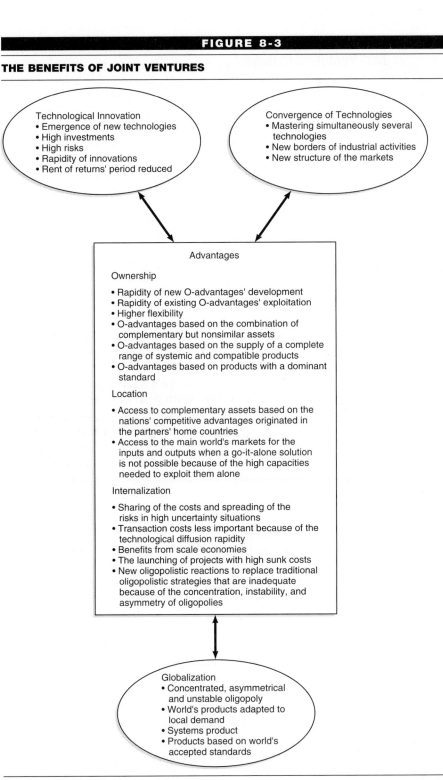

Technological Innovation
- Emergence of new technologies
- High investments
- High risks
- Rapidity of innovations
- Rent of returns' period reduced

Convergence of Technologies
- Mastering simultaneously several technologies
- New borders of industrial activities
- New structure of the markets

Advantages

Ownership

- Rapidity of new O-advantages' development
- Rapidity of existing O-advantages' exploitation
- Higher flexibility
- O-advantages based on the combination of complementary but nonsimilar assets
- O-advantages based on the supply of a complete range of systemic and compatible products
- O-advantages based on products with a dominant standard

Location

- Access to complementary assets based on the nations' competitive advantages originated in the partners' home countries
- Access to the main world's markets for the inputs and outputs when a go-it-alone solution is not possible because of the high capacities needed to exploit them alone

Internalization

- Sharing of the costs and spreading of the risks in high uncertainty situations
- Transaction costs less important because of the technological diffusion rapidity
- Benefits from scale economies
- The launching of projects with high sunk costs
- New oligopolistic reactions to replace traditional oligopolistic strategies that are inadequate because of the concentration, instability, and asymmetry of oligopolies

Globalization
- Concentrated, asymmetrical and unstable oligopoly
- World's products adapted to local demand
- Systems product
- Products based on world's accepted standards

Source: Philippe Gulger, "Building Transnational Alliances to Create Competitive Advantage," *Long Range Planning,* vol. 25, no. 1, 1992, p. 92. Copyright 1992, with permission from Pergamon Press Ltd., Headington Hill Hall, Oxford OX3 OBW, U.K.

Joint Venturing in Russia

Joint venturing is becoming an increasingly popular strategy for setting up international operations. Russia is particularly interested in these arrangements because of the benefits they offer for attracting foreign capital and helping the country tap its natural resource wealth. However, investors are finding that joint venturing in Russia and the other republics of the former Soviet Union can be fraught with problems. For example, Chevron, which has agreed to invest $10 billion over the next 25 years in developing the Tengiz oil field in Kazakhstan, recently found itself having to renegotiate the contract and drop its share of profits from 28 percent to under 20 percent. This became necessary because the original contract was negotiated with the Soviet Union under President Mikhail Gorbachev; after the breakup, the new government was unwilling to abide by the previous terms. Renegotiation is not the only problem facing joint-venture investors in Russia. Others include the following:

1. Many Russian partners view a joint venture as an opportunity to travel abroad and gain access to foreign currency; the business itself often is given secondary consideration.
2. Finding a suitable partner, negotiating the deal, and registering the joint venture often take up to a year, mainly because the Russians are unaccustomed to some of the basic steps in putting together business deals.
3. Russian partners typically try to expand joint ventures into unrelated activities, while foreign investors are more prone to minimizing risk and not overextending operations by getting into new areas.
4. Russians do not like to declare profits, because there is a 2-year tax holiday on profits that starts from the moment the first profits are declared. Foreign partners, on the other hand, are not influenced by this fact and often point out that because taxes must be paid in rubles, which have very little value, taxes are not a problem.
5. The government sometimes allows profits to be repatriated in the form of countertrade. However, much of what can be taken out of the country has limited value, because the government keeps control of those resources that are most salable in the world market.

These representative problems indicate why there is a growing reluctance on the part of some MNCs to enter into joint ventures in Russia. As one of them recently put it, "The country may well turn into an economic sink hole." As a result, many MNCs are very reluctant and are proceeding with caution.

---

accompanying sidebar, "Joint Venturing in Russia," illustrates some of the problems that need to be overcome for a joint venture to be successful.

Licensing Another way to gain market entry to implement strategy is to acquire the right to a particular product by getting an exclusive license to make and/or sell the good in a particular geographic locale. A *license* is an agreement that allows one party to use an industrial property right in exchange for payment to the other party. In a typical arrangement, the party giving the license (the licensor) will allow the other (the licensee) to use a patent, trademark, or proprietary information in exchange for a fee. The fee usually is based on sales, such as 1 percent of all revenues earned from an industrial motor sold in Asia. The licensor typically restricts licensee sales to a particular geographic locale and limits the time period covered by the arrangement. Therefore, the firm in this example may have an exclusive right to sell this patented motor in Asia for the next 5 years. This allows the licensor to seek licensees for other major geographic locales, such as Europe, South America, and Australia.

Licensing is used under a number of common conditions. For example, the product typically is in the mature stage of the product life cycle, competition is strong, and profit margins are declining. Under these conditions, the licensor is unlikely to want to spend money to enter foreign markets. However, if the company can find an MNC that is already there and willing to add the product to its own current offerings, both sides can benefit from the arrangement. A second common instance of licensing is when foreign governments require newly entering firms to make a substantial direct investment in the country. By licensing to a firm already there, the licensee avoids entry costs. A third condition is that the licensor usually is a small firm that lacks financial and managerial resources. Finally, companies that spend a relatively large share of their revenues on research and development (R&D) are likely to be licensors, and those who spend very little on R&D are more likely to be licensees. In fact, some small R&D firms make a handsome profit every year by developing and licensing new products to large firms with diversified product lines.

Some licensors use their industrial property rights to develop and sell goods in certain areas of the world and license others to handle other geographic locales. This provides the licensor with a source of additional revenues, but the licensee usually is not good for much more than a decade. This is a major disadvantage of licensing. In particular, if the product is very good, the competition will develop improvement patents that allow it to sell similar goods or even new patents that make the current product obsolete. Nevertheless, for the period during which the agreement is in effect, a license can be a very low-cost way of gaining and exploiting foreign markets. Table 8-5 provides some comparisons between licensing and joint ventures and summarizes the major advantages and disadvantages of each.

Franchising A *franchise* is a business arrangement under which one party (the franchisor) allows another (the franchisee) to operate an enterprise using its trademark, logo, product line, and methods of operation in return for a fee. Franchising is widely used in the fast-food and hotel/motel industries. The concept is very adaptable to the international arena, and with some minor adjustments for the local market, it can result in a highly profitable business. In fast foods, McDonald's, Burger King, and Kentucky Fried Chicken have used franchise arrangements to expand their markets from Paris to Tokyo and from Cairo to Caracas. In the hotel business, Holiday Inn, among others, has been very successful in gaining worldwide presence through the effective use of franchisees.

Franchise agreements typically require payment of a fee up front and then a percentage of the revenues. In return, the franchisor provides assistance and, in some instances, may require the purchase of goods or supplies to ensure the same quality of goods or services worldwide. Franchising can be beneficial to both groups: It provides the franchisor with a new stream of income and the franchisee with a time-proven concept and products or services that can be quickly brought to market.[55]

Export/Import Exporting or importing often are the only available choices for small firms wanting to go international. These choices also provide an avenue for larger firms that want to begin their international expansion with a minimum of investment. The paperwork associated with documentation and foreign-currency exchange can be turned over to an export management company to handle, or the firm can handle things itself by creating its own export department. The firm can

TABLE 8-5

PARTIAL COMPARISON OF GLOBAL STRATEGIC ALLIANCES

Strategy	Organization design	Advantages	Disadvantages	Critical success factors	Strategic human resources management
Licensing— manufacturing industries	Technologies	Early standardization of design Ability to capitalize on innovations Access to new technologies Ability to control pace of industry evolution	New competitors created Possible eventual exit from industry Possible dependence on licensee	Selection of licensee unlikely to become a competitor Enforcement of patents and licensing agreements	Technical knowledge Training of local managers on-site
Licensing— servicing and franchises	Geography	Fast market entry Low capital cost	Quality control Trademark protection	Partners compatible in philosophies/values Tight performance standards	Socialization of franchisees and licensees with core values
Joint ventures— specialization across partners	Function	Learning a partner's skills Economics of scale Quasivertical integration Faster learning	Excessive dependence on partner for skills Deterrent to internal investment	Tight and specific performance criteria Entering a venture as "student" rather than "teacher" to learn skills from partner Recognizing that collaboration is another form of competition to learn new skills	Management development and training Negotiation skills Managerial rotation
Joint venture— shared value-adding	Product or line of business	Strengths of both partners pooled Faster learning along value chain Fast upgrading of technologic skills	High switching costs Inability to limit partner's access to information	Decentralization and autonomy from corporate parents Long "courtship" period Harmonization of management styles	Team-building Acculturation Flexible skills for implicit communication

Source: David Lei and John W. Slocum, Jr., "Global Strategic Alliances: Payoffs and Pitfalls," *Organizational Dynamics*, Winter 1991, p. 48. Used with permission.

turn to major banks or other specialists who, for a fee, will provide a variety of services, including letters of credit, currency conversion, and related financial assistance.

A number of potential problems face firms that plan to export. For example, if a foreign distributor does not work out well, some countries have strict rules about dropping that distributor. Therefore, an MNC with a contractual agreement with the distributor could be stuck with the distributor. If the firm decides to get more actively involved, it may make direct investments in marketing facilities, such as warehouses, sales offices, and transportation equipment, without making a direct investment in manufacturing facilities overseas.

When importing goods, many MNCs make deals with overseas suppliers who can provide a wide assortment. It is common to find U.S. firms purchasing supplies and components from Korea, Taiwan, and Hong Kong. In Europe, there is so much trade between EU countries that the entire process seldom is regarded as "international" in focus by the MNCs that are involved.

Exporting and importing can provide easy access to overseas markets; however, the strategy usually is transitional in nature. If the firm continues to do international business, it will get more actively involved in terms of investment.[56]

The Role of the Functional Areas in Implementation

To implement strategies, MNCs must tap the primary functional areas of marketing, production, and finance. The following sections examine the roles of those functions in international strategy implementation.

Marketing   The implementation of strategy from a marketing perspective must be determined on a country-by-country basis. What works from the standpoint of marketing in one locale may not necessarily succeed in another.[57] In addition, the specific steps of a marketing approach often are dictated by the overall strategic plan, which in turn is based heavily on market analysis.

German auto firms in Japan are a good example of using marketing analysis to meet customer needs. Over the past 15 years, the Germans have spent millions of dollars to build dealer, supplier, and service-support networks in Japan, in addition to adapting their cars to Japanese customers' tastes. Volkswagen Audi Nippon has built a $320-million import facility on a deep-water port. This operation, which includes an inspection center and parts warehouse, can process 100,000 cars a year. Mercedes and BMW both have introduced lower-priced cars to attract a larger market segment, and BMW now offers a flat-fee, 3-year service contract on any new car, including parts. At the same time, German manufacturers work hard to offer first-class service in their dealerships. As a result, German automakers in recent years sell almost three times as many cars in Japan as their U.S. competitors do.[58]

The Japanese themselves also provide an excellent example of how the marketing process works. In many cases, Japanese firms have followed a strategy of first building up their market share at home and driving out imported goods. Then, the firms move into newly developed countries (e.g., Korea or Taiwan), honing their marketing skills as they go along. Finally, the firms move into fully developed countries, ready to compete with the best available. This pattern of implementing strategy has been used in marketing autos, cameras, consumer electronics, home appliances, petrochemicals, steel, and watches. For some products, however, such as computers, the Japanese have moved from their home market directly into fully developed countries and then on to the newly developing nations. Finally, the Japanese have gone directly to developed countries to market products in some cases, because the market in Japan was too small. Such products include color TVs, videotape recorders, and sewing machines. In general, once a firm agrees on the goods it wants to sell in the international marketplace, then the specific marketing strategy is implemented.

The implementation of marketing strategy in the international arena is built around the well-known "four Ps" of marketing: product, price, promotion, and place. As noted in the example of the Japanese, firms often develop and sell a product in local or peripheral markets before expanding to major overseas targets. If the product is designed specifically to meet an overseas demand, however, the process is more direct. Price largely is a function of market demand. For example, the Japanese have found that the U.S. microcomputer market is price-sensitive; by introducing lower-priced clones, the Japanese have been able to make headway, especially in the portable laptop market. The last two Ps, promotion and place, are dictated by local conditions and often left in the hands of those running the subsidiary or affiliate. Local management may implement customer sales incentives, for example, or make arrangements with dealers and salespeople who are helping to move the product locally.

Production Although marketing usually dominates strategy implementation, the production function also plays a role. If a company is going to export goods to a foreign market, the production process traditionally has been handled through domestic operations. In recent years, however, MNCs have found that whether they are exporting or producing the goods locally in the host country, consideration of worldwide production is important. For example, goods may be produced in foreign countries for export to other nations. Sometimes, a plant will specialize in a particular product and export it to all the MNC's markets; other times, a plant will produce goods only for a specific locale, such as Western Europe or South America. Still other facilities will produce one or more components that are shipped to a larger network of assembly plants. This latter option has been widely adopted by pharmaceutical firms and automakers such as Volkswagen and Honda.

If the firm operates production plants in different countries but makes no attempt to integrate its overall operations, the company is known as a *multidomestic.* A recent trend has been away from this scattered approach and toward global co-ordination of operations.[59] As Garland and Farmer explained, "the globally oriented firm tries to obtain the best inputs from around the world while producing components and products wherever it is most efficient to do so."[60]

If the product is labor-intensive, as in the case of microcomputers, then the trend is to farm the product out to low-cost sites such as Taiwan, Mexico, and Brazil, where the cost of labor is relatively low and the infrastructure (electric power, communications systems, transportation systems) is sufficient to support production. Sometimes, multiple sources of individual components are used; in other cases, only one or two are sufficient. In any event, careful co-ordination of the production function is needed when implementing the strategy, and the result is a product that is truly global in nature.

Finance   Use of the finance function to implement strategy normally is developed at the home office and carried out by the overseas affiliate or branch. When a firm went international in the past, the overseas operation commonly relied on the local area for funds, but the rise of global financing has ended this practice. MNCs have learned that transferring funds from one place in the world to another, or borrowing funds in the international money markets, often is less expensive than relying on local sources. Unfortunately, there are problems in these transfers.

Such a problem is representative of those faced by MNCs using the finance function to implement their strategies. One of an MNC's biggest recent headaches when implementing strategies in the financial dimension has been the re-evaluation of currencies. For example, in the late 1980s, the U.S. dollar dropped in value against the German mark and the Japanese yen; U.S. overseas operations that held these foreign currencies found their profits (in terms of dollars) rising sharply. Conversely, those that held pesos in Mexico or Argentina found that because of high inflation, the value of these currencies resulted in the operation's declaring lower profits (in terms of dollars).

When dealing with the inherent risk of volatile monetary exchange rates, some MNCs have bought currency options that (for a price) guarantee convertibility at a specified rate. Others have developed countertrade strategies, whereby they receive products in exchange for currency. For example, PepsiCo receives payment in vodka for its products sold in Russia. Countertrade continues to be a popular form of international business, especially in Third World countries and those with nonconvertible currencies.[61]

SUMMARY OF KEY POINTS

1. There is a growing need for strategic planning among MNCs. Some of the primary reasons include: foreign direct investment is increasing, planning is needed to co-ordinate and integrate increasingly diverse operations via an overall focus, and emerging international challenges require strategic planning.
2. A strategic plan can take on an economic focus, a political focus, a quality focus, an administrative co-ordination focus, or some variation of the four. In addition, an MNC typically is predisposed toward an ethnocentric, polycentric, regiocentric, or geocentric orientation. Companies may use a combination of these orientations in their strategic planning, but geocentric is the one employed most commonly by global companies.
3. Strategic planning is used by more MNCs every year, although no definitive evidence proves that this process always results in higher profitability. As with other aspects of international management, the particular situation largely will dictate the success of a strategic plan.
4. Strategy formulation consists of several steps. First, the MNC carries out external environmental scanning to identify opportunities and threats. Next, the firm conducts an internal resource analysis of company strengths and weaknesses. Strategic goals then are formulated in light of the results of these external and internal analyses.
5. Strategy implementation is the process of providing goods and services in accord with the predetermined plan of action. This implementation typically involves such considerations as: deciding where to locate operations, carrying out an entry and ownership strategy, and using functional strategies to implement the plan. Functional strategies focus on marketing, production, and finance.

KEY TERMS

strategic planning	environmental scanning
economic imperative	key factor for success (KFS)
political imperative	strategy implementation
quality imperative	fully owned subsidiary
administrative co-ordination	joint venture
ethnocentric predisposition	license
polycentric predisposition	franchise
regiocentric predisposition	multidomestic
geocentric predisposition	

REVIEW AND DISCUSSION QUESTIONS

1. Of the four imperatives discussed in this chapter—economic, political, quality, and administration—which would be most important to IBM in its efforts to make inroads in the Pacific Rim market? Would this emphasis be the same as that in the United States, or would IBM be giving primary attention to one of the other imperatives? Explain.

2. If a locally based manufacturing firm with sales of $350 million decided to enter the EU market by setting up operations in France, which orientation would be the most effective: ethnocentric, polycentric, regiocentric, or geocentric? Why? Explain your choice.

3. When a large MNC such as Ford Motor sets strategic goals, what areas are targeted for consideration? Incorporate the information from Table 8-4 in your answer. Would this list of strategic goals be very different from that formulated by the manufacturing firm in question 2 above? Why, or why not?

4. One of the most common entry strategies for MNCs is the joint venture. Why are so many companies opting for this strategy? Would a fully owned subsidiary be a better choice?

5. In recent years McDonald's has found that its international franchise operation has been producing more revenue per unit than its domestic operations. What might account for this? Is it likely that the firm will continue its international expansion? Why?

6. Mercedes recently changed its U.S. strategy by announcing that it is developing cars for the $30,000 to $45,000 price range (as well as its typical upper-end cars). What might have accounted for this change in strategy? In your answer, include a discussion of the implications from the standpoints of marketing, production, and finance.

PRACTICAL INTERNATIONAL MANAGEMENT ASSIGNMENT

Get recent copies (no more than 2 months old) of business magazines or newspapers, such as *Fortune, BusinessWeek*, the *New York Times* Sunday edition, or the *Wall Street Journal*, and find a story on a multinational corporation that is changing its international strategy. Carefully examine these changes, and determine how this new strategy will be beneficial. What KFSs will be needed for success? How will the specific strategy help to create or draw on these key factors? Also, why is the MNC making these strategy changes? Is the competition likely to make a countermove? Write a 2- to 3-page paper presenting your findings and conclusions.

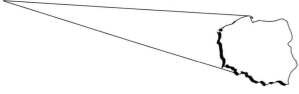

Toasting in Poland often plays a big part in both formal and informal dinners.

Poland

Poland is the sixth-largest country in Europe. It is bordered by Germany, the Czech Republic, and Slovakia in the west and south and by the former Soviet Union republics of the Ukraine in the south, Belarus in the east, and Lithuania in the northeast. The northwest section of the country is located on the Baltic Sea. Named after the Polane, a Slavic tribe that lived more than a thousand years ago, Poland has beautiful countryside and rapidly growing cities. Rolling hills and rugged mountains rise in southern Poland. There are approximately 40 million Poles, and GNP is around $200 billion. The country still is highly agricultural, and up to one-third of the population engages in farm work. The people have a rich heritage (at one point, the Poles ruled an empire that stretched across most of central Europe), many folk traditions (which the communist government discouraged), and strong loyalty to the Roman Catholic church. The government is now dominated by former communists (socialists), and Lech Walesa, the democratic hero, was defeated in the most recent presidential election. However, the socialists still are trying to establish a free-market system. Predictions are that the coming years will remain very difficult for the country as Poland tries to reestablish economic equilibrium and undo some of the major mistakes made by the communists.

The Poles indeed have overcome some major obstacles to make a viable economy for the years ahead. A medium-sized Canadian manufacturing firm has begun thinking about renovating a plant near Warsaw and building small power tools for the expanding Eastern European market. The company's logic is fairly straightforward. There appears to be no competition in this niche, because there has been little demand for power tools in this area. As these countries begin turning more and more toward a free-market model, however, they will have to increase their productivity if they hope to compete with Western European nations. Small power tools are one of the products they will need to accomplish this goal.

A second reason for the Canadian firm's interest in setting up operations in Poland is that the price of labor is fairly low. Other nearby countries have lower wage rates, but Warsaw, the company's specific choice, has a cadre of well-trained factory workers that could be transferred to this renovated factory. Product quality in the production of these tools is critical to success, so for this Canadian firm, Poland is an ideal location.

In addition, Poland likely will continue receiving economic support from Western Europe as well as Canada and the United States. Exporting from Poland to Western Europe or the United States therefore should be easier than from any other country in Eastern Europe. Moreover, the manufacturing firm is convinced that its proximity to Russia will open up that market as well.

Transportation costs to Russia will be low vis-à-vis competitors, and the Russians currently are looking for ways to increase their own worker productivity.

Finally, there likely will be little competition for the next couple of years, because small power tools do not carry a very large markup and no other manufacturer is attempting to tap what the Canadian firm views as "an emerging market for the twenty-first century." However, a final decision on this matter is going to have to wait until the company has made a thorough evaluation of the market and the competitive nature of the industry.

1. What are some current issues facing Poland? What is the climate for doing business in Poland today?
2. Is the Canadian manufacturing firm using an economic, political, or quality imperative approach to strategy?
3. How should the firm carry out the environmental scanning process? Would the process be of any practical value?
4. What are two key factors for success that will be important if this project is to succeed?

You Be the International Management Consultant

Go East, Young People, Go East

Amanda Brendhart, Jose Gutierrez, and Rhoda Schreiber founded and are partners in a small electronics firm, Electronic Visions, that has developed and patented some state-of-the-art computer components. Visions has had moderate success selling these components to large U.S.-based computer manufacturers. The biggest problem is that in recent months, the computer market has begun to turn soft, and many of the manufacturers are offering substantial discounts to generate sales. Therefore, although Visions has found an increasing demand for its product, it now is grossing less money than it was 4 months ago.

To increase both sales and profit, the partners have decided to expand into East Asia. Although this region is known for its low-cost computer production, the group believes that countries such as Japan, South Korea, and Taiwan soon will become more lucrative markets, because the U.S. government will make these countries open their doors to imports more fully. If trade barriers are removed, the partners are convinced that they can export the goods at very competitive prices. In addition, the partners intend to find a partner in each market so that they have someone to help with the marketing and financing of the product. Of course, if the components can be produced more cheaply with local labor, the partnership is willing to forgo exporting and have everything produced locally.

At present, the group is trying to answer three questions. First, what is the best entry strategy to use in reaching the East Asian markets? Second, what type of marketing strategy will be most effective? Third, if production must be co-ordinated between the United States and an overseas country, what is the best way to handle this? The partners believe that over the next 2 months, they will have a very good idea of what is going to happen regarding the opening of foreign markets. In the interim, they intend to work up a preliminary strategic plan that they can use to guide them.

1. What type of entry and ownership approach would you recommend? Defend your choice.
2. How could the partners use the four Ps of marketing to help implement strategy?
3. If production must be globally co-ordinated, will Visions have a major problem? Why, or why not?

CHAPTER 8 ENDNOTES

1. Robert L. Simpson and Oscar Suris, "Alex Trotman's Goal: To Make Ford No. 1 in World Auto Sales," *Wall Street Journal,* July 18, 1995, pp. A1, A8.

2. Also see Philip M. Rosenzweig, "The New 'American Challenge': Foreign Multinationals in the United States," *California Management Review,* Spring 1994, pp. 107–123.

3. See Daniel Sullivan and Alan Bauerschmidt, "The 'Basic Concepts' of International Business Strategy: A Review and Reconsideration," *Management International Review,* Special Issue 1991, pp. 111–124.

4. "Japanese Are Profiting from a New Leanness," *Wall Street Journal,* January 9, 1995, p. A1.

5. Cacilie Rohwedder, "Hugo Boss Looks Overseas for Factories and Customers," *Wall Street Journal,* July 10, 1995, p. B4.

6. Andrew Pollack, "Packard Bell Selling NEC a Big Stake," *New York Times,* July 6, 1995, pp. C1, C3.

7. "Siemens to Build Factory in England," *Globe and Mail,* August 7, 1995, p. B3.

8. Andrew Pollack, "Koreans Seen Buying More U.S. Concerns," *New York Times,* July 21, 1995, p. C5.

9. Anant R. Negandhi, *International Management* (Boston: Allyn & Bacon, 1987), p. 230.

10. James M. Hulbert and William K. Brandt, *Managing the Multinational Subsidiary* (New York: Holt, Rinehart and Winston, 1980), pp. 35–64.

11. Noel Capon, Chris Christodoulou, John U. Farley, and James Hulbert, "A Comparison of Corporate Planning Practice in American and Australian Manufacturing Companies," *Journal of International Business Studies,* Fall 1984, pp. 41–45.

12. Negandhi, *International Management,* pp. 235–236.

13. Martin K. Welge, "Planning in German Multinational Corporations," *International Studies of Management and Organization,* Spring 1982, pp. 6–37.

14. Martin K. Welge and Michael E. Kenter, "Impact of Planning on Control Effectiveness and Company Performance," *Management International Review,* vol. 20, no. 2, 1988, pp. 4–15.

15. See Rosalie L. Tung, "Strategic Management Thought in East Asia," *Organization Dynamics,* Spring 1994, pp. 55–65.

16. See Yves L. Doz, "Strategic Management in Multinational Companies," *Sloan Management Review,* Winter 1980, pp. 27–46.

17. A good example is provided in John Templeman and Gail E. Sachares, "A Hard U-Turn at VW," *BusinessWeek,* March 15, 1993, p. 47.

18. Jonathan B. Levine, "Everyone Loves a Bargain—Europeans Included," *BusinessWeek,* February 10, 1992, pp. 118–119.

19. "Bandag: Retreading the Tire Business," *BusinessWeek,* January 20, 1992, pp. 88–89.

20. Richard M. Hodgetts, *Blueprints for Continuous Improvement: Lessons from the Baldrige Winners* (New York: American Management Association, 1993).

21. For more on this topic, see Richard J. Schonberger, "Total Quality Management Cuts a Broad Swath—Through Manufacturing and Beyond," *Organizational Dynamics,* Spring 1992, pp. 16–28.

22. Sang M. Lee, Fred Luthans, and Richard M. Hodgetts, "Total Quality Management: Implications for Central and Eastern Europe," *Organizational Dynamics,* Spring 1992, pp. 44–45.

23. Erik Calonius, "Smart Moves by Quality Champs," *Fortune,* Special Edition 1991, pp. 24–25.

24. Doz, "Strategic Management," p. 29.

25. Also see Stephen J. Kobrin, "Is There a Relationship Between a Geographic Mind-Set and Multinational Strategy?" *Journal of International Business Studies,* Third Quarter 1994, pp. 493–511.

26. For insights to global strategy, see George S. Yip, *Total Global Strategy* (Englewood Cliffs, NJ: Prentice-Hall, 1995), Chapter 1.

27. Also see William H. Davidson, "The Role of Global Spanning in Business Planning," *Organizational Dynamics,* Winter 1991, pp. 5–16.

28. A good example is provided in Subrata N. Chakravarty, "Soap Opera Down Under," *Forbes,* February 15, 1993, pp. 140–146.

29. John Templeman et al., "How Mercedes Trumped Chrysler in China," *BusinessWeek,* July 31, 1995, pp. 50–51.

30. Jacques Neher, "A French Giant Stalks U.S. Telephone Market," *New York Times,* November 25, 1991, pp. C1–2.

31. John P. Wolkonowicz, "The EC Auto Industry Gears Up for Greater Competition," *Journal of European Business,* November/December 1991, p. 14.

32. Paul B. Carroll, "IBM to Sell PC Clone Made by Asian Firm," *Wall Street Journal,* March 11, 1992, pp. B1, B7.

33. Neil Gross, "Matsushita's Urgent Quest for Leadership," *BusinessWeek,* March 8, 1993, p. 52.

34. "On the Cutting Room Floor," *Economist,* April 8, 1995, p. 16.

35. "The Shock of the Yen," *Economist,* April 8, 1995, pp. 33–34.

36. For additional insights, see Christopher J. Clarke and Kieron Brennan, "Global Mobility—The Concept," *Long Range Planning,* vol. 25, no. 1, 1992, pp. 73–80.

37. Sea Jin Change, "International Expansion Strategy of Japanese Firms: Capacity Building Through

Sequential Entry," *Academy of Management Journal,* April 1995, p. 402.

38. See Harry Hammerly, "Matching Global Strategies with National Responses," *Journal of Business Strategy,* March/April 1992, pp. 8–12.

39. See Mark Alpert, "Wary Hope on Eastern Europe," *Fortune,* January 29, 1990, pp. 125–126; Shawn Tully, "What Eastern Europe Offers," *Fortune,* March 21, 1990, pp. 52–55.

40. Peter Waldman, "India Seeks to Open Huge Phone Market," *Wall Street Journal,* July 25, 1995, p. A9.

41. Miriam Jordan, "Indian Nationalists Pick the Next Targets," *Wall Street Journal,* August 22, 1995, p. A7.

42. See Pete Engardio, "Why Sweet Deals Are Going Sour in China," *BusinessWeek,* December 19, 1994, pp. 50–51.

43. John Garland and Richard N. Farmer, *International Dimensions of Business Policy and Strategy* (Boston: Kent Publishing, 1986), pp. 62–63.

44. See Mariah E. de Forest, "Thinking of a Plant in Mexico?" *Academy of Management Executive,* February 1994, pp. 33–40.

45. Harry I. Chernotsky, "Selecting U.S. Sites: A Case Study of German and Japanese Firms," *Management International Review,* vol. 23, no. 2, 1983, pp. 45–55.

46. Stephen Baker, David Woodruff, and Elizabeth Weiner, "Detroit South," *BusinessWeek,* March 16, 1992, pp. 98–103.

47. Richard N. Osborn and C. Christopher Baughn, "New Patterns on the Formation of US/Japanese Cooperative Ventures: The Role of Technology," *Columbia Journal of Business,* Summer 1987, pp. 57–65.

48. Allen R. Janger, *Organization of Organizational Joint Ventures* (New York: The Conference Board, 1980), pp. 7–8.

49. David P. Hamilton, "Japanese Chip Makers May Team to Develop Production Methods," *Wall Street Journal,* July 11, 1995, p. A12.

50. Timothy Aeppel, "GM Sets Venture with Poland's FSO to Build Opels," *Wall Street Journal,* March 2, 1992, p. A4.

51. "L. L. Bean Establishes Joint Venture to Open Retail Shop in Japan," *Wall Street Journal,* March 5, 1992, p. A12.

52. Steven A. Baumgarten and Richard J. Rivard, "The Evolution of Conditions for Joint Ventures in China," *Journal of Global Marketing,* vol. 5, nos. 1–2, 1991, p. 192.

53. See, for example, Steven Greenhouse, "Now Is the Time to Invest in the Soviet," *New York Times,* September 1, 1991, sec. 3, pp. 1, 6.

54. For additional insights, see William H. Newman, "'Focused Joint Ventures' in Transforming Economies," *Academy of Management Executive,* vol. 6, no. 1, 1992, pp. 67–75; Keith A. Rosten, "Soviet-U.S. Joint Ventures: Pioneers on a New Frontier," *California Management Review,* Winter 1991, pp. 88–108.

55. For more on this topic, see Eben Shapiro, "Overseas Sizzle for McDonald's," *New York Times,* April 17, 1992, p. C1.

56. For more on exporting, see Negandhi, *International Management,* pp. 403–407.

57. Hammerly, "Global Strategies."

58. Edith Hill Updike, "When in Japan, Do as the Germans Do," *BusinessWeek,* July 3, 1995, p. 43.

59. Martin K. Starr, "Global Production and Operations Strategy," *Columbia Journal of World Business,* Winter 1984, pp. 17–22.

60. Garland and Farmer, *Business Policy and Strategy,* p. 116.

61. Charles W. Neale, David D. Shipley, and J. Colin Dodds, "The Countertrading Experience of British and Canadian Firms," *Management International Review,* vol. 11, no. 1, 1991, pp. 19–35.

ORGANIZING INTERNATIONAL OPERATIONS

OBJECTIVES OF THE CHAPTER

The success of an international firm can be greatly affected by the overall structure and design of operations. There are a wide variety of organizational structures and designs from which to choose. Selecting the most appropriate structure depends on a number of factors, such as the desire of the home office for control over its foreign operations and the demands placed on the overseas unit by both the local market and the personnel who work there.

This chapter first presents and analyzes traditional organizational structures for effective international operations. Then, it explores some of the new, nontraditional organizational arrangements stemming from mergers, joint ventures, and the Japanese concept of *keiretsu*. The specific objectives of this chapter are:

1. **EXAMINE** the major types of organizational structure used in handling international operations.
2. **ANALYZE** the advantages and disadvantages of each type of organizational structure, including the conditions that make one preferable to others.
3. **DESCRIBE** the recent, nontraditional organizational arrangements coming out of mergers, joint ventures, and *keiretsus*.
4. **DISCUSS** the value of subsidiary boards of directors in overseas operations.
5. **EXPLAIN** how organizational characteristics such as formalization, specialization, and centralization influence how the organization is structured and functions.

ORGANIZATIONAL CHALLENGES

During the past decade, an increasing number of MNCs have been rethinking their approach to organizing international operations. A good example is Ford Motor, which recently decided to create a single, worldwide automotive operation with five vehicle centers. Four of these centers, located in the United States, will focus on larger cars, trucks, and sport-utility vehicles, while the fifth will be split between the company's design centers in Dunton, England, and Merkenich, Germany. The purpose of this new organizational design is to develop specific types of cars that will sell worldwide.[1]

This arrangement constitutes the most sweeping reorganization of Ford in over 25 years, and it is a bid to compete better not only in the company's established North American and European markets, but also in the potentially huge car and truck markets that now are emerging in Asia. As a result, Ford's North American Operations and Ford of Europe have been merged into a single operating unit, Ford Automotive Operations, that has a global reach.

This organizational approach goes well beyond cost-cutting. It is designed to transform Ford into a unified company that is a highly nimble, competitive MNC. By the year 2000, Ford intends to merge its South American and Asian operations into this organizational arrangement as well, and to eliminate duplication in product development while allowing the firm to rely on fewer global suppliers. Ford also intends to eliminate 20 percent of its top management and create multifunctional teams to design and market cars—thus effectively cutting its rigid bureaucracy and, among other things, approving new car proposals in less than 30 days![2]

Ford is not alone. The German MNC Mercedes-Benz has been reorganizing its operations and cutting costs sharply in an effort to become increasingly more competitive.[3] In 1993, Mercedes was producing cars that cost 30 percent more than competitive models such as Toyota's Lexus. Mercedes has responded by reorganizing operations, slashing payroll by 13 percent, and setting up auto-assembly sites in France and the United States. As a result, Mercedes has boosted productivity sharply; by 1995, it was able to produce 110,000 more cars per year with fewer people than 2 years earlier. This MNC also is revamping its supplier operations so that it can raise the percentage of components from outside operators from the current 55 percent to 60 percent by the end of the century. Additionally, these reorganizational efforts are helping Mercedes to launch new models and will be critical in ensuring that the firm increases annual production by 70 percent and reaches its goal of 1 million cars annually by the year 2000. In the process, Mercedes believes that it will be able to sell 200,000 A-Class cars per year in Europe at $14,300 or less, while also providing a wide array of more expensive vehicles at $35,000 and up. To a large degree, the success of this effort will depend on Mercedes' ability to continue its efficient reorganization efforts.

BASIC ORGANIZATIONAL STRUCTURES

The examples of Ford and Mercedes show how MNCs are dramatically reorganizing their operations to compete more effectively in the international arena. As with other MNCs following this strategic route, a number of basic organization structures need to be considered. In many cases, the designs are similar to those used domestically; however, significant differences may arise depending on the nature and scope of the overseas businesses and the home office's approach to

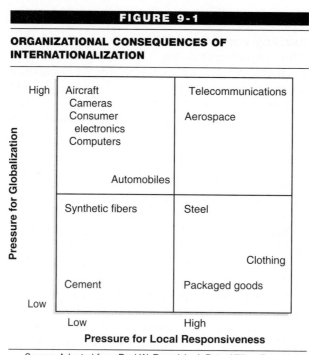

FIGURE 9-1

ORGANIZATIONAL CONSEQUENCES OF INTERNATIONALIZATION

Source: Adapted from Paul W. Beamish, J. Peter Killing, Donald J. LeCraw, and Harold Crookell, *International Management: Text and Cases* (Homewood, IL: Irwin, 1991), p. 99.

controlling the operation. Ideally, an overseas affiliate or subsidiary will be designed to respond to specific concerns, such as production technology or the need for specialized personnel. The overall goal, however, is to meet the needs of both the local market and the home-office strategy of globalization.

Figure 9-1 illustrates how the pressures for globalization versus local responsiveness play out in a host of industries. As an MNC tries to balance these factors, an if–then contingency approach can be used. *If* the strategy needed to respond quickly to the local market changes, *then* there will be accompanying change in the organizational structure. Despite the need for such a flexible, fast-changing, contingency-based approach, most MNCs still slowly evolve through certain structural arrangements in international operations. The following sections examine these structures, beginning with initial, preinternational patterns.[4]

Initial Division Structure

Many firms make their initial entry into international markets by setting up a subsidiary or by exporting locally produced goods or services. A subsidiary is a common organizational arrangement for handling finance-related businesses or other operations that require an on-site presence from the start. In recent years, many service organizations have begun exporting their expertise. Examples include architectural services,[5] legal services, advertising, public relations, accounting, and management consulting.[6] Research and development firms also fall into this category, exporting products that have been successfully developed and marketed locally.[7]

FIGURE 9-2

USE OF SUBSIDIARIES DURING THE EARLY STAGE OF INTERNATIONALIZATION

An export arrangement is a common first choice among manufacturing firms, especially those with technologically advanced products. Because there is little, if any, competition, the firm can charge a premium price and handle sales through an export manager. If the company has a narrow product line, this export manager usually reports directly to the head of marketing, and international operations are co-ordinated by this department. If the firm has a broad product line and intends to export a number of different products into the international market, the export manager will head a separate department and often report directly to the president. These two arrangements work well as long as the company has little competition and is using international sales only to supplement domestic efforts.

If overseas sales continue to increase, local governments often exert pressure in these growing markets for setting up on-site manufacturing operations. A good example is the recent General Motors joint venture in China. For now, the company will ship in parts for local assembly; however, before the end of the decade, between 30 and 40 percent of these parts will be made locally.[8] Additionally, many firms find themselves facing increased competition. Establishing foreign manufacturing subsidiaries can help the MNC to deal with both local government pressures and the competition. The overseas plants show the government that the firm wants to be a good local citizen. At the same time, these plants help the MNC greatly reduce transportation costs, thus making the product more competitive. This new structural arrangement often takes a form similar to that shown in Figure 9-2. Each foreign subsidiary is responsible for operations within its own geographic area, and the head of the subsidiary reports either to a senior executive who is co-ordinating international operations or directly to the home-office CEO.

International Division Structure

If international operations continue to grow, subsidiaries commonly are grouped into an *international division structure*, which handles all international operations

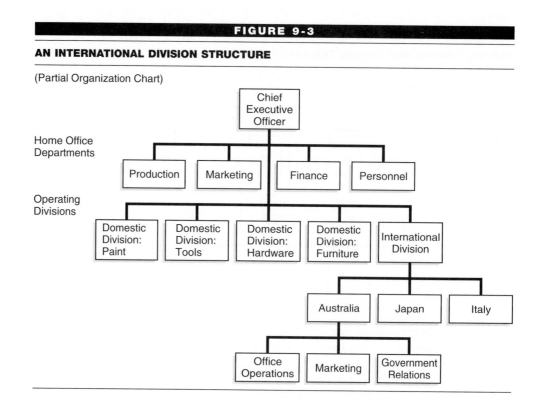

FIGURE 9-3

AN INTERNATIONAL DIVISION STRUCTURE

(Partial Organization Chart)

out of a division that is created for this purpose. This structural arrangement is useful as it takes a great deal of the burden off the chief executive officer for monitoring the operations of a series of overseas subsidiaries as well as domestic operations. The head of the international division co-ordinates and monitors overseas activities and reports directly to the chief executive on these matters. Figure 9-3 provides an example. PepsiCo reorganized its international soft-drink division into six such geographic business units covering 150 countries in which Pepsi does business. These geographic units each have self-sufficient operations and broad local authority.

Companies still in the developmental stages of international business involvement are most likely to adopt the international division structure.[9] Others that use this structural arrangement include those with small international sales, limited geographic diversity, or few executives with international expertise.

A number of advantages are associated with use of an international division structure. The grouping of international activities under one senior executive ensures that the international focus receives top management attention. The structural arrangement allows the company to develop an overall, unified approach to international operations, and the arrangement helps the firm to develop a cadre of internationally experienced managers.

Use of this structure does have a number of drawbacks, however. The structure separates the domestic and international managers, which can result in two different camps with divergent objectives. Also, as the international operation grows larger, the home office may find it difficult to think and act strategically and to allocate resources on a global basis; thus, the international division is penalized.

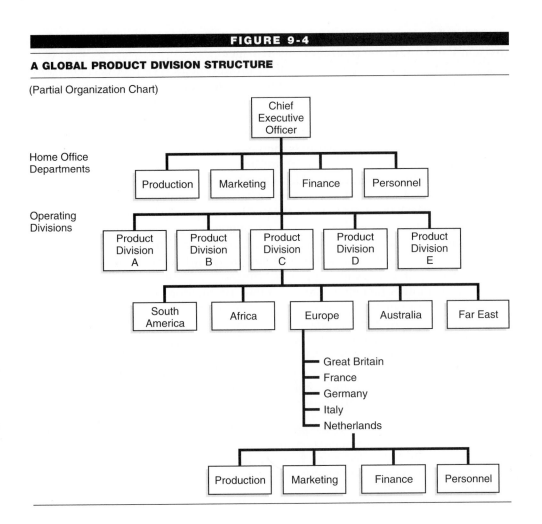

FIGURE 9-4

A GLOBAL PRODUCT DIVISION STRUCTURE

(Partial Organization Chart)

Finally, most research and development efforts are domestically oriented, so ideas for new products or processes in the international market often are given low priority.

Global Structural Arrangements

MNCs typically turn to global structural arrangements when they begin acquiring and allocating their resources based on international opportunities and threats.[10] This international perspective signifies a major change in management strategy, and it is supported by the requisite changes in organization structure.[11] Global structures come in three common types: product, area, and functional.

Global Product Division   A *global product division* is a structural arrangement in which domestic divisions are given worldwide responsibility for product groups. Figure 9-4 provides an illustration. As shown, the manager who is in charge of product division C has authority for this product line on a global basis. This manager also has internal functional support related to the product line. For example, all marketing, production, and finance activities associated with product division C are under the control of this manager.

The global product divisions operate as profit centers. The products generally are in the growth stage of the product life cycle, so they need to be promoted and marketed carefully. In doing so, global product division managers generally run the operation with considerable autonomy; they have the authority to make many important decisions. However, corporate headquarters usually will maintain control in terms of budgetary constraints, home-office approval for certain decisions, and mainly "bottom-line" (i.e., profit) results.

A global product structure provides a number of benefits. If the firm is very diverse (e.g., it produces products using a variety of technologies or has a wide variety of customers), the need to tailor the product to specific demands of the buyer becomes important.[12] A global product arrangement can help to manage this diversity. Another benefit is the ability to cater to local needs. If many geographic areas must have the product modified to suit their particular desires (e.g., foods, toys, or electric shavers), a global product division structure can be extremely important. Still another benefit is that marketing, production, and finance can be co-ordinated on a product-by-product global basis. Firms also use a product division structure when a product has reached the maturity stage in the home country or similar markets but is in the growth stage in others, such as Third World countries. An example might be color televisions or VCRs. These differing life cycles require close technologic and marketing co-ordination between the home and foreign market, which is best done by a product division approach. Other advantages of a global product division structure can be summarized as follows:

> It preserves product emphasis and promotes product planning on a global basis; it provides a direct line of communications from the customer to those in the organization who have product knowledge and expertise, thus enabling research and development to work on development of products that serve the needs of the world customer; and it permits line and staff managers within the division to gain an expertise in the technical and marketing aspects of products assigned to them.[13]

Unfortunately, the approach also has some drawbacks. One is the necessity of duplicating facilities and staff personnel within each division. A second is that division managers may pursue currently attractive geographic prospects for their products and neglect other areas with better long-term potential. A third is that many division managers spend too much time trying to tap the local rather than the international market, because it is more convenient and they are more experienced in domestic operations.

Global Area Division Instead of a global product division, some MNCs prefer to use a *global area division.* In this structure, global operations are organized based on a geographic rather than a product orientation. For example, the MNC may divide international operations into two groups: domestic and foreign, as shown in Figure 9-5. This approach often signals a major change in company strategy, because now international operations are put on the same level as domestic operations. In other words, European or Asian operations are just as important to the company as North American operations. For example, when British Petroleum recently purchased Standard Oil of Ohio, the firm revised its overall structure and adopted a global area division structure.[14]

FIGURE 9-5

A GLOBAL AREA DIVISION STRUCTURE

(Partial Organization Chart)

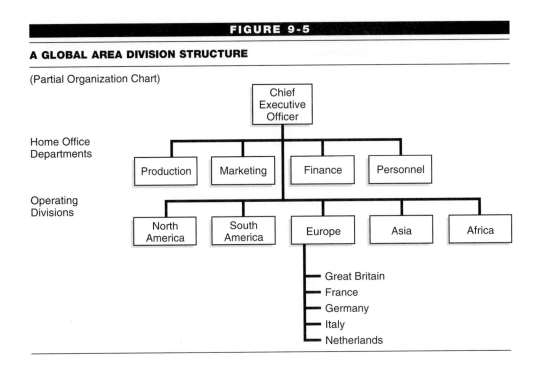

Under this arrangement, global division managers are responsible for all business operations in their designated geographic area. The chief executive officer and other members of top management are charged with formulating strategy that ensures the global divisions all work in harmony. For example, excess resources in one region are transferred to others that need them.

A global area division structure most often is used by companies that are in mature businesses and have narrow product lines. These product lines often are differentiated based on geographic area. For example, the product has a strong demand in Europe but not in South America, or the type of product that is offered in France differs from that sold in England. For example, the French want top-loading washing machines, but the British prefer front-loaders. Toys "R" Us stores in Japan feature a mix of roughly two-thirds Japanese toys and one-third imports.[15] In addition, the MNC usually seeks high economies of scale for production, marketing, and resource-purchase integration in that area. Thus, by manufacturing in this region rather than bringing the product in from somewhere else, the firm is able to reduce its cost per unit and bring the good to market at a very competitive price. Firms that produce autos, beverages, containers, cosmetics, food, or pharmaceuticals often use such a global area arrangement.

The geographic structure allows the division manager to cater to the tastes of the local market and make rapid decisions to accommodate environmental changes. A good example is food products. In the United States, soft drinks have less sugar than in South America, so the manufacturing process must be slightly different in these two locales. Similarly, in England, people prefer bland soups, but in France, the preference is for mildly spicy. In Turkey, Italy, Spain, and Portugal, people like dark, bitter coffee; in the United States, people prefer a milder, sweeter blend. In Europe, Canada, and the United States, people prefer less spicy food; in

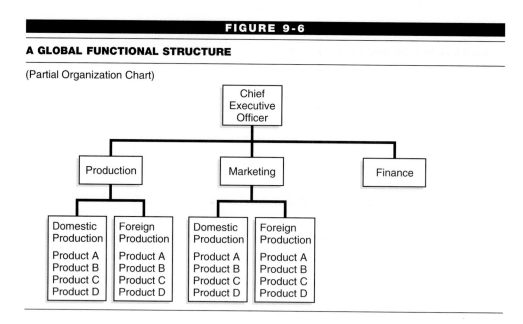

FIGURE 9-6

A GLOBAL FUNCTIONAL STRUCTURE

(Partial Organization Chart)

the Middle East and Asia, they like more heavily spiced food. A global area structure allows the geographic unit in a foods company to accommodate such local preferences.

The primary disadvantage of the global area division structure is the difficulty encountered in reconciling a product emphasis with a geographic orientation. For example, if a product is sold worldwide, a number of different divisions are responsible for sales. This lack of centralized management and control, however, can result in increased costs and duplication of effort on a region-by-region basis. A second drawback is that new research and development efforts often are ignored by division groups, because they are selling goods that have reached the maturity stage. Their focus is not on the latest technologically superior goods that will win in the market in the long run but on those that are proven winners and now are being marketed conveniently worldwide.

Global Functional Division   A *global functional division* organizes worldwide operations based primarily on function and secondarily on product. This approach is not widely used other than by extractive companies, such as oil and mining firms. Figure 9-6 provides an example.

A number of important advantages are associated with the global functional division structure. These include: (1) an emphasis on functional expertise; (2) tight centralized control; and (3) a relatively lean managerial staff. Some important disadvantages include: (1) co-ordination of manufacturing and marketing often is difficult; (2) managing multiple product lines can be difficult because of the separation of production and marketing into different departments; and (3) only the chief executive officer can be held accountable for the profits. As a result, the global functional process structure typically is favored only by those firms that need tight, centralized co-ordination and control of integrated production processes and those that are involved in transporting products and raw materials from one geographic area to another.

FIGURE 9-7

A MULTINATIONAL MATRIX STRUCTURE

(Partial Organization Chart)

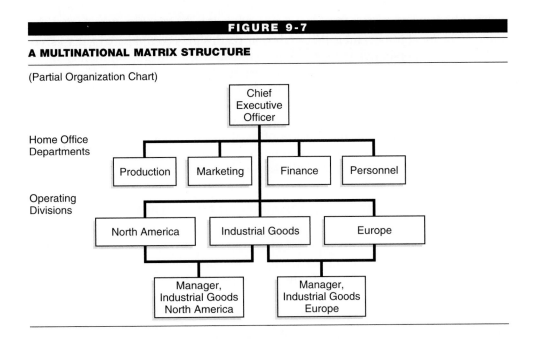

Home Office
Departments

Operating
Divisions

Mixed Organization Structures   Some companies find that neither a global product, area, or functional arrangement is satisfactory. They opt for a *mixed organization structure,* which combines all three into an MNC that supplements its primary structure with a secondary one and, perhaps, a tertiary (third) one. For example, if a company uses a global area approach, committees of functional managers may provide assistance and support to the various geographic divisions. Conversely, if the firm uses a global functional approach, product committees may be responsible for co-ordinating transactions that cut across functional lines. In other cases, the organization will opt for a matrix structure that results in managers' having two or more bosses. Figure 9-7 illustrates this structure. In this arrangement, the MNC co-ordinates geographic and product lines through use of a matrix design.[16]

In recent years, mixed organization structures have become increasingly popular. In one survey, more than one-third of responding firms indicated that they used this mixed organizational arrangement in contrast to others. In addition, respondents reported the following[17]:

International operations organized into national subsidiaries with local co-ordination for production/services, marketing, personnel, etc.	11.8%
International division structure with senior management reporting to the president or CEO of the company.	14.7%
One or more regional headquarters used to co-ordinate production/services, marketing, and personnel among national operations	20.6%
World-production or world-matrix structure used for co-ordination of international operations.	17.6%
Mixed forms of structure.	35.3%

Many advantages can be gleaned from a mixed organization structure. In particular, it allows the organization to create the specific type of design that best meets its needs. However, there are shortcomings associated with matrix structures.[18] The most important is that as the matrix design's complexity increases, coordinating the personnel and getting everyone to work toward common goals often become difficult. Too many groups are going their own way. Thus, many MNCs have not opted for a matrix structure; they are beginning to learn that simple, lean structures may be the best design. For example, well-known consultant Tom Peters claims international firms that became wedded to the matrix concept of organization only kept the illusion of local control intact; in reality, they put "New York-based, English-only-speaking, MBA-toting market modelers in charge of Thailand and Luxembourg and all stops in between."[19]

RECENT, NONTRADITIONAL ORGANIZATIONAL ARRANGEMENTS

In recent years, MNCs have increasingly expanded their operations in ways that differ from those used in the past. These include acquisitions, joint ventures, and *keiretsu*. These new organizational arrangements do not use traditional hierarchical structures and therefore cannot be shown graphically. The following sections describe how they work.

Organizational Arrangements from Mergers

A recent development in the way that MNCs are organized stems from the acquisition of other firms. For example, Siemens, the German electronics giant, purchased Nixdorf Computer of Great Britain, making Siemens the largest European-owned computer maker.[20] Nippon Mining of Japan purchased Gould, the American semiconductor equipment firm; Hoechst, the German chemical and pharmaceutic giant, purchased Marion Merrell Dow[21]; and LG Electronics acquired Zenith.[22] In other cases, MNCs have taken an equity position but have not purchased the entire company. For example, Ford Motor owns 75 percent of Aston Martin Lagonda of Britain, 49 percent of Autolatina of Brazil, and 25 percent of Mazda of Japan.[23] Other examples include Yamanouchi Pharmaceuticals' 29 percent ownership of Roberts Pharmaceuticals, Canon's 16.6 percent interest in Next Computers, and Mitsui's 5 percent ownership of Unisys.[24]

In each of these examples, the purchasing MNCs have fashioned a structural arrangement that promotes synergy while encouraging local initiative by the acquired firm. The result is an organization design that draws on the more traditional structures that have been examined here but still has a unique structure specifically addressing the needs of the two firms.

Organizational Arrangements from Joint Ventures

Another good example of recent organizational developments is joint-venture agreements, in which each party contributes to the undertaking but all parties coordinate their efforts for the overall good of the enterprise.[25] Samsung, the giant Korean MNC, provides a good example. This company now is melding heavy investment, acquisitions, and alliances to dominate markets for multimedia gear, cellular phones, and personal digital assistants. The MNC is very strong in the area of memory chips, but to become a broad-based technology giant, Samsung must rely on strategic alliances. Today, the company has an arrangement with

Motorola to develop the next generation of personal digital assistants based on Motorola's DragonBall microprocessor. Samsung also has alliances with AT&T to create pen-based computers, with Toshiba to make 64-megabyte flash memory chips, with USA Video to create video file servers, and with General Instrument to develop digital television.[26] Another recent example is the Morgan Stanley Group, which has entered a joint venture with the People's Construction Bank of China to create the China International Capital Corporation. Other partners in this venture include the Singapore government and a Hong Kong holding company. The objective is to help win deals involving project financing, direct investment, and both equity and bond offerings at a time when China needs to finance enormous infrastructure projects.[27]

Both of these joint ventures require carefully formulated structures that allow each partner to contribute what it does best and efficiently co-ordinate their efforts. In the case of Samsung, this calls for clearly spelling out the responsibilities of all parties and identifying the authority that each will have for meeting specific targets. In the case of China International Capital Corporation, the organizational structure will be used not only to raise capital but to network with the political structure.[28]

One of the main objectives in developing the structure for joint ventures is to help the partners address and effectively meld their different values, management styles, action orientation, and organization preferences. Figure 9-8 illustrates of how Western and Asian firms differ in terms of these four areas; the figure also is useful in illustrating the types of considerations that need to be addressed by MNCs from the same area of the world. Consider, for example, two Asian MNCs such as Korea's Samsung and Japan's NEC. Samsung has a joint-venture agreement with NEC for developing 256-megabyte DRAM chips. The two firms will need to structure their organizational interface carefully to ensure effective interaction, co-ordination, and co-operation. Simply put, in the case of both Samsung and its partners as well as the China International Capital Corporation and its partners, a mixed structure will be employed to ensure that the joint-venture partners are able to work both efficiently and harmoniously.[29]

Organizational Arrangements from *Keiretsus*

Still another type of newly emerging organizational arrangement is the *keiretsu*, which is a large, often vertically integrated group of companies that co-operate and work closely with each other.[30] A good example is the Mitsubishi Group, which is shown in Figure 9-9. This figure simply shows the members of the Mitsubishi *keiretsu*; it is not intended to be a matrix structure showing authority relationships. This *keiretsu* consists of 28 core members who are bound together not by authority relationships but rather by cross-ownership, long-term business dealings, interlocking directorates, and social ties (many of the senior executives are college classmates). As shown in Figure 9-9, there are three flagship firms in the group: Mitsubishi Corporation, which is a trading company; Mitsubishi Bank, which finances the *keiretsu's* operations; and Mitsubishi Heavy Industries, which is a leading worldwide manufacturer. In addition to the firms in Figure 9-9, hundreds of other Mitsubishi-related companies contribute to the power of the *keiretsu*.[31]

This form of organizational arrangement has been cited by some international management analysts as the reason why Japanese MNCs are so successful.[32] For

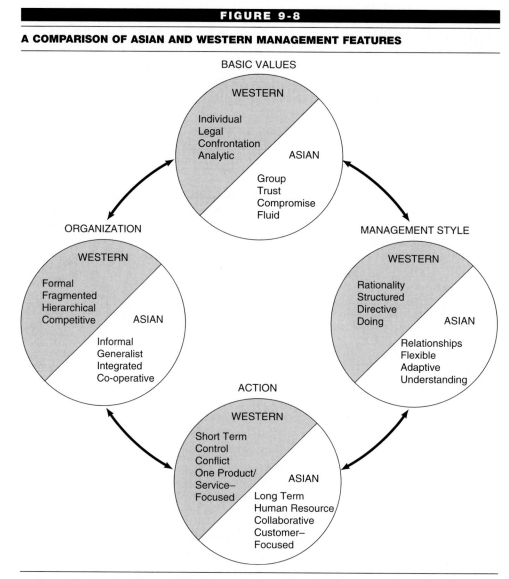

FIGURE 9-8

A COMPARISON OF ASIAN AND WESTERN MANAGEMENT FEATURES

BASIC VALUES

WESTERN
Individual
Legal
Confrontation
Analytic

ASIAN
Group
Trust
Compromise
Fluid

ORGANIZATION

WESTERN
Formal
Fragmented
Hierarchical
Competitive

ASIAN
Informal
Generalist
Integrated
Co-operative

MANAGEMENT STYLE

WESTERN
Rationality
Structured
Directive
Doing

ASIAN
Relationships
Flexible
Adaptive
Understanding

ACTION

WESTERN
Short Term
Control
Conflict
One Product/
Service—
Focused

ASIAN
Long Term
Human Resource
Collaborative
Customer—
Focused

Source: Reprinted from *European Management Journal,* June, Frederic Swierczek and Georges Hirsch, "Joint Ventures in Asia and Multicultural Management," p. 203, © 1994, with kind permission from Elsevier Sciences Ltd., The Boulevard, Langford Lane, Kidlington, OX5 IGB, U.K.

example, although *keiretsu* companies in Japan account for less than 1/10 of 1 percent of all Japanese firms, they account for over one-half of the value of all shares on the Tokyo Stock Exchange, as well as over 50 percent of all Japanese investments made in U.S. high-tech firms and over 50 percent of all Japanese-affiliated manufacturing facilities in California. Quite obviously, these *keiretsus* are very powerful. The Japanese are not the only ones using this organizational arrangement, however. Even large U.S. MNCs are creating their own type of *keiretsus.* Ford Motor, for example, now focuses its attention only on automotive and financial services and has divested itself of most other businesses. In the process of reorganizing, Ford has created a giant, *keiretsu*-like arrangement that includes

FIGURE 9-9

THE MITSUBISHI *KEIRETSU**

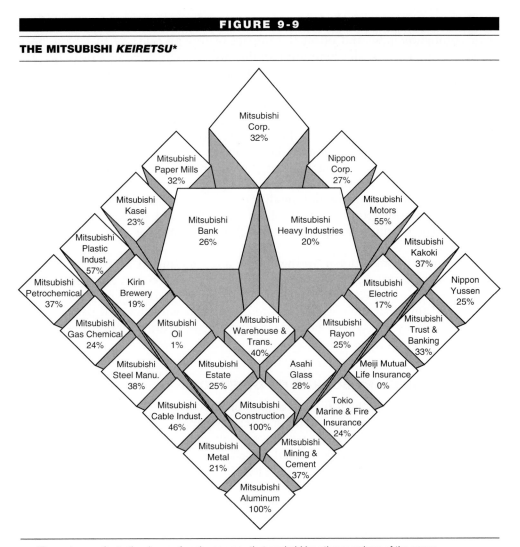

*Percentages refer to the shares of each company that are held by other members of the group.
Source: Adapted from William J. Holstein et al., "Mighty Mitsubishi Is on the Move," *BusinessWeek*, Sept. 24, 1990, pp. 98–104.

research and development (R&D), parts production, vehicle assembly, financial services, and marketing. For example, in R&D, Ford belongs to eight consortia that conduct research in areas such as improved engineering techniques, materials, and electric-car batteries. In parts production, Ford has equity stakes in Cummins (engines), Excel Industries (windows), and Decoma International (body parts, wheels), and it relies on these firms as major suppliers. In vehicle assembly, Ford has ownership interests in Europe, South America, and Asia and uses these arrangements to both manufacture and sell autos in these parts of the world. In financial services, Ford has seven wholly owned units that cover a wide gamut, from consumer credit to commercial lending. In the marketing area, Ford owns 49 percent of Hertz and uses this company as well as other rental car agencies as an outlet for its production.[33]

Ford is not alone. Today, more and more U.S. firms are co-operating to improve their competitiveness and offset the impact of foreign *keiretsus* that have been rapidly moving across the continuum of business activity, from upstream R&D to downstream marketing. For example, in the area of research, there now are more than 250 R&D consortia in the United States that are sharing both costs and information. The Big Three automakers are jointly working on new battery technology for electric cars. In design and production, manufacturers and suppliers are becoming partners; for example, at John Deere, workers now team up with their counterparts at suppliers such as McLaughlin Body Company to improve quality and cut costs. In the financing area, large companies such as Digital Equipment, IBM, and Novellus Systems are taking equity positions or lending money to their strategic suppliers to ensure high-quality parts and on-time delivery. In the marketing area, manufacturers and suppliers are selling and servicing each other's products. For example, Mazda buys vehicles from Ford for sale in the United States, and vice versa.[34]

These new organizational arrangements are resulting in a need for flexible structures that are designed to promote co-operation between enterprises.[35] As the positive effect of *keiretsu*-like arrangements begins to spread, more and more MNCs will find that their structures are interlinked with those of partners and suppliers.[36] The result will be a design that is difficult to draw on paper but that is very effective in practice.

USE OF SUBSIDIARY BOARDS OF DIRECTORS

Organizing begins on the top, with boards of directors. These boards are responsible for overseeing the corporation and ensuring that senior managers are operating in accord with the overall policies and objectives established by the board. As firms increase their international focus, many are finding that subsidiary boards of directors are useful in helping to shape and guide the activities of global operations.

A ***subsidiary board of directors*** oversees and monitors the operations of a foreign subsidiary. In recent years, this organizational arrangement has become increasingly popular. Some of the best-known multinationals use this arrangement, including Dow Chemical; Hewlett-Packard; Pilkington Bros., Ltd.; Honda Motor; and Matsushita Electric.

There are a number of reasons for this trend toward subsidiary boards. The main one is that as the external environment in which MNCs operate becomes extremely complex, rapid decision making gains in importance. To meet this need for immediate response, subsidiaries must be given more authority for local operations. At the same time, however, the corporate board would like to ensure that the subsidiary does not become too autonomous. The solution to this dilemma is a local board, which can play an important linking role between the two groups. The subsidiary board also can assist the unit in planning and controlling activities.

Four major areas in which MNCs use subsidiary boards have been identified. One is to advise, approve, and appraise local management. A second is to help the unit respond to local conditions. A third is to assist in strategic planning, and a fourth is to supervise the subsidiary's ethical conduct. These areas are spelled out in greater detail in Table 9-1, where survey responses from U.S., Canadian, Japanese, and European samples are provided. A close look at the table shows that the

TABLE 9-1				

IMPORTANCE OF SUBSIDIARY BOARDS OVER THE NEXT 5 TO 10 YEARS
Mean Ratings (1 = Low; 5 = High)

	United States (n = 31)	Canada (n = 9)	Japan (n = 14)	Europe, excluding Sweden (n = 28)	Sweden (n = 8)
Local management					
Advising local management	3.50	3.67	4.15	3.43	4.00
Approving budgets and short-term plans of the subsidiary	2.48	3.00	4.36	2.75	3.13
Monitoring operating performance and corrective measures in the subsidiary	2.81	3.00	4.00	2.71	3.38
Appraising the subsidiary's top management performance and top officers' compensation	2.10	2.33	3.64	2.46	2.63
Deciding the amount to remit as dividends	2.39	2.33	3.57	2.18	2.00
Local country contacts and conditions					
Facilitating the establishment of contacts with local leaders and institutions	2.90	3.56	3.62	3.32	3.88
Identifying and responding to concerned stakeholders (e.g., environmentalists and consumer groups)	2.10	1.44	3.50	1.68	1.00
Ensuring compliance with local legal requirements	3.50	2.67	4.23	3.00	3.75
Providing knowledge of local economic, political, and social conditions	3.48	3.44	4.00	3.39	4.25
Appraising and minimizing the subsidiary's political risk	3.00	2.89	3.79	2.57	2.57
Strategic plan					
Participating in drawing up the subsidiary's strategic plan	2.52	3.00	4.29	2.54	2.88
Ethical issues					
Supervising the subsidiary's ethical conduct	2.94	2.67	3.64	2.82	2.75

Source: Adapted from Mark P. Kriger and Patrick J. J. Rich, "Strategic Governance: Why and How MNCs Are Using Boards of Directors in Foreign Subsidiaries," *Columbia Journal of World Business,* Winter 1987, p. 43. Copyright 1987, reprinted with permission.

Japanese and the Swedes tend to place greater importance on these boards than Europeans and Americans, although all countries report important benefits from the use of these boards. Will the future see increasing use of this organizational arrangement? Very likely, the answer is yes.

ORGANIZATIONAL CHARACTERISTICS OF MNCs

Although MNCs have similar organizational structures, they do not all operate the same way. A variety of factors have been identified that help to explain the differences. These include overall strategy, employee attitudes, and local conditions. Of particular significance to this discussion are the organizational characteristics of formalization, specialization, and centralization.

Formalization

Formalization is the use of defined structures and systems in decision making, communicating, and controlling. Some countries make greater use of formalization than others; in turn, this affects the day-to-day organizational functioning. A recent large research study of Korean firms found that unlike employees in the United States, Korean workers perceive more positive work environments when expectations for their jobs are set forth more strictly and formally. In short, Koreans respond very favorably to formalization.[37] Korean firms tend to be quite formal, but this may not hold throughout Asia. For example, a study that investigated whether Japanese organizations are more formalized than U.S. organizations found that although Japanese firms tend to use more labor-intensive approaches to areas such as bookkeeping and office-related work than their U.S. counterparts, no statistical data support the contention that Japanese firms are more formalized.[38]

A more recent study of U.S. and Japanese firms in Taiwan divided formalization into two categories: objective and subjective.[39] Objective formalization was measured by things such as the number of different documents given to employees, organizational charts, information booklets, operating instructions, written job descriptions, procedure manuals, written policies, and work-flow schedules and programs. Subjective formalization was measured by the extent to which goals were vague and unspecified, use of informal controls, and use of culturally induced values in getting things done. The findings of this study are reported in Table 9-2.

Commenting on differences in the use of formalization, the researchers concluded that

> American and Japanese firms appear to have almost the same level of written goals or objectives for subordinates, written standards of performance appraisals, written schedules, programs, and work specifications, written duties, authority and accountability. However, managers in Japanese firms perceive less formalization than do managers in American firms. Less reliance on formal rules and structure in Japanese firms is also revealed by the emphasis on face-to-face or behavioral mode of control indicated by the ratio of foreign expatriates to total employees in subsidiaries.[40]

The study also found that U.S. MNCs tend to rely heavily on budgets, financial data, and other formalized tools in controlling their subsidiary operations. This contrasts with Japanese MNCs, in which wider use is made of face-to-face, informal controls. These findings reveal that although the outward structural design of overseas subsidiaries may appear to be similar, the internal functioning in characteristics such as formalization may be quite different.

In recent years, this formal/informal characteristic of organizations has become the focal point of increased attention.[41] One reason is because MNCs now realize there are two dimensions of formality/informality that must be considered: internal and external. Moreover, to a large degree, these formal/informal relationships require effective networking of a different type. As Yoshino and Rangan noted, there are

> two approaches that firms that must compete globally—and that includes most major firms—employ to achieve the layering of competitive advantages: (1) development of extensive *internal networks* of international subsidiaries in major national or regional markets and (2) forging *external networks* of strategic alliances with firms around the

---

TABLE 9-2

ORGANIZATIONAL CHARACTERISTICS OF U.S. AND JAPANESE FIRMS IN TAIWAN

Characteristics	U.S. firms ($n = 38$)	Japanese firms ($n = 85$)
Formalization (subjective)	3.54	3.47
Formalization (objective)	11.39	10.91
Horizontal specialization	12.89	10.02
Vertical specialization	7.04	7.75
Job routinization	2.25	2.86
Job autonomy	2.78	2.62
Foreign expatriates per 1000 employees	4.2	16.6
Ratio of firms using quality circles (in percentages)	24	32

Note: The highest score for the subjective formalization index, job routinization index, and autonomy index is 6; the lowest score is 1. The highest score for the objective formalization index is 19; the lowest score is 0. The highest score for the horizontal specialization index is 16; the lowest score is 0. Ratios of foreign expatriates to total employees are calculated on the basis of firms with 50 or more employees.

Source: Adapted from Rhy-song Yeh and Tagi Sagafi-nejad, "Organizational Characteristics of American and Japanese Firms in Taiwan," *National Academy of Management Proceedings,* 1987, p. 113. Used with permission.

TABLE 9-3

INTERNAL VS. EXTERNAL NETWORKS

Managerial dimensions	Internal network	External network
Shared vision	Yes	No
Animating mindset	Co-operation	Co-operation and competition
Organizational mandates	Clear	Ambiguous
Organizational objective	Global optimization	Develop win–win approaches
Emphasis on systems	More	Less
Emphasis on people	Less	More
Lines of authority	Clear	Ambiguous at best

Source: Information drawn from Michael Yoshino and N. S. Rangan, *Strategic Alliances* (Boston: Harvard Business School Press, 1995), p. 203.

world. These approaches are not mutually exclusive, and increasingly firms are striving to build both types of networks.[42]

What is particularly interesting about these networking relationships is that each places a different set of demands on the MNC. In particular, external networking with joint-venture partners often involves ambiguous organizational mandates, less emphasis on systems and more on people, and ambiguous lines of authority. This is a marked difference from internal networking characteristics, where formality is much stronger than informality and the enterprise can rely on a shared vision, clear organizational mandates, and well-developed systems and lines of authority.[43] Table 9-3 summarizes the characteristics of these internal and external networks.

Specialization

As an organizational characteristic, *specialization* is the assigning of individuals to specific, well-defined tasks. Specialization in an international context can be classified into horizontal and vertical specialization.

Horizontal specialization assigns jobs so that individuals are given a particular function to perform, and people tend to stay within the confines of this area. Examples include jobs in areas such as customer service, sales, recruiting, training, purchasing, and marketing research. When there is a great deal of horizontal specialization, personnel will develop functional expertise in one particular area.

Vertical specialization assigns work to groups or departments where individuals are collectively responsible for performance. Vertical specialization also is characterized by distinct differences between levels in the hierarchy such that those higher up are accorded much more status than those further down, and the overall structure usually is quite tall.

In the earlier, comparative study of 55 U.S. and 51 Japanese manufacturing plants, Japanese organizations had lower functional specialization of employees. Specifically, three-quarters of the functions listed were assigned to specialists in the U.S. plants, but less than one-third were assigned in the Japanese plants.[44] Later studies with regard to formalization have echoed this finding on specialization. As shown in Table 9-2, U.S. subsidiaries have more specialists than Japanese firms do.

By contrast, studies find that the Japanese rely more heavily on vertical specialization. They have taller organization structures in contrast to the flatter designs of their U.S. counterparts. Japanese departments and units also are more differentiated than those in U.S. organizations. Vertical specialization can be measured by the amount of group activity as well, such as in quality circles. Table 9-2 shows that Japanese firms make much greater use of quality circles than the U.S. firms. Vertical specialization also can result in greater job routinization. Because everyone is collectively responsible for the work, strong emphasis is placed on everyone's doing the job in a predetermined way, refraining from improvising, and structuring the work so that everyone can do the job after a short training period. Again, Table 9-4 shows that the Japanese organizations make much wider use of job routinization than U.S. organizations.

Centralization

Centralization is a management system in which important decisions are made at the top. In an international context, the value of centralization will vary according to the local environment and the goals of the organization. Many U.S. firms tend toward *decentralization,* pushing decision making down the line and getting the lower-level personnel involved. German MNCs centralize strategic headquarter-specific decisions independent of the host country and decentralize operative decisions in accordance with the local situation in the host country.[45] The accompanying sidebar, "Organizing in Germany," describes how relatively small German MNCs have been very successful with such a decentralization strategy. A comparative study found that Japanese organizations delegate less formal authority than their U.S. counterparts, but the Japanese permit greater involvement in decisions by employees lower in the hierarchy. At the same time, however, the

TABLE 9-4

MANAGERS' INFLUENCE IN U.S. AND JAPANESE FIRMS IN TAIWAN

Managers' work-related activity	U.S. firm average	Japanese firm average
Assigning work to subordinates	4.72	3.96
Disciplining subordinates	4.07	3.82
Controlling subordinates' work (quality and pace)	3.99	3.82
Controlling salary and promotion of subordinates	3.81	3.18
Hiring and placing subordinates	3.94	3.24
Setting the budget for own unit	3.45	3.16
Co-ordinating with other units	3.68	3.52
Influencing policy related to own work	3.22	2.85
Influencing policy not related to own work	2.29	1.94
Influencing superiors	3.02	3.00

Note: The highest score of means is 5 (very great influence); the lowest score is 1 (very little influence). The *T*-value for all scores is significant at the .01 level.

Source: Adapted from Rhy-song Yeh and Tagi Sagafi-nejad, "Organizational Characteristics of American and Japanese Firms in Taiwan," *National Academy of Management Proceedings*, 1987, p. 114. Used with permission.

Japanese manage to maintain strong control over their lower-level personnel by limiting the amount of authority given to the latter and carefully controlling and orchestrating worker involvement and participation in quality circles.[46] Other studies show similar findings.[47]

When evaluating the presence of centralization by examining the amount of autonomy that Japanese give to their subordinates, one study concluded:

> In terms of job autonomy, employees in American firms have greater freedom to make their decisions and their own rules than in Japanese firms. . . . Results show that managers in American firms perceive a higher degree of delegation than do managers in Japanese firms. Also, managers in American firms feel a much higher level of participation in the coordinating with other units, . . . in influencing the company's policy related to their work, and in influencing the company's policy in areas not related to their work.[48]

The finding related to influence is explained in more detail in Table 9-4; U.S. managers in Taiwanese subsidiaries felt that they had greater influence than did their Japanese counterparts. Moreover, when statistically analyzed, these data proved to be significant.

Putting Organizational Characteristics in Perspective

MNCs tend to organize their international operations in a manner similar to that used at home. If the MNC tends to have high formalization, specialization, and centralization at its home-based headquarters, these organizational characteristics probably will occur in the firm's international subsidiaries.[49] Japanese and U.S. firms are good examples. As the researchers of the comparative study in Taiwan concluded: "Almost 80 percent of Japanese firms and more than 80 percent of American firms in the sample have been operating in Taiwan for about ten years,

Organizing in Germany

By 1993, Europe was well into an economic slump that gave every indication of being both deep and prolonged. German labor unions, the most powerful in Europe, were having to give ground, and major corporations were scaling back operations and reporting losses. At the same time, a number of medium- and small-sized German companies continued to be some of the most successful in the world. Part of this success resulted from their carefully designed decentralized organization structures, a result of company efforts to remain close to the customer. The goal of these German MNCs is to establish operations in overseas locales, where they can provide on-site assistance to buyers. Moreover, these subsidiaries in most cases are wholly owned by the company and have centralized controls on profits.

A common practice among German MNCs is to overserve the market by providing more than is needed. For example, when the auto firm BMW entered Japan in 1981, its initial investment was several times higher than that required to run a small operation; however, its high visibility and commitment to the market helped to create customer awareness and build local prestige.

Another strategy is to leave expatriate managers in their positions for extended periods of time. In this way, they become familiar with the local culture and thus the market, and they are better able to respond to customer needs as well as problems. As a result, customers get to know the firm's personnel and are more willing to do repeat business with them.

Still another strategy the German MNCs use is to closely mesh the talents of the people with the needs of the customers. For example, there is considerable evidence that most customers value product quality, closeness to the customer, service, economy, helpful employees, technologic leadership, and innovativeness. The German firms will overperform in the area that is most important and thus further bond themselves to the customer.

A final strategy is to develop strong self-reliance so that when problems arise, they can be handled with in-house personnel. This practice is a result of German companies' believing strongly in specialization and concentration of effort. They tend to do their own research and to master production and service problems so that if there is a problem, they can resolve it without having to rely on outsiders.

How well do these German organizing efforts pay off? Many of these relatively small companies hold world market shares in the 70 to 90 percent range. These are companies that no one has ever heard about, such as Booder (fish-processing machines), Gehring (honing machines), Korber/Hauni (cigarette machines), Marklin & Cle (model railways), Stihl (chain saws), and Webasto (sunroofs for cars). Even so, every one of these companies is the market leader not only in Europe but also in the world, and in some cases, its relative market strength is up to 10 times greater than that of the nearest competitor.

but they maintain the traits of their distinct cultural origins even though they have been operating in the same (Taiwanese) environment for such a long time."[50]

These findings also reveal that many enterprises view their international operations as extensions of their domestic operations, thus disproving the widely held belief that convergence occurs between overseas operations and local customs. In other words, there is far less of an "international management melting pot" than many people realize. European countries are finding that as they attempt to unify and do business with each other, differing cultures (languages, religions, and values) are very difficult to overcome.

One challenge for the years ahead will be bringing subsidiary organizational characteristics more into line with local customs and cultures. Besides the countries of the EU, the Japanese firms operating in the United States provide another excellent example. Their failure to accept U.S. social values sometimes has resulted in employment and promotion discrimination lawsuits as well as backlashes from workers who feel they are being overworked and forced to abide by rules and regulations that were designed for use in Japan. For example, Honda of

America agreed to give 370 African-Americans and women a total of $6 million in back pay to resolve a federal discrimination complaint brought against the company.

SUMMARY OF KEY POINTS

1. A number of different organizational structures are used in international operations. Many MNCs begin by using an export manager or subsidiary to handle overseas business. As the operation grows or the company expands into more markets, the firm often will opt for an international division structure. Further growth may result in adoption of a global structural arrangement, such as a global production division, global area division structure, global functional division, or a mixture of these structures.

2. Although MNCs still use the various structural designs that can be drawn in an hierarchical manner, they recently have begun merging or acquiring other firms or parts of other firms, and the resulting organizational arrangements are quite different from those of the past. The same is true of the many joint ventures now taking place across the world. Perhaps the biggest change, however, stems from the Japanese concept of *keiretsu*, which involves the vertical integration and co-operation of a group of companies. Although the Mitsubishi Group, with its 28 core member firms, is the best example of this organizational arrangement, U.S. MNCs also are moving in this direction.

3. Some multinationals have subsidiary boards of directors that oversee and monitor the operations of a foreign subsidiary. As MNCs' worldwide operations increase, these boards likely will gain in popularity.

4. A variety of factors help to explain differences in the way that international firms operate. Three organizational characteristics that are of particular importance are formalization, specialization, and centralization. These characteristics often vary from country to country, so that Japanese firms will conduct operations differently from U.S. firms. When MNCs set up international subsidiaries, they often use the same organizational techniques they do at home without necessarily adjusting their approach to better match the local conditions.

KEY TERMS

international division structure
global product division
global area division
global functional division
mixed organization structure
keiretsu
subsidiary board of directors

formalization
specialization
horizontal specialization
vertical specialization
centralization
decentralization

REVIEW AND DISCUSSION QUESTIONS

1. A small manufacturing firm believes there is a market for hand-held tools that are carefully crafted for local markets. After spending 2 months in Europe, the president of this firm believes that his company can create a popular line of these tools. What type of organization structure would be of most value to this firm in its initial efforts to go international?

2. If the company in question 1 finds a major market for its products in Europe and decides to expand into Asia, would you recommend any change in its organization structure? If yes, what would you suggest? If no, why not?

3. If this same company finds after 3 years of international effort it is selling 50 percent of its output overseas, what type of organizational structure would you suggest for the future?

4. Why are *keiretsus* becoming so popular? What benefits do they offer? How can small international firms profit from this development? Give an example.

5. In what way do formalization, specialization, and centralization have an impact on MNC organization structures? In your answer, use a well-known firm such as IBM or Ford to illustrate the effects of these three characteristics.

PRACTICAL INTERNATIONAL MANAGEMENT ASSIGNMENT

Using Figures 9-2 through 9-7 as your point of reference, interview an international manager or foreign student with intimate knowledge of organizations in either South America, Canada, a European country, or an Asian country (other than Japan). Based on your information, what conclusions can you draw regarding the type of organization described. How does it relate to one (or more) of the designs found in Figures 9-2 through 9-7?

There is nothing an Australian likes better than to chat it up with a stranger at a pub.

In the International Spotlight

Australia

Australia is the smallest continent but the sixth-largest country in the world. It lies between the Indian and the Pacific Oceans in the southern hemisphere and has a land mass of almost 3 million square miles (around 85 percent the size of the United States). Referred to as being "down under" because it lies entirely within the southern hemisphere, it is a dry, thinly populated land. The outback is famous for its bright sunshine, enormous numbers of sheep and cattle, and unusual wildlife, such as kangaroos, koalas, platypuses, and wombats. Over 17 million people live in this former British colony, and 20 million are projected by the turn of the century. Although many British customs are retained, Australians have developed their own unique way of life. One of the world's most developed countries, Australia operates under a democratic form of government somewhat similar to that of Great Britain. Gross national product is over $400 billion, with the largest economic sectors being services, trade, and manufacturing.

A large financial-services MNC in the United States has been examining the demographic and economic data of Australia. This MNC has concluded that there will be increased demand for financial services in Australia during the next few years. As a result, the company is setting up an operation in the capital, Canberra, which is slightly inland from the two largest cities of Sydney and Melbourne.

This financial-service firm began in Chicago and now has offices in seven countries. Many of these foreign operations are closely controlled by the Chicago office. The overseas personnel are charged with carefully following instructions from headquarters and implementing centralized decisions. However, the Australian operation will be run differently. Because the country is so large and the population spread along the coast and to Perth in the west, and because of the "free spirit" cultural values of the Aussies, the home office feels compelled to give the manager of Australian operations full control over decision making. This manager will have a small number of senior-level managers brought from the United States, but the rest of the personnel will be hired locally. The office will be given sales and profit goals, but specific implementation of strategy will be left to the manager and his or her key subordinates on site.

The home office believes that in addition to providing direct banking and credit card services, the Australian operation should seek to gain a strong foothold in insurance and investment services. As the country continues to grow economically, this sector of the industry should increase relatively fast. Moreover, few multinational firms are trying to tap this market in Australia, and those that are doing so are from British Commonwealth countries. The CEO believes that the experience of the people being sent to Australia (the U.S. expatriates) will be particularly helpful in developing this market. He recently noted, "We know that the needs of the Australian market are not as sophisticated or complex as those in the United States, but we also know that they are moving in the same direction as we are. So we intend to tap our experience and knowledge and use it to garner a commanding share of this expanding market."

1. What are some current issues facing Australia? What is the climate for doing business in Australia today?

2. What type of organizational structure arrangement is the MNC going to use in setting up its Australian operation?

3. Can this MNC benefit from any of the new organizational arrangements, such as a joint venture or the Japanese concept of *keiretsu?*

4. Will this operation be basically centralized or decentralized?

You Be the International Management Consultant

Getting in on the Ground Floor

The EU currently is developing a strategy that will help member countries beat back the threat of U.S. and Japanese competition and develop a strong technological base for new product development. European multinational firms currently are strong in a number of different areas. For example, Germany's Hoechst and BASF and Switzerland's Sandoz and Hoffman-LaRoche are major companies in chemicals and pharmaceutics. Philips of the Netherlands invented compact discs and is dominant in the television market. Many strong European-based MNCs could provide a solid base for the EU to defend itself from outside economic invasion.

Ruehter Laboratories, a high-tech R&D firm located in New Jersey, holds a number of important pharmaceutic patents and would like to expand its operations worldwide. The company is considering buying a small, but highly profitable, Dutch insulin-maker. "This acquisition will help us enter the European market by getting in on the ground floor," noted the president.

Although the Dutch firm is quite small, it has strong R&D prowess and likely will play a major role in biotechnology research during the years ahead. Ruehter has talked to the Dutch firm, and the two have arrived at a mutually acceptable selling price. While waiting for the lawyers to work out the final arrangements, Ruehter intends to reorganize its overall operations so that the home-office management can work more closely with its new Dutch subsidiary. There are three areas that Ruehter intends to address in its reorganization efforts: (1) how the subsidiary will be structurally integrated into the current organization; (2) whether a subsidiary board will be an effective method of overseeing the Dutch operation; and (3) whether there can be any joint R&D efforts between the two groups.

1. What type of organization design would you recommend that Ruehter use?
2. Would a subsidiary board of directors be of any value in overseeing the Dutch operation?
3. If there were joint R&D efforts, would this be a problem?

CHAPTER 9 ENDNOTES

1. James Bennet, "Ford Revamps with Eye on the Globe," *New York Times*, April 22, 1994, p. C1.
2. James B. Treece, Kathleen Kerwin, and Heidi Hawley, "Ford: Alex Trotman's Daring Global Strategy," *BusinessWeek*, April 3, 1995, pp. 94–104.
3. John Templeman, "Mercedes Can't Shift into Cruise Control Yet," *BusinessWeek*, April 17, 1995, p. 58.
4. See George S. Yip, *Total Global Strategy* (Englewood Cliffs, NJ: Prentice-Hall, 1995), Chapter 8.
5. "Hong Kong Chooses Mott Connel Group to Design Airport," *The Wall Street Journal*, March 3, 1992, p. A6.
6. James D. Thayer, "Exporting Expertise: The Competitive Outlook for U.S. Service Firms in the EC," *Journal of European Business*, May/June 1991, pp. 19–25.
7. Pari Patel and Keith Kavitt, "Large Firms in the Production of the World's Technology: An Important Case of Non-Globalization," *Journal of International Business Studies*, vol. 22, no. 1, 1991, pp. 1–21.
8. Neal Templin, "GM to Assemble Trucks in China in a Joint Venture," *Wall Street Journal*, January 16, 1992, p. A8.
9. A. V. Phatak, *International Dimensions of Management*, 2nd ed. (Boston: PWS-Kent, 1989), p. 85.
10. James Bennet, "Eurocars: On the Road Again," *New York Times*, August 20, 1995, Section 3, pp. 1, 10.
11. See Karen Lowry Miller, "Siemens Shapes Up," *BusinessWeek*, May 1, 1995, pp. 52–53.
12. Valerie Reitman and Gabriella Stern, "Adapting a U.S. Car to Japanese Tastes," *Wall Street Journal*, June 26, 1995, pp. B1, B6.
13. Phatak, *International Dimensions*, pp. 92–93.
14. Peter Siddall, Keith Willey, and Jorge Tavares, "Building a Transnational Organization for BP Oil," *Long Range Planning*, vol. 25, no. 1, 1992, pp. 37–45.
15. Alan M. Rugman and Richard M. Hodgetts, *International Business* (New York: McGraw-Hill, 1995), p. 79.
16. For more on matrix organizations, see Andre Laurent, "Matrix Organizations and Latin Cultures," *International Studies of Management & Organization*, Winter 1980, pp. 101–114.
17. Reported in Peter J. Dowling, Randall S. Schuler, and Denice E. Welch, *International Dimensions of Human Resource Management*, 2nd ed. (Belmont, CA: Wadsworth Publishing, 1994), p. 33.
18. Christopher A. Bartlett and Sumantra Ghoshal, *Transnational Management: Text, Cases, and Readings in Cross-Border Management* (Homewood, IL: Irwin, 1992), pp. 517–518.
19. Tom Peters, *Thriving on Chaos* (New York: Alfred A. Knopf, 1987), p. 357.
20. Gail E. Shares, Jonathan B. Levine, and Peter Coy, "The New Generation at Siemens," *BusinessWeek*, March 9, 1992, p. 47.
21. Milt Freudenheim, "Hoechst to Pay $7.1 Billion for Dow Unit," *New York Times*, May 5, 1995, pp. C1, C5.
22. Laxmi Nakarmi, Richard A. Melcher, and Edith Updike, "Will Lucky Goldstar Reach Its Peak with Zenith?" *BusinessWeek*, August 7, 1995, p. 40.
23. *BusinessWeek*, January 27, 1992, p. 55.
24. *Fortune*, June 15, 1992, p. 116.
25. For some examples, see Paul Lawrence and Charalambos Vlachoutsicos, "Joint Ventures in Russia: Put the Locals in Charge," *Harvard Business Review*, January-February 1993, pp. 44–54; Jonathan B. Levine, "This Splice Could Be Golden," *BusinessWeek*, February 8, 1993, pp. 36–38; and Barnaby J. Feder, "Cummins Komatsu Form Pact," *The New York Times*, February 17, 1993, pp. C1, C6.
26. Laxmi Nakarmi, Kevin Kelly, and Larry Armstrong, "Look Out World—Samsung Is Coming," *BusinessWeek*, August 7, 1995, p. 53.
27. Seth Faison, "Morgan Stanley Establishes a Joint Venture in China," *New York Times*, August 12, 1995, p. 18.
28. For some insights regarding the importance of networking, see "The Battle for Ukraine," *Economist*, February 11, 1995, p. 56.
29. For an example of a venture in disarray, see Peter Galuszka and Susan Chandler, "A Plague of Disjointed Ventures," *BusinessWeek*, May 1, 1995, p. 55.
30. Robert L. Cutts, "Capitalism in Japan: Cartels and *Keiretsu*," *Harvard Business Review*, July-August 1992, pp. 48–55.
31. William J. Holstein et al., "Mighty Mitsubishi Is on the Move," *BusinessWeek*, September 24, 1990, pp. 98–104.
32. See Michele Kremen Bolton, Robert Malmrose, and William G. Ouchi, "The Organization of Innovation in the United States and Japan: Neoclassical and Relational Contracting," *Journal of Management Studies*, September 1994, pp. 653–679.
33. "Ford's *Keiretsu*," *BusinessWeek*, January 27, 1992, p. 55.
34. James B. Treece, Karen Lowrey Miller, and Richard A. Melcher, "The Partners," *BusinessWeek*, February 10, 1992, pp. 102–107.
35. For some additional insights, see Jon I. Martinez and J. Carlos Jarillo, "Cooperation Demands of International Strategies," *Journal of International Business Studies*, vol. 22, no. 3, 1992, pp. 429–444.
36. "*Keiretsu*, American Style," *BusinessWeek*, January 27, 1992, p. 110.

37. Steven M. Sommers, Seung-Hyun Bae, and Fred Luthans, "The Structure-Climate Relationship in Korean Organizations," *Asia Pacific Journal of Management*, vol. 12, no. 2, 1995, pp. 23–36.

38. James R. Lincoln, Mitsuyo Hanada, and Kerry McBride, "Organizational Structures in Japanese and U.S. Manufacturing," *Administrative Science Quarterly*, September 1986, p. 356.

39. Rhy-song Yeh and Tagi Sagafi-nejad, "Organizational Characteristics of American and Japanese Firms in Taiwan," *National Academy of Management Proceedings*, 1987, pp. 111–115.

40. Ibid., p. 113.

41. Abbass F. Alkhafaji, *Competitive Global Management: Principles and Strategies* (Delray Beach, FL: St. Lucie Press, 1995), pp. 390–391.

42. Michael Yoshino and N.S. Rangan, *Strategic Alliances* (Boston: Harvard Business School Press, 1995), p. 195.

43. For additional insights, see Anant K. Sundaram and J. Stewart Black, *The International Business Environment: Text and Cases* (Englewood Cliffs, NJ: Prentice-Hall, 1995), pp. 314–315.

44. Lincoln, Hanada, and McBride, "Organizational Structures," p. 349.

45. M. K. Welge, "A Comparison of Managerial Structures in German Subsidiaries in France, India, and the United States," *Management International Review*, vol. 21, no. 2, 1981, p. 12.

46. Lincoln, Hanada, and McBride, "Organizational Structures," p. 355.

47. Masumi Tsuda, "The Future of the Organization and the Individual to Japanese Management," *International Studies of Management & Organization*, Fall-Winter 1985, pp. 89–125.

48. Yeh and Sagafi-nejad, "Organizational Characteristics," p. 113.

49. Also see Valerie Reitman, "Toyota Names a New Chief Likely to Shake Up Global Auto Business," *Wall Street Journal*, August 11, 1995, pp. A1, A4.

50. Tsuda, "The Future of the Organization," p. 114.

INTERCULTURAL COMMUNICATION

OBJECTIVES OF THE CHAPTER

Communication takes on special importance in international management because of the difficulties in conveying meanings between parties from different cultures. The problems of misinterpretation and error are compounded in the international context. Chapter 10 examines how the communication process in general works, and it looks at the downward and upward communication flows that commonly are used in international communication. Then, the chapter examines the major barriers to effective international communication and reviews ways of dealing with these communication problems. The specific objectives of this chapter are:

1. **DEFINE** the term "communication," and examine some examples of external and internal communication.
2. **REVIEW** examples of explicit and implicit communication, and explain the importance of message interpretation.
3. **ANALYZE** the common downward and upward communication flows used in international communication.
4. **EXAMINE** the language, perception, culture, and nonverbal barriers to effective international communication.
5. **PRESENT** the steps that can be taken to overcome international communication problems.

TABLE 10-1

TOPICS OF CONVERSATION IN SELECT COUNTRIES

Country	Appropriate Topic	Inappropriate Topic
Austria	Cars, skiing, music	Money, religion, divorce/separation
France	Music, books, sports, theater	Prices of items; person's work, income, age
Germany	Travel abroad, hobbies, soccer, international politics	World War II, questions about personal life
Great Britain	History, architecture, gardening	Politics, money, prices
Japan	History, culture, art	World War II, government policies that help to exclude foreign competition
Mexico	Family, social concerns	Politics, debt or inflation problems, border violations

Source: Lillian H. Chaney and Jeanette S. Martin, *Intercultural Business Communication* © 1995, p. 102. Reprinted by permission of Prentice-Hall, Inc. Englewood Cliffs, New Jersey.

FIGURE 10-1

THE COMMUNICATION PROCESS

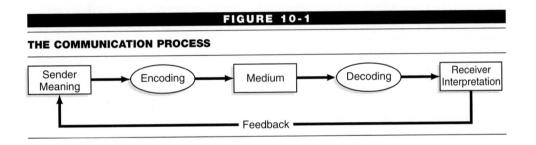

THE OVERALL COMMUNICATION PROCESS

Communication is the process of transferring meanings from sender to receiver. On the surface, this appears to be a fairly straightforward process. On analysis, however, there are a great many problems in the international arena that can result in the failure to transfer meanings correctly. One of these is the inability to effectively establish rapport with the other side. For example, many expatriates who have not been adequately trained will bring up conversation topics that more experienced international managers know should be avoided. Table 10-1 provides a brief list of some of do's and the don't's. When an inappropriate topic arises, communication breakdown likely will result, because the other party interprets the message differently from what was intended.[1]

In gaining some insights to this communication process, it is helpful to examine Figure 10-1. As shown, the sender of a message will determine what he or she wants to say and then encode the message to convey his or her meanings. The communiqué then is transmitted using some medium, such as telephone, letter, or face-to-face verbal interaction. Finally, the message is decoded and interpreted by the receiver. If the message is unclear or the receiver feels that a response is required, the process then is reversed: the receiver now becomes the sender, and the sender becomes the receiver. This reverse flow of information is achieved through feedback, which creates a two-way process. In practice, this back-and-forth flow of meanings is used to clarify, elaborate, and monitor actions by one or more parties to the communication. Unfortunately, this process often is interrupted by what is called "noise," which is the deliberate or nondeliberate distortion of the communication process. (This so-called "noise problem" is discussed later.)

External and Internal Communications

Organizational communication involves both the external and internal flow of information. In international management, this flow becomes particularly important, because parties to messages often are located in different geographic areas and/or have been born and raised in different cultures. This international context can create communication problems that are quite different from those faced by companies operating within one country.

Examples of External Communication   One major form of external communication during the years ahead will be government attempts to secure agreements with other nations regarding international trade. For example, the United States has been engaged in prolonged discussions with Japan regarding reciprocal trade agreements. The United States feels that Japan is not opening up for imports, is lagging behind in doing business with foreign firms, and is exporting goods to virtually every corner of the globe.

This perception of the problem greatly influences the way that the U.S. government communicates with Japan during trade negotiations. There are other interpretations of international trade strategy, however, and the Japanese have their own version. They believe that Americans are overrating the danger to their own economy and are failing to see that many of the steps being taken by U.S. business will make the United States a major economic power for the indefinite future.

Other external communication is more one-way in that it does not directly involve all the parties affected by the message. A good example is the EU's rules designed to ensure that member firms are not forced out of their home markets. The EU's Competition Directorate recently was empowered to approve mergers between large European firms.[2] This action will help to ensure that U.S. and Japanese companies do not dominate the European market. Another example of external communication involving the EU is the recent decision to place a floor on the price of computer chips. The Europeans have complained that other countries have produced chips and dumped them in Europe at below-cost prices. The result was that European firms were unable to compete, and some went out of business. This problem is unlikely to happen in the future. In recent years, European-made chips are now being protected from outside competition, a move that encourages foreign firms to establish operations in Europe.[3] Quite obviously, an understanding of external communication is critical to effective international management.

Examples of Internal Communication   Although the communication process is the same worldwide, its internal use often is influenced by cultural differences. How U.S. managers communicate may be quite different from how European or Asian managers do, and these differences are important to recognize. For example, a Harvard research team made a comparative study of the management of Russian and U.S. factories, and they found that Russian managers make greater use than U.S. managers of direct, face-to-face communications. U.S. managers rely more heavily on informal, written communication and the telephone.[4] On the other hand, a more recent observational study found both Russian and U.S. managers spend approximately one-third of their time carrying out communication activities.[5]

In another study, Pascale investigated communication techniques used by U.S. and Japanese managers operating both at home and in each other's country. He found that in some ways, the two national groups used similar communication techniques. For example, U.S. managers in the United States made an average of 37 phone calls daily, and U.S. managers in Japan averaged 34 calls a day. Japanese managers in Japan made 35 calls a day, and the Japanese managers in the United States averaged 30 calls daily. Therefore, use of the telephone to convey information really did not vary between the two groups; however, Pascale did find some important differences. For example, Japanese managers in Japan made much greater use of face-to-face contacts than U.S. or Japanese managers in the United States. Pascale's study also found greater use of upward and lateral communication in Japanese-based Japanese firms, but managers in U.S.-based Japanese firms used communication patterns similar to those used in U.S. firms.[6] Were there any perceived differences in the quality of decision making among the various groups of managers? Pascale found none. Each group gave itself a high score on decision quality; however, the Japanese-based Japanese firms perceived the quality of decision implementation as higher than that of the other three groups.[7]

Explicit and Implicit Communications

Besides the external and internal distinction, another major difference in the communication process is that some countries use very explicit (exact and precise) communiqués and others a highly implicit (not plainly expressed or implied) approach. In the United States, for example, managers are taught to say exactly what they mean. Objectives often are set forth in quantitative terms, and the date for their accomplishment is firmly established (e.g., "all overtime will be eliminated by July 1 of this year"). Figure 10-2 shows that in other countries, such as Japan, countries in Latin America, and Arab nations, managers often use a more implicit approach. For example, Ouchi makes the point in his best-selling book *Theory Z* that implicit communication is a key feature of decision making in Japan. He notes that Japanese managers are intentionally ambiguous when it comes to assigning responsibility for tasks, and foreigners who come to Japan to do business often are frustrated by their inability to figure out who is responsible for making the final decision. Ouchi describes it this way:

> Americans expect others to behave just as we do. Many are the unhappy and frustrated American businessmen or lawyers returning from Japan with the complaint that, "If only they would tell me who is really in charge, we could make some progress." The complaint displays a lack of understanding that, in Japan, no one individual carries responsibility for a particular turf. Rather, a group or team of employees assumes joint responsibility for a set of tasks. While we wonder at their comfortableness in not knowing who is responsible for what, they know quite clearly that each of them is completely responsible for all tasks, and they share that responsibility jointly. Obviously, this approach sometimes lets things "fall through the cracks" because everyone may think that someone else has a task under control. When working well, however, this approach leads to a naturally participative decision making and problem solving process.[8]

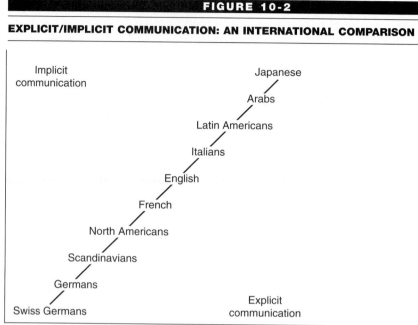

FIGURE 10-2

EXPLICIT/IMPLICIT COMMUNICATION: AN INTERNATIONAL COMPARISON

Source: Adapted from Martin Rosch, "Communications: Focal Point of Culture," *Management International Review,* vol. 27, no. 4, 1987, p. 60. Used with permission.

Implicitness of communication is carried so far in Japan that the courts have refused for years to allow spectators, including members of the press, to take notes during a trial unless given express permission by the judge. Only recently has the Japanese Supreme Court ruled that explicit note-taking is permissible. The case was resolved only after a long appeal process through the courts was conducted by a non-Japanese lawyer![9]

Interpretation of Communications

The effectiveness of communication in the international context typically is determined by how closely the sender and receiver have the same meaning for the same message.[10] If this meaning is different, effective communication will not occur. A good example was the U.S. firm that wanted to increase worker output among its Japanese personnel. This firm put an individual incentive plan into effect, whereby workers would be given extra pay based on their work output. The plan, which had worked well in the United States, was a total flop. The Japanese were accustomed to working in groups and to being rewarded as a group.[11] In another case, a U.S. firm offered a bonus to anyone who would provide suggestions that resulted in increased productivity. The Japanese workers rejected this idea, because they felt that no one working alone is responsible for increased productivity. It is always a group effort. When the company changed the system and began rewarding group productivity, it was successful in gaining support for the program.[12]

Another example has been provided by Adler, who points out that people doing business in a foreign culture often misinterpret the meaning of messages. As a

TABLE 10-2

DIALOGUE BETWEEN A U.S. PLANNER AND HIS COMPANY'S JAPANESE CEO

David:	The strategic plan is ready, Shintaro. We've focused on squeezing as much margin as possible out of each product. Our profit picture will be outstanding this year.
Shintaro:	That's good. I'm really delighted. But there is one small thing. How will we stand in terms of the budget imposed on us by Tokyo?
David:	We will achieve remarkable efficiencies through work force reductions and better co-ordination. I expect us to be 30 percent under budget.
Shintaro:	Oh, well, that is good. But what will Tokyo say?
David:	I don't understand. They will love us.
Shintaro:	Perhaps. But we may be sending the wrong signals. Tokyo may think we are cutting quality just to grab market share, which we will lose later to a Korean competitor that put more into production.
David:	I thought our goal was to increase market share.
Shintaro:	It is one goal, and an important one in a growth market. However, Mr. Fuji, our chairman, is a very traditional person. To him a budget is not just a limiting constraint. It embodies social thinking, too. We spend funds in response to our values about what our company should be doing in society to fulfill its destiny.
David:	I don't understand. What is our destiny?
Shintaro:	We must continue to be seen as a strong company creating quality products in the world. Sometimes our spending reflects our vision.
David:	This is mumbo-jumbo. We are in business to make money.
Shintaro:	Up to a point, of course. But we are really in business to serve society.

Source: Adapted by Jeremiah J. Sullivan, "Japanese Management Philosophies: From the Vacuous to the Brilliant," *California Management Review*, Winter 1992, pp. 74–75. Copyright 1992 by the Regents of the University of California. Reprinted by permission of the Regents.

result, they arrive at erroneous conclusions. She relates the following story of a Canadian doing business in the Middle East. The Canadian was surprised when his meeting with a high-ranking official was not held in a closed office and was constantly interrupted.

> Using the Canadian-based cultural assumptions that (a) important people have large private offices with secretaries to monitor the flow of people into the office, and (b) important business takes precedence over less important business and is therefore not interrupted, the Canadian interprets the . . . open office and constant interruptions to mean that the official is neither as high ranking nor as interested in conducting the business at hand as he had previously thought.[13]

The Canadian's interpretation of the office environment led him to lose interest in working in the Middle East. Table 10-2 provides another example, illustrating how the views of a Japanese CEO and a U.S. planner can differ regarding the purpose of the business.

COMMUNICATION FLOWS

Communication flows in international organizations, such as the one described earlier at IBM, move both down and up. However, as Figure 10-3 humorously, but in many ways accurately, portrays, there are some unique differences in organizations around the world.

FIGURE 10-3

COMMUNICATION EPIGRAMS

There are a number of different "organization charts" that have been constructed to depict international organizations. An epigram is a poem or line of verse that is witty or satirical in nature. The following organization designs are epigrams that show how communication occurs in different countries. In examining them, remember that each contains considerable exaggeration and humor, but also some degree of truth.

In America, everyone thinks he or she has a communication pipeline directly to the top.

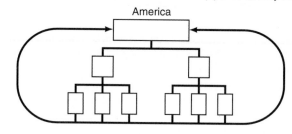

America

There are so many people in China that organizations are monolithic structures characterized by copious levels of bureaucracy. All information flows through channels.

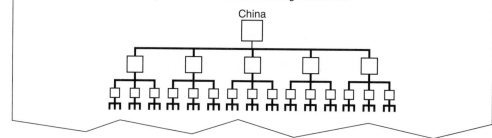

China

Downward Communication

Downward communication is the transmission of information from manager to subordinate. The primary purpose of the manager-initiated communication flow is to convey orders and information. Managers use this channel to let their people know what is to be done and how well they are doing. The channel facilitates the flow of information to those who need it for operational purposes.

In Asian countries, as noted earlier, downward communication is less direct than in the United States. Orders tend to be implicit in nature. Conversely, in some European countries, downward communication is not only direct but extends beyond business matters. For example, one early study surveyed 299 U.S. and French managers regarding the nature of downward communication and the managerial authority they perceived themselves as having. This study found that U.S. managers basically used downward communication for work-related matters. A follow-up study investigated matters that U.S. and French managers felt were within the purview of their authority.[14] The major differences involved work-related and nonwork-related activities: U.S. managers felt that it was within their authority to communicate or attempt to influence their people's social behavior only if it occurred on the job or it directly affected their work. For example, U.S. managers felt that it was proper to look into matters such as how much an

At the United Nations everyone is arranged in a circle so that no one is more powerful than anyone else. Those directly in front or behind others are philosophically aligned, and those nearby form part of an international bloc.

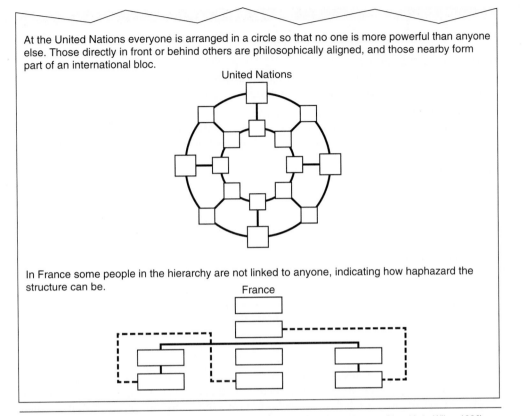

United Nations

In France some people in the hierarchy are not linked to anyone, indicating how haphazard the structure can be.

France

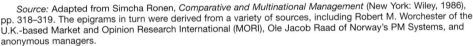

Source: Adapted from Simcha Ronen, *Comparative and Multinational Management* (New York: Wiley, 1986), pp. 318–319. The epigrams in turn were derived from a variety of sources, including Robert M. Worchester of the U.K.-based Market and Opinion Research International (MORI), Ole Jacob Raad of Norway's PM Systems, and anonymous managers.

individual drinks at lunch, whether the person uses profanity in the workplace, and how active the individual is in recruiting others to join the company. The French managers were not as supportive of these activities. The researcher concluded that "the Americans find it as difficult [as] or more difficult than the French to accept the legitimacy of managerial authority in areas unrelated to work."[15]

Upward Communication

Upward communication is the transfer of information from subordinate to superior. The primary purpose of this subordinate-initiated upward communication is to provide feedback, ask questions, or obtain assistance from higher-level management. In recent years, there has been a call for and a concerted effort to promote more upward communication in the United States. In other countries, such as in Japan, Hong Kong, and Singapore, upward communication has long been a fact of life. Managers in these countries have extensively used suggestion systems and quality circles to get employee input and always are available to listen to their people's concerns. For example, here are some observations from the approach the Japanese firm Matsushita uses in dealing with employee suggestions:

TABLE 10-3

MATSUSHITA'S PHILOSOPHY

Basic Business Principles

To recognize our responsibilities as industrialists, to foster progress, to promote the general welfare of society, and to devote ourselves to the further development of world culture.

Employees Creed

Progress and development can be realized only through the combined efforts and co-operation of each member of the Company. Each of us, therefore, shall keep this idea constantly in mind as we devote ourselves to the continuous improvement of our Company.

The Seven Spiritual Values

1. National service through industry
2. Fairness
3. Harmony and co-operation
4. Struggle for betterment
5. Courtesy and humility
6. Adjustment and assimilation
7. Gratitude

Source: Richard Tanner Pascale and Anthony G. Athos, *The Art of Japanese Management* (New York: Warner Books, 1981), p. 75.

Matsushita views employee recommendations as instrumental to making improvements on the shop floor and in the marketplace. [It believes] that a great many little people, paying attention each day to how to improve their jobs, can accomplish more than a whole headquarters full of production engineers and planners.

Praise and positive reinforcement are an important part of the Matsushita philosophy.... Approximately 90 percent of ... suggestions receive rewards; most only a few dollars per month, but the message is reinforced constantly: "Think about your job; develop yourself and help us improve the company." The best suggestions receive company-wide recognition and can earn substantial monetary rewards. Each year, many special awards are also given, including presidential prizes and various divisional honors.[16]

This company has used the same approach wherever it has established plants worldwide, and the approach has proved very successful. The company has all its employees begin the day by reciting its basic principles, beliefs, and values, which are summarized in Table 10-3, to reinforce in all employees the reason for the company's existence and to provide a form of spiritual fabric to energize and sustain them. All employees see themselves as important members of a successful team, and they are willing to do whatever is necessary to ensure the success of the group.

Outside these Asian countries, upward communication is not as popular. For example, in South America, many managers believe that employees should follow orders and not ask a lot of questions. German managers also make much less use of this form of communication. In most cases, however, evidence shows that employees prefer to have downward communication at least supplemented by upward channels. Unfortunately, such upward communication does not always occur because of a number of communication barriers.

TABLE 10-4

MULTILINGUALISM IN THE EU CLASSROOM

	Percentage of pupils in general secondary education learning English, French, or German as a foreign language, 1991–1992		
	English	**French**	**German**
Holland	96	65	53
Germany	93	23	—
Denmark	92	8	58
Spain	92	10	0.3
France	84	—	27
Belgium (Flemish)	68	98	22
Belgium (French)	58	1	6
Italy	61	33	3
Portugal	55	25	0.4
Britain	—	59	20
Ireland	—	69	24

Source: Eurostat, 1995.

COMMUNICATION BARRIERS

A number of common communication barriers are relevant to international management. The more important include language, perception, culture, and nonverbal communication.

Language Barriers

Knowledge of the home country's language (the language used at the headquarters of the MNC) is important for personnel placed in a foreign assignment. If managers do not understand the language that is used at headquarters, they likely will make a wide assortment of errors.[17] Additionally, many MNCs now prescribe English as the common language for internal communication, so that managers can more easily convey information to their counterparts in other geographically dispersed locales.[18] Despite such progress, however, language training continues to lag in many areas, although in an increasing number of European countries, more and more young people are becoming multilingual.[19] Table 10-4 shows the percentage of European students who are studying the major languages.

More recently, written communication has been getting increased attention, because poor writing is proving to be a greater barrier than poor talking. For example, Hildebrandt has found that among U.S. subsidiaries studied in Germany, language was a major problem when subsidiaries were sending written communications to the home office. The process often involved elaborate procedures associated with translating and reworking the report. Typical steps included: (1) holding a staff conference to determine what was to be included in the written message; (2) writing the initial draft in German; (3) rewriting the draft in German;

(4) translating the material into English; (5) consulting with bilingual staff members regarding the translation; and (6) rewriting the English draft a series of additional times until the paper was judged to be acceptable for transmission. The German managers admitted that they felt uncomfortable with writing, because their command of written English was poor. As Hildebrandt noted:

> All German managers commanding oral English stated that their grammatical competence was not sufficiently honed to produce a written English report of top quality. Even when professional translators from outside the company rewrote the German into English, German middle managers were unable to verify whether the report captured the substantive intent or included editorial alterations.[20]

Problems associated with the translation of information from one language to another have been made even clearer by Schermerhorn, who conducted research among 153 Hong Kong Chinese bilinguals who were enrolled in an undergraduate management course at a major Hong Kong university. The students were given two scenarios written in either English or Chinese. One scenario involved a manager who was providing information or assistance to a subordinate; the other involved a manager who was providing some form of personal support or praise for a subordinate. The research used the following procedures:

> [A] careful translation and back-translation method was followed to create the Chinese language versions of the research instruments. Two bilingual Hong Kong Chinese, both highly fluent in English and having expertise in the field of management, shared roles in the process. Each first translated one scenario and the evaluation questions into Chinese. Next they translated each other's Chinese versions back into English, and discussed and resolved translation differences in group consultation with the author. Finally, a Hong Kong professor read and interpreted the translations correctly as a final check of equivalency.[21]

The participants were asked to answer eight evaluation questions about these scenarios. A significant difference between the two sets of responses was found. Those who were queried in Chinese gave different answers from those who were queried in English. This led Schermerhorn to conclude that language plays a key role in conveying information between cultures, and that in cross-cultural management research, bilingual individuals should not be queried in their second language.

Cultural Barriers

Closely related to the language barriers are cultural barriers. For example, research by Sims and Guice compared 214 letters of inquiry written by native and nonnative speakers of English to test the assumption that cultural factors affect business communication. Among other things, the researchers found that nonnative speakers used exaggerated politeness, provided unnecessary professional and personal information, and made inappropriate requests of the other party. Commenting on the results and implications of their study, the researchers note that their investigation

> indicates that the deviations from standard U.S. business communication practices were not specific to one or more nationalities. The deviations did not occur among specific nationalities but were spread throughout the sample of nonnative letters used for the

study. Therefore, we can speculate that U.S. native speakers of English might have similar difficulties in international settings. In other words, a significant number of native speakers in the U.S. might deviate from the standard business communication practices of other cultures. Therefore, these native speakers need specific training in the business communication practices of the major cultures of the world so they can communicate successfully and acceptably with readers in those cultures.[22]

Research by Scott and Green has extended these findings, showing that even in English-speaking countries, there are different approaches to writing letters. In the United States, for example, it is common practice when constructing a bad-news letter to start out "with a pleasant, relevant, neutral, and transitional buffer statement; give the reasons for the unfavorable news before presenting the bad news; present the refusal in a positive manner; imply the bad news whenever possible; explain how the refusal is in the reader's best interest; and suggest positive alternatives that build goodwill."[23] In Great Britain, however, it is common to start out by referring to the situation, discussing the reasons for the bad news, conveying the bad news (often quite bluntly), and concluding with an apology or statement of regret (something that is frowned on by business-letter experts in the United States) designed to keep the reader's goodwill. Here is an example:

Lord Hanson has asked me to reply to your letter and questionnaire of February 12 which we received today.

As you may imagine, we receive numerous requests to complete questionnaires or to participate in a survey, and this poses problems for us. You will appreciate that the time it would take to complete these requests would represent a full-time job, so we decided some while ago to decline such requests unless there was some obvious benefit to Hanson PLC and our stockholders. As I am sure you will understand, our prime responsibility is to look after our stockholders' interests.

I apologize that this will not have been the response that you were hoping for, but I wish you success with your research study.[24]

U.S. MNC managers would seldom, if ever, send this type of letter; it would be viewed as blunt and tactless. However, the indirect approach that Americans use would be viewed by their British counterparts as overly indirect and obviously insincere.

Perceptual Barriers

Perception is a person's view of reality. How people see reality can vary and will influence their judgment and decision making. One example involves Japanese stockbrokers who recently have perceived that the chances of improving their career are better with U.S. firms, so they have changed jobs.[25] Another involves Hong Kong hoteliers who have begun buying U.S. properties, because they have the perception that if they can offer the same top-quality hotel service as back home, they can dominate their U.S. markets.[26] U.S. and Russian negotiators now are working to create a sweeping trade agreement that could be worth billions of dollars to the participants; the two sides perceive such a pact as a major breakthrough for East–West ventures.[27] These are all examples of how perceptions can play an important role in international management. Unfortunately, misperceptions also can become a barrier to effective communication. For example, when the Clinton administration recently decided to allow Taiwan President Lee Teng-hui to visit the United States, the Chinese (PRC) government perceived this as a threatening gesture and took actions of its own.[28] Besides conducting dangerous war games very near Taiwan's border as a warning not to become too bold in its quest for recognition as a sovereign nation, the PRC also snubbed U.S. car manufacturers and gave a much-coveted, $1 billion contract to Mercedes-Benz of Germany.[29] The following sections provide examples of such perception barriers in the international arena.

Advertising Messages   One way that perception can prove to be a problem in international management communication is when one person uses words that are misinterpreted by the other. Many firms have found to their dismay that a failure to understand home-country perceptions can result in disastrous advertising programs. Here are two examples:

> Ford . . . introduced a low cost truck, the "Fiera," into some Spanish-speaking countries. Unfortunately, the name meant "ugly old woman" in Spanish. Needless to say, this name did not encourage sales. Ford also experienced slow sales when it introduced a top-of-the-line automobile, the "Comet," in Mexico under the name "Caliente." The puzzling low sales were finally understood when Ford discovered that "caliente" is slang for a street walker.[30]

> One laundry detergent company certainly wishes now that it had contacted a few locals before it initiated its promotional campaign in the Middle East. All of the company's advertisements pictured soiled clothes on the left, its box of soap in the middle, and clean clothes on the right. But, because in that area of the world people tend to read from the right to the left, many potential customers interpreted the message to indicate the soap actually soiled the clothes.[31]

View of Others   Perception influences communication when it deals with how individuals "see" others. A good example is provided by the perception of foreigners who reside in the United States. Most Americans see themselves as extremely friendly, outgoing, and kind, and they believe that others also see them in this way. At the same time, many are not aware of what negative impressions they give to others. "International Management in Action: Foreign Perceptions" provides some insights into both of these assumptions and helps to illustrate the importance of communication in the international arena.

Another example of how the perceptions of others affect communication occurs in the way that some international managers perceive their subordinates. For example, a study examined the perceptions that German and U.S. managers had of the qualifications of their peers, managers, and subordinates in Europe and Latin America.[32] The findings showed that both the German and U.S. respondents perceived their subordinates to be less qualified than their peers. However, although the Germans perceived their managers to have more managerial ability than their peers, the Americans felt that their South American peers in many instances had equal or better qualifications than their own managers. Quite obviously, this perception will affect how U.S. expatriates communicate with their South American peers as well as how the expatriates communicate with their bosses.

Another study found that Western managers have more favorable attitudes toward women as managers than Asian or Saudi managers do.[33] This perception obviously affects the way these managers interact with their female counterparts.

INTERNATIONAL MANAGEMENT IN ACTION

Foreign Perceptions

How do people from overseas view Americans? One way of answering this question is by looking at how foreign college students studying in the United States perceive their hosts. A recent research study reported the results of 183 interviews that were conducted by U.S. students with foreign students from over 60 countries. The largest number of foreign students (16) came from Mexico. The next three largest groups, consisting of 10 students each, came from France, Germany, and India. In most cases (50) there were 5 or fewer students per country, so there was no chance that any one group was able to dramatically influence the overall responses of the 183 participants. One area the foreign students were asked to describe was their general impressions of the United States. The most commonly cited positive comments were these:

Description	Frequency of response
Friendly people—easy to get to know	64
Freedoms—open and free country	47
Job availability; career opportunities; entrepreneurship	27
Living conditions (housing, stores, easy parking, clothes); economy	25
Education/universities	24
Food	15
Modern technology	14
Entertainment; activities; parties	13
Beautiful women	11

The most commonly cited negative responses were these:

Description	Frequency of response
Weak family structure (families are not close, less family activities, a lack of respect for elders, high divorce rate, etc.)	20
Too money-conscious and materialistic	20
Ethnocentric people—arrogant, snobbish, individualistic, selfish	19
Prejudice against international people	18
Drugs and alcohol	13
High crime level; violence	12
Poor educational system—not rigorous; disrespectful of teachers	11
Rudeness	10

What makes these findings particularly important is that they differed substantially from what the U.S. students believed their foreign counterparts would say. Commenting on the results, one U.S. student noted, "Now I am more aware of the problems and difficult situations international people have when they come to the United States." Another said, "The assignment made me visualize how I would feel in another country and how I would want to be treated." Drawing together the overall results, the director of the project reported that the most unexpected and surprising reaction expressed by many students was "learning that international people perceive the United States differently than we perceive ourselves." If college students, often extremely sensitive to the world around them, have perception problems, one can only wonder how much greater this problem must be for adult, expatriate managers, who may be more set in their ways.

The same is true in the case of many Japanese managers, who according to one recent survey still regard women as superfluous to the effective running of their organizations and generally continue to treat women as second-class corporate citizens.[34]

The Impact of Culture

Besides language and perception, another major barrier to communication is culture, a topic that was given detailed attention in Chapter 4. Culture can affect communication in a number of ways, and one way is through the impact of cultural values.

Cultural Values One expert on Middle Eastern countries notes that people there do not relate to and communicate with each other in a loose, general way as those

TABLE 10-5	

U.S. PROVERBS REPRESENTING CULTURAL VALUES

Proverb	Cultural value
A penny saved is a penny earned	Thriftiness
Time is money	Time thriftiness
Don't cry over spilt milk	Practicality
Waste not, want not	Frugality
Early to bed, early to rise, makes one healthy, wealthy, and wise	Diligence; work ethic
A stitch in time saves nine	Timeliness of action
If at first you don't succeed, try, try again	Persistence; work ethic
Take care of today, and tomorrow will take care of itself	Preparation for future

Source: Drawn from Nancy J. Adler, *International Dimensions of Organizational Behavior,* 2nd ed. (Boston: PWS-Kent Publishing, 1991), pp. 79–80.

in the United States. Relationships are more intense and binding in the Middle East, and a wide variety of work-related values influence what people in the Middle East will and will not do.

> In North American society, the generally professed prevalent pattern is one of nonclass-consciousness, as far as work is concerned. Students, for example, make extra pocket money by taking all sorts of part-time jobs—manual and otherwise—regardless of the socioeconomic stratum to which the individual belongs. The attitude is uninhibited. In the Middle East, the overruling obsession is how the money is made and via what kind of job.[35]

These types of values indirectly, and in many cases directly, affect communication between people from different cultures. For example, one would communicate differently with a "rich college student" from the United States than with one from Saudi Arabia.

Another example is the way that people use time.[36] In the United States, people believe that time is an asset and is not to be wasted, which is an idea that often has limited meaning in other cultures. Various values are reinforced and reflected through the use of proverbs that Americans are taught from an early age. These proverbs help to guide people's behavior.[37] Table 10-5 lists some examples.

Misinterpretation Cultural differences can cause misinterpretations both in how others see expatriate managers and in how the latter see themselves. For example, U.S. managers doing business in Austria often misinterpret the fact that local businesspeople always address them in formal terms. They may view this as meaning that they are not friends or are not liked, but in fact, this formalism is the way that Austrians always conduct business. The informal, first-name approach used in the United States is not the style of the Austrians.

Many Americans also have difficulty interpreting the effect of national values on work behavior. For example, why do French and German workers drink alcoholic beverages at lunch time? Why are many European workers unwilling to work the night shift? Why do overseas affiliates contribute to the support of the

---

TABLE 10-6

COMMON FORMS OF NONVERBAL COMMUNICATION

1. Hand gestures, both intended and self-directed (autistic), such as the nervous rubbing of hands
2. Facial expressions, such as smiles, frowns, and yawns
3. Posture and stance
4. Clothing and hair styles (hair being more like clothes than like skin, both subject to the fashion of the day)
5. Interpersonal distance (proxemics)
6. Eye contact and direction of gaze, particularly in "listening behavior"
7. "Artifacts" and nonverbal symbols, such as lapel pins, walking sticks, and jewelry
8. Paralanguage (though often in language, just as often treated as part of nonverbal behavior—speech rate, pitch, inflections, volume)
9. Taste, including symbolism of food and the communication function of chatting over coffee or tea, and oral gratification such as smoking or gum chewing
10. Cosmetics: temporary—powder; permanent—tattoos
11. Time symbolism: what is too late or too early to telephone or visit a friend, or too long or too short to make a speech or stay for dinner
12. Timing and pauses within verbal behavior

Source: This information is found in J. C. Condon and F. S. Yousef, *An Introduction to Intercultural Communication* (Indianapolis, IN: Bobbs-Merrill, 1975), pp. 123–124.

---

employees' work council or donate money to the support of kindergarten teachers in local schools? These types of actions are viewed by some people as wasteful, but to those who know the culture of these countries, such actions promote the long-run good of the company. It is the outsider who is misinterpreting why these culturally specific actions are happening, and such misperceptions can become a barrier to effective communication.

Nonverbal Communication

Another major reason for perception problems is accounted for by *nonverbal communication,* which is the transfer of meaning through means such as body language and use of physical space. Table 10-6 summarizes a number of dimensions of nonverbal communication. The general categories that are especially important to communication in international management are kinesics and proxemics.

Kinesics *Kinesics* is the study of communication through body movement and facial expression. Primary areas of concern include eye contact, posture, and gestures. For example, when one communicates verbally with someone in the United States, it is good manners to look the other person in the eye. In some areas of the world, however, it is considered impolite to do this. Similarly, when Americans are engaged in prolonged negotiations or meetings, it is not uncommon for them to relax and put their feet up on a chair or desk, but this is insulting behavior in the Middle East. Here is just such an example from a classroom situation:

> In the midst of a discussion of a poem in the sophomore class of the English Department, the professor, who was British, took up the argument, started to explain the subtleties of the poem, and was carried away by the situation. He leaned back in his chair, put his

feet up on the desk, and went on with the explanation. The class was furious. Before the end of the day, a demonstration by the University's full student body had taken place. Petitions were submitted to the deans of the various faculties. The next day, the situation even made the newspaper headlines. The consequences of the act, that was innocently done, might seem ridiculous, funny, baffling, incomprehensible, or even incredible to a stranger. Yet, to the native, the students' behavior was logical and in context. The students and their supporters were outraged because of the implications of the breach of the native behavioral pattern. In the Middle East, it is extremely insulting to have to sit facing two soles of the shoes of somebody.[38]

Gestures also can be troublesome, because some have different meanings depending on the country. For example, in the United States, putting the thumb and index finger together to form an "O" is the sign for "okay." In Japan, this is the sign for money; in southern France, the gesture means "zero" or "worthless"; and in Brazil, it is regarded as a vulgar or obscene sign. In France and Belgium, snapping the fingers of both hands is considered vulgar; in Brazil, this gesture is used to indicate that something has been done for a long time. In Britain, the "V for victory" sign is given with the palm out; if the palm is in, this roughly means "shove it"; in non-British countries, the gesture means two of something and often is used when placing an order at a restaurant.[39] Gibson, Hodgetts, and Blackwell found that many foreign students attending school in the United States have trouble communicating, because they are unable to interpret some of the most common nonverbal gestures.[40] A survey group of 44 Jamaican, Venezuelan, Colombian, Peruvian, Thai, Indian, and Japanese students at two major universities were given pictures of 20 universal cultural gestures, and each was asked to describe the nonverbal gestures illustrated. In 56 percent of the choices the respondents either gave an interpretation that was markedly different from that of Americans or reported that the nonverbal gesture had no meaning in their culture. These findings help to reinforce the need to teach expatriates about local nonverbal communication.

Proxemics   *Proxemics* is the study of the way that people use physical space to convey messages. For example, in the United States, there are four "distances" people use in communicating on a face-to-face basis (see Figure 10-4.) ***Intimate distance*** is used for very confidential communications. ***Personal distance*** is used for talking with family and close friends. ***Social distance*** is used to handle most business transactions. ***Public distance*** is used when calling across the room or giving a talk to a group.

One major problem for Americans communicating with those from the Middle East or South America is that the intimate or personal distance zones are violated. Americans often tend to be moving away in interpersonal communication with their Middle Eastern or Latin counterparts, while the latter are trying to physically close the gap. The American cannot understand why the other is standing so close; the latter cannot understand why the American is being so reserved and standing so far away. The result is a breakdown in communication.

Office layout is another good example of proxemics. In the United States, the more important the manager, the larger the office, and often a secretary screens visitors and keeps away those whom the manager does not wish to see. In Japan, most managers do not have large offices, and even if they do, they

---

FIGURE 10-4

PERSONAL SPACE CATEGORIES FOR THOSE IN THE UNITED STATES

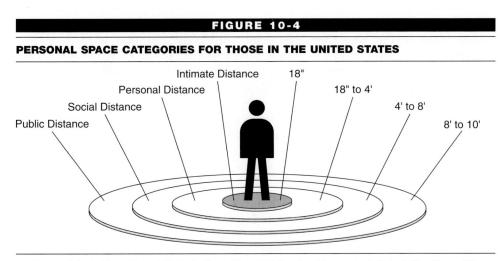

Source: Adapted from Richard M. Hodgetts and Donald F. Kuratko, *Management,* 2nd ed. (San Diego, CA: Harcourt Brace Jovanovich, 1991), p. 384.

spend a great deal of time out of it and with the employees. Thus, the Japanese have no trouble communicating directly with their superiors. A Japanese manager's staying in his office would be viewed as a sign of distrust or anger toward the group.

Another way that office proxemics can affect communication is that in many European companies, there is no wall between the space allocated to the senior-level manager and that of the subordinates. Everyone works in the same large room. These working conditions often are disconcerting to Americans, who tend to prefer more privacy.[41]

ACHIEVING COMMUNICATION EFFECTIVENESS

A number of steps can be taken to improve communication effectiveness in the international arena. These include providing feedback systems, providing language and cultural training, and increasing flexibility and co-operation.

Improve Feedback Systems

One of the most important ways of improving communication effectiveness in the international context is to open up feedback systems. Such feedback is particularly important between parent companies and their affiliates. There are two basic types of feedback systems: personal (e.g., meetings and telephone conversations) and impersonal (e.g., reports, budgets, and plans). Both of these systems help affiliates to keep their home office aware of progress and, in turn, help the home office to monitor and control affiliate performance as well as set goals and standards.

At present, there seem to be varying degrees of feedback between the home offices of MNCs and their affiliates. For example, one study evaluated the communication feedback between subsidiaries and home offices of 63 MNCs headquartered in Europe, Japan, and North America.[42] A marked difference was found between the way that U.S. companies communicated with their subsidiaries and the way that European and Japanese firms did. Over one-half of the U.S. subsidiaries responded that they received monthly feedback from their reports, in contrast to less than 10 percent of the European and Japanese subsidiaries. In addition, the Americans were much more inclined to hold regular management meetings on a regional or worldwide basis. Seventy-five percent of the U.S. companies had annual meetings for their affiliate top managers, compared with less than 50 percent for the Europeans and Japanese. These findings may help to explain why many international subsidiaries and affiliates are not operating as efficiently as they should. The units may not have sufficient contact with the home office. They do not seem to be getting continuous assistance and feedback that are critical to effective communication.

Based on his research among U.S. and German managers in Europe, Hildebrandt echoes such conclusions about the need for improved feedback systems. Some of his specific recommendations include holding more face-to-face meetings between parent and staff personnel and assigning someone as a liaison between the two groups.[43]

Provide Language Training

Besides improving feedback systems, another way to make communication more effective in the international arena is through language training. Many host-country managers cannot communicate well with their counterparts at headquarters. Because English has become the international language of business, those who are not native speakers of English should learn the language well enough so that face-to-face and telephone conversations are possible. If the language of the home office is not English, this other language also should be learned. As a U.S. manager working for a Japanese MNC recently told one of the authors, "The official international language of this company is English. However, whenever the home office people show up they tend to cluster together with their countrymen and speak Japanese. That's why I'm trying to learn Japanese. Let's face it. They say all you need to know is English, but if you want to really know what's going on you have to talk *their* language."

Written communication also is extremely important in achieving effectiveness. As noted earlier, when reports and letters are translated from one language to another, preventing a loss of meaning is virtually impossible. Moreover, if the communications are not written properly, they may not be given the attention they deserve. The reader will allow poor grammar and syntax to influence his or her interpretation and subsequent actions. Moreover, if readers cannot communicate in the language of those who will be receiving their comments or questions about the report, their messages also must be translated and likely will lose further meaning. Therefore, the process can continue on and on, each party failing to achieve full communication with the other. Hildebrandt has described the problems in this two-way process when an employee in a foreign subsidiary writes a report and then sends it to his or her boss for forwarding to the home office:

> The general manager or vice president cannot be asked to be an editor. Yet they often send statements along, knowingly, which are poorly written, grammatically imperfect,

or generally unclear. The time pressures do not permit otherwise. Predictably, questions issued from the States to the subsidiary and the complicated bilingual process now goes in reverse, ultimately reaching the original . . . staff member, who receives the English questions retranslated.[44]

Language training would help to alleviate such complicated communication problems.

Provide Cultural Training

It is very difficult to communicate effectively with someone from another culture unless at least one party has some understanding of the other's culture. Otherwise, communication likely will break down. This is particularly important for multinational companies that have operations throughout the world. Although there always are important differences between countries, and even between subcultures of the same country, firms that operate in South America find that the cultures of these countries have certain commonalities. These common factors also apply to Spain and Portugal. Therefore, a basic understanding of Latin cultures can prove to be useful throughout a large region of the world. The same is true of Anglo cultures, where norms and values tend to be somewhat similar from one country to another. When a multinational has operations in South America, Europe, and Asia, however, multicultural training becomes necessary. The sidebar "Communicating in Europe" provides some specific examples of cultural differences.

As Chapter 4 pointed out, it is erroneous to generalize about an "international" culture, because the various nations and regions of the globe are too different. Training must be conducted on a region- or country-specific basis. Failure to do so can result in continuous communication breakdown.

Increase Flexibility and Co-operation

Effective international communications require increased flexibility and co-operation by all parties. To improve understanding and co-operation, each party must be prepared to give a little. Take the case of International Computers Ltd., a mainframe computer firm that does a great deal of business in Japan. This firm urges its people to strive for successful collaboration in their international partnerships and ventures. To drive home the point of flexibility and co-operation, the company gives all its people who are involved in a joint partnership with an overseas firm a list of "dos" that are designed to make the arrangement work. These guidelines, listed in Table 10-7, are designed to ensure the requisite amount of flexibility and co-operation in intercompany interaction and negotiation. At the heart of this process is effective communication. As put by Kenichi Ohmae:

> We must recognize and accept the inescapable subtleties and difficulties of intercompany relationships. This is the essential starting point. Then we must focus not on contractual or equity-related issues but on the quality of the people at the interface between organizations. Finally, we must understand that success requires frequent, rapport-building meetings by at least three organizational levels: top management, staff, and line management at the working level.[45]

Communicating in Europe

In Europe, many countries are within easy commuting distance of their neighbors, so an expatriate who does business in France on Monday may be in Germany on Tuesday, Great Britain on Wednesday, Italy on Thursday, and Spain on Friday. Each country has its own etiquette regarding how to greet others and conduct oneself during social and business meetings. The following sections examine some of the things that expatriate managers need to know to communicate effectively.

France When one is meeting with businesspeople in France, promptness is expected, although tardiness of 5 to 10 minutes is not considered a major gaffe. The French prefer to shake hands when introduced, and it is correct to address them by title plus last name. When the meeting is over, a handshake again is proper manners.

French executives try to keep their personal and professional lives separate. As a result, most business entertaining is done at restaurants or country clubs. When gifts are given to business associates, they should appeal to intellectual or aesthetic pursuits as opposed to being something that one's company produces for sale on the world market. In conversational discussions, topics such as politics and money should be avoided. Also, humor should be used carefully during business meetings.

Germany German executives like to be greeted by their title, and one should never refer to someone on a first-name basis unless invited to do so. Business appointments should be made well in advance, and punctuality is important. Like the French, the Germans often entertain clients outside their house, so an invitation to a German manager's home is a special privilege and always should be followed with a thank-you note. Additionally, as is the case in France, one should avoid using humor during business meetings.

Great Britain In Britain, it is common to shake hands on the first meeting, and first names are always used in introductions. Unlike the custom in France and Germany, it is common practice in Britain to arrive a little late for business and social occasions, and invitations to British homes are more likely than in some other European cultures. A typical gift for the host is flowers or chocolates.

During business meetings, suits and ties are common dress; however, striped ties should be avoided if they appear to be a copy of those worn by alumni of British universities and schools or by members of military or social clubs. Additionally, during social gatherings it is a good idea not to discuss politics, religion, or gossip about the monarchy unless the British person brings the topic up first.

Italy In traditional companies, executives are referred to by title plus last name. It is common to shake hands when being introduced, and if the individual is a university graduate, the professional title *dottore* should be used.

Business appointments should be made well in advance, although punctuality is not essential. In most cases, business is done at the office, and when someone is invited to a restaurant, this invitation is usually done to socialize and not to continue business discussions. If an expatriate is invited to an Italian home, it is common to bring a gift for the host, such as a bottle of wine or a box of chocolates. During the dinner conversation, there is a wide variety of acceptable topics, including business, family matters, and soccer.

Spain It is common to use first names when introducing or talking to people in Spain, and close friends typically greet each other with an embrace. Appointments should be made in advance, but punctuality is not essential.

If one is invited to the home of a Spanish executive, flowers or chocolates for the host are acceptable gifts. If the invitation includes dinner, any business discussions should be delayed until after coffee is served. During the social gathering, some topics that should be avoided include religion, family, and work. Additionally, humor rarely is used during formal occasions.

TABLE 10-7

INTERNATIONAL COMPUTER LTD.'S GUIDELINES FOR SUCCESSFUL COLLABORATION

1. Treat the collaboration as a personal commitment. It's people that make partnerships work.

2. Anticipate that it will take up management time. If you can't spare the time, don't start it.

3. Mutual respect and trust are essential. If you don't trust the people you are negotiating with, forget it.

4. Remember that both partners must get something out of it (money, eventually). Mutual benefit is vital. This will probably mean you've got to give something up. Recognize this from the outset.

5. Make sure you tie up a tight legal contract. Don't put off resolving unpleasant or contentious issues until "later." Once signed, however, the contract should be put away. If you refer to it, something is wrong with the relationship.

6. Recognize that during the course of a collaboration, circumstances and markets change. Recognize your partner's problems and be flexible.

7. Make sure you and your partner have mutual expectations of the collaboration and its time scale. One happy and one unhappy partner is a formula for failure.

8. Get to know your opposite numbers at all levels socially. Friends take longer to fall out.

9. Appreciate that cultures—both geographic and corporate—are different. Don't expect a partner to act or respond identically to you. Find out the true reason for a particular response.

10. Recognize your partner's interests and independence.

11. Even if the arrangement is tactical in your eyes, make sure you have corporate approval. Your tactical activity may be a key piece in an overall strategic jigsaw puzzle. With corporate commitment to the partnership, you can act with the positive authority needed in these relationships.

12. Celebrate achievement together. It's a shared elation, and you'll have earned it!

Source: This information is found in Kenichi Ohmae, "The Global Logic of Strategic Alliances," *Harvard Business Review,* March-April 1989, p. 149.

SUMMARY OF KEY POINTS

1. Communication is the transfer of meaning from sender to receiver. This process can involve both the external and internal flow of information as well as explicit and implicit information. The key to the effectiveness of communication is how accurately the receiver interprets the intended meaning.

2. Communicating in the international context involves both downward and upward flows. Downward flows convey information from superior to subordinate; these flows vary considerably from country to country. For example, the downward system of organizational communication is much more prevalent in France than in Japan. Upward communication conveys information from subordinate to superior. In the United States and Japan, the upward system is more common than in South America or some European countries.

3. The international arena contains a number of communication barriers. Some of the most important are language, perception, culture, and nonverbal communication. Language, particularly in written communications, often loses considerable meaning during interpretation. Perception and culture can result in people's seeing and interpreting things differently, and as a result, communication can break down. Nonverbal communication such as body language, facial expressions, and use of physical space often varies from country to country and, if improper, often results in communication problems.

4. A number of steps can be taken to improve communication effectiveness. Some of the most important include improving feedback, providing language and cultural training, and encouraging flexibility and co-operation. These steps can be particularly helpful in overcoming communication barriers in the international context and can lead to more effective international management.

KEY TERMS

communication	proxemics
downward communication	intimate distance
upward communication	personal distance
perception	social distance
nonverbal communication	public distance
kinesics	

REVIEW AND DISCUSSION QUESTIONS

1. How does explicit communication differ from implicit communication? What is one culture that makes wide use of explicit communication? Implicit communication? Describe how one would go about conveying the following message in each of the two cultures you identified: "You are trying very hard, but you are still making too many mistakes."
2. One of the major reasons that foreign expatriates have difficulty doing business in the United States is that they do not understand American slang. A business executive recently gave the authors the following three examples of statements that had no direct meaning for her because she was unfamiliar with slang: He was laughing like hell. Don't worry; it's a piece of cake. Let's throw these ideas up against the wall and see if any of them stick. Why did the foreign expat have trouble understanding these statements, and what could be said instead?
3. Yamamoto Iron & Steel is considering setting up a minimill outside Atlanta, Georgia. At present, the company is planning to send a group of executives to the area to talk with local and state officials regarding this plant. In what way might misperception be a barrier to effective communication between the representatives for both sides? Identify and discuss two examples.
4. Diaz Brothers is a winery in Barcelona. The company would like to expand operations to the United States and begin distributing its products in the Chicago area. If things work out well, the company then will expand to both coasts. In its business dealings in the Midwest, how might culture prove to be a communication barrier for the company's representatives from Barcelona? Identify and discuss two examples.
5. Why is nonverbal communication a barrier to effective communication? Would this barrier be greater for Yamamoto Steel & Iron (question 3) or the Diaz Brothers (question 4)? Defend your answer.
6. For U.S. companies going abroad for the first time, which form of nonverbal communication barrier would be the greatest, kinesics or proxemics? Why? Defend your answer.

PRACTICAL INTERNATIONAL MANAGEMENT ASSIGNMENT

Interview a relevant manager from a company that does business with an overseas client, partner, or subcontractor. Ask the interviewee questions such as: (1) What forms of communication do you use to keep in touch with the other party? (2) What communication problems have you had in dealing with the other party? and (3) What steps have you taken, or do you plan to take, to overcome your communication problems? Be specific in your note-taking. Then, compare your answers with those of others in the class. In particular, what similarities and differences are there? Do firms doing business with Europeans have different problems from those doing business in East Asia or South America? What conclusions can you draw from your comparative analysis?

(For those who are unable to interview an international manager, foreign students on campus may be substituted. For example, the foreign students may be asked what communication problems they encountered when arriving in this country, and what specific steps they took to overcome these problems. When sharing this information with others in the class, similarities and differences by specific cultures should be noted.)

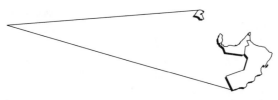

A guest should be careful not to admire an Arab host's possessions too much because one of them may be offered to you, and you may be forced to accept it as a gift rather than offend your host.

In the International Spotlight

Gulf States

The Gulf States comprise Bahrain, Kuwait, Oman, Qatar, and the United Arab Emirates (U.A.E.). These states lie along the eastern coast of the Arabian Peninsula, with Saudi Arabia bordering on the west and Iran on the east across the Arabian Gulf (called the Persian Gulf by Westerners). Each of the Gulf States countries is very small, but their desert land is strategically located in one of the largest oil-producing regions of the world.

Oil has made these nations some of the richest in the world, with very high per-capita income. They generally have free education, free health and social services, and no income tax. Because of the heat, business hours from May to October tend to be from 7 to 1 and from 4 to 7. During the rest of the year, the hours are from 8 to 2 and from 4 to 6. The largely government-owned oil industry dominates the economies but does not provide many jobs. The governments are trying to promote economic activities other than oil production to get their people off welfare.

Herman Kerdling's firm has had a very profitable business supplying the Gulf countries with oil-production machinery. Last month, Kerdling learned that he would be going to Oman for a 1-year assignment servicing the firm's contract. He was delighted, because he knows that all the top managers at headquarters have had similar international assignments. Moreover, Oman is one of the company's most important accounts. Kerdling was determined to be successful in this assignment.

Unfortunately, after several weeks in Oman, things have not worked out quite as he expected. Specifically, Kerdling is finding that doing business with the Arabs is difficult, because their approach is so different from that of Americans. One of the most disconcerting things is the fact that people stand so close when they talk. He often tries to back away and put some room between them, but the other person usually follows and closes the distance again.

Another problem is the way that meetings are conducted. Last week, Kerdling went to talk to an Arab customer about some new equipment that was to be delivered and installed within the next few weeks. He and the customer talked for about 5 minutes when someone in the next office suddenly barged in and interrupted the conversation. The customer talked to this individual for almost 5 minutes and then turned back to Kerdling and picked up the conversation where he had left off. Within a few minutes, however, someone else came in, and another interruption ensued. The meeting, which should have taken approximately 30 minutes, took over 2 hours to complete. As Kerdling left, he turned and saw another person start a conversation with the customer only to be interrupted by a third party. "How does anyone get anything done around here?" he wondered to himself.

A third problem are the letters and memos that Kerdling receives from his customers. These messages are translated by company-paid Arabic interpreters, and the interpreted copy is attached to the original. Herman sometimes has trouble with the interpretation, because the interpreters are not very good. Unfortunately, no one on the company's staff is fluent in Arabic, and no better interpreters can be found. There seems to be no way around this problem. Kerdling is convinced that there are many communication breakdowns caused by this lack of language fluency, but he is unsure of how to resolve the matter.

1. What are some current issues facing the Gulf States? What is the climate for doing business in the Gulf States today?
2. Why is Kerdling upset that his Arab hosts stand so close when they talk to him? What can he do about this?
3. Should Kerdling feel insulted when his conversation is interrupted by outsiders?
4. Is Kerdling right regarding communication breakdowns caused by a lack of language fluency? Can anything be done about the problem?

You Be the International Management Consultant

Foreign or Domestic?

Connie Hatley is a very successful businesswoman who has holdings in a wide variety of industries. Hatley recently was approached by one of the Big Three automakers and offered a multidealership arrangement. In return for investing $50 million in facilities, the auto manufacturer would be willing to give her five dealerships spread throughout the United States. These locations, for the most part, are in rural areas, but over the next decade, these locales likely will become much more populated. In addition, the company pointed out that a large percentage of new cars are purchased by individuals who prefer to buy in rural locations, because prices at these dealerships tend to be lower. Hatley has been seriously considering the offer, although she now has a competitive alternative.

A South Korean auto manufacturer has approached Hatley and offered her the same basic deal. Hatley indicated that she was wary of doing business with a foreign firm so far away, but the Korean manufacturer presented her with some interesting auto sales data, including: (1) between 1981 and 1996, the South Korean share of the U.S. auto market went from 0 to 2.4 percent; (2) South Korean automakers are capturing market share in the United States at a faster rate than any other competitor; (3) new technology is being incorporated into these Korean-built cars at an unprecedented rate, and the quality is among the highest in the industry; (4) although the Big Three (GM, Ford, and Chrysler) hold a large share of the U.S. auto market, their market among those 45 years of age or younger is declining and being captured by for-

eign competitors; and (5) the South Korean firm intends to increase its share of the U.S. market by 20 percent annually.

Hatley is very impressed with these data and forecasts. Last year, however, the Korean auto company's sales and market share slipped a little, and she is uneasy about having to deal with someone located halfway around the world. "If I don't receive scheduled deliveries, whom do I call?" She asked one of her vice presidents. "Also, we don't speak their language. If there is a major problem, how are we going to really communicate with each other? I like the proposal, and I'd take it if I were sure that we wouldn't have communication problems. However, $50 million is a lot of money to invest. If a mistake is made, I'm going to lose a fortune. They did experience some problems last year, and their sales were off that year. Of course, if the South Koreans are right in their long-range forecasts and I have no major problems dealing with them, my return on investment is going to be almost 50 percent higher than it will be with the U.S. manufacturer."

1. What specific types of communication problems might Hatley encounter in dealing with the South Koreans?

2. Can these communication problems be resolved, or are they insurmountable and will simply have to be tolerated?

3. Based on communication problems alone, should Hatley back away from the deal or proceed? Give your recommendation, then defend it.

CHAPTER 10 ENDNOTES

1. See Lillian H. Chaney and Jeanette S. Martin, *Intercultural Business Communication* (Englewood Cliffs, NJ: Prentice-Hall, 1995), p. 102.

2. Jonathan Kapstein, "Writing the New Rules for Europe's Merger Game," *BusinessWeek*, February 6, 1989, pp. 48–49.

3. Thane Peterson, "The EC Just Says No to Japan's Cheap Chips," *BusinessWeek*, January 30, 1989, pp. 46–47.

4. Paul R. Lawrence and Charalambos A. Vlachoutsicos, *Behind the Factory Walls: Decision Making in Soviet and U.S. Enterprises* (Cambridge, MA: Harvard University Press, 1990), p. 282. Also see James E. McLauchlin, "Communicating to a Diverse Europe," *Business Horizons*, January-February 1993, pp. 54–56.

5. See Fred Luthans, Dianne H. B. Welsh, and Stuart A. Rosenkrantz, "What Do Russian Managers Really Do? An Observational Study with Comparisons to U.S. Managers," *Journal of International Business Studies* 4th Quarter, 1993, pp. 741–761.; Fred Luthans, Richard Hodgetts, and Stuart A. Rosenkrantz, *Real Managers* (Cambridge, MA: Ballinger, 1988).

6. Richard Tanner Pascale, "Communication and Decision Making across Cultures: Japanese and American Comparisons," *Administration Science Quarterly*, March 1978, pp. 91–110.

7. Ibid., p. 103.

8. William G. Ouchi, *Theory Z* (New York: Avon Books, 1981), p. 39.

9. David E. Sanger, "U.S. Lawyer Makes Japan Sit Up and Take Note," *New York Times*, March 17, 1989, p. 24.

10. William C. Byham and George Dixon, "Through Japanese Eyes," *Training and Development Journal*, March 1993, pp. 33–36; Linda S. Dillon, "West Meets East," *Training and Development Journal*, March 1993, pp. 39–43.

11. Ouchi, *Theory Z*, p. 41.

12. Ibid., pp. 41–42.

13. Nancy J. Adler, *International Dimensions of Organizational Behavior*, 2nd ed. (Boston: PWS-Kent Publishing, 1991), pp. 75–76.

14. Giorgio Inzerilli, "The Legitimacy of Managerial Authority—A Comparative Study," *National Academy of Management Proceedings*, Detroit, 1980, pp. 58–62.

15. Ibid., p. 62.

16. Richard Tanner Pascale and Anthony G. Athos, *The Art of Japanese Management* (New York: Warner Books, 1981), pp. 82–83.

17. For some insights into this area, see Tachi Kiuchi, "How Japanese Can Speak to Americans," *Wall Street Journal*, March 4, 1992, p. A14.

18. Naoki Kameda, "Englishes' in Cross-Cultural Business Communication," *The Bulletin*, March 1992, p. 3.

19. See "Double or Quits," *Economist*, February 25, 1995, pp. 84–85.

20. H. W. Hildebrandt, "Communication Barriers between German Subsidiaries and Parent American Companies," *Michigan Business Review*, July 1973, p. 9.

21. John R. Schermerhorn, Jr., "Language Effects in Cross-Cultural Management Research: An Empirical Study and a Word of Caution," *National Academy of Management Proceedings*, 1987, p. 103.

22. Brenda R. Sims and Stephen Guice, "Differences between Business Letters from Native and Non-Native Speakers of English," *Journal of Business Communication*, Winter 1991, p. 37.

23. James Calvert Scott and Diana J. Green, "British Perspectives on Organizing Bad-News Letters: Organizational Patterns Used by Major U.K. Companies," *The Bulletin*, March 1992, p. 17.

24. Ibid., pp. 18–19.

25. Ted Holden, "Big Bucks vs. a Job for Life," *BusinessWeek*, January 9, 1989, p. 58.

26. Dori Jones Yang, "Hong Kong Hoteliers Start Colonizing the West," *BusinessWeek*, March 6, 1989, p. 44.

27. Peter Galuszka, Rose Brady, Richard A. Melcher, and Bill Javetski, "The Deal of the Decade May Get Done in Moscow," *BusinessWeek*, February 27, 1989, pp. 54–55.

28. Robert S. Greenberger, Bob Davis, and Kathy Chen, "Misperceptions Divide U.S. and China," *Wall Street Journal*, July 14, 1995, p. A8.

29. Joseph Kahn, "Fraying U.S.-Sino Ties Threaten Business," *Wall Street Journal*, July 7, 1995, p. A6; Nathaniel C. Nash, "China Gives Big Van Deal to Mercedes," *New York Times*, July 13, 1995, pp. C1, C5; and Seth Faison, "China Times a Business Deal to Make a Point to America," *New York Times*, July 16, 1995, pp. 1, 6.

30. David A. Ricks, *Big Business Blunders: Mistakes in Multinational Marketing* (Homewood, IL: Dow Jones-Irwin, 1983), p. 39.

31. Ibid., p. 55.

32. Edwin Miller, Bhal Bhatt, Raymond Hill, and Julian Cattaneo, "Leadership Attitudes of American and German Expatriate Managers in Europe and Latin America," *National Academy of Management Proceedings*, Detroit, 1980, pp. 53–57.

33. Abdul Rahim A. Al-Meer, "Attitudes Towards Women as Managers: A Comparison of Asians, Saudis and Westerners," *Arab Journal of the Social Sciences*, April 1988, pp. 139–149.

34. Sheryl WuDunn, "In Japan, Still Getting Tea and No Sympathy," *New York Times*, August 27, 1995, Section E, p. 3.

35. Fathi S. Yousef, "Cross-Cultural Communication: Aspects of the Contrastive Social Values between North Americans and Middle Easterners," *Human Organization*, Winter 1974, p. 385.

36. Richard Mead, *International Management: Cross Cultural Dimensions* (Cambridge, MA: Blackwell Publishers, 1994), pp. 176–177.

37. Alder, *International Dimensions of Organizational Behavior*, pp. 79–80.

38. Yousef, "Cross-Cultural Communication," p. 383.

39. See Roger E. Axtell (ed.), *Dos and Taboos around the World* (New York: Wiley, 1990), Chapter 2.

40. Jane Whitney Gibson, Richard M. Hodgetts, and Charles W. Blackwell, "Cultural Variations in Nonverbal Communication," *55th Annual Business Communication Proceedings*, San Antonio, November 8–10, 1990, pp. 211–229.

41. For more on proxemics, see Jane Whitney Gibson and Richard M. Hodgetts, *Organizational Communication: A Managerial Perspective*, 2nd ed. (New York: HarperCollins, 1991), pp. 124–129.

42. William K. Brandt and James M. Hulbert, "Patterns of Communications in the Multinational Corporation: An Empirical Study," *Journal of International Business Studies*, Spring 1976, pp. 57–64.

43. Hildebrandt, "Communication Barriers," pp. 13–14.

44. Ibid., p. 9.

45. Kenichi Ohmae, "The Global Logic of Strategic Alliances," *Harvard Business Review*, March-April 1989, p. 154.

DECISION MAKING AND CONTROLLING

OBJECTIVES OF THE CHAPTER

Although they are not directly related to internationalization, decision making and controlling are two management functions that play critical roles in international operations. In *decision making,* a manager chooses a course of action among alternatives. In *controlling,* the manager evaluates results in relation to plans or objectives and decides what action, if any, to take. How these functions are carried out is influenced by the international context. For example, the amount of decision-making authority given to subsidiaries is influenced by a number of international factors, such as the philosophy of the company and the amount of competition in the local environment. These factors may result in one international unit's having much more decision-making authority than another. Similarly, the tools and techniques that are used to control one subsidiary may differ from those used to control another.

This chapter examines the different decision-making and controlling management functions used by MNCs, notes some of the major factors that account for differences between these functions, and identifies the major challenges of the years ahead. The specific objectives of this chapter are:

1. **PROVIDE** comparative examples of decision making in different countries.
2. **PRESENT** some of the major factors affecting the degree of decision-making authority given to overseas units.
3. **COMPARE** and **CONTRAST** direct controls with indirect controls.
4. **DESCRIBE** some of the major differences in the ways that MNCs control operations.
5. **DISCUSS** some of the specific performance measures that are used to control international operations.

THE DECISION-MAKING AND CONTROLLING LINKAGES

Decision making and controlling are two vital and often interlinked functions of international management. For example, Fiat recently released its new Bravo and Brava models in Europe. These cars are aimed at the midsize market and incorporate technological sophistication and sleek styling. They offer newly designed five-cylinder engines, the latest in easy-to-use controls, and sound-proofing to muffle exterior noise.[1] Fiat needs these new offerings to bolster both sales and profitability, and if the cars do not generate the expected enthusiasm, the company could find itself in serious financial difficulty. Hopefully, the Fiat decision makers have made the right choices, and their control function will determine if they have.

Another recent example of decision making and control in action is IBM, which recently acquired Lotus and now is trying to position itself to meet the changing demands of the computer market place. The decision to make this acquisition gives IBM both Lotus' cc:Mail as well as Notes, which are top-selling packages for electronic-mail and groupware. IBM aims to make Notes a widespread "platform" for building networked information systems. This strategy also is important in preventing Microsoft from dominating networked computing the way that it currently rules desktop PCs. In fact, as the center of gravity continues to shift from desktop PCs to networks, operating systems such as Windows may no longer be the key strategic technology—thus, opening the door for IBM to get a big jump on Microsoft. The control function will tell whether this decision by IBM managers will re-establish this recently troubled firm as the major player in the industry and generate the increased sales and profits it seeks from this acquisition.[2]

Another example of the interlink between decision making and control in the computer industry is Dell Computer, which has learned the impact that poor decisions can have on the bottom line. In 1993, the firm had sales of $2 billion and managed to increase this total to $3 billion the next year. In the process of this sales growth, however, net income plunged from a $100 million profit to a $50 million loss! This company made a number of poor decisions, including going into the retail market and not being able to compete effectively with Compaq's strong brand name or Packard Bell's cutthroat pricing. Besides these decisions, however, Dell's phenomenal growth lacked the necessary controls to ensure financial liquidity and profitability. Dell was unable to track profits and losses by product type, technicians had thousands of dollars of spare parts sitting on their desks, and most of the response to customer orders was done in a reactionary, emergency mode. To counter these problems, the company brought in senior managers with a wide range of experience, and Dell now has reoriented itself. Today, the firm focuses on high-margin customers and has opted to sell exclusively through direct marketing rather than retailing. While its market share has declined from 5.6 percent to 4.6 percent, the company's profitability has been re-established. In 1995, sales were $3.5 billion, and outside analysts estimated that they would be $5 billion in 1996. At the same time, profitability in 1995 jumped to $150 million and was forecasted at $275 million for the following year. Stockholders also began to breathe a sigh of relief. The price per share, which plunged from $50 at the beginning of 1993 to $8 nine months later, slowly began to increase, and by late 1995, it stood at $75. Clearly, Dell Computer's decisions and controlling processes have helped to produce the desired results. Now it will be a matter of staying the course.[3]

Still another example of decision making and control is provided by the German automakers, who now are scrambling to cut their high costs to maintain world competitiveness. One reason for their problems is that between 1980 and 1994, the hourly cost for German auto workers almost doubled, reaching around $37 an hour. In contrast, Japanese and U.S. auto workers had average hourly wages of $29 and $27, respectively.[4] To control manufacturing costs, a number of German automakers are setting up operations in other countries. For example, Mercedes has operations in Vittoria, Spain; Hambach, France; and Tuscaloosa, Alabama. BMW has operations in Spartanburg, South Carolina; Volkswagen has facilities in Puebla, Mexico; and Opel has expanded its German-based operations to Antwerp, Belgium, and Luton, Britain, as well as into Poland and Austria. These decisions and follow-up control processes are designed to make these German automakers competitive in world markets.

THE DECISION-MAKING PROCESS

As shown in the previous examples, a number of decision-making areas currently are receiving attention in international management. MNCs manage the operation of their overseas subsidiaries or joint ventures through centralized or decentralized decision making. If centralized decision making is in place, most important decisions are made at the top; if decentralized decision making is in place, decisions are delegated to operating personnel. Another issue is how decision making is used to help the subsidiary respond to the economic and political demands of the country. Sometimes, these decisions are heavily economic in orientation and may concentrate on things such as return on investment for overseas operations. Other times, decisions are a result of cultural differences. For example, the performance evaluation decisions of local personnel by expatriate managers are greatly affected by the expatriate's cultural values. The best way to illustrate differences in decision-making styles in the international arena is to give some comparative examples.

Comparative Examples of Decision Making

Do decision-making philosophies and practices differ from country to country? Research shows that to some extent they do, although there also is evidence that many international operations, regardless of foreign or domestic ownership, use similar decision-making norms.

Most British organizations are highly decentralized. One major reason is that many upper-level managers do not understand the technical details of the business. Top-level managers depend heavily on middle managers to handle much of the decision making by decentralizing to their level.

The French use a different approach. One observer notes that many top French managers graduated from the Grand Écoles, and they often lack confidence in their middle managers.[5] As a result, decision making tends to be centralized.

In Germany, managers place a greater focus on productivity and quality of goods and services than they do on managing subordinates. In addition, management education is highly technical in focus, and a legal system called *codetermination* requires workers and their managers to discuss major decisions. As a result, German MNCs tend to be fairly centralized, autocratic, and hierarchical.

Scandinavian countries also have codetermination, but the Swedes focus much more on quality of work life and the importance of the individual in the organization. As a result, decision making is heavily decentralized and participative.

The Japanese are somewhat different from the Europeans. They make heavy use of a decision-making process called *ringisei*, or decision making by consensus. This approach can be described as follows:

> Under this system any changes in procedures and routines, tactics, and even strategies of a firm are organized by those directly concerned with those changes. The final decision is made at the top level after an elaborate examination of the proposal through successively higher levels in the management hierarchy, and results in acceptance or rejection of a decision only through consensus at every echelon of the management structure.[6]

Japanese consensus decision making is very time-consuming; however, it results in a high degree of commitment and acceptance by all involved parties. The approach combines both centralized and decentralized decision making. Top management still exercises a great deal of authority over what will be examined at the lower levels. Working within this framework, however, lower-level personnel have authority to review, analyze, critique, and recommend courses of action.

MNCs based in the United States tend to use fairly centralized decision making in managing their overseas units. This approach provides the necessary control for developing a worldwide strategy, because it ensures that all units are operating according to the overall strategic plan.

As shown in these examples, a number of decision-making approaches are used around the world. Most evidence, however, indicates that the overall trend currently is toward centralization. For example, in terms of both delegation and decision-making authority of overseas subsidiaries, there is evidence of a fair degree of centralization in areas such as marketing policies, financial matters, use of expatriate personnel, and decisions on production capacity. The results of a comparative study are summarized as follows:

> The convergence in organizational practices in general, and decision making in particular, is taking place rapidly. This can be seen from the results of our recent study of United States, German, British, Japanese, and Swedish multinational companies. The results showed the United States management practices concerning decision making are the norms being followed by other nations. Other countries' practices correlated strongly with those of United States practices.[7]

A number of reasons help to account for this trend toward centralized decision making in international management areas. One of the most important is the desire to increase economies of scale and to attain higher operational efficiency. Such centralized decision making, however, can stifle the creativity and flexibility needed by the subsidiary. In resolving this dilemma, effective MNCs try to evaluate each overseas operation on its own merits. A number of factors will influence international managers' conclusions about retaining or delegating decision making.

Factors Affecting Decision-Making Authority

A number of factors influence the decision-making authority that likely will give to a subsidiary. Table 11-1 lists some of the most important situational factors, and the following discussion looks at each in detail.

TABLE 11-1

FACTORS THAT INFLUENCE CENTRALIZATION OR DECENTRALIZATION OF DECISION MAKING IN SUBSIDIARY OPERATIONS

Encourage centralization	Encourage decentralization
Large size	Small size
Large capital investment	Small capital investment
Relatively high importance to MNC	Relatively low importance to MNC
Highly competitive environment	Stable environment
Strong volume-to-unit-cost relationship	Weak volume-to-unit-cost relationship
High degree of technology	Moderate to low degree of technology
Strong importance attached to brand name, patent rights, etc.	Little importance attached to brand name, patent rights, etc.
Low level of product diversification	High level of product diversification
Homogeneous product lines	Heterogeneous product lines
Small geographic distance between home office and subsidiary	Large geographic distance between home office and subsidiary
High interdependence between the units	Low interdependence between the units
Fewer highly competent managers in host country	More highly competent managers in host country
Much experience in international business	Little experience in international business

Company size influences decision making in that large organizations have a greater need for co-ordination and integration of operations. To ensure that all subsidiaries are effectively managed, the MNC will centralize the authority for a number of critical decisions. This centralization is designed to increase the overall efficiency of operations, and to the extent that centralization creates the desired uniformity and co-ordination, this is precisely what happens.

The greater the MNC's capital investment, the more likely that decision making will be centralized. The home office wants to keep a tight rein on its investment and ensure that everything is running smoothly. The subsidiary manager will be required to submit periodic reports, and on-site visits from home office personnel are quite common.

The more important the overseas operation is to the MNC, the closer the MNC will control it. Home-office management will monitor performance carefully, and the subsidiary manager usually will not be allowed to make any major decisions without first clearing them with the MNC senior management. In fact, in managing important overseas operations, the home office typically will appoint someone who they know will respond to their directives and will regard this individual as an extension of the central management staff.

In domestic situations, when competition increases, management will decentralize authority and give the local manager greater decision-making authority. This reduces the time that is needed for responding to competitive threats. In the international arena, however, just the opposite approach is used. As competition increases and profit margins are driven down, home-office management seeks to standardize product and marketing decisions to reduce cost and maintain profitability. More and more upper-level operating decisions are made by central management and merely implemented by the subsidiary.

If there is a strong volume-to-unit-cost relationship, firms that are able to produce large quantities will have lower cost per unit than those that produce smaller amounts. Under these conditions, home-office management typically will centralize decision making and assume authority over sourcing and marketing-related matters as well as overall strategy. This helps to ensure that the subsidiary's unit cost remains low.

The more sophisticated the level of technology, the greater the degree of centralized decision making. The MNC will attempt to protect these resources by making technology-related decisions at the home office. This is particularly true for high-tech, research-intensive firms such as computer and pharmaceutic companies, which do not want their technology controlled at the local level.

If strong importance is attached to brand name, patent rights, and so forth, decision making likely will be centralized. The MNC will want to protect its rights by making these types of decisions in the home office.

The greater the amount of product and service diversification, the greater the decentralization of the decision-making process, because the MNC typically will not have the staff or the resources for co-ordinating these diversified offerings on a worldwide basis. The home-office management will rely on the subsidiary management to handle this task. In addition, as the overseas unit becomes increasingly skilled in manufacturing and marketing products at the local level, the chance of the home management's recentralizing decision making becomes more remote.

If product and service lines are heterogeneous, differences often exist in the socioeconomic, political, legal, and cultural environments in the various countries where the firm is operating. These differences typically result in the MNC's turning over operating control to the local subsidiaries. In addition, the greater the differences in the environment between the home country and the subsidiary, the more likely the MNC will decentralize the decision-making process.

If the subsidiary and home office are far apart, decentralization is more likely than if the subsidiary is located near the home office. There is evidence that U.S. subsidiaries in North America are more closely controlled than those in South America and that those in the Far East are least controlled of all. The farther away the subsidiary, the more likely the home office will give it increased autonomy.

The greater the degree of interdependence among the units, typically the greater the centralization of decision making. The home office will want to co-ordinate and integrate the units into an effective system, usually from headquarters.

If the subsidiary has highly competent local managers, the chances for decentralization are increased, because the home office has more confidence in delegating to the local level and less to gain by making all the important decisions. Conversely, if the local managers are inexperienced or not highly effective, the MNC likely will centralize decision making and make many of the major decisions at headquarters.

If the firm has had a great deal of international experience, its operations likely will be more centralized. This finding is in accord with the research cited earlier, which shows a convergence toward more centralization by multinational firms.

In some areas of operation, MNCs tend to retain decision making at the top (centralization); other areas fall within the domain of subsidiary management (decentralization). It is most common to find finance, research and development, and strategic planning decisions being made at MNC headquarters, and the subsidiaries must work within the parameters established by the home office. In addition, when the subsidiary is selling new products in growing markets, centralized decision making is more likely. As the product line matures and the subsidiary managers gain experience, however, the company will start to rely more on decentralized decision making. These decisions involve planning and budgeting systems, performance evaluations, assignment of managers to the subsidiary, and use of co-ordinating committees to mesh the operations of the subsidiary with the worldwide operations of the MNC. The right degree of centralized or decentralized decision making can be critical to the success of the MNC.

A good example is Germany's *Mittelstand,* which is a term used to describe the approximately 2.5 million small- and medium-sized firms that account for two-thirds of the nation's economy and 80 percent of employment in the private sector. In recent years, these firms have been hard hit by large wage increases won by the unions. As a result, they now are fighting back, determined to survive at all costs. The owners have begun centralizing authority, trimming their work forces, moving more and more production out of Germany and to lower-wage countries in Southern and Central Europe as well as Asia, and using technology to increase productivity. These decisions are helping these firms to weather this latest economic storm and may well affect decision-making styles in larger German firms that also are struggling to remain competitive internationally.[8]

DECISION-MAKING ISSUES

There are a number of decision-making issues and challenges with which MNCs currently are being confronted. Three of the most prominent include total quality management decisions, use of joint ventures and other forms of co-operative agreements, and strategies for attacking competition in the international marketplace. The following examines some of the latest developments in each area.

Total Quality Management Decisions

To achieve world-class competitiveness as outlined in Chapter 3, MNCs are finding that a commitment to total quality management is critical. *Total quality management (TQM)* is an organizational strategy and accompanying techniques that result in delivery of high-quality products and/or services to customers.[9] The concept and techniques of TQM, which were introduced in Chapter 8 in relation to strategic planning, also are relevant to decision making and controlling.

One of the primary areas where TQM is having a big impact is in manufacturing.[10] For example, in recent years, U.S. automakers have greatly improved the quality of their cars, but the Japanese have continuous improvement of quality and thus still have the lead. A number of TQM techniques have been successfully applied to improve the quality of manufactured goods. One is the use of concurrent engineering/interfunctional teams in which designers, engineers, production specialists, and customers work together to develop new products.[11] This approach involves all the necessary parties and overcomes what used to be an all-too-common procedure: The design people would tell the manufacturing group what to produce, and the latter would send the finished product to retail stores for sale to the customer. Today, MNCs taking a TQM approach are customer-driven.

They use TQM techniques to tailor their output according to customer needs. A Toshiba executive recently noted: "In the past few years, we have strengthened our design review method by implementing a more thorough analysis of customer requirements in the product development stage. We have developed checklists that help us monitor every step of product development from planning and design through manufacturing, marketing and after-sales service."[12] IBM has followed a similar approach in developing its new AS/400 computer systems. Customer advisory councils were created to provide input, test the product, and suggest refinements. The result was one of the most successful product launches in the company's history.

A particularly critical issue is how much decision making to delegate to subordinates. TQM uses employee *empowerment,* which was discussed in Chapter 3. Individuals and groups are encouraged to generate ideas for improving quality and given the decision-making authority and necessary information to implement them. Many MNCs have had outstanding success with empowerment. For example, General Electric credits employee empowerment for cutting in half the time needed to change product-mix production of its dishwashers in response to market demand, and Kodak used the empowerment of its workers to increase productivity by teaching workers how to inspect their own work, keep track of their own performance, and even fix their own machines.

Another TQM technique that MNCs are successfully employing to develop and maintain world-class competitiveness is rewards and recognition. These range from increases in pay and benefits to the use of merit pay, discretionary bonuses, pay-for-skills and knowledge plans, plaques, and public recognition.[13] The important thing to realize is that the rewards and recognition approaches that work well in one country may be ineffective in another. For example, individual recognition in the United States may be appropriate and valued by workers, but in Japan, group rewards are more important as Japanese do not like to be singled out for personal praise. Similarly, although putting a picture or plaque on the wall to honor an individual is common practice in the United States, these rewards are frowned on in Finland as they remind the workers of how their neighbor, the Russians, used this system to encourage people to increase output (but not necessarily quality) and now the Russian economy is in shambles.[14]

Still another technique associated with TQM is the use of ongoing training to achieve continual improvement. This training takes a wide variety of forms, ranging from statistical quality control techniques to team meetings designed to generate ideas for streamlining operations and eliminating waste. In all cases, the objective is to apply what the Japanese call *kaizen,* or continuous improvement. By adopting a TQM perspective and applying the techniques discussed earlier, MNCs find that they can both develop and maintain a worldwide competitive edge.[15] A good example is Zytec, the world-class, Minnesota-based manufacturer of power supplies. The customer base for Zytec ranges from the United States to Japan to Europe. One way in which the firm ensures that it maintains a total quality perspective is to continually identify client demands and then work to exceed these expectations. Table 11-2 illustrates some of the targets this company aims to achieve before the end of this decade.

Indirectly related to TQM is ISO 9000. This refers to the International Standards Organization (ISO) certification to ensure quality products and services. Areas that are examined by the ISO certification team include design (product or service

TABLE 11-2

POWER SUPPLY PRODUCT CUSTOMER NEEDS: 1994–2000

Customer needs	1994 (typical)	2000 (typical)
Improved quality	400–2000 ppm[a]	3.4 ppm
Accelerated time to market for prototype	7–16 weeks	5–10 weeks
Increased efficiency/reduction in heat	70–75% efficient	75–90% efficient
Lower price	$0.35–$1.00/Watt	$0.20–$0.40/watt
Reduced output noise	2%	1%
Reduced operating voltages	3.3–5.0 Volts	1.5–5.0 Volts
Power supply intelligence	Limited intelligence	Integrated intelligence
Distributed power	Limited application	Increased application
Quality	>4 sigma[b]	>6 sigma[c]
Delivery frequency	Weekly	Daily
Repair on-time delivery	85%	97%
Repair cycle time	12 days	5 days
Product warranty	1–2 years	Lifetime
Product replacement	10–15 days	1-day exchange
Product locations	U.S. and Europe	Worldwide
Time to build first prototype	7–16 weeks	5–10 weeks
Time to build initial product	20–32 weeks	12–16 weeks
Geographic servicing	U.S. and Europe	North America, Europe, and East Asia

Notes: [a]parts per million; [b]6210 errors per million; [c]3.5 errors per million.
Source: Reported in Richard M. Hodgetts, *TQM in Small and Medium-Sized Organizations* (New York: AMACOM, 1996), p. 48.

specifications), process control (instructions for manufacturing or service functions), purchasing, service (e.g., instructions for conducting after-sales service), inspection and testing, and training. ISO 9000 certification is becoming a necessary prerequisite to doing business in the EU, but it also is increasingly used as a screening criterion for bidding on contracts or getting business in the United States and other parts of the world. For example, after a year of hard work, Foxboro Corporation, based in Massachusetts, obtained certification, and its business greatly increased.

Co-operative Ventures

Besides TQM, another area where decision making has a particular impact on MNCs is creating and nurturing co-operative ventures. One of the most common is *international joint ventures (IJVs),* which are formal arrangements with foreign partners who typically, although not always, are located in the country where the business will be conducted. In the case of Ford and Mazda, whose IJV was described in Chapter 9, each has operations in the other's country. In some cases, however, two foreign firms will team up to provide goods or services in a third country; one example is Davidson Instrument Panel, a U.S. firm, and Marley, a British company, which have teamed up to produce instrument panels in Born, the Netherlands, then ship them to a Ford Motor plant in Belgium.[16]

IJVs and other co-operative agreements are becoming extremely popular because of the benefits they offer to both parties. In particular, they provide large firms with an opportunity to gain a foothold in new markets. For example, Daewoo Motor of Korea recently invested $1.1 billion in Fabryka Samochodow Osobowych (FSO), a state-owned, Polish auto factory. The firm's 60 percent ownership stake helps strategically position Daewoo in the Eastern European auto market. This is all part of a master strategy that also has seen Daewoo invest $340 million in Fabryka Samochodow Lublinie (FSL), another Polish automaker, and $156 million in a joint venture to build its Ciselo family car with Romania's Automobile Craiova SA. Poland and Romania are Central and Eastern Europe's two most attractive auto markets, with a significant population and six people for every automobile. Internationally, this geographic region has a growth potential similar to that of South Korea's own robust auto sector.[17]

Another example of IJVs is Chevron-Kazakhstan (a former republic in the U.S.S.R. in Central Asia). This joint venture currently is producing 40,000 to 50,000 barrels of oil a day, and it is looking to expand this volume. As a result, the joint venture now is negotiating with Iran for an oil swap that would result in the Chevron group delivering 30,000 to 40,000 barrels of oil per day to Iran by the joint venture, Tengiz-chevroil (TCO). In turn, Iran would give the joint venture oil from its own giant Tengiz field or its supply on Kharg Island in the Persian Gulf. Interestingly, this arrangement would allow the Kazakhstan government to export Iranian oil to the world market. Currently, this cannot be done, because the Kazakhstan oil must be piped to the Caspian Sea, and there is a political deadlock over construction of the needed pipeline. If the joint-venture partners can work out a satisfactory solution, all parties may well prosper.[18]

As shown in these examples, multinationals are and will be making a host of decisions related to IJVs. In Russia, the current trend is to renegotiate many of the old agreements and seek smaller deals that entail less bureaucratic red tape and are easier to bring to fruition.[19] At the same time, the U.S. administration is trying to create a plan for providing assistance to the former Soviet republics, and this likely will generate increased interest in the use of IJVs.[20]

Besides the former Soviet Union, other areas of the world that also were previously closed to foreign investment are beginning to open up. A good example is Vietnam. Japan's Idemitsu Oil Development Company has signed a deal with the Vietnamese government that will give this company the rights to explore an offshore oil and gas field in the Gulf of Tonkin. U.S. firms are beginning to take advantage of opportunities in Vietnam as well. For example, Citibank and Bank of America both have been approved for branch status in Vietnam. The bulk of their business will be wholesale banking and, in the case of Bank of America, advising the government on financing the rebuilding of Vietnam's crippled power sector.[21] Other U.S. firms with interest in Vietnam include AT&T, Coca-Cola, General Electric, Mobil, and Ralston Purina, to name but a few of the most visible. Over the next few years, more and more multinationals will seek to tap the economic potential of formerly isolated nations that now are prepared to modify their political agendas to improve the standard of living for their people.

Decisions for Attacking the Competition

Another series of key decisions relates to MNC actions that are designed to attack the competition and gain a foothold in world markets.[22] The accompanying box,

INTERNATIONAL MANAGEMENT IN ACTION

Kodak Goes Digital, Making Film Obsolete

Kodak has been attacking the competition in a number of ways. One has been to file a complaint with the U.S. government accusing its main competitor, Fuji, of blocking Kodak growth in the Japanese market and asking the administration to take steps to correct this situation. This is only a short-term strategy designed to increase the growth of Kodak film in one country, however. Of far more future importance are technological developments such as the emergence of inexpensive cameras that use digital technology, which will make film obsolete.

Under its current CEO, George Fisher, who was hired away from Motorola, Kodak is in the throes of reorganizing and focusing its efforts on new growth areas while continuing to extract as much sales and profit as possible from its current product lines. For example, Fisher recently created a dital imaging unit, thus gathering most of the firm's digital talent into one division. Before this, efforts at digital product development were spread through the divisions. At the same time, Kodak is working to reignite overall growth by focusing on the Asian market. The company believes that it can double its growth rate in photography, a tough challenge given that the world market is growing very slowly.

The real focus of Fisher's effort is in digital technology, however, and the company's strategy in this area finally ap-

pears to be getting into focus. Still, this digital thrust will not be easy, because of both the difficulty in generating research and development breakthroughs and in marketing the new products. Some of Kodak's earlier efforts were anything but spectacular. For example, the photo-CD, which is a compact disk that Kodak developed to store photographs for viewing on TV screens or PC monitors, flopped as a consumer product. Buyers balked at paying $500 for a player that plugs into a TV plus $20 per disk. Fortunately, the company did find a ready market among small businesses such as desktop publishers and real-estate agents, which used the unit to display their offerings. The lesson is clear: Creating a new technologic product is not enough; it also is important to carefully identify the market where it can be sold successfully.

Kodak knows that the industry will go digital and the film business eventually will die out. Therefore the company must be prepared to meet the future with new products such as the digital camera. In the interim, the firm also must push ahead in the film business and with new camera offerings such as its single-use, throwaway camera, which really is nothing more than an inexpensive cardboard-and-plastic box with a roll of film inside. Kodak also has extended this line to include telephoto, panoramic, portrait, and underwater versions of the camera. The firm hopes that all these efforts will help them to attack the competition successfully while continuing to develop and perfect digital products that will appeal to the masses.

International Management in Action: "Kodak Goes Digital, Making Film Obsolete" gives an example. Another is the Deutsche Bank's recent decision to expand its operations in North America and to offer more services. Although this German MNC traditionally has confined its activities to lending money, it now has moved into trading and financial advisory services for large corporations and wealthy individuals. It is drawing heavily on its familiarity with European security markets to offer U.S. clients investment assistance as well as to sell U.S. securities overseas.[23]

Another interesting way of attacking the competition is the decision by the Japanese government to help U.S. firms sell goods in Japan. The logic is simple: By increasing sales of U.S. MNCs, the Japanese hope to blunt criticism that their markets are closed to outsiders. To promote U.S. MNC success in Japan, the government has created an organization known as the Japan External Trade Organization, or "Jetro," for short. Jetro has advisors in the United States who are paid to help encourage and promote exports. These advisors serve as intermediaries, bringing together U.S. firms that want to sell with Japanese firms that are looking for suppliers and products. To date, a number of U.S. firms have done quite well thanks to Jetro. For example, Crane National Vendors of Bridgeton, Missouri, has sold $4 million of its computerized vending machines in Japan. Marlink, Inc., of Rocky Mount, North Carolina, has sold over $1.3 million of its log cabins in Japan.

Andermac, Inc., of Yuba City, California, has designed hospital beds specifically for the Japan market and has sales of over $500,000 to the Japanese.

THE CONTROLLING PROCESS

As indicated in the introduction to this chapter, controlling involves evaluating results in relation to plans or objectives and deciding what action to take. An excellent illustration is Mitsubishi's purchase of 80 percent of Rockefeller Center in the late 1980s. The Japanese firm paid $1.4 billion for this choice piece of Manhattan real estate, and it looked like a very wise decision. Over the next 6 years, however, depressed rental prices and rising maintenance costs resulted in Mitsubishi sinking an additional $500 million into the project. Finally, in late 1995, the company decided it had had enough and announced that it was walking away from the investment. Mitsubishi passed ownership to Rockefeller Center Properties Inc., the publicly traded, real-estate investment trust that holds the mortgage on the Center. The cost of keeping the properties was too great for the Japanese firm, which decided to cut its losses and focus efforts on more lucrative opportunities elsewhere.[24]

Another example is IBM, which has been trying very hard to resurrect its troubled PC division. In doing so, the firm has taken a number of control steps, including slashing the personal computer work force by 20 percent, cutting costs by $400 million, increasing inventory turnover by 25 percent, reducing the number of different components in its PCs by an average of 50 percent, and increasing worldwide shipments by 22 percent. However, there still is more to do. As of 1995, gross profit margins still trail those of Apple, Compaq, and Dell. More products must be developed in the $1500 to $2000 range, which is the "sweet spot" for increasing market share. Additionally, the IBM PC division needs to streamline development to get new models into high-volume manufacturing faster and tighten its product shipments so that orders are sent out within days rather than weeks.[25] Such efforts throughout the corporation should help to increase revenue, which has been fairly stable over the last few years, as well as net income, which now has begun to turn around but could go much higher.[26]

In many ways, the control function is conceptually and practically similar to decision making. Like decision-making approaches, the approaches used by multinationals in controlling their operations have long been an area of interest. Of particular concern has been how companies attempt to control their overseas operations to become an integrated, co-ordinated unit. Unfortunately, a number of control problems arise. Examples include: (1) the objectives of the foreign operation and the corporate objectives conflict; (2) the objectives of joint-venture partners and corporate management conflict; (3) amount of experience and competence in planning are widely diverse among foreign CEOs; and (4) basic philosophic conflicts exist about objectives and policies of foreign operations, largely because of cultural differences between home- and host-country managers. The following discussion examines the various types of and approaches to control to help overcome such problems.

Types of Control

Control functions that can be used by MNCs commonly are classified into two broad types: direct and indirect.[27] MNCs make wide use of both.

Direct Controls *Direct controls* involve face-to-face or personal meetings to monitor operations. A good example is International Telephone and Telegraph (ITT), which holds monthly management meetings at its New York headquarters. These meetings are run by the CEO of the company, and reports are submitted by each ITT unit manager throughout the world. Problems are discussed, goals set, evaluations made, and actions taken that will help the unit to improve its effectiveness.

Another common form of direct control is visits by top executives to overseas affiliates or subsidiaries. During these visits, top managers can learn firsthand the problems and challenges facing the unit and offer assistance.

A third form is the staffing practices of MNCs. By determining who to send overseas to run the unit, the corporation can directly control how the operation will be run. The company will want the manager to make operating decisions and handle day-to-day matters, but the individual also will know which decisions should be cleared with the home office. In fact, this approach to direct control sometimes results in a manager who is more responsive to central management than to the needs of the local unit.

A fourth form is the organizational structure itself. By designing a structure that makes the unit highly responsive to home-office requests and communications, the MNC ensures that all overseas operations are run in accord with central management's desires. This structure can be established through formal reporting relationships and chain of command (who reports to whom).

Indirect Controls *Indirect controls* use reports and other written forms of communication to control operations. One of the most common examples is the use of monthly operating reports that are sent to the home office. Other examples, which typically are used to supplement the operating report, include financial statements, such as balance sheets, income statements, cash budgets, and financial ratios, that provide insights into the unit's financial health. The home office uses these operating and financial data to evaluate how well things are going and make decisions regarding necessary changes. Three sets of financial statements usually are required from subsidiaries: (1) statements prepared to meet the national accounting standards and procedures prescribed by law and other professional organizations in the host country; (2) statements prepared to comply with the accounting principles and standards required by the home country; and (3) statements prepared to meet the financial consolidation requirements of the home country.[28]

Indirect controls are particularly important in international management because of the great expense associated with direct methods. Typically, MNCs will use indirect controls to monitor performance on a monthly basis, whereas direct controls are used semiannually or annually. This dual approach best provides the company with effective control of its operations at a price that also is cost-effective.

Approaches to Control

International managers can employ many different approaches to control. These approaches typically are dictated by the MNC's philosophy of control, the economic environment in which the overseas unit is operating, and the needs and desires of the managerial personnel who staff the unit. Working within control parameters, MNCs will structure their processes so that they are as efficient and effective as possible. As one analysis notes, "selected tools must be used to manage data, to manage managers, and to manage conflicts; and . . . the successful companies blend an array of tools into a consistent management process."[29] Typically, these tools give the unit manager the autonomy needed to adapt to changes in the market and attract competent local personnel. The tools also provide for coordination of operations with the home office so that the overseas unit is in harmony with the MNC's strategic plan.

Some control tools are universal. For example, all MNCs use financial tools in monitoring overseas units. This was true as long as two decades ago, when the following was reported:

> The cross-cultural homogeneity in financial control is in marked contrast to the heterogeneity exercised over the areas of international operations. American subsidiaries of Italian and Scandinavian firms are virtually independent operationally from their parents in functions pertaining to marketing, production, and research and development; whereas, the subsidiaries of German and British firms have limited freedom in these areas. Almost no autonomy on financial matters is given by any nationality to the subsidiaries.[30]

Some Major Differences   MNCs control operations in many different ways, and these often vary considerably from country to country. For example, how British firms control their overseas operations often is different from how German or French firms do. Similarly, U.S. MNCs tend to have their own approach to controlling that differs from both European and Japanese approaches. When Horovitz examined the key characteristics of top management control in Great Britain, Germany, and France, he found that British controls had four common characteristics: (1) financial records were sophisticated and heavily emphasized; (2) top management tended to focus its attention on major problem areas and did not get involved in specific, detailed matters of control; (3) control was used more for general guidance than for surveillance; and (4) operating units had a large amount of marketing autonomy.[31]

This model was in marked contrast to that of German managers, who employed very detailed control and focused attention on all variances large and small. These managers also placed heavy control on the production area and stressed operational efficiency. In achieving this centralized control, managers used a large central staff for measuring performance, analyzing variances, and compiling quantitative reports for senior executives. Overall, the control process in the German firms was used as a policing and surveillance instrument. French managers employed a control system that was closer to that of the Germans than to the British, however. Control was used more for surveillance than for guiding operations, and the process was centrally administered. Even so, the French system was less systematic and sophisticated.[32]

How do U.S. MNCs differ from their European counterparts? One comparative study found that a major difference is that U.S. firms tend to rely much more heavily on reports and other performance-related data. Americans make greater use of output control, and Europeans rely more heavily on behavioral control. Commenting on the differences between these two groups, the researcher noted: "This pattern appears to be quite robust and continues to exist even when a number of common factors that seem to influence control are taken into account."[33] Some specific findings from this study include:

1. Control in U.S. MNCs focuses more on the quantifiable, objective aspects of a foreign subsidiary, whereas control in European MNCs tends to be used to measure more qualitative aspects. The U.S. approach allows comparative analyses between other foreign operations as well as domestic units; the European measures are more flexible and allow control to be exercised on a unit-by-unit basis.

2. Control in U.S. MNCs requires more precise plans and budgets in generating suitable standards for comparison. Control in European MNCs requires a high level of companywide understanding and agreement regarding what constitutes appropriate behavior and how such behavior supports the goals of both the subsidiary and the parent firm.

3. Control in U.S. MNCs requires large central staffs and centralized information-processing capability. Control in European MNCs requires a larger cadre of capable expatriate managers who are willing to spend long periods of time abroad. This control characteristic is reflected in the career approaches used in the various MNCs. Although U.S. multinationals do not encourage lengthy stays in foreign management positions, European MNCs often regard these positions as stepping stones to higher offices.

4. Control in European MNCs requires more decentralization of operating decisions than control in U.S. MNCs.

5. Control in European MNCs favors short vertical spans or reporting channels from the foreign subsidiary to responsible positions in the parent.[34]

As noted earlier in the discussion of decision making, these differences help to explain why many researchers have found European subsidiaries to be more decentralized than U.S. subsidiaries. On the one hand, Europeans rely on the managerial personnel they assign from headquarters to run the unit properly. Americans tend to hire a greater percentage of local management people and control operations through reports and other objective, performance-related data. The difference results in Europeans' relying more on socioemotional control systems and Americans' opting for task-oriented, objective control systems.

Evaluating Approaches to Control   Is one control approach any better than the other? At present, each seems to work best for its respective group. Some studies predict that as MNCs increase in size, however, they likely will move toward the objective orientation of the U.S. MNCs. Commenting on the data gathered from large German and U.S. MNCs, the researchers concluded:

> Control mechanisms have to be harmonized with the main characteristics of management corporate structure to become an integrated part of the global organization concept and to meet situational needs. Trying to explain the differences in concepts of control we have to consider that the companies of the U.S. sample were much larger and more diversified.... Accordingly, they use different corporate structures, combining operational units into larger units and integrating these through primarily centralized, indirect, and task-oriented control.... The German companies have not (yet) reached this size and complexity, so a behavioral model of control seems to be fitting.[35]

Approaches to control also differ between U.S. and Japanese firms. For example, one study surveyed the attitudes of a large sample of Japanese and U.S. controllers and line managers. Respondents were drawn from the 500 largest industrial firms in both countries, and some of the results are presented in Table 11-3.

TABLE 11-3

SELECTED BELIEFS RELATED TO PLANNING AND CONTROL

	Statement of results—average responses[a]			
	Japan		United States	
	Managers	Controllers	Managers	Controllers
To be useful in performance evaluation of managers, a budget must be revised continuously throughout the year.	3.07	3.14	2.70	2.48
It is important that budgets be very detailed.	3.38	3.31	2.93	2.97
It is appropriate to charge other activities when budgeted funds are used up.	3.01	2.91	1.96	1.52
Budgets should be developed from the bottom up rather than from the top down.	3.13	3.01	3.68	3.96
Budgets are useful in communicating the goal and planned activities of the company.	4.54	4.68	4.11	4.23
Budgets are useful in coordinating activities of various departments.	4.24	4.46	3.78	4.02
A manager who fails to attain the budgets should be replaced.	2.56	2.67	2.00	1.92
Top management should judge a manager's performance mainly on the basis of attaining budget profit.	3.25	3.38	2.27	2.07
It is important that executive compensation depend on a comparison of actual and budgeted performance.	3.18	3.18	3.55	3.56
It is important that managers who perform exceptionally well receive more money than other managers in similar positions.	3.84	3.92	4.28	4.14
It is important for a manager to have quantitative or analytic skills as opposed to people skills.	3.12	3.15	2.04	1.96
The best way to determine the value of capital projects is through the use of quantitative analysis.	3.61	3.80	3.23	3.37

Note: [a]The response scale was as follows:
strongly disagree	1
disagree	2
neutral	3
agree	4
strongly agree	5

Source: Adapted from Lane Daley, James Jiambalvo, Gary L. Sundem, and Yasumasa Kondo, "Attitudes toward Financial Control Systems in the United States and Japan," *Journal of International Business Studies*, Fall 1985, pp. 100–102. Used with permission.

One overall finding of the research was that Japanese controllers and managers prefer less participation in the control process than their U.S. counterparts do. In addition, the Japanese have longer-term planning horizons, view budgets as more of a communication device than a controlling tool, and prefer more slack in their budgets than the Americans. These results are extremely important in terms of adapting U.S. approaches to Japanese-owned subsidiaries. The study results suggest the following:

> U.S. managers who wish to design control systems for foreign divisions in Japan (or vice-versa) may wish to consider modifications to the typical domestic system, or they should at least be aware of the potential differences in responses to the system in the areas of budget development, evaluation against budgets, long-run/short-run orientation of budgets, the use of budget slack, and the use of analytic tools in developing inputs to the budget process to name a few.[36]

TABLE 11-4	
CHARACTERISTICS OF TYPE A AND TYPE Z ORGANIZATIONS	
Type A **(traditional U.S. firm)**	**Type Z** **(modified U.S. firm)**
Short-term employment	Long-term employment
Individual decision making	Consensual decision making
Individual responsibility	Individual responsibility
Rapid evaluation and promotion	Slow evaluation and promotion
Explicit, formalized control	Implicit, informal control with explicit, formalized measures
Specialized career path	Moderately specialized career path
Segmented concern	Holistic concern, including family

Source: Adapted from Alfred M. Jaeger, "Contrasting Control Modes in the Multinational Corporation: Theory, Practice, and Implications," *International Studies of Management & Organization,* Spring 1982, p. 63. Used with permission.

A number of researchers have focused on this concept of adapting control techniques to suit the culture of the foreign enterprise. One particularly interesting approach has been the investigation of whether a bureaucratic approach is more effective than a cultural control system. One researcher investigated this by contrasting the approaches of two firms. One used a typical U.S. bureaucratic approach, following what is commonly referred to as "Theory A" (see Table 11-4). The other used a modified U.S. approach that incorporates elements of Japanese management, commonly referred to as "Theory Z."

There were benefits and drawbacks to each approach. For example, the Type A subsidiary had more freedom to carry out its activities in accord with local practices. The Type Z subsidiary worked to introduce its own culture and get the local personnel to accept it. Therefore, the Type A approach was more effective in adjusting to local demands from both the personnel and the government. The Type Z subsidiary remained in closer contact with headquarters, however, and because of its humanistic approach to managing the personnel (e.g., no layoffs), it was more highly regarded by the workers than the Type A subsidiary was. So, in deciding which form of control to use, MNCs must determine whether they want a more bureaucratic or a more cultural control approach. From the cultural perspective, it must be remembered that this control will vary across subsidiaries.[37]

CONTROL TECHNIQUES

A number of performance measures are used for control purposes. Three of the most common types are those related to financial performance, quality performance, and personnel performance.

Financial Performance

Financial performance evaluation of a foreign subsidiary or affiliate usually is based on profit and return on investment. *Profit* is the amount remaining after all expenses are deducted from total revenues. *Return on investment (ROI)* is measured through dividing profit by assets; some firms use profit divided by owners' equity (returns on owners' investment, or ROOI) in referring to the return-on-investment performance measure. In any case, the most important part of the ROI calculation is profits, which often can be manipulated by management. Thus, the amount of profit directly relates to how well or how poorly a unit is judged to perform. For example, if an MNC has an operation in both country A and country B and taxes are lower in country A, the MNC may be able to benefit if the two units have occasion to do business with each other. This benefit can be accomplished by having the unit in country A charge higher prices than usual to the unit in country B, thus providing greater net profits to the MNC. Simply put, sometimes differences in tax rates can be used to maximize overall MNC profits. This same basic form of manipulation can be used in transferring money from one country to another, which can be explained as follows:

> Transfer prices are manipulated upward or downward depending on whether the parent company wishes to inject or remove cash into or from a subsidiary. Prices on imports by a subsidiary from a related subsidiary are raised if the multinational company wishes to move funds from the receiver to the seller, but they are lowered if the objective is to keep the funds in the importing subsidiary. . . . Multinational companies have been known to use transfer pricing for moving excess cash from subsidiaries located in countries with weak currencies to countries with strong currencies in order to protect the value of their current assets.[38]

The so-called "bottomline (i.e., profit) performance" of subsidiaries also can be affected by a devaluation or revaluation of local currency. For example, if a country devalues its currency, then subsidiary export sales will increase, because the price of these goods will be lower for foreign buyers, whose currencies now have greater purchasing power. If the country revalues its currency, then export sales will decline because the price of goods for foreign buyers will rise, because their currencies now will have less purchasing power in the subsidiary's country. Likewise, a devaluation of the currency will increase the cost of imported materials and supplies for the subsidiary, and a revaluation will decrease these costs because of the relative changes in the purchasing power of local currency. Because devaluation and revaluation of local currency are outside the control of the overseas unit, bottom-line performance sometimes will be a result of external conditions that do not accurately reflect how well the operation actually is being run.

Of course, not all bottom-line financial performance is a result of manipulation or external environmental conditions. Comparing results from country to country sometimes is difficult, however, because the situations are not similar. For example, managers of South American subsidiaries would have been faced with inflation 100 times or more than inflation elsewhere during the late 1980s. The fluctuating value of the South American country's currency would have made it difficult to use profitability of the unit as a measure for evaluating management. Using financial performance alone when controlling a subsidiary for effective performance can be misleading.

Quality Performance

Just as quality has become a major focus in decision making, as discussed earlier under TQM, it also is a major dimension of the modern control process of MNCs. The term "quality control" (QC) has been around for a long time, and it is a

---

FIGURE 11-1

CLOSED-CYCLE MODEL OF A QUALITY CONTROL PROCESS FLOW

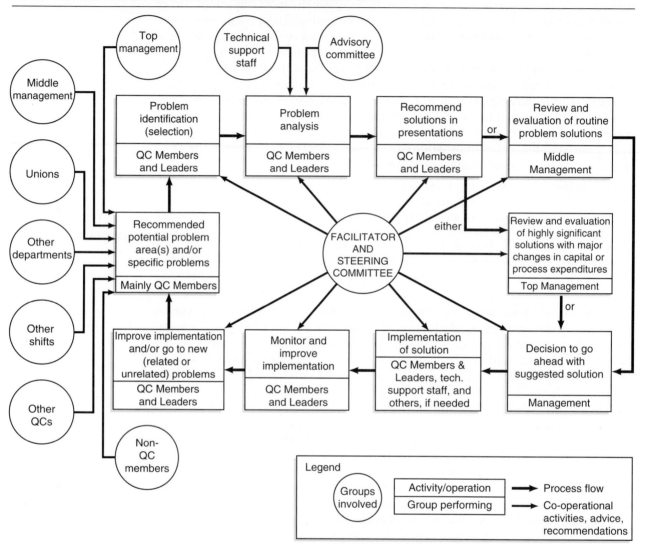

Source: Adapted from H. J. Bocker and H. O. Overgard, "Japanese Quality Circles: A Managerial Response to the Productivity Problem," *Management International Review,* vol. 2, no. 2, 1982, p. 14. Used with permission.

major function of production and operations management. Besides the TQM techniques of concurrent engineering/interfunctional teams, employee empowerment, reward/recognition systems, and training, which were discussed under decision making, another technique more directly associated with the control function is the use of quality circles, which have been popularized by the Japanese. A *quality control circle (QCC)* is a group of workers who meet on a regular basis to discuss ways of improving the quality of work. Figure 11-1 shows what is involved in a quality circle approach to the control process. This approach has helped many MNCs to improve the quality of their goods and services dramatically.

How the Japanese Do Things Differently

There are a number of things that Japanese firms do extremely well. One is to train their people carefully, a strategy that many successful U.S. firms also employ. Another is to try and remain on the technological cutting edge. A third, and increasingly important because of its uniqueness to the Japanese, is to keep a keen focus on developing and bringing to market goods that are competitively priced.

In contrast to Western firms, many Japanese companies use what is called a "target cost" approach. Like other multinational firms, Japanese companies begin the new product development process by conducting marketing research and examining the characteristics of the product to be produced. At this point, however, the Japanese take a different approach. The traditional approach used by MNCs around the world is next to go into designing, engineering, and supplier pricing, then to determine if the cost is sufficiently competitive to move ahead with manufacturing. Japanese manufacturers, on the other hand, first determine the price that the consumer most likely will accept, and then they work with design, engineering, and supply people to ensure that the product can be produced at this price. The other major difference is that after most firms manufacture a product, they will engage in periodic cost reductions. The Japanese, however, use a *kaizen* approach, in which there are continuous cost-reduction efforts.

The critical difference between the two systems is that the Japanese get costs out of the product during the planning and design stage. Additionally, they look at profit in terms of product lines rather than just individual goods, so a consumer product that would be rejected for production by a U.S. or European firm because its projected profitability is too low may be accepted by a Japanese firm because the product will attract additional customers to other offerings in the line. A good example is Sony, which decided to build a smaller version of its compact personal stereo system and market it to older consumers. Sony knew that the profitability of the unit would not be as high as usual, but it went ahead because the product would provide another market niche for the firm and strengthen its reputation. Also, a side benefit is that once a product is out there, it may appeal to an unanticipated market. This was the case with Sony's compact personal stereo system. The unit caught on with young people, and Sony's sales are 50 percent greater than anticipated. Had Sony made its manufacturing decision solely on "stand alone" profitability, the unit never would have been produced.

These approaches are not unique to Japanese firms. Foreign companies operating in Japan are catching on and use them as well. A good example is Coca-Cola Japan. Coke is the leading company in the Japanese soft-drink market, which sees the introduction of more than 1000 new products each year. Most offerings do not last very long, and a cost accountant might well argue that it is not worth the effort to produce them. However, Coca-Cola introduces one new product a month. Most of these sodas, soft drinks, and cold coffees survive less than 90 days, but Coke does not let the short-term bottom line dictate the decision. The firm goes beyond quick profitability and looks at the overall picture. Result: Coca-Cola continues to be the leading soft-drink firm in Japan despite competition that often is more vigorous than that in the United States.

Why are Japanese-made goods of higher quality than those of many other countries? The answer cannot rest solely on technology, because many MNCs have the same or superior technology or the financial ability to purchase it. There must be other causal factors. The accompanying sidebar, "How the Japanese Do Things Differently," gives some details on these factors. One study attempted to answer the question by examining the differences between Japanese and U.S. manufacturers of air conditioners.[39] In this analysis, many of the commonly cited reasons for superior Japanese quality were discovered to be inaccurate. One theory was that Japanese focus their production processes on a relatively limited set of tasks and narrow product lines, but this was not so. Nor was support found for the commonly held belief that single sourcing provided Japanese firms with cost advantages over those using multiple sourcing; the firms studied regularly relied on a number of different suppliers. So, what were the reasons for the quality differences?

One reason was the focus on keeping the workplace clean and ensuring that all machinery and equipment was properly maintained. The Japanese firms were more careful in handling incoming parts and materials, work-in-process, and finished products than their U.S. counterparts. Japanese companies also employed equipment fixtures to a greater extent than U.S. manufacturers in ensuring proper alignment of parts during final assembly.

The Japanese minimized worker error by assigning new employees to existing work teams or pairing them with supervisors. In this way, the new workers gained important experience under the watchful eye of someone who could correct their mistakes.

Another interesting finding was that the Japanese made effective use of QCCs. Quality targets were set, and responsibility for their attainment then fell on the circle while management provided support assistance. This was stated by the researcher as follows:

> In supporting the activities of their QCC's, the Japanese firms in this industry routinely collected extensive quality data. Information on defects was compiled daily, and analyzed for trends. Perhaps most important, the data were made easily accessible to line workers, often in the form of publicly posted charts. More detailed data were available to QCC's on request.[40]

This finding pointed out an important difference between Americans and Japanese. The Japanese pushed data on quality down to the operating employees in the quality circles, whereas Americans tended to aggregate the quality data into summary reports aimed at middle- and upper-level management.

Another important difference is that the Japanese tend to build in early warning systems so that they know when something is going wrong. A good example is that incoming field data are reviewed immediately by the quality department, and problems are assigned to one of two categories: routine or emergency. Special efforts then are made to resolve the emergency problems as quickly as possible. High failure rates attributable to a single persistent problem are identified and handled much faster than in U.S. firms.

Management attitudes toward quality also were quite different. The Japanese operate under the philosophy of "anything worth doing in the area of quality is worth overdoing." Workers are trained for all jobs on the line, even though they eventually are assigned to a single workstation. This method of "training overkill" ensures that everyone can perform every job perfectly and results in two important outcomes: (1) if someone is moved to another job, he or she can handle the work without any additional assistance; and (2) the workers realize that management puts an extremely high value on the need for quality. When questioned regarding whether their approach to quality resulted in spending more money than was necessary, the Japanese managers disagreed. They believed that quality improvement was technically possible and economically feasible. They did not accept the common U.S. strategy of building a product with quality that was "good enough."

These managers were speaking only for their own firms, however. Some evidence shows that at least in the short run, an overfocus on quality may become economically unwise. Even so, firms must remember that in the long run, quality goods and services lead to repeat business, which translates into profits and growth. From a control standpoint, however, the major issue is how to identify

FIGURE 11-2

SOLVING A QUALITY PROBLEM: TAGUCHI METHOD VS. TRADITIONAL METHOD

■ Trying to find the cause of defects in the paint of a minivan hood, engineers identified seven possible causes. In a traditional approach (top), extensive experiments in which each possibility is investigated one by one would be conducted, involving as many as 500 different hoods. In actuality, there would be many more boxes (or steps) in the traditional method, making it very slow and tedious. With the Taguchi method (bottom), a brainstorming session is followed by a few experiments with about 40 hoods in which several factors are changed simultaneously, their selection based on statistical techniques. ■

Traditional Method Possible causes are studied one by one while holding the other factors constant.

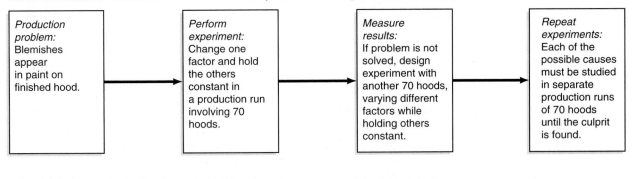

Taguchi Method Brainstorming and a few bold experiments seek to quickly find the problem.

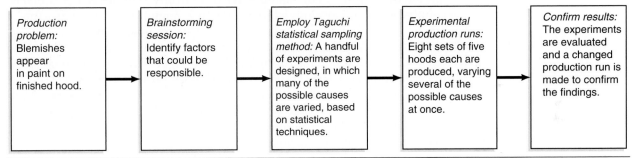

Source: From information reported in John Holusha, "Improving Quality, the Japanese Way," *New York Times*, July 20, 1988, p. 35.

quality problems and resolve them as efficiently as possible. One approach that has been gaining acceptance in the United States is that proposed by Genichi Taguchi, one of the world's foremost authorities on quality control. Taguchi's approach is to dispense with highly sophisticated statistical methods unless more fundamental ways do not work. Figure 11-2 provides an example of how his approach was used to identify the cause of defects in the paint on a minivan hood. This approach to solving quality control problems is proving to be so effective that many MNCs are adopting it. They also are realizing that the belief that Japanese firms will correct quality control problems regardless of the cost is not true. As Taguchi puts it, "the more efficient approach is to identify the things that can be controlled at a reasonable cost in an organized manner, and simply ignore those too expensive to control."[41] To the extent that U.S. MNCs can do this, they will be able to close the quality gap.

TABLE 11-5		

PERFORMANCE EVALUATIONS BY JAPANESE AND U.S. MANAGERS IN U.S.-BASED JAPANESE MANUFACTURING FIRMS

Group	Average score[a]	Frequency
U.S. rater's ratings of U.S. subordinates	5.10	139
U.S. rater's ratings of Japanese subordinates	5.04	27
Japanese rater's ratings of U.S. subordinates	4.71	65
Japanese rater's ratings of Japanese subordinates	5.53	30
Total sample	5.05	261

Note: [a]On a 7-point Likert scale.
Source: Adapted from Golpira Eshgi, "Nationality Bias and Performance Evaluations in Multinational Corporations," *National Academy of Management Proceedings*, 1985, p. 96. Used with permission.

Personnel Performance

Besides financial techniques and the emphasis on quality, another key area of control is personnel performance evaluation. This can take a number of different forms. One of the most common is the periodic appraisal of work performance. Although the objective is similar from country to country, how performance appraisals are done differs. For example, what is effective employee performance in one country is not always judged to be effective in another. This is particularly important when expatriate managers evaluate local managers based on home-country standards. A good example came out of a survey that found Japanese managers in U.S.-based manufacturing firms gave higher evaluations to Japanese personnel than to Americans. The results, which are provided in Table 11-5, led the researcher to conclude: "It seems that cultural differences and diversified approaches to management in MNCs of different nationalities will always create a situation where some bias in performance appraisal may exist."[42] Dealing with these biases is a big challenge facing MNCs.

Another important difference is how personnel performance control actually is conducted. A study that compared personnel control approaches used by Japanese managers in Japan with those employed by U.S. managers in the United States found marked differences.[43] For example, when Japanese work groups were successful because of the actions of a particular individual, the Japanese manager tended to give credit to the whole group. When the group was unsuccessful because of the actions of a particular individual, however, the Japanese manager tended to perceive this one employee as responsible. In addition, the more unexpected the poor performance, the greater the likelihood that the individual would be responsible. In contrast, individuals in the United States typically were given both the credit when things went well and the blame when performance was poor.

Other differences relate to how rewards and monitoring of personnel performance are handled. Both U.S. and Japanese managers offered greater rewards and more freedom from close monitoring to individuals when they were associated with successful performance, no matter what the influence of the group on the performance. The Americans carried this tendency further than the Japanese in the case of rewards, however, including giving high rewards to a person who is a "lone wolf."[44]

A comparison of these two approaches to personnel evaluation shows that the Japanese tend to use a more social or group orientation, while the Americans are more individualistic. The researchers found that overall, however, the approaches were quite similar, and that the control of personnel performance by Japanese and U.S. managers is far more similar than different.

Such similarity also can be found in assessment centers used to evaluate employees. An *assessment center* is an evaluation tool that is used to identify individuals with the potential to be selected or promoted to higher-level positions. Used by large U.S. MNCs for many years, these centers also are employed around the world. A typical assessment center would involve simulation exercises such as: (1) in-basket exercises that require managerial attention; (2) a committee exercise in which the candidates must work as a team in making decisions; (3) business decision exercises in which participants compete in the same market; (4) preparation of a business plan; and (5) a letter-writing exercise. Table 11-6 provides an example of dimensions used in an assessment center in the United Kingdom. These forms of evaluation are beginning to gain support, because they are more comprehensive than simple checklists or the use of a test to interview and thus better able to identify those managers who are most likely to succeed when hired or promoted.

SUMMARY OF KEY POINTS

1. Decision making involves choosing from among alternatives. Some countries tend to use more centralized decision making than others, so that more decisions are made at the top of the MNC than are delegated to the subsidiaries and operating levels.
2. A number of factors help to influence whether decision making will be centralized or decentralized, including company size, amount of capital investment, relative importance of the overseas unit to the MNC, volume-to-unit-cost relationship, level of product diversification, distance between the home office and the subsidiary, and the competence of managers in the host country.
3. There are a number of decision-making issues with which MNCs currently are being confronted. Three of the most important include total quality management (TQM) decisions, use of joint ventures and other forms of co-operative agreements, and strategies for attacking the competition.
4. Controlling involves evaluating results in relation to plans or objectives, then taking action to correct deviations. MNCs control their overseas operations in a number of ways. Most combine direct and indirect controls. Some prefer heavily quantifiable methods, and others opt for more qualitative approaches. Some prefer decentralized approaches; others opt for greater centralization.
5. Three of the most common performance measures used to control subsidiaries are in financial, quality, and personnel areas. Financial performance typically is measured by profit and return on investment. Quality performance often is controlled through quality circles. Personnel performance typically is judged through performance evaluation techniques.

TABLE 11-6

DIMENSIONS ASSESSED IN A U.K. ASSESSMENT CENTER

Dimensions	In-basket	Committee I (presentation)	Committee II (discussion)	Business decisions (1)	Business decisions (2–5)	Business decisions (6–8)	Presentation (business plan)	Letter writing
Analytic ability	*			*	*		*	
Administrative ability	*			*	*		*	
Business sense	*			*	*	*	*	
Written communication	*							*
Oral communication		*	*				*	
Perceptive listening			*	*				
Vigor	*		*	*		*		
Emotional adjustment		*	*		*		*	
Social skill			*		*	*		*
Ascendancy		*	*		*	*	*	
Flexibility			*		*	*		
Relations with subordinates	*		*					*

Source: Adapted from Clive A. Fletcher and Victor Dulewicz, "An Empirical Study of a U.K.-Based Assessment Center," *Journal of Management Studies*, January 1984, pp. 84–97. Used with permission.

KEY TERMS

decision making
controlling
codetermination
ringisei
total quality management (TQM)
empowerment
international joint ventures (IJVs)

direct controls
indirect controls
profit
return on investment (ROI)
quality control circle (QCC)
assessment center

REVIEW AND DISCUSSION QUESTIONS

1. A British computer firm is acquiring a smaller competitor located in Frankfurt. What are two likely differences in the way these two firms carry out the decision-making process? How could these differences create a problem for the acquiring firm? Give an example in each case.
2. Would the British firm in the question above find any differences between the way it typically controls operations and the way that its German acquisition carries out the control process?
3. How do U.S. and Japanese firms differ in the way they go about making decisions and controlling operations? How are the two similar? In each case, provide an example.
4. How are U.S. multinationals trying to introduce total quality management (TQM) into their operations? Give two examples. Would a U.S. MNC doing business in Germany find it easier to introduce these concepts into German operations, or would there be more receptivity to them back in the United States? Why? What if the U.S. multinational were introducing these ideas into a Japanese subsidiary?
5. What are some common control approaches used by U.S. firms at home that may not work well in Europe? Identify and describe three. In your answer, be sure to explain how U.S. multinationals must change their approach in each of these examples.
6. Why are Japanese firms likely to have trouble using their personnel performance evaluation techniques in the United States? Cite two reasons. What do these firms need to realize to make the necessary adjustments in their approach? Are these changes possible, or will the Japanese firms continue to have trouble?

PRACTICAL INTERNATIONAL MANAGEMENT ASSIGNMENT

Interview two foreign subsidiary managers in two different MNCs. (You may do this either in person or by telephone.) Discuss with these managers the amount of decision-making authority they have and the types of controls that are used to monitor their performance. Compare and contrast the two answers. Then, compare your findings with those of your classmates. What conclusions can you draw regarding decision-making and controlling methods used by MNCs?

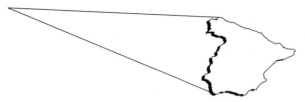

Spaniards consider bull-fighting to be more an art than a sport.

Spain

Spain, which covers 195,000 square miles, is located on the Iberian peninsula at the southwest corner of Europe; its southernmost tip is directly across from Morocco. The country has a population of approximately 40 million and a gross national product of about $490 billion ($12,250 per capita). Until the mid-1990s, Spain, known for its sunny climate, colorful bull-fights, and storybook castles, was one of the most underdeveloped countries in Western Europe. Now, it is an industrialized country whose economy relies heavily on trade, manufacturing, and agriculture. Many of the old Spanish customs, such as taking a siesta (nap or rest) after lunch, are disappearing. The democratic government uses a constitutional monarchy, which was adopted in 1978, in which the king is head of state and commander-in-chief of the armed forces, but the legislative power rests in a bicameral parliament consisting of a Congress of Deputies and a Senate.

Investors Limited, a partnership based in Hong Kong and headed by Stanley Wong, owns 17 medium and large hotels throughout Asia and a total of 9 others throughout the United Kingdom, France, and Germany. The group now plans on buying a large hotel in Madrid. This hotel was built at the turn of the century but was completely refurbished in 1985 at a cost of HK$16 million. The current owners have since decided that the return on investment, which has been averaging 5.2 per-

cent annually, is too small to justify continuing the operation. They have offered the hotel to the Wong group for HK$50 million. One-half is payable immediately, and the rest will be paid in equal annual installments over 5 years.

Stanley Wong believes that this is a good investment and has suggested to his partners they accept the offer. "Europe is going to boom during the 1990s," he told them, "and Spain is going to be an excellent investment. This hotel is one of the finest in Madrid, and we are going to more than triple our investment by the end of the decade."

In the past, the partnership has handled all hotel investments in the same way. A handful of company-appointed managers are sent in to oversee general operations and monitor financial performance, and all other matters continue to be handled by those personnel who have been with the hotel before acquisition. The investment group intends to handle the Madrid operation in the same way. "The most important thing," Stanley noted recently, "is that we keep control of key areas of performance such as costs and return on investment. If we do that and continue to offer the best possible service, we'll come out just fine."

1. What are some current issues facing Spain? What is the climate for doing business in Spain today?

2. Do you think the Wong group, in running the hotel, should use centralized or decentralized decision making?

3. What types of direct controls might the Wong group use? What types of indirect control might be employed?

4. What are some likely differences between the control measures that the Wong group would use and those that typically are used in countries such as Spain?

You Be the International Management Consultant

Expansion Plans

Kranden & Associates is a very successful porcelain-manufacturing firm. The company has six world-renowned artists who design fine-crafted porcelain statues and plates that are widely regarded as collectibles. Each year, the company offers a limited edition of new statues and plates. Last year, the company made 30 new offerings. On average, 2500 of each line are produced, and they usually are sold within 6 months. The company does not produce more than this number to avoid reducing the value of the line to collectors; however, the firm does believe that additional statues and plates could be sold in some areas of the world without affecting the price in North America. In particular, the firm is thinking about setting up production facilities in Rio de Janeiro, Brazil, and Paris, France.

The production process requires skilled personnel, but there are people in both Rio de Janeiro and Paris who can do this work. The basic methods can be taught to these people by trainers from the U.S. plant, because the production process will be identical.

The company intends to send three managers to each of its overseas units to handle setup operations and get the production process off the ground. This should take 12 to 18 months. Once this is done, one person will be left in charge, and the other two will return home.

The company believes that it will be able to sell just as much of the product line in Europe as it does in the United States. The South American market is estimated to be one-half that of the United States. Over the last 5 years, Kranden has had a return on investment of 55 percent. The company charges premium prices for its porcelain but still has strong demand for its products because of the high regard collectors and investors have for the Kranden line. The quality of its statues and plates is highly regarded, and the firm has won three national and two international awards for creativity and quality in design and production over the past 18 months. Over the last 10 years, the firm has won 27 such awards.

1. In managing its international operations, should the firm use centralized or decentralized decision making?
2. Would direct or indirect controls be preferable in managing these operations?
3. What kinds of performance measures should the company use in controlling these international operations?

CHAPTER 11 ENDNOTES

1. Christina Bennett, "The Bravo Could Put Fiat in Overdrive," *BusinessWeek,* September 11, 1995, p. 60.
2. Amy Cortese and Ira Sager, "Gerstner at the Gates," *BusinessWeek,* June 19, 1995, pp. 36–37.
3. Rahual Jacob, "The Resurrection of Michael Dell," *Fortune,* September 18, 1995, pp. 117–128.
4. Nathaniel C. Nash, "Luxuries They Can't Afford," *New York Times,* September 13, 1995, p. C1.
5. Raghu Nath, *Comparative Management: A Regional View* (Cambridge, MA: Ballinger Publishing, 1988), p. 126.
6. Ibid., pp. 74–75.
7. Anant R. Negandhi, *International Management* (Boston: Allyn & Bacon, 1987), p. 193.
8. Karen Lowrey Miller, "The *Mittelstand* Takes a Stand," *BusinessWeek,* April 10, 1995, pp. 94–95.
9. Sang M. Lee, Fred Luthans, and Richard M. Hodgetts, "Total Quality Management: Implications for Central and Eastern Europe," *Organizational Dynamics,* Spring 1992, p. 45.
10. For additional insights into this area, see Jerry Flint, "The Myth of U.S. Manufacturing's Decline," *Forbes,* January 18, 1993, pp. 40–42.
11. Joseph B. White, Gregory A. Patterson, and Paul Ingrassia, "American Auto Makers Need Major Overhaul to Match the Japanese," *Wall Street Journal,* January 10, 1992, pp. A1, A10.
12. Jerry Bowles, "Is American Management Really Committed to Quality?" *Management Review,* April 1992, pp. 44–45.
13. For more on this topic, see Richard J. Schonberger, "Total Quality Management Cuts a Broad Swath—through Manufacturing and Beyond," *Organizational Dynamics,* Winter 1992, pp. 21–23; Thomas H. Berry, *Managing the Total Quality Transformation* (New York: McGraw-Hill, 1991), pp. 159–170.
14. Schonberger, "Total Quality Management," p. 23.
15. For more on this topic and the challenges it presents, see Larry J. Kerr, "Achieving World Class Performance Step by Step," *Long Range Planning,* vol. 25, no. 1, 1992, pp. 46–52; Gilbert Fuchsberg, "Quality Programs Show Shoddy Results," *Wall Street Journal,* May 14, 1992, pp. B1, B9.
16. Randall S. Schuler et al., "Formation of an International Joint Venture: Davidson Instrument Panel," *Human Resource Planning,* vol. 14, no. 1, 1991, pp. 51–59.
17. Steve Glain, "Daewoo Purchase of Polish Plant Shows Firm's Contrarian Strategy," *Wall Street Journal,* August 18, 1995, p. 7C.
18. James Tanner, "Chevron Venture Talking with Iran About an Oil Swap," *Wall Street Journal,* September 12, 1995, p. A6.
19. Rose Brady et al., "Let's Make a Deal—But a Smaller One," *BusinessWeek,* January 20, 1992, pp. 44–45.
20. See, for example, Amy Borrus, Patricia Kranz, and Rose Brady, "From Bush, Reluctant Turnaround on Aid," *BusinessWeek,* January 20, 1992, p. 49; Robert S. Greenberger, "Baker Is Wooing Central Asian Republics," *Wall Street Journal,* February 14, 1992, p. A8.
21. "Vietnam Branch Status for Two U.S. Banks," *Financial Times,* November 11, 1994, p. 5.
22. See, for example, John Templeman, "Mercedes is Downsizing—and That Includes the Sticker," *BusinessWeek,* February 8, 1993, p. 38.
23. Michael Quint, "Deutsche Banks Pursue Diversity for Its U.S. Unit," *New York Times,* May 6, 1992, p. C5.
24. Stephanie Strom, "Japanese Scrap $2 Billion Stake in Rockefeller," *New York Times,* September, 12, 1995, pp. A1, C8; Richard D. Hylton, "Behind the Fall of Rockefeller Center," *Fortune,* July 10, 1995, pp. 82–85.
25. Ira Sager, "The Man Who's Rebooting IBM's PC Business," *BusinessWeek,* July 24, 1995, pp. 68–72.
26. "IBM: Why the Good News Isn't Good Enough," *BusinessWeek,* January 23, 1995, pp. 72–73.
27. See Arvind Phatak, *International Dimensions of Management,* 2nd ed. (Boston: PWS-Kent, 1989), pp. 150–153. Many of the examples are taken from this discussion.
28. Ibid., p. 152.
29. Yves Doz and C. K. Prahalad, "Patterns of Strategic Control within Multinational Corporations," *Journal of International Studies,* Fall 1984, p. 55.
30. John D. Daniels and Jeffrey Arpan, "Comparative Home Country Influences on Management Practices Abroad," *Academy of Management Journal,* September 1972, p. 310. Also see Magoroh Maruyama, "Some Management Considerations in the Economic Reorganization of Eastern Europe," *Academy of Management Journal,* May 1990, pp. 90–91.
31. Jacques H. Horovitz, "Management Control in France, Great Britain and Germany," *Columbia Journal of World Business,* Summer 1978, pp. 17–18.
32. Ibid., p. 18.
33. William G. Egelhoff, "Patterns of Control in U.S., U.K., and European Multinational Corporations," *Journal of International Business Studies,* Fall 1984, p. 81.
34. Ibid., pp. 81–82.
35. M. Kreder and M. Zeller, "Control in German and U.S. Companies," *Management International Review,* vol. 28, no. 3, 1988, pp. 64–65.

36. Lane Daley, James Jiambalvo, Gary L. Sundem, and Yasumasa Kondo, "Attitudes toward Financial Control Systems in the United States and Japan," *Journal of International Business Studies,* Fall 1985, pp. 91–110.

37. Anil K. Gupta and Vijay Govindarajan, "Knowledge Flows and the Structure of Control within Multinational Corporations," *Academy of Management Journal,* December 1991, pp. 768–792.

38. Phatak, *International Dimensions of Management,* p. 154.

39. David A. Garvin, "Japanese Quality Management," *Columbia Journal of World Business,* Fall 1984, pp. 3–12.

40. Ibid., p. 6

41. Cited in John Holusha, "Improving Quality, the Japanese Way," *New York Times,* July 20, 1988, p. 25.

42. Golpira Eshgi, "Nationality Bias and Performance Evaluations in Multinational Corporations," *National Academy of Management Proceedings,* 1985, p. 95.

43. Jeremiah Sullivan, Teruhiko Suzuki, and Yasumasa Kondo, "Managerial Theories and the Performance Control Process in Japanese and American Work Groups," *National Academy of Management Proceedings,* 1985, pp. 98–102.

44. Ibid.

PART FOUR

ORGANIZATIONAL BEHAVIOR AND HUMAN RESOURCES MANAGEMENT

MOTIVATION ACROSS CULTURES

OBJECTIVES OF THE CHAPTER

Motivation is closely related to the performance of human resources in modern organizations. When motivation is applied to international management, it must be remembered that although the motivation process may be the same across cultures, the content of what motivates people often is culturally based. What motivates employees in the United States may only be moderately effective in Japan, France, or Nigeria. Therefore, although motivation is the concept of choice for analyzing employee performance, an international context requires country-by-country, or at least regional, examination of differences in motivation.

This chapter examines motivation as a psychological process and how motivation can be used in understanding and improving employee performance. It also identifies and describes internationally researched work motivation theories and discusses their relevance for international human resource management. The specific objectives of this chapter are:

1. **DEFINE** "motivation," and explain it as a psychological process.

2. **EXAMINE** the hierarchy-of-needs motivation theory, and assess its value to international human resource management.

3. **DISCUSS** the two-factor theory of motivation and how an understanding of employee satisfaction can be useful in human resource management throughout the world.

4. **DESCRIBE** achievement motivation theory, and illustrate how this type of motivation can help to motivate employees in the international arena.

5. **RELATE** the importance of job design and work centrality in understanding how to motivate employees in an international context.

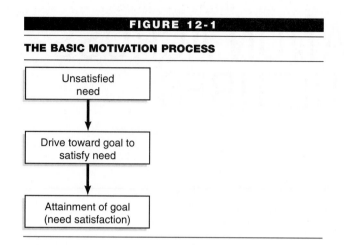

FIGURE 12-1

THE BASIC MOTIVATION PROCESS

Unsatisfied need

↓

Drive toward goal to satisfy need

↓

Attainment of goal (need satisfaction)

THE NATURE OF MOTIVATION

Motivation is a psychological process through which unsatisfied wants or needs lead to drives that are aimed at goals or incentives. Figure 12-1 shows this motivation process. The three basic elements in the process are needs, drives, and goal-attainment. A person with an unsatisfied need will undertake goal-directed behavior to satisfy the need. A simple example is a person working to earn money so that she or he can put a down payment on a house. This individual will be motivated or driven to earn this money as quickly as possible and might look for overtime work or a second job to supplement her or his regular salary. Once the down payment is made, the person then might drop the overtime or second job and not be as driven as before. The individual also might have another goal, such as a new car, and the process would begin anew.

Motivation is an important topic in international human resource management, because many MNC managers assume they can motivate their overseas personnel with the same approaches that are used in the home country. Is this true, or do major differences require tailor-made, country-by-country motivation programs? As described in earlier chapters (especially Chapter 4), there obviously are some motivational differences caused by culture. The major question is: Are these differences highly significant, or can an overall theory of work motivation apply throughout the world? Considerable research on motivating human resources has looked at motivation in a large number of countries; however, before reviewing these findings, two generally agreed-on starting assumptions about work motivation in the international arena should be made.

The Universalist Assumption

The first assumption is that the motivation *process* (not content) is universal. All people are motivated to pursue goals they value—what the work-motivation theorists call goals with "high valence" or "preference." Although the process is universal, however, the specific content and goals that are pursued will be influenced by culture. For example, one recent analysis suggests that the key incentive for many U.S. workers is money; for Japanese employees, it may be respect and power; and for Latin American workers, it may be an array of factors, including family considerations, respect, job status, and a good personal life. Similarly, the primary interest of the U.S. worker is him- or herself; for the Japanese, it is group interest; and for the Latin American employee, it is the interest of the employer.[1] Simply put, motivation differs across cultures. Adler sums up the case against universality of motivation as follows:

> Unfortunately, American as well as non-American managers have tended to treat American theories as the best or only way to understand motivation. They are neither. American motivation theories, although assumed to be universal, have failed to provide consistently useful explanations outside the United States. Managers must therefore guard against imposing domestic American theories on their multinational business practices.[2]

In the United States, personal achievement is an important need, and individual success through promotions and more money may be an important goal. In China, however, group affiliation is an important need, and harmony becomes an important goal. Therefore, the ways to motivate U.S. employees may be quite different from those used on Chinese workers. The motivational process is the same, but the needs and goals are different because of differences between the two cultures. This conclusion recently was demonstrated in a study by Welsh, Luthans, and Sommer that examined the value of extrinsic rewards, behavioral management, and participative techniques among Russian factory workers. The first two motivational approaches worked well to increase worker performance, but the third did not. The researchers noted that

> this study provides at least beginning evidence that U.S.-based behavioral theories and techniques may be helpful in meeting the performance challenges facing human resources management in rapidly changing and different cultural environments. We found that two behavioral techniques—administering desirable extrinsic rewards to employees contingent upon improved performance, and providing social reinforcement and feedback for functional behaviors and corrective feedback for dysfunctional behaviors—significantly improved Russian factory workers' performance. By the same token, the study also points out the danger of making universalist assumptions about U.S.-based theories and techniques. In particular, the failure of the participative intervention does not indicate so much that this approach just won't work across cultures, as that historical and cultural values and norms need to be recognized and overcome for such a relatively sophisticated theory and technique to work effectively.[3]

The Assumption of Content and Process

The second starting assumption is that work-motivation theories can be broken down into two general categories: content, and process. *Content theories* explain work motivation in terms of what arouses, energizes, or initiates employee behavior. *Process theories* of worker motivation explain how employee behavior is initiated, redirected, and halted.[4] Most research in international human resource management has been content-oriented, because these theories examine motivation in more general terms and are more useful in creating a composite picture of employee motivation in a particular country or region. Process theories are more sophisticated and tend to focus on individual behavior in specific settings. Thus, they have less value to the study of employee motivation in international settings, although there has been some research in this area as well.[5] By far, the majority of research in the international arena has been content driven, and this chapter focuses on those findings.

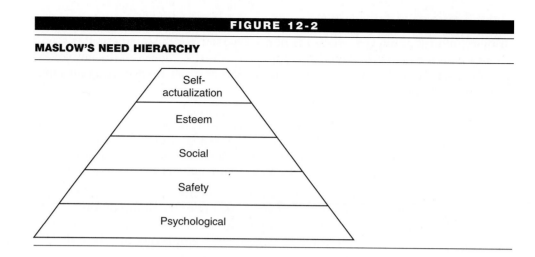

FIGURE 12-2

MASLOW'S NEED HIERARCHY

The following sections examine work motivation in an international setting by focusing on three content theories that have received the greatest amount of attention: the hierarchy-of-needs theory, the two-factor motivation theory, and the achievement motivation theory. Each offers important insights regarding international human resource management.

THE HIERARCHY-OF-NEEDS THEORY

The hierarchy-of-needs theory is based primarily on work by Abraham Maslow, a well-known U.S. psychologist now deceased.[6] Maslow's hierarchy of needs has received a great deal of attention from international management researchers, who have attempted to identify its value in understanding employee motivation throughout the world.[7]

The Maslow Theory

Maslow postulated that everyone has five basic needs, which constitute a need hierarchy. In ascending order, beginning with the most basic, they are physiological, safety, social, esteem, and self-actualization needs. Figure 12-2 illustrates this hierarchy.

Physiological needs consist of food, clothing, shelter, and other basic physical needs. Maslow contended that if someone were deprived of all need satisfaction, the individual's drive to satisfy these physiological needs would be greater than the drive to satisfy any other need. Applied to work motivation, these physiological needs often are satisfied through the wages and salaries paid by the organization.[8]

Safety needs include the desire for security, stability, and absence of pain. Organizations typically help personnel to satisfy these needs through safety programs and equipment and by providing security through medical insurance, unemployment and retirement plans, and similar benefits.[9]

Social needs include the need to interact and affiliate with others and the need to feel wanted by others. This desire for "belongingness" often is satisfied on the job through social interaction within the work group, in which people give and receive friendship. Besides the formally assigned work group, the formation of informal groups and acquaintanceships also is typical.

Esteem needs involve the needs for power and status. These result in individuals' needing to feel important and receive recognition from others. Promotions, awards, and feedback from the boss lead to feelings of self-confidence, prestige, and self-importance.

Self-actualization needs are desires to reach one's full potential by becoming everything that one is capable of becoming. Although less is known about this highest-level need, most closely associated would be the ideas concerning human potential. In the organization, this may not be a promotion but instead may involve mastering one's environment as well as setting and achieving attainable goals.[10]

Maslow's theory, translated over the years, includes a number of basic assumptions. One is that lower-level needs must be satisfied before higher-level needs become motivators. A second is that once a need is satisfied, it no longer serves as a motivator. A third is that there are more ways to satisfy higher-level than lower-level needs. Some of these assumptions came from Maslow's original work, some from others' work, and some have been modified by Maslow. These assumptions have driven much of the international research on the theory.

International Findings on Maslow's Theory

Do people throughout the world have needs that are similar to those described in Maslow's need hierarchy? Research generally shows that they do. For example, in a classic study undertaken by Haire, Ghiselli, and Porter, a sample of 3641 managers from 14 countries was surveyed. This study is quite dated but still the most comprehensive and relevant for showing the different cultural impacts on employee motivation. Countries in this survey included the United States, Argentina, Belgium, Chile, Denmark, England, France, Germany, India, Italy, Japan, Norway, Spain, and Sweden.[11] With some minor modification, the researchers examined the need satisfaction and need importance of the four highest-level needs in the Maslow hierarchy. The esteem need was divided into two groups: esteem and autonomy. The first examined the importance of self-esteem and prestige; the second examined the importance of authority and the opportunity for independent thought and action.

The results of this study showed that all these needs were important to the respondents across cultures. It should be remembered, however, that the subjects in this huge international study were managers, not rank-and-file employees. Upper-level needs were of particular importance to these managers. These findings, for select country clusters (Latin Europe, United States/United Kingdom, and Nordic Europe), show that autonomy and self-actualization were the most important needs for the respondents. Interestingly, these same managers also reported that these needs were those with which they were *least* satisfied , which led Haire and his associates to conclude:

> It appears obvious, from an organizational point of view, that business firms, no matter what country, will have to be concerned with the satisfaction of these needs for their managers and executives. Both types of needs were regarded as relatively quite important by managers, but, at the present time at least, the degree to which they were fulfilled did not live up to their expectations.[12]

Since this classic study, a number of others have examined management groups from other countries. One follow-up study surveyed managers in eight East Asian countries and found that autonomy and self-actualization in most cases ranked high; however, the degree of satisfaction/dissatisfaction varied much more widely than that reported by Haire and his associates. Some East Asian managers apparently are quite dissatisfied with their ability to satisfy autonomy and self-actualization needs.

Both research studies indicate the value of examining motivation of human resources (in this case, managers) in terms of country or geographic clusters. Each country or geographic region appears to have its own need-satisfaction profile. In using this information to motivate managers, MNCs would be wise to consider the individual country's or region's profile and adjust their approach accordingly.

Some researchers even have suggested modifying Maslow's hierarchy by reranking the order of needs.[13] Nevis believes that the Maslow hierarchy reflects a culture that is Western-oriented and focused on the inner needs of individuals. Obviously, not all cultures function this way. Eastern cultures emphasize the needs of society. As a result, Nevis suggested that the Chinese hierarchy of needs has four levels, which from lowest to highest are: (1) belonging (social); (2) physiological; (3) safety; and (4) self-actualization in the service of society. If this is true, MNCs attempting to do business in China must consider this revised hierarchy and determine how they can modify their compensation and job-design programs to accommodate the requisite motivational needs. In any event, Nevis's idea is worth considering, because it forces the multinational firm to address work motivation based on those cultural factors that are unique to it.

The discussion so far indicates that even though it is culturally specific, the need-hierarchy concept is a useful way to study and apply work motivation internationally. Others such as the well-known Dutch researcher Geert Hofstede, however, have suggested that need-satisfaction profiles are *not* a very useful way of addressing motivation, because there often are so many different subcultures within any given country that it may be difficult or impossible to determine which culture variables are at work in any particular work setting. The Haire and follow-up studies dealt only with managers, but Hofstede has found that job categories are a more effective way of examining motivation. He reported a linkage between job types and levels and the need hierarchy. Based on survey results from over 60,000 people in more than 50 countries who were asked to rank a series of 19 work goals (see Tables 12-1 and 12-2), he found that:

- Professionals ranked all four top goals corresponding to "high" Maslow needs.
- Clerks ranked all four top goals corresponding to "middle" Maslow needs.
- Unskilled workers ranked all four top goals corresponding to "low" Maslow needs.
- Managers and technicians showed a mixed picture—with at least one goal in the "high" Maslow category.[14]

The tables from Hofstede's research show that self-actualization and esteem needs rank highest for professionals and managers. Conversely, security, earnings, benefits, and physical working conditions are most important to low-level, unskilled workers. These findings illustrate that job categories and levels may have

TABLE 12-1

TOP-RANKING GOALS FOR PROFESSIONAL TECHNICAL PERSONNEL FROM A LARGE VARIETY OF COUNTRIES

Rank	Goal	Questionnaire wording
1	Training	Have training opportunities (to improve your present skills or learn new skills)
2	Challenge	Have challenging work to do—work from which you can get a personal sense of accomplishment
3	Autonomy	Have considerable freedom to adopt your own approach to the job
4	Up-to-dateness	Keep up-to-date with the technical developments relating to your job
5	Use of skills	Fully use your skills and abilities on the job
6	Advancement	Have an opportunity for advancement to higher-level job
7	Recognition	Get the recognition you deserve when you do a good job
8	Earnings	Have an opportunity for high earnings
9	Co-operation	Work with people who co-operate well with one another
10	Manager	Have a good working relationship with your manager
11	Personal time	Have a job which leaves you sufficient time for your personal or family life
12	Friendly department	Work in a congenial and friendly atmosphere
13	Company contribution	Have a job which allows you to make a real contribution to the success of your company
14	Efficient department	Work in a department which is run efficiently
15	Security	Have the security that you will be able to work for your company as long as you want to
16	Desirable area	Live in an area desirable to you and your family
17	Benefits	Have good fringe benefits
18	Physical conditions	Have good physical working conditions (good ventilation and lighting, adequate work space, etc.)
19	Successful company	Work in a company which is regarded in your country as successful

Source: Geert H. Hofstede, "The Colors of Collars," *Columbia Journal of World Business,* September 1972, p. 74. Used with permission.

a dramatic effect on motivation and may well offset cultural considerations. As Hofstede noted, "There are greater differences between job categories than there are between countries when it comes to employee motivation."[15]

In deciding how to motivate human resources in different countries or help them to attain need satisfaction, researchers such as Hofstede recommend that MNCs focus most heavily on giving physical rewards to lower-level personnel and on creating a climate in which there is challenge, autonomy, the ability to use one's skills, and co-operation for the middle- and upper-level personnel. Of course, this does not mean that executives are unmotivated by large compensation packages. As seen in "International Management in Action: Up, Up, and Away," these packages are starting to get larger and larger.

Overall, there seems to be little doubt that need-hierarchy theory is useful in helping to identify motivational factors for international human resource management. This theory alone is not sufficient, however. Other content theories, such as the two-factor theory, add further understanding and effective practical application for motivating personnel.

TABLE 12-2

THE FOUR MOST IMPORTANT GOALS RANKED BY OCCUPATIONAL GROUP AND RELATED TO THE NEED HIERARCHY

Goals ranked in "need hierarchy"	Professionals (research laboratories)	Professionals (branch offices)	Managers	Technicians (branch offices)	Technicians (manufacturing plants)	Clerical workers (branch offices)	Unskilled workers (manufacturing plants)
High—Self-actualization and esteem needs:							
Challenge	1	2		3	3		
Training		1	1	1			
Autonomy	3	3	2				
Up-to-dateness	2	4		4			
Use of skills	4						
Middle—Social needs:							
Co-operation			3/4			1	
Manager			3/4		4	2	
Friendly department						3	
Efficient department						4	
Low—Security and physiologic needs:							
Security				2	1		2
Earnings					2		3
Benefits							4
Physical conditions							1

Source: Geert H. Hofstede, "The Colors of Collars," *Columbia Journal of World Business*, September 1972, p. 78. Used with permission.

INTERNATIONAL MANAGEMENT IN ACTION

Up, Up, and Away

Is money a motivator? Many argue that it is and point to ever-increasing executive compensation packages and the rising salaries of managers in general. Some of the latest data reveal that CEOs in major companies make very high salaries, and here are some select examples of the average salary, bonus, and long-term incentives for typical CEOs of top firms:

United States	$700,000
France	$500,000
Italy	$490,000
Great Britain	$480,000
Germany	$430,000
Holland	$350,000

U.S. CEOs remain at the top, although European managers are beginning to close the gap. Japanese CEOs, for whom recent data were unavailable, often rank much lower than their U.S. or European counterparts; however, Japanese CEOs also have very lucrative benefit allowances, including free housing, golf memberships, and unlimited entertainment accounts.

The most recent data show that between 1984 and 1992, the total remuneration of chief executives of large U.S. firms (annual sales of $250 million or greater) more than doubled. In second place were French executives, whose average pay tripled during this time. Surprisingly, perhaps, the pay of other managers in all these companies remained comparable, indicating a big gap between the CEO and other management staff in many firms around the world.

Additionally, CEOs now are having to work even harder for their remuneration. Base salaries in some countries have risen by less than total remuneration, thus indicating that a larger part of the pay package now comes from long-term performance incentives such as productivity and market share growth. U.S. firms have led the way in this area, with long-term incentives accounting for almost one-third of the total pay package. These incentives also have increased in popularity in France and Britain—but not in Germany and Japan.

At the same time, employee benefits are on the rise. For example, Mexico now requires that in the event of disability or retirement, employees with at least 15 years of service receive 12 paid days of salary for each year of employment. If the person is being terminated, the individual is entitled to severance pay of 3 months' salary plus 20 paid days for each year of service. In Europe, termination benefits also are quite high. A typical 45-year-old Spanish or Italian manager with 20 years of service and a $50,000 salary would be entitled to termination benefits ranging from $94,000 to $130,000. In Japan, permanent staff members who are terminated involuntarily can receive as much as $600,000. These statistics help to explain why money is one of the most important motivators around the world.

THE TWO-FACTOR THEORY OF MOTIVATION

The two-factor theory was formulated by well-known work-motivation theorist Frederick Herzberg and his colleagues. Similar to Maslow's theory, Herzberg's has been a focus of attention in international human resource management research over the years. This two-factor theory is closely linked to the need hierarchy.

The Herzberg Theory

The *two-factor theory of motivation* holds that two sets of factors influence job satisfaction: hygiene factors and motivators. The data from which the theory was developed were collected through a critical incident methodology that asked the respondents to answer two basic types of questions: (1) When did you feel particularly good about your job? and (2) When did you feel exceptionally bad about your job? Responses to the first question generally related to job content and included factors such as achievement, recognition, responsibility, advancement, and the work itself. Herzberg called these job-content factors *motivators.* Responses to the second question related to job context and included factors such as salary, interpersonal relations, technical supervision, working conditions, and company

TABLE 12-3

HERZBERG'S TWO-FACTOR THEORY

Hygiene factors	Motivators
Salary	Achievement
Technical supervision	Recognition
Company policies and administration	Responsibility
Interpersonal relations	Advancement
Working conditions	The work itself

TABLE 12-4

THE RELATIONSHIP BETWEEN MASLOW'S NEED HIERARCHY AND HERZBERG'S TWO-FACTOR THEORY

Maslow's need hierarchy	Herzberg's two-factor theory
Self-actualization	Motivators
	Achievement
	Recognition
	Responsibility
Esteem	Advancement
	The work itself
Social	Hygiene factors
	Salary
	Technical supervision
Safety	Company policies and administration
	Interpersonal relations
Physiologic	Working conditions

policies and administration. Herzberg called these job-context variables *hygiene factors.* Table 12-3 lists both groups of factors; a close look at the two lists shows that the motivators are heavily psychological and relate to Maslow's upper-level needs but that hygiene factors are environmental in nature and relate more to Maslow's lower-level needs. Table 12-4 illustrates this linkage.

The two-factor theory also holds that these two sets of factors relate to employee satisfaction. This relationship is more complex than the traditional view that employees are either satisfied or dissatisfied; according to the two-factor theory, if hygiene factors are not taken care of or are deficient, there will be dissatisfaction (see Figure 12-3). Importantly, however, if hygiene factors are taken care of, there may be no dissatisfaction, but there also may not be satisfaction. Only by providing the motivators will there be satisfaction. In short, hygiene factors help to prevent dissatisfaction (thus the term "hygiene," as it is used in the health field), but only motivators lead to satisfaction. Therefore, according to this theory, motivating human resources must include recognition, a chance to achieve and grow, advancement, and interesting work.

FIGURE 12-3

VIEWS OF SATISFACTION/DISSATISFACTION

Traditional View

Satisfaction ——————————————— Dissatisfaction

Two-factor View

(hygiene factors)

Absent ———————————————— Present
(dissatisfaction)   (no dissatisfaction)

(motivators)

Absent ———————————————— Present
(no satisfaction)   (satisfaction)

Before examining the two-factor theory in the international arena, it is important to note that Herzberg's theory has been criticized by some organizational-behavior academics. One criticism surrounds the classification of money as a hygiene factor and not as a motivator. There is no universal agreement on this point, and some researchers report that salary is a motivator for some groups, such as blue-collar workers, or those for whom money is important for psychological reasons, such as a score-keeping method for their power and achievement needs.

A second line of criticism is whether Herzberg has developed a total theory of motivation. Some argue that his findings actually support a theory of job satisfaction. In other words, if a company gives its people motivators, they will be satisfied; if it denies them motivators, they will not be satisfied; and if the hygiene factors are deficient, they may well be dissatisfied. Much of the international research on the two-factor theory discussed next is directed toward the satisfaction/dissatisfaction concerns rather than complex motivational needs, drives, and goals.

International Findings on Herzberg's Theory

International findings related to the two-factor theory fall into two categories. One consists of replications of Herzberg's research in a particular country; that is, do managers in country X give answers similar to those in Herzberg's original studies? The other consists of cross-cultural studies that focus on job satisfaction; that is, what factors cause job satisfaction and how do these responses differ from country to country? The latter studies are not a direct extension of the two-factor theory, but they do offer insights regarding the importance of job satisfaction in international human resource management.

Two-Factor Replications   A number of research efforts have been undertaken to replicate the two-factor theory, and in the main, they support Herzberg's findings. George Hines, for example, surveyed 218 middle managers and 196 salaried employees in New Zealand using ratings of 12 job factors and overall job satisfaction.

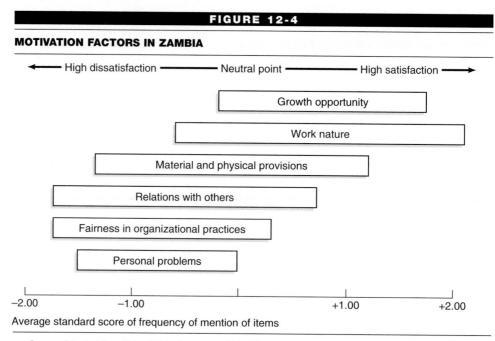

FIGURE 12-4

MOTIVATION FACTORS IN ZAMBIA

← High dissatisfaction ——— Neutral point ——— High satisfaction →

Growth opportunity

Work nature

Material and physical provisions

Relations with others

Fairness in organizational practices

Personal problems

−2.00 −1.00 +1.00 +2.00

Average standard score of frequency of mention of items

Source: Adapted from Peter D. Machungwa and Neal Schmitt, "Work Motivation in a Developing Country," *Journal of Applied Psychology,* February 1983, p. 41. Used with permission.

Based on these findings, he concluded that "the Herzberg model appears to have validity across occupational levels."[16]

Another similar study was conducted among 178 managers in Greece who were Greek nationals. Overall, this study found that Herzberg's two-factor theory of job satisfaction generally held true for these managers. The researchers summarized their findings as follows:

> As far as job dissatisfaction was concerned, no motivator was found to be a source of dissatisfaction. Only categories traditionally designated as hygiene factors were reported to be sources of dissatisfaction for participating Greek managers. . . . Moreover . . . motivators . . . were more important contributors to job satisfaction than to dissatisfaction . . . (66.8% of the traditional motivator items . . . were related to satisfaction and 31.1% were related to dissatisfaction). Traditional hygiene factors, as a group, were more important contributors to job dissatisfaction than to job satisfaction (64% of the responses were related to dissatisfaction and 36% were related to satisfaction).[17]

Another study tested the Herzberg theory in an Israeli kibbutz.[18] Motivators there tended to be sources of satisfaction and hygiene factors sources of dissatisfaction, although interpersonal relations (a hygiene factor) were regarded more as a source of satisfaction than of dissatisfaction. The researcher was careful to explain this finding as a result of the unique nature of a kibbutz, however, where interpersonal relations of a work and nonwork nature are not clearly defined, thus making difficult the separation of this factor on a motivator/hygiene basis. Commenting on the results, the researcher noted, "the findings of this study support Herzberg's two-factor hypothesis: Satisfactions arise from the nature of the work itself, while dissatisfactions have to do with the conditions surrounding the work."[19]

TABLE 12-5

THE RESULTS OF ADMINISTERING THE JOI TO FOUR CROSS-CULTURAL GROUPS

	Relative rankings			
	United States (*n* = 49)	Australia (*n* = 58)	Canada (*n* = 25)	Singapore (*n* = 33)
Achievement	2	2	2	2
Responsibility	3	3	3	3
Growth	1	1	1	1
Recognition	10	10	8	9
Job status	7	7	4	7
Relationships	5	5	10	6
Pay	8	8	6	8
Security	9	9	9	10
Family	6	6	7	5
Hobby	4	4	4	4

Source: G. E. Popp, H. J. Davis, and T. T. Herbert, "An International Study of Intrinsic Motivation Composition," *Management International Review*, vol. 26, no. 3, 1986, p. 31. Used with permission.

Similar results on the Herzberg theory have been obtained by research studies in developing countries. For example, one study examined work motivations in Zambia, employing a variety of motivational variables, and work motivation was a result of six factors: work nature, growth and advancement, material and physical provisions, relations with others, fairness/unfairness in organizational practices, and personal problems. These variables are presented in Figure 12-4. They illustrate that in general, the two-factor theory of motivation was supported in this African country.[20]

Cross-Cultural Job-Satisfaction Studies   A number of cross-cultural studies related to job satisfaction also have been conducted in recent years. These comparisons show that Herzberg-type motivators tend to be of more importance to job satisfaction than hygiene factors. For example, one study administered the Job Orientation Inventory (JOI) to M.B.A. candidates from four countries.[21] As seen in Table 12-5, the relative ranking placed hygiene factors at the bottom of the list and motivators at the top. What also is significant is that although Singapore students do not fit into the same cultural cluster as the other three groups in the study, their responses were similar. These findings provide evidence that job-satisfaction-related factors may not be culturally bound.[22]

Another, more comprehensive study of managerial job attitudes investigated the types of job outcomes that are desired by managers in different cultures. Data were gathered from lower- and middle-management personnel who were attending management development courses in Canada, the United Kingdom, France, and Japan.[23] The researchers sought to identify the importance of 15 job-related outcomes and how satisfied the respondents were with each one.

The results indicated that job content is more important than job context. Organizationally controlled factors (*job context factors,* such as conditions, hours, earnings, security, benefits, and promotions) for the most part did not receive as high a ranking as internally mediated factors (*job content factors*, such as responsibility, achievement, and the work itself). The data also show that managers from the four countries differ significantly regarding both the perceived importance of job outcomes and the level of satisfaction experienced on the job with respect to these outcomes. These differences are useful in shedding light on what motivates managers in these countries and, in the case of MNCs, in developing country-specific human resource management approaches. The most striking contrasts were between the French and the British. Commenting on the applicability of this research to the formulation of motivational strategies for effective human resource management, the researchers noted the following:

> The results suggest . . . that efforts to improve managerial performance in the UK should focus on job content rather than on job context. Changes in the nature of the work itself are likely to be more valued than changes in organizational or interpersonal factors. Job enrichment programs which help individuals design their own goals and tasks, and which downplay formal rules and structure, are more likely to improve performance in an intrinsically oriented society such as Britain, where satisfaction tends to be derived from the job itself, than in France, where job context factors such as security and fringe benefits are more highly valued. The results suggest that French managers may be more effectively motivated by changing job situation factors, as long as such changes are explicitly linked to performance.[24]

In summary, Herzberg's two-factor theory appears to reinforce Maslow's need hierarchy through its research support in the international arena. As with the application of Maslow's theory, however, MNCs would be wise to apply motivation–hygiene theory on a country-by-country or a regional basis. Although there are exceptions, such as France, there seems to be little doubt that job content factors are more important than job context factors in motivating not only managers but also lower-level employees around the world, as Hofstede pointed out.

ACHIEVEMENT MOTIVATION THEORY

Besides the need-hierarchy and two-factor theories of work motivation, the achievement motivation theory has been given a relatively great amount of attention in the international arena. Achievement theory actually has been more applied to the actual practice of management than the others, and it has been the focus of some interesting international research.

The Background of Achievement Motivation Theory

Achievement motivation theory holds that individuals can have a need to get ahead, to attain success, and to reach objectives. Note that like the upper-level needs in Maslow's hierarchy or like Herzberg's motivators, the need for achievement is learned. Therefore, applied to the international scene, in the United States, where entrepreneurial effort is encouraged and individual success promoted, the probability is higher that there would be more people with high needs for achievement than, for example, in China, Russia, or other Eastern European countries,[25] where cultural values have not traditionally supported individual, entrepreneurial efforts.

Researchers such as the well-known Harvard psychologist David McClelland have identified a characteristic profile of high achievers.[26] First, they like situations in which they take personal responsibility for finding solutions to problems. They want to win based on their own efforts and not on luck or chance. Second, they tend to be moderate risk-takers rather than high or low risk-takers. If a decision-making situation appears to be too risky, they will learn as much as they can about the environment and try to reduce the probability of failure. In this way, they turn a high-risk situation into a moderate-risk situation. If the situation is too low-risk, however, there usually is an accompanying low reward, and they tend to avoid these situations with insufficient incentive.

Third, high achievers want concrete feedback on their performance. They like to know how well they are doing, and they use this information to modify their actions. High achievers tend to gravitate into vocations such as sales, which provide them with immediate, objective feedback of how they are doing. Finally, and this has considerable implications for human resource management, these high achievers tend to be loners. They genuinely do not like or get along well with other people. They do not form warm, close relationships, and they have little empathy for others' problems. This last characteristic may distract from their effectiveness as managers of people.

Researchers have discovered a number of ways to develop high achievement needs in people. These involve teaching the individual to do the following: (1) obtain feedback on performance, and use this information to channel one's efforts in areas where success likely will be achieved; (2) emulate people who have been successful achievers; (3) develop an internal desire for success and challenge; and (4) daydream in positive terms by picturing oneself as successful in the pursuit of important objectives.[27] In other words, this suggests that the need for achievement can be taught and learned.

International Findings on Achievement Motivation Theory

A number of international researchers have investigated the role and importance of high achievement needs in human resource management.[28] One study, discussed under the two-factor theory, used the JOI scale and found that achievement or a sense of accomplishment ranked as the second most important work-reward factor.[29] Remember, however, that these results were obtained with M.B.A. students from various countries who were studying in the United States. It should not be surprising that these respondents who came to the United States for advanced study of business, regardless of their home country, would have a high need for achievement. The question remains as to what degree people throughout the world have this need.

Early research among Polish industrialists found that many of them were high achievers.[30] The average high-achievement score was 6.58, which was quite close to that of the U.S. managers' score of 6.74. This led some to conclude there is evidence that managers in countries as diverse as the United States and those of Eastern European have high needs for achievement.[31] More recently, however, researchers have *not* found a high need for achievement in Eastern European countries. One study, for example, surveyed Czech industrial managers and found that the average high-achievement score was 3.32, considerably lower than that of U.S. managers.[32] Because the need for achievement is learned, differences in these

TABLE 12-6

STANDARDIZED SCORES ON WORK GOALS FOR MANAGERS FROM FOUR COUNTRIES

Variables	People's Republic of China	Hong Kong	Taiwan	Singapore
Making a contribution	671	—	—	—
Coworkers who cooperate	635	579	571	624
Autonomy	603	512	480	532
Training	583	596	657	611
Efficiency	578	—	—	—
Skills	—	555	577	536
Challenge	515	548	548	571
Working relationship with manager	483	522	524	551
Earnings	454	567	442	552
Security	450	452	506	437
Recognition	446	487	487	442
Benefits	439	323	363	439
Area	—	477	438	362
Favorable physical conditions	433	436	407	432
Promotion	364	640	630	593
Time for nonwork activities	345	307	372	348

Note: Data, except those for the People's Republic, are from Geert Hofstede's book *Culture's Consequences: International Differences in Work-Related Values* (Beverly Hills: Sage, 1980). For the variables for the People's Republic, included are the skills goals in the training goal; the area goal is irrelevant in the context of the People's Republic.

Source: Oded Shenkar and Simcha Ronen, "Structure and Importance of Work Goals among Managers in the People's Republic of China," *Academy of Management Journal*, September 1987, p. 571. Used with permission.

samples can be attributed to cultural differences. By the same token, given the dramatic, revolutionary changes that occurred in Eastern Europe at the end of the 1980s, one could argue that the achievement needs of Eastern Europeans, once they are allowed to be freely expressed, may well be high today.[33] The important point, however, is that because achievement is a learned need and thus largely determined by the prevailing culture, it is not universal and may change over time.

China is a good example of a country where a high need for achievement has largely been absent. In recent years, however, a growing segment of the population, especially younger people, such as those who demonstrated at Tiananmen Square, seem to have this need. In high-achieving societies, work goals such as autonomy, challenge, promotions, and earnings are valued. The need for affiliation and safety rank far down the list; the high achiever is not very interested in these. In China, achievement-oriented goals traditionally have not ranked very high, although recent government-sponsored economic programs may be changing this.[34] Table 12-6 reports standardized scores on work goals for four East Asian countries.[35] Note that there are five variables to which high achievers would tend to give high scores: autonomy, challenge, earnings, recognition, and promotion. The managers from the People's Republic of China gave high scores to only one of these: autonomy. On the other four high-achievement responses, two were the lowest and the other two second lowest. Conversely, high achievers would not give high scores to affiliation or security-related goals such as co-operation with coworkers, security, benefits, physical working conditions, and time for nonwork activities. Yet most of these are rated relatively high for the Chinese sample.

On the other hand, as China's economy continues to grow and the government allows more market-based efforts, the achievement motivation drive likely will increase among the general population. This finding has been reinforced by a recent study of Chinese and U.S. businesses that found Chinese employees were economically oriented and favored reward systems giving more to some individuals than to others. Conversely, U.S. employees were more humanistically oriented and preferred a more equal distribution of material rewards. Among other things, the study concluded that, "The Chinese differential preferences . . . are consistent with efforts to encourage individual responsibility and to link reward to performance . . ."[36] So, the seeds of the achievement motivation drive now appear to be taking root in China.

These examples show there is considerable cultural impact on achievement motivation theory. The ideal profile for high-achieving societies can be described in terms of the cultural dimensions examined in Chapter 4. In particular, two basic cultural dimensions identified by Hofstede in Chapter 4 best describe high-achieving societies. First, these societies tend to have the cultural dimension of low uncertainty avoidance. Those in high-achieving societies are not afraid to take at least moderate risks or to live with ambiguity. Second, they tend to have the cultural dimension of moderate to high masculinity (Hofstede's term), as measured by the high importance assigned to the acquisition of money and other physical assets and the low value given to caring for others and quality of work life. This combination is found almost exclusively in Anglo countries or in nations that have been closely associated with them through colonization or treaty, such as India, Singapore, and Hong Kong (countries that have been associated with Great Britain) and the Philippines (which has been associated with the United States).

Countries that fall into one of the other three quadrants in Figure 12-5 will not be very supportive of the high need for achievement. MNCs in these geographic regions would be wise to formulate a human resource management strategy for either changing the situation or adjusting to it. If they decide to change the situation, they must design jobs to fit the needs of their people or put people through an achievement motivation training program to create high-achieving managers and entrepreneurs.

A number of years ago, McClelland was able to demonstrate the success of such achievement motivation training programs with underdeveloped countries. For example, in India, he conducted such a program with considerable success. In following up these Indian trainees over the subsequent 6 to 10 months, he found that two-thirds were unusually active in achievement-oriented activities. They had started new businesses, investigated new product lines, increased profits, or expanded their present organizations. For example, the owner of a small radio store opened a paint and varnish factory after completing the program. McClelland concluded that this training appeared to have doubled the natural rate of unusual achievement-oriented activity in the group studied.[37]

If international human resource managers cannot change the situation or train the participants, then they must adjust to the specific conditions of the country and formulate a motivation strategy that is based on those conditions. In many

FIGURE 12-5

SELECTED COUNTRIES ON THE UNCERTAINTY AVOIDANCE AND MASCULINITY SCALES

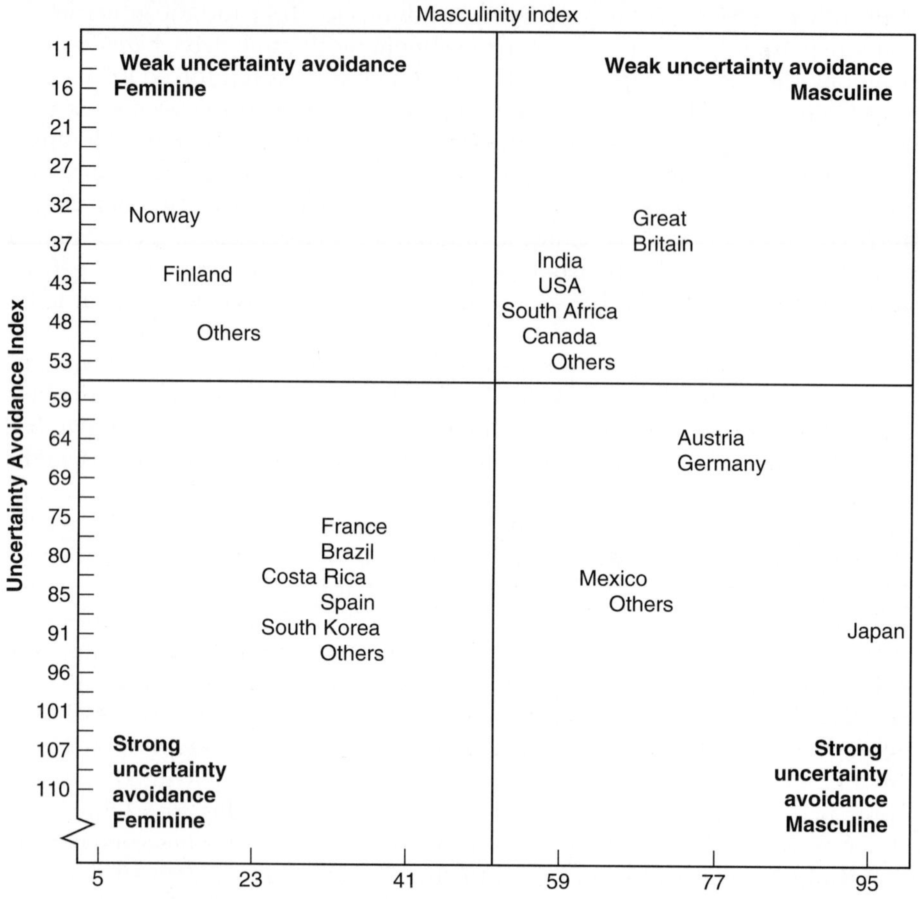

Masculinity index

Uncertainty Avoidance Index		
11	**Weak uncertainty avoidance**	**Weak uncertainty avoidance**
16	**Feminine**	**Masculine**
21		
27		
32	Norway	Great
37		Britain
43	Finland	India / USA
48	Others	South Africa / Canada
53		Others
59		
64		Austria
69		Germany
75	France	
80	Brazil	
85	Costa Rica / Spain	Mexico / Others
91	South Korea	Japan
96	Others	
101		
107	**Strong**	**Strong**
110	**uncertainty**	**uncertainty**
	avoidance	**avoidance**
	Feminine	**Masculine**

5   23   41   59   77   95

Source: Adapted from Geert Hofstede, "The Cultural Relativity of Organizational Practices and Theories," *Journal of International Business Studies,* Fall 1983, p. 86. Used with permission.

cases, this requires consideration of a need-hierarchy approach blended with an achievement approach. Hofstede offers such advice in dealing with the countries in the various quadrants of Figure 12-5.

> The countries on the feminine side . . . distinguish themselves by focusing on quality of life rather than on performance and on relationships between people rather than on money and things. This means *social motivation:* quality of life plus security and quality of life plus risk.[38]

In the case of countries that are attempting to introduce changes that incorporate values from one of the other quadrants in Figure 12-5, the challenge can be even greater.

In summary, achievement motivation theory provides additional insights into the motivation of personnel around the world. Like the need-hierarchy and two-factor theories, however, achievement motivation theory must be modified to

TABLE 12-7

CULTURAL DIMENSIONS IN JAPAN, SWEDEN, AND THE UNITED STATES

	Degree of dimension		
Cultural dimension	High/strong X ←	Moderate X—	Low/weak → X
Uncertainty avoidance	J	USA	S
Individualism	USA S	J	
Power distance	J USA	S	
Masculinity	J	USA	S

Source: Adapted from Geert Hofstede, "The Cultural Relativity of the Quality of Life Concept," *Academy of Management Review*, July 1984, pp. 391, 393. Used with permission.

meet the specific needs of the local culture. The culture of many countries does not support high achievement. However, the cultures of Anglo countries and those that reward entrepreneurial effort would support achievement motivation, and their human resources would be managed accordingly.

MOTIVATION APPLIED: JOB DESIGN AND WORK CENTRALITY

Although content theories provide important insights into how to motivate human resources in international management, two areas of application that have received a great deal of recent attention are job design and the role of work in people's lives, or what is called "work centrality."

Job Design

Job design consists of a job's content, the methods that are used on the job, and the way in which the job relates to others in the organization. The job design typically is a function of the work to be done and the way in which management wants the job to be carried out. These factors help to explain why the same type of work may have a different impact on the motivation of human resources in various parts of the world and result in different quality of work life.

Quality of Work Life: The Impact of Culture

Quality of work life (QWL) is not the same throughout the world. For example, assembly line employees in Japan will work at a rapid pace for hours and have very little control over their work activities. In Sweden, assembly line employees work at a more relaxed pace and have a great deal of control over their work activities. U.S. assembly line employees are somewhere in between; they typically work at a pace that is less demanding than that in Japan but more structured than that in Sweden.

What accounts for these differences? One answer is found in the culture of the country. QWL is directly related to culture. Table 12-7 compares the three industrialized nations mentioned earlier using the four cultural dimensions described in Chapter 4. A brief look shows that each country has a different cultural profile, helping to explain why similar jobs may be designed quite differently from country to country. Assembly line work is a good comparative example.

In Japan, there is strong uncertainty avoidance. The Japanese like to structure tasks so there is no doubt regarding what is to be done and how it is to be done. Individualism is low, so there is strong emphasis on security and individual risk-taking is discouraged. The power distance index is high, so Japanese workers are accustomed to taking orders from those above them. The masculinity index for the Japanese is high, which shows that they put a great deal of importance on money and other material symbols of success. In designing jobs, the Japanese structure tasks so that the work is performed within these cultural confines. Japanese managers work their employees extremely hard. Although Japanese workers contribute many ideas through the extensive use of quality circles, Japanese managers give them very little say in what actually goes on in the organization (in contrast to the erroneous picture often portrayed by the media, which presents Japanese firms as highly democratic and managed from the bottom up[39]) and depend heavily on monetary rewards, as reflected by the fact that the Japanese rate money as an important motivator more than the workers in any other industrialized country do.

In Sweden, however, uncertainty avoidance is low, so job descriptions, policy manuals, and similar work-related materials are more open-ended or general as opposed to the detailed procedural materials developed by the Japanese. In addition, Swedish workers are encouraged to make decisions and take risks. Swedes exhibit a moderate to high degree of individualism, which is reflected in their emphasis on individual decision making (in contrast to the collective or group decision making of the Japanese). They have a weak power distance index, which means that Swedish managers use participative approaches in leading their people. Swedes score low on masculinity, which means that interpersonal relations and the ability to interact with other workers and discuss job-related matters are important. These cultural dimensions result in job designs that are markedly different from those in Japan.

Cultural dimensions in the United States are closer to those of Sweden than to those of Japan. In addition, except for individualism, the U.S. profile is between that of Sweden and Japan (again see Table 12-7). This means that job design in U.S. assembly plants tends to be more flexible or unstructured than that of the Japanese but more rigid than that of the Swedes.

This same pattern holds for many other jobs in these countries. All job designs tend to reflect the cultural values of the country. The challenge for MNCs is to adjust job design to meet the needs of the host country's culture. For example, when Japanese firms enter the United States, they often are surprised to learn that people resent close control. In fact, there is evidence that the most profitable Japanese-owned companies in the United States are those that delegate a high degree of authority to their U.S. managers.[40] Similarly, Japanese firms operating in Sweden find that quality of work life is a central concern for the personnel and that a less structured, highly participative management style is needed for success. Some of the best examples are provided by sociotechnical job designs.

Sociotechnical Job Designs

Sociotechnical designs are job designs that blend personnel and technology. The objective of these designs is to integrate new technology into the workplace so that workers accept and use these developments to increase overall productivity. Because technology often requires people to learn new methods and, in some cases, work faster, employee resistance is typical. Effective sociotechnical design can overcome these problems. There are a number of good examples, and perhaps the most famous is that of Volvo, the Swedish automaker. Sociotechnologic changes that were reflective of the cultural values of the workers were introduced at the firm's Kalmar plant. Autonomous work groups were formed and given the authority to elect their own supervisors as well as to schedule, assign, and inspect their own work. Each group was allowed to work at its own pace, although there was an overall output objective for the week and each group was expected to attain this goal.[41] The outcome was very positive and resulted in Volvo's recently building another plant that employs even more sophisticated sociotechnical job design concepts.

Similar sociotechnical projects have been instituted by other firms outside Sweden. A well-known U.S. example is General Foods, which set up autonomous groups at its Topeka, Kansas, plant to produce Gaines pet food. Patterned after the Volvo example, the General Foods project allowed workers to share responsibility and work in a highly democratic environment. Other U.S. firms also have opted for a self-managed team approach. In fact, recent research reports that the concept of multifunctional teams with autonomy for generating successful product innovation is more widely used by successful U.S., Japanese, and European firms than any other form of teamwork concept.[42] Its use must be tempered by the cultural situation, however. Volvo-type designs are far more likely to be used effectively during the 1990s in Scandinavian countries than in the auto plants of, say, Japan, Korea, or Taiwan. Even the widely publicized General Foods project at Topeka in the United States had some problems. Some former employees there indicate that the approach has steadily eroded and that some managers were openly hostile because it undermined their power, authority, and decision-making flexibility. The most effective job design will be a result of both the job to be done and the cultural values that support a particular approach.[43] For MNCs, the challenge will be to make the fit between the design and the culture.

At the same time, it is important to realize that functional job descriptions now are being phased out in many MNCs and replaced by more of a process approach. This new approach is explained as follows:

> Process management differs from managing a function in three ways. First, it uses external objectives. Old-line manufacturing departments, for example, tend to be measured on unit costs, an intradepartmental number that can lead to overlong production runs and stacks of unsold goods. By contrast, an integrated manufacturing and shipping process might be rated by how often it turns over its inventory—a process-wide measurement that reveals how all are working together to keep costs down. Second, in process management, employees with different skills are grouped to accomplish a complete piece of work. . . . Third, information moves straight to where it's needed, unfiltered by a hierarchy. If you have a problem with people upstream from you, you deal with them directly, rather than asking your boss to talk to theirs.[44]

The result is a more horizontal network that relies on communication and teamwork.[45] This approach also is useful in helping to create and sustain partnerships with other firms.[46]

Work Centrality

Work centrality, which can be defined as the importance of work in an individual's life relative to his or her other areas of interest (family, church, leisure), provides important insights into how to motivate human resources in different cultures.[47] After conducting a review of the literature, Bhagat and associates found that Japan has the highest level of work centrality, followed by moderately high levels for the former Yugoslavia and Israel, average levels for the United States and Belgium, moderately low levels for the Netherlands and Germany, and low levels for Britain.[48] In other words, these findings would indicate that successful multinationals in Japan must realize that although work is an integral part of the Japanese lifestyle, work in the United States must be more balanced with a concern for other interests.

Additional areas also could be evaluated in terms of helping to determine the role of work in the scheme of things. For example, in the United States there recently has been a pronounced increase in the number of hours worked annually, while the number in Japan has shrunk considerably.[49] The average American now is adding 9 hours annually to the time that he or she spends on the job.[50] Work is becoming a greater part of the U.S. employee's life and a lesser part among Japanese workers.[51] Moreover, this is occurring at a time when according to the Japanese Ministry of Labor, U.S. productivity per hour is running 62 percent higher than that of Japan when adjusted for purchasing power parity.[52]

Value of Work   Although work is an important part of the lifestyles of most people, there still are a large number of misconceptions. For example, one reason that Japanese work such long hours is that the cost of living is very high and hourly employees cannot afford to pass up the opportunity for extra money. Among salaried employees who are not paid extra, most Japanese managers expect their subordinates to stay late at work, and this has become a requirement of the job. Moreover, there is recent evidence that Japanese workers may do far less work in a business day than outsiders would suspect.[53] On the other hand, it is equally true that many Japanese do accept work as an integral part of their lifestyle, and in some cases, this is resulting in serious physical maladies. A recent survey by the Japanese prime minister's office found that 63 percent of those who were surveyed complained of being chronically tired, and 53 percent felt emotionally stressed. Additionally, only 26 percent said they were very healthy, compared with 48 percent in 1979.[54] In fact, as seen in the accompanying sidebar, "*Karoshi,* or Stressed Out in Japan," the effects of overwork are beginning to be recognized as a problem in Japan. At the same time, some Japanese traditionally have had lifetime employment and thus feel committed to their firm because of everything that it has done for them. Most Japanese were never given lifetime employment, however, and with the downturn in the Japanese economy, those who are ensured of continued employment feel that they are special and, in turn, respond with dedication and fervor. Quite simply, they value work as an integral part of their existence.[55]

Job Satisfaction   In addition to the implications that value of work has for motivating human resources across cultures, another interesting contrast is job satisfaction. For example, one current study has revealed that Japanese office workers may be much less satisfied with their jobs than their U.S., Canadian, and EU counterparts are. The Americans, who reported the highest level of satisfaction in this

Karoshi, or Stressed Out in Japan

Doing business in Japan can be a real killer. Overwork, or *karoshi* as it is called in Japan, claims 10,000 lives annually in this hard-driving, competitive economic society according to Hiroshi Kawahito, a lawyer who has founded the National Defense Council for Victims of Karoshi.

One of the latest cases is Jun Ishii of Mitsui & Company. Ishii was one of the firm's only speakers of Russian. In the year before his death, Ishii made 10 trips to Russia, totaling 115 days. No sooner would he arrive home from one trip than the company would send him out again. The grueling pace took its toll. While on a trip, Ishii collapsed and died of a heart attack. His widow filed a lawsuit against Mitsui & Company, charging that her husband had been worked to death. Tokyo labor regulators ruled that Ishii had indeed died of *karoshi,* and the government now is paying annual worker's compensation to the widow. The company also co-operated and agreed to make a one-time payment of $240,000.

The reason that the case received so much publicity is that this is one of the few instances in which the government has ruled that a person died from overwork. Now regulators are expanding *karoshi* compensation to salaried as well as hourly workers. This development is receiving the attention of the top management of many Japanese multinationals, and some Japanese MNCs are beginning to take steps to prevent the likelihood of overwork. For example, Mitsui & Company is assessing its managers based on how well they set overtime hours, keep subordinates healthy, and encourage workers to take vacations. Matsushita Electric is extending vacations from 16 days annually to 23 days and is requiring all workers to take this time off. One branch of Nippon Telegraph & Telephone has found that stress is making some workers irritable and ill, so the company is initiating periods of silent meditation. Other companies are following suit, although there still are many Japanese who work well over 2500 hours a year and feel both frustrated and burned out by job demands.

Fortunately, the Ishii case likely will bring about some improvements in working conditions for many Japanese employees. Experts admit, however, that it is difficult to determine if *karoshi* is caused by work demands or by private, late-night socializing that may be work-related. Other possible causes include high stress, lack of exercise, and fatty diets, but whatever the cause, one thing is clear: More and more Japanese families no longer are willing to accept the belief that *karoshi* is a risk that all employees must accept. Work may be a killer, but this outcome can be prevented through more carefully implemented job designs and work processes.

study, were pleased with job challenges, opportunities for teamwork, and ability to make a significant contribution at work. Japanese workers, however, were least pleased with these three factors.[56] Similar findings also were found in an earlier study by the coauthor (Luthans and colleagues) of this text, who reported that U.S. employees had higher organizational commitment than Japanese or Korean workers in this cross-cultural study. What makes these findings particularly interesting is that a large percentage of the Japanese and Korean workers were supervisory employees, who could be expected to be more committed to their organization than nonsupervisory employees, and a significant percentage of these employees also had lifetime guarantees.[57] This study also showed that findings related to job satisfaction in the international arena often are different than expected.[58]

Conventional wisdom not always being substantiated was reinforced recently by research in cross-cultural studies that found Japanese workers who already were highly paid compared with their colleagues, and who then received even higher wages, experienced decreased job satisfaction, morale, commitment, and intention to remain with the firm. This contrasts sharply with U.S. workers, who did not experience these negative feelings.[59] These findings show that the motivation approaches used in one culture may have limited value in another.[60]

Recent research by Kakabadse and Myers also has brought to light findings that are contradictory to commonly accepted beliefs. These researchers surveyed managers from several European countries such as the United Kingdom, France, Belgium, Sweden, and Finland and, among other things, examined job satisfaction among managerial levels. It has long been assumed that satisfaction is highest at the upper levels of organizations; however, this study found varying degrees of satisfaction among managers, depending on the country. The researchers reported that

> senior managers from France and Finland display greater job dissatisfaction than the managers from the remaining countries. In terms of satisfaction with and commitment to the organization, British, German and Swedish managers display highest levels of commitment. Equally, British and German managers highlight that they feel stretched in their job, but senior managers from French organizations suggest that their jobs lack sufficient challenge and stimulus. In keeping with the job related views displayed by French managers, they equally indicate their desire to leave their job because of their unsatisfactory work-related circumstances.[61]

On the other hand, current research also reveals that some of the conditions that help to create organizational commitment among U.S. workers also have value in other cultures. For example, a very recent, large study of Korean employees ($n = 1192$ in 27 companies in eight major industries) found that consistent with U.S. studies, Korean employees' position in the hierarchy, tenure in their current position, and age all related significantly to organizational commitment. Also, like previous studies in the United States, as the size of the Korean organizations increased, commitment decreased, and the more positive the climate perceptions, the more the commitment.[62] In other words, there is at least beginning evidence that the theoretic constructs predicting organizational commitment may hold across cultures.

Also related to motivation are job attitudes toward quality of work life. Recent research reports that EU workers see a strong relationship between how well they do their jobs and the ability to get what they want out of life. U.S. workers were not as supportive of this relationship, and Japanese workers were least likely to see any connection.

In conclusion, it should be remembered that work is important in every society. The extent of importance will vary, however, and much of what is "known" about work as a motivator often is culture-specific. The lesson to be learned for international management is that although the process of motivation may be the same, the content may change from one culture to another.

SUMMARY OF KEY POINTS

1. Two basic types of theories explain motivation: content, and process. Content motivation theories have been given much more attention in international management research, because they provide the opportunity to create a composite picture for motivation of human resources in a particular country or region of the world. In addition, content theories apply more directly to providing ways for managers to improve the performance of their human resources.
2. Maslow's hierarchy-of-needs theory has been studied in a number of different countries. Researchers have found that regardless of country, managers have to be concerned with the satisfaction of these needs for their human resources.

3. Some researchers have suggested that satisfaction profiles are not very useful for studying motivation in an international setting, because there are so many different subcultures within any country or even at different levels of a given organization. These researchers have suggested that job categories are more effective for examining motivation, because job level (managers versus operating employees) and the need hierarchy have an established relationship.

4. Like Maslow's theory, Herzberg's two-factor theory has received considerable attention in the international arena, and his original findings from the United States have been replicated in other countries. Cross-cultural studies related to job satisfaction also have been conducted. The data show that job content is more important than job context to job satisfaction.

5. The third content motivation theory that has received a great amount of attention in the international arena is the need for achievement. Some current findings show that this need is not as widely held across cultures as was previously believed. In some parts of the world, however, such as Anglo countries, cultural values support people to be high achievers. In particular, Dutch researcher Geert Hofstede has suggested that an analysis of two cultural dimensions, uncertainty avoidance and masculinity, helps to identify high-achieving societies. Once again, it can be concluded that different cultures will support different motivational needs, and that international managers developing strategies to motivate their human resources for improved performance must recognize cultural differences.

6. Although content theories provide important insights into the motivation of human resources, two additional areas that have received a great deal of recent attention in the application of motivation are job design and the role of work in people's lives, or work centrality. Job design is influenced by culture as well as the specific methods that are used to bring together the people and the work. Work centrality helps to explain the importance of work in an individual's life relative to other areas of interest. Research reveals that in recent years, work has become a relatively greater part of the average U.S. employee's life and perhaps less a part of the average Japanese worker's life. Recent evidence also indicates that Japanese office workers may be much less satisfied with their jobs than U.S., Canadian, and EU workers are. These findings suggest that MNCs should design motivation packages that address the specific needs of different cultures.

KEY TERMS

motivation	motivators
content theories	hygiene factors
process theories	job context factors
physiological needs	job content factors
safety needs	achievement motivation theory
social needs	job design
esteem needs	sociotechnical designs
self-actualization needs	work centrality
two-factor theory of motivation	*karoshi*

REVIEW AND DISCUSSION QUESTIONS

1. Do people throughout the world have needs similar to those described in Maslow's need hierarchy? What does your answer reveal about using universal assumptions regarding motivation?

2. Is Herzberg's two-factor theory universally applicable to human resource management, or is its value limited to Anglo countries?

3. What are the dominant characteristics of high achievers? Using Figure 12-5 as your point of reference, determine which countries likely will have the greatest percentage of high achievers. Why is this so? Of what value is your answer to the study of international management?

4. A U.S. manufacturer is planning to open a plant in Sweden. What should this firm know about the quality of work life in Sweden that would have a direct effect on job design in the plant? Give an example.

5. What does a U.S. firm setting up operations in Japan need to know about work centrality in that country? How would this information be of value to the multinational? Conversely, what would a Japanese firm need to know about work centrality in the United States? Explain.

PRACTICAL INTERNATIONAL MANAGEMENT ASSIGNMENT

Using the library or interviews with relevant, knowledgeable people as resources, gather information regarding how Japanese managers attempt to motivate their human resources in their organizations located in Japan. What forms of compensation do they offer? Then, find out the type of compensation that Japanese companies offer to their employees in the United States. Are the two approaches the same, or do the Japanese provide different forms of compensation for their U.S. workers? Based on your findings, what conclusions can you draw regarding how Japanese MNCs try to motivate their overseas personnel vis-à-vis their own people?

The streets of Singapore are extremely clean because of harsh penalties against littering.

Singapore

Singapore is an island city-state that is located at the southern tip of the Malay Peninsula. The small country covers 239 square miles and is connected by train across the Johore Strait to West Malaysia in the north. The Strait of Malacca to the south separates Singapore from the Indonesian island of Sumatra. There are approximately 3.0 million people in Singapore, resulting in a population density per square mile of almost 15,000 people. About three-fourths of Singaporeans are of Chinese descent, 15 percent are Malays, and the remainder are Indian and European. The gross national product of this thriving country is over $100 billion, and per-capita GNP is around $33,000. One of the so-called newly industrialized countries or Four Tigers (along with Korea, Taiwan, and Hong Kong), Singapore in recent years has seen tremendous economic growth, and prices have remained moderately stable. The very clean and modern city has become the major commercial and shipping center of Southeast Asia. The government of this former British colony consists of a cabinet headed by Prime Minister Goh Chok Tong and a parliament of 81 members, who are elected by universal suffrage.

For the last 6 months, the Madruga Corporation of Cleveland has been producing small electronic toys in Singapore. The small factory has been operated by local managers, but Madruga now wants to expand the Singapore facilities as well as integrate more expatriate managers into the operation. The CEO explained: "We do not want to run this plant as if it were a foreign subsidiary under the direct control of local managers. It is our plant and we want an on-site presence. Over the last year we have been staffing our Canadian and European operations with headquarters personnel, and we are now ready to turn attention to our Singapore operation." Before doing so, however, the company intends to conduct some on-site research to learn the most effective way of managing the Singapore personnel. In particular, the Madruga management team is concerned with how to motivate the Singaporeans and make them more productive. One survey has already been conducted among the Singapore personnel; this study found a great deal of similarity with the workers at the U.S. facilities. Both the Singapore and U.S. employees expressed a preference for job content factors such as the chance for growth, achievement, and increased responsibility, and they listed money and job security toward the bottom of the list of things they looked for in a job.

Madruga management is intrigued by these findings and believes that it might be possible to use some of the same motivation approaches in Singapore as it does in the United States. Moreover, one of the researchers sent the CEO a copy of an article showing that people in Singapore have weak uncertainty avoidance and a general cultural profile that is fairly similar to that of the United States. The CEO is not sure what all this means, but she does know that motivating workers in Singapore apparently is not as "foreign" a process as she thought it would be.

1. What are some current issues facing Singapore? What is the climate for doing business in Singapore today?
2. Based on the information in this case, determine the specific things that seem to motivate human resources in Singapore.
3. Would a knowledge of the achievement motive be of any value to the expatriate managers who are assigned to the Singapore operation?
4. If you were using Figure 12-5 to help explain how to motivate the Singapore human resources effectively, what conclusions could you draw that would help provide guidelines for the Madruga management team?

You Be the International Management Consultant

Motivation Is the Key

Over the last 5 years, Corkley & Finn, a regional investment brokerage house, has been extremely profitable. Some of its largest deals have involved co-operation with investment brokers in other countries. Realizing that the world economy is likely to grow vigorously over the next 25 years, the company has decided to expand its operation and open overseas branches. In the beginning, the company intends to work in co-operation with other local brokerages; however, the company believes that within 5 years, it will have garnered enough business to break away and operate independently. For the time being, the firm intends to set up a small office in London and another in Tokyo.

The firm plans on sending four people to each of these offices and recruiting the remainder of the personnel from the local market. These new branch employees will have to spend time meeting potential clients and building trust. This will be followed by the opportunity to put together small financial deals and, it is hoped, much larger ones over time.

The company is prepared to invest whatever time or money is needed to make these two branches successful. "What we have to do," the president noted, "is establish an international presence and then build from there. We will need to hire people who are intensely loyal to us and use them as a cadre for expanding operations and becoming a major player in the international financial arena. One of our most important challenges will be to hire the right people and motivate them to do

the type of job we want and stay with us. After all, if we bring in people and train them how to do their jobs well and then they don't perform or they leave, all we've done is spend a lot of money for nothing and provide on-the-job training for our competitors. In this business, our people are the most important asset, and clients most often are swayed toward doing business with an investment broker with whom they think they can have a positive working relationship. The reputation of the firm is important, but it is always a function of the people who work there. Effective motivation of our people is the key to our ultimate success in these new branches."

1. In motivating the personnel in London and Tokyo, would the company find that the basic hierarchical needs of the workers were the same? Why or why not?
2. How could an understanding of the two-factor theory of motivation be of value in motivating the personnel at both of these locations? Would hygiene factors be more important to one of these groups than to the other? Would there be any difference in terms of the importance of motivators?
3. Using Figure 12-5 as a point of reference, what recommendation would you make regarding how to motivate the personnel in London? In Tokyo? Are there any significant differences between the two? If so, what are they? If not, why not?

CHAPTER 12 ENDNOTES

1. Abbass F. Alkhafaji, *Competitive Global Management* (Delray Beach, FL: St. Lucie Press, 1995), p. 118.
2. Nancy J. Adler, *International Dimensions of Organizational Behavior*, 2nd ed. (Boston: PWS-Kent, 1991), p. 160.
3. Dianne H. B. Welsh, Fred Luthans, and Steven Sommer, "Managing Russian Factory Workers: The Impact of U.S.-Based Behavioral and Participative Techniques," *Academy of Management Journal*, February 1993, p. 75.
4. For a more detailed discussion, see Fred Luthans, *Organizational Behavior*, 7th ed. (New York: McGraw-Hill, 1995), Chapter 6.
5. Ken I. Kim, Hun-Joon Park, and Nori Suzuki, "Reward Allocations in the United States, Japan, and Korea: A Comparison of Individualistic and Collectivistic Cultures," *Academy of Management Journal*, March 1990, pp. 188–198. Also see Miyo Umeshima and Ron Dalesio, "More Like Us," *Training and Development Journal*, March 1993, pp. 26–31.
6. A. H. Maslow, "A Theory of Human Motivation," *Psychological Review*, July 1943, pp. 390–396.
7. For more information on this topic, see Richard Mead, *International Management Cross-Cultural Dimensions* (Cambridge, MA: Blackwell Publishers, 1994), pp. 209–212.
8. See, for example, Igor Reichlin et al., "Long Days, Low Pay, and a Moldy Cot," *BusinessWeek*, January 27, 1992, pp. 44–45; Luis R. Gomez-Mejia, "Compensation Strategies in a Global Context," *Human Resource Planning*, vol. 14, no. 1, 1991, pp. 29–41; and "Japanese Firms Perfume Offices," *Wall Street Journal*, February 27, 1992, p. A7.
9. See "In Europe, Cash Eases the Pain of Getting Fired," *BusinessWeek*, March 16, 1992, p. 26; Stewart Toy et al., "Europe Gets in Shape by Pushing Out Pink Slips," *BusinessWeek*, March 2, 1992, pp. 52–54; and Alan S. Blinder, "How Japan Puts the 'Human' in Human Capital," *BusinessWeek*, November 11, 1991, p. 22.
10. See Richard M. Hodgetts, *Modern Human Relations at Work*, 6th ed. (Hinsdale, IL: Dryden Press, 1996), Chapter 2; and John Dobbs, "The Empowerment Environment," *Training and Development Journal*, March 1993, pp. 55–57.
11. Mason Haire, Edwin E. Ghiselli, and Lyman W. Porter, *Managerial Thinking: An International Study* (New York: John Wiley & Sons, 1966).
12. Ibid., p. 75.
13. Edwin C. Nevis, "Cultural Assumption and Productivity: The United States and China," *Sloan Management Review*, Spring 1983, pp. 17–29.
14. Geert H. Hofstede, "The Colors of Collars," *Columbia Journal of World Business*, September 1972, pp. 77–78.
15. Ibid., p. 72.
16. George H. Hines, "Cross-Cultural Differences in Two-Factor Motivation Theory," *Journal of Applied Psychology*, December 1973, p. 376.
17. Donald D. White and Julio Leon, "The Two-Factor Theory: New Questions, New Answers," *National Academy of Management Proceedings*, 1976, p. 358.
18. D. Macarov, "Work Patterns and Satisfactions in an Israeli Kibbutz: A Test of the Herzberg Hypothesis," *Personnel Psychology*, Autumn 1972, pp. 483–493.
19. Ibid., p. 492.
20. Peter D. Machungwa and Neal Schmitt, "Work Motivation in a Developing Country," *Journal of Applied Psychology*, February 1983, pp. 31–42.
21. G. E. Popp, H. J. Davis, and T. T. Herbert, "An International Study of Intrinsic Motivation Composition," *Management International Review*, vol. 26, no. 3, 1986, pp. 28–35.
22. Also see Rabi S. Bhagat et al., "Cross-Cultural Issues in Organizational Psychology: Emergent Trends and Directions for Research in the 1990s," in C. L. Cooper and I. Robertson (eds.), *International Review of Industrial and Organizational Psychology* (New York: John Wiley & Sons, 1990), p. 76.
23. Rabindra N. Kanungo and Richard W. Wright, "A Cross-Cultural Comparative Study of Managerial Job Attitudes," *Journal of International Business Studies*, Fall 1983, pp. 115–129.
24. Ibid., pp. 127–128.
25. Fred Luthans, "A Paradigm Shift in Eastern Europe: Some Helpful Management Development Techniques," *Journal of Management Development*, vol. 12, no. 8, 1993, pp. 53–60.
26. For more information on the characteristics of high achievers, see David C. McClelland, "Business Drive and National Achievement," *Harvard Business Review*, July-August 1962, pp. 99–112.
27. For more detail on the achievement motive, see Luthans, *Organizational Behavior*, pp. 144–146.
28. Fred Luthans, Brooke R. Envick, and Mary F. Sully, "Characteristics of Successful Entrepreneurs: Do They Fit the Cultures of Developing Countries?" *Proceeding of the Pan Pacific Conference*, 1995, pp. 25–27.
29. For an earlier example of similar findings using sample groups of male Australian M.B.A. candidates and University of California-Berkeley M.B.A. candidates, see Theodore T. Herbert, Gary E. Popp, and Herbert J. Davis, "Australian Work-Reward Preferences," *National Academy of Management Proceedings*, 1979, pp. 289–292.

30. These data were reported in David C. McClelland, *The Achieving Society* (Princeton, NJ: Van Nostrand, 1961), p. 294.

31. E. J. Murray, *Motivation and Emotion* (Englewood Cliffs, NJ: Prentice-Hall, 1964), p. 101.

32. David J. Krus and Jane A. Rysberg, "Industrial Managers and N ach: Comparable and Compatible?" *Journal of Cross-Cultural Psychology,* December 1976, pp. 491–496.

33. For example, see Henry Grunwald, "New Challenges to Capitalism," *Fortune,* May 7, 1990, pp. 138–144; Shawn Tully, "What Eastern Europe Offers," *Fortune,* March 12, 1990, pp. 52–55.

34. See James McGregor, "China Wants Urban Workers to Purchase Their Homes, Abandoning Mao's Vision of Nearly Cost-Free Shelter," *Wall Street Journal,* January 23, 1992, p. A13.

35. Oded Shenkar and Simcha Ronen, "Structure and Importance of Work Goals among Managers in the People's Republic of China," *Academy of Management Journal,* September 1987, pp. 564–576.

36. Chao C. Chen, "New Trends in Rewards Allocation Preferences: A Sino-U.S. Comparison," *Academy of Management Journal,* April 1995, p. 425.

37. David C. McClelland, "Achievement Motivation Can Be Developed," *Harvard Business Review,* November-December 1965, p. 20.

38. Geert Hofstede, "Motivation, Leadership, and Organization: Do American Theories Apply Abroad?" *Organizational Dynamics,* Summer 1980, pp. 55–56.

39. For a systematic analysis of this and other myths of Japanese management, see Richard M. Hodgetts and Fred Luthans, "Japanese HR Management Practices," *Personnel,* April 1989, pp. 42–45.

40. "Japanese Employers Are 'Locking Out' Their U.S. Managers," *Business Week,* May 7, 1990, p. 24.

41. For more on this topic, see Noel M. Tichy and Thore Sandstrom, "Organizational Innovations in Sweden," *Columbia Journal of World Business,* Summer 1974, pp. 18–28; Fred Luthans, *Organizational Behavior,* 5th ed. (New York: McGraw-Hill, 1989), pp. 273–274.

42. "Product Innovation Gains Worldwide Importance," *HR Focus,* March 1992, p. 12.

43. Eric Sundstrom, Kenneth P. DeMeuse, and David Futrell, "Work Teams: Applications and Effectiveness," *American Psychologist,* February 1990, pp. 120–133.

44. Thomas A. Stewart, "The Search for the Organization of Tomorrow," *Fortune,* May 18, 1992, p. 95.

45. For some interesting insights on horizontal networking, see Larry Hirschhorn and Thomas Gilmore, "The New Boundaries of the 'Boundaryless' Company," *Harvard Business Review,* May-June 1992, pp. 104–115.

46. See, for example, Akio Morita, "Partnering for Competitiveness: The Role of Japanese Business," *Harvard Business Review,* May-June 1992, pp. 76–83.

47. See Lillian H. Chaney and Jeanette S. Martin, *Intercultural Business Communication* (Englewood Cliffs, NJ: Prentice-Hall, 1995), pp. 46–47.

48. Bhagat et al., "Cross-Cultural Issues," p. 72.

49. Tim W. Ferguson, "Japan's Buffeted Banks—and U.S. Opportunity: Long on Jobs," *Wall Street Journal,* February 25, 1992, p. A15.

50. John Conston, "More Work, Less Play Is the Rule of the Day," *Wall Street Journal,* February 14, 1992, p. A9.

51. Also see Christopher J. Chipello, "Japan's Quality of Life," *Wall Street Journal,* January 28, 1992, p. A9.

52. Andrew Tanzer and Gale Eisenstodt, "Rich Country, Poor Japanese," *Forbes,* May 25, 1992, p. 45.

53. Urban C. Lehner, "Is It Any Surprise the Japanese Make Excellent Loafers?" *Wall Street Journal,* February 28, 1992, pp. A1, A10.

54. "Stress Takes Toll on Japanese," *Wall Street Journal,* February 4, 1992, p. A11.

55. Eamonn Fingleton, "Jobs for Life: Why Japan Won't Give Them Up," *Fortune,* March 20, 1995, pp. 119–125.

56. "Satisfaction in the USA, Unhappiness in Japanese Offices," *Personnel,* January 1992, p. 8.

57. Fred Luthans, Harriette S. McCaul, and Nancy G. Dodd, "Organizational Commitment: A Comparison of American, Japanese, and Korean Employees," *Academy of Management Journal,* March 1985, pp. 213–219.

58. For additional insights, see Abdul Rahim A. Al-Meer, "Organizational Commitment: A Comparison of Westerners, Asians, and Saudis," *International Studies of Management and Organization,* Summer 1989, pp. 74–84.

59. David I. Levine, "What Do Wages Buy?" *Administrative Science Quarterly,* September 1993, pp. 462–483.

60. David Heming, "What Wages Buy in the U.S. and Japan," *Academy of Management Executive,* November 1994, pp. 88–89.

61. Andrew Kakabadse and Andrew Myers, "Qualities of Top Management: Comparisons of European Manufacturers," *Journal of Management Development,* vol. 14, no. 1, 1995, p. 6.

62. Steven M. Sommer, Seung-Hyun Bae, and Fred Luthans, "Organizational Commitment across Cultures: The Impact of Antecedents on Korean Employees," *Human Relations,* 1996, vol. 49 (in press).

LEADERSHIP ACROSS CULTURES

OBJECTIVES OF THE CHAPTER

Leadership often is credited for the success or failure of international operations. Note that like the other topics discussed so far, effective leadership styles and practices in one culture are not necessarily effective in others. For example, the leadership approach used by effective U.S. managers would not necessarily be the same as that employed in other parts of the world. Even within the same country, effective leadership tends to be very situation-specific; however, also like the other areas studied in international management, certain leadership styles and practices transcend international boundaries. This chapter examines these leadership differences and similarities.

First, the basic foundation for the study of leadership is reviewed. Next, leadership in various parts of the world, including Europe, East Asia, the Middle East, and Third World countries are examined. The specific objectives of this chapter are:

1. **DESCRIBE** the basic philosophic foundation and styles of managerial leadership.
2. **EXAMINE** the attitudes of European managers toward leadership practices.
3. **COMPARE** and **CONTRAST** leadership styles in Japan with those in the United States.
4. **COMPARE** and **CONTRAST** leadership approaches in Middle Eastern and developing countries with those in the economic powers of the world.

FOUNDATION FOR LEADERSHIP

When one realizes that much of history, political science, and the behavioral sciences is either directly or indirectly concerned with leadership, the statement that more concern and research has focused on leadership than on any other topic becomes believable. With all this attention over the years, however, there still is no generally agreed-on definition, let alone firm answers to which approach is more effective than others in the international arena. For present purposes, however, *leadership* can be defined as the process of influencing people to direct their efforts toward achievement of some particular goal or goals.[1] Leadership is widely recognized as being very important in the study of international management, but relatively little effort has gone to systematically studying and comparing leadership approaches throughout the world.[2] Most international research efforts on leadership have been directed toward a specific country or geographic area.

The following two comparative areas provide a foundation for understanding leadership in the international arena: (1) the philosophic grounding of how leaders view their subordinates; and (2) leadership approaches as reflected through use of autocratic-participative characteristics and behaviors of leaders. The philosophies and approaches used in the United States often are quite different from those employed by leaders in overseas organizations, although these differences often are not as pronounced as is commonly believed.

Philosophical Background: Theories X and Y

One primary reason that leaders behave as they do is their philosophy or beliefs regarding how to direct their subordinates most effectively. Managers who believe their people are naturally lazy and work only for money will use a leadership style that is different from those who believe their people are self-starters and enjoy challenge and increased responsibility. Douglas McGregor, the pioneering leadership theorist, labeled these two sets of philosophic assumptions with the terms "Theory X" and "Theory Y."

A *Theory X manager* believes that people are basically lazy and that coercion and threats of punishment must be used to get them to work. The specific philosophic assumptions that Theory X leaders feel are most descriptive of their subordinates are:

1. By their very nature, people do not like to work and will avoid it whenever possible.
2. Workers have little ambition, try to avoid responsibility, and like to be directed.
3. The primary need of employees is job security.
4. To get people to attain organizational objectives, it is necessary to use coercion, control, and threats of punishment.[3]

A *Theory Y manager* believes that under the right conditions, people not only will work hard but seek increased responsibility and challenge. In addition, a great deal of creative potential basically goes untapped, and if these abilities can be tapped, workers will provide much higher quantity and quality of output. The specific philosophic assumptions that Theory Y leaders feel are most descriptive of their subordinates are:

1. The expenditure of physical and mental effort at work is as natural to people as resting or playing.
2. External control and threats of punishment are not the only ways of getting people to work toward organizational objectives. If people are committed to the goals, they will exercise self-direction and self-control.
3. Commitment to objectives is determined by the rewards that are associated with their achievement.
4. Under proper conditions, the average human being learns not only to accept but to seek responsibility.
5. The capacity to exercise a relatively high degree of imagination, ingenuity, and creativity in the solution of organizational problems is widely distributed throughout the population.
6. Under conditions of modern industrial life, the intellectual potential of the average human being is only partially tapped.[4]

The reason behind these beliefs, however, will vary by culture. U.S. managers believe that to motivate workers, it is necessary to satisfy their higher-order needs. This is done best through a Theory Y leadership approach. In China, Theory Y managers act similarly—but for different reasons. After the 1949 revolution, two types of managers emerged: Experts, and Reds. The Experts focused on technical skills and primarily were Theory X advocates. The Reds, skilled in the management of people and possessing political and ideologic expertise, were Theory Y advocates. The Reds also believed that the philosophy of Chairman Mao supported their thinking (i.e., all employees had to rise together both economically and culturally). Therefore, both U.S. and Chinese managers support Theory Y, but for very different reasons.[5]

These philosophic assumptions help to dictate the leadership approach that is used. They most easily are seen in behaviors used by managers, such as giving orders, getting and giving feedback, and creating an overall climate within which the work will be done.

Leadership Behaviors and Styles

Leader behaviors can be translated into three commonly recognized styles: (1) authoritarian; (2) paternalistic; and (3) participative. *Authoritarian leadership* is the use of work-centered behavior that is designed to ensure task accomplishment. As shown in Figure 13-1, this leader behavior typically involves the use of one-way communication from superior to subordinate. The focus of attention usually is on work progress, work procedures, and roadblocks that are preventing goal attainment. Although this leadership style often is effective in handling crises, some leaders employ it as their primary style regardless of the situation. It also is widely used by Theory X managers, who believe that a continued focus on the task is compatible with the kind of people they are dealing with.

Paternalistic leadership uses work-centered behavior coupled with a protective employee-centered concern. This leadership style can be best summarized by the statement, "work hard and the company will take care of you." This approach was described in Figure 12-5 and perhaps is best supported by cultures such as those found in Japan. Paternalistic leaders expect everyone to work hard; in turn, the employees will be guaranteed employment and given security benefits such

FIGURE 13-1

LEADER–SUBORDINATE INTERACTIONS

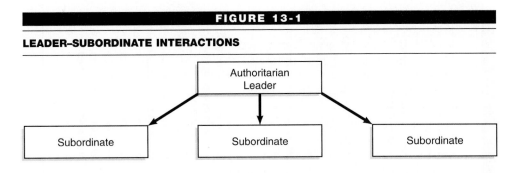

One-way downward flow of information and influence from authoritarian leader to subordinates.

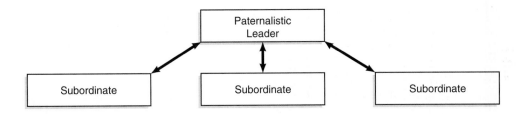

Continual interaction and exchange of information and influence between leader and subordinates.

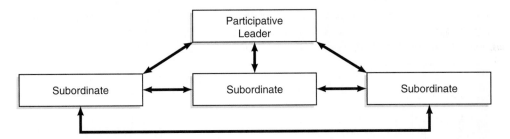

Continual exchange of information and influence between leader and subordinates and/or between subordinates themselves.

Source: Adapted from Richard M. Hodgetts, *Modern Human Relations at Work,* 6th ed. (Hinsdale, IL: Dryden, 1996) p. 280.

as medical and retirement programs. Paternalistic leaders often are referred to as "soft" Theory X leaders because of their strong emphasis on strictly controlling their employees coupled with concern for their welfare. They often treat their employees as strict but caring parents would their children.

One way of contrasting authoritative and paternalistic leaders is in terms of Likert's management systems or leadership styles, as presented in Table 13-1. As shown, an authoritarian leader is characterized by Likert's system 1, and a paternalistic leader is characterized by system 2.

TABLE 13-1

LIKERT'S SYSTEMS OR STYLES OF LEADERSHIP

Leadership characteristic	System 1 (exploitive autocratic)	System 2 (benevolent autocratic)	System 3 (participative)	System 4 (democratic)
Leadership processes used (extent to which superiors have confidence and trust in subordinates)	Have no confidence and trust in subordinates	Have condescending confidence and trust, such as master has in servant	Substantial but not complete confidence and trust, still wish to keep control of decisions	Complete confidence and trust in all matters
Character of motivational forces (underlying motives tapped)	Physical security, economic needs, and some use of the desire for status	Economic needs and moderate use of ego motives (e.g., desire for status, affiliation, and achievement)	Economic needs and considerable use of ego and other major motives (e.g., desire for new experiences)	Full use of economic, ego, and other major motives such as motivational forces arising from group goals
Character of communication process (amount of interaction and communication aimed at achieving organization's objectives)	Very little	Little	Quite a bit	Much, with both individuals and groups
Character of interaction influence process (amount and character of interaction)	Little interaction and always with fear and distrust	Little interaction and usually with some condescension by superiors; fear and caution by subordinates	Moderate interaction, often with fair amount of confidence and trust	Extensive friendly interaction with high degree of confidence and trust
Character of decision-making process (at what level in organization are decisions formally made)	Bulk of decisions at top of organization	Policy at top; many decisions within prescribed framework made at lower levels but usually checked with top before action is taken	Broad policy decisions at top; more specific decisions at lower levels	Decision making widely done throughout organization, although well integrated through linking process provided by overlapping groups
Character of goal setting or ordering (manner in which usually done)	Orders issued	Orders issued, opportunity to comment may exist	Goals are set or orders issued after discussion with subordinates of problems and planned action	Except in emergencies, goals are usually established by group participation

Source: Adapted from Rensis Likert, *The Human Organization* (New York:McGraw-Hill, 1967). Used with permission.

FIGURE 13-2

THE MANAGERIAL GRID

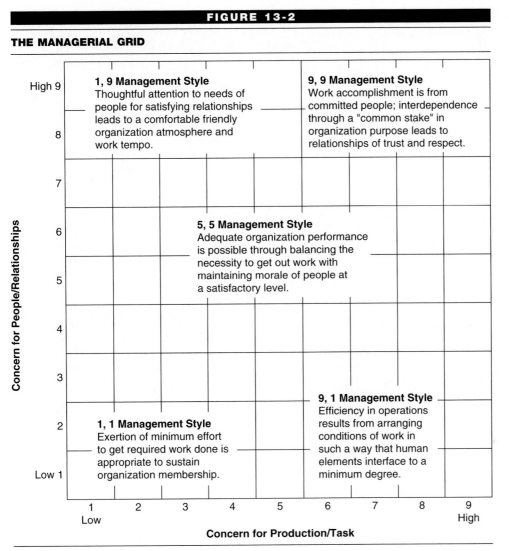

Source: Adapted from Robert S. Blake and Jane S. Mouton, "Managerial Facades," *Advanced Management Journal,* July 1966, p. 31.

Participative leadership is the use of both a work-centered and people-centered approach. Participative leaders typically encourage their people to play an active role in assuming control of their work, and authority commonly is highly decentralized. In terms of Likert's four systems shown in Table 13-1, participative leaders are characterized by system 3. (Likert's system 4 leaders are fully democratic and go beyond the participative style.) Another way of characterizing participative leaders is in terms of the managerial grid, which is a traditional, well-known method of identifying leadership style. As shown in Figure 13-2, participative leaders are on the 9,9 position of the grid. This is in contrast to paternalistic leaders, who tend to be about 9,5, and autocratic leaders, who are more of a 9,1 position on the grid. Participative leadership is very

INTERNATIONAL MANAGEMENT IN ACTION

The Jury Is Still Out

International management is becoming increasingly important for those pursuing a master's degree in business administration (M.B.A.). In fact, many universities now are rethinking their M.B.A. curriculum and adding new courses that are designed to give the student a global perspective. M.B.A. students of the 1990s, at least at leading U.S. business schools, will take courses related to ethics, negotiation, communication, and technology. "For better or worse, students will get more of what educators call experiential learning, in which they act as consultants, intern in the United States and overseas, and join in activities such as mock negotiations and Outward Bound trips." The biggest change, however, may be that of a required foreign language.

U.S. M.B.A. students tend to be very parochial, believing that English will always be the international language of business. Although this may be true, students in an increasing number of programs are going to get a semester or two of Japanese, Spanish, German, or a similarly important foreign language that will better prepare them for international business. Some schools are going even further and offering a course on formal entertaining so that the students understand how to conduct themselves properly in social settings. Another major curriculum change will be a stronger focus on the behavioral area. More emphasis will be given to people skills, such as communication, motivation, and leadership in an international setting.

The M.B.A. student of the 1990s may be more of a generalist in the true sense of the word. The strong functional emphasis that traditionally has been given to educating future business leaders in areas such as accounting, finance, production, personnel, and marketing may be replaced by a broader, more general education that better prepares them to manage in the global economy.

Will all business education move in this direction? It is too early to tell. The answer will depend heavily on the amount of support that is provided by both the faculty and the business community. Faculty members have been educated to focus on specialized functional areas applied to their own country. Now, they will have to start thinking in more macro, global terms. The business community, meanwhile, is sitting on the sidelines. If businesses like the new business school products, they likely will provide financial support for these types of business programs. If they do not like what they see, the universities may end up going it alone. Academic administrators and faculty members who now are implementing these revised business education programs for future business leaders are betting that their product will be accepted with open arms by the business community and that they will receive the necessary support to continue their efforts. Right now, the jury is still out.

popular in many technologically advanced countries. Such leadership has been widely espoused in the United States, England, and other Anglo countries, and it currently is very popular in Scandinavian countries as well. For example, at General Electric, managers are encouraged to use a participative style that delivers on commitment and shares the values of the firm, which is an approach that also is common in these other nations.[6] The remainder of the chapter gives more details and research results relating leadership styles by country and area of the world.

LEADERSHIP IN THE INTERNATIONAL CONTEXT

How do leaders in other countries attempt to direct or influence their subordinates? Are their approaches similar to those used in the United States? Research shows that there are both similarities and differences, which in many cases are a result of culture.[7] Most international research on leadership has focused on Europe, East Asia, the Middle East, and on developing countries such as India, Peru, Chile, and Argentina. The accompanying box, "International Management in Action: The Jury is Still Out," takes a look at how the international management leaders of the future are being educated.

Attitudes of European Managers toward Leadership Practices

In recent years, much research has been directed at leadership approaches in Europe.[8] Most effort has concentrated on related areas, such as decision making, risk-taking, strategic planning, and organization design, that have been covered in previous chapters. Some of this previous discussion is relevant to an understanding of leadership practices in Europe. For example, British managers tend to use a highly participative leadership approach. This is true for two reasons: (1) the political background of the country favors such an approach; and (2) because most top British managers are not highly involved in the day-to-day affairs of the business, they prefer to delegate authority and let much of the decision making be handled by middle- and lower-level managers. This preference contrasts sharply with that of the French and the Germans,[9] who prefer a more work-centered, authoritarian approach. In fact, if labor unions did not have legally mandated seats on the boards of directors, participative management in Germany likely would be even less pervasive than it is, a problem that currently confronts firms like Volkswagen that are trying to reduce sharply their overhead to meet increasing competition in Europe.[10] Scandinavian countries, however, make wide use of participative leadership approaches, with worker representation on the boards of directors and high management–worker interaction regarding workplace design and changes.

As a general statement, most evidence indicates that European managers tend to use a participative approach. They do not entirely subscribe to Theory Y philosophical assumptions, however, because an element of Theory X thinking continues. This was made clear by the now-classic Haire, Ghiselli, and Porter study of 3641 managers from 14 countries.[11] (The motivation-related findings of this study were reported in the previous chapter.) The leadership-related portion of this study sought to determine whether these managers were basically traditional (Theory X, or system 1/2) or democratic-participative (Theory Y, or system 3/4) in their approach. Specifically, the researchers investigated four areas relevant to leadership:

1. *Capacity for leadership and initiative.* Does the leader believe that employees prefer to be directed and have little ambition (Theory X), or that characteristics such as initiative can be acquired by most people regardless of their inborn traits and abilities (Theory Y)?
2. *Sharing information and objectives.* Does the leader believe that detailed, complete instructions should be given to subordinates and that subordinates need only this information to do their jobs, or does the leader believe that general directions are sufficient and that subordinates can use their initiative in working out the details?
3. *Participation.* Does the leader support participative leadership practices?
4. *Internal control.* Does the leader believe that the most effective way to control employees is through rewards and punishment or that employees respond best to internally generated control?

Overall Results of Research on Attitudes of European Managers Responses by managers to the four areas covered in the Haire, Ghiselli, and Porter study, as noted in the last chapter, are quite dated, but these responses still are the most comprehensive available and are relevant to the current discussion of leadership

TABLE 13-2

CLUSTERS OF COUNTRIES IN THE HAIRE, GHISELLI, AND PORTER STUDY

NORDIC-EUROPEAN COUNTRIES	ANGLO-AMERICAN COUNTRIES
Denmark	England
Germany	United States
Norway	
Sweden	DEVELOPING COUNTRIES
LATIN-EUROPEAN COUNTRIES	Argentina
Belgium	Chile
France	India
Italy	
Spain	JAPAN

similarities and differences across cultures. The specifics by country may have changed somewhat over the years, but the leadership processes revealed should not be out of date. The clusters of countries studied by these researchers are shown in Table 13-2. Results indicate that none of the leaders from various parts of the world, on average, were very supportive of the belief that individuals have a capacity for leadership and initiative. The researchers put it this way: "In each country, in each group of countries, in all of the countries taken together, there is a relatively low opinion of the capabilities of the average person, coupled with a relatively positive belief in the necessity for democratic-type supervisory practices."[12]

An analysis of standard scores compared each cluster of countries against the others, and it revealed that Anglo leaders tend to have more faith in the capacity of their people for leadership and initiative than do the other clusters. They also believe that sharing information and objectives is important; however, when it comes to participation and internal control, the Anglo group tends to give relatively more autocratic responses than all the other clusters except developing countries. Interestingly, Anglo leaders reported a much stronger belief in the value of external rewards (pay, promotion, etc.) than did any of the clusters except that of the developing countries. These findings clearly illustrate that attitudes toward leadership practices tend to be quite different in various parts of the world.

The Role of Level, Size, and Age on European Managers' Attitudes Toward Leadership The research of Haire and associates provided important additional details within each cluster of European countries. These findings indicated that in some countries, higher-level managers tended to express more democratic values than lower-level managers; however, in other countries, the opposite was true. For example, in England, higher-level managers responded with more democratic attitudes on all four leadership dimensions, whereas in the United States, lower-level managers gave more democratically oriented responses on all four. In the Scandinavian countries, higher-level managers tended to respond more democratically; in Germany, lower-level managers tended to have more democratic attitudes.

Company size also tended to influence the degree of participative-autocratic attitudes. There was more support among managers in small firms than in large ones regarding the belief that individuals have a capacity for leadership and initiative; however, respondents from large firms were more supportive of sharing information and objectives, participation, and use of internal control.

Those from large U.S. companies were most supportive of the first three attitudes, and those from small firms were more supportive of internal control.

There were findings that age also had some influence on participative attitudes. Younger managers were more likely to have democratic values when it came to capacity for leadership and initiative and so sharing information and objectives, although on the other two dimensions of leadership practices older and younger managers differed little. In terms of specific countries, however, some important differences were found. For example, younger managers in both the United States and Sweden espoused more democratic values than their older counterparts; in Belgium, just the opposite was true.

Conclusions About European Leadership Practices   Although now quite dated, as already mentioned, data from this classic Haire and associates study do nevertheless show differences in the attitudes toward leadership practices between European managers. In most cases, these leaders tend to reflect more participative and democratic attitudes, but not in every country. In addition, organizational level, company size, and age seem to greatly influence attitudes toward leadership. Because many of the young people in this study now are middle-aged, European managers in general are highly likely to be more participative than their older counterparts of the 1960s and 1970s; however, no empirical evidence proves that each generation of European managers is becoming more participative than the previous one. Also, just because they express favorable attitudes toward participative leadership does not mean that they actually practice this approach, although it is certainly true that boards of directors of U.S. multinationals operating in Europe are becoming more international and that this multicultural mix may indeed promote participative management.[13] More research that actually observes today's European managers' style in their day-to-day jobs is needed before any definitive conclusions can be drawn.

Japanese Leadership Approaches

Japan is well known for its paternalistic approach to leadership. As noted in Figure 12-5, Japanese culture promotes a high safety or security need, which is present among home country–based employees as well as MNC expatriates. For example, one study examined the cultural orientations of 522 employees of 28 Japanese-owned firms in the United States and found that the native Japanese employees were more likely to value paternalistic company behavior than their U.S. counterparts.[14] Another study found that Koreans also value such paternalism.[15] However, major differences appear in leadership approaches used by the Japanese and those in other locales.

For example, the comprehensive Haire, Ghiselli, and Porter study found that Japanese managers have much greater belief in the capacity of subordinates for leadership and initiative than do managers in most other countries.[16] In fact, in the study, only managers in Anglo-American countries had stronger feelings in this area. The Japanese also expressed attitudes toward the use of participation to a greater degree than others. In the other two leadership dimensions, sharing information and objectives and using internal control, the Japanese respondents were above average but not distinctive. Overall, however, this classic study found that the Japanese respondents scored highest on the four areas of leadership

TABLE 13-3

JAPANESE VS. U.S. LEADERSHIP STYLES

Philosophical dimensions	Japanese approach	U.S. approach
Employment	Often for life; layoffs are rare	Usually short-term; layoffs are common
Evaluation and promotion	Very slow; big promotions may not come for the first 10 years	Very fast; those not quickly promoted often seek employment elsewhere
Career paths	Very general; people rotate from one area to another and become familiar with all areas of operations	Very specialized; people tend to stay in one area (accounting, sales, etc.) for their entire careers
Decision making	Carried out via group decision making	Carried out by the individual manager
Control mechanism	Very implicit and informal; people rely heavily on trust and goodwill	Very explicit; people know exactly what to control and how to do it
Responsibility	Shared collectively	Assigned to individuals
Concern for employees	Management's concern extends to the whole life, business and social, of the worker	Management concerned basically with the individual's work life only

Source: Adapted from William Ouchi, *Theory Z: How American Business Can Meet the Japanese Challenge* (Reading, MA: Addison-Wesley, 1981).

combined. In other words, although these findings are quite dated, they do provide evidence that Japanese leaders have considerable confidence in the overall ability of their subordinates and use a style that allows their subordinates to actively participate in decisions.

Differences between Japanese and U.S. Leadership Styles

In a number of ways, Japanese leadership styles differ from those in the United States. For example, the Haire and associates study found that except for internal control, large U.S. firms tend to be more democratic than small ones, whereas in Japan, the profile is quite different.[17] A second difference is that younger U.S. managers appear to express more democratic attitudes than their older counterparts on all four leadership dimensions, but younger Japanese fall into this category only for sharing information and objectives and in the use of internal control.[18] Simply put, evidence points to some similarities between U.S. and Japanese leadership styles, but major differences also exist.

A number of reasons have been cited for these differences. One of the most common is that Japanese and U.S. managers have a basically different philosophy of managing people. Table 13-3 provides a comparison of seven key characteristics that come from the work of William Ouchi, author of the widely recognized *Theory Z*, which combines Japanese and U.S. assumptions and approaches. Note in the table that the Japanese leadership approach is heavily group-oriented, paternalistic, and concerned with the employee's work and personal life. The U.S. leadership approach is almost the opposite.[19]

TABLE 13-4

JAPANESE AND U.S. SENIOR MANAGEMENT APPROACHES TO PROCESSING INFORMATION

Japanese senior management approach (variety amplification)	U.S. senior management approach (variety reduction)
State a policy that all phenomena are relevant	State a policy that focuses only on relevant issues and sources of information
Require all employees to be identifiers of corporate problems and opportunities	Identify specific employees who will identify problems and opportunities
Seek a large quantity of information from the environment	Seek only high-quality information from the environment
State a desire for the firm to attain an idea—a dream	State a desire for the firm to attain a realistic level—a goal
Focus on creating challenges—barriers to hurdle and problems to solve	Focus on taking advantage of opportunities—holes in the barrier to crawl through
Vitalize people	Direct people

Source: Adapted from Jeremiah J. Sullivan and Ikujiro Nonaka, "The Application of Organizational Learning Theory to Japanese and American Management," *Journal of International Business Studies*, Fall 1986, pp. 130–131. Used with permission.

Another difference between Japanese and U.S. leadership styles is how senior-level managers process information and learn. Japanese executives are taught and tend to use *variety amplification,* which is the creation of uncertainty and the analysis of many alternatives regarding future action. By contrast, U.S. executives are taught and tend to use *variety reduction,* which is the limiting of uncertainty and the focusing of action on a limited number of alternatives.[20] Some specific characteristics of these two approaches are shown in Table 13-4.

When this study of processing information and learning examined the leadership styles used by Japanese and U.S. senior managers, it found that the Japanese focused very heavily on problems while the U.S. managers focused on opportunities.[21] The Japanese were more willing to allow poor performance to continue for a time so that those who were involved would learn from their mistakes, but the Americans worked to stop poor performance as quickly as possible. Finally, the Japanese sought creative approaches to managing projects and tried to avoid relying on experience, but the Americans sought to build on their experiences.[22]

Still another major reason accounting for differences in leadership styles is that the Japanese tend to be more ethnocentric than their U.S. counterparts. The Japanese think of themselves as Japanese managers who are operating overseas; most do not view themselves as international managers. As a result, even if they do adapt their leadership approach on the surface to that of the country in which they are operating, they still believe in the Japanese way of doing things and are reluctant to abandon it.

Similarities between Japanese and U.S. Leadership Styles

Although differences exist and get considerable attention in both research and the popular media, important similarities in leadership approaches also exist between the Japanese and the Americans. For example, a somewhat dated, but still relevant, study examined the ways in which leadership style could be used to influence the achievement motivation of Japanese subjects.[23] Achievement motivation was measured among a series of participants, and two major groups were created: one consisted of Japanese high achievers, the other of Japanese low achievers. Four smaller groups of high-achieving participants and four more of low-achieving participants then were created. Each high-achieving group was assigned a supervisor who used a different leadership style. The same pattern was used with the low-achieving groups.

In each of the two major clusters (high achievers and low achievers), one group was assigned a leader who focused on performance (called "P supervision" in the study). The supervisor used a 9,1 (high on task, low on people) type of style on the managerial grid (see Figure 13-2, which identifies all the styles on the grid). This supervisor was work-centered, took the initiative in solving problems that impeded performance, and ensured that all rules were followed, exhorting the workers to "hurry up," "work more quickly," and "don't fool around; get to work." The supervisor also compared this group with the others, related how far behind they were, and pressed them to catch up.

In a second group within each major cluster, the supervisor's leadership style focused on maintaining and strengthening the group (called "M supervision" in the study). The individual used a 1,9 (low on task, high on people) leadership style on the managerial grid. The supervisor was open to suggestions, never pushed personal opinions on the workers, and encouraged a warm, friendly environment. This supervisor often said, "Let's be pleasant and cheerful," and "Let's be more friendly." The supervisor also was sympathetic when things did not go well and worked to improve interpersonal relations by reducing tensions and increasing the sociability of the environment.

In a third group within each major cluster, the supervisor focused on both performance and maintenance (called "PM supervision" in the study). This supervisor put pressure on the workers to do their work but, at the same time, offered encouragement and support to the workers. In other words, this supervisor used a 9,9 leadership style from the managerial grid.

In the fourth group within each major cluster, the supervisor focused on neither performance nor maintenance (called "pm supervision" in the study). This supervisor simply did not get very involved in either the task or the people side of the group being led. In other words, the supervisor used a 1,1 leadership style on the grid.

The results of these four leadership styles among the high-achieving and low-achieving groups are reported in Figures 13-3 and 13-4. In the high-achieving groups, the PM (or 9,9) leadership style that emphasized both the task and human dimensions was the most effective throughout the entire experiment, and the pm (or 1,1) leadership style was consistently ineffective. The P (or 9,1 [high on task, low on people]) leadership style was the second most effective during the early and middle phases of the study, but it was supplanted by the M (or 1,9 [low on task, high on people]) leadership style in the later phases. Among the low-achieving groups, the P (or 9,1) supervision was most effective. The M (or 1,9) leadership style was the second most effective during the early sessions, but it soon tapered off and produced negative results in later sessions. The PM (or 9,9) style was moderately ineffective during the first three sessions but improved rapidly and

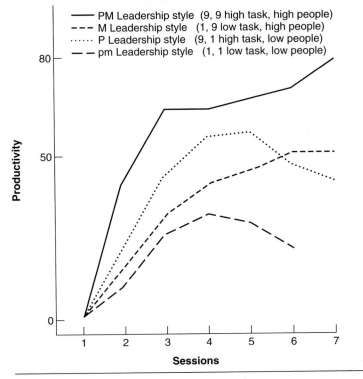

FIGURE 13-3

PRODUCTIVITY OF JAPANESE GROUPS WITH HIGH-ACHIEVEMENT
MOTIVATION UNDER DIFFERENT LEADERSHIP STYLES

——— PM Leadership style (9, 9 high task, high people)
– – – M Leadership style (1, 9 low task, high people)
······· P Leadership style (9, 1 high task, low people)
— — pm Leadership style (1, 1 low task, low people)

Source: Adapted from Jyuji Misumi and Fumiyasu Seki, "Effects of Achievement Motivation on the Effective-ness of Leadership Patterns," *Administrative Science Quarterly,* March 1971, p. 57. Used with permission.

was the second most effective by the end of the seventh session. The pm (or 1,1) leadership style was consistently effective until the fifth session, then productiv-ity began to level off.

The results of this study are similar to those that would be expected among high- and low-achieving groups of U.S. managers. In addition, the study showed that high-achieving groups of Japanese tend to be more productive than low-achieving groups. Thus, this study shows some degree of convergence or similar-ity between Japanese and U.S. managers regarding the most effective types of leadership styles given the achievement motivation of the group members.

Recent findings support these conclusions and suggest they can be extended to other countries as well. For example, in the United States the Saturn recently has proved to be one of General Motors' most successful new auto offerings. The ap-proach used in managing workers in the Saturn plant is quite different from that employed in other GM plants. Strong attention is given to allowing workers a voice in all management decisions, and pay is linked to quality, productivity, and profitability.[24] Japanese firms such as Sony use a similar approach, encouraging personnel to assume authority, use initiative, and work as a team.[25] Major empha-sis also is given to developing communication links between management and the

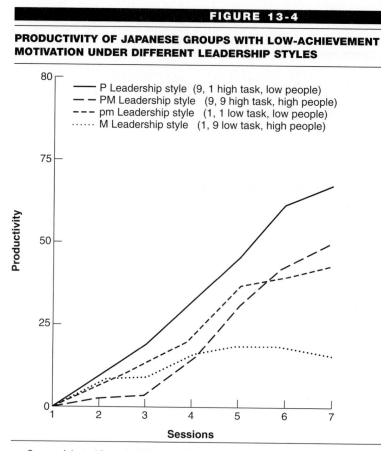

FIGURE 13-4

PRODUCTIVITY OF JAPANESE GROUPS WITH LOW-ACHIEVEMENT MOTIVATION UNDER DIFFERENT LEADERSHIP STYLES

Source: Adapted from Jyuji Misumi and Fumiyasu Seki, "Effects of Achievement Motivation on the Effectiveness of Leadership Patterns, *Administrative Science Quarterly,* March 1971, p. 57. Used with permission.

employees[26] and to encouraging people to do their best.[27] Korean firms also are relying more heavily on a 9,9 leadership style. Sang Lee and associates recently reported that among Korea's largest firms, a series of personality criteria are used in screening employees, and many of these directly relate to 9,9 leadership: harmonious relationships with others, creativeness, motivation to achieve, future orientation, and a sense of duty.[28] For example, at the big Korean MNC LG Electronics (formerly Lucky Goldstar), more and more authority now is being delegated down the line to the middle-management ranks.

Another common trend is the movement toward team orientation and away from individualism. The accompanying sidebar, "Global Teams," illustrates this point.

Leadership in the Middle East

Research also has been conducted on Middle East countries to determine the similarities and differences in managerial attitudes toward leadership practices. For example, in a follow-up study to that of Haire and associates, mid-level managers from Arab countries were surveyed and found to have higher attitude scores for

Global Teams

International leaders now put increasing focus on developing global teams that are capable of overcoming cultural barriers and working together in an efficient, harmonious manner. At Dallas-based Maxus Energy (a wholly owned subsidiary of YPF, the largest Argentinean corporation in the world), teams consist of Americans, Dutch, British, and Indonesians who have been brought together to pursue a common goal: maximize oil and gas production. Capitalizing on the technical expertise of the members and their willingness to work together, the team helped the company to achieve its objective and add oil reserves to its stockpiles—an almost unprecedented achievement. This story is only one of many that help to illustrate the way in which global teams are being created and used to achieve difficult international objectives.

In developing effective global teams, companies are finding there are four phases in the process. In phase one, the team members come together with their own expectations, culture, and values. In phase two, members go through a self-awareness period, during which they learn to respect the cultures of the other team members. Phase three is characterized by a developing trust among members, and in phase four, the team begins working in a collaborative way. How are MNCs able to create the environment that is needed for this metamorphosis? Several specific steps are implemented by management, including:

1. The objectives of the group are carefully identified and communicated to the members.

2. Team members are carefully chosen so that the group has the necessary skills and personnel to reinforce and complement each other.

3. Each person learns what he or she is to contribute to the group, thus promoting a feeling of self-importance and interdependency.

4. Cultural differences between the members are discussed so that members can achieve a better understanding of how they may work together effectively.

5. Measurable outcomes are identified so that the team can chart its progress and determine how well it is doing. Management also continually stresses the team's purpose and its measurable outcomes so that the group does not lose sight of its goals.

6. Specially designed training programs are used to help the team members develop interpersonal, intercultural skills.

7. Lines of communication are spelled out so that everyone understands how they can communicate with the other members of the group.

8. Members are continually praised and rewarded for innovative ideas and actions.

MNCs now find that global teams are critical to their ability to compete successfully in the world market. As a result, leaders who are able to create and lead these interdisciplinary, culturally diverse groups are finding themselves in increasing demand by MNCs.

---

capacity for leadership and initiative than those from any of the other countries or clusters reported in Table 13-2.[29] The Arab managers' scores for sharing information and objectives, participation, and internal control, however, all were significantly lower than those of managers in the other countries and clusters reported in Table 13-2. The researcher concluded that his results were accounted for by the culture of the Middle East region. Table 13-5 summarizes not only the leadership differences between Middle Eastern and Western managers but also other areas of organization and management. The researcher noted that

> management should recognize the Middle Eastern executive's desire to have the opportunity to become more of an integral part of the management team. His democratic attitude towards individual's capacity for leadership and, yet, classical attitude towards other management practices (participation, sharing information and internal control) are largely a function of his cultural values, and to a much lesser degree, of western influence in education and work setting and their countries' stage of economic development.[30]

TABLE 13-5		

DIFFERENCES IN MIDDLE EASTERN AND WESTERN MANAGEMENT

Management dimensions	Middle Eastern management	Western management
Leadership	Highly authoritarian tone, rigid instructions. Too many management directives.	Less emphasis on leader's personality, considerable weight on leader's style and performance.
Organizational structures	Highly bureaucratic, over centralized, with power and authority at the top. Vague relationships. Ambiguous and unpredictable organization environments.	Less bureaucratic, more delegation of authority. Relatively decentralized structure.
Decision making	Ad hoc planning, decisions made at the highest level of management. Unwillingness to take high risk inherent in decision making.	Sophisticated planning techniques, modern tools of decision making, elaborate management information systems.
Performance evaluation and control	Informal control mechanisms, routine checks on performance. Lack of vigorous performance evaluation systems.	Fairly advanced control systems focusing on cost reduction and organizational effectiveness.
Personnel policies	Heavy reliance on personal contacts and getting individuals from the "right social origin" to fill major positions.	Sound personnel management policies. Candidates' qualifications are usually the basis for selection decisions.
Communication	The tone depends on the communicants. Social position, power, and family influence are ever-present factors. Chain of command must be followed rigidly. People relate to each other tightly and specifically. Friendships are intense and binding.	Stress usually on equality and a minimization of difference. People relate to each other loosely and generally. Friendships not intense and binding.

Source: Adapted from M. K. Badawy, "Styles of Mid-Eastern Managers," *California Management Review,* Spring 1980, p. 57. Copyright 1980 by the Regents of the University of California. Reprinted by permission of the Regents.

More recent research provides some evidence that there may be much greater similarity between Middle Eastern leadership styles and those of Western countries.[31] In particular, the observation was made that Western management practices are very evident in the Arabian Gulf region because of the close business ties between the West and this oil-rich geographic area.

This study used a questionnaire survey among 381 managers in the two top levels of 10 multinational organizations that were engaged in either production or marketing in the Persian Gulf region.[32] The questionnaire was designed to determine which of Likert's leadership styles or systems these Middle Eastern managers were using. (See Table 13-1 for Likert's systems or styles.) Organization climate characteristics that were measured included communication flows, decision-making practices, concern for employees, influence on departments, and motivation of employees. The findings showed that almost all managers were operating in a system 3 (participative) style, the same approach that was used by their U.S. counterparts.[33] These findings indicate more similarity between leadership styles of Middle Eastern and Western managers than previously thought. Once again, we see the danger of generalizations and stereotypes in international management.

Leadership Approaches in Developing Countries

Some research has focused on leadership styles in developing countries such as India, Peru, Chile, and Argentina. These studies have examined leadership in terms of Likert's systems or styles (see Table 13-1) and the managerial attitudes toward the four dimensions of leadership practice from the Haire, Ghiselli, and Porter study.

Because of India's long affiliation with Great Britain, leadership styles in India would seem more likely to be participative than those in the Middle East or other developing countries. Haire and associates found some degree of similarity between leadership styles in India and Anglo-American countries, but it was not significant. The study found Indians to be similar to the Anglo-Americans in terms of managerial attitudes toward capacity for leadership and initiative, participation, and internal control. The difference is in sharing information and objectives. The Indian managers' responses tend to be quite similar to those of managers in other developing countries.[34]

Other early research on leadership styles in India found that a highly controlling superior had a positive effect on subordinates' job satisfaction.[35] Other research that focused more on Indian industrial firms, however, indicates that the most effective leadership style used by Indian managers often is a more participative one. One study, for example, found that the job satisfaction of Indian employees increases as leadership style becomes more participative.[36] Still another study reached similar conclusions based on interviews and surveys conducted with managers in a cross-section of industries in northern and western India using a questionnaire that identified Likert systems or styles of leadership.[37] Of the 120 respondents, 14 percent classified their organization as operating under exploitive autocratic leadership (system 1), 63 percent as benevolent autocratic (system 2), and 23 percent as consultative participative (system 3). None viewed their firm as operating under fully democratic leadership (system 4). In addition, this study found that the more autocratic the leadership style (systems 1 and 2), the lower the level of job satisfaction.[38]

These findings from India show that participative leadership style may be more common and more effective in developing countries than has been reported previously. Over time, developing countries (as also shown in the case of the Persian Gulf nations) may be moving toward a more participative leadership style.[39]

A similar situation exists in Peru. There is little reason to believe that managerial attitudes toward leadership practices would have been any different from those reported by Haire and associates for other South American countries, such as Argentina or Chile. The results from the Haire and associates study for those two developing countries were similar to those for India.[40] More recent research, however, has found that leadership styles in Peru may be much closer to those in the United States than was previously assumed.

Stephens conducted research among three large textile plants in an urban area in Peru.[41] These three Peruvian plants were matched with three U.S. plants of similar size in urban settings in the southwest United States. Because these Peruvian and U.S. firms all were in the same industry and faced similar competitive pressures, this study was an excellent opportunity to compare intercultural leadership profiles and identify any significant differences. Using the same four dimensions of leadership practice that were used in the Haire and associates study, Stephens found that the leadership profiles of the Peruvian and U.S. managers were similar. Commenting on the results, he noted that

> there is little reason to conclude that leader styles are much different in Peru than in the U.S. Absolutely, U.S. leaders appear to perceive workers as having more initiative, being more internally motivated, and therefore more capable of meaningful participation. However, the differences for initiative and locus of control were not statistically significant and differences for sharing of information and objectives showed Peruvians to be statistically more inclined to share than U.S. managers. Taken in total, this does not suggest a more participative, democratic leader style in the U.S. and an authoritarian, external control oriented style in Peru.[42]

As in the case of Middle Eastern managers, these findings in South America indicate there indeed may be more similarities in international leadership styles than previously assumed. As countries become more economically advanced, participative styles may well gain in importance. Of course, this does not mean that MNCs can use the same leadership styles in their various locations around the world. There still must be careful contingency application of leadership styles (different styles for different situations); however, many of the more enlightened participative leadership styles used in the United States and other economically advanced countries, such as Japan, also may have value in managing international operations even in developing countries as well as the emerging Eastern European countries.[43]

SUMMARY OF KEY POINTS

1. Leadership is a complex and controversial process that can be defined as influencing people to direct their efforts toward the achievement of some particular goal or goals. Two areas warrant attention as a foundation for the study of leadership in an international setting: philosophical assumptions about people in general, and leadership styles. The philosophical foundation is heavily grounded in Douglas McGregor's Theories X and Y. Leadership styles relate to how managers treat their subordinates and incorporate authoritarian, paternalistic, and participative approaches. These styles can be summarized in terms of Likert's management systems or styles (systems 1 through 4) and the managerial grid (1,1 through 9,9).

2. The attitudes of European managers toward dimensions of leadership practice, such as the capacity for leadership and initiative, sharing information and objectives, participation, and internal control, were examined in a classic study by Haire, Ghiselli, and Porter. They found that Europeans, as a composite, had a relatively low opinion of the capabilities of the average person coupled with a relatively positive belief in the necessity for participative leadership styles. The study also found that these European managers' attitudes were affected by hierarchical level, company size, and age. Overall, however, European managers espouse a participative leadership style.

3. The Japanese managers in the Haire and associates study had a much greater belief in the capacity of subordinates for leadership and initiative than managers in most other countries. The Japanese managers also expressed a more favorable attitude toward a participative leadership style. In terms of sharing information and objectives and using internal control, the Japanese responded above average but were not distinctive. In a number of ways, Japanese leadership styles differed from those of U.S. managers. Company size and age of the managers are two factors that seem to affect these differences. Other reasons include the basic philosophy of managing people, how information is processed, and the high degree of ethnocentrism by the Japanese. However, some often

overlooked similarities are important, such as how effective Japanese leaders manage high-achieving and low-achieving subordinates.

4. Leadership research in the Middle East traditionally has stressed the basic differences between Middle Eastern and Western management styles. More recent research, however, shows that many managers in multinational organizations in the Persian Gulf region operate in a Western-oriented Likert system 3 (participative) style. Such findings indicate that there may be more similarities of leadership styles between Western and Middle Eastern parts of the world than has previously been assumed.

5. Leadership research also has been conducted among managers in developing countries, such as India, Peru, Chile, and Argentina. These studies show that Likert's system 3 (participative) leadership styles are more in evidence than traditionally has been assumed. Although there always will be important differences in styles of leadership between various parts of the world, participative leadership styles may become more prevalent as countries develop and become more economically advanced.

KEY TERMS

leadership	paternalistic leadership
Theory X manager	participative leadership
Theory Y manager	variety amplification
authoritarian leadership	variety reduction

REVIEW AND DISCUSSION QUESTIONS

1. Using the results of the classic Haire and associates study as a basis for your answer, compare and contrast managers' attitudes toward leadership practices in Nordic-European and Latin-European countries. (The countries in these clusters are identified in Table 13-2.)

2. Is there any relationship between company size and the attitude toward participative leadership styles by European managers?

3. Using the Haire and associates study results and other supporting data, determine what Japanese managers believe about their subordinates. How are these beliefs similar to those of U.S. and European managers? How are these beliefs different?

4. A U.S. firm is going to be opening a subsidiary in Japan within the next 6 months. What type of leadership style does research show to be most effective when leading high-achieving Japanese? Low-achieving Japanese? How are these results likely to affect the way that U.S. expatriates should lead their Japanese employees?

5. A British firm is in the process of setting up operations in the Middle East Gulf States. What Likert system or style of leadership do managers in this region seem to use? Is this similar to that used by Western managers?

6. What do U.S. managers need to know about leading in the international arena? Identify and describe three important guidelines that can be of practical value.

PRACTICAL INTERNATIONAL MANAGEMENT ASSIGNMENT

Gather recent information on joint ventures between the United States and one of the Eastern European countries. What type of leadership style generally is being used with employees in the Eastern European country? How does this style differ from that used by U.S. managers? What conclusions can you draw regarding how this information can be valuable to MNCs looking to do business in Eastern Europe?

Germans greatly respect titles such as "doktor" and never jump to a first-name basis until invited.

Germany

A unified Germany has become a major event of modern times. Although problems remain, Germany has become a major economic power in the world. The single Germany is big but still only about the size of the state of Nevada in the United States, and with a population of about 82 million, Germany has about three times the population of California. In addition, the one Germany still is only 60 percent of the economic size of Japan and 25 percent that of the United States in the mid-1990s. Because Germany has rebuilt almost from the ground up since World War II, however, many feel that Germany, along with Japan, is an economic miracle of modern times. Unified Germany's GNP is behind that of both the United States and Japan, but Germany exports more than Japan, its gross investment as a percent of GNP is higher than that of the United States, and its average compensation to workers is higher than that of the United States or Japan. It is estimated that Germany has direct control of about one-fourth of Western Europe's economy, which gives it considerable power in Europe. The German people are known for being thrifty, hard-working, and obedient to authority. They love music, dancing, good food and beer, and fellowship. The government is a parliamentary democracy headed by a chancellor.

For the last 13 years the Wiscomb Company has held a majority interest in a large retail store in Bonn. The store has been very successful and also has proved to be an excellent training ground for managers whom the company wanted to prepare for other overseas assignments. First, the managers would be posted to the Bonn store and, then, after 3 or 4 months of international seasoning, they would be sent on to other stores in Europe. Wiscomb has holdings in the Netherlands, Luxembourg, and Austria. The Bonn store has been the primary training ground because it was the first one the company had in Europe, and the training program was created with this store in mind.

A few months ago, the Wiscomb management and its German partners decided to try a new approach to selling. The plan called for some young U.S. managers to be posted to the Bonn store for a 3-year tour while some young German managers were sent stateside. Both companies hoped that this program would provide important training and experience for their people; however, things have not worked out as hoped. The U.S. managers have reported great difficulty in supervising their German subordinates. Three of their main concerns are: (1) their subordinates do not seem to like to participate in decision making, preferring to be told what to do; (2) the German nationals in the store rely much more heavily on a Theory X approach to supervising than the Americans are accustomed to using, and they are encouraging their

U.S. counterparts to follow their example; and (3) some of the German managers have suggested to the young Americans that they not share as much information with their own subordinates. Overall, the Americans believe that the German style of management is not as effective as their own, but they feel equally ill at ease raising this issue with their hosts. They have asked if someone from headquarters could come over from the United States and help to resolve their problem. A human resources executive is scheduled to arrive next week and meet with the U.S. contingent.

1. What are some current issues facing Germany? What is the climate for doing business in Germany today?
2. Are the leadership styles used by the German managers really much different from those used by the Americans?
3. Do you think the German managers are really more Theory X–oriented than their U.S. counterparts? Why, or why not?
4. Are the German managers who have come to the United States likely to be having the same types of problems?

You Be the International Management Consultant

An Offer from Down Under

The Gandriff Corporation is a successful retail chain in the U.S. Midwest. The St. Louis-based company has had average annual growth of 17 percent over the last 10 years and would like to expand to other sections of the country. Last month, however, it was made a very interesting offer by a group of investors from Australia. The group is willing to put up $100 million to help Gandriff set up operations Down Under. The Australian investors believe that Gandriff's management and retailing expertise could provide it with a turnkey operation. The stores would be built to Gandriff's specifications, and the entire operation would be run by Gandriff. The investors would receive 75 percent of all profits until they recovered their $100 million plus an annual return of 10 percent. At this point the division of profits will then become 50-50.

Gandriff management likes the idea but feels there is a better chance for higher profit if they were to set up operations in Europe. The growth rate in European countries, it is felt, will be much better than that in Australia. The investors, all of whom are Australian, are sympathetic and have promised Gandriff that they will invest another $100 million in Europe, specifically England, France, and Germany, within 3 years if Gandriff agrees to first set up and get an Australian operation running. The U.S. firm believes this would be a wise move but is delaying a final decision, because it still is concerned about the ease with which it can implement its current approach in foreign markets. In particular, the management is concerned as to whether the leadership style used in the United States will be successful in Australia and in European countries. Before making a final decision, management has decided to hire a consultant specializing in leadership to look into the matter.

1. Will the leadership style used in the United States be successful in Australia, or will the Australians respond better to another?
2. If the retailer goes into Europe, in which country will it have the least problem using its U.S.-based leadership style? Why?
3. If the company goes into Europe, what changes might it have to make in accommodating its leadership approach to the local environment? Use Germany as an example.

CHAPTER 13 ENDNOTES

1. This definition is given in Richard M. Hodgetts, *Modern Human Relations at Work,* 6th ed. (Hinsdale, IL: Dryden Press, 1996), p. 270.
2. See Nancy J. Adler, *International Dimensions of Organizational Behavior,* 2nd ed. (Boston: PWS-Kent, 1991), pp. 147–152.
3. Douglas McGregor, *The Human Side of Enterprise* (New York: McGraw-Hill, 1960), pp. 33–34.
4. Ibid., pp. 47–48.
5. Adler, *International Dimensions of Organizational Behavior,* p. 150.
6. James C. Hyatt, "GE Is No Place for Autocrats, Welch Decrees," *Wall Street Journal,* March 3, 1992, pp. B1, B6; Brian Dumaine, "The New Non-Manager Managers," *Fortune,* February 22, 1993, pp. 80–84.
7. A good example is provided by Geert Hofstede, "Cultural Constraints in Management Theories," paper presented at the National Academy of Management, August 1992.
8. See, for example, Karen Lowry Miller, "Siemens Shapes Up," *BusinessWeek,* May 1, 1995, pp. 52–53.
9. Karen Lowry Miller, "The Toughest Job in Europe," *BusinessWeek,* October 9, 1995, pp. 52–53.
10. Ferdinand Protzman, "New Leadership for Volkswagen," *New York Times,* March 30, 1992, pp. C1–2, John Templeman, "A Hard U-Turn at VW," *BusinessWeek,* March 15, 1993, p. 47.
11. Mason Haire, Edwin E. Ghiselli, and Lyman W. Porter, *Managerial Thinking: An International Study* (New York: John Wiley & Sons, 1966).
12. Ibid., p. 21.
13. See Joann S. Lublin, "More U.S. Companies Venture Overseas for Directors Offering Fresh Perspectives," *Wall Street Journal,* January 22, 1992, p. B1.
14. James R. Lincoln, Mitsuyo Hanada, and Jon Olson, "Cultural Orientations and Individual Reactions to Organizations: A Study of Employees of Japanese-Owned Firms," *Administrative Science Quarterly,* March 1981, pp. 93–115; also see Karen Lowry Miller, "Land of the Rising Jobless," *BusinessWeek,* January 11, 1993, p. 47.
15. Sangjin Yoo and Sang M. Lee, "Management Style and Practice of Korean Chaebols," *California Management Review,* Summer 1987, pp. 95–110.
16. Haire, Ghiselli, and Porter, *Managerial Thinking,* p. 29.
17. Ibid., p. 140.
18. Ibid., p. 157.
19. For more on this topic, see Edgar H. Schein, "SMR Forum: Does Japanese Management Style Have a Message for American Managers?" *Sloan Management Review,* Fall 1981, pp. 55–68.
20. Jeremiah J. Sullivan and Ikujiro Nonaka, "The Application of Organizational Learning Theory to Japanese and American Management," *Journal of International Business Studies,* Fall 1986, pp. 127–147.
21. Ibid., pp. 130–131.
22. Ibid. Also see Emily Thornton, "Japan's Struggle to Be Creative," *Fortune,* April 19, 1993, pp. 129–134.
23. Jyuji Misumi and Fumiyasu Seki, "Effects of Achievement Motivation on the Effectiveness of Leadership Patterns," *Administrative Science Quarterly,* March 1971, pp. 51–59.
24. David Woodruff et al., "Saturn," *BusinessWeek,* August 17, 1992, pp. 88–89.
25. Brenton R. Schlender, "How Sony Keeps the Magic Going," *Fortune,* February 24, 1992, pp. 75–84, Rabi S. Bhagat et al., "Cross-Cultural Issues in Organizational Psychology: Emergent Trends and Directions for Research in the 1990s," in C. L. Cooper and I. Robertson (eds.), *International Review of Industrial and Organizational Psychology* (New York: John Wiley & Sons, 1990), p. 83.
26. Robert Neff and William J. Holstein, "The Harvard Man in Mitsubishi's Corner Office," *BusinessWeek,* March 23, 1992, p. 50.
27. See Gary Hatzenstein, "Japanese Management Style beyond the Hype: What to Try, What to Toss," *Working Woman,* February 1991, pp. 49, 98–101.
28. Sang M. Lee, Sangjin Yoo, and Tosca M. Lee, "Korean Chaebols: Corporate Values and Strategies," *Organizational Dynamics,* Spring 1991, p. 41.
29. M. K. Badawy, "Managerial Attitudes and Need Orientations of Mid-Eastern Executives: An Empirical Cross-Cultural Analysis," *National Academy of Management Proceedings,* 1979, pp. 293–297.
30. Ibid., p. 297.
31. Abdulrahman Al-Jafary and A. T. Hollingsworth, "An Exploratory Study of Management Practices in the Arabian Gulf Region," *Journal of International Business Studies,* Fall 1983, pp. 143–152.
32. Ibid.
33. Ibid., p. 146.
34. Haire, Ghiselli, and Porter, *Managerial Thinking,* p. 22.
35. Robert D. Meade, "An Experimental Study of Leadership in India," *Journal of Social Psychology,* June 1967, pp. 35–43.
36. Sudhir Kakar, "Authority Patterns and Subordinate Behavior in Indian Organizations," *Administrative Science Quarterly,* September 1971, pp. 298–307.
37. Bikki Jaggi, "Job Satisfaction and Leadership Style in Developing Countries: The Case of India," *International Journal of Contemporary Sociology,* October 1977, pp. 230–236.

38. Ibid., p. 233.
39. For more information on this topic, see Jai B. P. Sinha, "A Model of Effective Leadership Styles in India," *International Studies of Management & Organization,* Summer-Fall 1984, pp. 86–98.
40. Haire, Ghiselli, and Porter, *Managerial Thinking,* p. 22.
41. D. B. Stephens, "Cultural Variations in Leadership Style: A Methodological Experiment in Comparing Managers in the U.S. and Peruvian Textile Industries," *Management International Review,* vol. 21, no. 3, 1981, pp. 47–55.
42. Ibid., p. 54.
43. See Pete Engardio, Dexter Roberts, and Bruce Einhorne, "China's New Elite," *BusinessWeek,* June 5, 1995, pp. 48–51.

HUMAN RESOURCE SELECTION AND REPATRIATION

OBJECTIVES OF THE CHAPTER

MNCs annually select thousands of people to staff not only their home-country facilities but also their subsidiaries around the world. Who should be selected for a foreign assignment, and how are they handled when they get back? Chapter 14 focuses on potential human resources that can be used for overseas assignments, criteria that are used in the selection process, and how MNCs handle repatriation of the managers back to their country of origin (in most cases, home-country managers are returning to headquarters or to local operations). The specific objectives of this chapter are:

1. **IDENTIFY** the three basic sources that MNCs can tap in filling management vacancies in overseas operations.
2. **SET FORTH** some of the most common selection criteria used in identifying the best people for overseas assignments.
3. **DESCRIBE** the selection procedures used in making the final decisions on the part of both the organization and the individual manager.
4. **DISCUSS** the reasons for people's returning from overseas assignments and present some of the strategies used in ensuring a smooth transition back into the local operation.

SOURCES OF HUMAN RESOURCES

There are three basic sources that MNCs can tap for overseas positions: (1) home-country nationals; (2) host-country nationals; and (3) third-country nationals. The following sections analyze each of these major sources.

Home-Country Nationals

Home-country nationals are managers who are citizens of the country where the MNC is headquartered. In fact, sometimes the term "headquarters nationals" is used. These managers commonly are called *expatriates,* or simply "expats," which refers to those who live and work away from their home country. Historically, MNCs have staffed key positions in their foreign affiliates with home-country nationals or expatriates. Based on research in U.S., European, and Japanese firms, Rosalie Tung found that U.S. and European firms used home-country nationals in less-developed regions but preferred host-country nationals in developed regions. The Japanese, however, made considerably more use of home-country personnel in all geographic areas, especially at the middle- and upper-level ranks.[1]

There are a variety of reasons for using home-country nationals.[2] Tung found that the most common reason for using home-country nationals (given by 70 percent of the respondents) was to start up operations. MNCs prefer to have their own people launch a new venture. The second most common reason (cited by 68 percent of the respondents) was that the home-country people had the necessary technical expertise. Other reasons for using home-country nationals include

> the desire to provide the company's more promising managers with international experience to equip them better for more responsible positions; the need to maintain and facilitate organizational coordination and control; the unavailability of managerial talent in the host country; the company's view of the foreign operation as short lived; the host country's multiracial population, which might mean that selecting a manager of either race would result in political or social problems; the company's conviction that it must maintain a foreign image in the host country; and the belief of some companies that a home country manager is the best person for the job.[3]

Host-Country Nationals

Host-country nationals are local managers who are hired by the MNC.[4] For a number of reasons, many multinationals use host-country managers at the middle- and lower-level ranks: Many countries expect the MNC to hire local talent, and this is a good way to meet this expectation.[5] Also, even if it wanted to staff all management positions with home-country personnel, the MNC is unlikely to have this many available managers, and the cost of transferring and maintaining them in the host country would be prohibitive.

Although top management positions typically are filled by home-country personnel, this is not always the case. For example, many U.S. MNCs use home-country managers to get the operation started, then they turn things over to host-country managers. However, there are exceptions even to this pattern.[6] An early study found that U.S. managers often were put in charge of subsidiaries in MNCs that were in the process of marketing a product worldwide.[7] As the product was introduced into each new country, however, the local manager was replaced by a home-country manager. Then, when the international effort was completed, host-country managers were again put in charge.[8]

This traditional pattern of managerial positions filled by home- and host-country personnel illustrates why it is so difficult to generalize about staffing patterns in an international setting.[9] An exception would be in those cases where government regulations dictate selection practices and mandate at least some degree of "nativization." In Brazil, for example, two-thirds of the employees in any foreign subsidiary traditionally had to be Brazilian nationals. In addition, many countries exert real and subtle pressures to staff the upper-management ranks with nationals. In the past, these pressures by host countries have led companies such as Standard Oil to change their approach to selecting managers.[10]

In European countries, home-country managers who are assigned to a foreign subsidiary or affiliate often stay in this position for the remainder of their career. Europeans are not transferred back to headquarters or to some other subsidiary, as is traditionally done by U.S. firms. Another approach, although least common, is always to use a home-country manager to run the operation. The Japanese are an exception; they tend to use this approach. As a recent report noted:

> Japanese almost always occupy the highest office in their overseas divisions, including the sales operation. "If anyone has a problem with it, he goes to work for another company," says Thomas Elliott, a senior vice president of Honda Motor Co. of America. Thomas Mignanelli, an executive vice president of Nissan Motor Corp., says, "They tell you up front there will always be a Japanese president."[11]

U.S. firms, on the other hand, rely much more on host-country managers. Tung has identified four reasons that U.S. firms tend to use host-country managers: (1) these individuals are familiar with the culture; (2) they know the language; (3) they are less expensive than home-country personnel; and (4) hiring them is good public relations. European firms who use host-country managers gave the two major reasons of familiarization with the culture and knowledge of the language, whereas Japanese firms gave the reason that the host-country national was the best-qualified individual for the job.[12] The accompanying box, "International Management in Action: Important Tips on Working for Foreigners," gives examples of how Americans can better adapt to foreign bosses.[13]

Third-Country Nationals

Third-country nationals are managers who are citizens of countries other than the one in which the MNC is headquartered or the one in which they are assigned to work by the MNC. Available data on third-country nationals are not as extensive as those on home- or host-country nationals. Tung found that the two most important reasons that U.S. MNCs use third-country nationals were that these people had the necessary expertise or were judged to be the best ones for the job. European firms gave only one answer: The individuals were the best ones for the job. Japanese firms, she found, do not hire third-country nationals.[14]

Phatak reports that U.S. MNCs use third-country nationals only from highly developed countries, and this is the ultimate promotion for this person.[15] Unlike U.S. managers, who commonly are put in a foreign position to gain experience before being routed back to headquarters, the third-country national assigned to head a foreign subsidiary or affiliate will tend to remain there indefinitely.

INTERNATIONAL MANAGEMENT IN ACTION

Important Tips on Working for Foreigners

As the Japanese, South Koreans, and Europeans continue to expand their economic horizons, increased employment opportunities will be available worldwide. Is it a good idea to work for foreigners? Those who have done so have learned that there are both rewards and penalties associated with this career choice. Here are some useful tips that have been drawn from the experiences of those who have worked for foreign MNCs.

First, although most U.S. managers are taught to make fast decisions, most foreign managers take more time and view rapid decision making as unnecessary and sometimes bad. In the United States, we hear the cliché that "the effective manager is right 51 percent of the time." In Europe, this percentage is perceived as much too low, which helps to explain why European managers analyze situations in much more depth than most U.S. managers do. Americans working for foreign-owned firms have to focus on making slower and more accurate decisions.

Second, most Americans are taught to operate without much direction. In Latin countries, managers are accustomed to giving a great deal of direction, and in East Asian firms, there is little structure and direction. Americans have to learn to adjust to the decision-making process of the particular company.

Third, most Americans go home around 5 p.m. If there is more paperwork to do, they take it with them. Japanese managers, on the other hand, stay late at the office and often view those who leave early as being lazy. Americans have to either adapt or convince the manager that they are working as hard as their peers but in a different physical location.

Fourth, many international firms say that their official language is English. However, important conversations always are carried out in the home-country's language, so it is important to learn that language.

Fifth, many foreign MNCs make use of fear to motivate their people. This is particularly true in manufacturing work, where personnel are under continuous pressure to maintain high output and quality. For instance, those who do not like to work under intense conditions would have a very difficult time succeeding in Japanese auto assembly plants. Americans have to understand that humanistic climates of work may be the exception rather than the rule.

Finally, despite the fact that discrimination in employment is outlawed in the United States, it is practiced by many MNCs, including those operating in the United States. Women seldom are given the same opportunities as men, and top-level jobs almost always are reserved for home-office personnel. In many cases, Americans have accepted this ethnocentric (nationalistic) approach, but as Chapter 17 will discuss, ethics and social responsibilities are a major issue in the international arena and these challenges must be met now and in the future.

Third-country nationals more typically are found in MNCs that have progressed through the initial and middle stages of internationalization and now are in the more advanced stages.[16] Figure 14-1 shows that the number of third-country subsidiary managers in the U.S. companies studied was greatest during the stable growth period and into the stage characterized by political and competitive threat. Among European firms, a somewhat different pattern was found. Beginning with the initial manufacturing stage, these European MNCs began using third-country managers and continued to do so until political and competitive threats were faced (stage 6). At this point, as for the U.S. firms, use of third-country managers began to decline; they were replaced by host-country nationals.

A number of advantages have been cited for using third-country nationals. One is that the salary and benefit package usually is less than that of a home-country national, yet in recent years, the salary gap between the two has begun to diminish. A second reason is that the third-country national may have a very good working knowledge of the region and/or speak the same language as the local people. This helps to explain why many U.S. MNCs have hired English or Scottish managers for the top positions at subsidiaries in former British colonies such as Jamaica, India, the West Indies, and Kenya. It also explains why successful multinationals such as Gillette, Coca-Cola, and IBM recruit local managers and train them to run overseas subsidiaries.[17]

MNC INTERNATIONALIZATION

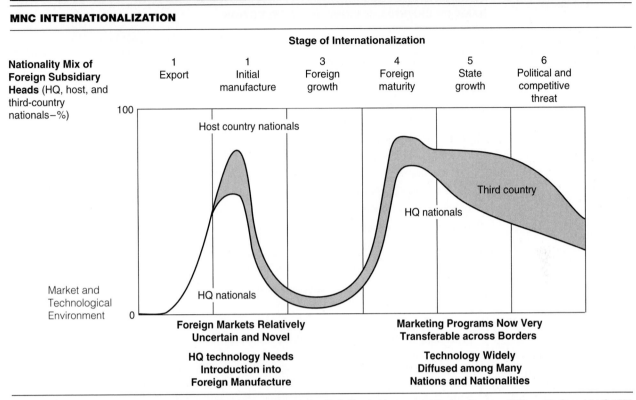

Source: Lawrence G. Franco, "Who Manages Multinational Enterprises?" *California Management Review*, Summer 1973, p. 33. Copyright © 1973 by the Regents of the University of California. Reprinted by permission of the Regents.

Today, a new breed of multilingual, multiexperienced, so-called "global managers" has emerged.[18] These new managers are part of a growing group of international executives who can manage across borders and do not fit the traditional third-country nationals mold. With a unified Europe and other such developments in North America and Asia, these global managers are in great demand. Additionally, with labor shortages developing in certain regions of the world, there is a wave of migration from regions with an abundance of personnel to those where the demand is strongest.[19]

SELECTION CRITERIA FOR INTERNATIONAL ASSIGNMENTS

Making an effective selection decision for an overseas assignment can prove to be a major problem.[20] Typically, this decision is based on *international selection criteria,* which are factors used to choose international managers.[21] These selections are influenced by the MNC's experience and often are culturally-based. For example, Hoecklin has noted that in

Anglo-Saxon cultures, what is generally tested is how much the individual can contribute to the tasks of the organization. In these cultures, assessment centres, intelligence tests and measurements of competencies are the norm. In Germanic cultures, the emphasis is more on the quality of education in a particular function. The recruitment

TABLE 14-1

RANK OF CRITERIA IN EXPATRIATE SELECTION

	Australian managers $n = 47$	Expatriate managers[a] $n = 52$	Asian managers $n = 15$
1. Ability to adapt	1	1	2
2. Technical competence	2	3	1
3. Spouse and family adaptability	3	2	4
4. Human relations skill	4	4	3
5. Desire to serve overseas	5	5	5
6. Previous overseas experience	6	7	7
7. Understanding of host country culture	7	6	5
8. Academic qualifications	8	8	8
9. Knowledge of language of country	9	9	9
10. Understanding of home country culture	10	10	10

Note: [a]U.S., British, Canadian, French, New Zealand, or Australian managers working for an MNC outside their home countries.
Source: Raymond J. Stone, "Expatriate Selection and Failure," *Human Resource Planning*, vol. 14, no. 1, 1991, p. 10. Used with permission.

process in Latin and Far Eastern cultures is very often characterized by ascertaining how well the person "fits in" with the larger group. This is determined in part by the elitism of higher educational institutions, such as the *grandes ecoles* in France or the University of Tokyo in Japan, and in part by their interpersonal style and ability to network internally. If there are tests in Latin cultures, they will tend to be more about personality, communication and social skills than about the Anglo-Saxon notion of "intelligence."[22]

Sometimes as many as a dozen criteria are used, although most MNCs give serious consideration to only five or six.[23] Table 14-1 reports the importance of some of these criteria as ranked by Australian, expatriate, and Asian managers from 60 leading Australian, New Zealand, British, and U.S. MNCs with operations in South Asia.

General Criteria

Some selection criteria are given a great deal of weight; others receive, at best, only lip service. A company sending people overseas for the first time often will have a much longer list of criteria than will an experienced MNC that has developed a "short list." For example, in one study, Tung found that personnel sent overseas by MNCs could be grouped into four categories—chief executive officer, functional head, troubleshooter, and operative—and each category had its own criteria for selection.[24] Chief executive officers had to be good communicators, and they had to have management talent, maturity, emotional stability, and the ability to adapt to new environmental settings. Functional heads had to be mature and have emotional stability and technical knowledge about their job. Troubleshooters had to have technical knowledge of their business and be able to exercise initiative and creativity. Operatives had to be mature, emotionally stable, and respectful of the laws and people in the host country. In short, the nature of the job determined the selection factors.

Typically, both technical and human criteria are considered. Firms that fail to consider both often find that their rate of failure is quite high. For example, Tung investigated both U.S. and Japanese companies and found that many U.S. firms had poor success in choosing people for overseas assignments; meanwhile, the Japanese firms were quite successful. The primary difference between the two was that the Americans tended to focus most heavily on technical considerations, whereas the Japanese also considered behavioral or relational skills, such as the ability of the managers to deal with clients, customers, superiors, peers, and subordinates.[25] The following sections examine more specific commonly used criteria in choosing overseas managers.

Adaptability to Cultural Change

Overseas managers must be able to adapt to change.[26] They also need a degree of cultural toughness.[27] Research shows that many managers are exhilarated at the beginning of their overseas assignment. After a few months, however, a form of culture shock creeps in, and they begin to encounter frustration and feel confused in their new environment. One analysis noted that many of the most effective international managers suffer this cultural shock.[28] This may be a good sign, because it shows that the expatriate manager is becoming involved in the new culture and not just isolating himself or herself from the environment. Here is an example provided by a North American who was assigned to the Middle East:

> My third day in Israel, accompanied by a queasy stomach, I ventured forth into the corner market to buy something light and easy to digest. As yet unable to read Hebrew, I decided to pick up what looked like a small yogurt container that was sitting near the cheese. Not being one hundred percent sure it contained yogurt, I peered inside; to my delight, it held a thick white yogurt-looking substance. I purchased my "yogurt" and went home to eat—soap, liquid soap. How was I to know that soap came in packages resembling yogurt containers, or that market items in Israel were not neatly divided into edible and inedible sections, as I remembered them in the United States. My now "clean" stomach became a bit more fragile and my confidence waned.[29]

As this initial and trying period comes to an end, an expatriate's satisfaction with conditions tends to increase.[30] In fact, as seen in Figure 14-2, after the first 2 years, most people become more satisfied with their overseas assignment than when they first arrived. Research also shows that men tend to adjust a little faster than women, although both sexes exhibit a great deal of similarity in terms of their degree of satisfaction with overseas assignments. In addition, people over 35 years of age tend to have slightly higher levels of satisfaction after the first year, but managers under 35 have higher satisfaction during the next 3 to 4 years. In all cases, however, these differences are not statistically significant.[31]

Organizations examine a number of characteristics in determining whether an individual is sufficiently adaptable. Examples include work experiences with cultures other than one's own, previous overseas travel, a knowledge of foreign languages (fluency generally is not necessary), and recent immigration background or heritage.[32] Others include: (1) the ability to integrate with different people, cultures, and types of business organizations; (2) the ability to sense developments in the host country and accurately evaluate them; (3) the ability to solve problems within different frameworks and from different perspectives; (4) sensitivity to the fine print of differences of culture, politics, religion, and ethics, in addition to

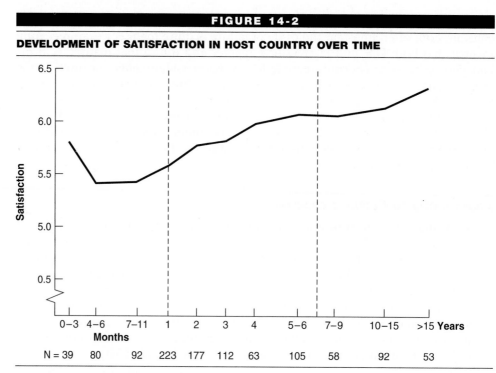

FIGURE 14-2

DEVELOPMENT OF SATISFACTION IN HOST COUNTRY OVER TIME

Note: Satisfaction scale: 1 = extremely low; 7 = extremely high.
Source: Ingemar Torbiorn, *Living Abroad* (New York: John Wiley & Sons, 1982), p. 98. Copyright 1982 by John Wiley & Sons. Used with permission.

individual differences; and (5) flexibility in managing operations on a continuous basis despite lack of assistance and gaps in information.[33]

Independence and Self-Reliance

In many overseas assignments, managers must carry out responsibilities and functions at levels higher than those to which they are accustomed. At the same time, managers have fewer people to call on for assistance and guidance. At company headquarters, a large staff of technical advisors may be available to provide assistance and guidance. In foreign assignments, managers often must be more self-reliant. One analysis reports that some of the determinants of independence and self-reliance include prior field experience (domestic or foreign), special project or task force experience, a hobby or avocation that requires a high degree of self-reliance, and a record of extracurricular college activities or community service activities.[34]

Physical and Emotional Health

Most organizations require that their overseas managers have good physical and emotional health. Some examples are fairly obvious. An employee with a heart condition would be rejected for overseas assignment; likewise, an individual with a nervous disorder would not be considered.

The psychological ability of individuals to withstand culture shock also would be considered, as would the current marital status as it affects the individual's ability to cope in a foreign environment. For example, one U.S. oil company operating in the Middle East considers middle-aged men with grown children to be the best able to cope with cultural shock, and for some locations in the desert, people from Texas or southern California make better risks than those from New England.[35]

Age, Experience, and Education

Most MNCs strive for a balance between age and experience. There is evidence that younger managers are more eager for international assignments. These managers tend to be more "worldly" and have a greater appreciation of other cultures than older managers do. By the same token, young people often are the least developed in terms of management experience and technical skills; they lack real-world experience. To gain the desired balance, many firms send both young and seasoned personnel to the same overseas post. As Blue and Haynes put it, "Ideally, that team should be selected for both its youth and its experience, taking into consideration reporting relationships, specific responsibilities, authority and professional judgment as the determinants of whether youth or experience is best suited to a specific job."[36]

Many companies consider an academic degree, preferably a graduate degree, to be of critical importance to an international executive; however, universal agreement regarding the ideal type of degree is nonexistent. As one expert observed:

> Companies with highly technical products tend to prefer science degrees. Other firms feel that successful management requires depth, drive, imagination, creativity, and character—and that the type of person exemplified by these traits is more likely to be produced by a liberal arts education. But the overall prize-winning combination seems to be an undergraduate degree combined with a graduate business degree from a recognized business school.[37]

MNCs, of course, use formal education only as a point of departure for their own training and development efforts. For example, Siemens of Germany gives its international management team specific training designed to help them deal more effectively with the types of problems they will face on the job.[38]

Language Training

One recognized weakness of many MNCs is that they do not give sufficient attention to the importance of language training. English is the primary language of international business, and most expatriates from all countries can converse in English. Those who can speak only English are at a distinct disadvantage when doing business in non-English-speaking countries, however. One study asked 1100 Swedish expatriates how satisfied they were with knowledge of the local language. These Swedish managers expressed particular dissatisfaction with their understanding of Japanese and Middle Eastern languages.[39] In other words, language can be a very critical factor, and international experts have referred to it as "a most effective indirect method of learning about a country . . . as well as the value systems and customs of its people."[40]

Traditionally, U.S. managers have done very poorly in the language area. For example, a recent survey of 1500 top managers worldwide faulted U.S. expatriates for minimizing the value of learning foreign languages. Executives in Japan, Western Europe, and South America, however, placed a high priority on speaking more than one language. The report concludes that "these results provide a poignant indication of national differences that promise to influence profoundly the success of American corporations."[41]

Motivation for a Foreign Assignment

Although individuals being sent overseas should have a desire to work abroad, this usually is not sufficient motivation. International management experts contend that the candidate also must believe in the importance of the job and even have something of an element of idealism or a sense of mission. Applicants who are unhappy with their current situation at home and are looking to get away seldom make effective overseas managers.

Some experts believe that a desire for adventure or a pioneering spirit is an acceptable reason for wanting to go overseas. Other motivators that often are cited include the desire to increase one's chances for promotion and the opportunity to improve one's economic status.[42] For example, many U.S. MNCs regard international experience as being critical for promotion to the upper ranks. In addition, thanks to the supplemental wage and benefit package, U.S. managers sometimes find that they can make, and especially save, more money than if they remained stateside.

Spouses and Dependents

Spouses and dependents are another important consideration when a person is to be chosen for an overseas assignment. If the family is not happy, the manager often performs poorly. In a recent survey of 80 U.S. MNCs assessing the reasons for expatriate failure, the number-one reason was the inability of the manager's spouse to adjust to a different physical or cultural environment.[43] For this reason, some firms interview both the spouse and the manager before deciding whether to approve the assignment.[44]

One popular approach in appraising the family's suitability for an overseas assignment is called *adaptability screening.* This process evaluates how well the family is likely to stand up to the rigors and stress of overseas life. The company will look for a number of things in this screening, including how closely knit the family is, how well it can withstand stress, and how well it can adjust to a new culture and climate. The reason this family criterion receives so much attention is that MNCs have learned that an unhappy executive will be unproductive on the job and the individual will want to transfer home long before the tour of duty is complete. In both cases, the firm stands to lose a great deal of money.[45]

Leadership Ability

The ability to influence people to act in a particular way, commonly called "leadership," is another important criterion in selecting managers for an international assignment. Determining whether a person who is an effective leader in the home country will be equally effective in an overseas environment can be difficult, however. In determining whether an applicant has the desired leadership ability, many firms look for specific characteristics, such as maturity, emotional stability, the ability to communicate well, independence, initiative, creativity, and good health. If these characteristics are present and the person has been an effective leader in the home country, MNCs assume that the individual also will do well overseas.[46]

Other Considerations

Applicants also can take certain steps to prepare themselves better for international assignments. Tu and Sullivan have suggested the applicant can carry out a number of different phases.[47] In phase one, they suggest focusing on self-evaluation and general awareness. This includes answering the question: Is an international assignment really for me? Other questions in the first phase include finding out if one's spouse and family support the decision to go international and collecting general information on the available job opportunities.

Phase two is characterized by a concentration on activities that should be completed before being selected. Some of these include: (1) conducting a technical skills match to ensure that one's skills are in line with those that are required for the job; (2) starting to learn the language, customs, and etiquette of the region where one will be posted; (3) developing an awareness of the culture and value systems of this geographic area; and (4) making one's superior aware of this interest in an international assignment.

The third phase consists of activities to be completed after being selected for an overseas assignment. Some of these include: (1) attending training sessions provided by the company; (2) conferring with colleagues who have had experience in the assigned region; (3) speaking with expatriates and foreign nationals about the assigned country; and (4) if possible, visiting the host country with one's spouse before the formally scheduled departure.[48]

INTERNATIONAL HUMAN RESOURCE SELECTION PROCEDURES

Besides considering the selection criteria discussed so far, MNCs use a number of selection procedures. The two most common are tests and interviews. Some international firms use one; a smaller percentage employ both. Recently, theoretical models containing the variables that are important for adjusting to an overseas assignment have been developed. These adjustment models can help contribute to more effective selection of expatriates. The following sections examine traditional testing and interviewing procedures, then present an adjustment model.

Testing Procedures

Some evidence suggests that although testing is used by some firms, it is not extremely popular. For example, an early study found that almost 80 percent of the 127 foreign operations managers who were surveyed reported that their companies used no tests in the selection process.[49] This contrasts with the more widespread testing these firms use when selecting domestic managers. A number of comments were offered regarding why testing was not used. Here is a sampling of the reasons:

Tests are too expensive and you have to be a mathematical and psychological wizard to construct and interpret them. What you get for your money and effort is not worth it.

Testing and predicting success are inseparable partners. We know this and selectors in other firms know this. However, measuring managerial performance in overseas operations is something that is taking time to pinpoint. Thus, until we make progress in measuring success it is our belief that there is no reason why we should become involved in constructing tests for overseas managerial candidates.

We have used tests in the past and found that they did not improve the selection process. If something does not pay its own way we discard it. Testing did not pay and had to be eliminated as a screening device. We now use the candidate's domestic record and our personal opinions about his adaptability potential. We think that our overseas experience enables us to be excellent judges about a candidate's probability of succeeding abroad.[50]

More recently Tung uncovered similar findings.[51] Only a small percentage of the U.S., Japanese, and Western European MNCs that she surveyed used tests to determine a candidate's technical competence. Things were not much better when it came to relational abilities—only 5 percent of the U.S. firms and 21 percent of the German firms used testing for this purpose, and none of the Japanese firms did. The U.S. firms used a combination of approaches when testing, but the Germans relied most heavily on psychological testing.

Interviewing Procedures

Many firms use interviews to screen people for overseas assignments. One expert notes: "It is generally agreed that extensive interviews of candidates (and their spouses) by senior executives still ultimately provide the best method of selection."[52] Tung's research supports these comments. For example, 52 percent of the U.S. MNCs she surveyed reported that in the case of managerial candidates, MNCs conducted interviews with both the manager and his or her spouse, and 47 percent conducted interviews with the candidate alone. For technically oriented positions, 40 percent of the firms interviewed both the candidate and the spouse, and 59 percent conducted interviews with the candidate alone. German MNCs follow a pattern similar to that of U.S. companies. In the case of management positions, 41 percent interviewed both the candidate and the spouse, and 59 percent interviewed the candidate only. For technically oriented positions, these percentages were 62 and 39, respectively. Concerning these findings, Tung concluded:

These figures suggest that in management-type positions which involve more extensive contact with the local community, as compared to technically oriented positions, the adaptability of the spouse to living in a foreign environment was perceived as important for successful performance abroad. However, even for technically oriented positions, a sizable proportion of the firms did conduct interviews with both candidate and spouse. This lends support to the contention of other researchers that MNCs are becoming increasingly cognizant of the importance of this factor to effective performance abroad.[53]

An Adjustment Model

In recent years, international human resource management scholars have developed theoretical models that help to explain the factors involved in effectively

FIGURE 14-3

A THEORETIC MODEL FOR EXPLAINING INTERNATIONAL ADJUSTMENT OF EXPATRIATES

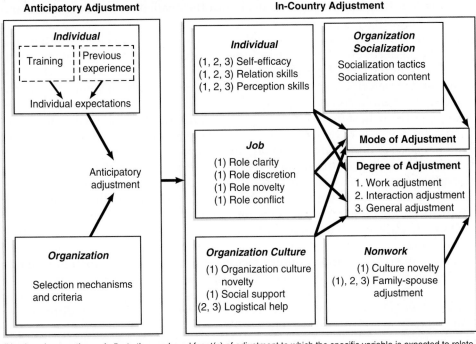

(Numbers in parentheses indicate the numbered facet(s) of adjustment to which the specific variable is expected to relate.)

Source: J. Stewart Black, Mark Mendenhall, and Gary Oddou, "Toward a Comprehensive Model of International Adjustment: An Integration of Multiple Theoretical Perspectives," *Academy of Management Review,* April 1991, p. 303. Used with permission.

adjusting to overseas assignments.[54] These adjustment models help to identify the theoretical underpinnings of effective selection of expatriates. Figure 14-3 provides an example of one such adjustment model.

As shown, there are two major types of adjustments that an expatriate must make when going on an overseas assignment. One is the anticipatory adjustment. This is carried out before the expat leaves for the assignment. The other is the in-country adjustment, which takes place on-site.

The anticipatory adjustment is influenced by a number of important factors. One individual factor is the predeparture training that is provided. This often takes the form of cross-cultural seminars or workshops, and it is designed to acquaint expats with the culture and work life of the country to which they will be posted. Another individual factor affecting anticipatory adjustment is the previous experience the expat may have had with the assigned country or those with similar cultures. These two individual factors, training and previous experience, help to determine the accuracy of the expat's expectations.

The organizational input into anticipatory adjustment is most directly related and concerned with the selection process. Traditionally, MNCs relied on only one important selection criteria for overseas assignments: technical competence.

Obviously, technical competence is important, but it is only one of a number of skills that will be needed. If the MNC concentrates only on technical competence as a selection criterion, then it is not properly preparing the expatriate managers for successful adjustment in overseas assignments. Expats are going to go abroad believing that they are prepared to deal with the challenges awaiting them, and they will be wrong.

Once the expatriate is on-site, a number of factors will influence his or her ability to adjust effectively. One factor includes the expat's ability to maintain a positive outlook in the face of a high-pressure situation, to interact well with host nationals, and to perceive and evaluate the host country's cultural values and norms correctly. A second factor is the job itself, as reflected by the clarity of the role the expat plays in the host management team, the authority the expat has to make decisions, the newness of the work-related challenges, and the amount of role conflict that exists. A third factor is the organizational culture and how easily the expat can adjust to it. A fourth input is nonwork factors, such as the toughness with which the expatriate faces a whole new cultural experience and how well his or her family can adjust to the rigors of the new assignment. A fifth and final factor identified in the adjustment model is the expat's ability to develop effective socialization tactics and to understand "what's what" and "who's who" in the host organization.

These anticipatory and in-country factors will influence the expatriate's mode and degree of adjustment to an overseas assignment. As identified in Figure 14-3, these factors cover a wide continuum of considerations. They can help to explain why effective selection of expatriates is multifaceted and can be very difficult and challenging.

THE COMPENSATION ISSUE

One of the first questions that MNCs will answer in the selection process is: How much will it cost to post a home- or third-country national to an overseas assignment? In recent years, many MNCs have been using fewer nonlocals, because the expense is so high. Housing is a good example; here are some of the most recent monthly rents for a nice two-bedroom apartment in select cities[55]:

Sydney	$1100
Cairo	$1200
Buenos Aires	$1500
Paris	$2150
New York	$2300
London	$2950
Moscow	$5000
Shanghai	$6300
Tokyo	$7100
Hong Kong	$7200

Common Elements of Compensation Packages

The overall compensation package often will vary from country to country. As Bailey has noted:

Compensation programs implemented in global organization will not mirror an organization's domestic plan because of differences in legally mandated benefits, tax laws, cultures, and employee expectations based on local practices. The additional challenge in compensation design is the requirement that excessive costs be avoided and at the same time employee morale be maintained at high levels.[56]

There are, however, four common elements in the typical expatriate compensation package. These include base salary, benefits, allowances, and taxes.

Base Salary   Base salary is the amount of money that an expatriate normally receives in the home country. In the United States this was around $150,000 for upper-middle managers in the mid-1990s, and this rate was similar to that paid to managers in both Japan and Germany. In the past, upper-middle managers in both Japan and Germany made less than their U.S. counterparts, but in recent years, the Japanese yen and German mark have strengthened against the U.S. dollar, thus effectively eliminating the salary gap.

Expatriate salaries typically are set according to the base pay of the home countries. Therefore, a German manager working for a U.S. MNC and assigned to Spain would have a base salary that reflects the salary structure in Germany. U.S. expatriates have salaries tied to U.S. levels. The salaries usually are paid in home currency, local currency, or a combination of the two. The base pay also serves as the benchmark against which bonuses and benefits are calculated.

Benefits   Approximately one-third of compensation for regular employees is benefits. These benefits compose a similar, or even larger, portion of expat compensation. A number of thorny issues surround compensation for expatriates, however. These include:

1. whether MNCs should maintain expatriates in home-country benefit programs, particularly if these programs are not tax-deductible;
2. whether MNCs have the option of enrolling expatriates in host-country benefit programs and/or making up any difference in coverage;
3. whether host-country legislation regarding termination of employment affects employee benefits entitlements;
4. whether the home or host country is responsible for the expatriates' social security benefits;
5. whether benefits should be subject to the requirements of the home or host country;
6. which country should pay for the benefits;
7. whether other benefits should be used to offset any shortfall in coverage; and
8. whether home-country benefits programs should be available to local nationals.[57]

Most U.S.-based MNCs include expatriate managers in their home-office benefits program at no additional cost to the expats. If the host country requires expats to contribute to their social security program, the MNC typically picks up the tab. Fortunately, several international agreements between countries recently have eliminated such dual coverage and expenses.

Additionally, MNCs often provide expatriates with extra vacation and with special leaves. The MNC typically will pay the airfare for expats and their families to make an annual visit home, for emergency leave, and for expenses when a relative in the home country is ill or dies.

Allowances   Allowances are an expensive feature of expatriate compensation packages. One of the most common parts is a cost-of-living allowance—a payment for differences between the home country and the overseas assignment. This allowance is designed to provide the expat with the same standard of living that he or she enjoyed in the home country, and it may cover a variety of expenses, including relocation, housing, education, and hardship.

Relocation expenses typically involve moving, shipping, and storage charges that are associated with personal furniture, clothing, and other items that the expatriate and his or her family are (or are not) taking to the new assignment. Related expenses also may include cars and club memberships in the host country, although these perks commonly are provided only to senior-level expats.

Housing allowances cover a wide range. Some firms provide the expat with a residence during the assignment and pay all associated expenses. Others give a predetermined housing allotment each month and let expats choose their own residence. Additionally, some MNCs help those going on assignment with the sale or lease of the house they are leaving behind; if the house is sold, the company usually pays closing costs and other associated expenses. Firms such as General Motors encourage their people to retain ownership and rent their houses. In these cases, it is common to find the MNC paying all rental management fees and reimbursing the employees for up to 6 months of rent if the houses are unoccupied.

Education allowances for the expat's children are another integral part of the compensation package. These expenses cover costs such as tuition, enrollment fees, books, supplies, transportation, room, board, and school uniforms. In some cases, expenses to attend postsecondary schools also are provided.

Hardship allowances are designed to induce expats to work in hazardous areas or an area with a poor quality of life. Those who are assigned to Eastern Europe, China, and some Middle Eastern countries sometimes are granted a hardship premium. These payments may be in the form of a lump sum ($10,000 to $50,000) or a percentage (15% to 50%) of the expat's base compensation.

Taxes   The other major component of expatriate compensation is tax equalization. For example, an expat may have two tax bills, one from the host country and one from the U.S. Internal Revenue Service, for the same pay. IRS Code Section 911 permits a deduction of up to $70,000 on foreign-earned income. Top-level expats often earn far more than this, however; thus, they may pay two tax bills for the amount by which their pay exceeds $70,000.

Usually, MNCs pay the extra tax burden. The most common way is by determining the base salary and other extras (e.g., bonuses) that the expat would make if based in the home country. Taxes on this income then are computed and compared with the taxes due on the expat's income. Any taxes that exceed what would have been imposed in the home country are paid by the MNC, and any windfall is kept by the expat as a reward for taking the assignment.

Tailoring the Package

Working within the four common elements just described, MNCs will tailor-make compensation packages to fit the specific situation. For example, senior-level managers in Japan are paid only around four times as much as junior staff members. This is in sharp contrast to the United States, where the multiple is much higher.[58] A similar situation exists in Europe, where many senior-level managers make far less than their U.S. counterparts and stockholders, politicians, and the general public oppose U.S.-style affluence. For example, the head of British Gas recently received a 76 percent salary raise, to $760,000, while 25,000 workers were facing layoffs in a cost-cutting move. This led to protests at the annual stockholder meeting. In Sweden, the head of L.M. Ericsson, the giant telecom equipment company, received a 100 percent pay hike, to $1.5 million dollars, and the country's politicians were outraged. What makes this even more interesting is that the company's pretax earnings had jumped by 81 percent in the previous year and the executive had received a host of lucrative job offers from other firms.[59]

These developments pinpoint a thorny problem: Can a senior-level U.S. expat be paid a salary that is significantly larger than local senior-level managers in the overseas subsidiary, or will this create morale problems? This is a difficult question to answer and must be given careful consideration. One solution is to link pay and performance to attract and retain outstanding personnel.[60] For example, at Salomon Brothers, the U.S. investment bank, employees are well paid if they do well and penalized if they do poorly—and this system is acceptable to all concerned. As a recent report noted:

> The result is that in exceptionally good years Salomon's new system appears to offer its employees exceptional returns, but it will be less generous than at present when times are hard. The firm's aim is to make staff behave as if they own the business, rather than merely work for it. It is a big gamble. Some of the firm's most profitable traders may be tempted away by fatter bonuses elsewhere. Alan Howard, one of its top traders in London, left Salomon after the pay deal was confirmed, moving to Japan's Tokai Bank for a two-year package reputedly worth a guaranteed [$7.5 million].[61]

In formulating the compensation package, a number of approaches can be used. The most common is the *balance sheet approach,* which involves ensuring that the expat is "made whole" and does not lose money by taking the assignment. A second, and often complementary approach, is negotiation, which involves working out a special, ad hoc arrangement that is acceptable to both the company and the expat. A third approach is called *localization* and involves paying the expat a salary that is comparable to those of local nationals. This approach most commonly is used with individuals early in their careers and who are being given long-term overseas assignment. A fourth approach is the *lump sum method,* which involves giving the expat a predetermined amount of money and letting the individual make his or her own decisions regarding how to spend it. A fifth is the *cafeteria approach,* which entails giving expats a series of options and then letting them decide how to spend the available funds. For example, if expats have children, they may opt for private schooling; if expats have no children, they may choose a chauffeur-driven car or an upscale apartment. A sixth method is the *regional system,* under which the MNC sets a compensation system for all expats who are assigned to a particular region. Therefore, everyone going to Europe falls under one particular system, and everyone being assigned to South America is covered by a different system.[62]

The most important thing to remember about global compensation is that the package must be cost effective and fair. If it meets these two characteristics, it likely will be acceptable to all parties.[63]

TABLE 14-2

GOAL RANKING AMONG OVERSEAS PERSONNEL

Rank	Goal	Questionnaire wording
1	Training	Have training opportunities (to improve your present skills or learn new skills)
2	Challenge	Have challenging work to do—work that gives you a personal sense of accomplishment
3	Autonomy	Have considerable freedom to adopt your own approach to the job
4	Earnings	Have opportunity for high earnings
5	Advancement	Have an opportunity for advancement to higher-level jobs
6	Recognition	Get the recognition you deserve for doing a good job
7	Security	Have job security (steady work)
8	Friendly department	Work in a department where the people are congenial and friendly to one another
9	Personal time	Have a job which leaves you sufficient time for your personal and/or family life
10	Company contribution	Have a job which allows you to make a real contribution to your company's success

Source: Adapted from David Sirota and J. Michael Greenwood, "Understand Your Overseas Work Force," *Harvard Business Review*, January-February 1971, p. 55.

INDIVIDUAL AND HOST-COUNTRY VIEWPOINTS

Until now, we have examined the selection process mostly from the standpoint of the MNC: What will be best for the company? However, two additional perspectives for selection warrant consideration: (1) that of the individual who is being selected; and (2) that of the country to which the candidate will be sent. Research shows that each has specific desires and motivations regarding the expatriate selection process.

Candidate Motivations

Why do individuals accept foreign assignments? One answer is a greater demand for their talents abroad than at home. For example, a growing number of senior U.S. managers have moved to Mexico because of Mexico's growing need for experienced executives. In another recent case, a U.S. engineering professor quit his job and moved to Japan to learn Japanese and to work in a Fujitsu manufacturing plant, learning how the company operates. Today, he has been promoted into the management ranks and is helping to run a plant back in the United States.[64]

A number of researchers have investigated overall candidate motivations. One early study administered an opinion questionnaire to 13,000 employees of a large electrical equipment manufacturing firm with operations in 46 countries. There were 200 multiple-choice items in the questionnaire, and the instrument was translated into 12 foreign languages to accommodate all groups of people.[65] Fourteen goals were found to have varying degrees of importance. These extended from a desire for training to the need to work for a successful company. Table 14-2 presents a brief description of the 10 most important goals.

TABLE 14-3

GOAL RANKING BY OCCUPATION

	Average rank		
Goal	**Salespeople**	**Technical personnel**	**Service personnel**
Training	2	1	1
Challenge	1	2	2.5
Autonomy	3	3	7
Earnings	4	4.5	4
Advancement	5	6	5
Recognition	6	4.5	9
Security	10	11	2.5
Friendly department	9	8	8
Personal time	11	7	6
Company contribution	7.5	9.5	10

Source: Adapted from David Sirota and J. Michael Greenwood, "Understand Your Overseas Work Force," *Harvard Business Review*, January-February 1971, p. 56.

This study found that the importance of each goal was somewhat influenced by the individual's occupation. Table 14-3 shows this breakdown. The most important objectives related to achievement; the least important related to what the organization gives to its employees.

In drawing together their findings, these researchers grouped the participating countries into clusters: Anglo (Australia, Austria, Canada, India, New Zealand, South Africa, Switzerland, United Kingdom, and United States); Northern European (Denmark, Finland, Norway); French (Belgium and France); northern South American (Colombia, Mexico, and Peru); southern South American (Argentina and Chile); and Independent (Brazil, Germany, Israel, Japan, Sweden, and Venezuela). Based on these groupings, they were able to identify major motivational differences. Some of their findings included:

1. The Anglo cluster was more interested in individual achievement and less interested in the desire for security than any other cluster.
2. The French cluster was similar to the Anglo cluster, except that less importance was given to individual achievement and more to security.
3. Countries in the Northern European cluster were more oriented to job accomplishment and less to getting ahead; considerable importance was assigned to jobs not interfering with personal lives.
4. In South American clusters, individual achievement goals were less important than in most other clusters. Fringe benefits were particularly important to South American groups.
5. Germans were similar to those in the South American clusters, except that they placed a great emphasis on advancement and earnings.
6. The Japanese were unique in their mix of desires. They placed high value on earnings opportunities but low value on advancement. They were high on challenge but low on autonomy. At the same time, they placed strong emphasis on

working in a friendly, efficient department and having good physical working conditions.[66]

A more recent study also investigated the reasons why personnel accept overseas positions.[67] The study sampled 135 U.S. expatriate managers at the upper-middle ranks of three foreign subsidiaries of three major U.S. MNCs. Four major sets of variables explained why people go overseas. The most important reason was the enhancement of one's international business career. This included things such as increased promotion potential, the opportunity to improve career mobility, and the opportunity for greater responsibility. The second most important reason was the attraction to overseas assignments. This included the opportunity to go overseas, the desire to live in a particular locale, and encouragement from one's family to take the assignment. The third most important reason was technical competence. The individual had knowledge of the particular job to be done and/or had proven performance or capability in this area of work. The fourth was that the assignment was viewed as necessary for one's career. For example, some candidates felt that all managers who wanted to reach the upper ranks had to have international experience and/or these jobs were necessary in gathering knowledge and experience for future assignments.

Another interesting focus of attention has been on those countries that expatriates like best. The Torbiorn study cited earlier found that the 1100 Swedish expatriates surveyed were at least fairly well satisfied with their host country, and in some cases were very satisfied. Figure 14-4 reports these findings. In particular, the expatriates were more satisfied in countries that had the same general living standard or level of industrial development as their own. Similar language and religion also were important factors.[68]

Host-Country Desires

Although many MNCs try to choose people who fit in well, little attention has been paid to the host country's point of view. Whom would it like to see put in managerial positions? One study surveyed over 100 host-country organizations (HCOs) in five countries: Germany ($n = 38$), England ($n = 33$), France ($n = 16$), Holland ($n = 16$), and Belgium ($n = 8$). The respondents were either chief executive officers of the HCO or heads of departments that interacted extensively with expatriate managers heading the subsidiary. Data were collected via a questionnaire survey and a comprehensive interview. The 200-item questionnaire was designed to determine both present and desired personnel policies and patterns of managerial behavior.[69] The findings are presented in Table 14-4.

The results showed that in the main, accommodating the wishes of HCOs can be very difficult. They are highly ethnocentric in orientation. They want local managers to head the subsidiaries; and they set such high levels of expectation regarding the desired characteristics of expatriates that anyone sent by the MNC is unlikely to measure up. These findings help to explain why many MNCs welcome input from their host-country nations regarding staffing decisions but do not let themselves be totally swayed by these opinions. Quite obviously, many MNCs are as guilty of ethnocentric behavior as their host-country counterparts. The accompanying sidebar, "Recruiting Managers in Japan," provides a detailed example of Japanese ethnocentricity.

FIGURE 14-4

EXPATRIATE SATISFACTION IN VARIOUS HOST COUNTRIES

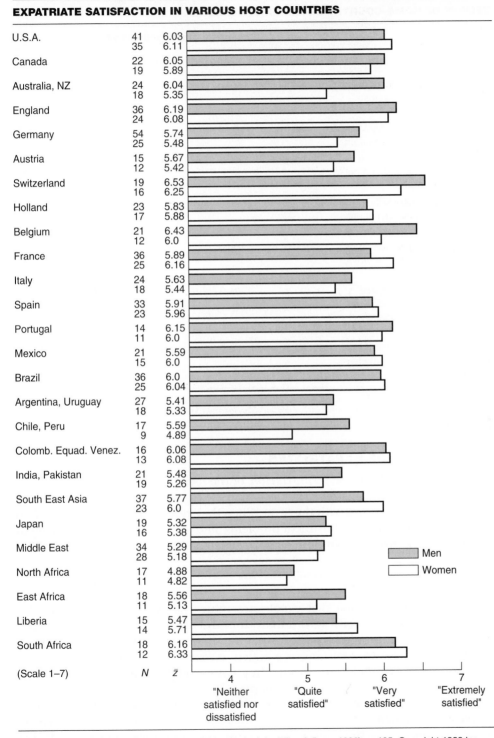

	N	z̄
U.S.A.	41	6.03
	35	6.11
Canada	22	6.05
	19	5.89
Australia, NZ	24	6.04
	18	5.35
England	36	6.19
	24	6.08
Germany	54	5.74
	25	5.48
Austria	15	5.67
	12	5.42
Switzerland	19	6.53
	16	6.25
Holland	23	5.83
	17	5.88
Belgium	21	6.43
	12	6.0
France	36	5.89
	25	6.16
Italy	24	5.63
	18	5.44
Spain	33	5.91
	23	5.96
Portugal	14	6.15
	11	6.0
Mexico	21	5.59
	15	6.0
Brazil	36	6.0
	25	6.04
Argentina, Uruguay	27	5.41
	18	5.33
Chile, Peru	17	5.59
	9	4.89
Colomb. Equad. Venez.	16	6.06
	13	6.08
India, Pakistan	21	5.48
	19	5.26
South East Asia	37	5.77
	23	6.0
Japan	19	5.32
	16	5.38
Middle East	34	5.29
	28	5.18
North Africa	17	4.88
	11	4.82
East Africa	18	5.56
	11	5.13
Liberia	15	5.47
	14	5.71
South Africa	18	6.16
	12	6.33

(Scale 1–7)

Legend: Men, Women

Scale: 4 "Neither satisfied nor dissatisfied", 5 "Quite satisfied", 6 "Very satisfied", 7 "Extremely satisfied"

Source: Ingemar Torbiorn, *Living Abroad* (New York: John Wiley & Sons, 1982), p. 125. Copyright 1982 by John Wiley & Sons. Used with permission.

TABLE 14-4

BELIEFS OF HOME-COUNTRY ORGANIZATION EXPATS

Beliefs	Percentage of respondents who agree				
	Holland	England	Germany	Belgium	France
All top managers of foreign subsidiaries should be host-country nationals.	87.5	78.0	35.1	42.9	81.3
Expatriate managers should be of West European ethnic origin.	90.0	95.5	96.3	100.0	58.3
Expatriate managers should be thoroughly familiar with the culture of the host country.	93.8	90.3	78.9	100.0	81.3
Expatriate managers should adhere to local managerial patterns of behavior.	87.5	96.9	73.7	100.0	93.3
Expatriate managers should be proficient in the host-country language.	100.0	100.0	100.0	100.0	100.0
Expatriate managers should have a working knowledge of the host country's social characteristics.	93.3	96.9	84.2	100.0	100.0
Expatriate managers should be thoroughly familiar with the history of the host country.	93.3	83.9	81.6	100.0	100.0

Source: Adapted from Y. Zeira and M. Banai, "Attitudes of Host-Country Organizations toward MNCs' Staffing Policies: A Cross-Country and Cross-Industry Analysis," *Management International Review,* vol. 21, no. 2, 1981, p. 42. Used with permission.

REPATRIATION OF EXPATRIATES

For most overseas managers, *repatriation,* or the return to one's home country, occurs within 5 years of the time they leave.[70] Few expatriates remain overseas for the duration of their stay with the firm. When they return, these expatriates often find themselves facing readjustment problems, and some MNCs now are trying to deal with these problems through use of transition strategies.

Reasons for Returning

The most common reason that expatriates return home from overseas assignments is that their formally agreed-on tour of duty is over. Before they left, they were told that they would be posted overseas for a predetermined period, often 2 to 3 years, and now are returning as planned. A second common reason is that expatriates want their children educated in a home-country school, and the longer they are away, the less likely this will happen.[71]

A third reason that expatriates return is because they are not happy in their overseas assignment. Managers with families who return home early often do so because the spouse or children do not want to stay, and the company feels that the loss in managerial productivity is too great to be offset by short-term personal

Recruiting Managers in Japan

Recruiting managers in host countries can be a very difficult chore. For example, small U.S. firms in Japan report that local managers often do not want to work for them because they are unfamiliar with the company and do not want to run the risk of joining a business that may be around for only a short time. Larger, highly visible MNCs, such as IBM, Coca-Cola, and Ford Motor, do not have this problem, but there are other recruiting challenges for human resources management in Japan that are just as formidable.

One of these challenges facing an MNC in Japan is the significant amount of time it takes to recruit a Japanese manager. In the United States, when an MNC wants to hire an identified manager from another company, it will either have a headhunter contact the individual or have someone from the MNC do it. In either case, the MNC doing recruiting in the United States will quickly find out if the person is interested in changing jobs. If the answer is yes, a tentative offer will be made, and negotiations will begin. Quite often, the entire process will take only two or three meetings spread over a few weeks. Managers are recruited quite differently in Japan. There, the recruitment process is very slow and very deliberate, often taking 6 months to a year. The extended time is necessary, because there are a number of rules of business etiquette that must be followed.

A multinational doing recruiting in Japan typically goes through the following steps. A top manager from the multinational that is seeking to hire a manager away from a Japanese firm will first meet with that person's manager, and perhaps even the person's family, and request permission to negotiate with the individual. The MNC will have to provide assurances regarding this person's future position, security, and opportunities. Only then will meetings and negotiations with the manager begin. Moreover, the higher up the organization the recruited manager is located, the more delicate and slow-moving the process tends to be. There is little that the multinational can do, however, because it needs to recruit the top local talent.

The primary reason why it is so important for MNCs doing business in Japan to have local managers is because the Japanese are extremely ethnocentric. Japanese consumers and firms prefer to buy from Japanese businesses. They prefer local products to imports. In selecting people, MNCs in Japan typically put a Japanese national in charge of the subsidiary or make the individual the number-two person. They also recruit a large percentage of the managerial work force from the local market and do everything they can to give their subsidiary a "local look." In fact, in many Japanese subsidiaries of MNCs, there are no visible foreign managers.

One of the most important things that MNCs have learned about doing business in Japan is that they must be regarded as a local firm if they hope to succeed. MNCs such as IBM have done this so well that they are regarded as "Japanese" by the locals. As a result, many of the barriers that prevent other multinationals from doing business in Japan do not exist for companies such as IBM, which clearly understands the value of recruiting managers in Japan.

---

unhappiness. Therefore, the individual is allowed to come back even though typically the cost is quite high.[72]

A fourth reason that people return is failure to do a good job. Such failure often spells trouble for the manager. As a director of employee relations of a large U.S. MNC put it: "If a person flunks out overseas . . . we bring him home . . . He's penalized indirectly because the odds are that if he flunked out over there, he's in trouble over here. But we bring him back and, generally, he has a tough row to hoe."[73]

Readjustment Problems

After returning to the home country, some expatriates have readjustment problems. In fact, on occasion, the re-entry problems are greater than the adjustment problems faced overseas. Sometimes, expatriates feel that their international

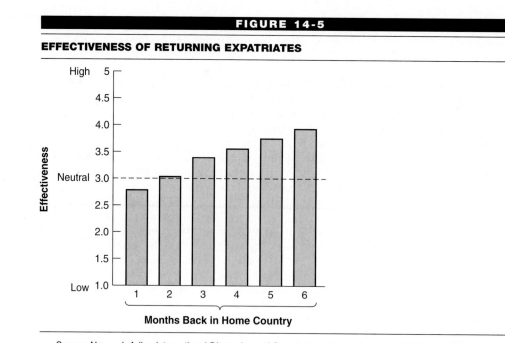

FIGURE 14-5

EFFECTIVENESS OF RETURNING EXPATRIATES

Source: Nancy J. Adler, *International Dimensions of Organizational Behavior,* 2nd ed. (Boston: PWS-Kent, 1991), p. 238. Copyright © 1991 by Wadsworth, Inc. Reprinted by permission of PWS-Kent Publishing Company, a division of Wadsworth, Inc.

experience is not highly regarded by the company. For some, their current job has less responsibility and is boring when compared with the challenge of their overseas position. Here are some representative expatriate comments that describe these frustrations:

> My colleagues react indifferently to my international assignment. . . . They view me as doing a job I did in the past; they don't see me as having gained anything while overseas.

> I had no specific reentry job to return to. I wanted to leave international and return to domestic. Working abroad magnifies problems while isolating effects. You deal with more problems, but the home office doesn't know the details of the good or bad effects. Managerially, I'm out of touch.

> I'm bored at work. . . . I run upstairs to see what [another returning colleague] is doing. He says, "Nothing." Me, too.[74]

A recent study by Tung found that in general, the longer the duration of an offshore assignment, the more problem the expatriate has being reabsorbed into the home office. Here are the major reasons:

1. The "out of sight, out of mind" syndrome is common.
2. Organizational changes made during the time the individual was abroad may make his or her position in the parent headquarters redundant or peripheral.
3. Technological advances in the parent headquarters may render the individual's existing skills and knowledge obsolete.[75]

Still another problem is adjusting to the new job back home. It sometimes takes from 6 months to 1 year before managers are operating at full effectiveness. Figure 14-5 provides an illustration.

Other readjustment problems are more personal in nature. Many expatriates find that the salary and fringe benefits to which they have become accustomed in the foreign assignment now are lost, and adjusting to this lower standard of living is difficult. In addition, those who sold their houses and now must buy new ones find that the monthly cost often is much higher than when they left. The children often are placed in public schools, where classes are much larger than in the overseas private schools. Many also miss the cultural lifestyles, as in the case of an executive who is transferred from Paris, France, to a medium-sized city in the United States,[76] or from any developed country to an underdeveloped country.

Recent research supports the findings noted here and offers operative recommendations for action. Based on questionnaires completed by 174 respondents who recently had been repatriated from four large U.S. MNCs, Black found the following:

1. With few exceptions, individuals whose expectations were met had the most positive levels of repatriation adjustment and job performance.
2. In the case of high-level managers in particular, expatriates whose job demands were greater, rather than less, than expected reported high levels of repatriation adjustment and job performance. Those having greater job demands may have put in more effort and had better adjustment and performance.
3. Job performance and repatriation adjustment were greater for individuals whose job constraint expectations were undermet than for those individuals whose expectations were overmet. In other words, job constraints were viewed as an undesirable aspect of the job and having them turn out to be less than expected was a pleasant surprise that helped adjustment and performance.
4. When living and housing conditions turned out to be better than expected, general repatriation adjustment and job performance were better.
5. Individuals whose general expectations were met or overmet had job evaluations that placed them 10 percent higher than those whose general expectations were unmet.[77]

Transition Strategies

To help smooth the adjustment from an overseas to a stateside assignment, some MNCs have developed *transition strategies,* which can take a number of different forms. One is the use of *repatriation agreements,* whereby the firm tells the individual how long she or he will be posted overseas and promises to give the individual, on return, a job that is mutually acceptable. This agreement typically does not promise a specific position or salary, but the agreement may state that the person will be given a job that is equal to, if not better than, the one held before leaving.

Some firms also rent or otherwise maintain expatriates' homes until they return. The Aluminum Company of America and Union Carbide both have such plans for managers going overseas. This plan helps to reduce the financial shock that often accompanies home shopping by returning expatriates.

A third strategy is to use senior executives as sponsors of managers abroad, as described here:

It is the responsibility of a sponsor to monitor the performance, compensation, and career paths of expatriate managers who are under their wings, and to plan for their return. Sponsors begin scouting anywhere from six months to a year prior to an

TABLE 14-5

ASSESSMENT OF REPATRIATE EXPERIENCE

Survey categories	Mean score[a]
Cultural re-entry	
1. The transition back to the American lifestyle was very easy.	3.71
2. I do not miss the people I worked with in the overseas assignment.	5.27
3. I felt comfortable giving up the friendships that I had developed overseas.	4.69
4. *If my spouse and/or children joined me overseas*, their transition back to the American lifestyle was very easy.	4.10
5. My family and friends back in the U.S. were interested in hearing about my experiences living overseas.	3.93
6. *If my spouse and/or children joined me overseas*, their friends in the U.S. were interested in hearing about the overseas experience.	4.23
7. Life back in the States seems exciting in comparison with the cultural experience I had during my overseas assignment.	4.95
8. My company provided me with help regarding relocation problems like housing and transportation.	3.44
Financial implications	
1. The total financial package that I received in my new U.S. job assignment was better than my total financial package overseas.	5.42
2. The salary offer in the U.S. job assignment was better than my salary overseas.	4.20
3. The fringe benefits in the new U.S. job assignment were better than when I was working overseas.	5.65
4. *If you did not own your house or apartment in the U.S. while working overseas*, the cost of buying one upon returning from overseas was very reasonable.	5.87
5. My personal finances since returning from overseas are in better shape than was true *before* I left for the overseas assignment.	3.23
6. My company provided me bridge loans or other interim financial assistance when I returned from overseas.	5.31
7. My company provided me with considerable accounting advice/financial planning upon my return from overseas.	5.40

expatriate's return for a suitable position that he or she can come back to. Union Carbide and IBM are two companies who make use of such sponsors, but there are others as well.[78]

Still another approach is to keep expatriate managers apprised of what is going on at corporate headquarters and to plug these managers into projects at the home office whenever they are on leave in the home country. This helps maintain the person's visibility and ensures the individual is looked on as a regular member of the management staff.

In the final analysis, a proactive strategy that provides an effective support system to allay expatriate concerns about career issues while serving abroad may work best. Tung found that the successful U.S., European, Japanese, and Australian MNCs that she studied had: (1) mentor programs (one-on-one pairing of an expatriate with a member of home-office senior management); (2) a separate

TABLE 14-5 Continued

ASSESSMENT OF REPATRIATE EXPERIENCE

Survey categories	Mean score[a]
Nature of job assignment	
1. It was clear to me what permanent job I would have when I first returned from overseas.	3.42
2. I experienced more autonomy in my new job than had been the case in my overseas assignment.	5.37
3. My job status is less in my new job than had been the case in my overseas assignment.	4.54
4. I have less political influence in the company in my new job than had been the case in my overseas assignment.	4.69
5. *If it applies,* my mentor was helpful in apprising me of company developments when I first returned from overseas.	4.92
6. *If it applies,* my mentor helped in finding a good job assignment for me when I returned from overseas.	4.50
7. The present job is less challenging than the one I held overseas.	4.38
8. I consider that the company was fair with me in terms of identifying a suitable job assignment for me when I returned from overseas.	3.68
9. I view my present job assignment as very permanent.	3.96
10. I feel a high sense of job (employment) security with my present company.	3.02
11. Looking back at it, I consider that the overseas assignment benefitted me in terms of career opportunities in the company.	3.41
12. Overall, the managerial skills I gained overseas are being utilized by my employer now that I am working back in the U.S.	4.20
13. I was placed in a "holding pattern" when I first returned from the overseas assignment.	2.76
14. My company was helpful in providing me with career counseling when I returned from overseas.	5.88
15. My company provided my spouse with considerable help with career counseling when I returned from overseas.	6.51

[a]1 = strongly agree; 7 = strongly disagree.
Source: Nancy K. Napier and Richard B. Peterson, "Expatriate Re-entry: What Do Expatriates Have to Say?" *Human Resource Planning,* vol. 14, no. 1, 1991, pp. 26–27. Used with permission.

organization unit with primary responsibility for the specific needs of expatriates; and/or (3) maintenance of constant contacts between the home office and the expatriate.[79]

Recent research supports and expands these findings. One study surveyed 99 employees and managers with international experience in 21 corporations.[80] The reactions of the respondents to statements regarding the repatriation experience are provided in Table 14-5. The findings reveal that cultural re-entry, financial implications, and the nature of job assignments are three major areas of expatriate concern. In particular, some of the main problems of repatriation identified in this study include: (1) adjusting to life back home; (2) facing a financial package that is not as good as that overseas; (3) having less autonomy in the stateside job than in the overseas position; and (4) not receiving any career counseling from the company. To the extent that the MNC can address these types of problems and others presented in Table 14-5, the transition will be smooth, and the expatriate's performance effectiveness once home will increase quickly. Some additional steps suggested by experts in this area include:

1. Arrange an event to welcome and recognize the employee and family, either formally or informally.
2. Establish support to facilitate family reintegration.
3. Offer repatriation counseling or workshops to ease the adjustment.
4. Assist the spouse with job counseling, resume writing, and interviewing techniques.
5. Provide educational counseling for the children.
6. Provide the employee with a thorough debriefing by a facilitator to identify new knowledge, insights, and skills and to provide a forum to showcase new competencies.
7. Offer international outplacement to the employee and re-entry counseling to the entire family if no positions are possible.
8. Arrange a postassignment interview with the expatriate and spouse to review their view of the assignment and address any repatriation issues.[81]

SUMMARY OF KEY POINTS

1. MNCs can use three basic sources for filling overseas positions: home-country nationals (expatriates), host-country nationals, and third-country nationals. The most common reason for using home-country nationals, or expatriates, is to get the overseas operation under way. Once this is done, many MNCs turn the top management job over to a host-country national who is familiar with the culture and language and who often commands a lower salary than the home-country national. The primary reason for using third-country nationals is that these people have the necessary expertise for the job.
2. Many criteria are used in selecting managers for overseas assignments. Some of these include adaptability, independence, self-reliance, physical and emotional health, age, experience, education, knowledge of the local language, motivation, the support of spouse and children, and leadership.
3. Those who meet selection criteria then are given some form of screening. Some firms use psychological testing, but this approach has lost popularity in recent years. More commonly, candidates are given interviews. A recent development, theoretic models that identify important anticipatory and in-country dimensions of adjustment, offers help in effective selection.
4. Compensating expatriates can be a difficult problem, because there are many variables to consider. However, most compensation packages are designed around four common elements: base salary, benefits, allowances, and taxes. Working within these elements, the MNC will tailor-make the package to fit the specific situation. In doing so, there are six different approaches that can be used, including the balance sheet approach, the complementary approach, localization, lump sum method, the cafeteria approach, and the regional method. Whichever one (or combination) is used, the package must be both cost-effective and fair.
5. A manager might be willing to take an international assignment for a number of reasons, including: increased pay, promotion potential, the opportunity for greater responsibility, the chance to travel, and the ability to use his or her talents and skills. Research shows that most home countries prefer that the individual who is selected to head the affiliate or subsidiary be a local manager, even though this often does not occur.

6. At some time, most expatriates return home, usually when the predetermined tour is over. Sometimes, managers return because they want to leave early; other times, they return because of poor performance on their part. In any event, readjustment problems can happen back home, and the longer the managers have been gone, the bigger the problems usually are. Some firms now are developing transition strategies to help expatriates adjust to their new environments.

KEY TERMS

home-country nationals
expatriates
host-country nationals
third-country nationals
international selection criteria
adaptability screening
balance sheet approach

localization
lump sum method
cafeteria approach
regional system
repatriation
transition strategies
repatriation agreements

REVIEW AND DISCUSSION QUESTIONS

1. A New York–based MNC is in the process of staffing a subsidiary in New Delhi, India. Why would it consider using expatriate managers in the unit? Local managers? Third-country managers?
2. What selection criteria are most important in choosing people for an overseas assignment? Identify and describe the four that you judge to be of most universal importance, and defend your choice.
3. Building on your answer to the question above, discuss some theoretical dimensions that may affect anticipatory and in-country adjustment of expats. How can these be turned into selection criteria?
4. What are the major common elements in an expat's compensation package? Besides base pay, which would be most important to you? Why?
5. Why are individuals motivated to accept international assignments? Which of these motivations would you rank as positive reasons? Which would you regard as negative reasons?
6. Why do expatriates return early? What can MNCs do to prevent this from happening? Identify and discuss three steps they can take.
7. What kinds of problems do expatriates face when returning home? Identify and describe four of the most important. What can MNCs do to deal with these repatriation problems effectively?

PRACTICAL INTERNATIONAL MANAGEMENT ASSIGNMENT

Review recent issues of popular business magazines such as *Fortune, BusinessWeek,* and *Forbes,* and identify three firms that are beginning (or have just begun) new overseas ventures. Examine the types of businesses they are in and the specific activities in which they will engage. Then, using the selection criteria provided in this chapter, identify the three criteria that you believe would be most important in choosing managers for each venture. Finally, note whether the head of the overseas branch would be a home-country, host-country, or third-country national. Be sure to explain your reasoning. When you are finished, compare your findings with those of other class members.

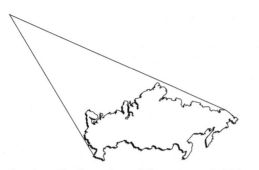

Russians like the sayings: "The eyes are afraid, but the hands do the work" and "The dream is frightful, but God is merciful."

In the International Spotlight

Russia

Russia is by far the largest republic in the former Soviet Union. Russia stretches from Eastern Europe across northern Asia and to the Pacific Ocean. The 150 million people consist of 83 percent Russians, 4 percent Tartars, and a scattering of others. The largest city and capital is Moscow, with about 9 million people. At present, there is both social and economic turmoil in Russia. In 1991, hard-line communists unsuccessfully attempted to overthrow Mikhail Gorbachev; the failed coup led to the end of communist rule and the emergence of Boris Yeltsin as president. Although Yeltsin received popular support in a referendum in the spring of 1993, he still faces more than political and social turmoil. As of 1996 the economy still was poor, but improving. Although prices no longer are controlled and privatization has begun, the GNP and the value of the ruble both have deteriorated. At the same time, the country has been scurrying to meet payments to its international creditors and faces political uncertainty.

Despite poor economic conditions and the difficulty of attracting foreign investors, Russia still is considered to be an attractive place to do business by some MNCs. One that has been extremely interested in the country is Earth, Inc. (EI), a farm-implement company that is headquartered in Birmingham, Alabama. EI recently entered into an agreement with the government of Russia to set up operations near Moscow in a factory that was op-erating at about one-half of capacity. The factory will produce farm implements for the newly emerging Eastern European market. EI will supply the technical know-how and product design as well as assume responsibility for marketing the products. The Russian plant will build the equipment and package it for shipping.

The management of the plant operation will be handled on a joint basis. EI will send a team of five management and technical personnel from the United States to the Russian factory site for a period of 12 to 18 months. After this time, EI hopes to send three of them home, and the two who remain would continue to provide ongoing assistance. At the same time, EI intends to hire four middle-level managers and eight first-level supervisors from Italy and Germany, because the operation will need Europeans who are more familiar with doing manufacturing in this part of the world. Very few locals have inspired EI with confidence that they can get the job done. However, over a 2-year period, EI intends to replace the third-country nationals with trained local managers. "We need to staff the management ranks with knowledgeable, experienced people," the CEO explained, "at least until we get the operation up and running successfully with our own people. Then we can turn more and more of the operation over to local management, and run the plant with just a handful of headquarters people on site."

This arrangement has been agreed to by the Russian government, and EI currently is identifying and recruiting managers both in the United States and Europe. Initially, the firm thought that this would be a fairly simple process, but screening and selecting is taking much longer than anticipated. Nevertheless, EI hopes to have the plant operating within 12 months.

1. What are some current issues facing Russia?

What is the climate for doing business in Russia today?

2. What are some of the benefits of using home-country nationals in overseas operations? What are some of the benefits of using host-country nationals?

3. Why would a multinational such as EI be interested in bringing in third-country nationals?

4. What criteria should EI use in selecting personnel for the overseas assignment in Russia?

You Be the International Management Consultant

A Selection Decision

The Star Corporation is a Hong Kong manufacturing firm that is going to do business in mainland China. The company's contract with the Chinese government calls for it to supply technical know-how and machinery for producing consumer electronics. These products are not state-of-the-art, but they will be more than adequate for the needs of the Chinese consumers. Star has agreed to sell the Chinese its plant, which was being closed because it no longer was competitive.

The Chinese will pay to move all the machinery and equipment to their country and install it in a factory that currently is being modified for this purpose. The two then will become partners in the venture. Star will provide the management and technical expertise to run the plant, and the Chinese will provide the workers and be responsible for paying for all output. Star will receive an annual fee of $3 million and 5 percent of all sales.

The Star management is very pleased with the arrangement. Although they are of Chinese descent, they have lived in Hong Kong all their lives and know relatively little about doing business either with or in China. To provide Star with the necessary information and assistance, a native of China, educated there but living in Hong Kong the past 5 years, was brought in. The individual told the company the following facts about China:

- Chinese managers do not plan. They usually are told what to do and they do it. Planning is handled by others and simply passed on to them.
- Chinese managers are not concerned with profit or loss. They simply do their jobs and let the government worry about whether the operation is making money.
- No rewards are given to workers who perform well; everyone is treated the same. If there is no work, the workers are still paid, although they may not be required to come to the factory.
- There is a basic aversion to individual decision making; most decisions are collective efforts.
- The current government of China would like its managers to learn how to run a profit-oriented operation and eventually eliminate the need for foreign managerial assistance.
- When outsiders tell the Chinese how to do things, they have to be careful not to insult or offend the Chinese, who often are sensitive about the way they are treated.

1. What selection criteria would you recommend to Star when deciding whom to send to China?
2. What procedures should the company use in making the final selection?
3. What type of repatriation agreement would you recommend the firm use? Be specific regarding some things you would suggest be contained in the agreement.

CHAPTER 14 ENDNOTES

1. Rosalie L. Tung, "Selection and Training Procedures of U.S., European and Japanese Multinationals," *California Management Review,* Fall 1982, p. 59.
2. Ingemar Torbiorn, "Operative and Strategic Use of Expatriates in New Organizations and Market Structures," *International Studies of Management & Organization,* vol. 24, no. 3, 1994, pp. 5–17.
3. Arvind V. Phatak, *International Dimensions of Management,* 2nd ed. (Boston: PWS-Kent Publishing, 1989), p. 106.
4. Also see Charlene Marmer Solomon, "Learning to Manage Host-Country Nationals," *Personnel Journal,* March 1995, pp. 60–67.
5. Also see Jan Selmer, Inn-Lee Kang, and Robert P. Wright, "Managerial Behavior of Expatriate versus Local Bosses," *International Studies of Management & Organization,* vol. 24, no. 3, 1994, pp. 48–63.
6. See, for example, Peter J. Dowling and Denise E. Welsh, "The Strategic Adaptation Process of International Human Resource Management: A Case Study," *Human Resource Planning,* vol. 14, no. 1, 1991, pp. 61–69.
7. Lawrence G. Franco, "Who Manages Multinational Enterprises?" *Columbia Journal of World Business,* Summer 1973, pp. 30–42.
8. See Charles M. Vance and Peter Smith Ring, "Preparing the Host Country Workforce for Expatriate Managers: The Neglected Other Side of the Coin," *Human Resource Development Quarterly,* Winter 1994, pp. 337–352.
9. H. Scullion, "Strategic Recruitment and Development of the 'International Manager,'" *Human Resource Management Journal,* vol. 3, no. 1, 1992, pp. 57–69.
10. Cecil G. Howard, "The Multinational Corporation: Impact on Nativization," *Personnel,* January-February 1972, pp. 138–145.
11. Faye Rice, "Should You Work for a Foreigner?" *Fortune,* August 1, 1988, p. 134.
12. Tung, "Selection and Training Procedures," pp. 61–62.
13. See Oded Shenkar and Mee-Kau Nyaw, "The Interplay of Human Resources in Chinese-Foreign Ventures," in Oded Shenkar, *Global Perspectives of Human Resource Management* (Englewood Cliffs, NJ: Prentice-Hall, 1995), pp. 280–285.
14. Tung, "Selection and Training Procedures," pp. 61–62.
15. Phatak, *International Dimensions of Management,* p. 107.
16. Franko, "Who Manages Multinational Enterprises?" p. 33.
17. Jennifer J. Laabs, "The Global Talent Search," *Personnel Journal,* August 1991, pp. 38–40; Richard M. Hodgetts and Fred Luthans, "U.S. Multinationals' Expatriate Compensation Strategies," *Compensation and Benefits Review,* January-February 1993, pp. 57–62.
18. Shawn Tully, "The Hunt for the Global Manager," *Fortune,* May 21, 1990, pp. 140–144.
19. Raphael Pura, "Many of Asia's Workers Are on the Move," *Wall Street Journal,* March 5, 1992, p. A13.
20. Michael Selz, "For Many Small Firms, Going Abroad Is No Vacation," *Wall Street Journal,* February 27, 1992, p. B2; David C. Bangert and Jozsef Poor, "Human Resource Management in Foreign Affiliates in Hungary," in Oded Shenkar (ed.), *Global Perspectives of Human Resource Management* (Englewood Cliffs, NJ: Prentice-Hall, 1995), pp. 258–266.
21. A. Haslberger and L. K. Strok, "Development and Selection of Multinational Expatriates," *Human Resource Development Quarterly,* Autumn 1992, pp. 287–293.
22. Lisa Hoecklin, *Managing Cultural Differences* (Workingham, England: Addison-Wesley, 1994), p. 124.
23. Winfred Arthur, Jr., and Winston Bennett, Jr., "The International Assignee: The Relative Importance of Factors Perceived to Contribute to Success," *Personnel Psychology,* Spring 1995, pp. 99–114.
24. Rosalie L. Tung, "U.S. Multinationals: A Study of Their Selection and Training Procedures for Overseas Assignments," *National Academy of Management Proceedings,* Atlanta, 1979, pp. 298–299. For more on this topic, see Yoram Zeira and Moshe Banai, "Selection of Expatriate Managers in MNCs: The Host-Environment Point of View," *International Studies of Management & Organization,* Spring 1985, pp. 33–51.
25. Rosalie L. Tung, "Human Resource Planning in Japanese Multinationals: A Model for U.S. Firms?" *Journal of International Business Studies,* Fall 1984, p. 141.
26. Jean E. Heller, "Criteria for Selecting an International Manager," *Personnel,* May-June 1980, p. 48.
27. Mark Mendenhall and Gary Oddou, "Acculturation Profiles of Expatriate Managers: Implications for Cross-Cultural Training Programs," *Columbia Journal of World Business,* Winter 1986, p. 76.
28. Indrei Ratiu, "Thinking Internationally: A Comparison of How International Executives Learn," *International Studies of Management & Organization,* Spring-Summer 1983, pp. 139–150.
29. Nancy J. Adler, *International Dimensions of Organizational Behavior,* 2nd ed. (Boston: PWS-Kent Publishing, 1991), pp. 228–229.
30. Ingemar Torbiorn, *Living Abroad* (New York: John Wiley, 1982), pp. 97–99.
31. Ibid., pp. 100–101.

32. Jeffrey L. Blue and Ulric Haynes, Jr., "Preparation for the Overseas Assignment," *Business Horizons,* June 1977, p. 62.

33. Phatak, *International Dimensions of Management,* p. 114.

34. Blue and Haynes, "Preparation for the Overseas Assignment," p. 63.

35. Richard M. Hodgetts, *Management Theory, Process, and Practice,* 5th ed. (San Diego: Harcourt Brace Jovanovich, 1990), chapter 19.

36. Blue and Haynes, "Preparation for the Overseas Assignment," p. 65.

37. Heller, "Criteria for Selecting an International Manager," p. 50.

38. Paul E. Schares, "Looking for a Few Good Managers," *BusinessWeek,* March 9, 1992, p. 48.

39. Torbiorn, *Living Abroad,* p. 128.

40. Blue and Haynes, "Preparation for the Overseas Assignment, p. 64."

41. The survey was conducted by executive recruiters for Korn-Ferry International and the Columbia Business School. Excerpts were reported in "Report: Shortage of Executives Will Hurt U.S.," *Omaha World Herald,* June 25, 1989, p. 1G.

42. Torbiorn, *Living Abroad,* p. 48; Ford S. Worthy, "The Good Life of Yanks in Asia," *Fortune,* April 23, 1990, pp. 156–161.

43. Rosalie L. Tung, "Expatriate Assignments: Enhancing Success and Minimizing Failure," *Academy of Management Executive,* May 1987, p. 117.

44. Blue and Haynes, "Preparation for the Overseas Assignment," p. 64.

45. For more on this topic, see "Gauging a Family's Suitability for a Stint Overseas," *BusinessWeek,* April 16, 1979, pp. 127–128.

46. See, for example, Heller, "Criteria for Selecting an International Manager," pp. 50–51.

47. Howard Tu and Sherry E. Sullivan, "Preparing Yourself for an International Assignment," *Business Horizons,* January-February 1994, p. 68.

48. Ibid.

49. James C. Baker and John M. Ivancevich, "The Assignment of American Executives Abroad: Systematic, Haphazard or Chaotic?" *California Management Review,* Spring 1971, p. 41.

50. Ibid.

51. Tung, "Selection and Training Procedures," p. 64.

52. Heller, "Criteria for Selecting an International Manager," p. 53.

53. Tung, "Selection and Training Procedures," p. 65.

54. This section is based on J. Stewart Black, Mark Mendenhall, and Gary Oddou, "Toward a Comprehensive Model of International Adjustment: An Integration of Multiple Theoretical Perspectives," *Academy of Management Review,* April 1991, pp. 291–317.

55. Seth Faison, "Our Man in Shanghai Rents a Pad," *New York Times,* July 9, 1995, Section E, p. 4.

56. Elaine K. Bailey, "International Compensation," in Oded Shenkar (ed.), *Global Perspectives of Human Resource* (Englewood Cliffs, NJ: Prentice-Hall, 1995), p. 148.

57. See Hodgetts and Luthans, *Compensation & Benefits Review,* pp. 58–59.

58. Eamonn Fingleton, "Jobs For Life: Why Japan Won't Give Them Up," *Fortune,* March 20, 1995, p. 122.

59. Julia Flynn and Farah Nayeri, "Continental Divide Over Executive Pay," *BusinessWeek,* July 3, 1995, pp. 40–41.

60. See, for example, Fred Luthans, "A Paradigm Shift in Eastern Europe: Some Helpful Management Development Techniques," *Journal of Management Development,* vol. 12, no. 1, 1993, pp. 55–56.

61. "Bonus Points," *Economist,* April 15, 1995, pp. 71–72.

62. See Dennis R. Briscoe, *International Human Resource Management* (Englewood Cliffs, NJ: Prentice-Hall, 1995), pp. 111–120.

63. Charlene Marmer Solomon, "Global Compensation: Learn the ABCs," *Personnel Journal,* July 1995, pp. 70–76.

64. Jacob M. Schlesinger, "A U.S. Professor Takes an Unusual Course—In a Japanese Factory," *Wall Street Journal,* March 30, 1992, pp. A1, 5.

65. David Sirota and J. Michael Greenwood, "Understand Your Overseas Work Force," *Harvard Business Review,* January-February 1971, pp. 53–60.

66. Ibid., pp. 59–60.

67. Edwin L. Miller and Joseph L. C. Cheng, "Circumstances That Influenced the Decision to Accept an Overseas Assignment," *National Academy of Management Proceedings,* Kansas City, 1976, pp. 336–429; Edwin L. Miller and Joseph L. C. Cheng, "A Closer Look at the Decision to Accept an Overseas Position," *Management International Review,* vol. 18, no. 3, 1978, pp. 25–33.

68. Torbiorn, *Living Abroad,* p. 127.

69. Y. Zeira and M. Banai, "Attitudes of Host-Country Organizations toward MNCs' Staffing Policies: A Cross-Country and Cross-Industry Analysis," *Management International Review,* vol. 21, no. 2, 1981, pp. 38–47.

70. Also see Anders Edstrom and Jay Galbraith, "Alternative Policies for International Transfers of Managers," *Management International Review,* vol. 34, Special Issue, 1994, pp. 71–82.

71. Torbiorn, *Living Abroad,* p. 41.

72. Zeira and Banai, "Selection of Expatriate Managers," p. 34.

73. John S. McClenahan, "The Overseas Manager: Not Actually a World Away," *Industry Week*, November 1, 1976, p. 53.

74. Adler, *International Dimensions of Organizational Behavior*, p. 236.

75. Rosalie L. Tung, "Career Issues in International Assignments," *The Academy of Management Executive*, August 1988, p. 242.

76. D. W. Kendall, "Repatriation: An Ending and a Beginning," *Business Horizons*, November-December 1981, p. 23.

77. J. Stewart Black, "Coming Home: The Relationship of Expatriate Expectations with Repatriate Adjustment and Job Performance," *Human Relations*, vol. 45, no. 2, 1992, p. 188.

78. Phatak, *International Dimensions of Management*, p. 126.

79. Tung, "Career Issues in International Assignments," p. 243.

80. Nancy K. Napier and Richard B. Peterson, "Expatriate Re-entry: What Do Expatriates Have to Say?" *Human Resource Planning*, vol. 14, no. 1, 1991, pp. 19–28.

81. Charlene Marmer Solomon, "Repatriation: Up, Down or Out?" *Personnel Journal*, January 1995, p. 32.

HUMAN RESOURCE DEVELOPMENT ACROSS CULTURES

OBJECTIVES OF THE CHAPTER

Firms doing international business need to be particularly concerned with training and organization development to better prepare their personnel for overseas assignments. This chapter examines how successful multinational organizations prepare personnel to go overseas. A specific focus is the reasons for training and development and the various types of training that commonly are offered. Training by use of cultural assimilators is discussed, and their value in providing effective acculturation is analyzed. Broader-based organization development also is considered—how it works as well as its value in helping to resolve human problems in an international setting. The specific objectives of this chapter are:

1. **IDENTIFY** the training process as used in international management, and note that people from different cultures often have different learning styles.
2. **DISCUSS** the most common reasons for training and the types of training that often are provided.
3. **EXPLAIN** how cultural assimilators work and why they are so highly regarded.
4. **IDENTIFY** the term "organization development," and discuss its use in international management.

The Cultural Integrator

In recent years, some international management experts have suggested that firms use a cultural integrator to deal with the cultural differences they face overseas. The basic concept of integration is not new; MNCs long have tested their products in foreign markets to ensure that any necessary modifications are made before full-scale selling begins. Similarly, many of these firms have trained and developed their people before sending them to foreign assignments. In most cases, however, the personnel are not totally prepared to deal with the day-to-day cultural challenges, because they lack field experience. This is where the cultural integrator enters the picture.

The integrator is responsible for helping handle problems between the subsidiary and host cultures. Among other things, the person advises management about the consequences of those actions that can negatively affect its position in the host country and market, and he or she works with management in developing an appropriate response.

Some companies send the cultural integrator from the home office. Many choose a host-country national who has intimate knowledge of the multinational's culture and can view operations from both sides. Quite often, the individual holds a staff position and can only advise and recommend courses of action; the person has no authority to demand implementation of such actions. For this reason, the integrator needs proficiency in both conceptual and human relations skills. He or she must be able to envision the relationships between the MNC and host country that will result in the best "fit" for both. At the same time, the individual must be able to persuade line managers to accept her or his point of view.

Will the 1990s see greater use of cultural integrators? This trend appears to be very likely.

As more corporations expand internationally, there is a greater need to integrate their operations into foreign societies. It cannot be expected that an international manager can function effectively in all host societies. Nor can it be expected that a manager will remain in a society long enough to gain the cultural familiarity necessary to function effectively there, since one of the competitive advantages of an international firm is its managerial mobility. The cultural integrator offers a clear resolution to this dilemma, allowing international organizations to achieve their full potential.

TRAINING IN INTERNATIONAL MANAGEMENT

Training is the process of altering employee behavior and attitudes in a way that increases the probability of goal attainment.[1] This training process is particularly important in preparing employees for overseas assignments.[2] For example, most expatriates (defined in Chapter 14 as those who live and work away from their home country and who are citizens of the country in which the MNC is headquartered) are unfamiliar with the customs, cultures, and work habits of the local people. As a result, they often make critical mistakes. Here is such a blunder:

> An American company eager to do business in Saudi Arabia sent over a sales manager to "get something going." The salesman began calling contacts soon after his arrival on Monday . . . After many disappointing appointments, the salesman ran into an old buddy who gave him an introduction to some basic rules of Saudi etiquette and how to do business with the Arabs. The salesman learned that he had repeatedly insulted his contacts by his impatience, refusal of coffee, the "all business talk" attitude and aggressive selling. Even incidental acts such as handing people papers with his left hand and exposing the side of his shoe while sitting on the floor were improper Saudi customs.[3]

The simplest training, in terms of preparation time, is to place a cultural integrator in each foreign operation. This individual is responsible for ensuring that the operation's business systems are in accord with those of the local culture. The integrator advises, guides, and recommends actions needed to ensure this synchronization.[4] The "International Management in Action: The Cultural Integrator," accompanying box, describes in detail the use of such a person.

Unfortunately, although using an integrator can help, it seldom is sufficient. The other expatriates also must have a working knowledge of local customs and be aware of how to handle themselves in business transactions. To accomplish this, firms need a well-designed training program that is administered before individuals leave for their overseas assignment (and, in some cases, also on-site) and then evaluated later to determine its overall effectiveness.[5] One recent review found that cross-cultural training, which can take many forms, is becoming increasingly popular. A recent survey of 228 companies found the following:

1. Of organizations with cultural programs, 58 percent offer training only to some expatriates, while 42 percent offer it to all of them.
2. Ninety-one percent offer cultural orientation programs to spouses, and 75 percent offer them to dependent children.
3. The average duration of the cultural training programs is 3 days.
4. Cultural training is continued after arrival in the assignment location 32 percent of the time.
5. Thirty percent offer formal cultural training programs.
6. Of those without formal cultural programs, 37 percent plan to add such training.[6]

The most common topics covered in cultural training include social etiquette, customs, economics, history, politics, and business etiquette. The MNC's overall philosophy of international management and demands of the specific cultural situation are the starting point.[7]

The Impact of Overall Management Philosophy on Training

The type of training that is required of expatriates is influenced by the firm's overall philosophy of international management. For example, some companies prefer to send their own people to staff an overseas operation; others prefer to use locals whenever possible. Briefly, four basic philosophic positions of multinational corporations (MNCs) can influence the training program:

1. An *ethnocentric MNC* puts home-office people in charge of key international management positions. The MNC headquarters group and the affiliated world company managers all have the same basic experiences, attitudes, and beliefs about how to manage operations. Many Japanese firms follow this practice.
2. A *polycentric MNC* places local nationals in key positions and allows these managers to appoint and develop their own people. MNC headquarters gives the subsidiary managers authority to manage their operations just as long as these operations are sufficiently profitable. Some MNCs use this approach in East Asia, Australia, and other markets that are deemed too expensive to staff with expatriates.
3. A *regiocentric MNC* relies on local managers from a particular geographic region to handle operations in and around that area. For example, production facilities in France would be used to produce goods for all EU countries. Similarly, advertising managers from subsidiaries in Italy, Germany, France, and Spain would come together and formulate a "European" advertising campaign for the company's products. A regiocentric approach often relies on regional group cooperation of local managers. The Gillette MNC uses a regiocentric approach.
4. A *geocentric MNC* seeks to integrate diverse regions of the world through a global approach to decision making. Assignments are made based on qualifi-

cations, and all subsidiary managers throughout the structure are regarded as equal to those at headquarters. IBM is an excellent example of an MNC that attempts to use a geocentric approach.

All four of these philosophical positions can be found in the multinational arena, and each puts a different type of training demand on the MNC. For example, ethnocentric MNCs will do all training at headquarters, but polycentric MNCs will rely on local managers to assume responsibility for seeing that the training function is carried out.

The Impact of Different Learning Styles on Training

Another important area of consideration is learning styles.[8] *Learning* is the acquisition of skills, knowledge, and abilities that results in a relatively permanent change in behavior. A great deal of research has been conducted on the various types and theories of learning.[9] The application of these ideas in an international context often can be quite challenging, however, because cultural differences can affect learning.

As one group of researchers recently noted, "Two countries may be very similar in ecology and climate and, for example, through a common legacy of colonialism, have a similar language and legal, educational and governmental infrastructure but may be markedly different in terms of beliefs, attitudes and values."[10] Moreover, research shows that people with different learning styles prefer different learning environments, and if there is a mismatch between the preferred learning style and the work environment, dissatisfaction and poor performance can result.[11]

One study recently investigated learning styles by giving a learning style questionnaire to British middle managers, Indian midcareer managers, and East African midcareer managers. Two dimensions of learning style were measured: analysis and action. The analysis dimension measures the extent to which the learner adopts a theory-building and test approach as opposed to using an intuitive approach. The action dimension measures the extent to which the learner uses a trial-and-error approach as opposed to employing a contemplative or reflective approach.[12] The researchers found important differences in learning style between the three cultures. Indian managers were much higher on analysis than the other two groups. British managers were much higher on action. East African managers were the lowest on both analysis and action scores. The results were summarized as follows:

> The results of this study advance the argument . . . and raise questions about not only the aims and content of management development activities in different cultures but also about the nature of the learning process and the design of learning environments employed. . . . It may well be that the kind of learning environments and activities which promote effective learning in some cultures may not promote the same outcomes in other cultures where different learning styles predominate. This could have important implications for the design of learning environments, the composition of training groups and the location of training (in host country, regional center or home country) undertaken by transnational organizations.[13]

In addition to these conclusions, those responsible for training programs must remember that even if learning does occur, the new behaviors will not be used if they are not reinforced.[14] For example, if the head of a foreign subsidiary is highly ethnocentric and believes that things should be done the way they are in the home country, new managers with intercultural training likely will find little reward or reinforcement for using their ideas. This cultural complexity also extends to the way in which the training is conducted.[15] A corporate trainer and specialist for Esso Production Malaysia recently offered the following advice for training in cross-cultural settings:

> Start with a problem-oriented approach—avoid using complicated theories and defini-tions. Focus on here and now and "how to's." For teaching in cross-cultural settings, start with affirming the values of the participants, especially those which are part of their cultural heritage and are the basis of their shared practices. Once these values are identified, begin to look for gaps in performance and create an awareness of what is needed. The trainer will then focus on the steps to be taken to develop the new skills repertoire. A word of caution—if the skills have to do with interpersonal skills, it is bet-ter to have some contribution from the local participants. In this instance the trainer's task is to inform not to instruct.[16]

Reasons for Training

Training programs are useful in preparing people for overseas assignments for many reasons. These reasons can be put into two general categories: organiza-tional and personal.

Organizational Reasons Organizational reasons for training relate to the enter-prise at large and its efforts to manage overseas operations more effectively. One primary reason is to help overcome *ethnocentrism,* the belief that one's way of do-ing things is superior to that of others. Ethnocentrism is common in many large MNCs where managers believe that the home office's approach to doing business can be exported intact to all other countries, because this approach is superior to anything at the local level. Training can help home-office managers to understand the values and customs of other countries so that when they are transferred over-seas, they have a better understanding of how to interact with local personnel. This training also can help managers to overcome the common belief among many personnel that expatriates are not as effective as host-country managers. This is particularly important given that an increasing number of managerial po-sitions now are held by foreign managers in U.S. MNCs.[17]

Another organizational reason for training is to improve the flow of commu-nication between the home office and the international subsidiaries and branches. Quite often, overseas managers find that they are not adequately informed re-garding what is expected of them while the home office places close controls on their operating authority. This is particularly true when the overseas manager is from the host country. Effective communication can help to minimize these problems.

Finally, another organizational reason for training is to increase overall effi-ciency and profitability. Research shows organizations that closely tie their train-ing and human resource management strategy to their business strategy tend to outperform those that do not.[18]

Personal Reasons Although there is overall organizational justification, the pri-mary reason for training overseas managers is to improve their ability to interact effectively with local people in general and their personnel in particular.[19] One early study that surveyed 75 organizations in England, Holland, Belgium, and Germany found that some of the biggest complaints about managers by their personnel revolved around personal shortcomings in areas such as politeness, punctuality, tactfulness, orderliness, sensitivity, reliability, tolerance, and empathy.[20] As a result, an increasing number of training programs now address social topics such as how to take a client to dinner, effectively apologize to a customer, appropriately address one's overseas colleagues, communicate formally and politely with others, and learn how to help others "save face."[21] These programs also focus on dispelling myths and stereotypes by replacing them with facts about the culture. For example, in helping expatriates better understand Arab executives, the following guidelines are offered:

1. There is a close relationship between the Arab executive and his environment. The Arab executive is looked on as a community and family leader, and there are numerous social pressures on him because of this role. He is consulted on all types of problems, even those far removed from his position.
2. With regard to decision making, the Arab executive likely will consult with his subordinates, but he will take responsibility for his decision himself rather than arriving at it through consensus.
3. The Arab executive likely will try to avoid conflict. If there is an issue that he favors but is opposed by his subordinates, he tends to impose his authority. If it is an issue favored by the subordinates but opposed by the executive, he will likely let the matter drop without taking action.
4. The Arab executive's style is very personal. He values loyalty over efficiency. Although some executives find that the open-door tradition consumes a great deal of time, they do not feel that the situation can be changed. Many executives tend to look on their employees as family and will allow them to bypass the hierarchy to meet them.
5. The Arab executive, contrary to popular beliefs, puts considerable value on the use of time. One thing he admires most about Western or expatriate executives is the use of their time, and he would like to encourage his own employees to make more productive use of time.[22]

Another growing problem is the belief that foreign language skills are not really essential to doing business overseas.[23] Effective training programs can help to minimize these personal problems.

A particularly big personal problem that managers have in an overseas assignment is arrogance. This is the so-called "Ugly American" problem that U.S. expatriates have been known to have. Many expatriate managers find that their power and prestige are much greater than they were in their job in the home country. This often results in improper behavior, especially among managers at the upper and lower positions of overseas subsidiaries. This arrogance takes a number of different forms, including rudeness to personnel and inaccessibility to clients. Zeira and Harari made the following observations:

> Another manifestation of expatriate managers' arrogance is their widespread tendency to ignore invitations to become participant observers in HCOs [host-country organizations]. The underlying idea behind these invitations involves rotating expatriate managers in various HCO departments to enable them to observe patterns of organizational behavior at various hierarchical levels. The purpose of this observation is to familiarize expatriate managers, especially those new in their jobs or about to begin to

assume them, with the goals, policies, procedures, formal and informal norms, and expectations of HCOs regarding expatriate managers and their respective subsidiaries.[24]

Another common problem is expatriate managers' overruling of decisions, often seen at lower levels of the hierarchy. When a decision is made by a superior who is from the host country and the expatriate does not agree with it, the expatriate may appeal to higher authority in the subsidiary. Host-country managers obviously resent this behavior, because it implies that they are incompetent and can be second-guessed by expatriate subordinates.

Still another common problem is the open criticizing by expatriate managers of their own country or the host country. Many expatriates believe that this form of criticism is regarded as constructive and shows them to have an open mind. Experience has found, however, that most host-country personnel view such behavior negatively and feel that the manager should refrain from such unconstructive criticism. It just creates bad feelings and lack of loyalty.

In addition to helping deal with these types of personal problems, training can be useful in improving overall management style.[25] Research shows that many host-country nationals would like to see changes in some of the styles of expatriate managers, including their leadership, decision making, communication, and group work. In terms of leadership, the locals would like to see their expatriate managers be more friendly, accessible, receptive to subordinate suggestions, and encouraging to subordinates to make their best efforts. In decision making, they would like to see clearer definition of goals, more involvement in the process by those employees who will be affected by the decision, and greater use of group meetings to help make decisions. In communication, they would like to see more exchange of opinions and ideas between subordinates and managers. In group work, they would like to see more group problem-solving and teamwork. When Harari and Zeira researched the attitudes in six subsidiaries of non-Japanese MNCs, three in Japan and three from outside (United States, France, and Israel), they found that all host-country nationals wanted to see the use of more behavioral management techniques.[26]

The specific training approach used must reflect both the industrial and the cultural environment. For example, there is some evidence that Japanese students who come to the United States to earn an M.B.A. degree often find this education of no real value back home. One graduate noted that when he tactfully suggested putting to use a skill he had learned during his U.S. M.B.A. program, he got nowhere. An analysis of Japanese getting an outside education concluded:

> Part of the problem is the reason that most Japanese workers are sent to business schools. Whatever ticket the M.B.A. degree promises—or appears to promise—Americans, the diploma has little meaning within most Japanese companies. Rather, companies send students abroad under the life-time employment system to ensure that there will be more English speakers who are familiar with Western business practices. Some managers regard business schools as a kind of high-level English language school, returning students say, or consider the two years as more or less a paid vacation.[27]

TYPES OF TRAINING PROGRAMS

There are many different types of multinational management training programs. Some last only a few hours; others last for months. Some are fairly superficial; others are extensive in coverage.[28] Figure 15-1 shows some of the key considerations that influence development of these programs.

FIGURE 15-1

A MODEL FOR THE DEVELOPMENT OF MULTINATIONAL MANAGERS

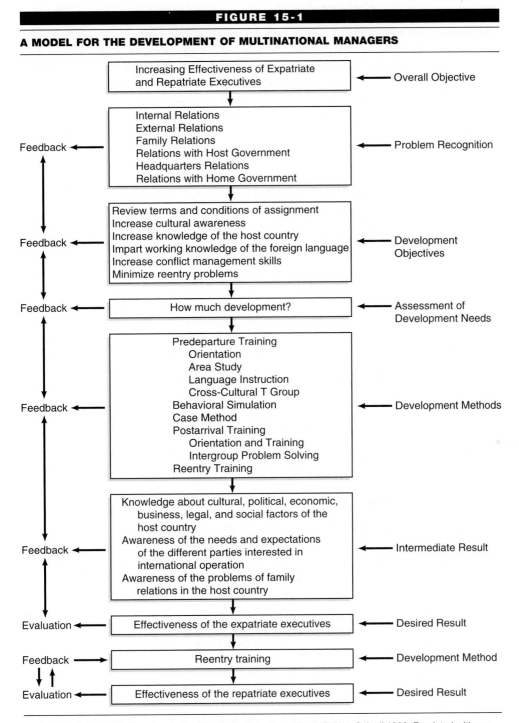

Standardized vs. Tailor-Made

Some management training is standard, or generic. For example, participants often are taught how to use specific decision-making tools, such as quantitative analysis, and regardless of where the managers are sent in the world, the application is the same. These tools do not have to be culturally specific. For example, successful Japanese MNCs tend to provide all their personnel with a common training and development program.[29] Similarly, basic behaviorally oriented concepts such as communication, motivation, and leadership often initially are taught with a generic program, then a tailor-made program is created so that the material can be made country- or region-specific. Research shows that small firms usually rely on standard training programs and larger MNCs design their own. Some of the larger MNCs are increasingly turning to specially designed video programs for their training and development needs.[30]

Tailor-made training programs are created for the specific needs of the participants. Input for these offerings usually is obtained from managers who currently are working (or have worked) in the country to which the participants will be sent as well as from local managers and personnel who are citizens of that country. These programs often are designed to provide a new set of skills for a new culture.[31] Quite often, the offerings are provided before the individuals leave for their overseas assignment; however, there also are postdeparture training programs that are conducted on-site. These often take the form of systematically familiarizing the individual with the country through steps such as meeting with government officials and other key personnel in the community; becoming acquainted with managers and employees in the organization; learning the host-country nationals' work methods, problems, and expectations; and taking on-site language training.[32]

A good example is provided by Underwriters Laboratories, Inc., which has developed a 2-day, in-house training program for professional members of its staff who travel to Japan to work with clients on projects and for staff members who deal extensively with Japanese clients in the United States.[33] The program is designed around a series of minilectures that cover topics ranging from how to handle introductions to the proper way to exchange gifts to the correct way of interpreting Japanese social and business behavior. The 2-day program consists of lectures, case studies, role plays, language practice, and a short test on cultural terminology; it concludes with a 90-minute question-and-answer period. At the end of the program, participants have a fundamental understanding of how to communicate with the Japanese. More importantly, they know the types of information they lack and how to go about learning more on becoming more effective intercultural communicators.

One of the most common types of training in both standard and tailor-made packages is that of self-evaluation. Participants in such training are provided personal insights about their behaviors. For example, managers will be given tests to determine if their managerial style is basically factual, intuitive, analytical, or normative. A *factual manager* looks at the available information and makes decisions based on the data. An *intuitive manager* is imaginative, innovative, and can jump from one idea to another. An *analytical manager* is systematic, logical, and carefully weighs alternatives to problems. A *normative manager* is idealistic and concerned with how things should be done. Every manager will be some combination of all four types, but by learning their individual preferences, participants gain insights into their own approach to dealing with people.

		TABLE 15-1		

CULTURAL CHARACTERISTICS OF MANAGERIAL STYLES AND ACTIVITIES

Activity	Factual style	Intuitive style	Analytical style	Normative style
Planning	Focus on the present, on the here-and-now. The manager clarifies the existing situation, what is.	Focus on the future. The manager sets up objectives.	Relate past, present, and future. The manager works on strategies and tactics.	Focus on the past. The manager reviews and assesses what has been done to direct new action.
Performance appraisal	Deal with skills. (Register the facts.)	Concentrate on potential. (Look for possibilities.)	Assess performance according to several factors. (The individual, the situation, the manager, the environment.)	Insist on the performance appraisal process, the relationship, the sharing of perceptions. (To understand each other is the aim.)
Decision making	Decisions are based on facts and on thorough investigations; they are always well documented.	Decisions are related to hunches, imagination, guesses, trial and error, risk-taking.	Decisions are the result of a systematic way to identify options, alternatives and weigh them according to a set of well-analyzed pros and cons.	Decisions are closely linked to the value systems which exist in the team, organization, or culture concerned.
Coaching	Each individual has to find his or her own way. The manager can only facilitate the process by clarifying the facts.	The manager motivates the employee in describing a "could be" situation appealing to him or her.	Coaching is systematically organized, in a kind of step-by-step approach: "This is what has to be done to change what is into what should be."	The basic assumption that underlines the evaluative approach toward coaching is that weaknesses and strengths should be fairly evaluated and taken care of.

Source: This information is found in Pierre Casse, *Training for the Multicultural Manager* (Washington, DC: Society for Intercultural Education, Training and Research, 1982), p. 41.

Table 15-1 shows how managerial style will influence the way that an individual plans, appraises performance, makes decisions, and coaches. In many cases, this personal style also will be analyzed on a cultural basis. For example, Table 15-2 describes the four approaches in terms of how they would be carried out on a cultural basis. This integration on a geographic basis helps the participants better understand the intercultural effect of their management style.

As emphasized, the specific training program used will depend on the needs of the individual. Tung surveyed managers in Europe, Japan, and the United States and found six major types of cross-cultural training programs:

1. Environmental briefings used to provide information about things such as geography, climate, housing, and schools
2. Cultural orientation designed to familiarize the individual with cultural institutions and value systems of the host country
3. Cultural assimilators using programmed learning approaches designed to provide the participants with intercultural encounters
4. Language training
5. Sensitivity training designed to develop attitudinal flexibility
6. Field experience, which sends the participant to the country of assignment to undergo some of the emotional stress of living and working with people from a different culture[34]

TABLE 15-2

MANAGEMENT STYLES APPLIED TO FIVE CULTURES

Management style	European cultures	North American cultures	African cultures	Asian cultures	South American cultures
Factual	• Meanings are in individuals • Theoretic as opposed to practical • Inconsistent	• Individuals rely on the spoken words • Professional experiences are perceived as important • Pragmatic	• Meanings come from the environment • Time is viewed as flexible; it is not rigid • "Things" are alive	• Meanings are everywhere; in people, things • No clear-cut separation between the internal and external worlds • Sensing is an illusion	• Touching is an important part of the communication process • Sensual • Attracted to poetry, art, literature
Intuitive	• Like to play with ideas • Creative and imaginative • Enjoy exploring new avenues	• Look for ideas which can be used • Enjoy learning • Can be perceived as "naive" at times (simplistic ideas)	• Superstitious • Ideas come from group interactions • What is perceived is at least as important as what is	• Highly "spiritual" • A great sense of unity is shared by many people • Metaphysical	• Enjoy disagreements on principles, ideas; the stimulation of an exchange of opinions • Jump from one idea to another • Emotional when talking about possibilities and opportunities
Analytical	• Deductive • Rigid organizational structures • Centralized decision-making process	• Inductive • Flexible organization cultures • Decentralized decision-making process	• Are process oriented • Thinking is highly internalized (visual thinking) • Thinking is assimilated to "feeling"	• Accept ambiguity • Open to many options (there is not just "one way") • Integrate polarities and contradictions	• A certain fatalism (faith is valued) • *Mañana* concept • Disorganized and highly centralized
Normative	• Overcritical • Quality of life is highly valued • Conflicts are enjoyable	• Getting the job done is the priority • People like to be liked at the same time that they "push" people around • Self-esteem is based largely on professional accomplishments	• The concept of kinship is highly valued • Friendship comes before business and is lasting • Interpersonal relationships are based on sincerity	• Simplicity and humility are highly valued • Peacefulness is what counts above all • Enjoy flowing with situational forces	• *Machismo* (conservative) • *Dignita* • *Personalismo*

Source: This information is found in Pierre Casse, *Training for the Multicultural Manager* (Washington, DC: Society for Intercultural Education, Training and Research, 1982), p. 43.

Surprisingly, Tung found that only 32 percent of the U.S. firms she surveyed had formal training programs to prepare individuals for foreign assignments. This contrasted sharply with the 57 percent of Japanese firms and 69 percent of European companies that had formal programs. Table 15-3 reports the findings based on type of program and functional task. She concludes the following:

TABLE 15-3

FREQUENCY OF TRAINING PROGRAMS IN U.S., EUROPEAN, AND JAPANESE SAMPLES (percent)

Training programs	CEO			Functional head			Troubleshooter			Operating personnel		
	U.S.	Eur.	Japan.	U.S.	Eur.	Japan.	U.S.	Eur.	Japan.	U.S.	Eur.	Japan.
Environmental briefing	52	57	67	54	52	57	44	38	52	31	38	67
Cultural orientation	42	55	14	41	52	14	31	31	19	24	28	24
Culture assimilator	10	21	14	10	17	14	7	10	14	9	14	19
Language training	60	76	52	59	72	57	36	41	52	24	48	76
Sensitivity training	3	3	0	1	3	0	1	3	5	0	3	5
Field experience	6	28	14	6	24	10	4	3	10	1	7	24

Source: Rosalie L. Tung, "Selection and Training Procedures of U.S., European, and Japanese Multinationals," *California Management Review,* Fall 1982, p. 66. © 1982 by the Regents of the University of California. Reprinted from the *California Management Review*, vol. 25, no. 1. By permission of the Regents.

Results indicate that for both the U.S. and West European samples, most of the firms that had training programs recognized the need for more rigorous training for the CEOs and functional heads than for trouble-shooters and operatives. In contrast, the Japanese firms that sponsored training programs appear to provide slightly more rigorous training for operatives. This could arise from the fact that since CEOs have more extensive records of overseas work experience, the need to subject them to the more rigorous programs was perceived as less important.[35]

Some organizations now have extended this idea to include cross-cultural training of family members, especially children who will be accompanying the parents. The accompanying sidebar, "U.S.-Style Training for Expats and Their Teenagers," explains how this approach to cultural assimilation is carried out.

In addition to training expats and their families, effective MNCs also are developing carefully crafted programs for training personnel from other cultures who are coming into their culture. These programs, among other things, have materials that are specially designed for the target audience. Some of the specific steps that well-designed cultural training programs follow include:

1. Local instructors and a translator, typically someone who is bicultural, observe the pilot training program and/or examine written training materials.
2. The educational designer then debriefs the observation with the translator, curriculum writer, and local instructors.
3. Together, the group examines the structure and sequence, ice breaker, and other materials that will be used in the training.
4. The group then collectively identifies stories, metaphors, experiences, and examples in the culture that will fit into the new training program.
5. The educational designer and curriculum writer make the necessary changes in the training materials.

U.S.-Style Training for Expats and Their Teenagers

One of the major reasons why expatriates have trouble with overseas assignments is that their teenage children are unable to adapt to the new culture, and this has an impact on the expat's performance. To deal with this acculturation problem, many U.S. MNCs now are developing special programs for helping teenagers assimilate into new cultures and adjust to new school environments. A good example is provided by General Electric Medical Systems Group (GEMS), a Milwaukee-based firm that has expatriates in France, Japan, and Singapore. As soon as GEMS designates an individual for an overseas assignment, this expat and his or her family are matched up with those who have recently returned from this country. If the family going overseas has teenage children, the company will team them up with a family that had teenagers during its stay abroad. Both groups then discuss the challenges and problems that must be faced. In the case of teenagers, they are able to talk about their concerns with others who already have encountered these issues, and the latter can provide important information regarding how to make friends, learn the language, get around town, and turn the time abroad into a pleasant experience. Coca-Cola uses a similar approach. As soon as someone is designated for an overseas assignment, the company helps initiate cross-cultural discussions with experienced personnel. Coke also provides formal training through use of external cross-cultural consulting firms who are experienced in working with all family members.

A typical concern of teenagers going abroad is that they will have to go away to boarding school. In Saudi Arabia, for example, national law forbids expatriate children's attending school past the ninth grade, so most expatriate families will look for European institutions for their children. GEMS addresses these types of problems with a specially developed education program. Tutors, schools, curricula, home-country requirements, and host-country requirements are examined, and a plan and specific program of study are developed for each school-age child before he or she leaves.

Before the departure of the family, some MNCs will subscribe to local magazines about teen fashions, music, and other sports or social activities in the host country, so that the children know what to expect when they get there. Before the return of the family to the United States, these MNCs provide similar information about what is going on in the United States, so that when the children return for a visit or come back to stay, they are able to quickly fit into their home-country environment once again.

An increasing number of MNCs now give teenagers much of the same cultural training they give their own managers; however, there is one area in which formal assistance often is not as critical for teens as for adults: language training. While most expatriates find it difficult and spend a good deal of time trying to master the local language, many teens find that they can pick it up quite easily. They speak it at school, in their social groups, and out on the street. As a result, they learn not only the formal language but also clichés and slang that help them communicate more easily. In fact, sometimes their accent is so good that they are mistaken for local kids. Simply put: The facility of teens to learn a language often is greatly underrated. A Coca-Cola manager recently drove home this point when he declared: "One girl we sent insisted that, although she would move, she wasn't going to learn the language. Within two months she was practically fluent."

A major educational benefit of this emphasis on teenagers is that it leads to an experienced, bicultural person. So when the young person completes college and begins looking for work, the parent's MNC often is interested in this young adult as a future manager. The person has a working knowledge of the MNC, speaks a second language, and has had overseas experience in a country where the multinational does business. This type of logic is leading some U.S. MNCs to realize that effective cross-cultural training can be of benefit for their work forces of tomorrow as well as today.

6. The local instructors are trained to use the newly developed materials.
7. After the designer, translator, and native-language trainers are satisfied, the materials are printed.
8. The language and content of the training materials are tested with a pilot group.[36]

In developing the instructional materials, culturally specific guidelines are carefully followed so that the training does not lose any of its effectiveness. For example, inappropriate pictures or scenarios that might prove to be offensive to the audience must be screened out. Handouts and other instructional materials that are designed to enhance the learning process are provided for all participants. If the trainees are learning a second language, generous use of visuals and live demonstrations will be employed.

Cultural Assimilators

The cultural assimilator has become one of the most effective approaches to cross-cultural training. A *cultural assimilator* is a programmed learning technique that is designed to expose members of one culture to some of the basic concepts, attitudes, role perceptions, customs, and values of another.[37] These assimilators are developed for each pair of cultures. For example, if an MNC is going to send three U.S. managers from Chicago to Caracas, a cultural assimilator would be developed to familiarize the three Americans with Venezuelan customs and cultures. If three Venezuelan managers from Caracas were to be transferred to Singapore, another assimilator would be developed to familiarize the managers with Singapore customs and cultures.

In most cases, these assimilators require the trainee to read a short episode of a cultural encounter and choose an interpretation of what has happened and why. If the trainee's choice is correct, he or she goes on to the next episode. If the response is incorrect, the trainee is asked to reread the episode and choose another response. Table 15-4 provides an example.

Choice of Content of the Assimilators   One of the major problems in constructing an effective cultural assimilator is deciding what is important enough to include. Some assimilators use critical incidents that are identified as being important. To be classified as a critical incident, a situation must meet at least one of the following conditions:

1. An expatriate and a host national interact in the situation.
2. The situation is puzzling or likely to be misinterpreted by the expatriate.
3. The situation can be interpreted accurately if sufficient knowledge about the culture is available.
4. The situation is relevant to the expatriate's task or mission requirements.[38]

These incidents typically are obtained by asking expatriates and host nationals with whom they come in contact to describe specific intercultural occurrences or events that made a major difference in their attitudes or behavior toward members of the other culture. These incidents can be pleasant, unpleasant, or simply nonunderstandable occurrences.

Validation of the Assimilator   The term *validity* refers to the quality of being effective, of producing the desired results. It means that an instrument—in this case, the cultural assimilator—measures what it is intended to measure.[39] After the cultural assimilator's critical incidents are constructed and the alternative responses

TABLE 15-4

A CULTURAL ASSIMILATOR SITUATION

Sharon Hatfield, a school teacher in Athens, was amazed at the questions that were asked of her by Greeks whom she considered to be only casual acquaintances. When she entered or left her apartment, people would ask her where she was going or where she had been. If she stopped to talk, she was asked questions like, "How much do you make a month?" or "Where did you get that dress you are wearing?" She thought the Greeks were very rude.

Page X-2

Why did the Greeks ask Sharon such "personal" questions?

1. The casual acquaintances were acting like friends do in Greece, although Sharon did not realize it.

Go to page X-3

2. The Greeks asked Sharon the questions in order to determine whether she belonged to the Greek Orthodox Church.

Go to page X-4

3. The Greeks were unhappy about the way in which she lived and they were trying to get Sharon to change her habits.

Go to page X-5

4. In Greece such questions are perfectly proper when asked of women, but improper when asked of men.

Go to page X-6

Page X-3

You selected 1: The casual acquaintances were acting like friends do in Greece, although Sharon did not realize it.

Correct. It is not improper for in-group members to ask these questions of one another. Furthermore, these questions reflect the fact that friendships (even "casual" ones) tend to be more intimate in Greece than in America. As a result, friends are generally free to ask questions which would seem too personal in America.

Go to page X-1

Page X-4

You selected 2: The Greeks asked Sharon the questions in order to determine whether she belonged to the Greek Orthodox Church.

No. This is not why the Greeks asked Sharon such questions. Remember, whether or not some information is "personal" depends upon the culture. In this case, the Greeks did not consider these questions too "personal." Why? Try again.

Go to page X-1

Page X-5

You selected 3: The Greeks were unhappy about the way in which she lived and they were trying to get Sharon to change her habits.

No. There was no information given to lead you to believe that the Greeks were unhappy with Sharon's way of living. The episode states that the Greeks were acquaintances of Sharon.

Go to page X-1

Page X-6

You selected 4: In Greece such questions are perfectly proper when asked of women, but improper when asked of men.

No. Such questions are indeed proper under certain situations. However, sex has nothing to do with it. When are these questions proper? Try to apply what you have learned about proper behavior between friends in Greece. Was Sharon regarded as a friend by these Greeks?

Go to page X-1

Source: Adapted from Fred E. Fiedler, Terence Mitchell, and Harry C. Triandis, "The Culture Assimilator: An Approach to Cross-Cultural Training," *Journal of Applied Psychology,* April 1971, pp. 97–98.

are written, the process is validated. Making sure that the assimilator is valid is the crux of its effectiveness. One way to test an assimilator is to draw a sample from the target culture and ask these people to read the scenarios that have been written and choose the alternative they feel is most appropriate. If a large percentage of the group agrees that one of the alternatives is preferable, this scenario is used in the assimilator. If more than one of the four alternatives receives strong support, however, either the scenario and/or the alternatives are revised until there is general agreement or the scenario is dropped.

A second validation step is to ask the sample group to rate how important each episode is. This helps to identify those incidents that should be included and those that are of only marginal value and can be omitted.

After the final incidents are chosen, they are sequenced in the assimilator booklet. Similar cultural concepts are placed together and presented, beginning with simple situations and progressing to more complex ones. Most cultural assimilator programs start out with 150 to 200 incidents, of which 75 to 100 eventually are included in the final product.

The Cost–Benefit Analysis of Assimilators   The assimilator approach to training can be quite expensive. A typical 75- to 100-incident program often requires approximately 800 hours to develop. Assuming that a training specialist is costing the company $50 an hour including benefits, the cost is around $40,000 per assimilator. This cost can be spread over many trainees, however, and the program may not need to be changed every year. An MNC that sends 40 people a year to a foreign country for which an assimilator has been constructed is paying only $200 per person for this programmed training. In the long run, the costs often are more than justified. In addition, the concept can be applied to virtually all cultures. Many different assimilators have been constructed, including Arab, Thai, Honduran, and Greek, to name but four. Most importantly, research shows that these assimilators improve the effectiveness and satisfaction of those being trained as compared with other training methods.[40]

Other Approaches

In addition to assimilators, a variety of other approaches are used in preparing managers for international assignments. These include visits to the host country, briefings by host-country managers, in-house management programs, and training in local negotiation techniques.[41]

The best "mix" of training often is determined by the individual's length of stay. The longer that a person will be assigned to an international locale, the greater the depth and intensity of the training should be. Figure 15-2 illustrates this idea. Using the model in this figure, if the expected level of interaction is low and the degree of similarity between the individual's culture and the host culture is high, the length of the training should be less than a week, and methods such as area and cultural briefings should be used. Conversely, if the level of interaction is going to be high and the individual will be gone for 1 to 3 years, use of assessment centers, field experiences, and simulations should be considered. The degree, type, and length of training is a result of expected integration and length of stay. Simply put, today's MNCs use a contingency approach in developing their training strategy.

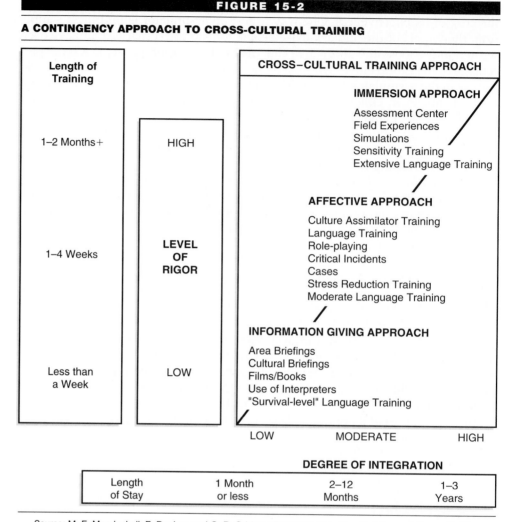

FIGURE 15-2

A CONTINGENCY APPROACH TO CROSS-CULTURAL TRAINING

Source: M. E. Mendenhall, E. Dunbar, and G. R. Oddou, "Expatriate Selection, Training and Career-Pathing: A Review and Critique," *Human Resource Management,* Fall 1987, p. 338. Used with permission. © 1987. Reprinted by permission of John Wiley & Sons, Inc.

ORGANIZATION DEVELOPMENT

Organization development (OD) has been broadly defined as the deliberate and reasoned introduction, establishment, reinforcement, and spread of change for the purpose of improving an organization's effectiveness and health. The OD process has been widely used in the United States and Western Europe to help organizations identify problems that are associated with change and to formulate effective solutions.

Nature of OD

A basic purpose of OD is to reconcile individual-group-organization differences. Two of the most common reasons for this reconciliation are: (1) individual or group conflicts in the organization are resulting in a loss of overall effectiveness;

and (2) the organization is introducing changes, such as new technology, and efforts must be made to gain acceptance by the personnel.

Most OD efforts are led by an individual who is skilled in the behavioral sciences and knows how to guide and facilitate the introduction and implementation of change effectively. This OD change agent typically will use one or more OD interventions. *OD intervention* is a catch-all term used to describe the structured activity in which targeted individuals, groups, or units engage in accomplishing task goals that relate to organization development. There are many examples of OD interventions. Some are fairly simple and designed to improve individual or interpersonal behavioral skills. Others are more sophisticated and involve large groups or even the entire organization. Some of the most common interventions include the following:

- *Team building.* An extension of classic T-groups (training groups) and sensitivity training, which were designed to help the participants better understand themselves and each other, team building is geared more to improving organizational effectiveness through co-operation and a "team" effort by key personnel.
- *Management by objectives (MBO).* A management system for the joint setting of subordinate goals, coaching and counseling the personnel, and providing feedback on their performance.
- *Confrontation meetings.* The gathering and analysis of information related to intra- or intergroup conflict, followed by formulation of a plan of action by the participants to resolve these problems.
- *Third-party peacemaking.* The diagnosis of group conflict followed by use of an outside party (usually the OD change agent) to facilitate a constructive resolution of the situation.
- *Survey feedback.* Often more detailed and long-range than the confrontation meeting, this intervention involves the gathering and analysis of information related to group behavior and problems and the feeding back of this information to develop effective action plans.

Table 15-5 provides a classification of the interventions just described as well as other common interventions. Note that these interventions can focus on the individual, groups of two or three people, large groups, intergroup relations, or the total organization. The OD intervention that is used will be determined by the particular problems that are uncovered after an OD change agent analyzes the situation.

Research shows that in most cases, success of an OD intervention depends on a number of important conditions. These include:

1. Use of an outside OD consultant who will collect the data, determine how best to deal with the problem, and lead the intervention.
2. Support for the effort from all levels of management.
3. Proper implementation of the OD intervention.
4. Follow-up to ensure that once things are improved, they do not slip back.

OD in International Settings

Can OD techniques be applied successfully in international settings? Researchers have found that although OD interventions can be useful, some limitations are

TABLE 15-5

CLASSIFICATION OF OD INTERVENTIONS BY TARGET GROUPS

Target Group	Types of interventions
Interventions designed to improve the effectiveness of INDIVIDUALS	Life- and career-planning activities Role analysis technique Coaching and counseling T-group (sensitivity training) Education and training to increase skills, knowledge in the areas of technical task needs; relationship skills; process skills; decision-making, problem-solving, planning, and goal-setting skills Grid OD phase 1 (leadership style training) Some forms of job enrichment Gestalt OD (wholistic, systems approach) Transactional analysis
Interventions designed to improve the effectiveness of DYADS/TRIADS	Process consultation Third-party peacemaking Grid OD phases 1, 2 (leadership style training) Gestalt OD (wholistic, systems approach) Transactional analysis
Interventions designed to improve the effectiveness of TEAMS and GROUPS	Team building—Task-directed Process-directed Family T-group (sensitivity training) Survey feedback Process consultation Role analysis technique "Start-up" team-building activities Education in decision making, problem solving, planning, and goal setting in group settings Some forms of job enrichment and MBO (management by objectives) Sociotechnical systems (technical-human interaction)
Interventions designed to improve the effectiveness of INTERGROUP RELATIONS	Intergroup activities—Process-directed Task-directed Organizational mirroring (three or more groups) Structural interventions Process consultation Third-party peacemaking at group level Grid OD phase 3 (leadership style training) Survey feedback
Interventions designed to improve the effectiveness of the TOTAL ORGANIZATION	Technostructural activities such as collateral organizations Confrontational meetings Strategic planning activities Grid OD phases 4, 5, 6 Survey feedback Interventions based on Lawrence and Lorsch's contingency theory Interventions based on Likert's Systems 1–4 Physical settings

Source: Wendell L. French and Cecil H. Bell, Jr., *Organization Development*, 4th ed. © 1990, p. 122. Reprinted by permission of Prentice-Hall, Inc., Englewood Cliffs, N.J.

caused by cultural barriers. Bourgeois and Boltvinik, for example, note that in South America, egalitarian social principles do not attract as much support as in the United States. This results in a lack of democratic management, communication, and trust among the personnel and personal willingness to participate in decision making. They observe:

Authoritarian management styles are not only accepted, but practically demanded by both Latin American workers and subordinate managers. Recent research has confirmed that, at least among Mexican managers, the perceived need to share information and objectives with subordinates is less than it typically is among American managers; there is also less belief in participative management styles. Any offer made to a Latin American subordinate to participate in decision making would not only be met with bewilderment but would result in a lowering of respect for the superior. With the acceptance of autocratic style comes complete faith in the superior's competence and wisdom. Any request for subordinate input would erode this faith and be perceived as a sign of weakness.[42]

Another major problem is language. Some of the words and concepts that are used in OD do not translate into Spanish. For example, although there in concept, the actual word *compromise* does not exist in Spanish. As a result, there may be confusion and many of the conditions critical to the success of OD change efforts are missing. Thus, many OD techniques will not work well in South American cultures.

There also are problems in applying OD in regions such as Europe, Asia, and Australia. As noted in Chapter 4, four cultural dimensions are given major attention. Two of these are power distance and uncertainty avoidance. In a typical OD intervention, participants are asked to share information, be open and honest in their communications, listen to what is being said by others, and work as a team to identify and resolve problems. This process requires the individuals to let down their guard and take the chance that they will be embarrassed or have their egos bruised. Participants who do these things must have low power distance. They must be willing to treat everyone else as an equal and not allow hierarchical rank or status to affect their interaction with the other individuals.

At the same time, participants must have low uncertainty avoidance. They must be able to live with ambiguity. Hofstede's research shows that few countries have these two dimensions of low power distance and low uncertainty avoidance. He found the four countries that best fit this cultural pattern are Denmark, Sweden, Ireland, and Great Britain. Jamaica also is a good candidate because of its low uncertainty avoidance, although it does have moderately high power distance. The United States, Canada, Australia, and others in that cluster also are good candidates for OD, although not as good as the Denmark cluster.[43] The overall conclusion is fairly obvious: OD interventions in many cases do not work well overseas, because the culture does not lend itself to these techniques. This is particularly true of unstructured interventions such as team building.[44]

Even management by objectives, which is so popular in the United States, has not been widely accepted. Comparing its success in the United States with that in Germany and France, Jaeger has noted that

in Germany, which scores quite a bit higher on uncertainty avoidance, MBO has become management by joint goal setting, mitigating some of the risk and emphasizing the team approach, which is in line also with the lower individualism present in the German culture.

In France, MBO has generally run into problems. . . . The original DPO (Director par Objectifs) became DPPO (Direction Participative par Objectifs) after the 1968 student revolts: "anything that fostered participation and decentralization was welcomed." Nevertheless, the high power distance to which the French are accustomed from childhood ultimately has thwarted the successful utilization of MBO as a truly participative process. Trepo notes that the problem is not necessarily with MBO per se but its implementation by French managers. He describes examples of managers who are unaware that they are trying to exert control through the implementation of the objectives of MBO almost by fiat.[45]

Similarly, the confrontation meeting, with its strong emphasis on low uncertainty avoidance and power distance, is particularly, inappropriate in areas such as South America, the Mediterranean, Japan, Pakistan, Iran, Thailand, and Taiwan.[46] However, some OD interventions do seem to have value. Third-party peacemaking is particularly compatible in many cultures, and if handled correctly, survey feedback could be used in countries with high uncertainty avoidance and power distance. Jaeger comments:

> Survey feedback generates data that at first may be looked at in a dispassionate way, without generating uncertainty or raising questions that would overstep the boundaries of hierarchy. Thus, an evaluation of the data can proceed slowly and not reach sensitive issues very quickly, if at all. With survey feedback one also has some control over the type of data generated, as the consultant can decide which questions are asked. A culturally sensitive consultant can therefore put together a questionnaire that generates data in such a way that a problem can be defined and discussed without upsetting the power relationships present. Hence, survey feedback could be an appropriate intervention even in those countries . . . that have high uncertainty avoidance and high power distance.[47]

In addition, OD practitioners can improve the chances of effectively using these techniques by accepting that cross-cultural OD interventions must be adapted to local conditions. Joint efforts with local practitioners can be of particular value. OD practitioners also need to learn the language of the country where the intervention is used to facilitate the exchange of information between participants and the OD change agent. The change agent can gain participant assistance in modifying the intervention for local use. As Bourgeois and Boltvinik have noted: "The straightforward transfer of American organizational development technologies to an alien cultural setting could have deleterious consequences for both the focal organization and the individuals in it if a concerted effort is not made to recognize and compensate for the potential conflicts inherent in applying its value-laden techniques in foreign organizations."[48]

Global Leadership Development

Another current trend of human resource development is to focus on leadership.[49] Tichy has noted that a number of leadership training approaches can be used. As shown in Figure 15-3, these range from awareness to cognitive and conceptual understanding to the development of skills and then on to new problem-solving approaches and, ultimately, fundamental change. In this process, management development becomes deeper, involves greater risk, incorporates a longer-term time horizon, and focuses on organization (rather than just individual) change.

At the same time, effective MNCs now encourage strong leadership in the areas of both hard and soft organizational issues. Examples of hard issues include the budget, manufacturing, marketing, distribution, and finance; soft issues address values, culture, vision, leadership style, and innovative behavior. In exercising strong leadership on hard organizational issues, attention is focused on becoming a low-cost provider of goods and services. In exercising strong leadership on soft organizational issues, the emphasis is on developing and maintaining innovativeness.

FIGURE 15-3

THE TICHY DEVELOPMENT MATRIX

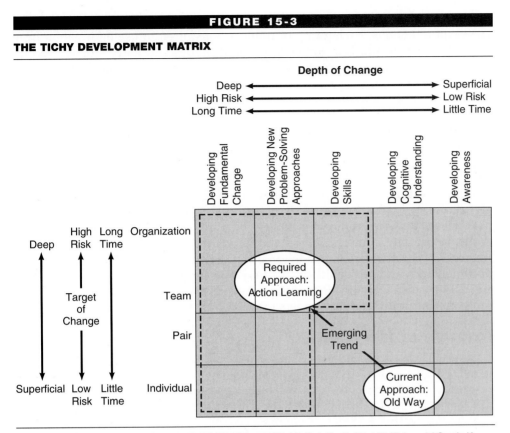

Source: Reported in Noel M. Tichy, "Global Development," in Vladimir Pucik, Noel M. Tichy, and Carole K. Barnett (eds.), *Globalizing Management* (New York: John Wiley, 1993), pp. 206–224.

GLP Program   One of the best examples of the emerging leadership development program used by MNCs is the Global Leadership Program (GLP), which is a consortium of leading U.S., European, and Japanese firms, global faculty, and participating host countries. Here is how the GLP has been described:

> The companies are part of an ongoing partnership started in 1988 jointly committed to research and development on issues of globalization. The program design, facilities, and support staff are directed by core faculty from universities in the United States, Europe, and Japan. The members of the consortium participate in a research partnership and in an intensive 5-week Global Leadership Program designed for senior executives with CEO potential.[50]

The GLP is designed to provide participants with an intensive international experience to develop a global mindset, instill cross-cultural competency, and provide the opportunity for global networking. The program is 5 weeks in duration, but before attending, each person is given specially prepared briefing materials about the country that he or she will visit. At the beginning, participants are asked to complete the survey instruments that are designed to assess the individual's perceptions regarding the characteristics of a global organization, dimensions of global leadership, and the way that managers carry out their global responsibilities.

The core of the program is a 2-week, on-site, country assessment carried out by cross-cultural teams. Each group of trainees is required to use information from the assessment to produce investment opportunities and entry strategy recommendations as well as video documentaries as part of their country assessment. Among other things, each team of trainees spends 2 weeks preparing for the country assessment by working on its personal global leadership capabilities and its global mindset and team skills. Preparation also includes a weekend at an Outward Bound school and a 2-day assessment in Washington, DC.

The GLP is designed to blend rigorous intellectual development of global leaders, beginning with each individual's map of his or her own personal global mindset. Then, these are shared with the members of each team, who then are responsible for creating an analytical framework to guide its assessment of a major geopolitical region of the world. By the second week of the program, the teams have started on their country assessment. During the third and fourth weeks, the participants split up and travel to their respective countries. During the fifth and last week of the program, the individuals write their reports and make their video documentaries and presentations. Because of its strong emphasis on involvement and action learning, the GLP has become one of the best recognized development programs for training global leaders for MNCs.

SUMMARY OF KEY POINTS

1. Training is the process of altering employee behavior and attitudes to increase the probability of goal attainment. Many expatriates need training before (as well as during) their overseas stay. A number of factors will influence a company's approach to training. One is the basic type of MNC: ethnocentric, polycentric, regiocentric, or geocentric. Another factor is the learning style of the trainees.

2. There are two primary reasons for training: organizational and personal. Organizational reasons include overcoming ethnocentrism, improving communication, and validating the effectiveness of training programs. Personal reasons include improving the ability of expatriates to interact locally and increasing the effectiveness of leadership styles. There are two types of training programs: standard and tailor-made. Research shows that small firms usually rely on standard programs and larger MNCs tailor their training. The six major types of training include environmental briefings, cultural orientation, cultural assimilators, language training, sensitivity training, and field experience.

3. A cultural assimilator is a programmed learning approach that is designed to expose members of one culture to some of the basic concepts, attitudes, role perceptions, customs, and values of another. Assimilators have been developed for many different cultures. Their validity has resulted in the improved effectiveness and satisfaction of those being trained as compared with other training methods.

4. Organization development (OD) is the deliberate and reasoned introduction, establishment, reinforcement, and spread of change for the purpose of improving an organization's effectiveness. The basic purpose of OD is to reconcile individual-group-organization differences, often accomplished through the use of OD interventions such as team building, MBO, confrontation meetings, third-party peacemaking, and survey feedback.

5. Research shows that OD interventions often are less effective in international settings. One primary reason is that many cultures do not have low power distance or low uncertainty avoidance, which are two key dimensions for successful OD efforts. This is why team building has not worked well and MBO has been greatly modified. On the other hand, third-party peacemaking and survey feedback have been successful, because they can be adapted to the two cultural dimensions of power distance and uncertainty avoidance.

KEY TERMS

training

ethnocentric MNC

polycentric MNC

regiocentric MNC

geocentric MNC

learning

ethnocentrism

factual manager

intuitive manager

analytical manager

normative manager

cultural assimilator

validity

organization development (OD)

OD intervention

team building

management by objectives (MBO)

confrontation meetings

third-party peacemaking

survey feedback

REVIEW AND DISCUSSION QUESTIONS

1. How do the following types of MNCs differ: ethnocentric, polycentric, regiocentric, and geocentric? Which most likely would provide international management training to its people? Which would least likely provide international management training to its people?
2. IBM is planning on sending three managers to its Zurich office, two to Madrid, and two to Tokyo. None of these individuals has any international experience. Would you expect the company to use a standard training program or a tailor-made program for each group?
3. Ford Motor now is in the process of training managers for overseas assignments. Why might this MNC want to learn the managerial styles (factual, intuitive, analytical, and normative) of each person? Of what value would this be in the training process? Give two examples.
4. Zygen, Inc., a medium-sized manufacturing firm, is planning to enter into a joint venture in China. Would training be of any value to those managers who will be part of this venture? If so, what types of training would you recommend?
5. Hofstadt & Hoerr, a German-based insurance firm, is planning on expanding out of the EU and opening offices in Chicago and Buenos Aires. How would a cultural assimilator be of value in training the MNC's expatriates? Is the assimilator a valid training tool?
6. Why would an MNC be interested in using OD techniques? What are their benefits? What are their limitations? On balance, how useful are they?

PRACTICAL INTERNATIONAL MANAGEMENT ASSIGNMENT

Contact local organizations to see if they have been involved in an organizational development program. What has their success been? How could such a program be applied in a European operation? What modifications would have to be made for such an application of OD?

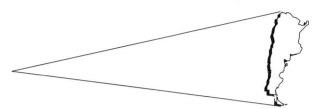

In Argentina, men, when meeting after a long absence, hug each other, while women clasp hands with both hands and kiss each other on the cheek.

In the International Spotlight

Argentina

Argentina occupies most of the southern part of South America. The country covers a triangular area of approximately 1.1 million square miles. It is bordered on the west by Chile, on the north by Bolivia and Paraguay, and on the east by Uruguay and the Atlantic Ocean. There are approximately 34 million people in the country (in South America, only Brazil is larger and has more people). People from many European countries settled Argentina, but most came from Spain and Italy. The urban Argentines thus have European customs and continue to draw from them in terms of fashion, art, literature, and architecture. Much of the country's wealth comes from the land (Argentina exports more beef than any other country). The economy during the 1980s had many problems, but in recent years, it has been improving. Both GDP and capital investments are increasing, and the inflation rate has gone from an unbelievable 3103 percent in 1989 to double digits today. As noted in one recent report, Argentine shopkeepers now dare to label prices in ink. The economic outlook for the future remains risky, but hopeful.

Despite the shaky economic conditions in Argentina, for the last 2 years Warren Worthy's U.S.-based company has been operating two shopping malls in Buenos Aires and one in Cordoba. The operations have not been as profitable as the company would like, but they are making money, un-like most of the rest of the retail industry in the country.

Earlier this year, Warren sent one of his senior-level management people, Paul Flexner, to look over the mall operations and see if there were any changes that might be made. Paul was met at the airport by one of the eight U.S. managers who held the top jobs in the Buenos Aires and Cordoba operations. Paul was accompanied by an interpreter. During his stay, Paul had an opportunity to look over the operations of the shopping malls and talk to many relevant parties. Paul was able to put together a number of recommendations that he was convinced could be useful. Overall, the major problem he felt was that the Americans being sent down from the United States did not have enough training or orientation to Argentinean culture and language. When Paul asked one of the expatriate managers about this, he was tersely told, "Oh, we pick up things as we go along. If there's something I don't understand, I ask my interpreter. These guys are worth their weight in gold down here."

Paul also noticed that the U.S. managers remained aloof in terms of involvement. Their style was to give orders and then depend on the Argentineans who worked for them to implement the decisions. Paul believes that the reason for this approach is that the Americans are not really sure of how to do things, so they prefer not to get too involved. On his return to the United States, Paul is going to recommend that a detailed training program be put together and that no one be sent to Argentina until he or she has successfully completed this course. In particular, Paul wants to see major emphasis given to culture and language training. Before leaving, he mentioned some of his ideas to one of the U.S. managers, but the expatriate did not seem very receptive. "Oh, it's not necessary to go through all of that trouble," he told Paul. "We're doing just fine by relying on interpreters."

1. What are some current issues facing Argentina? What is the climate for doing business in Argentina today?
2. Do you agree with Paul that language training is needed?
3. Should the firm develop a standardized or a tailor-made training program?
4. What are some things that Americans need to know about management styles in South America? In your answer, incorporate data from Table 15-2.

You Be the International Management Consultant

A Southern Expansion

A small but rapidly growing U.S. irrigation equipment company is thinking about expanding its operations into the South American market. Founded 8 years ago, the firm has annual sales of $25 million and is growing at a 25 percent annually compounded rate. Most of these sales are in the United States, although the company has been trying to penetrate the Indian market and had sales of $1 million there last year.

The company sells a patented piece of irrigation equipment that has proven performance capabilities. The biggest problem for the firm is that many buyers prefer better-known companies' products, so it has to compete vigorously based on price. Thus, the board of directors is considering entering markets that are not as competitive. "There is very little irrigation equipment selling in South America," the chair of the board recently told top management. "Why don't we look into this market and see if we can develop a foothold. Admittedly, the agricultural community down there won't be as knowledgeable as they are in the states, but we could end up getting in on the ground floor."

Following up this suggestion, the company sent three representatives to South America to investigate the market. These individuals all agreed that there is a large, untapped potential in the region that could be the base for a very profitable foreign venture. As a result, the company has drafted a preliminary plan of action for doing business in Argentina, Brazil, Chile, and Colombia. If sales are sufficient in these four countries, the firm will then expand to other South American locations. The company wants to enter into a business arrangement with foreign partners whereby the firm provides the equipment and the partners handle the selling activities. Each country would have a central sales office that would serve as the link between the firm and its local foreign-run outlets. The head of this sales office would be a U.S. American appointed by company headquarters' senior management. This individual would be responsible for providing assistance to the local outlets and keeping headquarters' senior management informed about developments in the region. The sales office head would have a small staff consisting of two expatriates and three locals.

Initial plans call for setting up the first unit in each country within the next 18 months and, if things go according to plan, expanding coverage to an average of three outlets per country within the first 3 years. In each case, the company will set up the initial units in the country's agricultural centers and then slowly expand into other areas.

1. What type of training would you recommend for the expatriate managers?
2. Would you recommend the use of cultural assimilators? If no, why not? If yes, for whom?
3. If there are operating problems, would it be possible to use OD techniques to resolve them?

CHAPTER 15 ENDNOTES

1. Richard M. Hodgetts and Donald F. Kuratko, *Management*, 3rd ed. (San Diego: Harcourt Brace Jovanovich, 1991), p. 329.

2. Richard Mead, *International Management* (Cambridge, MA: Blackwell Publishers, 1994), Chapter 16.

3. Lennie Copeland, "Making Costs Count in International Travel," *Personnel Administrator*, July 1984, p. 47.

4. Robert C. Maddox and Douglas Short, "The Cultural Integrator," *Business Horizons*, November-December 1988, pp. 57–59.

5. Chris Brewster and Juana Pickard, "Evaluating Expatriate Training," *International Studies of Management and Organization*, vol. 24, no. 3, 1994, pp. 18–35.

6. Charlene Marmer Solomon, "Global Operations Demand that HR Rethink Diversity," *Personnel Journal*, July 1994, p. 50.

7. J. Stewart Black and Mark Mendenhall, "Cross Cultural Training Effectiveness: A Review and a Theoretical Framework for Future Research," *Academy of Management Review*, January 1990, pp. 113–136.

8. Brian O'Reilly, "How Execs Learn Now," *Fortune*, April 5, 1993, pp. 52–55.

9. Fred Luthans, *Organizational Behavior*, 7th ed. (New York: McGraw-Hill, 1995), Chapter 8.

10. J. Hayes and C. W. Allinson, "Cultural Differences in the Learning Styles of Managers," *Management International Review*, vol. 28, no. 3, 1988, p. 76.

11. Ibid., p. 79.

12. Ibid., pp. 75–80.

13. Ibid., p. 79.

14. Also see Joel Cutcher-Gershenfeld et al., "Japanese Team-Based Work Systems in North America: Explaining the Diversity," *California Management Review*, Fall 1994, pp. 42–64.

15. See Kalburgi M. Srinivas, "Globalization of Business and the Third World," *Journal of Management Development*, vol. 14, no. 3, 1995, pp. 44–46; Donna L. Wiley, "Developing Managers in the Former Soviet Union," *International Studies of Management & Organization*, vol. 24, no. 4, 1994, pp. 64–82.

16. John R. Schermerhorn, "Intercultural Management Training: An Interview with Asma Abdullah," *Journal of Management Development*, vol. 13, no. 3, 1994, pp. 60–61.

17. Also see Schon Beechler and John Zhuang Yang, "The Transfer of Japanese-Style Management to American Subsidiaries: Contingencies, Constraints, and Competencies," *Journal of International Business Studies*, Third Quarter 1994, pp. 467–491.

18. Allan Bird and Schon Beechler, "Links Between Business Strategy and Human Resource Management Strategy in U.S.-Based Japanese Subsidiaries: An Empirical Investigation," *Journal of International Business Studies*, First Quarter 1995, p. 40.

19. Phillip C. Wright, "The Expatriate Family Firm and Cross-Cultural Management Training: A Conceptual Framework," *Human Resource Development Quarterly*, vol. 5, no. 2, 1994, pp. 153–167.

20. Yoram Zeira and Ehud Harari, "Host-Country Organizations and Expatriate Managers in Europe," *California Management Review*, Spring 1979, p. 42.

21. For more on this, see Tomoko Yoshida and Richard W. Breslin, "Intercultural Skills and Recommended Behaviors," in Oded Shenkar (ed.), *Global Perspectives of Human Resource Management* (Englewood Cliffs, NJ: Prentice-Hall, 1995), pp. 112–131.

22. Alan M. Barrett, "Training and Development of Expatriates and Home Country Nationals," in Oded Shenkar, *Global Perspectives of Human Resource Management* (Englewood Cliffs, NJ: Prentice-Hall, 1995), p. 135.

23. "Ready to Travel?" *BusinessWeek*, March 2, 1992, p. 46.

24. Zeira and Harari, "Host-Country Organizations," p. 43.

25. Also see Clinton O. Longenecker and Serguei Popovski, "Managerial Trials of Privatization: Retooling Russian Managers," *Business Horizons*, November-December 1994, pp. 35–43.

26. For more on this topic, see Ehud Harari and Yoram Zeira, "Training Expatriates for Managerial Assignments in Japan," *California Management Review*, Summer 1978, pp. 56–62.

27. Yukimo Ono, "Japanese Firms Don't Let Masters Rule," *Wall Street Journal*, May 4, 1992, p. B1.

28. Mark E. Mendenhall and Gary Oddou, "The Overseas Assignment: A Practical Look," *Business Horizons*, September-October 1988, p. 13.

29. Karen J. Lindberg, "The Intricacies of Training and Development in Japan," *Human Resource Development Quarterly*, vol. 2, no. 2, 1991, pp. 101–114; Sam Stern, "Invited Reaction: Training and Development in Japan—the Basis for Relationships," *Human Resource Development Quarterly*, vol. 2, no. 2, 1991, pp. 115–120.

30. Peter R. Schleger, "Making International Videos: An Odyssey," *Training and Development Journal*, February 1992, pp. 25–32.

31. Gary W. Hogan and Jane R. Goodson, "The Key to Expatriate Success," *Training and Development Journal*, January 1990, pp. 50–52.

32. Also see C. B. Derr and G. Oddou, "Internationalizing Managers: Speeding Up the Process," *European Management Journal*, December 1993, pp. 435–441.

33. Robert Cyr, "Client Relations in Japan," *Training and Development Journal,* September 1990, pp. 83–85.

34. Rosalie L. Tung, "Selection and Training Procedures of U.S., European, and Japanese Multinationals," *California Management Review,* Fall 1982, p. 65.

35. Ibid., pp. 66–67.

36. Michael J. Marquardt and Dean W. Engel, *Global Human Resource Management* (Englewood Cliffs, NJ: Prentice-Hall, 1995), p. 44.

37. Fred E. Fiedler, Terence Mitchell, and Harry C. Triandis, "The Culture Assimilator: An Approach to Cross-Cultural Training," *Journal of Applied Psychology,* April 1971, p. 95.

38. Ibid., p. 97.

39. For more on this topic, see Luthans, *Organizational Behavior,* pp. 34–37.

40. Fiedler, Mitchell, and Triandis, "The Culture Assimilator," p. 102.

41. Peter J. Dowling, Randall S. Schuler, and Denice E. Welch, *Human Resource Management,* 2nd ed. (Belmont, CA: Wadsworth Publishing Company, 1994), p. 134.

42. L. J. Bourgeois III and Manuel Boltvinik, "OD in Cross-Cultural Settings: Latin America," *California Management Review,* Spring 1981, p. 77.

43. Geert Hofstede, "The Cultural Relativity of Organizational Practices and Theories," *Journal of International Business Studies,* Fall 1983, p. 84.

44. Alfred M. Jaeger, "The Applicability of Organization Development Overseas: Reality or Myth?" *National Academy of Management Proceedings,* Boston, August 12–15, 1984, pp. 95–104.

45. Alfred M. Jaeger, "Organization Development and National Culture: Where's the Fit?" *Academy of Management Review,* January 1986, p. 185.

46. Ibid.

47. Alfred M. Jaeger, "The Appropriateness of Organization Development outside North America," *International Studies of Management & Organization,* Spring 1984, p. 32.

48. Bourgeois and Boltvinik, "OD in Cross-Cultural Settings," p. 80.

49. Noel M. Tichy, "Global Development," in Vladimir Pucik, Noel M. Tichy, and Carole K. Barnett (eds.), *Globalizing Management* (New York: John Wiley, 1993), pp. 206–224.

50. Ibid., p. 219.

LABOR RELATIONS AND INDUSTRIAL DEMOCRACY

OBJECTIVES OF THE CHAPTER

Besides personnel selection and repatriation (Chapter 14) as well as training and organization development (Chapter 15), another critical part of managing human resources in the international arena is how the MNC handles its labor relations. How domestic firms deal with their labor relations and determine union contracts can differ significantly from country to country. A second challenge, especially for those MNCs operating in Europe and Asia, is industrial democracy, which is much more prevalent there than in other parts of the world. A third challenge is the need to co-ordinate worldwide efforts through formulation of an effective labor relations strategy.

This chapter addresses these challenges. Initially, it examines labor relations in the international arena using the United States as the point of comparison. Next, the internationalism of labor unions is explored. The chapter then looks at the various approaches to industrial democracy that are employed in Europe and Asia. Finally, how MNCs attempt to integrate industrial relations into their overall strategy is reviewed. The specific objectives of this chapter are:

1. **DEFINE** "labor relations," and examine the approaches used in the United States and other countries.

2. **REVIEW** the international structure of labor unions.

3. **EXAMINE** the nature of industrial democracy, and note some of the major differences that exist throughout the world.

4. **DESCRIBE** the philosophical views and strategic approaches that are used by MNCs in managing international industrial relations.

451

TABLE 16-1			
PERCENTAGE OF THE WORK FORCE THAT IS UNIONIZED BY COUNTRY			
Country	Percentage	Country	Percentage
Sweden	85.3	India	28.0
Denmark	73.2	Taiwan	28.0
Norway	65.0	Mexico	26.0
Austria	61.0	Venezuela	25.0
Belgium	53.0	Japan	25.0
Ireland	52.4	Greece	25.0
Luxembourg	49.7	Netherlands	25.0
United Kingdom	42.0	Lebanon	20.0
Australia	41.0	South Korea	18.0
Italy	40.0	Singapore	16.5
Poland	40.0	Spain	16.0
Canada	35.0	France	12.0
Germany	35.0	United States	12.0
Portugal	30.0		

Source: M. Rothman, D. Briscoe, and R. Nacamulli (eds), *Industrial Relations Around the World* (Berlin: Walter de Gruyter, 1993); J. Visser, "Trade Union in Western Europe: Present Situation and Prospects," *Labour and Society,* vol. 13, no. 2, 1988, pp. 125–182; OECD, *Employment Outlook,* Paris 1991; and Dennis R. Briscoe, *International Human Resource Management* (Englewood Cliffs, NJ: Prentice-Hall, 1995), p. 154.

LABOR RELATIONS IN THE INTERNATIONAL ARENA

The term *labor relations* can be defined as the process through which management and workers identify and determine the job relationships that will be in effect at the workplace. These relationships often are communicated verbally, but in some cases, they also are written in the form of a contract, particularly when workers are represented by a union and a management–labor contract is negotiated and agreed to by both parties. As shown in Table 16-1, the percentage of workers who are union members varies widely by country. In Sweden, over 85 percent are unionized, while in France and the United States, only 12 percent are unionized.[1] Therefore, depending on the countries where it does business, an MNC will face varying degrees of organized labor challenges.

As in other areas of international human resource management, the specific approaches to labor relations will vary from country to country. Some nations employ a labor negotiation process similar to that in the United States, in which both sides have power; others are characterized by either a strong management group or a highly powerful union. This is true in terms of the way that labor agreements are negotiated and enforced as well as the way industrial conflicts are resolved. Using the U.S. approach to labor relations as a benchmark, the following sections discuss how this labor relations process is carried out in selected countries around the globe.

The U.S. Approach to Labor Relations

In the United States, formal labor agreements result from *collective bargaining,* in which union and management representatives negotiate wages, hours, and conditions of employment and administer the labor contract. A *union* is an organization that represents the workers and, in collective bargaining, has the legal authority to negotiate with the employer and to administer the labor contract. How collective bargaining is carried out in the United States often differs from how it is done in other countries because of the nature of U.S. labor laws.

For a work group to unionize in the United States, 30 percent of the workers must first sign authorization cards requesting that a specific union represent them in bargaining with the employer. If this percentage is met, the union can petition the National Labor Relations Board (NLRB) to hold an election. When this is done, it will be certified as the bargaining agent if the union receives more than 50 percent of the workers' votes. The two sides then will meet and hammer out a labor contract. This agreement typically remains in effect for 2 to 3 years. When it expires, a new agreement is negotiated, and assuming that the union continues to represent the workers, the cycle continues anew. If the workers are dissatisfied with their representation, they can vote out the union and go back to things the way they were before.[2]

Note that if the workers support the union but that union is unable to negotiate a labor agreement that is acceptable to them, the workers may go on strike to pressure management to agree to their terms. Management, however, can bring sanctions of its own, including locking out employees or hiring strike breakers (called "scabs" by union members) to fill the positions of those who refuse to work. This happened in the highly publicized air traffic controllers strike when President Reagan replaced the striking controllers and broke the union. Unlike those in most other countries, however, labor strikes in the United States almost always are confined to periods when the contract is being renegotiated. Strikes seldom are used in the middle of the labor contract agreement, because mechanisms such as a grievance procedure can be employed.

Steps of a Grievance Procedure   A *grievance* is a complaint brought by an employee who feels that he or she has been treated improperly under the terms of the labor agreement. In the United States, efforts are made to solve these problems at the lowest level of the hierarchy and as quickly as possible. The contract will spell out the specific steps in the grievance procedure. The first step usually involves a meeting of the union representative at the operating level (commonly called the "shop steward") and the supervisor, who attempt to agree on how to solve the grievance. If it is not solved at this level, the grievance may go to the next steps, involving union officials and higher-level management representatives. These conciliatory approaches usually solve the grievance to the satisfaction of both parties. Sometimes, however, the matter ends up in the hands of a mediator or an arbitrator.[3]

Mediation and Arbitration   A *mediator* brings both sides together and helps them to reach a settlement that is mutually acceptable. An *arbitrator* provides a solution to a grievance that both sides have been unable to resolve themselves and that both sides agree to accept. A number of arbitration approaches typically are used. In resolving wage-related issues, for example, three of the most common include: (1) splitting the difference between the demands of the two parties; (2) using an either–or approach, in which one side's position is fully supported and the other side's rejected; and (3) determining a fair wage based on market conditions.

INTERNATIONAL MANAGEMENT IN ACTION

They're Leading the Pack

Many believe that MNCs are attracted to Third World locations because of labor relations policies that are conducive to co-operation, low wages, and productivity. In truth, the United States is still proving to be one of the most attractive locations for international firms. Although the power of U.S. labor unions is declining, the labor relations climate is conducive to rising productivity. Today, the United States is not only the most productive nation in the world, its overall productivity is increasing faster than that of the other major industrial powers, such as Japan, Germany, and France. The Japanese economy has been having trouble since the early 1990s, and the surging value of the yen has reduced its international competitiveness. Despite having some of the most successful MNCs in the world (e.g., Hitachi, Mitsubishi, Sony, and Toyota), Japan is experiencing some difficulties. The same is true in Europe. Many MNCs on the continent now are engaged in painful restructuring that is designed to make them more efficient and competitive in world markets. Their governments fight such downsizing, however, because of the negative impact on employment. As a result, firms such as Daimler Benz and Volkswagen in Germany and Alcatel Alsthom in France continue to face the challenge of becoming more efficient on the one hand and accommodating government directives to hire more people on the other. These are problems that U.S. MNCs do not yet face, and it helps them to maintain high productivity. There also are other reasons why U.S. productivity is doing so well relative to the rest of the world.

One is that the U.S. work ethic seems to be stronger than ever. For example, U.S. workers now are working more hours per week than they did 20 years ago. Other major economic powers such as Germany and Japan are finding just the opposite; their people are working shorter workweeks than at any time in the past. In Japan, for example, the average manufacturing worker today puts in approximately 20 percent fewer hours than in 1960, and this downward trend likely will continue. A couple of reasons are that many Japanese feel they already make enough money to take care of their needs, and many claim that they are fed up with hard work. Even Japanese union members oppose lengthening the workweek, despite efforts from their leadership to co-operate with the companies and put in more hours. Part of this opposition is a belief among the rank-and-file Japanese workers that the union represents the company's interests rather than their interests.

A second factor is that labor costs in the United States actually are lower in recent years than in most other major industrial countries. Thanks to union–management co-operation, U.S. companies have been able to introduce high-tech, efficient machinery. As a result, firms such as Ford and Chrysler now can manufacture cars at lower prices than foreign competitors can. Moreover, as Ford and Chrysler continue closing outmoded plants and running others at close to capacity, costs per car should decline even further. Much of this outcome is a result of effective labor relations strategies and shows that U.S. manufacturers not only are back in the ballgame but, in many cases, may be leading the pack.

Importance of Positive Labor Relations   Labor relations are important, because they directly determine labor costs, productivity, and eventually, even profits. The accompanying box, "International Management in Action: They're Leading the Pack," gives details on some of the benefits from healthy labor relations. If the union and management do not have good relations, the organization's cost of doing business likely will be higher than it otherwise would be. In fact, in recent years, many MNCs entering the United States have been looking for sites where they can set up nonunion plants. They are convinced that unions make them less competitive. This conviction certainly is debatable, although some MNCs have been particularly effective in keeping out unions. One example is the Japanese Nissan plant in Smyrna, Tennessee, which to date has continually defeated union efforts.

Labor Relations in Other Countries

Because labor relations strategies vary greatly from country to country, MNCs find that the strategy used in one country sometimes is irrelevant or of limited value in another. A number of factors can account for this. One is the economic development of the country, given that general labor relations strategies often change as a country's economic situation changes. In addition, entry strategies often must be modified as the firm begins to settle in. Changes in the political environment also must be taken into consideration. For example, under the Thatcher government, British labor unions had a difficult time; in fact, prounion recognition provisions that were legislated in the mid-1970s were repealed in the 1980s. With the recent election of John Major as prime minister, the conservatives continue to dominate. As a result, British unions continue to lose power.

Still another factor is strike activity. Unions in many countries often call strikes in the middle of a contract period. These strike decisions often catch the company unprepared and result in lost productivity and profit as the firm tries to negotiate with the union and/or transfer work to other geographic locales and minimize the economic effect.

Other differences are more regional in nature. For example, labor relations throughout Europe are somewhat similar, but they differ sharply from those in the United States. Some of these differences in European labor relations include:

1. In Europe, firms typically negotiate their agreements with unions at the national level, through employer associations representing their particular industries, even when there also is local, within-company negotiations. This national agreement establishes certain minimum conditions of employment that frequently are augmented through bargaining with the union at the firm or the local level.
2. Unions in many European countries have more political power than those in the United States, so when employers deal with their union(s), they in effect often are dealing directly or indirectly with the government. Unions often are allied with a particular political party—generally referred to as the labor party, although in some countries these alliances are more complex, such as a number of different political parties, each supported and primarily identified with a particular union or set of unions.
3. There is a greater tendency in Europe for salaried employees, including those at managerial levels, to be unionized, often in a union of their own.
4. Unions in most European countries have existed longer than those in the United States. Consequently, they occupy a more accepted position in society and are less concerned about gaining approval.[4]

The following sections examine industrial relations approaches in a number of selected countries.

Great Britain   In contrast to the situation in the United States, the labor agreement in Great Britain is not a legally binding contract. It is merely an "understanding" among the parties that sets forth the terms and conditions of employment that are acceptable at present. Violations of the agreement by the union or management carry no legal penalties, because the contract cannot be enforced in court.

Labor agreements in Great Britain typically are less extensive than those in the United States. These understandings usually contain provisions that define the structure of the relationships among the parties and set forth procedures for handling complaints. Typically, however, there is no provision for arbitration of disagreements or grievances, although both mediation and arbitration on occasion are used.

Germany   Traditionally, unions and management in Germany have had a more co-operative relationship than those in the United States, where an adversarial relationship often has existed. While some observers believe that the unification of West and East Germany will increase labor conflict,[5] much of this pessimism is a result of the government's failure to formulate an overall blueprint for integrating the two countries.[6] As this integration is fully accomplished, labor harmony should improve. Certainly, on an overall basis, there is a spirit of co-operation between German management and labor brought about by, among other things, the use of industrial democracy, in which workers serve on the board of directors and ensure that the rank and file are treated fairly. A detailed discussion of industrial democracy is given toward the end of this chapter.

Union power in Germany is quite strong. Although union membership is voluntary, there generally is one union in each major industry. This powerful industry union will negotiate a contract with the employers' federation for the industry, and the contract will cover all major issues, including wages and terms of employment. All firms that are members of the employers' federation then will pay the agreed-on wages. Firms that are not members of the federation typically will use the contract as a guide to what they should pay their people. Although a minority of the labor force is organized, unions set the pay scale for about 90 percent of the country's workers, with wages determined by job classifications. If an individual is replaced because of automation or laid off because of declining business, the worker's wage settlement also is handled according to the previously determined agreement. Still other agreements are hammered out to cover general working conditions, work hours, overtime pay, personal leave, and vacations.

If there is a conflict over interpretation or enforcement of the agreement, the situation typically is negotiated between the company and the worker with participation of a union representative and/or work council. If an impasse is reached, the situation can be referred to a German labor court for final settlement.

In recent years, some German unions have become more adversarial. For example, IG Metall union has been adopting an approach in dealing with employers that is more like that used in the United States.[7] Overall, however, the labor relations climate in Germany traditionally is much more serene than in the United States, and most unions lack the firepower to engage in prolonged strikes.[8] One primary reason is that the rights of workers are addressed more carefully by management. A second is that even though they are covered by a labor contract, individual workers are free to negotiate either individually or collectively with management to secure wages and benefits that are superior to those in the agreement.

Japan   Unions and management have a co-operative relationship in Japan. One reason is social custom, which dictates nonconfrontational union–management behavior. The provisions in Japanese labor agreements usually are general and vague, although they are legally enforceable. Disputes regarding the agreement often are settled in an amicable manner. Sometimes, they are resolved by third-party mediators or arbitrators. Labor commissions have been established by law, and these groups, as well as the courts, can help to resolve negotiations impasses.

Japanese unions are most active during the spring and again at the end of the year, because these are the two periods during which bonuses are negotiated. Recently, Japanese unions, like the German unions, have been trying to extend wage bargaining to cover all firms in a particular industry. This would provide the union with greater negotiating power over the individual firms within the industry. Their success in this industrywide bargaining strategy would have particular impact on MNCs operating in Japan. Compared with those of most other industrialized countries, however, Japanese unions remain relatively weak.

How Industrial Conflict Is Handled around the World

When the union and management reach an impasse in contract negotiations or over some issue, conflict results. The union may call for a strike, or management may have a lockout. A *strike* is a collective refusal to work to pressure management to grant union demands. In recent years, strikes have been less common in most countries; however, when measured in terms of working days lost per 1000 employees, strikes are still a powerful weapon in dealing with industrial conflict. Figure 16-1 presents some of the latest strike-related data for major industrial nations. A *lockout* is the company's refusal to allow workers to enter the facility. Other typical union strategies resulting from conflict include slowdowns, sabotage, sit-ins, and boycotts. The following sections show how these approaches are handled around the world.

United States   Most U.S. labor contracts have a specific provision that outlaws strikes; thus, sudden or unauthorized strikes (commonly called "wildcat strikes") are uncommon. If either party to the contract feels that the other is not acting in good faith or living up to the terms, the grievance procedure is used to resolve the matter peacefully. However, once the contract period is over and if a new one is not successfully negotiated, the workers may strike or continue to work without a contract while threatening to walk out. On the other side, management also may lock out the workers, although this is much more rare. The modern position of more and more U.S. unions is that a philosophy of "us against them" is not as conducive to the long-range welfare of the union as is a strategy of working together to find common ground. In this regard, U.S. unions are moving closer to the approach that is used by many unions in other countries.

Great Britain   In Great Britain, labor unions are relatively powerful (although this power has been eroded in recent years), and strikes are more prevalent than in the United States. Labor agreements typically do not prohibit strikes, and the general public is more used to and tolerant of them. Strikes in Britain often are brief, however, and do not involve a large number of people, although British miners did have prolonged strikes during the 1980s.

Some labor experts believe that industrial conflict in Britain results in more problems than in the United States, because the system is not geared toward the efficient resolution of problems. For example, many in the British general public as well as the workers believe that it is management's job to look after workers, and failure to do so is a breach of management's social responsibility. This climate often results in hard feelings and impedes rapid solutions. In addition, the procedure for handling grievances, in contrast to that used in the United States, often is informal, cumbersome, and sometimes results in fragmented efforts with the outcome costly in terms of both time and money. Sometimes, management uses the lockout to vent its frustration over the bureaucratic delays in resolving labor-related problems. Although things have been changing for the better in recent

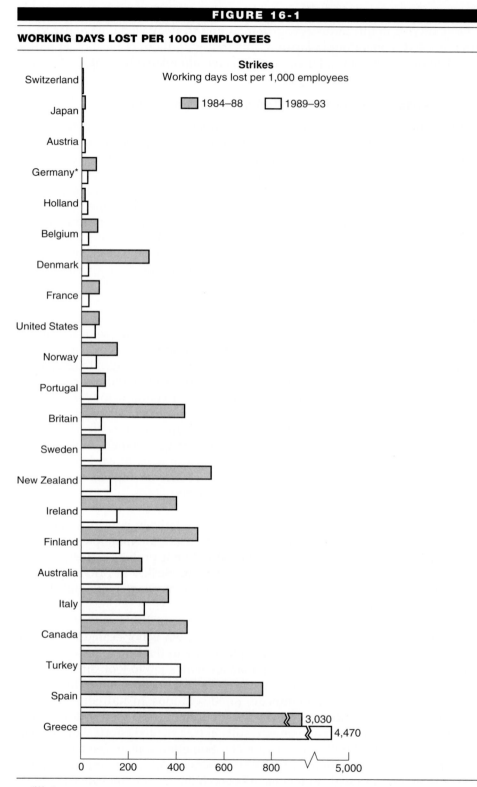

FIGURE 16-1

WORKING DAYS LOST PER 1000 EMPLOYEES

*Western.
Source: United Kingdom Department of Employment, 1994.

years, the British in general still appear willing to accept conflict with resulting strikes and lockouts as the price of protecting the rights of the workers.

Germany   A number of similarities exist between the United States and Germany in terms of managing labor conflicts. As in the United States, strikes and lockouts are prohibited in Germany during the period when a labor agreement is in effect. A strike is legal, however, when the contract has run out and a new one has not yet been ratified by the workers. Although German unions tend to be industrywide, quite often several agreements are in force in a particular company, and these agreements do not have the same termination dates. Therefore, one group of workers may be striking or working without a contract while another is working under contract. In addition, different terms and conditions of employment exist for different groups of workers, just as in the United States. Similarly, there sometimes are strikes in the middle of a contract period in clear violation of the labor agreement, indicating that the German preference for orderly and well-defined work relationships is not always present. Overall, however, there tends to be a fair amount of co-operation between management and labor because of the way labor relations are legally structured, although the situation may change with the influence of and the reaction to the East Germans.

Japan   Strikes and lockouts in Japan are very rare. Following World War II, there was a period of severe labor unrest coupled with massive, and sometimes crippling, labor strikes. Today, however, strikes are of short duration and used only to drive home a particular, minor point, not to cripple an industry or inconvenience the public. One knowledgeable observer has explained it this way:

> Since threats are generally unnecessary, a strike in Japan is merely a way to embarrass management, and thus may last from a couple of hours to a couple of days, with those of a week or more considered very long. But an equally important reason for strikes' being so short is the strong social pressure to keep the conflict quiet and resolve it quickly and quietly without having to resort to the law. In Japan the law is regarded as the instrument with which the state imposes its will. Hence, the Japanese do not like the law and will try to stay as far away from it as possible.[9]

Sometimes, strikes occur when a Japanese union is negotiating with management during industrywide negotiations. These strikes are aimed at showing that the workers support their union and are not designed to indicate any particular grievance or complaint with management. This is understood by both sides. The issues over which both sides might disagree are fairly limited. This is true for two reasons: (1) An individual's term of employment never exceeds those provided for in the labor contract, because this would indicate that this worker was more important than the other members of the work group; and (2) the law establishes standards for minimum wages, hours, overtime, rest periods, vacations, sick leaves, sanitary conditions, and discharge. Therefore, individual needs or desires are not given a great deal of attention by the union; however, Japanese unions still try to gain benefits for their people, as seen in recent efforts to win wage increases[10] and cuts in working hours.[11]

An insight into Japanese labor relations is provided by the cultural value of *Wa*, which implies that individuals should subordinate their interests and identities to those of the group. This cultural value helps to account for a great deal of the harmony that exists between management and labor in Japan.

INTERNATIONAL STRUCTURE OF UNIONS

So far, this discussion has centered on the international implications of labor relations, but the structure of unions themselves also has important implications. Most labor unions are locally or nationally based, but some are internationally active. Union internationalization has been achieved in three basic ways: (1) through use of intergovernmental organizations; (2) through use of transnational union affiliations; and (3) through extension of domestic contracts.

Intergovernmental Organizations

There are two important intergovernmental organizations. The *International Labour Office (ILO)* is a United Nations affiliate that consists of government, industry, and union representatives. The ILO has worked to define and promote fair labor standards regarding health and safety, working conditions, and freedom of association for workers throughout the world. In the early 1970s, the ILO published a study of social policy implications of MNCs.[12] Some topics in that study included investment concentration by area and industry, capital and technology transfers, international trade, work force efforts, working conditions, and industrial relations effects. The study concluded by noting the different views and concerns of employers and workers, and it recommended that the social problems and benefits specific to MNCs be identified and studied further.

Later in the decade, the ILO conducted a series of industry-specific studies on MNCs in Western Europe, and in the early 1980s, the ILO published a series of country studies on the employment effects of MNCs, including jobs lost and gained as a result of MNCs as well as the quality of jobs within MNCs. Some of its important conclusions were: (1) jobs were growing faster in MNCs than in non-MNCs; (2) white-collar positions were increasing at the expense of blue-collar jobs; and (3) one key reason for this employment growth was the R&D intensity of MNCs.

The *Organization for Economic Cooperation and Development (OECD)* is a government, industry, and union group that was founded in 1976 and that has established a voluntary set of guidelines for MNCs. These guidelines include MNCs' obligation to respect the laws and regulations of foreign countries, and in turn, these foreign countries are obliged to provide national treatment to MNCs within their borders. In recent years, these guidelines have been used to help countries regulate the operations of MNCs within their national boundaries.

Transnational Union Affiliations

There are four basic types of international trade affiliations: global, regional, specialized, and industrial operations. *Global international trade affiliations* cut across regional and industrial groups and are heavily concerned with political activities. The *International Confederation of Free Trade Unions (ICFTU)* is the most important global international for MNCs. Most of the *regional internationals* are subdivisions of the globals, and the regionals' activities are applications of the globals' activities. *Specialized internationals,* such as the ILO, the Trade Union Advisory Committee in the OECD, and the European Trade Union Congress, which represents workers' interests at the European Community level, function as components of intergovernment agencies and lobby within these agencies. The *industrial internationals* also are affiliates of the global internationals. In the ICFTU, they are called International Trade Secretaries (ITS), and there is an individual ITS for each major industry group.

Also of transnational interest are worldwide company councils that have been formed under the auspices of the International Trade Secretaries (ITS). For example, there is a General Motors Council, which consists of union representatives from GM plants throughout the world. This council meets periodically to share information about collective bargaining, working conditions, and other developments that can be valuable to unions in gaining comparable treatment for their people in country-level bargaining.

The international structure of the ITS provides a union vehicle that is parallel to the international structure of an MNC. On occasion, an ITS representative has sought to intervene at the global headquarters of an MNC on behalf of a member union having difficulty in its dealings with a subsidiary of the MNC at the national level. Some labor relations experts believed that when worldwide company councils were developing during the 1970s, they would become vehicles for transnational collective bargaining with MNCs; however, the diverse legal and cultural environments of the various countries have been a major barrier to this development.

Extensions of Domestic Contracts

Some U.S. unions have sought to deal with MNCs by bargaining with them on a global basis. The International Union of Electrical (IUE) workers, for example, invited union representatives from General Electric's overseas plants to participate in its collective bargaining. These foreign representatives were only observers, however, because U.S. labor law limits collective bargaining to matters that relate to the U.S. labor unit. In another action, the IUE contended that GE was transferring work overseas and charged that this was an unfair labor practice under the provisions of the collective bargaining agreements; however, the general counsel for the National Labor Relations Board rejected the charge and held that the union had not substantiated its claim. Overall, unions have been unsuccessful in attempting to prevent companies from transferring work overseas, although this certainly will continue to be a major focal point in the years ahead.

INDUSTRIAL DEMOCRACY

Industrial democracy involves the rights of employees to participate in significant management decisions. This participation by labor includes areas such as wage rates, bonuses, profit sharing, vacations and holiday leaves, work rules, dismissals, and plant expansions and closings. Industrial democracy is not widely used in the United States, where management typically refuses to relinquish or share its authority (commonly called "managerial prerogatives") to make major decisions. In many other countries, however, and especially in Europe, the right of industrial democracy is guaranteed by national law. This right can take a number of different forms.

Common Forms of Industrial Democracy

As the EU consolidates its goal of unification, the head of the European Commission has stated that a primary objective is to obtain a minimum threshold of social rights for workers, to be negotiated between a "European union" and employers. At present, several forms of industrial democracy exist in European countries and elsewhere. In some countries, one form may be more prevalent than others, but it is common to find a number of these forms existing simultaneously.

Codetermination   Codetermination, which was discussed briefly in Chapter 11, involves the participation of workers on boards of directors. The idea began right after World War II in Germany to prevent the re-emergence of Nazism in the coal and steel industries. By the mid-1970s, European countries besides Germany, such as Austria, Denmark, the Netherlands and Sweden, all had legally mandated codetermination. In most cases, boards of directors had to consist of one-third worker representatives. In the late 1970s, Germany increased this to 50 percent for private companies with 2000 or more employees. Despite such efforts, some researchers report that the workers are not greatly impressed with codetermination; many regard such participation on boards as merely a cosmetic attempt to address the substantive issue of true industrial democracy.

Work Councils   To varying degrees, work councils exist in all European countries. These councils are a result of either national legislation or collective bargaining at the company–union level. Their basic function is to improve company performance, working conditions, and job security. In some firms, these councils are worker- or union-run, whereas in others, members of management chair the group. Workers typically are elected to serve on the council, and management representatives are appointed by the company. The amount of council power will vary. In England, France, and Scandinavia, the groups tend not to be as powerful as in Germany, the Netherlands, and Italy.

Shop Floor Participation   A wide number of approaches are used to achieve shop floor participation. Some of the most common include worker involvement programs, quality circles, and other forms of participative management discussed in earlier chapters. QWL (quality of work life) programs such as those used in the Scandinavian countries and currently very popular in manufacturing and assembly plants throughout Europe and the United States are excellent examples.

Financial Participation   Financial participation takes a number of forms. One of the most common is profit sharing between management and workers. In some cases, productivity sharing plans are used, whereby management shares productivity gains in a predetermined ratio, such as 50-50, with the workers. This motivates workers to recommend efficiency measures and develop shortcuts to doing their jobs in return for a share of the increased profits. Overall, financial participation has not been widely adopted overseas, although it has gained a foothold in a number of U.S. industries.

Collective Bargaining   If no specific forms of industrial democracy are in effect, collective bargaining itself can become the mechanism to obtain industrial democracy for workers. As noted previously, the ability of unions to bargain collectively is legally restricted in some countries (e.g., a majority vote of the bargaining unit is required in the United States) and is not widely used in others. However, some nations, such as Sweden, require collective bargaining and allow many matters that in the United States are considered to be managerial prerogatives and not applicable to bargaining, such as work rules and standards, to be open for negotiation with the workers.

Industrial Democracy in Selected Countries

Industrial democracy takes a number of different forms depending on the country. For example, the approach used in the United States differs from those used in Europe and Asia. The following discussion briefly highlights some of these differences.

United States   In the United States, the most common form of industrial democracy is collective bargaining, whose guidelines are spelled out by law. A union that is certified by the NLRB becomes the exclusive bargaining agent for employees in the unit and is authorized to represent workers in the negotiation and administration of a labor–management contract. During the last decade, other forms of industrial democracy have gained ground, most notably shop floor participation in the form of problem-solving teams, special purpose teams, and self-managing teams.

Problem-solving teams meet weekly to discuss ways of improving quality, efficiency, and the overall work environment. While they generally are not empowered to implement their ideas, their suggestions often result in more efficient operations. These teams have begun to gain widespread support, as found in the growth of quality circle groups.

Special purpose teams design and introduce work reforms and new technology. In unionized firms, both management and labor will collaborate on operational decisions at all levels. This involvement often creates the necessary environment for both quality and productivity improvements. These teams are continuing to gain popularity, especially in unionized operations.

Self-managing teams consist of individuals who learn all the tasks of all group members, which allows them to rotate from job to job. These teams also take over supervisory duties such as scheduling work, ordering materials, and determining vacation times. These teams have been so effective that in some cases, productivity has increased and quality has risen dramatically. In recent years, these teams have become increasingly popular, and the future will apparently see even greater use of them.[13]

The three types of industrial democracy described here represent a radical departure from the way that U.S. firms traditionally have been managed. The old approach of a top-down management holding on to all the authority now is being replaced with an industrial democracy philosophy of sharing power with the workers. This approach is bringing U.S. firms more into step with the approach taken by firms in other countries over the years.

Great Britain   Industrial democracy is not new to England. Self-governing workshops (worker co-operatives) existed as early as the 1820s; however, Great Britain has not become the hub of industrial democracy in the twentieth century.

For example, unlike many workers in Germany and Scandinavia, British workers are not legally mandated to have seats on the board of directors. During the mid-1970s, it appeared that this would happen, but by the early 1990s, indications were that it would not occur in the near future, if at all. As in the United States, however, there is industrial democracy in Great Britain in the form of collective bargaining and worker representation on the shop floor.

Work groups within a British company or plant will elect a chief spokesperson or steward from their ranks to act as their interface with management. If the employees are unionized, a union council will represent them. These councils help to ensure that workers are treated fairly by management. Unfortunately, this sometimes creates a problem, because spokespersons or stewards in the firm may not agree with the union councils.

During the coming years, British firms likely will begin relying more heavily on participative approaches such as those used in the United States and Northern Europe. The primary reason is that competitive nations have been able to show that shop floor democracy is a key element in reducing production costs and increasing product quality. However, legally mandated industrial democracy measures are unlikely in Great Britain any time in the near future.

Germany   Industrial democracy and codetermination are very strong in Germany, especially in the steel and auto industries. Although the union is charged with handling the collective bargaining, internal boards have been established by law for ensuring codeterminism in the workplace. As noted earlier, the full impact of unifying with East Germany is yet to be determined, but all firms with 2000 or more employees (1000 or more in the steel industry) presently must have boards composed of workers. One supervisory board is made up of an equal number of representatives who are elected by both the shareholders and the employees, and of one additional, neutral person. This supervisory board in German companies is similar to the board of directors in U.S. firms. The other type of board in German firms is the management board, which is responsible for daily operation. Employees in each plant also elect a plant work council; if it is a multiplant company, members of the plant work council serve on a company work council as well.

Work councils perform a number of important functions, including negotiating wage rates above the contractually established minimums, negotiating benefits, setting wage rates for new jobs, and re-evaluating pay when workers are transferred between jobs. In multiplant operations, these councils sometimes have difficulty finding out what is happening at the shop floor, so they rely heavily on meetings with employees and communications with shop stewards. As a result, German workers have two groups working for them: the union, which is bargaining collectively with management; and the work council, which is negotiating employment issues relating to that particular plant.

Because of the strong degree of codeterminism, some German managers have argued that the process undermines their ability to operate efficiently. They contend that the legally established industrial democracy hampers their efforts; however, research does not support such a position. For example, Scholl conducted a study of both managers and work councils to determine whether codetermination results in more complex, and thus slower, decision making.[14] He focused on decisions that related to both investment and personnel matters. In general, the study found that the ability of German firms to make decisions is not hampered

FIGURE 16-2

EMPLOYEE PARTICIPATION IN ALL LEVELS OF DANISH FIRMS

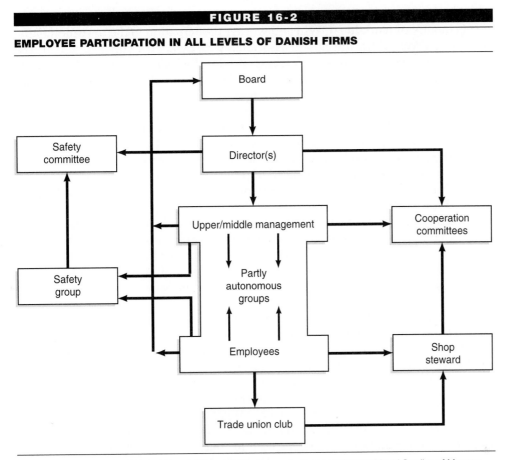

Source: Adapted from Reinhard Lund, "Industrial Democracy in Denmark," *International Studies of Management & Organization,* Summer 1987, p. 18. Used with permission.

by codeterminism. The coming years likely will see even greater efforts toward codeterminism in a unified Germany.

Denmark   Industrial democracy ensures that Danish workers participate in the management of their firms both directly and indirectly. The direct form includes use of semiautonomous work groups that provide ideas on enhancing productivity and quality and on scheduling the work. The indirect form includes use of shop stewards on the work floor, representation on boards of directors, co-operation committees consisting of worker and manager representatives, safety groups made up of a supervisor and an elected employee representative, and participation on safety committees that are headed by a manager. Figure 16-2 provides an organizational illustration of these employee participation and industrial democracy arrangements.

Unlike the situation in Germany, where the participation of workers on boards of directors is perceived as cosmetic, co-operation committees of firms in Denmark seem particularly important in ensuring a true feeling of industrial democracy on the part of Danish workers. For example, one study found that most Danish workers felt the co-operation committees contributed heavily to openness, co-ordination of effort, and a feeling of importance.

Sweden Industrial democracy in Sweden is directed very heavily toward ensuring quality of work life (QWL) and worker participation in the operation of the enterprise. QWL efforts are closely associated with Sweden's Volvo approach. The creation of semiautonomous work teams and development of a co-operative spirit between management and workers are key elements in Volvo and the Swedish approach to industrial democracy. In addition, councils and committees encourage employee involvement in identifying and implementing changes, which lead to improved QWL, which helps to sustain high morale and positive attitudes of workers and to improve productivity and quality of products and services. There is some recent evidence, however, that the early, glowing reports from Volvo may have been overstated, and that instead of returning dignity to the workers, the assembly lines are just more efficient and not really reaching the standards that are required for world-class competition.[15]

Swedish firms also have workers who are members of the board of directors. To ensure that these worker board participants are competent in handling their tasks, they typically are given formal training and spend time with other workers on the board in learning how to do things such as analyze and evaluate financial statements, read reports, and focus on both long-range and short-range issues.

China China has the largest work force in the world, but even now, little is known to outsiders about how industrial democracy really works there. Similar to the situation in Eastern Europe, many changes have occurred in China recently.[16] Unlike what has happened in Eastern Europe, many of the reforms and Westernized policies and practices in China, including the nature of industrial democracy, are closely related to the current political climate.[17]

Chinese enterprises traditionally had two policy-making committees; one contained Communist party leaders and members, and the other included managers and worker representatives. Which committee had more power depended on the political climate, but after reforms in the 1980s, the workers (not the party members) represented industrial democracy in communist countries; however, worker participation in management decision making is less open than Westerners may expect. One recent study of a variety of enterprises in Beijing found that the number of employees who participate in management decisions is not very high but that the scope was quite broad and important (sales and business plans, production operations decisions, wages and bonuses, employee benefits, housing allocations, transfer of funds, and termination of problem employees).[18] Only time will tell what course industrial democracy will take in China.[19]

Japan Unlike the situation in Europe and China, industrial democracy in Japan is not closely tied to political philosophy. It is oriented more to the operating philosophy of enhancing worker performance. The best example is quality circles, in which Japanese workers are encouraged to identify and help solve job-related problems that are associated with quality and flow of work. Management is particularly receptive to workers' ideas that will produce bottom-line results. Except for a few unusual cases, however, such as the Tokyo-based consulting and advertising firm of ODS—where all workers have a say in everything from office smoking, hours, and tardiness rules to the approval of board members, salaries of managers, and allocation of profits—Japan has very little industrial democracy in the European sense. This is reflected by the basic nature of Japanese union–management relations.

There are over 70,000 unions in Japan, and most of them are *enterprise unions,* which means that they represent both the hourly and salaried employees of the particular company. Including salaried employees is a marked departure from labor unions in other countries. Employees join the union because they are members of the firm and union membership is expected; however, they do not expect the union to negotiate and win big salary increases for them. A major reason that Japanese unions are relatively weak is because many are company-dominated, a practice that is outlawed in the United States. In the large firms such as Toyota, for example, the president of the union typically is a middle-level manager who has been nominated by the company and elected by the membership. This arrangement ensures that the unions act in harmony with the company's wishes and undermines industrial democracy.

Although there sometimes are labor strikes in Japan, as noted earlier, they usually are short-lived and have little effect on company operations. In fact, these strikes often are just ceremonial in nature and designed to encourage the workers to think of themselves as union employees. In truth, most workers think of themselves as company employees who are simply associated with the union. Moreover, it is not uncommon to find a union strike in a company with two or three work shifts and no loss of work output. This is because when the strikers are done picketing or marching, they go to work and the group coming out of the factory takes up the strike activity. In a factory with three shifts, a line employee will work a full shift, picket for a while, go home to eat and sleep, and then return to the factory for her or his shift.

Of all the industrialized nations, Japan faces the greatest challenge from industrial democracy during the years ahead. Japanese MNCs in Europe, and to a growing degree in the United States, will find that they must relinquish more control over operations to the workers if they hope to achieve the same productivity results they have at home.[20] Conversely, MNCs in Japan report that Japanese white-collar workers are too used to working in a disciplined, corporate environment and fail to make decisions and take initiative.[21] Therefore, changes are needed at home as well.

STRATEGIC MANAGEMENT OF INTERNATIONAL LABOR RELATIONS

The strategic management of international labor relations will be a major challenge facing MNCs in the years ahead, because so many different approaches can be taken. The approach used in U.S. firms may not be the same as that employed in other countries, including Anglo nations. In Great Britain, as noted earlier, unions do not have the power they once had. In many other European countries, such as Germany, however, unions continue to be quite strong, and especially as the Eastern European traditions of industrial democracy become infused in the EU, the workers will continue to have a great deal of authority in determining what the firm will do. It also is important to realize that those strategies benefitting unions in one country may have no value in others. This sometimes can be a conflict between international unions. For example, when Ford Motor felt that the labor climate in Britain was unfavorable to further investing, the company was approached by a group of Dutch businesspeople and urged to consider the Netherlands for future investment. Despite the strong criticism of British unions, the leadership of the Dutch trade unions did not object to these suggestions that investment funds be transferred to their country.[22]

The Philosophical Backdrop

As noted in earlier chapters, MNCs can use a number of philosophies as a starting point for their approach to management functions, including labor relations. For instance, under an ethnocentric philosophy, the MNC will take an approach to labor relations in other countries that is identical to its approach at home. Cultural, legal, and economic factors of the host country will not be considered in industrial relations efforts. This approach, quite obviously, generally is not effective and can even have disastrous results; as companies begin going international, they soon abandon such an approach.

A second approach is to use a polycentric philosophy in managing international industrial relations. Under this philosophy, the MNC will evaluate each country or geographic region as a separate entity. The MNC's international industrial relations strategy will be a series of different approaches depending on the country.

A third approach is a geocentric philosophy that is characterized by an effort to understand the interrelationships between the various geographic locations and a strategy to link them with a unifying thread and a composite industrial relations approach. The primary difference between a polycentric and a geocentric philosophy is that the latter considers the interrelationships between the various groups. Here are some examples of how industrial relations in one country can affect those in others:

1. Opel (General Motors' German subsidiary) negotiates an *increase* in the basic workweek hours with Belgian unions as it adds a second shift at its Belgian assembly plant. The intent of management is to keep the costs of production there competitive with those at a similar Opel plant in Germany. The intent of the Belgian workers is to expand employment and enhance job security.
2. A U.S. electronics firm cuts back its U.S. manufacturing output by 10 percent through laying off a like percentage of its U.S. workers. Its French subsidiary picks up the resulting product market slack. By cutting back employment in the United States, the firm avoids the large payments to workers that French law would have required if the cutback had been made by the French subsidiary.
3. Workers at a German company's British subsidiary go out on strike to support their demand for improved wages. Operations at the company's German plants continue, providing substantial cash inflows (revenues) to the entire system. The British workers completely forgo their cash inflows—their wages—during the strike. The company is less severely pressed financially than these workers are and can sustain a long strike if need be.
4. Ford of Europe integrates production among several European subsidiaries. For certain models of cars, the engines are British-made, the power train and some stampings are German-made, the wheels and other stampings are Belgian-made, and so on. A strike by workers in Belgium could shut down plants in Britain, Germany, and elsewhere. This gives the Belgian workers operational leverage vis-à-vis management and enhances their power in collective bargaining.[23]

The Japanese also make an interesting case study of the need for a geocentric philosophy toward industrial relations. Japanese auto firms long have realized that auto capacity is outstripping demand both in North America and Europe. As Japan continues to increase its foothold in North America, it will have to pay greater attention to its industrial relations approaches and modify them to meet the local labor market. Japan also will need to co-ordinate its worldwide holdings with a carefully formulated geocentric strategy toward labor relations. At the same time, Japanese auto producers are buying into Europe. One of the latest acquisitions has been Honda's 20 percent purchase of the Rover Group, best known for its production of the Sterling, which competes with the Volvo, Saab, BMW, and lower-priced Mercedes. This development also will require a well-focused, geocentrically based labor relations strategy.

Compensation Policies

Another major area of consideration in formulating an international labor relations strategy is compensation.[24] Wages that are paid in one country often differ considerably from those paid in other countries for the same job. Here are some examples of average hourly wages in the early 1990s in U.S. dollars[25]:

Germany	$25.14	Japan	$18.40
Switzerland	$24.12	France	$16.60
Italy	$20.11	United States	$15.88
Netherlands	$19.95	Britain	$14.14
Belgium	$19.70	Spain	$13.98
Denmark	$19.39	Greece	$6.92
Canada	$18.42	Portugal	$4.89

There also are wide gaps in the benefits and other perks that are provided to employees. The accompanying sidebar, "Unions Do Well in Germany," highlights some of these differences.

Organizing International Industrial Relations

In organizing international industrial relations, a number of factors help to explain the relative degree of centralized and decentralized control that is exercised. The following compares the organizational dimensions of U.S. and European MNCs that are critical to labor relations:

1. A number of studies have shown that compared with European MNCs, U.S. firms tend to concentrate authority at corporate headquarters, with greater emphasis on formal management controls and a close reporting system (particularly within the area of financial control) to ensure that planning targets are met.

2. European MNCs tend to deal with labor unions at the industry level (frequently via employer associations) rather than the company level. The opposite is more typical for U.S. firms. In the United States, employer associations have not played a key role in the industrial relations system, and company-based labor relations policies are the norm.

3. A final factor is the extent of the home product market. If domestic sales are large relative to overseas operations (as is the case with many U.S. companies), it is more likely that overseas operations will be regarded by the parent company as an extension of domestic operations. This is not the case for many European MNCs, whose international operations represent the major part of their business.[26]

In addition, when compared with British firms, U.S. MNCs are much more likely to be involved in collective bargaining and strike settlement issues of their overseas subsidiaries. British firms tend to adopt a more "hands off" approach

Unions Do Well in Germany

Unions in Germany are becoming more confrontational, although they certainly are a great deal more co-operative with management than their counterparts in the United States. On the other hand, many observers wonder if it is necessary for German unions to get tough with employers given that these unions have done so well in recent years. Perhaps a soft-sell approach is indeed best. Certainly, there are a number of key statistics that bear out the success of German union efforts. One is the high cost of hourly labor. In manufacturing, for example, German workers make considerably more than U.S. workers, and they are paid more than any other workers in the world. Moreover, if benefits are added into the calculation, the hourly rate of German workers rises even higher, far ahead of Japan and the United States.

A second interesting statistic is the annual increase in manufacturing unit labor costs. Not only is Germany leading the world in hourly wages, the yearly increase during the period 1985 to 1990 inclusive was a whopping 15.6 percent. Simply put, German salaries are high and getting significantly higher. Japan also is having problems with these costs, as seen by the fact that annual increases during this 6-year period averaged 10.3 percent. On the other hand, the United States had manufacturing unit labor costs fall by 0.1 percent annually during this same period.

These statistics help to explain one other important fact: Union membership in Germany is strong. While union membership so far in the 1990s has declined by 42 percent in France, 32 percent in Spain, and 16 percent in the United States, it went down a mere 3 percent in Germany. In fact, one great fear of German economists is that union demands will drive employers from high-wage countries to low-wage ones and will lead to a restructuring of jobs to eliminate waste and gain the productivity needed to meet new wage demands. In the case of Daimler-Benz Dasa, for example, the company recently cut 9000 jobs and is in the process of selling at least three of its German plants. The powerful German union IG Metall, however, has been very successful in getting its way with most employers. This union's most recent contract with Volkswagen (VW) ensures that the company's 100,000 workers will receive an estimated 2.5 percent annual wage increase and a gurantee of their jobs until the end of 1997. This is very good news indeed for the union members, because VW currently is a high-cost, inefficient producer and needs to take steps to reduce waste and streamline operations. Its latest union contract, in the view of many industry observers, simply postpones the day of reckoning. On the other hand, company spokespeople point out that the firm was able to extract some important concessions from the union, including increasing the maximum workweek from 28.8 hours to 38.8 hours, cutting hourly rest breaks from 5 minutes back to 2 1/2 minutes, and cutting the overtime bonus from 50 percent down to 30 percent. The big question is whether these concessions will be sufficient to keep VW competitive on a worldwide basis.

Today, labor relations and its costs continue to be a major concern for MNCs doing business in Germany. This helps to explain why the United States and other countries are becoming more attractive to German firms, many of whom are beginning to set up overseas operations and export the goods back to Germany. To a large extent, labor relations is proving to be a major part of MNC strategy in Germany.

and confine themselves to giving advice and guidance to their subsidiaries, allowing local management to deal with day-to-day industrial relations matters.[27] These examples point out that industrial relations practices differ from country to country, and MNCs need to be concerned with co-ordinating these activities.

A number of alternative approaches can be used in managing labor relations in different cultures. For example, one study found that labor relations often is delegated to the local management, except in the case of pension issues, which are handled by the MNC headquarters.[28] The foreign subsidiary is not totally on its own when it comes to labor relations, however. A great deal of guidance and advice still comes from the home office, and hiring and staffing policies also ensure that headquarters plays a role in industrial relations. In addition, many expatriate subsidiary managers use the same industrial relations approach, or a modified version of the approach, that they used back home.

The linkage between the subsidiary and headquarters often is handled by a home-based industrial relations staff, which provides advice and assistance. This industrial relations staff typically gathers information related to wages, benefits, and working conditions around the world as well as at the location of the particular subsidiary. This helps local managers to determine the labor contract that should be negotiated or, in the case of nonunionized operations, the level of wages and benefits that should be paid.

The MNC industrial relations staff also provides assistance in dealing with labor disputes and grievances. The staff can provide information as to how similar problems have been handled in other locales and can be of particular importance to the subsidiary. Many local managers may be unaware of the variety of approaches that can be used in negotiating labor agreements and resolving related problems.

Information provided by the MNC headquarters industrial relations staff can be used by upper-level management in determining when and where to make changes in production work worldwide as well. For example, if wage rates in France go up 10 percent next year, will this reduce the MNC's competitiveness in that market? If it will, what costs are associated with moving some of this work to the MNC's plant in Barcelona? The industrial relations staff at headquarters can help to answer this question in terms of wages, salaries, and benefits. When this information is coupled with that provided by the staffs in manufacturing, marketing, and legal, the MNC then is in a position to make a final decision regarding the wisdom of transferring the work to another locale. An example would be McDonnell Douglas, which agreed to build a large percentage of 40 new jetliners in China, the country that ordered the planes.[29]

SUMMARY OF KEY POINTS

1. Labor relations is the process through which management and workers identify and determine the job relationships that will be in effect at the workplace. In the United States, these agreements result from negotiations at the union–management bargaining table. In other countries, the approach is different. For example, the labor agreement in Great Britain is not a binding contract. In Germany, however, it is binding, and the unions are particularly influential in determining wages, salaries, and working conditions. In Japan, labor agreements usually are general and vague, although they are legally enforceable.

2. From time to time, industrial conflicts result from disagreements between management and the union. In the United States, these often are solved through use of a grievance procedure, the steps of which are spelled out in the union contract. In Great Britain, the conflict resolution process often is fragmented and costly, because the system is not designed to deal with such problems. The approach in Germany is similar to that in the United States. In Japan, industrial conflict is minimal because of the way that unions are formed and led.

3. Unions have attempted to become internationally active in three basic ways. One is through use of intergovernmental organizations such as the ILO (International Labour Office) and the OECD (Organization for Economic Cooperation and Development). Another is through transnational union affiliations. A third is by extending domestic contracts into the international arena.

4. Industrial democracy is the rights that employees have to participate in significant management decisions. Such decisions include wage rates, bonuses, profit sharing, vacations and holiday leaves, work rules, dismissals, and plant expansions and closings. Industrial democracy is not as widespread in the United States as it is in other countries, especially in Germany and the Scandinavian countries. Some of the most common forms

of industrial democracy include codetermination, work councils, shop floor participation, financial participation, and collective bargaining.

5. In formulating a strategy and managing international industrial relations, MNCs can draw on a number of philosophies. The most effective tends to be a geocentric philosophy that is characterized by an effort to understand the interrelationships between the various geographic locations and a strategy to link them with a composite, unifying theme. This approach to labor relations can be helpful in dealing with compensation policy issues as well as in providing assistance to the worldwide subsidiaries on labor issues or challenges that they face.

KEY TERMS

labor relations

collective bargaining

union

union grievance

mediator

arbitrator

strike

lockout

International Labour Office (ILO)

Organization for Economic Cooperation and Development (OECD)

global international trade affiliations

International Confederation of Free Trade Unions (ICFTU)

regional internationals

specialized internationals

industrial internationals

industrial democracy

problem-solving teams

special purpose teams

self-managing teams

enterprise unions

REVIEW AND DISCUSSION QUESTIONS

1. What are three major differences between the way that labor–management agreements are reached in the United States and in Great Britain? Germany? Japan? Compare and contrast the process in all four countries.
2. How are industrial conflicts handled in the United States? Great Britain? Germany? Japan? Compare and contrast the process in all four countries.
3. A U.S. MNC is considering opening a plant in Germany. What are three labor relations and industrial democracy developments that this firm needs to know about? Identify and describe each.
4. A French firm is talking to state officials in Indiana about setting up a new plant in Terre Haute. What types of labor relations issues should the company be investigating so that it can have the most efficient and effective operation?
5. How would each of the following philosophical views affect the formulation of strategy and the management of international industrial relations: ethnocentric, polycentric, and geocentric?
6. A Japanese MNC is considering setting up a manufacturing plant east of Los Angeles. How is the firm likely to organize and control the industrial relations strategies and practices of this overseas subsidiary? Are there any particular problems the home office is likely to confront? Be complete in your answer.

PRACTICAL INTERNATIONAL MANAGEMENT ASSIGNMENT

From the library or by interviewing local labor union officials, find out what a given union does internationally. Does it have members in other countries? How does collective bargaining differ in these countries? What role, if any, does industrial democracy play in the philosophy and practice of unionism now? What role, if any, will it play in the future?

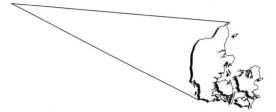

In the International Spotlight

Denmark

Toasting with a "skoal"—directly to an individual or to the whole group—is common in Denmark.

Denmark is a small kingdom in Northern Europe that is surrounded by water except for a 42-mile border shared with Germany to the south. The country is approximately 17,000 square miles of small green farms, blue lakes, and white coastal beaches. The population is 5.2 million, one-fourth of whom live in Copenhagen. Although poor in natural resources, the Danes are famous for their dairy products, processed foods, and beautifully designed manufactured goods, including furniture and silverware. Since the time of the Vikings, the Danes have been a seafaring people. Denmark maintains large shipping and fishing industries. The prosperous Danes have a high standard of living, and the economy is fairly stable and moderately strong. Consumer prices rose about two-thirds during the 1980s, but this increase was less than that of other Scandinavian countries, and during the 1990s, prices have been fairly stable. Denmark has been a constitutional monarchy for over 130 years. Legislative power is in the hands of a parliament whose members are elected for 4-year terms, and a prime minister heads the government.

Two months ago, a medium-sized, high-tech firm based in Seattle, called Seattle Tech, Inc. (STI), entered into a joint venture with a Danish electronics manufacturing firm. STI is going to invest $1.4 million and give its Danish partner the right to use its patents to manufacture a portable facsimile machine. The Danish company is going to renovate one wing of its factory and devote this area to the production of these machines.

There are two reasons that STI wanted to enter into this agreement: One is that the arrangement provides it entry into the EU. A second is an analysis that indicated overall costs for producing the fax machines in Denmark would be about 25 percent less than if they were made in the United States and shipped over. Cost is a very important factor in STI's decision. Control also is important. STI insists that the units be produced according to the master blueprint that is being provided. "Quality is a key factor in the success of these machines," the vice president of production noted, "and this means that we must produce them to a strict manufacturing tolerance. We can't have anyone making arbitrary changes in the process."

Everything appeared to be going well until earlier this week, when the CEO of STI was talking to the top management of the Danish company in Copenhagen. There, for the first time, he learned that the board of directors consists of seven members of management and six members of the union. Moreover, to his surprise, he learned that Danish workers often get involved in shop floor decision making and make recommendations regarding how to change production flows and techniques to increase productivity and quality. The president is happy to learn that the workers are so interested in trying to improve output and quality, but he is concerned that any tinkering with the production process for the facsimile machines could result in major quality problems. He explained these concerns to his counterpart in the Danish firm, but he feels that his points were not well received. "We may have made a major mistake," the CEO of STI told his assistant when they returned from their meeting in Copenhagen. "It may be necessary for us to back out of this venture and look for a different partner."

1. What are some current issues facing Denmark? What is the climate for doing business in Denmark today?
2. Do the workers have to be included on the board of directors? Can the company force them off?
3. How important is worker participation in decision making in Denmark?
4. What would you recommend that STI do at this point?

You Be the International Management Consultant

Helping Them Make a Comeback

During the 1970s, Volkswagen was the leading U.S. foreign car importer. In 1979, the firm sold 300,000 cars and held 2.8 percent of the total market. The next year saw sales slip to 275,000 units, but because of the general decline of industry sales, Volkswagen's share of the U.S. market rose to 3 percent. Since then, however, things have not looked very good for this firm. By 1982, sales had slipped to 160,000 units, and market share was down to 1.8 percent. The firm rebounded slightly during the middle of the decade, but by the early 1990s, the company was selling only 150,000 units annually in the United States, and market share had slipped to 1.3 percent. Quite obviously, the firm was being overrun in the United States by the other imports, including Japanese models and revitalized German lines such as Mercedes.

Despite this trend, the company is not quitting. At present, Volkswagen intends to continue shrinking its U.S. work force and keeping costs to a minimum. In 1988, the firm closed its U.S. manufacturing plant in Pennsylvania and now is reducing U.S. operations from its peak of 6000 workers before the shutdown to 1600 employees. Despite these cutbacks, the United States will remain a key market for Volkswagen. As one observer put it:

> Because Volkswagen builds more than three million cars and trucks a year worldwide, its financial performance in this country constitutes a small fraction of its overall results. But with increased competition [in] Europe . . . and Japanese rivals poised to intensify their threat, the company sees the American market as an important battleground in a larger struggle that includes Europe and South America. VW believes a return to a mass-market strategy in the United States will help it gird for fierce battles on its home turf.

1. What was the logic behind Volkswagen's decision to close its U.S. plant?
2. How critical will labor relations be in helping Volkswagen regain its market share in the United States? Defend your answer.
3. What would you recommend that Volkswagen do in co-ordinating its worldwide labor operations so as to produce the lowest-price car and thus increase its competitiveness?

CHAPTER 16 ENDNOTES

1. See "Getting Their Dues," *Economist*, March 25, 1995, pp. 68, 73.

2. For more on this topic, see Richard M. Hodgetts and K. Galen Kroeck, *Personnel/Human Resource Management* (Fort Worth, TX: HBJ/Dryden, 1992), pp. 480–483.

3. See Fred Luthans and Richard M. Hodgetts, *Business Today: Functions and Challenges* (Houston, TX: Dame Publishing, 1995), p. 218.

4. Dennis R. Briscoe, *International Human Resource Management* (Englewood Cliffs, NJ: Prentice-Hall, 1995), p. 159.

5. Lindley H. Clark, Jr., "Germany: Beyond Strikes, Another Challenge," *Wall Street Journal*, May 5, 1992, p. A16; "German Labor Conflicts Seen," *Wall Street Journal*, January 29, 1992, p. A40.

6. Herbert Henzler, "Managing the Merger: A Strategy for the New Germany," *Harvard Business Review*, January-February 1992, pp. 24–29.

7. Audrey Choi, "Steelworkers of Germany Endorse Strike," *Wall Street Journal*, February 3, 1992, p. A6.

8. Audrey Choi, "Steelmakers in Germany Set Labor Pact," *Wall Street Journal*, February 4, 1992, p. A11; Gail E. Schaves, "Germany's Mighty Unions Are Being Forced to Bend," *BusinessWeek*, March 1, 1993, pp. 52–56.

9. Keith Atkinson, "State of the Unions," *Personnel Administrator*, September 1986, p. 58.

10. Masayoshi Kanabayashi, "Japan's Unions Settle for Rise of 5% in Wages," *Wall Street Journal*, March 27, 1992, p. A6.

11. Masayoshi Kanabayashi, "Japan's Workers Could Win Cuts in Working Hours," *Wall Street Journal*, February 27, 1992, p. A6.

12. *Multinational Enterprises and Social Policy* (Geneva: International Labour Office, 1973).

13. John Hoerr, "The Payoff from Teamwork," *BusinessWeek*, July 10, 1989, p. 57; Brian Dumaine, "Who Needs a Boss?" *Fortune*, May 7, 1990, pp. 52–60.

14. Wolfgang Scholl, "Codetermination and the Ability of Firms to Act in the Federal Republic of Germany," *International Studies of Management & Organization*, Summer 1987, pp. 27–37.

15. For additional insights, see Steven Prokesch, "Edges Fray on Volvo's Brave New Humanistic World," *New York Times*, July 6, 1991, p. F5.

16. See, for example, Shanthi Kalathil, "In China, Investors Flock Inland from Costly Coast," *Wall Street Journal*, October 25, 1995, p. A11.

17. See, for example, Keith Bradsher, "Senate Backs Curbs on Beijing's Access to Markets in U.S.," *New York Times*, February 26, 1992, pp. A1, A5.

18. See Irene Hall-Siu Chow and Oded Shenkar, "HR Practices in the People's Republic of China," *Personnel*, December 1989, pp. 41–47.

19. Also see Dinah Lee et al., "China's Ugly Export Secret: Prison Labor," *BusinessWeek*, April 22, 1991, pp. 42–46.

20. For example, see "Japanese Employers Are 'Locking Out' Their U.S. Managers," *BusinessWeek*, May 7, 1990, p. 24.

21. "Japanese Workers Criticized," *Wall Street Journal*, February 24, 1992, p. A10.

22. Peter J. Dowling, Randall S. Schuler, and Denice E. Welch, *International Dimensions of Human Resource Management*, 2nd ed. (Belmont, CA: Wadsworth, 1994), pp. 198.

23. Robert Grosse and Duane Kujawa, *International Business: Theory and Managerial Applications* (Homewood, IL: Irwin, 1988), p. 447.

24. See, for example, Damon Darlin, "U.S. Firms Take Chances in South Korea," *Wall Street Journal*, June 15, 1992, pp. B1, B5.

25. Reported in *Wall Street Journal*, May 15, 1992, p. A8.

26. Reported in Dowling, Schuler, and Welch, *International Dimensions*, p. 188.

27. Malcolm Warner and Riccardo Peccei, "Worker-Participation and Multi-National Companies," *Management International Review*, Special Issue 1994, p. 84.

28. Grosse and Kujawa, *International Business*, pp. 463–464.

29. Richard W. Stevenson, "McDonnell Douglas in $1 Billion Chinese Deal," *New York Times*, June 29, 1992, pp. C1–2.

PART FIVE

INTERNATIONAL MANAGEMENT HORIZONS

ETHICS AND SOCIAL RESPONSIBILITY

OBJECTIVES OF THE CHAPTER

The current concern that all businesses and the general public have for ethical behavior and social responsibility is not restricted to the domestic situation. In this era of a global economy, MNCs must be concerned with how they carry out their business and their social role in host countries. This chapter examines business ethics and social responsibility in the international arena, and it looks at some of the critical social issues that will be confronting MNCs in the years ahead. The discussion includes ethical decision making in various countries, regulation of foreign investment, and current responses to social responsibility by today's multinationals. The specific objectives of this chapter are:

1. **EXAMINE** some of the major ethical issues and problems confronting MNCs in selected countries.
2. **EXPLAIN** some of the ways that host countries are attempting to regulate foreign investments and why reciprocity is such an important trade issue.
3. **DISCUSS** some of the actions being taken by selected industrialized countries to be more socially responsive to world problems.

ETHICS AROUND THE WORLD

The ethical behavior of business has become a major issue. In the United States, insider trading scandals, bribes, and the MAD syndrome (*M*ergers, *A*cquisitions, and *D*ivestitures) have received considerable media attention and aroused the public's concern about ethics in international business.

Ethics is the study of morality and standards of conduct. Ethics is important in the study of international management, because ethical behavior in one country sometimes is viewed as unethical behavior in other countries. Considerable attention has been given in the management literature to ethical problems in the United States; not so well known are the ethical issues in other parts of the world. The following sections examine some of the ethical problems that occur in international business in selected countries.

Ethical Problems and Concerns in Japan

In terms of both internal and external business relations, Japan, like the United States, has had more than its share of ethical problems in recent years. Some of the most devastating and widely publicized have occurred in both the political and business arenas.

Political and Business Scandals Several years ago, Japan was rocked by a bribery scandal involving the Recruit Company. In an effort to curry favor, this firm had been giving politicians and influential businesspeople an opportunity to buy cut-rate stock in a Recruit real estate subsidiary. The shares eventually were listed on the public stock exchange, and the early stockholders, many of whom were these targeted people, made large returns on their investment. When this information became public, some members of the cabinet, including the prime minister, were forced to resign.[1]

Since this time, there have been additional scandals. One of the more recent has been a bribery scandal involving ruling-party politicians. In this case, Japanese politicians received money from a property developer in return for helping to resolve legal problems arising from a contract linked to building a factory.[2] In another case, the official charged with running the ruling Liberal Democratic party admitted that he took campaign contributions from the head of a trucking concern and failed to report these funds.[3]

Another major scandal in Japan has involved stock brokers, politicians, and mafia (or "yakuza") members. Some of the country's largest brokerages have been accused of giving inside stock tips to important politicians in return for favors. Another charge has been that of reimbursing influential customers for losses in the stock market. A third charge leveled at one brokerage was that it did special favors, such as manipulating stocks owned by members of the mob and financing their fees for golf club applications. These charges resulted in resignation of the heads of two of the largest securities firms in the country.[4]

More recently, some security firms have been investigated for allegedly agreeing to buy stocks at an inflated price, with the understanding that these securities would be bought back by the original seller at a higher price.[5] In still another case, five former officials of a Japanese futures investment firm were arrested for allegedly defrauding customers of almost $100 million by withholding funds intended for investment in Hong Kong sugar futures.[6] In a third case, Japan's Fair

---

INTERNATIONAL MANAGEMENT IN ACTION

Fighting Back

An increasing number of working women in Japan feel they are victims of sexual harassment. For example, one female executive at a prestigious Tokyo service company found notes on her desk alluding to her sex life. Male colleagues pinned up a nude centerfold resembling the woman, and on another occasion, they wrote the woman's name at the top of a diagram of a human brain, indicating which lobes drove her sexual obsessions. When the woman protested, she was transferred to another post, and the men were not disciplined. Commenting on the problem, the female executive noted that she spent half of her energy trying to cope with the humiliation, while her bosses acted as though the situation was something she would have to solve by herself. This story is only representative of what many Japanese women have faced over the years. In fact, a recent Labor Ministry poll reveals that 43 percent of all women in management positions complain of sexual harassment. Only recently have they spoken out and tried to do something. Now, there are a growing number of lawsuits charging firms with *sekuhara*, sexual harassment and sexual discrimination.

In addition to the legal action being taken by Japanese women against their employers, female employees from other countries who work for Japanese-based multinationals also are beginning to fight back. For example, some Japanese firms in the United States have been hit with sexual harassment charges. Sumitomo Corporation, the giant trading firm, faces a complaint before the Equal Employment Opportunity Commission that its Chicago office abused a female U.S. employee who worked as a sales assistant. The woman charges that Japanese managers allowed pornographic materials to be circulated and that one manager continually asked her for pictures of herself in a bathing suit. The woman also has charged the firm with giving her only token promotions. In another case, C. Itoh & Company is now trying to reach an out-of-court settlement with female employees at its New York office. The U.S. women employees have initiated a class action suit charging the Japanese firm with sex discrimination.

The lawsuits in the United States are more damaging to Japanese multinationals, because they are being filed in a country where sexual harassment is frowned on and courts are prepared to assess heavy damages against companies that break the law. In Japan, however, many firms still believe that this issue is not a serious one. One Japanese lawyer recently stated that companies in Japan are likely to try to handle the problem without making any significant changes in the way things are done. If this is true, complaints, lawsuits, and pressure on corporate Japan will undoubtedly continue until equality in the workplace receives more attention and steps are taken to rectify a very real problem.

Trade Commission began an investigation into allegations that the country's major makers of printing ink had conspired to raise prices.[7]

Changing Social Climate in Japan   The developments noted earlier have helped to focus the attention of many MNCs on the changing social environment in Japan. The role of business ethics in the coming years likely will differ sharply from what it has been in the past. Previously, Japanese politicians and businesspeople thought nothing of giving favors to each other and looking for reciprocity, but this behavior appears to be changing. Influence peddling (trying to influence others through reciprocal favors) in Japan now is serious business, and everyone from the president of a foreign MNC to the head of huge domestic corporations such as NTT will be held to the same high standard of ethical behavior.

Prejudice and Discrimination in Japan   Another area where Japan has faced ethical problems is that of prejudice and discrimination. One of the most common examples is sexual harassment in the workplace, an issue on which more and more Japanese women are fighting back, as discussed in the accompanying box, "International Management in Action: Fighting Back." In one recent case, a woman won a judgment of $12,500 from her company. This was the first lawsuit ever filed in Japan charging sexual harassment, and it set off a wave of concern.[8]

Within 48 hours of the verdict, the government had issued 10,000 copies of a booklet on sexual harassment, and all were quickly snapped up.

Besides sex discrimination, some Japanese firms also are having problems dealing with minority workers. Comments made by Japanese political figures about African-Americans and Hispanics, for example, have been criticized for their discriminatory meaning.[9] Japanese businesses also have been known to engage in insensitive racial stereotypes. For example, a Japanese department store drew fire a few years ago for displaying mannequins with distorted stereotypes of black faces, and an entertainment company provoked protests by selling Little Black Sambo dolls.[10]

The biggest furor, however, has been created by Japanese firms' attempts to keep minority hiring to a minimum. For example, evidence shows Japanese firms that set up operations in the United States tend to favor areas where minorities in general, and African-Americans in particular, are not situated.[11] Most people live within 30 miles of their job site, and national census data show that the propensity to commute declines rapidly once one goes beyond this limit. One analysis found that Japanese assembly plants and supplier plants in North America are less likely to set up operations within 30 miles of areas inhabited by minorities. The researchers made observations such as the following:

> In the course of our research, we heard Japanese managers specifically explain their decisions on plant siting in such terms. . . . Des Rosiers, who has carried out several site studies for Japanese auto companies, added: "They ask for profiles of the community by ethnic background, by religious background, by professional make-up. . . . There are demographic aspects that they like. They like a high German content. . . . [The Japanese] probably don't like other types of profiles." In a similar vein, a midwestern state official responsible for recruiting Japanese firms to his state in the early 1980s reported to us that "many Japanese companies at the time specifically asked to stay away from areas with high minority populations."[12]

This study provided further evidence for prejudice and discrimination when the percentage of African-Americans in the local area was compared with the percentage that were employed by Japanese firms. The results showed that African-Americans were consistently underrepresented in the Japanese plants. Legal action stemming from discriminatory employment practices has been successful against some Japanese firms in the United States. For example, several years ago, Honda of America Manufacturing, Inc., agreed to give 370 African-Americans and women a total of $6 million in back pay to resolve a federal discrimination complaint, and Sumitomo Bank's U.S. operation was handed a $2.6 million sex discrimination verdict.

These examples and empirical evidence indicate that Japanese firms in the United States have had more than their share of problems in dealing with the hiring and treatment of minorities and women. More important, unless Japanese firms change their approach, these problems will grow worse during the coming years, because equality in the workplace continues to be a central social issue and indicator for social responsibility of business in the United States.[13] In fairness to the Japanese, however, it should be noted that they are making an effort to improve equality in employment, and their concern for the safety and health of workers may be unmatched anywhere in the world.[14]

Social Responsibility Implications from Lobbying   Another area of growing ethical concern is the Japanese lobbying effort in the United States.[15] Japan, more than other countries, spends millions of dollars every year for lobbying in Washington. For this money, Japanese firms have been able to hire very savvy, effective lobbyists, and these investments seem to be getting results. For example, when the Japanese firm Toshiba sold defense-sensitive, high-tech milling equipment to the former Soviet Union, the Japanese lobby in Washington was able to defuse the issue effectively. The lobbyists persuaded those writing sanctions into a final trade bill to water down the penalties for Toshiba.

The Japanese also have been very effective in lobbying at the state and local levels. Here are two examples:

> In Illinois, where Mitsubishi Corp. opened a $650 million auto plant with Chrysler Corp., Mitsubishi executives became a driving force behind the month-long Festival of Japan. Working through the Chicago Japanese Chamber of Commerce and the Japan-America Society, in cooperation with the Japanese consul-general, they raised $1.2 million for the festival. The highlight of the event: a visit by then Prime Minister Noboru Takeshita to meet Illinois Governor James R. Thompson and other luminaries.
>
> In the southeast, Japan's regional effort is assisted by former Georgia Governor George Busbee, a founder of the Japan/U.S. Southeast Assn., which groups top Japanese and Southeastern political and business leaders. When a Washington problem arises, these regional networks are in place to help Japan. Says TRW's Choate [a well-known trade expert], "The Japanese government and Japanese companies are infinitely more effective in lobbying in this town [than U.S. companies]."[16]

Is it ethical for Japanese firms to hire bank-rolled, well-connected, talented lobbyists to argue their case in Washington? Is it ethical for former U.S. cabinet officers and elected officials to become lobbyists for Japan? Recall the furor over ex-President Reagan's receiving millions of dollars for his speaking engagements in Japan soon after he left office. Certainly, these activities are legal. Many Americans feel that the interests of the United States and Japan are not the same when it comes to business dealings, however, and that Americans are being shortchanged in the process. To the extent that these feelings (some would call them latent racism)[17] persist, Japanese lobbying will continue to be an area of ethical concern during the years ahead.

The Status of Women Managers in Japan   The number of women in managerial positions in Japan has been increasing in recent years, but statistics reveal that these opportunities still are quite limited and, similar to the U.S., a "glass ceiling" exists. For example, in 1979, as part of the background research for the forthcoming Japanese Equal Employment Opportunity Law, a cabinet-level commission surveyed companies listed on the stock exchange and special corporations in three major urban centers. The data revealed that of the 1497 companies surveyed, the average firm had 3321 employees, and of these, 242 were in management positions. Women, however, constituted 23 percent of the work force of these large firms—but only 0.3 percent of those in decision-making positions.

Since then, follow-up studies have tried to determine whether Japanese women were making any headway in large firms. In 1981, the same cabinet-level commission found that the number of women employees had grown to 40 percent of the work force in these large firms—but still only 0.5 percent of the management group. A 1984 study found a very slight improvement, but women still represented less than 1 percent of management. In a 1989 update, the Women's Bureau surveyed 7000 Japanese companies with 30 or more employees. This study was conducted 3 years after the Equal Employment Opportunity Law went into effect.

In the largest firms, the Bureau found that 12 percent of companies with more than 5000 workers and 6.7 percent of those with 1000 to 4999 workers had woman at the division-head level. For women at the section-head level, the rates were 45 percent for companies with over 5000 workers and 25 percent for those with 1000 to 4999 workers. For women at the first supervisory level, which represents the pool from which managerial personnel will be selected in the future, the rates were 72 percent of companies with 5000 or more employees and 52 percent of companies with 1000 to 4999 employees. Overall, the Japanese Women's Bureau concluded:

> These figures are a remarkable improvement over the situation reported in 1984. They all refer, however, to the percentage of companies that report having any women at all in their managerial ranks. The actual percentage of women in these positions remains minuscule. According to the national wage census for 1989, in companies employing 1,000 or more persons, only 0.36 percent of division heads and 0.13 percent of section heads were women, but women held 3.6 percent of the . . . subsection-head positions. By the most generous measure, women occupied only 2.2 percent of managerial positions in companies with 1000 or more employees.[18]

There are a number of reasons for the lack of progress among women in large Japanese firms. One is that they often are excluded from transfers to branch offices or posts far away from their homes. As a result, they are unable to acquire the range of experience needed for promotion to upper-level managerial positions.

Among those Japanese women who have been able to achieve managerial rank in large corporations, there is evidence that they have done so only after long service to the company and often at the expense of marriage and motherhood. The fastest road to the top for Japanese women appears to be in small businesses, where they are able to play an important role and are recognized for their achievements. The opportunities do not seem to be as promising in large firms, despite the enactment of the Equal Employment Opportunity Law that was supposed to help reduce barriers to promotion. In fact, under current interpretations of this law, firms can require women to commit themselves at the time of hiring to either: (1) a traditional track with good benefits but no promotion opportunities; or (2) a career track with more rigorous standards and opportunities ostensibly equivalent to those offered to male permanent employees. Since most women are unwilling to opt for the latter track, businesses feel they can legitimately refuse to promote them to higher level positions. Moreover, because few women work in government ministries that could put political pressure on companies to alter their current practices, there appears to be little likelihood that things will change in the near future. About the only major development that could change this bleak picture for Japanese women may be the increasing demand for skilled employees and the growing labor shortage now being brought about by declining birth rates. Commenting on this development in Japan, Steinhoff and Tanaka recently predicted:

> The labor shortage will not only increase employment opportunities for women in large companies but will at the same time lead to changes in the way large companies utilize their managerial employees. The companies assume that women are unwilling or unable to meet the high time and energy commitments the current managerial system demands, but young men are also increasingly reluctant to pay the price. As the companies reduce working hours, social demands, and arbitrary transfers in order to keep their male managers, they will also be creating a more favorable working environment

for women. Thus Japan appears to be at a turning point, with several factors converging to change both the opportunity structure and the work environment for women in management.[19]

Ethical Problems and Concerns in Europe

Ethical behavior in European countries is an important area of interest in international management, because in some respects, these countries differ sharply from Japan and the United States.[20] France and Germany are good representative examples.

One study surveyed 124 U.S., 72 French, and 70 German managers.[21] Each was asked to respond to a series of five vignettes that examined ethical situations related to coercion and control, conflict of interest, the physical environment, paternalism, and personal integrity. In most cases, the U.S. managers' responses were quite different from those of their European counterparts. The following is an example of one of the vignettes:

> Rollfast Bicycle Company has been barred from entering the market in a large Asian country by collusive efforts of the local bicycle manufacturers. Rollfast could expect to net 5 million dollars per year from sales if it could penetrate the market. Last week a businessman from the country contacted the management of Rollfast and stated that he could smooth the way for the company to sell in his country for a price of $500,000.

The executives from the three countries were asked how they would respond to the request for payment. The Americans were opposed to paying the money; 39 percent of them said that a bribe was unethical or illegal under the Foreign Corrupt Practices Act. Only 12 percent of the French managers felt that way, and none of the Germans agreed. However, 55 percent of the French and 29 percent of the Germans said that paying the money was not unethical but merely the price to be paid for doing business.

Part of the reason for these answers is that to date, neither France nor Germany has laws that make it a crime to bribe or corrupt a public or private official of another country.[22] Legal restrictions are not the only reasons for the differences in managerial views of ethical behavior, however. Here is the conflict-of-interest vignette that was presented to the managers:

> Jack Brown is vice president of marketing for Tangy Spices, a large spice manufacturer. Jack recently joined a business venture with Tangy's director of purchasing to import black pepper from India. Jack's new company is about to sign a five year contract with Tangy to supply their black pepper needs. The contract is set at a price 3 cents per pound above the current market price for comparable black pepper imports.[23]

Should Brown sign the contract? Once again, the managers were divided regarding what should be done and why. Most U.S. managers felt that signing the contract would be dishonest or a conflict of interest. Many of the French managers agreed, but only one-third of the Germans indicated that they would not sign the agreement.

Summing up the responses of the managers to all five vignettes, the researchers concluded:

> If one were to generalize, the U.S. managers were noticeably more concerned with ethical and legal questions. Their French and German counterparts appeared to worry

more about maintaining a successful business posture. To be sure, there was some overlapping of responses; however, the differences remained.[24]

This cross-national research on ethical behavior shows that MNCs must be aware that the ethical practices of their home country may be quite different from those of countries where they do business. A number of reasons account for these differences, including culture, personal values, incentives, and the obvious legal restrictions.

The Status of Women Managers in Europe

Because most European countries have experienced only limited population growth in recent years, integration of women into the work force has become a critical goal. Similar to the United States and Japan, however, European women have encountered equal opportunity problems and a "glass ceiling" in the managerial ranks. The following discussion examines the current status of women managers in three major European nations: France, Germany, and Great Britain.

France   The proportion of French women in the labor force from 1900 until 1970 remained at about 35 percent. Since then, however, more than 2 million women have entered the work force, compared with less than 200,000 men. This trend would seem to indicate that women now should be gaining a greater foothold in the managerial ranks—and to a degree, this is true. Over the last 35 years, the number of women managers has increased almost ninefold, while the number of managerial positions has increased fivefold. The greatest gains have been in product promotion and sales, import-export, sales administration, real estate, urban planning and architecture, socioeconomic studies, and chemistry. Table 17-1 provides some of the latest available data on French managers by function.

Although French women are making strides in the management ranks, they still are underrepresented in corporate management. Table 17-1 shows that women still are far behind men in terms of corporate management and the traditional functions of manufacturing and sales. A number of reasons are given for this underrepresentation. One is that promotion into top management depends on more than diplomas, abilities, and ambitions.[25] As in the United States and Japan, French women face many obstacles when trying to break the glass ceiling. As one analysis of women managers in France notes:

> Being a manager includes having to work long hours, travel, make difficult decisions, motivate people, and achieve high objectives—most often with limited resources and strong business competitors. For women managers, it also often means fighting within their own company to establish a reputation as a leader—since women are rarely spontaneously seen as leaders, avoiding or responding appropriately to sexist criticisms, motivating employees to accept and execute their decisions, and sometimes hiding their family problems. Women frequently have more difficulty than men getting access to information necessary to make wise career decisions. Although it is important for women to understand the organization's career criteria, few companies in France provide such information through either equal opportunity managers or assertiveness courses.[26]

From a legal standpoint, French law guarantees equal treatment and equal professional opportunities. Enforcement of these guarantees is fairly weak, however, and organizations that could be valuable to women generally are uninvolved. For example, unions have generally resisted taking on women's issues, and there are

TABLE 17-1

FRENCH WOMEN AND MEN MANAGERS BY FUNCTION: 1989

Function	Percentage of women	Percentage of men
Corporate management	2.9	6.6
Manufacturing, construction	2.2	10.7
Manufacturing support services	2.4	8.5
Research, development	7.9	12.9
Marketing, sales	19.9	27.1
Banking, insurance, real estate, tourism, transportation	4.0	4.4
Administration	18.4	6.1
Finance, accounting, control	8.6	5.7
Information systems	7.8	9.7
Personnel, education	7.7	2.7
Communications	8.7	1.8
Medical, social, culture	6.3	2.4
Others	2.8	1.4
Total	100.0	100.0

The total is less than 100 because of rounding.
Source: Helene Alexandre, *Les Femmes Cadres* [Women Managers]. Paris: APEC, 1990.

no organizations in France comparable to the Coalition of Labor Union Women in the United States that could promote equal opportunity issues. Even French associations of women managers are limited in their efforts and, for the most part, focus primarily on social networking. So, while some French companies have promoted women into higher-level positions and have affirmative action programs in place, these firms unfortunately still are the exception rather than the rule. As one analyst recently put it, "Companies' needs for the best possible managers will favor highly qualified women; but to succeed, these women will most likely have to accept even more difficult working conditions."[27]

Germany   Before unification, 47 percent of working-age women in West Germany and 91 percent of those in East Germany were in the work force. In both West and East, however, women held few top management positions. Studies of large West German firms found that 5.9 percent of top managers and 7.8 percent of managers at the next level were women, but only 0.7 percent were members of managing boards of public companies. In East Germany, one-third of all management positions were held by women, but these primarily were low-level jobs. With the unification of Germany, the status of women in management does not look any more promising. One reason is that professional qualifications appear to relate inversely to hierarchical position. Antal and Krebsbach-Gnath explained this seeming paradox as follows:

> The higher the position, the less significance the organization attaches to . . . "objective" criteria. The factors that receive more weight in promotion decisions for senior management positions are both less objective and more often based on traditional male career patterns. In effect, therefore, they discriminate against women. Among the factors listed

in one study for promotion into upper-level management were professional competence, effectiveness, professional experience, length of experience, time with the company, commitment to the job, and professional and regional mobility. To the extent that "objective" factors and qualifications, such as education and training that women can consciously acquire, play a lesser role in decision making, other sociopsychological and systemic factors assume increasing importance and create less easily surmountable barriers to career development for women.[28]

Unlike some other countries, Germany in the last decade has introduced laws that mandate equal opportunity and the creation of equal opportunity positions throughout the public sector. Today, all German states must ensure that their legislation provides for equal treatment of men and women in the workplace. On the other hand, use of quotas are unacceptable, and this makes the legislation difficult to enforce. Additionally, those individuals who are designated as equal opportunity officers typically have difficulty carrying out their tasks, because they often lack the needed authority to enforce their decisions.

In the private sector, there has been some progress toward increasing the number of women in upper-level management positions through the introduction of voluntary equal opportunity programs. Some German firms also have nominated individuals or groups and assigned them the responsibility of ensuring equal opportunity for all personnel. Another, and more recent, development is the conclusion of company-level, work-family agreements between employers and workers' representatives regarding parental leave and return plans. These plans allow employees to take a longer parental leave than is granted by law, and to attract these employees back, these plans guarantee an equivalent job on returning from the extended leave.

Some analysts indicate that Germany's growing need for competent managers likely will increase the number of women in management and the opportunity for them to achieve higher-level positions. On the other side, critics argue this is wishful thinking and that what is needed is stronger legislation. Still others contend that until there is a fundamental change in the way that male managers view the role and status of women, nothing significant will happen. These arguments all point to one conclusion: Opportunities for women managers in Germany remain limited and do not seem likely to improve significantly before the turn of the century.

Great Britain   By the beginning of the 1990s, approximately 12 million women were in the British work force, which was about 44 percent of the country's total work force. As shown in Table 17-2, the number of women in management and related occupations has been steadily increasing over the last two decades. Once again, however, as in other countries, British women are not well represented at the highest levels of most organizations. As one analyst notes:

> If membership in the Institute of Directors is an indicator, the proportion of women at the most senior levels in both the public and private sector remains very small. There are no woman chief executives among Britain's top 100 companies, as listed in *The Times*, and a 1989 report found that among members of company boards in the 200 largest industrial companies in the United Kingdom, only 21 had women board members. In total, 24 women were appointed, but the majority, eighteen, were either part-time or nonexecutive directors. Several of the appointed women had a family connection to the company or a title—that of lady or baroness.[29]

TABLE 17-2

BRITISH WOMEN IN MANAGEMENT AND RELATED OCCUPATIONS

Category	Women as a percentage of all employees in category		
	1975	1986	1991
General management	9.7	10.4	—
Management positions, excluding general management	10.9	16.4	—
Professional and related supporting management and administrative positions	12.0	20.3	—
Managers and administrators	—	—	30.6
Professional occupations	—	—	38.3
Associate professional and technical occupations	—	—	49.3
Total, all management and related occupations	11.3	17.4	37.9

Source: New Earnings Survey 1975, Part E, Table 138; *New Earnings Survey 1986,* Part E, Table 138, London: HMSO; M. Naylor and E. Purdie, "Results of the 1991 Labour Force Survey," *Employment Gazette,* April 1992.

Most women managers in Britain are employed in retail distribution, hotel and catering, banking, finance, medical and other health services, and food, drink, and tobacco. Almost all of these women managers are at the lowest levels, and they have a long way to go if they hope to reach the top. Legislation designed to prevent discrimination in the work place is proving to be of limited value; however, a number of steps are being taken to help British women attain equal opportunity in employment.

In recent years, British women have been setting up their own associations, such as the Women's Engineering Society, to develop sources for networking and to increase their political lobbying power. There also is a national association, known as The 300 Group, that campaigns for women seeking election to Parliament. In addition, women have become very active in joining management and professional associations, such as the Hotel, Catering and Institutional Management Association; the Institute of Personnel Management; and the Institute of Health Service Management. Women now constitute 50 percent or more of the membership in these professional associations.

At the same time, a growing number of British companies are proactively trying to recruit and promote women into the management ranks. They are introducing career development programs specifically for women and are prepared to take whatever steps are necessary to ensure that outstanding women remain with the company. For example, the National Westminster Bank allows women managers to leave for up to 5 years to raise their children and then return to a management position at their previous level. Firms also are designing strategies to ensure that equal opportunities are, in fact, being implemented. Chief executives and directors of leading companies recently have formed a group known as Opportunity 2000. One of the group's goals is to provide a wide range of assistance to women who are interested in business careers; in particular, the focus is on helping firms to demonstrate a commitment to these goals, change their old ways of doing business, communicate their desires to potential women managers, and make the necessary financial and time commitments that are needed to ensure success. While it is still too early to say how successful Opportunity 2000 will be, these efforts do appear to be on the right track. One analysis summed up the current status and future direction as follows:

> Recent forecasts of the economy in Britain have highlighted the increased dependence that companies will have on women in the twenty-first century. It forecasts that there will be greater need for managers, professionals, and associated staff and that women will generally represent an increasing proportion of that workforce. It remains to be seen whether initiatives such as Opportunity 2000 will enable the number of women managers to reach a self-sustaining critical mass. Women managers have made strides forward in the last decade. Perhaps with many companies waking up to the necessity of retaining all good employees, more will also learn to use the full potential of their women as managers in order to benefit both the corporate and the national economies.[30]

Ethical Problems and Concerns in China

Along with the tremendous market opportunities in China are some ethical problems for MNCs doing business there. After the violent, June 1989 crackdown on the student protestors in Beijing's Tiananmen Square, many questioned whether any business should be conducted there until more freedom and human rights were restored. As a result, many MNCs pulled out or have not gone into China.[31]

Despite the ethical implications stemming from Tiananmen Square, many MNCs were, and still are, attracted to the competitive advantages offered by China. One of these advantages is the low cost of labor. Companies as nearby as Hong Kong and as far away as the United States have found this cheap labor attractive. In the case of Hong Kong, a severe labor shortage and strict labor laws have made it difficult to meet mounting work demands in industries such as clothing and toy making. In the case of U.S. manufacturers, many toy makers have subcontracted their work to the Chinese, because labor is such a large percentage of their overall costs.

Factory workers in China are not well paid, and to meet the demand for output, they often are forced to work 12 hours a day, 7 days a week. In some cases, children are used for this work and are paid very little, usually only one-half of an adult's wages. The government also has been using prison labor to produce goods for the export market.[32] In addition, since China recently has opened up to the outside world and there has been a rush to get rich under the market economy reforms, there has been a dramatic increase in crime and illegal business activities.[33]

These developments have led to friction between the U.S. Congress and China, and they have resulted in continual efforts by the Senate to impose conditions on the renewal of China's favorable trade status with the United States.[34] During the 1990s, the personal support of Presidents Bush and Clinton have been needed to ensure that China's most favored nation trade status remained intact.[35]

Piracy and Counterfeit Problems   The U.S. government is taking a harder line on Chinese piracy of intellectual property. In the case of music recordings, pirated sales in recent years were 265 percent greater than retail sales of these products, as shown in Figure 17-1. This makes China the largest pirate of this intellectual property in the world. Industry analysts also believe that 90 percent of computer software in China has been pirated from U.S. firms; the same is true for a host of

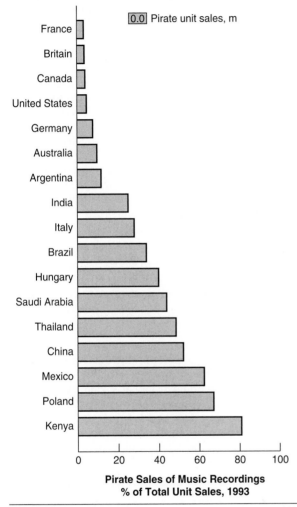

FIGURE 17-1

PIRATE SALES OF MUSIC RECORDINGS AS A PERCENTAGE OF TOTAL UNIT SALES; 1993

Pirate Sales of Music Recordings % of Total Unit Sales, 1993

Source: International Federation of the Phonographic Industry, 1994.

other electronic and technological offerings. The accompanying sidebar, "Getting Tough . . . Or Else," gives some specific examples of this huge pirating problem. Although, to date, words are louder than actions, the Chinese government keeps promising to crack down on piracy, and a number of high-ranking people within China want to see copyright laws enforced. One recent report noted:

Reformist officials have told American businessmen privately that they would like China's copyright laws enforced. This camp includes officials at the influential State Science and Technology Commission as well, presumably, as the foreign-trade minister, Wu Li. These people have little quarrel with America's demands that China's customs officials should be given more power, that taskforces should be created in the provinces to deal with property, and that the intellectual-property courts should be

Get Tough . . . or Else

A growing number of multinationals are very concerned about doing business in China, and they have good reason to be. Within hours of the time their goods are on the street, many find that counterfeiters are already working on developing their own version of the product—and in many cases, these clones look just like the original. Today, there are fake cans of Coca-Cola, fake McDonald's hamburger restaurants, fake versions of the Jeeps that Chrysler manufactures with a joint-venture partner in Beijing, and fake Gillette razor blades.

One of the most disconcerting things for foreign MNCs in China is that counterfeiters often are blatantly obvious in their efforts. One good example is a fast-food restaurant in downtown Shanghai about 100 yards from a McDonald's outlet. This restaurant uses a sign with golden arches on a red background in a way that makes it look like a McDonald's. Lawyers for McDonald's say they are looking into taking legal action.

Even more disconcerting is that when counterfeiters are caught, the Chinese government often does very little about it. The Gillette Razor Blade Company is a good example of this. The Huaxing Razor Blade Factory was producing Gillette look-alike blades and packaging them in the same blue package as that used by Gillette. After Chinese authorities raided the factory, they fined the company $3500 and told management that it was illegal to produce counterfeit blades and they were to stop. Five months later, when it became evident that the company was still manufacturing the blades, there was a second raid, followed by a fine of $3300. At that time, the manager was asked why he not only kept producing the blades but also used the same packaging as before. He remarked that he did not want to throw away packaging that had already been printed. "We didn't want to waste it," he said.

Will such a "slap on the wrist" type of enforcement stop the counterfeiting? This is unlikely, because the fines are small compared with the revenues being generated. The Chinese government also does not seem to be very interested in taking sterner measures. In fact, in some cases when MNCs have complained that counterfeiters have gone back to their old ways, inspectors have refused to take any additional action, arguing that "we already addressed that issue and we are now moving on to other matters." Such an attitude worries MNCs, because they feel there is no protection for their intellectual properties. A lawyer who has represented several U.S. companies in trademark disputes in China put it this way:

> In most countries, if you have 10 pirates, you can go after one, expect seven to stop, and then figure out how to get the remaining two. But in China, when you go after one the other nine see exactly what you're doing. Not only do they keep pirating, but you invite 10 more to join in.

Unless the government of China takes more stringent steps to do something about pirating and counterfeiting, MNCs likely will take action of their own. One of the most commonly mentioned steps is to demand that Chinese exports to the United States be limited and that levies be assessed on these goods to offset the loss of revenues being sustained by the U.S. MNCs. In the final analysis, it appears that China will have to get tough on pirates and counterfeiters . . . or else.

---

made friendlier to the plaintiff. They know that China's own companies, such as software producers, need protection from pirates.[36]

Until safeguards such as these become a reality, China will continue to be a hot bed of pirating and counterfeit activities—and MNCs will proceed with caution when doing business there.

The Status of Women Managers in China   As in other countries, women managers in China confront a "glass ceiling" when trying to reach top management ranks. There are a number of reasons for this, including cultural stereotypes, restricted opportunities, and of course, discrimination.

Cultural stereotypes are deep-rooted and very prevalent in China, and they go a long way toward hindering women's preparation for managerial roles as well as their more direct opportunities for promotion. Women have been socialized to be shy and unassertive. As a result, they often are viewed as being unprepared to assume leadership positions. A common stereotype is that Chinese women are disorganized, narrow-minded, and hard to work with compared to men.[37] Such widespread thinking greatly inhibits the advancement of women in management.

Coupled with this are restricted opportunities. For example, Chinese women are not well represented in the Communist party, which is one of the fastest ways to gain upward mobility. Additionally, Chinese women are less likely to be chosen for education and training programs, again restricting their opportunity to enter the upper-managerial ranks. In particular, women typically are required to have higher test scores on university entrance exams to ensure their admission. They also face segregation on the job and, as a result, often end up with the less meaningful tasks. For example, men typically operate the high-tech equipment and processes, while women do the routine work.

Discrimination in the work place is both blatant and subtle. For example, women often are given additional workplace favors, such as extra rest periods, but in turn, these serve as the basis for bypassing them for promotions, which go instead to men who work longer hours. Additionally, women are required to retire at the age of 60, while men can work until 65. This inhibits their career advancement and helps to prevent them from reaching senior management positions. Drawing together many of these perceptions and stereotypes, Korabik has summed up the series of interviews that she conducted with women managers in the People's Republic of China by noting:

> Stereotypes in China are particularly insidious because no research exists to show them to be inaccurate. Many Chinese therefore believe them to represent the "true" nature of women and men. Government campaigns to eradicate such stereotypes have been largely ineffective, and their consequences are often not redressed because they are not viewed as discriminatory. Thus, despite many laws intended to insure equality in the workplace, Chinese women managers are still at a disadvantage compared to men.[38]

REGULATING FOREIGN INVESTMENT

The regulation of foreign investment is another area of international business that has at least indirect implications for ethics and social responsibility. Many countries have a growing concern regarding the ethics of an MNC's gaining an economic foothold and then taking the resources and profits back home. This concern focuses on reciprocity between the home country of MNCs and the host country. The United States again provides a good example. The latest available data reveal that foreigners have invested triple-digit billions in the United States, and U.S. investments abroad also are in triple-digit billions. Moreover, foreign investors have put more money into this country than U.S. investors have put overseas.

The rapid increase of foreign investment in the United States has raised ethical concerns among many Americans, who believe that such foreign investment needs to be regulated more closely.[39] In addition, some are concerned that countries like Japan seem much more interested in selling to the United States than in buying from U.S. firms. These concerns have ethical and social responsibility implications, and they have led to regulation of acquisitions and reciprocal trade agreements in the United States.[40] Other countries are following the U.S. lead by also looking more closely at these two areas and how they affect their own country.

Regulation of Acquisitions

In the United States, under preliminary regulations published by the Treasury Department, most foreign investors now must obtain formal approval before acquiring a U.S. company. The primary exceptions are industries such as toys and games, food products, hotels and restaurants, and legal services. Acquisition requests are reviewed by the interagency Committee on Foreign Investment, which is made up of eight agencies and headed by the Treasury Department. The stated objective of the regulation is to prevent foreign firms from gaining control of U.S. businesses that are important to U.S. security.

Although at first glance this regulation might appear to be a major barrier to acquisitions by overseas investors, its scope is really quite restricted, and it applies to only a small number of deals. The Treasury Department estimates that fewer than 170 acquisitions a year are covered by this regulation; however, as noted in the following analysis, there can be far-reaching consequences:

> The proposed regulations subject acquisitions, including those that have already been completed since the bill was passed, to divestiture over an indefinite period. They provide that a transaction could be dissolved any time should a foreign investor fail to notify the Government, provide false and misleading information or omit material information. Foreign investors could also become subject to the law if under an acquisition loan agreement, a default would allow them to step in and control the company.[41]

Other countries are following the U.S. lead and implementing similar regulatory practices. For example, many Third World nations now refuse to allow MNCs to establish new operations or purchase ongoing businesses unless they first obtain governmental clearance. This ensures that the government remains in control of the economy and is not overly reliant on foreign companies. In practice, however, many of these countries need MNC operations and are willing to accede to most requests for setting up, acquiring, or expanding local operations.

The countries in the European Union also are beginning to limit the business dealings of foreign multinationals. In particular, in the EU new regulations are making it more difficult for MNCs not located in Europe to do business there.[42] The EU, except for England, is particularly sensitive to the rise of Japanese industrialism and the likelihood that Japanese auto manufacturers will dominate the world market. The EU also is trying to support local companies by mandating that certain parts and equipment, such as computer chips, that are to be sold in Europe also be built there by firms from the EU.

These regulatory developments show that countries around the globe are concerned about the increasingly large amount of foreign investment being made in their economies. This is particularly true in the case of those nations that are viewed as *nonreciprocal trade partners,* or those which sell goods to others but do not buy from them.

The Implications of Reciprocity

Is there an ethical and social responsibility to engage in reciprocal trade? This question is at the forefront of current trade talks between many countries, but especially between the United States and Japan. How much of an obligation does Japan have to import U.S. goods and services in light of its tremendous volume of exports to the United States? Every year, the Japanese have massive trade surpluses with the United States. The 1990s provide an excellent example. Despite some success in reducing barriers in areas such as tobacco and telecommunications and the weakening of the dollar against the yen, the annual trade deficit remained in the $50 to $60 billion range in the mid 1990s.

In recent years, the executive branch has undertaken a review of U.S.-Japanese trade relations. One primary source of information for the analysis was a voluminous report prepared by a special task force consisting of members from both government and business. The group recommended a 1-year trial period during which trade negotiations would be conducted with Japan. If no substantive results were achieved, the group suggested using Super 301, which is a provision of the Omnibus Trade and Competitiveness Act of 1988 that allows for sanctions against "unfair traders."

In the past few years, the United States has targeted Japan and Brazil, among others, for retaliatory action. Whether or not retaliatory action will work, the important thing to remember is that the United States feels it is unethical and irresponsible for countries such as Japan and Brazil to behave in trade relations as they do. Most European countries disagree with the United States and believe there are more effective ways of negotiating trade problems than the use of sanctions. However, as long as the U.S. administration believes that the United States is not being treated ethically in the international trade arena, retaliation will continue to be a means to obtain reciprocity in international trade.

Remember that many critics of Japan point to the fact that Japan deserves such retaliation, that Japan refuses to do business with many outside companies, and that Japan stacks the deck so that all the cards are favorable to its self-interests. A second argument in favor of a retaliatory stance against Japan focuses on the fact that the Japanese often buy foreign businesses such as hotels. Then, when the Japanese travel abroad, they stay at these hotels and Japan recaptures funds that otherwise would flow into the international community. One report described this process as follows:

> Japan's well-heeled travelers . . . prefer neatly wrapped package tours when they go abroad. The Tokyu group, another retailing conglomerate, provides such services by funneling vacationers through an affiliated travel agency to Tokyu's 15 Pacific Basin resorts, hotels, and condominiums. An airline partially owned by Tokyu flies vacationers to the holiday complexes. Joining the retailers in going global are Japan's airlines. In addition to managing 23 Nikko hotels, JAL uses its reservations network to book passengers into 90 other affiliated Nikko hotels. The airline is also developing five overseas resorts. Rival All Nippon Airways manages seven overseas hotels, from China to California, and is scouting for more. . . . And a hefty chunk of profits will end up in Japanese coffers.[43]

Another reason to support retaliation against Japan is that many countries already have sought and reached joint trade agreements with the United States. The argument goes that if Japan were serious in its efforts, it would have done so as well. For example, as early as 1987, South Korea had reached an agreement with the United States to increase imports from the United States by $2.6 billion and to buy a wide range of products, from supercomputers to grain. South Korea also allowed the import of U.S. computers a year ahead of schedule, cut financing to exporters to restrain exports, and pledged to create a service network for imported U.S. machinery. Similarly, Taiwan cut tariffs on a wide variety of products, from farm goods to footwear. Taiwan also allowed U.S. insurance companies to enter its market, liberalized restrictions on foreign banks, and gave some U.S. firms contracts for building the Taipei subway.[44] By offering concessions, countries are more likely to placate the United States, which often is their largest international market, and to ensure there is no trade backlash. There is recent evidence that the years of U.S. pressure on Japan are beginning to pay off. By the mid 1990s, with only a few exceptions, such as rice imports, foreign companies no longer are totally excluded by law, regulation, or tariff from doing business in Japan.[45]

RESPONSE TO SOCIAL OBLIGATIONS

So far, the discussion has focused on differences in ethical standards between countries and why nations such as the United States are concerned about trade reciprocity. However, many countries are responsive to their international social obligations. For example, the United States is leading the way in pushing for higher ethical codes, and others, such as Italy, which has had a tradition of corruption, are putting forth considerable effort to clean things up.[46] Japan is working hard to help Third World countries deal with their economic problems as well.

Foreign Corrupt Practices Act

During the special prosecutor's investigation of the Watergate scandal in the early 1970s, a number of questionable payments made by U.S. corporations to public officials abroad were uncovered. These bribes became the focal point of investigation by the Internal Revenue Service, the Securities and Exchange Commission (SEC), and the Justice Department. Concern over bribes in the international business arena eventually culminated in the passage of the *Foreign Corrupt Practices Act (FCPA)* of 1977, which makes it illegal to influence foreign officials through personal payment or political contributions. The objectives of the FCPA were to stop U.S. MNCs from initiating or perpetuating corruption in foreign government and to upgrade the image both of the United States and U.S. businesses abroad.[47]

Some critics of this legislation feared the loss of sales to foreign competitors, especially in those countries where bribery is viewed as a way of doing business. Nevertheless, the U.S. government pushed ahead and attempted to enforce the act. Some of the countries that were named in early bribery cases included Algeria, Kuwait, Saudi Arabia, and Turkey, although the State Department strived to convince the SEC and the Justice Department not to reveal the names of countries or foreign officials involved in its investigations for fear of creating internal political problems for U.S. allies. Although, for the most part, this political sensitivity was justified, a couple of interesting developments were: (1) MNCs found they could live within the guidelines set down by the FCPA; and (2) many foreign governments actually applauded these investigations under the FCPA, because it helped them crack down on corruption in their own country.

One analysis reported that since passage of the FCPA, U.S. exports to "bribe prone" countries actually have increased.[48] Investigations reveal that once bribes were removed as a key competitive tool, more MNCs were willing to do business in that country. This proved to be true even in the Middle East, where many U.S. MNCs always had assumed that bribes were required to ensure contracts.

On the other hand, this does not mean that bribery is a thing of the past. A recent report issued by the U.S. Commerce Department contends that since 1994, foreign companies have used bribes to edge out U.S. MNCs on some $45 billion of international business deals. The report describes a case of bribery involving the contract for a power-generating plant in Central Europe as follows:

> A European company was awarded the multimillion-dollar contract even though the Central European government's own review board had recommended the contract be awarded to a U.S. firm. The report says there was clear evidence that a power-company official had been given a cash bribe by the European company that won the contract. The company used the same practice to win other contracts in Eastern and Central Europe, according to the report.[49]

These recent experiences reveal that bribery continues to be a problem for U.S. MNCs. At the same time, to comply with the provisions of the FCPA, U.S. firms must be careful not to follow suit and resort to bribery themselves.[50] This advice also is useful for multinational managers doing business in the United States. The U.S. government has been vigorous in its prosecution of bribery and kickback schemes, and one example would be the recent case of Honda employees who were officials of American Honda. They were involved in an illegal program to solicit bribes from Honda auto dealers in exchange for ensuring that the dealers had a steady supply of cars. The scheme, which lasted from the late 1970s until 1992, involved American Honda executives who received cash, Rolex watches, and swimming pools in exchange for their awarding franchises or larger allotments of hot-selling Accords and other cars. The highest-ranking executive in the scheme was given 5 years in federal prison and fined $364,000; other convicted employees received lesser, but still significant, sentences.[51]

International Assistance

Besides fighting corruption, another way to meet social responsibilities has been to provide assistance to underdeveloped countries. For many years, this foreign aid has taken the form of food, machinery, and equipment to help feed the people of Third World countries and stimulate their economies. During the 1970s in particular, many less-developed countries attempted to improve their conditions by borrowing large sums of money for economic development. In most cases, the monies were not wisely spent, and the countries now are having difficulty meeting their debt obligations. Poland, for example, has foreign debts in double-digit billions and very little hope of paying back this money. Mexico and South American countries such as Peru, Argentina, and Brazil are no better off. As a result, some of the economic superpowers recently have been calling for assistance to these countries. Two primary avenues are under investigation: (1) debt reduction or renegotiation; and (2) direct grants.

The United States and Japan are the two leading proponents of international aid. Some Americans have called for a Third World debt reduction plan, and the Japanese government has proposed a package worth $43 billion designed to improve the global environment and spur economic growth in countries suffering under the burden of poverty and indebtedness.[52] Some specific parts of the Japanese package include: (1) low-interest loans to other countries; (2) grants to specific nations in sub-Saharan Africa; and (3) a 3-year program of grants and credits for environmental needs, including tree planting and helping poor people to find alternatives to cutting down trees for fuel and fodder.[53] These decisions will affect

MNCs, because they will help to stimulate world economies and open up markets for more goods and services.

Another form of aid is being carried out by MNCs themselves. Multinationals are beginning to realize that they must take steps to ingratiate themselves in the countries where they do business. A philanthropic role can pragmatically help protect their investments, improve their corporate image, and help meet their social responsibilities. The Japanese are a good example. When Prime Minister Nakasone made derogatory remarks about U.S. African-Americans and Hispanics, Japanese foundations and companies in the United States tried to minimize the damage by increasing their donations to funds that help to promote African-American college students and similar groups. Honda, which was the target of a racial discrimination suit over hiring practices in Ohio, became a big donor to organizations such as the Clara Hale House in Harlem and has provided a scholarship for minority students at Duke University. Mazda has been giving $70,000 annually to the United Way, and Hitachi America has given $30,000 to a local library. Quite clearly, these Japanese MNCs understand the long-run benefits of philanthropy. As one observer pointed out: "In coming years, Japan's role as philanthropist in the U.S. is destined to grow, perhaps even to explode. Clearly, the tracks needed to roll out major fundraising drives and manage large projects have been laid down. American institutions are certain to benefit, and Corporate Japan should, too."[54]

U.S. and European multinationals follow similar philanthropy patterns. Quite clearly, MNC assistance directed at host countries is a two-way street. Each side stands to benefit economically through MNCs' meeting their social responsibilities.

SUMMARY OF KEY POINTS

1. Ethics is the study of morality and standards of conduct. It is important in the study of international management because ethical behavior often varies from one country to another. For example, in recent years in Japan, political and business scandals and apparent cases of avoiding minority hiring have drawn attention to the need for another look at ethical and socially responsible behavior. Japan's lobbying efforts in Washington also have been questioned from an ethical standpoint.

2. Research in France and Germany reveals that European and U.S. MNCs seem to have different standards of ethics that result in different types of decisions and business practices. For example, U.S. MNCs do not believe in bribing businesspeople or politicians to gain favors, while some studies find that more respondents in samples of both German and French managers were not as concerned with bribes as being unethical and instead felt payoffs were merely a cost of doing business. In the area of equal opportunity for women, the Europeans have goals for fully integrating women into the work force and even recent EU legislation to ensure equal pay and equal treatment in employment. However, similar to U.S. women, European women are still being deprived of equal opportunities and are underrepresented in the managerial ranks of European firms, although some progress is being made.

3. Ethics also is a problem in countries such as China. Since the violent crackdown at Tiananmen Square, many MNCs have questioned whether they should do any business with the Chinese. Those that found the low labor cost attractive too often overlooked the fact that the Chinese factory employees work long hours for very low pay and that some of these workers are political prisoners. These types of exploitive practices have ethical implications. So, too, does the status of women managers. As in many other countries,

women managers in China face a "glass ceiling" blocking their advancement into top management. Three of the main reasons are cultural stereotypes, restricted opportunities, and discrimination.

4. A more indirect area of ethics and social responsibility deals with the regulation of foreign investment. In the United States, for example, the interagency Committee on Foreign Investment, which involves eight agencies headed by the Treasury Department, was set up to curb the indiscriminant buying of U.S. firms by foreign investors. The committee regulates the acquisition of U.S. companies by foreign multinationals. A similar, indirect area of ethics and social responsibility is reciprocal trade and the desire of countries such as the United States to get trading partners such as Japan to open their markets to U.S. goods.

5. During the 1990s, multinationals likely will become more concerned about being socially responsive, and legislation such as the U.S. Foreign Corrupt Practices Act is forcing the issue. Other countries also are passing laws to regulate the ethical practices of their MNCs. MNCs are being more proactive (often because they realize it makes good business sense) in providing international assistance in the form of philanthropy and direct community involvement as well.

KEY TERMS

ethics

nonreciprocal trade partners

Foreign Corrupt Practices Act (FCPA)

REVIEW AND DISCUSSION QUESTIONS

1. What lessons can U.S. multinationals learn from the political and bribery scandals in Japan that can be of value to them in doing business in this country? Discuss two.

2. In recent years, some prominent spokespeople have argued that those who work for the U.S. government in trade negotiations should be prohibited for a period of 5 years from accepting jobs as lobbyists for foreign firms. Is this a good idea? Why?

3. How do ethical practices differ among the United States and European countries such as France and Germany? What implications does your answer have for U.S. multinationals operating in Europe?

4. Why are many MNCs reluctant to produce or sell their goods in China? What role can the Chinese government play in helping to resolve this problem?

5. In what way is trade reciprocity an ethics or social responsibility issue? How important is this issue likely to become during the current decade?

6. Why are MNCs getting involved in philanthropy and local communities? Are they displaying a sense of social responsibility, or is this merely a matter of good business? Defend your answer.

PRACTICAL INTERNATIONAL MANAGEMENT ASSIGNMENT

Choose any ethical or social responsibility–related topic from this chapter, then go to the library and update the topic by finding out what has taken place in recent months. Write a brief essay describing your findings, and share them with the other students in the class. What conclusions can you draw as a result of your investigation?

Saudi Arabia

In Saudi Arabia, they go by lunar time (watches are set differently), and the year is counted from Mohammad's death (about 622 A.D.).

Saudi Arabia is a large Middle Eastern country covering 865,000 square miles. Part of its east coast rests on the Persian Gulf, and much of the west coast rests along the Red Sea. One of the countries on its borders is Iraq. After Iraq's military takeover of Kuwait in August 1990, Iraq next threatened to invade Saudi Arabia. This, of course, did not happen, but only time will tell what will happen next in this explosive part of the world.

There are approximately 17 million people in Saudi Arabia, and the per-capita income is around $8,000. This apparent prosperity is misleading, because most Saudis are poor farmers and herders who tend their camels, goats, and sheep. In recent years, however, more and more have moved to the cities and have jobs connected to the oil industry. Nearly all are Arab Muslims. The country has the two holiest cities of Islam: Mecca, and Medina. The country depends almost exclusively on the sale of oil (it is the largest exporter of oil in the world) and has no public debt. The government is a monarchy, and the king makes all important decisions but is advised by ministers and other government officials. Royal and ministerial decrees account for most of the promulgated legislation. There are no political parties.

Earlier this week, Robert Auger, the executive vice president of Skyblue, a large commercial aircraft firm based in Kansas City, had a visit with a Saudi minister. The Saudi official explained to Auger that the government planned to purchase 10 aircraft over the next 2 years. A number of competitive firms were bidding for the job. The minister went on to explain that despite the competitiveness of the situation, several members of the royal family were impressed with Auger's company. The firm's reputation for high-quality performance aircraft and state-of-the-art technology gave it the inside track. A number of people are involved in the decision, however, and in the minister's words, "anything can happen when a committee decision is being made."

The Saudi official went on to explain that some people who would be involved in the decision had recently suffered large losses in some stock market speculations on the London Stock Exchange. "One relative of the King, who will be a key person in the decision regarding the purchase of the aircraft, I have heard, lost over $200,000 last week alone. Some of the competitive firms have decided to put together a pool of money to help ease his burden. Three of them have given me $100,000 each. If you were to do the same, I know that it would put you on a par with them, and I believe it would be in your best interests when the decision is made." Auger was stunned by the suggestion and told the minister that he would check with his people and get back with the minister as soon as possible.

As soon as he got back to his temporary office, Auger sent a coded message to headquarters asking management what he should do. He expects to have an answer within the next 48 hours. In the interim, he has had a call from the minister's office, but Auger's secretary told the caller that Auger had been called away from the office and would not be returning for at least 2 days. The individual said he would place the call again at the beginning of this coming week. In the interim, Auger has talked to a Saudi friend whom he had known back in the United States who was currently an insider in the Saudi government. Over dinner, Auger hinted at what he had been told by the minister. The friend seemed somewhat puzzled about what Auger was saying and indicated that he had heard nothing about any stock market losses by the royal family or pool of money being put together for certain

members of the decision-making committee. He asked Auger, "Are you sure you got the story straight, or as you Americans say, is someone pulling your leg?"

1. What are some current issues facing Saudi Arabia? What is the climate for doing business in Saudi Arabia today?
2. Is it legal for Auger's firm to make a payment of $100,000 to help ensure this contract?
3. Do you think other firms are making these payments, or is Auger's firm being singled out? What conclusion can you draw from your answer?
4. What would you recommend that Skyblue do?

You Be the International Management Consultant

It Sounds a Little Fishy

For the past 2 years, the Chicago-based Brattle Company has been thinking about going international. Two months ago, Brattle entered into negotiations with a large company based in Paris to buy one of its branches in Lyon, France. This would give Brattle a foreign subsidiary. Final arrangements on the deal should be completed within a month, although a few developments have occurred that concern the CEO of Brattle, Angela Scherer.

The most serious concern resulted from a conversation that Scherer had with one of the Lyon firm's largest customers. This customer had been introduced to Scherer during a dinner that the Paris headquarters gave in her honor last month. After the dinner, Scherer struck up a conversation with the customer to assure him that when Brattle took over the Lyon operation, they would provide the same high-quality service as their predecessor. The customer seemed interested in Scherer's comments and then said, "Will I also continue to receive $10,000 monthly for directing my business to you?" Scherer was floored; she did not know what to say. Finally she stammered, "That's something I think you and I will have to talk about further." With that, the two shook hands and the customer left. Scherer has not been back in touch with the customer since the dinner and is unsure of what to do next.

The other matter that has Scherer somewhat upset is a phone call from the head of the Lyon operation last week. This manager explained that his firm was very active in local affairs and donated approximately $5000 a month to charitable organizations and philanthropic activities. Scherer is impressed with the firm's social involvement but wonders whether Brattle will be expected to assume these obligations. She then told her chief financial officer, "We're buying this subsidiary as an investment and we are willing to continue employing all the local people and paying their benefits. However, I wonder if we're going to have any profits from this operation after we get done with all the side payments for nonoperating matters. We have to cut back a lot of extraneous expenses. For example, I think we have to cut back much of the contribution to the local community, at least for the first couple of years. Also, I can't find any evidence of payment of this said $10,000 a month to that large customer. I wonder if we're being sold a bill of goods, or have they been paying him under the table? In any event, I think we need to look into this situation more closely before we make a final decision on whether to buy this operation."

1. If Scherer finds out that the French company has been paying its largest customer $10,000 a month, should Brattle back out of the deal? If Brattle goes ahead with the deal, should it continue to make these payments?
2. If Scherer finds out that the customer has been making up the story and no such payments were actually made, what should she do? What if this best customer says he will take his business elsewhere?
3. If Brattle buys the French subsidiary, should Scherer continue to give $5000 monthly to the local community? Defend your answer.

CHAPTER 17 ENDNOTES

1. For some insights into the Recruit scandal, see Susan Chira, "Another Top Official in Japan Loses Post in Wake of Scandal," *New York Times,* January 25, 1989, pp. 1, 5; "Bribery Trial to Challenge Japanese Ways," *Omaha World Herald,* November 24, 1989, p. 4; and "Remember the Recruit Scandal? Well . . . ," *BusinessWeek,* January 8, 1990, p. 52.
2. "More Japanese Politicians Named in Bribery Scandal," *Wall Street Journal,* January 17, 1992, p. A8.
3. James Sterngold, "A Top Politician in Japan Quits, Admitting He Took Illegal Funds," *New York Times,* August 28, 1992, pp. A1, A6.
4. James Sterngold, "Stock Scandal in Japan Runs Deep," *New York Times,* February 2, 1991, pp. 17, 23; Bill Powell, Hideko Takayama, and Kay Itoi, "Tokyo's Power Club," *Newsweek,* July 8, 1991, pp. 40–42.
5. Quentin Hardy, "Securities Firms in Japan Face Another Probe," *Wall Street Journal,* February 29, 1992, p. A10.
6. "Arrests in Japan Futures Case," *Wall Street Journal,* March 3, 1992, p. A6.
7. "Japan Is Investigating Alleged Collusion Plot by Ink Manufacturers," *Wall Street Journal,* March 3, 1992, p. A6.
8. Steven R. Weisman, "Landmark Harassment Case in Japan," *New York Times,* April 17, 1992, p. A3.
9. Also see Urban C. Lehner and Masayoshi Kanabayashi, "Politicians' Anti-U.S. Remarks Greeted with Silent Approval by Many Japanese," *Wall Street Journal,* January 23, 1992, p. A12.
10. James B. Treece, "What the Japanese Must Learn about Racial Tolerance," *BusinessWeek,* September 5, 1988, p. 41.
11. Robert E. Cole and Donald R. Deskins, Jr., "Racial Factors in Site Location and Employment Patterns of Japanese Auto Firms in America," *California Management Review,* Fall 1988, p. 11.
12. Ibid., pp. 17–18.
13. Fred Luthans, Richard M. Hodgetts, and Kenneth R. Thompson, *Social Issues in Business,* 6th ed. (New York: Macmillan, 1990).
14. Richard E. Wokutch, "Corporate Social Responsibility Japanese Style," *Academy of Management Executive,* May 1990, pp. 56–74.
15. Pat Choate, *Agents of Influence* (New York: Knopf, 1991).
16. Steven J. Dryden and Douglas Harbrecht, "When Japan's Lobbyists Talk, Washington Doesn't Just Listen," *BusinessWeek,* July 11, 1989, p. 68.
17. See Ellis Cose, "Yellow-Peril Journalism," *Time,* November 27, 1989, p. 79; Lee Smith, "Fear and Loathing of Japan," *Fortune,* February 26, 1990, pp. 50–60.
18. Patricia G. Steinhoff and Kazuko Tanaka, "Women Managers in Japan," in Nancy J. Adler and Dafna N. Izraeli (eds.), *Competitive Frontiers: Women Managers in a Global Economy* (Cambridge, MA: Blackwell Publishing, 1994), p. 86.
19. Ibid., p. 97.
20. See, for example, Richard C. Morais, "People in Glass Houses Throwing Stones," *Forbes,* May 25, 1992, pp. 84–93.
21. Helmut Becker and David J. Fritzsche, "A Comparison of the Ethical Behavior of American, French, and German Managers," *Columbia Journal of World Business,* Winter 1987, pp. 87–95.
22. Ibid., p. 90.
23. Ibid., p. 94.
24. Ibid.
25. Evelyne Serdjenian, "Women Managers in France," in Nancy J. Adler and Dafna N. Izraeli (eds.), *Competitive Frontiers: Women Managers in a Global Economy* (Cambridge, MA: Blackwell Publishing, 1994), p. 199.
26. Ibid., pp. 199–200.
27. Ibid., p. 204.
28. Ariane Berthoin Antal and Camilla Krebsbach-Gnath, "Women in Management in Germany: East, West, and Reunited," in Nancy J. Adler and Dafna N. Izraeli (eds.), *Competitive Frontiers: Women Managers in a Global Economy* (Cambridge, MA: Blackwell Publishing, 1994), pp. 210–211.
29. Valerie Hammond and Viki Holton, "The Scenario for Women Managers in Britain in the 1990s," in Nancy J. Adler and Dafna N. Izraeli (eds.), *Competitive Frontiers: Women Managers in a Global Economy* (Cambridge, MA: Blackwell Publishing, 1994), p. 230.
30. Ibid., p. 241.
31. Denis Fred Simon, "After Tiananmen: What Is the Future for Foreign Business in China?" *California Management Review,* Winter 1990, pp. 106–110.
32. Dinal Lee et al., "China's Ugly Export Secret: Prison Labor," *BusinessWeek,* April 22, 1991, pp. 42–46.
33. Pete Engardio, "The Wild, Wild East," *BusinessWeek,* December 28, 1992, pp. 50–51.
34. Keith Bradsher, "Senate Backs Curbs on Beijing's Access to Markets in U.S.," *New York Times,* February 26, 1992, pp. A1, A5.
35. See "Making War on China's Pirates," *Economist,* February 11, 1995, p. 33.
36. Ibid.
37. Karen Korabik, "Managerial Women in the People's Republic of China: The Long March Continues," in Nancy J. Adler and Dafna N. Izraeli (eds.),

Competitive Frontiers: Women Managers in a Global Economy (Cambridge, MA: Blackwell Publishers, 1994), p. 118.

38. Ibid., p. 124.

39. See Badiul A. Majumdar, "Foreign Ownership of America: A Matter of Concern," *Columbia Journal of World Business,* Fall 1990, pp. 13–21.

40. See Paul Magnusson and Blanca Riemer, "Carla Hills, Trade Warrior," *BusinessWeek,* January 22, 1990, pp. 50–55.

41. Clyde H. Farnsworth, "Proposal on Foreign Investors," *New York Times,* July 15, 1989, p. 20.

42. Heinz Weihrich, "Europe 1992: What the Future May Hold," *Academy of Management Executive,* May 1990, pp. 7–18.

43. Amy Borrus and Mark Maremont, "The Japanese Go Globe-Trotting, but the Yen Stays Home," *BusinessWeek,* October 17, 1988, pp. 45–46.

44. Steven J. Dryden, Maria Shao, and Laxmi Nakarmi, "Where Sanctions against Japan Are Really Working," *BusinessWeek,* May 11, 1987, pp. 61–62.

45. Carla Rapoport, "You Can Make Money in Japan," *Fortune,* February 12, 1990, pp. 85–92.

46. John Rossant, "The Cleanup of Italy Inc.," *BusinessWeek,* March 1, 1993, pp. 50–51.

47. Kate Gillespie, "Middle East Response to the U.S. Foreign Corrupt Practices Act," *California Management Review,* Summer 1987, p. 9.

48. John Graham, "Foreign Corruption Practices Act: A Manager's Guide," *Columbia Journal of World Business,* Fall 1983, p. 93.

49. Robert S. Greenberger, "Foreigners Use Bribes to Beat U.S. Rivals in Many Deals, New Report Concludes," *Wall Street Journal,* October 12, 1995, pp. A3, A17.

50. For insights into ethics and the law, see Lillian H. Chaney and Jeanette S. Martin, *Intercultural Business Communication* (Englewood Cliffs, NJ: Prentice-Hall, 1995), pp. 226–228.

51. James Bennet, "4 Former Honda Employees Sentenced in Kickback Case," *New York Times,* August 26, 1995, p. 19.

52. Steven R. Weisman, "Japan to Propose a Package of Aid Worth $43 Billion," *New York Times,* July 12, 1989, pp. 1, 24.

53. Ibid.

54. Amy Borrus et al., "Japan Digs Deep to Win the Hearts and Minds of America," *BusinessWeek,* July 11, 1988, p. 75.

FUTURE OF INTERNATIONAL MANAGEMENT

OBJECTIVES OF THE CHAPTER

Clearly, international management is a dynamic and exciting field of study and practice. As we enter the twenty-first century, even more attention will be given to international management, and the current trend toward borderless economies should accelerate. Unified Germany and the EU as a whole are examples.[1] So are the United States, Canada, and Mexico, which are eliminating trade barriers and forming an economic entity based on NAFTA, and other nations in South America, including Chile, likely will contribute to a borderless situation in this part of the world.[2] Japan, South Korea, and other Asian countries, including Singapore, Taiwan, Hong Kong, and China, are becoming another borderless region of the global economy. By the turn of the century, other regions, such as India, the Middle East, and Africa, also will become increasingly important to international management.[3] These and other dramatic changes serve as the context for this concluding chapter on the future of international management.

Specifically, this chapter reviews the type of global perspective that will permeate management thinking in all countries and all types of organizations in the years ahead. The chapter then focuses on how transition strategies to become a truly transnational corporation must be formulated and carried out. The objectives of this chapter are:

1. **EXAMINE** the trend toward a true global perspective by multinational companies.
2. **DESCRIBE** some of the specific steps in formulating and implementing transition strategies for becoming a transnational corporation.

A GLOBAL PERSPECTIVE

What does the future hold for international management? One certain development is that managers from all countries in all types of organizations will become much more global in their perspective. Instead of looking on their firms as U.S. or German or Japanese companies that happen to be doing business in various areas of the world, future international managers will view their companies as organizations that sell goods and services throughout the globe and just happen to be headquartered in, say, New York, Bonn, or Tokyo. This global perspective is critical to the development of a genuine international management strategy for the years ahead.

To meet the challenges that are inherent in a global perspective requires a series of strategic capabilities that seldom are possessed by any one manager. Bartlett and Ghoshal have identified these needed capabilities as: (1) the ability to build worldwide efficiency and competitiveness; (2) the ability to understand and interpret local markets, build local resources and capabilities, and contribute to the development of global strategy; and (3) the ability to transfer expertise from one unit to another through use of benchmarking information, cross-pollination among groups, and the championing of innovations with worldwide applications.[4] Because no single manager has all these capabilities to the degree needed, it is becoming increasingly important that groups of specialized managers be developed. These groups should be capable of integrating the assets, resources, and people in culturally diverse operating units. Additionally, international managers taking a global perspective must consider their companies as "boundaryless." However, this may be easier said than done:

> These new boundaries are more psychological than organizational. They aren't drawn on a company's organizational chart but in the minds of its managers and employees. And instead of being reflected in a company's structure, they must be "enacted" over and over again in a manager's relationships with bosses, subordinates, and peers. Because these new boundaries are so different from the traditional kinds, they tend to be invisible to most managers. Yet knowing how to recognize these new boundaries and use them productively is the essence of management in the flexible organization. And managers can find help in doing so from an unexpected place: their own gut feelings about work and the people with whom they do it.[5]

Those global managers who are able to accept and be part of this philosophical change in the global perspective of their company will be well on their way to understanding the nature of MNCs of the twenty-first century.

A World Market View: TNCs

Some MNCs, or *transnational corporations (TNCs)* as they are coming to be known, view the world as one market. National boundaries are irrelevant in the efforts of TNCs to find the best sources of materials, produce goods at the lowest price, and raise capital for operations. Even location of the headquarters is immaterial; if a TNC is conducting most of its business in Asia and the operation needs a top management presence there, the TNC will move its headquarters.

What has caused this change in perspective? Domestic markets often are too small to support the investments that are necessary to bring a product or service to market. For example, during the 1970s, pharmaceutical firms found that a new drug took 4 to 5 years to develop, and the cost was around $16 million. By the late 1980s, the time for development had more than doubled, and many drugs cost in the neighborhood of $250 million. These expenses require the drug firm to sell its product internationally to recoup the investment as quickly as possible.[6] Of course, not every product can be sold worldwide, because the demand often is insufficient or the market is fragmented. Then, the company must focus its efforts on a select number of countries. Many businesses are finding a global approach to be extremely profitable, however. One analysis, for example, has identified 136 industries, from accounting to zippers, where successful firms use a global approach. Specific industrial examples include autos, banking, consumer electronics, entertainment, publishing, travel services, and washing machines.[7]

Most MNCs have not yet really become purely global enterprises—TNCs. However, some are well on their way. U.S.-based IBM is a good candidate. So, too, is Whirlpool, which purchased Philips' $2 billion-a-year appliance business in Europe and is integrating its operation into a worldwide appliance business. Here is a close look at some representative examples of those MNCs making the transition to TNCs:

1. *General Motors,* even though it has undergone severe problems domestically, is becoming increasingly transnational. This TNC is credited to John F. Smith, the previous head of GM Europe, who was brought back as president of GM. Smith now is trying to replicate the European success companywide by integrating operations worldwide, copying successful strategies used by other divisions, and tailoring approaches to meet the needs of local customers. Now the company sources its parts worldwide and buys based on quality as well as price. At the same time, GM has linked its British plants to its pan-European production system and can export cars from Britain to the Continent to meet growing demand. Meanwhile, company research and development (R&D) centers work closely to create new product offerings and get them to worldwide markets. Result: Over the past 5 years, GM's share of the U.S. market may have bottomed out, but importantly, the firm's European profits are at an all-time high, and the company is making inroads in the Asian market as well.[8] A good example is GM's success in China, where it recently was chosen by the government to build sedans.[9] This project is valued at more than $1 billion and is only one of many GM business deals in China. Others include: (1) a dozen ventures by its Delphi Automotive Systems unit to make car parts; (2) a $40 million investment in five technology institutes to teach the design of car parts, engines, and transmissions; and (3) the renegotiation of a $30 million joint venture with First Auto Works to build pickup trucks.[10]

2. *Apple* is developing a TNC by combining its talents with those of other computer makers, using joint ventures to help develop and market its products everywhere. For example, Apple has entered into agreements with IBM to jointly conduct research and manufacturing and uses Sharp Electronics to produce the Newton, its electronic pager.[11] Such strategies appear to be paying off.[12]

3. *Asea Brown Boveri* (ABB) is a Swiss/Swedish firm that has more than 70 companies throughout Europe and the United States. The global electrical equipment giant is larger than Westinghouse and often competes head-to-head with such multinational giants as General Electric and Siemens. The firm has 250 global managers and a work force of 210,000 employees, but only 150 people

are at headquarters. The rest are out in the field in operational jobs. ABB sources its materials and supplies worldwide while managing local operations with local boards of directors. Unlike most other MNCs, ABB uses a matrix structure that allows it to swap technology, products, and ideas between the geographically dispersed units. In this way, the $30 billion firm is moving toward transnational status. For example, ABB is aggressively moving into Asia, where demand for electric power is growing four times faster than in Europe and North America. Between 1992 and 1994, ABB increased its power-generation sales from $1 billion to $3 billion, and this growth likely will continue throughout the decade.[13]

4. *Coca-Cola*, with annual revenues of over $16 billion and profits approaching $3 billion, is one of the world's most successful MNCs.[14] A large part of this success results from the company's international operations, which account for most of its sales and profits and likely will continue doing so. Over the last decade, Coca-Cola has increased its international presence in both Europe and Asia, and in the process, it has begun to implement a new international strategy that in the words of the company's president, is to be "fast and flexible."[15] A good example is the company's Japanese operations, its most profitable market. Product development in Japan is fast and furious. New offerings are rushed to market and, when their appeal fades, quickly withdrawn and replaced by others. Consider a drink called "Ambasa Whitewater," which initially sold millions of cases; when market demand slackened, the product was pulled to make room for new offerings. Another example of this "fast and flexible" strategy is the rapidity with which decisions are made. In a recent meeting with managers in Hanoi, a senior-level Coke executive made a quick decision to double the size of the firm's new plant with a $10 million investment, even though the Vietnamese market was still untested. In Eastern Europe, the company's newfound agility has helped it to surpass Pepsi and become the number-one soft drink in this newly emerging market. By spending more than $1.5 billion in former communist bloc countries to bring in manufacturing, distribution, and marketing operations, Coca-Cola now is seen as the "milk of capitalism" in Eastern Europe. Quite obviously, the company's transition to a TNC is paying off handsomely.

5. *Boeing*, the giant U.S. aircraft manufacturer, has annual revenues in excess of $21 billion.[16] Well over one-half of Boeing's sales are from international orders.[17] One reason for the company's success overseas is that it is widely regarded as the premier aircraft maker in the world, so as the fleets of airlines around the world continue to expand and/or replace old aircraft, Boeing's plan is to be the company of first choice. This world-class image has a lot to do with Boeing's commitment to view its market as worldwide in scope. A good recent example is the firm's major contract from Singapore Airlines for what could be as many as 77 of its 777 mid-sized commercial jets, which are wide-body, twin-jet aircraft that can carry 300 to 400 people on long flights at lower costs than current jumbo aircraft.[18] The total value of the Singapore order is in the neighborhood of $13 billion. In the past, Singapore had split its purchase orders between Boeing and Airbus Industrie, the European consortium, but this time Boeing was the clear winner. The current contract is a firm order for 34 of the 777s and an option for an additional 43.[19] A number of reasons account for Boeing's success in the international arena. One is its ability to negotiate effectively. For example, in addition to providing a state-of-the-art aircraft to Singapore Airlines,

Boeing also has agreed to buy back the planes at a future date at a predetermined price. A second reason is the company's ability to work well with other firms by co-ordinating activities effectively. In the case of the 777s, for example, the jet engines will be built by Rolls-Royce, so the two firms will have to mesh their plans closely to provide the aircraft by the promised delivery date. A third reason is Boeing's ability to develop new markets. This is clearly seen by the fact that it now has locked up 230 firm orders for its 777 and has options for an additional 150. In addition to Singapore Airlines, other Asian carriers that have ordered this new plane include All Nippon Airways, Thai Airways International, Japan Airlines, Cathay Pacific Airways, China Southern, Japan Air System, and Korean Air Lines. While it is more difficult to generate sales in Europe because of the strong competition from Airbus, Boeing also has its sights set on this market as well as Latin American. The company realizes that its future rests in the growing world demand for aircraft, and it is continuing to move in this direction.

An Objective Approach to Globalization

Effective globalization often is characterized by objective analysis of data and decisions based on the bottom line of the enterprise. If a company can cut its cost by 15 percent through moving production to an offshore facility, this step is likely even if some current domestic personnel must be reassigned or let go. The company will not necessarily abandon its social responsibilities to all groups involved, but it will not allow sentimentality or emotional nationalism to override economic considerations. Thus, the link between the new transnationals and their home country is beginning to diminish.

Loosening the Links   Many U.S. MNCs are good examples of global enterprises whose success no longer is tied to the economics of their country. Many are setting up operations overseas, because it is more profitable to do so. As shown in Table 18-1, the 20 largest U.S. exporters obtain well over $100 billion in revenue from their international sales, and in some cases, these overseas sales account for more than one-third of their total revenue. This business that U.S. firms are doing abroad in turn can reduce the amount of U.S. exports and compound trade-deficit problems for the United States. Under the new transnational perspective, however, these firms do not consider the decrease in exports and increased deficit to be their problem. As the chief financial officer of Colgate-Palmolive has declared: "The United States does not have an automatic call on our resources. There is no mind-set that puts this country first."[20] In fact, TNCs tend to follow their market wherever it takes them.

This trend of weakening ties with the home country is not without severe social consequences. For example, unemployment often results. Here is how the argument that globalization actually may hurt the home country typically is presented:

> The leading critics of globalization are union leaders, trying to save American jobs, and some economists and politicians, who assert that any manufacturing operation creates wealth for the host country. The argument is that industry is not only a source of jobs, but also of income for researchers who develop new products, for parts suppliers and for lawyers, accountants, and many other service workers.[21]

TABLE 18-1

THE 20 LARGEST U.S. EXPORTERS

Company	Major export	1994 Export revenues (in U.S. $ millions)	Percent of total revenues
General Motors	Motor vehicles and parts, locomotives	16,127	10.4
Ford Motor	Motor vehicles and parts	11,892	9.3
Boeing	Commercial aircraft	11,844	54.0
Chrysler	Motor vehicles and parts	9,400	11.9
General Electric	Jet engines, turbines, plastics, medical systems, locomotives	8,110	12.5
Motorola	Communications equipment, semiconductors	7,370	33.1
International Business Machines	Computers and related equipment	6,336	9.9
Philip Morris	Tobacco, beer, food products	4,942	9.2
Archer Daniels Midland	Protein meals, vegetable oils, flour, alcohol, grain	4,675	41.1
Hewlett-Packard	Measurement, computation, communication products and systems	4,653	18.6
Intel	Microcomputer components, modules, systems	4,561	39.6
Caterpillar	Engines, turbines, construction, mining, and agricultural machinery	4,510	31.5
McDonnell Douglas	Aerospace products, missiles, electronic systems	4,235	32.1
E.I. DuPont de Nemours	Chemicals, polymers, fibers, specialty products	3,625	10.4
United Technologies	Jet engines, helicopters, cooling equipment	3,108	14.7
Eastman Kodak	Imaging products	2,600	15.4
Lockheed	Aerospace products, missiles, electronic systems	2,079	15.8
Compaq Computer	Computers and related equipment	2,018	18.6
Raytheon	Electronic systems, engineering and construction projects	1,867	18.6
Digital Equipment	Computers, software, related equipment	1,830	13.6

Source: Company records, 1995.

Changing Demographics   Another significant influence on transnational decision making is the changing demographics of the world population. Two primary demographic dimensions will receive a great deal of attention in the years ahead. One is consideration of real gross domestic/national product growth rates; the other is labor force growth rates.

Doing Business in India

For over four decades, India has been shunned by most MNCs. The political and bureaucratic red tape was more than most multinationals could take. Those firms that did venture in found that getting approval of any project typically took years. For example, in 1985, PepsiCo applied for approval of its soft drinks, snack foods, and food-processing project. It took until 1990 before all hurdles finally were overcome. Texas Instruments faced a similar fate. The company set up operations in 1985 and had to work its way through 43 agencies for approval to start the project and export computer software. Other firms such as Coca-Cola pulled out of the Indian market in the late 1970s, unwilling to deal with such time-delaying procedures. Then, things began to change markedly.

The turn of events can be traced to the government of Prime Minister Rao, who took over the reins in June 1991. The new government has decided to tear down many of the barriers to doing business, eliminate red tape, and streamline the economy. Result: Many MNCs interested in doing business in India indicated that the government was making good on its promises. For example, Coca-Cola re-entered the market and was able to get such approval within 90 days of application. Motorola applied for permission to set up a software-development operation to serve businesses in other countries. It took less than a year from proposal to implementation, and the firm soon had 13 projects totaling $150 million in various stages, ranging from cellular telephones and paging systems to semiconductor assembly and a worldwide satellite-based personal communications system.

General Electric is another good example. The company has a joint venture with Wipro Corporation, the second-largest computer manufacturer in India. The group's new Wipro GE Medical Systems manufactures CAT scanners and ultrasound machines for the medical market as well as other equipment for the mass market. In addition, GE recently signed new deals for plastics, appliances, and lighting. Approval of the Wipro GE venture took a mere 9 months.

Unfortunately, beginning in 1995, old problems began to reappear, and some major political opposition groups began a strong backlash against multinationals. For example, the giant Enro power plant outside Bombay was put on hold. This project, which was the crown jewel of a budding new business relationship between India and the United States, sent a message to other MNCs: Invest with caution. The major question that now confronts the multinationals is whether the government will stay the course and continue promoting foreign investment in the face of opposition, or whether it will buckle under to those who want to go back to the 1970s, when Prime Minister Indira Gandhi forced Coca-Cola, IBM, and other big companies out of India and drove away foreign investment for a generation. With his Congress Party facing tough elections, Prime Minister Rao to date has appeared reluctant to support the MNCs. In turn, more of these firms are beginning to wonder if they should cancel their future plans for India and focus on developing Asian countries where the business climate is more favorable.

Many industrialized nations such as the United States and the EU do not always focus their efforts in the fastest-growing economic regions of the world. Research shows that a large percentage of U.S. firms concentrate their attention on Europe, the United Kingdom, Canada, and the Pacific Rim. These are areas where many U.S. MNCs feel comfortable; however, these companies may be overlooking some other fast-growing areas, such as India (see the accompanying sidebar, "Doing Business in India") and China. As discussed in Chapter 1, these two countries constitute the two largest untapped sources of economic growth for many MNCs. Both also present considerable political risks, but given their future potential, an increasing number of multinationals now believe these two countries warrant serious investment consideration.

A second demographics-related change is occurring in the labor force growth rates of the world. As seen in Table 18-2, the world's growth rate during the latter half of the 1980s was 9.2 percent, but this will increase to 16.5 percent during the

---

TABLE 18-2

THE WORLD'S WORK FORCE: 1985–2000

(Population figures in thousands)

	1985	1990	2000	Change 1985–1990		Change 1990–2000	
World	2,163,664	2,363,547	2,752,524	199,903	9.2%	388,977	16.5%
North America	129,592	135,438	146,561	5,846	4.5%	11,123	8.2%
Canada	12,723	13,360	14,461	637	5.0%	1,101	8.2%
United States	116,800	122,005	132,017	5,205	4.5%	10,012	8.2%
Caribbean	12,287	13,813	16,732	1,526	12.4%	2,919	21.1%
Latin America	140,249	158,285	199,959	18,036	12.9%	41,674	26.3%
Central America	34,186	40,007	53,631	5,821	17.0%	13,624	34.1%
Europe	226,373	231,702	238,186	5,329	2.4%	6,484	2.8%
Eastern Europe	58,036	59,336	62,946	1,300	2.2%	3,610	6.1%
Northern Europe	40,596	41,363	42,226	767	1.9%	863	2.1%
Southern Europe	56,888	59,019	61,742	2,131	3.7%	2,723	4.6%
Western Europe	70,852	71,984	71,272	1,132	1.6%	(712)	−1.0
Asia	1,292,138	1,436,522	1,680,559	144,384	11.2%	244,037	17.0%
China	617,906	679,900	760,917	61,994	10.0%	81,017	11.9%
Japan	59,772	62,202	64,352	2,430	4.1%	2,150	3.5%

Source: International Labor Office, *Economically Active Population Estimates and Projections, 1950–2025,* vols. IV and V, 3rd ed. (Geneva, 1986). Reported in *Inc.'s Guide to International Business,* 1988, p. 45.

1990s. The largest increase will occur in Central America, South America, the Caribbean, and Asia. These population statistics have two important implications for emerging transnationals. First, there are expanding markets for specific types of goods and services. For example, as Figure 18-1 shows, Mexico, Brazil, India, and Malaysia will have more than one-third of their population under the age of 14 during the 1990s. This contrasts with nations such as Germany, Switzerland, Sweden, Italy, and the Netherlands, where less than 20 percent of the population will be in this age group during this time.

A related development will be the increase of the middle class in countries such as India (although only 7 percent of the population is considered to be middle class, this figure still represents more people than the entire population of France). Second, as the population increases, so will the number of people in the work force. More people will be looking for work, and transnationals seeking low-cost labor sources likely will find them in countries with expanding populations. By the same token, labor-intensive industries will move out of those countries where the work force is shrinking, employees demand higher salaries, and social costs are very high. Europe is a good example of the impact of a shrinking work force. As one report noted:

> Europe's "demographic winter,". . . suggests problems ahead for the continent's economy. As the work force shrinks and the number of pensioners soars, Europe must place more and more of its resources into such things as health care and social services. By the year 2000, for instance, 100 German workers will support 31 elderly dependents; in contrast, the same number of Singaporeans will support 13 dependents.[22]

Even the United States is being affected by demographic developments, particularly in the form of immigration. In the 1980s alone, 8.7 million people came into

FIGURE 18-1

POPULATION UNDER THE AGE OF 14 IN SELECTED COUNTRIES

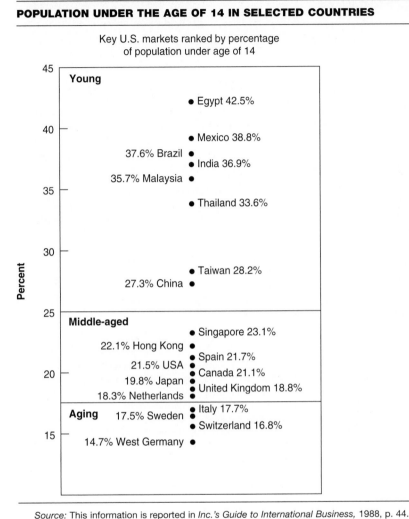

Source: This information is reported in *Inc.'s Guide to International Business*, 1988, p. 44.

the country, matching the great immigration decade of 1900 through 1910; and in 1990, the number was over 1 million. Moreover, most of these people are from Asia (35 percent), Mexico (24 percent), the Caribbean (13 percent), and Central and South America (11 percent), in contrast to the situation in previous decades, when most immigrants came from Europe.[23] This development means that MNCs doing business in the United States will need to consider revising their strategies, because there are new, growing ethnic markets. Simply stated, studying the demographics of the world population may help TNCs to make those decisions that are best for the bottom line rather than those that fit traditionally preconceived notions. In other words, objective analysis will supplant subjective evaluation. Objective analyses will require training in customs and cultures for expatriates. Chapters in Part Four stressed such training, and the accompanying box, "International Management in Action: It's the Little Things that Count," gives some further insights.

INTERNATIONAL MANAGEMENT IN ACTION

It's the Little Things that Count

One of the most important ways to prepare for an overseas assignment is to know the customs and cultures of the local situation. It's often the little things that count in doing business overseas. The following are some basic guidelines that are useful in selected geographic areas:

Canada Business dress is more conservative than that in the United States, so pack some business suits. When you converse with customers or clients, it is all right to talk about French-Canadian relations, but be careful not to get the provinces mixed up. Have a general understanding of where each is located, and do not ask people from Edmonton if they get many storms off the Great Lakes. If the people you are working with prefer to speak French, find out in advance and have an interpreter on hand.

Great Britain Be on your best behavior in public, because people assume that this also is the way that you will do business in private. Be courteous, say please and thank you, and when you accept a dinner invitation, be sure to reply with a handwritten thank-you note. Dinner usually occurs at 7:30; you can be a few minutes late but do not be early. Most topics are acceptable for dinner conversation, but stay away from gossip about the royal family as well as the situation in Northern Ireland.

Hong Kong Businesspeople in this country like to get things done. Some experts claim they can get more accomplished in Hong Kong over lunch than in a week of effort in other countries. However, customs are still important. Therefore, when dressing for dinner or a business meeting, be sure to avoid the classic navy blue suit with the white shirt. In Hong Kong, blue and white connote mourning.

Italy Stay away from discussions about politics, because these generally result in spirited debate in which a visitor does not want to get involved. Italians are style conscious, so business suits should be trendy or exquisitely tailored. When you are invited to dinner at someone's home, it is acceptable to bring a bottle of wine, a wrapped box of chocolates, or flowers. If the latter approach is used, stay away from chrysanthemums and calla lilies, because they are used only for funerals.

Mexico Business usually proceeds at a leisurely pace. Lunch sometimes never takes place, and dinner that is scheduled for 9 sometimes does not start until midnight. Mexicans like to stand close to the person with whom they are speaking, and they shake hands enthusiastically. Eye contact is important, because it implies sincerity and interest. It also helps a lot to know someone with authority, because visitors who are "well connected" often are able to achieve a great deal more than those who are not.

Japan The key to doing business successfully with the Japanese is to gain their trust and respect. In negotiations, it is permissible to bring a translator but not a lawyer. When the time comes to close a deal, a handshake is enough, and the formalities involving lawyers can come later. Another hint is not to use humor or make sarcastic remarks during a business meeting. Be prepared to attend an after-hours get-together (without the spouse), wait for a toast before drinking, and allow the host to choose what to discuss. One Japanese executive summed it up when he said, "I could not agree with him, but I'll still give him my business because he has earned my respect."

TRANSITION STRATEGIES FOR TNCs

In addition to a global perspective, the transition to an effective TNC must be driven by strategy formulation and implementation. The important steps in this transition strategy involve evaluating the environment and then making the right moves, emulating only what works, and being prepared to do business. The following sections explain what these seemingly simple but important steps mean and also provide some specific examples.

Making the Right Moves

Making the right moves depends on making a correct analysis of two major areas: customer needs and competitive responses. What goods and services does the customer currently want, and what will these individuals want over the next 1 to 3 years? What are the major strengths and weaknesses of the competition in this market, and how are these likely to change over the next 1 to 3 years? These two questions are critical in helping transnationals to make the right moves. In responding to the answers, TNCs likely will implement three basic strategies: (1) reduction of overcapacity; (2) differentiation of product offerings to address the specific needs of the market; and (3) the rapid exploitation of the learning curve.[24]

Reduction of Overcapacity   Many industries have overcapacity. In Europe, for example, turbine producers operate at only 60 percent of capacity. In the locomotive manufacturing industry, companies operate between 50 and 80 percent of capacity. In Japan, the United States, and Europe, major automakers all operate well below full capacity.[25] During the years ahead, management will have to choose between two courses of action: (1) close facilities or (2) increase demand. Electrolux has opted for the first and has closed or refocused the efforts of every factory it has purchased over the last 10 years. Today, Electrolux manufactures all front-loading washing machines in its Italian plant, all top-loading washing machines in its French plant, and all microwave ovens in its British plant.[26]

Other transnationals will have to opt for the second course and attempt to increase demand by introducing more cost-efficient technology and passing the savings on to the customer through lower prices. To date, this strategy has been most effective in industries where substantial savings can be achieved through centralized production and efficient export procedures and where the product can be internationally standardized. Good examples include television and auto manufacturing firms.

Differentiation Where Necessary   Matsushita, for example, has been able to dominate the world television market, because this product required very little, if any, differentiation on a country-by-country basis. Many products, however, do require differentiation to meet local tastes. Even within the EU, where commonality is being encouraged and even legislated, local differences still are likely to remain major barriers to the sale of standardized products. One observer commented on this European situation as follows:

> The persistence of local tastes and preferences . . . will prevent most companies from operating as genuine pan-European entities. . . . The differences are clear enough. The French eat 33 kilograms per capita of beef each year, while the Portuguese eat only 10 kg. The Spanish eat 22 kg of poultry each year, while the Germans eat only 9.5 kg. The French want top-loading washing machines, while the British prefer front-loaders. Such differences will not erode overnight.[27]

Exploiting Learning   Another important dimension that will help to ensure that a TNC will make the right moves involves learning how to take advantage of information or learning. For example, many high-tech industries will need to develop state-of-the-art technology that can be used to produce new, innovative products. These firms cannot rest on their laurels, however. They must then attempt to standardize the technology and use it to produce goods for other markets. In this way, the companies can maximize profit while increasing market share.[28]

Cellular phone technology is a good example. This technology first was used in manufacturing expensive auto phones. Then, "walk around" models were developed. Today, car phones are less expensive, and a growing number of MNCs, from Motorola to Ericsson to Nippon Telegraph and Telephone, have developed more affordable models in their attempt to capture a larger share of this world market. In other words, as firms begin to learn how to manufacture and sell a product, they then try to exploit this knowledge in the international marketplace. This pattern of "learn and then exploit" should be of increasing importance to transnationals during the years ahead.

Another good example is Nissan, which has built a factory specifically designed to reduce job difficulty and stress. This new plant has eliminated many of the old ways of assembling cars, including squatting on the floor, stretching across the seat or the hood, and ducking under the auto. Even conveyor belts have been taken out. Now, cars are placed on motor-driven dollies, which can be raised or lowered so that workers do not have to stretch or squat. Additionally, if it takes longer than usual to complete a particular task, workers can simply push the dolly up to the next station as soon as they are finished. Other differences between this plant and traditional ones include the use of natural sunlight filtering through skylights, air-conditioning, and use of robots to perform the dirtiest and most difficult jobs. Nissan believes that this new plant will reduce absenteeism and turnover and increase productivity.[29]

In summary, TNCs that make the right moves will depend on a combination of efficiency, responsiveness, and learning. In the meantime, TNCs also must fashion organization designs such as those covered in Chapter 9 that will help them to implement these strategies. This will include, among other things, monitoring what the competition does and deciding what is worth copying and what is not.

Emulating Only What Works

In the last 10 years, much attention has been given to Japanese-style management and its value for other firms around the globe. Will transnationals adopt Japanese management practices during the coming decade? Probably the best answer is yes, but only on a limited basis, because it now is clear that far too many problems are associated with blind acceptance of the Japanese approach.[30] Moreover, recent evidence reveals that many managers are quite mistaken regarding why the Japanese have been so successful. In contrast to the majority of popular thinking, much of Japan's success may *not* be a result of its culture. Obviously, many reasons explain the recent success of Japanese MNCs. One analysis points out the Japanese advantage of being a follower in industries rather than a leader:

> Most of the institutions Japan has invented derive not from culture but from its experience of late industrialization. As a follower or "catching-up" nation in the process of industrialization, Japan avoided some of the rigidities of the early industrializers and put together the institutions of capitalism in novel ways.
>
> As a follower nation, Japan learned something about labor and its relationship to production that is obscured in Western economic theory. Rather than regarding labor as a separate factor of production, as Western textbooks tell us that it is, the Japanese came to regard labor as a form of capital. They did not hit on this insight all at once but only over time, in the process of trying to create an industrial relations system that avoided the class conflict and labor unrest associated with industrialization in the West. But many important consequences follow from this insight.[31]

Recognizing that Japanese management may not be *the* answer helps to explain why many non-Japanese multinationals are reluctant to follow the tenets of Japanese-based Theory Z.[32] The situation faced by the Japanese is not the same as that faced by many TNCs going into the next century. Moreover, Japanese firms do not employ a universal strategy. Instead, like successful enterprises from other countries around the globe, the Japanese alter their strategy to suit the demands of the specific environment.

If a Japanese firm operating in the United States believes that the key to success is effective human resource management, the firm typically will use Japanese-style techniques such as quality circles, because this approach will work the best. However, this does not mean that they maintain close control over the host-country nationals. In fact, one recent study found that the most profitable Japanese-owned companies in the United States were those that delegate a high degree of authority to their U.S. managers.[33] By the same token, if a Japanese company believes that success is determined by technological processes, the firm may place its own people in key positions but de-emphasize Japanese-style human resource management. Japanese managers recognize that there is little to be gained by overemphasizing their approaches in this latter situation. As another example, if the Japanese firm is product-centered and has little competition, the firm typically will supply components made at home and use the local plant as a simple assembly operation. If the assembly process is labor-intensive and the costs are high, however, as in the case of automobiles or motorcycles, then Japanese human resource management techniques will be given relatively more importance.[34] In other words, successful MNCs do not automatically use home-country management techniques in all their overseas operations. Instead, these firms copy only what works, and the Japanese again are a good example.

In recent years, the Japanese have revised some of their thinking about how to improve operations and done a 180-degree turnaround. Some of the new thinking in Japanese management includes:

1. Continuous improvement in the form of small, incremental gains no longer is sufficient. As international competition increases, attention now is being directed toward setting high targets and making radical changes for achieving them.
2. Instead of re-engineering the processes used in making products, attention now is being focused on re-engineering the products themselves, because product design often accounts for as much as 80 percent of total production costs.
3. Simplification of product design is critical to cost containment. Therefore, the emphasis now is on taking things out of the product design and making it easier to manufacture. This is in contrast to the old approach of adding more to the product design.
4. Product variety is being reduced sharply, because the cost of producing fewer versions of a product will cut costs sharply and these savings can be passed on to the customer in the form of lower prices.
5. Consensus decision making is being de-emphasized, because it is time-consuming and often inefficient. Lone workers in the field, aided by high-tech information systems, often can make better choices than groups of employees who collectively review data and arrive at a decision that is acceptable to everyone.[35]

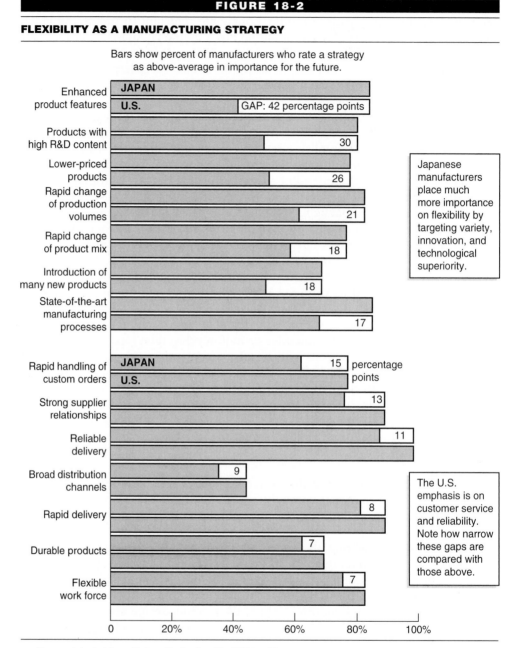

FIGURE 18-2

FLEXIBILITY AS A MANUFACTURING STRATEGY

Bars show percent of manufacturers who rate a strategy as above-average in importance for the future.

Japanese manufacturers place much more importance on flexibility by targeting variety, innovation, and technological superiority.

The U.S. emphasis is on customer service and reliability. Note how narrow these gaps are compared with those above.

Source: Adapted from *Forbes*, September 21, 1992, p. 63.

Another good example is the way that Japanese MNCs are trying to deal with the fact that U.S. multinationals are closing the quality gap. As shown in Figure 18-2, Japanese manufacturers now are placing more emphasis on flexibility, producing in small lots and changing models quickly.[36] Undoubtedly, U.S. MNCs soon will emulate this strategy.

Being Prepared to Do Business

Being prepared to do business as applied to a transition strategy focuses on two areas: (1) training personnel to do business in different cultures and (2) learning how to identify the best locations for new operations.

Training in Ways of Doing Business and Negotiating The specific ways in which MNCs can train, and in some cases have trained, their personnel were discussed in Chapter 15. With an eye toward the future, however, managers must recognize that training will become an important strategic factor, especially with regard to understanding how managers in other countries conduct operations.[37] For example, when an MNC is involved in a joint venture with Russia, what are the most important areas of consideration? For instance, one point to remember is that Russians are very concerned with the amount of Western currency the contract will generate. They need hard currency to help rebuild their economy, so a business venture that calls for new investment likely will require the outside partners to invest dollars. Similarly, a deal that allows the Russians to sell goods in the West is preferable to one that simply involves sales within Russia, because the outside market will provide a flow of funds into their economic system.

Other countries present a different set of priorities when MNCs are negotiating contracts. For example, in pre–Tiananmen Square China, an analysis rank-ordered these priorities as follows: price, technology protection, valuation of capital contributions for joint ventures, training, delivery schedules, penalty clauses, warranty protection, and determining technical specifications.[38] International managers who are unfamiliar with how to negotiate effectively with the Chinese likely would have ranked these in a different order, and found that this mistake had cost them lots of time and effort. Price seemed far and away to be the single most difficult matter to resolve in dealing with the Chinese. Moreover, the Chinese negotiator who was determining the price often was not the end user. As a result, this negotiator may well have settled on a price that did not provide training for the users or warranty coverage of the product. If something went wrong, it was the end user's problem. Therefore, warranty protection was a very low priority for Chinese negotiators. In the years ahead, TNCs will need to train their people in effective negotiating tactics.

The importance to U.S. international managers of learning how to do business overseas becomes even clearer when we realize that other countries often send their people to the United States to learn how to negotiate and interact effectively with Americans. The Japanese, for example, try to give their people both in-house intercultural training and hands-on experience. When the Japanese discuss a joint venture with a U.S. firm, the Americans commonly send four or five people to Japan to discuss the matter, while the Japanese send three or four times as many to the United States to study the situation and decide how to proceed. As a result, the Japanese learn a great deal about how to do business with Americans in addition to finding out how their U.S. partners manage operations. This practice of international exposure and learning is invaluable in helping Japanese managers to compete on a worldwide basis, and this practice will be increasingly important to all TNCs.

Unfortunately, training often has not received the necessary attention. Adler and Bartholomew have reported that many MNCs have developed strategies that far outdistance the capabilities of their people.[39] In fact, human resource strategies

---

TABLE 18-3

TRANSNATIONALLY COMPETENT MANAGERS

Transnational skills	Transnationally competent managers	Transnational international managers
Global perspective	Understand worldwide business environment from a global perspective	Focus on a single foreign country and on managing relationships between headquarters and that country
Local responsiveness	Learn about many cultures	Become an expert on one culture
Synergistic learning	Work with and learn from people from many cultures simultaneously	Work with and coach people in each foreign culture separately or sequentially
	Create a culturally synergistic organizational environment	Integrate foreigners into the headquarters' national organizational culture
Transition and adaptation	Adapt to living in many foreign cultures	Adapt to living in a foreign culture
Cross-cultural interaction	Use cross-cultural interaction skills on a daily basis throughout one's career	Use cross-cultural interaction skills primarily on foreign assignments
Collaboration	Interact with foreign colleagues as equals	Interact within clearly defined hierarchies of structural and cultural dominance
Foreign experience	Transportation for career and organization development	Expatriation or inpatriation primarily to get the job done

Source: Nancy J. Adler and Susan Bartholomew, "Managing Globally Competent People," *Academy of Management Executive*, May 1992, p. 54. Used with permission.

are significantly *less* global than MNC business strategies. Table 18-3 illustrates this discrepancy. Additionally, there are fresh approaches emerging for doing business in the global marketplace. Strategies related to developing core competencies, re-engineering MNC systems, and employing time-based competition will be critical to success in the years ahead. In short, there still is a great deal more to be done by multinationals in becoming transnational in their approach.

A good example of becoming more transnational is the way in which MNCs now are extending their knowledge of how to deal with domestic markets by modifying it to accommodate the international arena. For example, U.S. managers have been trained for decades in the classical "4-Ps" of marketing: product, price, place, and promotion. Now, they are learning the "4-Ps" of international marketing:

- *Pre-emption.* It is important to be the first company to introduce a new product or service, because this often is critical to getting and holding the largest market position.
- *Proximity.* It is important to introduce new goods and services worldwide at approximately the same time rather than waiting for markets to mature, despite the fact that there may be more demand for the new offering in the United States than in Japan and more in Japan than in Belgium.
- *Predisposition.* It is critical to develop a strong international reputation so that when potential customers hear about a new good or service that is being offered by the firm, they will be predisposed to buy it because they have had success with the company's goods and services in the past.
- *Propagation.* Everyone in the company must get behind and support new products and services so that the international sales force is pushing just as hard for the success of offering as is the domestic group.[40]

These four guidelines are being followed by an increasing number of MNCs. Especially relevant to international management, they are finding that proximity is extremely important. In the past, most U.S.-based MNCs would roll out their new products in the U.S. market and maybe in one or two other economically advanced countries. Over the next 3 to 4 years, they gradually would begin offering these products in more of the world market, and perhaps a decade later, they would offer them everywhere. The problem with this strategy was that by the time the MNC finally started moving into the second group of countries, the competition already was firmly entrenched. The product introduction guideline for the twenty-first century has become: Roll out new offerings on a worldwide basis, and grow the market from there. Rosabeth Kanter recently explained it this way:

> Years ago there used to be fairly long time lags between a product introduction in one country, such as the United States, and the time it was finally introduced, say, in Latin America. But now these time lags are closing. Data on consumer electronics have shown a 12-year time lag between the introduction of black and white television in the United States and when they finally were introduced in smaller, less economically advanced nations. However, by the time we got to the FAX machines, it was everywhere almost instantly.[41]

Identifying the Best Locales   Where should MNCs set up their operations? In Chapter 8, location considerations were addressed in macroenvironmental terms; however, recent research shows that a host of other factors, many of them microenvironmental, also warrant attention. After examining more than 37 companies operating in 15 countries, Kanter and colleagues found that related to the location of a business are three criteria for success:

1. *Concepts* are the first criterion and refer to leading-edge ideas, designs, or formulations for products or services that create value for customers. For example, when an MNC with a high-technology emphasis locates in the United States, it needs to be near a source of high-technology ideas. This is where concepts enter the picture.

2. *Competence* is the second criterion and involves the ability to translate ideas into applications for customers and to execute these requirements into the highest standards. For example, if an MNC is looking to manufacture products, it needs to find a locale where there is a high degree of competence, such as an experienced labor pool that can be trained to produce the desired goods.

3. *Connections* are the third criterion of success and refer to the alliances among businesses that can help to leverage core capabilities, create more value for customers, or simply open doors and widen horizons. If the MNC is looking to use location as a springboard to the rest of the country, or even for cross-border activity, it needs to find a locale where local businesspeople are well connected with other markets and can provide the MNC with ready access.[42]

These three criteria are important in helping MNCs to succeed in global markets, because they emphasize innovation (concepts), learning (competence), and collaboration (connections). In particular, these three criteria can be implemented as follows:

1. *Organize around customer logic:* rapidly feed customer needs and desires into new product and service concepts, and transform the overall concept of the business when technologies and markets shift.

2. *Set high goals:* try to be the world standard in the niches that are pursued, and seek to "redefine the category" with each new offering.
3. *Select people who are broad, creative thinkers:* define jobs broadly rather than narrowly, encourage personnel to become multiskilled at working across territories, and give them the best tools for those jobs.
4. *Encourage enterprise:* empower people to seek new product and service concepts, let them act on their ideas, and provide abundant recognition for initiative.
5. *Collaborate with partners:* combine the best of one's own personnel and their partners' expertise for customized customer applications.[43]

MNCs that employ the above are helping to create what is being called the "global shopping malls" of the future. In the process, they are becoming world class, focused outward rather than inward, steeped in the latest knowledge, and comfortable operating across the boundaries of countries, industries, communities, and companies.

How can MNCs go about finding locales where the needed criteria for success (concepts, competencies, and connections) are present? The answer is that geographic locales often readily distinguish themselves in these categories, and a careful review of location sites can identify them. Following Kanter, for the sake of simplicity: (1) those locales that are superior in providing concepts could be called "thinkers"; (2) those that lead the way in competencies could be called "makers"; and (3) those that are superior in connections could be called "traders."

An example of a location of thinkers is Boston, which is a magnet for brainpower. The area has 65 colleges and universities, and one-half the population attends college. In addition, this brainpower attracts research dollars that are used for a variety of investigations, from computers to environmental medicine and from manufacturing processes to textile research. While the emphasis of thinkers is on research and the generation of new knowledge, however, these individuals also are active in translating concepts into commercialization and for attracting industry to the area. The basis of their competence is intellectual, but they go beyond being thinkers by using this strength to help them become better makers and traders.

Makers are characterized by their ability to produce best-in-class output. A good example is the Spartanburg and Greenville areas of South Carolina, which have been extraordinarily successful in attracting foreign manufacturing companies. There are a number of strengths on which makers rely. These include the active solicitation of foreign investment, creation of a hospitable business climate and strong work ethic, a focus on continual improvement in training and education, and the ability to collaborate with both government and business. Like thinkers, makers go beyond just their primary area of strength. They use thinking concepts for attracting businesses to their region, and they trade ideas to connect agencies and firms that can help to improve the process.

Traders have the skills and infrastructure for connecting with other regions and cultures and for leveraging these connections in a multitude of major industries. Miami is an excellent example. The city is multicultural and multilingual; over one-half the population is Cuban-American. The city also has a giant seaport that provides it with a connection to Latin America and Europe. Best of all, many businesspeople in Miami have close connections with firms throughout Latin America and Europe. Based on her interviews with Cuban businesspeople in this city, Kanter has noted:

While Miami Cubans built dense interpersonal connections within their own commu-nity, they were also well connected outward. Cuban communities sprang up in Europe, in Paris, London, and throughout Spain; in Venezuela, Puerto Rico, Canada, and Mex-ico; and in other large U.S. cities. This created a vast network . . . an ethnic network with Miami at its center. "One reason Miami today is such an important international center of trade, communications, and finance is that so many Cubans did *not* settle there," an observer commented.[44]

At the same time, Miami has been able to attract thinkers, as evidenced by the growth of its educational base. In addition to the University of Miami and Miami Dade Community College, both of which are well known throughout the country, Florida International University came into existence in the early 1970s and cur-rently is the 35th largest urban university in the United States. Collectively, these three institutions graduate over 25,000 students annually. Miami also has been ac-tive as a maker, as evidenced by the large percentage of the population that are owner-entrepreneurs.

During the remainder of this decade and well into the twenty-first century, MNCs will seek locations that will help them to extend their international reach. In doing so, they will look to identify communities that primarily are thinkers, makers, or traders. At the same time, communities will try to establish themselves in one of these categories to attract multinationals.

A FINAL WORD

In this book, a great deal has been said about how to manage international oper-ations. In closing, two points merit consideration: the inevitability of joint part-nering, and the need for ongoing research.

Joint Partnering

Current trends leave no doubt that the world of international management will be one of joint partnerships and agreements. Transnationals will be boundaryless companies in the twenty-first century, because this is the only way that they will be able to survive. Sometimes called a *virtual corporation,* defined as a network of companies that come together to exploit fast-changing opportunities and share costs, skills, and access to global markets,[45] good examples would be IBM, Toshiba, and Siemens. These TNCs created a joint venture to develop state-of-the-art, "benchmark" (best in the world) memory chips that may well be the mainstay of computers in the next century. These chips will be able to store 256 million bits of data each, which is equivalent to 10,000 pages of typed text. Large-capacity chips will make it much easier for businesses to store information as well as open the door for computer scientists to achieve breakthroughs in areas such as com-puter speech recognition, machine vision, and computer reasoning.[46]

One main reason for this joint venture is to help control the expenses of re-search and production. In the early 1990s, it cost approximately $500 million to build a manufacturing plant capable of producing the most advanced chips, which at one time could store 16 million bits of information. As the decade pro-gresses, the cost of these high-tech plants will rise sharply and is predicted to be in the neighborhood of $1 billion by 1999. No computer firm can afford to take such a large risk, hence the need for a joint venture. These types of arrangements will become increasingly prevalent during this decade.

Another reason for partnering is that the success of TNCs depends heavily on a strong worldwide economy, a genuine commitment to helping nations improve the well-being of their citizens, and a willingness to share success with other businesses, TNCs and local firms alike. Akio Morita, chairman of Sony and a leading proponent of worldwide partnering, has suggested that Japanese TNCs take the following steps:

- Manufacture more products locally in the United States—reducing exports from Japan and creating high-quality jobs for U.S. workers.
- Discover and develop more parts and components suppliers among U.S. firms in the United States.
- Augment U.S. "human capital" by training workers in the most advanced aspects of Japanese production processes, and do advanced R&D locally.
- Build business partnerships, including technology exchanges and transfers, with like-minded U.S. corporations.
- Practice "borderless" policies within Japanese corporations—internationalizing management as much as possible and offering equal training and promotional opportunities to all employees.
- Participate fully as "corporate citizens" in community activities and philanthropic endeavors in the United States, with special attention to supporting education, skills training, and scientific research.
- Work to reduce trade-related imbalances by identifying high-quality companies and products in the United States that can be introduced to the Japanese market.[47]

Such suggestions clearly reinforce the need for co-operation and joint partnering. They also illustrate that the international environment now is, and in the years ahead will be, markedly different from that of past decades.

Continued Research

A great many theories have relevance to the study of international management. Many have been discussed in this book, but all must be continually subjected to review, analysis, and reformulation. A good example is the theory of lifetime employment in Japan. For many years, international management experts have argued that lifetime employment creates a highly motivated work force and that Western organizations should emulate this approach. More recent research, however, reveals that lifetime employment is less useful as a motivator than as a control tool for ensuring worker loyalty and performance. In return for guaranteed employment, the personnel stay with the firm for their entire career, work hard, and are compliant to management's wishes. Based on an analysis of empirical data collected on this topic, two researchers recently concluded: "Lifetime employment is offered within a . . . context of loyalty and benevolence based on cultural values. Its impact, however, is to increase the control of Japanese employees by managers."[48] Moreover, these researchers found that lifetime employment was not widely used by firms in tight labor markets, because it was not possible to control the workers, who could easily find jobs with other companies and derived little motivation from such guarantees.

International management research also is important because it generates new hypotheses for testing. For example, as workers in large companies with guaranteed lifetime employment near retirement (55 to 60 years of age), will management replace them with younger people who are not given such guarantees? As the competitive environment increases, will MNCs stop offering these guarantees because they reduce the firms' flexibility in responding to changing conditions? Will young workers entering the Japanese work force during this decade be motivated by such guarantees, or will they turn them down because they are unwilling to commit their career to one firm in return for job security?[49] These types of questions must be focal points for international management research, because changing economic, cultural, and social environments are creating new conditions in which TNCs must compete. Research can help to shed light on the effect of these changes. A recent summary of research on Japanese management practices concluded the following:

1. The cultural underpinnings of Japanese society are shifting toward Western values, although this shift is not uniform across culture and is not rapid in all sectors.
2. Industrial organization in Japan, especially the *keiretsu*, will continue to provide competitive advantages and is being extended internationally.
3. Long-range planning is becoming more formal and moving toward a Western style, although it will retain a more visionary perspective.
4. Manufacturing productivity per employee in the United States is rapidly approaching or exceeding parity with Japan. Advantages for Japanese companies appear in certain areas such as R&D and product design, but these appear to be heavily supported by governmental and vertical alliances.
5. The Japanese possess some advantages in the management of quality processes; however, the gap between Japanese and U.S. quality management is closing, though perhaps more slowly than the productivity gap.
6. In neutral countries, the quality image of Japanese products continues to slightly exceed those of the United States, largely because of distribution, promotion, and service advantages.
7. The Japanese will continue to invest more heavily in R&D than U.S. firms and to introduce new products both faster and more economically than the United States by using superior organizational, communicative, and integrative arrangements, discriminatory patent protection, superior governmental funding, and exceptional support by *keiretsus*. These advantages will be aggressively protected and enhanced in the future.
8. Traditional Japanese human resource management practices, including lifetime employment, seniority-based systems, and company unions, are rapidly disappearing and cannot be relied on to produce future competitive advantage. Transplanted Japanese organizations have had limited success in implementing these practices and will make fewer attempts to do so in the future.
9. Because of the rapidly converging parity of U.S. and Japanese productivity and quality, as well as diminishing human resource management advantages, future competitive advantages of the Japanese, if they persist, will derive largely from managerial and organization learning excellence, strengthened by structural systems that promote information amplification, and bolstered by even greater reliance on the *keiretsu* and the Ministry of International Trade and Industry.[50]

Only time will tell how accurate these predictions prove to be, but such information is valuable to the field of international management.

Research also will play an increasing role in helping to uncover how and why multinationals succeed. In particular, greater attention must be given to strategy research designed to explain why some firms do better than others and how these strategies are changing. For example, during the 1970s, traditional international business strategy gave strong support to the concept of *strategic fit,* in which an organization must align its resources in such a way as to mesh with the environment. Auto firms had to design and build cars that were in demand, and this might mean a variety of models and accessories depending on the number of markets being served. Analogously, electronics firms had to maintain state-of-the-art technology to meet consumer demands for new, high-quality, high-performance products. Today, successful multinationals do much more than attempt to attain a strategic fit. The rapid pace of competitive change requires linkages between all segments of the business, from manufacturing on down to point-of-purchase selling, and in every phase of operation, there must be attention to value-added concepts.

Recently, the concept of strategic fit is being supplemented by the concept of *strategic stretch,* which is the creative use of resources to achieve ever more challenging goals.[51] It is important for MNCs to employ strategic stretch, because without it, they find that what is immediately feasible drives out what is ultimately desirable. Without strategic stretch, Percy Barnevik never would have been able to build ABB into a global giant, and Ted Turner never would have dared to dream of creating CNN. Those multinationals with the greatest amount of resources today will not be the leaders in tomorrow's international arena if they fail to use the creative judgement that is fundamental to strategic stretch. Scarcity of resources can be offset by creativity and risk-taking, and this can make all the difference in besting competitors whose primary strength is an abundance of resources. Commenting on this, Hamel and Prahalad have noted:

> We believe that companies like NEC, Charles Schwab, CNN, Sony, Glaxo, Canon, and Honda were united more by the unreasonableness of their ambitions and the creativity exhibited in getting the most from the least than they were by a common cultural or institutional heritage. If further evidence is needed, consider the less-than-sterling performance of Japan's largest banks and brokerages in world markets. Almost unique among Japan's multinationals, these firms possessed immense resource advantages where they entered world markets. Yet material advantages have proved to be a poor substitute for the strategic creativity engendered by resource scarcity.[52]

Of course, it is unlikely there will ever be agreement on all aspects of international management strategy, if only because the specific environmental demands made on one company or industry will require a response different from that needed in another. However, there will continue to be efforts to find overriding strategic principles that have broad value and can be used by most transnationals. A good example was provided by Sullivan and Bauerschmidt, who surveyed managers of large multinationals in an effort to discover those international management strategy principles that were of most value. They found that three were of critical importance to large MNCs: (1) the ability to optimize efficiency; (2) rapid response to environmental changes; and (3) the ability to develop distinct, proprietary advantages.[53] In the case of small firms, major emphasis was needed on innovation, because this helps to make up for the companies' lack of expertise in international manufacturing and marketing.

These findings help to explain how to apply strategy on a practical level. They also illustrate that international research and practice can be brought together in a meaningful way. During the years ahead, we likely will see a great deal more of such investigations, because this is the only way to ensure that international management efforts are based on fact and not intuitive generalizations. The field of international management will continually change, and those organizations and managers willing to continually rethink and reformulate their approaches based on emerging data will be the big winners. The paradigms of international management are changing. TNCs that hope to be successful in the twenty-first century must not only adapt but anticipate and stay ahead of this change.[54]

SUMMARY OF KEY POINTS

1. One major development in the future of international management will be a more global perspective. Corporations will become transnationals (TNCs), no longer concerned with traditional national borders, and view the world as one giant market. Ties will loosen between TNCs and their home countries, and changing market conditions, such as demographic changes in terms of population, age, culture, and product demands, will receive more attention.

2. A second, and complementary, development will be a focus on transitional strategies—how they are formulated and implemented. The right moves include adopting strategies that reduce overcapacity, differentiating product offerings, and allowing for the rapid exploitation of the learning curve, watching the competition, and emulating only what works. Another important area of change should involve training managers in the customs and cultures of those geographic areas where they will be working and being able to choose the best worldwide locations for setting up operations.

3. Finally, current trends point to the inevitability of joint partnering and the need for ongoing research. The joint venture will become a way for TNCs to compete effectively in the global economy, and continued international research is needed to learn and innovate for future success.

KEY TERMS

transnational corporations
virtual corporation

strategic fit
strategic stretch

REVIEW AND DISCUSSION QUESTIONS

1. How does a TNC view the world? How does this view differ from that of an MNC? In light of your answer, how would IBM of the 1980s differ from IBM of the 1990s?

2. What are some changing demographics that will be of major importance to TNCs during the coming years? Identify and discuss two of them.

3. Effective strategy formulation and implementation in the future will require attention to areas such as reducing overcapacity, differentiating product offerings, and exploiting the learning curve. How can this be done by firms such as General Motors? Apple Computer? Coca-Cola?

4. One rule of international strategy is: Emulate only what works. How does this rule apply to the use of a Japanese-based Theory Z approach in U.S. firms? Defend your answer.

5. The "4-Ps" of traditional marketing have been replaced by the "4-Ps" of international marketing. What are these, and which one is most relevant to international management? Why?

PRACTICAL INTERNATIONAL MANAGEMENT ASSIGNMENT

Choose an international manufacturing-related industry such as automobiles, industrial equipment, or consumer goods. Do library research on the general economic condition of this industry, and identify those firms that seem to be most profitable. How closely are they following the three guidelines set forth in this chapter: reduce overcapacity, differentiate product lines to address local tastes, and exploit the learning curve? Based on your answers, what conclusions can you offer regarding successful strategies in this industry during the years ahead?

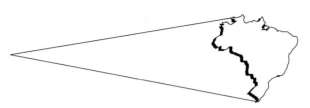

In the International Spotlight

Brazil

In Spanish-speaking countries, the father's name comes first in people's surnames, but in Portuguese-speaking Brazil, it is the other way around, with the mother's name first.

Brazil covers an area of 3.3 million square miles (about 90 percent the size of the United States) and is the largest country in South America and fifth-largest in the world. It is located on the east coast of the continent and borders every country in South America except Ecuador and Chile. There are 165 million people in Brazil, and over 9 million of them live in São Paulo. There is a wide range of living standards, from the very rich to the poor who live in huts with mud walls and thatched roofs in the country and in deplorable slums in the cities. This gap between rich and poor is a serious problem, but the middle class—made up of teachers, businesspeople, and government employees—is growing. The country has a Portuguese heritage and still maintains these customs and language. The major sectors of the economy are manufacturing, services, trade, and agriculture. The last several years have been difficult economic times for the country. The military ran the government until 1985, when civilian rule was re-established, but has suffered from scandal and instability. In recent years, there has been triple-digit inflation and, in some periods, even higher rates. In addition, the country is saddled with an enormous foreign debt that is the largest of any developing nation.

Hobart and Henderson (H&H) is a multiproduct manufacturing firm located in the northeast part of the United States. Very few people have heard of H&H, but the company has been extremely suc-

cessful by following what it calls its "Japanese strategy." The firm waits for a successful Japanese product to hit the market and then reverse-engineers the product. In other words, after figuring out how the Japanese produced the product in the first place, H&H then works on improving the product, getting its own patent, and then producing and marketing the good at a lower price in the international market. As the CEO of H&H recently put it, "As long as the Japanese keep coming out with new products, we'll never run out of things to produce and sell."

The latest product that H&H is reverse-engineering is a hand-held computer game. The company believes that within 4 months it will have the technology and skills to produce these games at 70 percent of what it is costing the Japanese. Of course, the Japanese are having them mass produced in low-cost areas of the world, but H&H intends to follow suit by having them produced in Rio de Janeiro. The operation will be set up by local Brazilians, but H&H will install its own top management staff and make them responsible for overall productivity and profitability. At present, only two additional areas remain for the company to address before proceeding with the Brazilian venture. The first is whether any international managerial training will be needed before sending the expatriate managers to Rio. The second is whether these expatriates should be kept there indefinitely or whether the company should pull them out as soon as possible and turn the entire operation over to local Brazilian management. Decisions on both matters are expected within the next 10 days, and the company hopes to have the operation up and going within 4 months.

1. What are some current issues facing Brazil? What is the climate for doing business in Brazil today?

2. How effective is a strategy of copying what works for other firms?

3. Should H&H give its expatriates international management training?

4. Should H&H plan on removing its own top-level management team from the Rio plant and turning things over to local Brazilian management?

You Be the International Management Consultant

Going in Two Directions at the Same Time

Hackworth & Franklin (H&F) is a moderately large manufacturing firm that produces farm machinery and equipment. Although the company has a limited product line, two factors account for its international success. First, the firm's two stateside plants are among the most efficient in the industry. Because worldwide demand is so strong for H&F products, the factories operate at capacity, and both are running two shifts a day. At the same time, the company has a very attractive productivity-sharing plan that encourages personnel to develop new cost-cutting procedures and look for ways of redesigning facilities or changing work flows so that the jobs can be done more efficiently. Second, H&F has developed some revolutionary products thanks to its high-caliber research and development staff, and these products are tailored for their local markets. These two factors have helped the firm increase annual sales by 25 percent over each of the last 5 years.

Despite its high efficiency, H&F is beginning to realize that transportation costs are eroding a large percentage of its profits. The company now is thinking about setting up two plants, one in Europe and one in East Asia. These plants will handle some existing business but mainly will handle new business and, within 3 years, should be operating at capacity. H&F management already has made preliminary inquiries and identified local facilities that can be converted into operating plants within 6 months. If the company proceeds with this plan, over 60 percent of its sales will be handled by the overseas plants by 1999.

The basic idea is attractive to the senior managers of H&F, although they are concerned that the firm eventually will have to relinquish much of its control over operations, because local decisions will have to be decentralized. There also is concern over expanding operations into two countries, at opposite ends of the world, at the same time. Some senior-level executives are suggesting that H&F open a plant in Europe first, learn what it is like to go international, then use this knowledge and experience to open a plant in East Asia. An equal number on the top management team, including the chair of the board, believe that the firm should build both plants at the same time. Here is how the head of the board explained her point of view:

> We know that within the next 5 years we are going to have to develop better machinery and equipment if we hope to continue our world dominance in selective agricultural markets. We also know that the costs of exporting are becoming prohibitive. We can continue to do our research and development here in the United States. However, if we want to be successful in the European Union and the Pacific Rim countries, we are going to have to have a physical presence there. And I think the longer we procrastinate, the more difficult it is going to become for us. I know that it is best to concentrate your attention and energies on one thing at a time. But in this case, I think we're best off going in two directions at the same time.

1. Will this new strategy result in a change in the way the firm views its market, or is the proposed plan simply an extension of management's current strategy?
2. Are there any benefits to the firm in continuing its current export strategy? What are the benefits of setting up locations worldwide? Which of the two approaches—going to Europe first and then East Asia, or going to both at the same time—would you recommend to the company? Defend your answer.

CHAPTER 18 ENDNOTES

1. Shawn Tully, "Europe 1992: More Unity Than You Think," *Fortune*, August 24, 1992, pp. 136–142.
2. Roberto E. Batres, "One Market for the Americas," *Journal of Business Strategy*, March/April 1992, pp. 13–14.
3. See Keith Bradsher, "As Global Talks Stall, Regional Trade Pacts Multiply," *New York Times*, August 23, 1992, p. F5.
4. Christopher A. Bartlett and Sumantra Ghoshal, "What Is a Global Manager?" *Harvard Business Review*, September-October 1992, pp. 124–132.
5. Larry Hirschhorn and Thomas Gilmore, "The New Boundaries of the 'Boundaryless' Company," *Harvard Business Review*, May-June 1992, p. 105.
6. Jeremy Main, "How to Go Global—and Why," *Fortune*, August 28, 1989, p. 70.
7. Ibid., p. 71.
8. Paul Ingrassia and Timothy Aeppel, "Worried by Japanese, Thriving GM Europe Vows to Get Leaner," *Wall Street Journal*, July 27, 1992, pp. A1, A6. For an analysis of GM's current problems, also see Carol Loomis, "Dinosaurs?" *Fortune*, May 3, 1993, pp. 36–42.
9. Joseph Kahn and Gabriella Stern, "GM Wins Bidding for China Auto Project," *Wall Street Journal*, October 24, 1995, p. A3.
10. Keith Naughton et al., "How GM Got the Inside Track in China," *BusinessWeek*, November 6, 1995, pp. 56–57.
11. Neil Gross and Kathy Rebello, "Apple? Japan Can't Say No," *BusinessWeek*, June 29, 1992, pp. 32–33.
12. John Markoff, "Defying Skeptics, Apple Raises Its Market Share," *New York Times*, November 1, 1995, pp. C1–C2.
13. "Asia Delivers an Electric Shock," *Economist*, October 28, 1995, pp. 77–78.
14. *Fortune*, August 7, 1995, p. F30.
15. Robert Frank, "Coca-Cola Is Shedding Its Once-Stodgy Image with Swift Expansion," *Wall Street Journal*, August 22, 1995, pp. A1, A5.
16. *Fortune*, August 7, 1995, p. F38.
17. *Fortune*, November 13, 1995, p. 74.
18. Lawrence M. Fisher, "Boeing Gets Record $12.7 Billion Order," *New York Times*, November 15, 1995, pp. C1, C7.
19. Jeff Cole, "Boeing Is Victor in Battle for Singapore Air Order," *Wall Street Journal*, November 15, 1995, p. A3.
20. Louis Uchitelle, "U.S. Businesses Loosen Link to Mother Country," *New York Times*, May 21, 1989, p. 1.
21. Ibid., p. 12.
22. *Inc's Guide to International Business*, 1988, p. 45.
23. Michael J. Mandel et al., "The Immigrants," *BusinessWeek*, July 13, 1992, pp. 114–122.
24. For additional insights, see John F. Magee, "1992: Moves Americans Must Make," *Harvard Business Review*, May-June 1989, pp. 78–84.
25. Also see Emily Thornton, "How Japan Got Burned in the U.S.A.," *Fortune*, June 15, 1992, pp. 114–116.
26. Eric G. Friberg, "1992: Moves Europeans Are Making," *Harvard Business Review*, May-June 1989, p. 88.
27. Ibid., pp. 88–89.
28. Also see Rita Koselka, "A Tight Ship," *Forbes*, July 20, 1992, pp. 141–144.
29. Andrew Pollack, "Assembly-Line Amenities for Japan's Auto Workers," *New York Times*, July 20, 1992, pp. A1, C5.
30. See, for example, S. Prakash Sethi, Nobuaki Namiki, and Carl L. Swanson, "The Decline of the Japanese System of Management," *California Management Review*, Summer 1984, pp. 35–45; Richard M. Hodgetts and Fred Luthans, "Japanese HR Management Practices: Separating Fact from Fiction," *Personnel*, April 1989, pp. 42–45.
31. Chalmers Johnson, "Japanese-Style Management in America," *California Management Review*, Summer 1988, p. 41.
32. Akio Morita, "Why Japan Must Change," *Fortune*, March 9, 1992, pp. 66–67; Andrew Pollack, "Japan's Slump Imperils Lifetime Jobs," *New York Times*, September 14, 1992, p. C8.
33. "Japanese Employers Are 'Locking Out' Their U.S. Managers," *BusinessWeek*, May 7, 1990, p. 24.
34. Johnson, "Japanese-Style Management in America," p. 37.
35. Ronald Henkoff, "New Management Secrets from Japan—Really," *Fortune*, November 27, 1995, pp. 135–146.
36. Thomas A. Stewart, "Brace for Japan's Hot New Strategy," *Fortune*, September 21, 1992, pp. 62–74.
37. Joann S. Lublin, "Companies Use Cross-Cultural Training to Help Their Employees Adjust Abroad," *Wall Street Journal*, August 4, 1992, pp. B1, B6.
38. John Frankenstein, "Trends in Chinese Business Practice: Changes in the Beijing Wind," *California Management Review*, Fall 1986, pp. 148–160.
39. Nancy J. Adler and Susan Bartholomew, "Managing Globally Competent People," *Academy of Management Executive*, May 1992, pp. 52–65. Also see Michael J. Marquardt and Dean W. Engle, *Global Human Resource Development* (Englewood Cliffs, NJ: Prentice-Hall, 1993).

40. Gary Hamel and C. K. Prahalad, *Competing for the Future* (Boston: Harvard Business School Press, 1994), pp. 246–263.
41. Richard M. Hodgetts, "A Conversation with Rosabeth Moss Kanter," *Organization Dynamics*, Summer 1995, p. 58.
42. For more, see Rosabeth Moss Kanter, "Thriving Locally in the Global Economy," *Harvard Business Review*, September-October 1995, pp. 151–160.
43. Rosabeth Moss Kanter, *World Class: Thriving Locally in the Global Economy* (New York: Simon & Schuster, 1995), p. 59.
44. Ibid., p. 289.
45. John Byrne, "The Virtual Corporation," *Business-Week*, February 8, 1993, pp. 98–102.
46. Also see Ray Grenier and George Metes, *Going Virtual* (Upper Saddle River, NJ: Prentice-Hall, 1995).
47. Akio Morita, "Partnering for Competitiveness: The Role of Japanese Business," *Harvard Business Review*, May-June 1992, p. 78.
48. Jeremiah J. Sullivan and Richard B. Peterson, "A Test of Theories Underlying the Japanese Lifetime Employment System," *Journal of International Business Studies*, First Quarter 1991, p. 79.
49. Robert Neff, "Fixing Japan," *BusinessWeek*, March 29, 1993, pp. 68–74.
50. J. Bernard Keys, Luther Trey Denton, and Thomas R. Miller, "The Japanese Management Theory Jungle—Revisited," *Journal of Management*, vol. 20, no. 2, 1994, pp. 373–402.
51. Hamil and Prahalad, *Competing for the Future*, p. 23.
52. Ibid., p. 156.
53. Daniel Sullivan and Alan Bauerschmidt, "The 'Basic Concepts' of International Business Strategy: A Review and Reconsideration," *Management International Review*, Special Issue 1991, pp. 111–124.
54. Also see Richard W. Wright and David A. Ricks, "Trends in International Business Research: Twenty-Five Years Later," *Journal of International Business Studies*, Fourth Quarter 1994, pp. 687–701.

INTERNATIONAL MANAGEMENT CASES

MOTOROLA: AN INTERNATIONAL COMPETITOR

In 1993, George Fisher, then Chair of the Board and CEO, left Motorola to head Eastman Kodak. Most of his management team remained in place. T. L. Tooker, the former president, became vice-chair and chief executive officer, and Chris Galvin, the grandson of founder Paul Galvin, became president and chief operating officer. Today, Motorola continues to be the global leader in wireless communication equipment.

Early History and Background

Paul Galvin started what now is Motorola in 1928 making battery eliminators for household radios. The Galvin Manufacturing Corporation soon found a new name by producing commercialized car radios. The name *Motorola* was derived from the combination of motor and the victrola (i.e., the old record player). Bob Galvin, a graduate of Notre Dame and the University of Chicago, joined Motorola in 1940, and in 1959, when his father died, he assumed senior leadership of the company. At that time, Motorola had a leading position in military and commercial communications and also had its first semiconductor-production facility in operation.

In the 1960s, Galvin lead his company into international markets. He also moved the firm away from consumer electronics and focused more attention on high-technology markets. This required him to be more savvy not only in business but politics as well. In 1970, he accepted a seat on the President's Commission for International Trade & Investment, and from 1982 to 1985, he chaired the Industry Policy Advisory Committee to the U.S. Special Representative to the Multilateral Trade Negotiations. He is credited with being a key architect of the plan that opened the Japanese semiconductor market in 1986.

By 1996, the company was competing in a wide array of sectors, including:

Source: This case was written specially for this book with the assistance of M. A. Boney and Josette Hagel.

Sector	Product line
General systems	Cellular infrastructure and telephone subscriber units
Semiconductor products	Semiconductor devices for consumer and industrial applications
Communications products	Land mobile products, paging products, wireless data products
Government and Space technology	U.S. government products, including the iridium satellite
Other products	Automotive and energy

Competition from Japan

In the early to mid-1980s Motorola's virtual lock on the U.S. market for pagers and cellular phones was shattered by better-quality products from Japan. The company's Phoenix-based Semiconductor Products sector suffered a dramatic blow by being forced out of the dynamic random access memory (DRAMs) business, which was the largest-selling chip at that time. In a few short years, Motorola slipped from being number two in worldwide chip sales to lagging behind NEC, Toshiba, Hitachi, and its archrival Texas Instruments. By 1986, Motorola was considering merging its semiconductor business with Toshiba Corporation; however, instead of joining with the Japanese, Motorola leadership decided to improve its own operations. This job fell to George Fisher, who had come to Motorola from AT&T in 1975 to join the mobile radio unit. Motorola embraced the tactics of its Japanese competitors, such as driving relentlessly for market share, sharply upgrading quality, and constantly honing manufacturing processes to pare costs. New goals were set for the company in 1981: a 10-fold improvement in quality in 5 years, and a doubling of market share every 5 years.

Improvements in Quality

From 1985 to 1986, a group of Motorola executives in the Communication Products sector toured Japanese plants, which at that time were considered the best in the world in consumer goods such as watches, television sets, videocassette recorders, calculators, and so on. The Motorola group wanted to find out first-hand why these Japanese companies had earned such a reputation for high quality. They discovered that these factories had process defect rates 500 to 1000 times better than ordinary electronics companies, and their costs were lower than their competitors! Most U.S. executives had the mindset that outstanding quality costs money and does not save money. Based on this new information, Motorola redoubled its efforts to increase quality.

Motorola also learned from the Japanese that product defects represented only 5 to 10 percent of the cost of improving a company's performance. Other factors such as quicker response to customer, faster cycle times for initial designs, and the order-to-delivery process were even more important. Mistakes in billing, credit, and back ordering were as likely as poor product quality to keep a company from its objective of meeting or exceeding customers' total quality expectations. Preventive or in-process controls were the best ways to ensure that products met customers' expectations. For instance, customer complaint cards were found to be useless as a control device in measuring quality service, because most customers did not complain. They simply took their business to a competitor.

Taking into account the lessons learned from the Japanese, Motorola launched into a massive education and training program in 1985 for all of its 105,000 employees. The purpose was to explore global competitiveness and risk-taking and to hone their practical skills on process control and ways to reduce cycle times. Promotions, bonuses, and raises were specifically tied to quality improvement. For the 3 years ending in 1988, quality gains amounted to 3 percent of Motorola's total payroll. In that same year, Motorola won the Malcolm Baldrige Award for quality; this was the inaugural year for this prestigious national award. At that time, the number of defects had dropped from 3000 per million in 1983 to less than 200 per million. New goals for quality were set: the company was to have six-sigma quality (3.4 errors per million) by 1992.

The results of Motorola's quality improvement effort are demonstrated by reductions in cycle time. In 1988, the time required for receiving, processing, and delivering an order for a two-way radio decreased to 3 days (from 30 days only 18 months before). The time from the start of the design phase to the beginning of the production of the next radio was reduced from 3 years to 15 months in 1985, and Operation Bandit was launched to improve an existing product, the Bravo pager. As a result of this project, 17 minutes after an order is placed from anywhere in the country, a bar code is placed on a blank circuit board. This bar code contains all the information the factory needs to make the pager, and as the board goes down the line, each robot reads the bar code and executes the proper instructions. Another success story is the company's Micro TAC telephone, which weighs approximately 11.5 ounces and contains about 12 percent as many parts as in Motorola's first portable cellular phone in 1978. The original phone took 40 hours to assemble in 1985; today, it takes 2 hours.

Motorola also shook off its not-invented-here (NIH) bias to become an ardent supporter of Sematech, a research and development (R&D) consortium started as a last-ditch effort to stave off Japanese companies by developing the best chipmaking technologies available. Motorola also forged strategic alliances with firms in both the United States and Japan. In 1987, Motorola formed a pact with Toshiba to re-enter the DRAM business. It also linked up with IBM to develop cutting-edge chipmaking methods and with Apple as well, in a three-way consortium, to develop the PowerPC, which is mounting a credible alternative to Intel's Pentium microprocessor.

During this period Motorola's focus was changed and greater emphasis placed on the customer. The company also broke down barriers between departments to improve operations. One example was development of the microprocessor for Canon's best-selling camera. In 1983, Nobuhiko Shinoda, then a section chief for Canon, sought out Motorola because he had read that the company had developed a specialized microprocessor for the automotive market. Motorola not only tailored the chip for Canon, its engineers also invented other key components.

Expansion into Japan

Motorola decided not only to adopt the best Japanese methods of achieving quality in manufacturing but also to exploit areas in which the Japanese were weak, such as marketing and software development. The company decided to challenge Japan both in the U.S. and the Japanese markets. In both 1982 and 1984, Motorola convinced the U.S. Commerce Department that Japanese companies were illegally dumping pagers and cellular phones in the U.S. market. Washington penalized the Japanese with tariffs of 106 percent; also, at Motorola's prodding, the Commerce Department forced the Japanese to make good on a promise they previously had made to establish additional radio-spectrum frequencies. This allowed Motorola's cellular phone system to operate in the densely populated Tokyo–Nagoya corridor. This was a major coup, because Japan represents the second largest pager market outside the United States, estimated at 11 million pagers in 1996.

In 1993, Japan's Ministry of Posts and Technology adopted Motorola's new paging technology as the national standard for the next generation of pagers. This pager is marketed in Japan by Nippon Motorola Ltd.'s Paging Products Division. The system is based on technology developed by Motorola and NTT (Nippon Telegraph and Telephone), Japan's domestic telephone company. NTT licensed the technology and buys the equipment from Motorola. This arrangement has proven to be mutually beneficial for both companies. It gives Motorola a wider presence in a market that has been difficult for U.S. telecommunications firms to penetrate, and it gives NTT access to more customers as the technology accommodates more users on the nation's limited number of paging channels.

Expansion into China

Business opportunities are growing rapidly in China, and while the Chinese government has earmarked vast amounts to add telephone lines and switching equipment, they simply cannot keep up with the demand for communication equipment to accommodate this growth. For example, in 1996, there were approximately 400 million city dwellers in China, but only 11 million pagers were in use; however, this still is about one-and-a-half times the number of pagers there were in 1992. Motorola holds about one-third of the pager market, but it faces stiff competition from Japan's NEC, which has manufacturing facilities in the southern province of Guongdong. Motorola's main manufacturing base for the Asia-Pacific region is in Singapore. In 1992, however, the company invested $120 million to establish a manufacturing base in Tianjin, a northern city in China, and already has produced over 1 million pagers at this plant.

In November 1993, Motorola established Motorola China Electronic Ltd. in Beijing. It is headquartered in a six-story building that houses the corporate headquarters, sales office, marketing, and engineering for China.

In March 1994, Motorola won a $100 million contract with the Beijing municipal government to provide them with a digital communication system. In May 1994, the company received three major contracts for a paging system in China (in Zhejiang, Liaoning, and Hubei provinces) worth more than $15 million. Later that same year, the company received a $57 million order from two northeastern provinces and a $12 million order to expand and upgrade its analog cellular system in Hellonjiang province.

Global Communication

In 1990, Motorola began raising funds for a global telephone system. It formed a subsidiary called Iridium to launch 66 small satellites and build a $3.4 billion system. This system will connect users through pocket-sized telephones anywhere in the work with no intermediary land-based systems. Motorola will be paid by Iridium to build the system, and its primary goal is to supply all the equipment required.

In 1994, Motorola completed raising all the required capital for the system, and it holds a 28 percent stake in the operation. Iridium's largest investors are from Japan. The DDI Corporation, Japan's second largest telephone company, is the dominant partner in a consortium of 17 Japanese firms that invested $235 million. Other Japanese investors include Sony, Mitsubishi, and Mitsui. In Germany, Veba A.G., which owns electric utilities and local telephone services, has invested $140 million. In South America, Motorola signed up a consortium led by a Brazilian construction company, Inepar. In Korea, Korean Mobile Telecommunications put up $70 million. In the United States, Sprint decided to invest $70 million, and both Raytheon, which is building the satellite antenna assemblies, and Lockheed, which is building the satellite chassis, invested around $35 million each.

There are a number of competitors, however, and many have systems that are expected to be cheaper to build. The most serious is a small company called Qualcomm. The firm has a plan to manufacture a global satellite system called GlobalStar. Qualcomm's 1994 annual revenue was only $271 million, and its entire income was generated from one source: a satellite tracking system for truck fleets. Therefore, the company does not have the resources to become a major wireless communication system competitor. The firm may be able to overcome this through joint ventures with companies like Japan's NEC, although raising the $1.7 billion in capital that it needs to begin the project will be extremely difficult.

While many competitors have developed lower-cost plans, none will be able to achieve worldwide communication without an interconnecting cellular system. And while cellular systems are in rapid development around the world, this still is not likely to occur for some time.

In any event, the Iridium subsidiary will have the capability of switching between the satellite mode and the cellular mode as needed. Motorola is banking that an elite niche of business travelers will be willing to pay the price, which may be upwards of $3 a minute, to have the freedom to roam at will without changing their telephone number. The magnitude of the investment required for this project as well as Motorola's ability to put it together has made one thing obvious: Motorola has earned the respect not only of its Japanese competitors but of the rest of business as one of the best companies in the world.

1. What generic business is Motorola in?
2. What are the major risks with which Motorola should be concerned?
3. What is Motorola's international strategy?
4. What are two things that Motorola should do to maintain its leadership position in the world as it enters the twenty-first century?

ISRAEL: A UNIQUE MEMBER OF THE GLOBAL COMMUNITY

Israel frequently finds itself in the world news. Despite playing an active role in modern history, its economy is relatively small, and the size of its consumer market is considered to be small and unattractive for many Western MNCs. Still, the Israeli economy has been growing rapidly in recent years, and after reaching more than 400 percent in the mid-1980s, inflation has been brought under control.

Human, Not Natural Resources

Being short of natural resources, the greatest asset that Israel possesses is an educated and skilled pool of scientific and technically trained human resources. The country has the highest per-capita ratio of research scientists in the work force worldwide. This wealth of human resources has been cited by many foreign companies as the primary reason for investing in Israel. The recent mass immigration from the former Soviet Union has further enhanced the quality of Israel's labor force.

Even though Israel has a quality work force, wages are relatively low compared with other industrialized economies such as the United States, Japan, and most European countries. The average gross salary of an electrical engineer in Israel amounts to about $18,000 per year, while counterparts in the United States and other industrialized countries earn between $28,600 and $53,600 annually.

Trade Agreements Provide a Competitive Advantage

Israel has signed free trade agreements (FTAs) with the United States and the European Union (EU). These FTAs eliminate most of the customs, duties, and other trade barriers. Israel also has signed reciprocal trade agreements with Canada, Japan, Australia, and New Zealand, which provide Israel with a preferred status. Although Israel is always in the political "hotseat," since the end of the Persian Gulf war in mid-1991, it has gained full diplomatic relations with emerging markets such as China and India and obtained most-favored-nation status with the republics of Eastern Europe (except Russia). More important, relations have thawed between Israel and the Pacific Rim countries.

These trade agreements are very beneficial to Israel. For example, the European FTA potentially may provide a significant competitive advantage to Israeli manufacturers and exporters. U.S. businesses trying to penetrate "Fortress Europe" face significant trade barriers and may find it beneficial to use Israel as an exporting bridge to bypass them. Outside MNCs placing production facilities in Israel may take advantage of Israel's inexpensive skilled labor as well as compete successfully in Europe by exploiting the advantages provided by these FTAs. Currently, Israel is the only country that has FTAs with both the United States and the EU. The fact that Israel is a geographic bridge and crossroads connecting Africa, Asia, and Europe increases the country's attractiveness to foreign investors.

Investment Incentives

The Israeli government has adopted a set of goals to create more jobs and increase exports. To achieve these goals, the government offers a wide range of incentive programs that include grants, government-backed loan guarantees, subsidies, free trade zones, and tax benefits. These incentives are offered to enterprises that create more jobs (especially in the nation's less populated and industrialized areas), increase exports, and contribute to research and development (R&D) as well as new product development. In fact, the Israeli government will help any venture that will have an overall effect of improving the nation's economy.

Source: This case was written specially for this book with the assistance of Erez Hasdai and Elizabeth Novick.

The government has created Yozma Venture Capital Ltd., a state-owned investment company that offers investors opportunities to form joint-venture funds or invest directly in high-tech companies on favorable terms. Another funding source is the Israel–U.S. Bi-National Research and Development Foundation (Bird-F), which funds joint ventures that engage in R&D and product development.

Strategies for Doing Business

Israel's strategy is that the operational benefits of international diversification will be higher for firms possessing intangible, firm-specific assets (e.g., R&D technology) that they want to exploit in other national markets. Indeed, most corporations that engage in business with Israel possess at least one intangible asset, usually technological innovation capacity. Intel was a pioneer in this regard, opening a semiconductor-design center in Israel over 20 years ago. Since then, Israel has witnessed a flood of foreign hardware, software, and telecommunication companies using the Israeli skilled, technical work force.

Typical Israeli companies have a well-defined niche market. Their technological expertise generally is strong enough to offset their lack of capital resources, marketing skills, and distance from major markets. In the classic form of strategic alliance, the Israeli side typically develops the products while the foreign investor supplies product identification and marketing skills. This formula combines the strengths of both parties to reduce the product's cycle time, thus providing the customer with a better and/or cheaper product much faster. Not only does this approach allow foreign companies to tap Israeli resources without building facilities or hiring employees, it also fits Israel's own economic goals.

In contrast to many other developing countries, the main reason for investing in Israel, according to U.S. executives, is to gain access to its quality technical talent. The influx of immigrants that escaped the Nazi regime in Europe during the 1940s and, more recently, from the former Soviet Union has provided Israel with a large pool of talents that are of particular interest to electronic companies. These include expertise in digital signal processes, communication theory, electro-optics, and software designs. In the 1980s, the Israelis developed great products that they did not know how to sell. Today, most local companies combine innovative technology with low cost, ease of installation, and excellent service. Foreign venture capital can give these companies the management and marketing expertise they lack.

Another form of investment in Israel is wholly owned development and manufacturing centers. This strategy was used by prominent MNCs such as Intel, IBM, Motorola, and DEC. The strategy is consistent with recent trends in international trading markets. The global marketplace consists of large numbers of small-scale ventures that are very focused in scope and a relatively small number of widely known, large multinational manufacturers of consumer goods, such as Sony, Volkswagen, GM, DEC, and so on. These large, multinational manufacturers are the major customers of the small-scale ventures that typically concentrate on the development and production of a limited number of components and parts and possess little, if any, marketing skills. Similarly, MNCs expanding to Israel have enormous resources to spend on designing and customizing their products. More important, they have the market knowledge and the muscle in distribution channels. No Israeli company has this kind of marketing advantage, no matter how great its end product.

U.S. MNCs in Israel

Semiconductor giants such as Intel and Motorola have made major investments in Israel during recent years, thus giving local engineers the chance to develop leading-edge components and parts that are driving the entire computer and communication industry. Soft-drink giants Coca-Cola and Pepsi also have a presence in Israel.

Intel Dov Fruman, Intel's CEO, believes that the Israeli work force is the primary reason the company decided to enter this country. He is quoted as calling the Israelis "improvisors and networkers." Another reason for Intel's investment is that overall costs run 10 percent below U.S. operations.

Intel has designed coprocessors in Haifa for 21 years and also has produced microprocessors, including the 386 and 486, at its $300 million Jerusalem lab since 1986. The expansion of the Har Hahotzevim industrial zone in Jerusalem is the largest single investment ever made in Israel. Recently, the Israeli government approved a $380 million grant to support a major upgrading of the Jerusalem plant. Spread over 7 years, this money was approved under the law authorizing state grants covering 38 percent of high-technology business ventures in the city.

Motorola Motorola Israel is a wholly owned subsidiary of Motorola, Inc. Like Intel, Motorola expanded to Israel to take advantage of its highly skilled work force and to exploit its R&D capabilities. Motorola, Inc., provides funding and marketing expertise to develop its products, while the Israeli subsidiary concentrates on bringing out new and improved products.

Originally, Motorola only had design centers in Israel but later built production facilities to exploit the economic benefits of having these facilities close to design centers located in Tel Aviv and the southern city of Arad. The company develops and exports digital signal processors, radio communication, remote systems, cellular radio telephones, and data transmission devices. It also develops, manufactures, markets, and exports communications, water control and irrigation, and paging systems.

Motorola Israel won the Prize for Quality from Motorola, Inc., for a communications process that it developed for UPS. In 1994, Motorola Israel received Motorola, Inc.'s, "International Mandate" to be the exclusive developer, manufacturer, and marketer of the international company's wireless transmitters.

Pepsi and Coca-Cola Coca-Cola was the first soft-drink firm to enter the Israeli market (in 1968). As a pioneer in this market, Coca-Cola created entry barriers, mainly brand identity and access to distribution channels, that provided it with a competitive advantage.

Initially, Coca-Cola had to make a strategic choice: whether to enter the Israeli or the Arab market. Having chosen Israel, the company was placed on the Arab League's "Blacklist" of international companies doing business with the Jewish state and therefore was barred from most of these Arab markets.

Coca-Cola brought in the most recent and advanced manufacturing technology and built a fully automated plant in Tel Aviv. All operations, production, and support functions are entirely computerized. Coke also employed its famous marketing competencies to secure market share. This strategy is consistent with Coke's highly touted global marketing philosophy, which involves aggressive advertising and promotion campaigns to maintain existing brand loyalty. For example, passengers arriving in Israel are served Coca-Cola products on board El Al (the Israeli government-owned airline) and are exposed to heavy advertising at the airport and on all major highways leading to the big cities. At present, Coca-Cola controls approximately two-thirds of the Israeli soft-drink market.

While Coca-Cola was setting up operations in Israel, Pepsi was targeting the Arab markets, which are more lucrative in terms of market potential. Recently, Pepsi expanded into Israel and is trying to obtain shelf space in supermarkets, which sell over one-half of Israel's beverages. With its "first-in-the-market" advantage, Coca-Cola possesses solid shelf space in virtually every retail chain in the country. To meet its goal of getting into the stores, Pepsi has developed a tracing and tracking system to convince supermarket owners to allocate space shelf for its products. Another strategy that Pepsi is pursuing is to distribute products through "mom-and-pop" outlets, which also sell a large amount of Israel's soft drinks.

Soon after entering the Israeli market, Pepsi faced a major crisis that forced the company to re-evaluate its marketing strategy. Ultraorthodox religious groups objected to Pepsi's advertisement campaign that included a billboard poster of an ape dragging its fists on the ground and the caption "Ten million years before the choice." The religious objection was not only the implication that man evolved from the ape, which runs counter to their belief in God's creation of man, but also to the reference of "10 million years," which contradicts the Jewish tradition holding that creation occurred only 5755 years ago. The influential religious group threatened to withdraw the kosher seal from Pepsi's products, which could have meant a significant blow to sales. In addition, the ultraorthodox claimed that Pepsi was violating traditional Jewish values by sponsoring rock concerts on Saturday evenings (Shabat), a sacred day in the Jewish religion. In response, Pepsi decided to modify the advertising campaign, removing the reference to "10 million years" and the ape, leaving only a Neanderthal man to hint at evolution. Despite this, the ultraorthodox group declared that the attitude behind Pepsi's advertising campaign contradicted their beliefs. Regarding the Pepsi-sponsored concerts, Reuven Avital, general manager of Pepsi Israel, said: "They came and said of our marketing campaign, 'Gentlemen, this is unacceptable,' and we said 'We can't do without it, the young generation wants concerts, wants this music, and it is our target market.' This was a macro issue, a philosophical issue, a conceptual issue." As it stands now, the conflict between Pepsi and the orthodox religious group is unresolved.

1. What important issues should MNCs take into consideration when investing and operating in Israel?
2. In what ways can outside high-tech companies successfully integrate their operations into Israel?
3. What are the major challenges that Pepsi is facing in Israel? What would you recommend that Pepsi do to solve its problems?
4. According to Hofstede's research, what cultural dimensions should foreign companies consider when entering Israel?

VIETNAM: AN EMERGING MARKET IN THE GLOBAL ECONOMY

Mentioning Vietnam to most Americans brings visions of unpleasant memories from recent history. Yes, the war is long over, and what is left are crowds of people in the cities hurrying around on bicycles and motor scooters and peasants in the countryside tending their fields. To an increasing number of MNCs around the world, however, this picture of Vietnam also represents an untapped market with enormous long-term growth potential. For example, U.S. automakers predict that the Vietnamese market very soon will have a high demand for automobiles. As the standard of living continues to rise, more and more of the new Vietnamese middle class will be able to purchase vehicles. The "Big Three" U.S. automakers are responding to this anticipated demand by trying to enter this emerging market.

Historical Barriers Overcome

U.S. MNCs have been anxiously awaiting the opportunity to enter the Vietnamese market for a number of years; however, the ill-fated history between these two countries has been difficult to overcome. Following the "no-win" war, the United States was determined to prevent the economic development of Vietnam. By invoking the Trading with the Enemy Act and putting political pressure on other countries and international investment agencies such as the International Monetary Fund and World Bank, the United States effectively averted much of the economic development loans and both direct and indirect foreign investments from entering Vietnam. In addition to the political and economic pressure from the

United States, the Vietnamese government's unwillingness to break its ties with communist ideology and its unlawful occupation of Cambodia also dissuaded foreign investors from entering this potentially lucrative market.

Because of the international political and economic isolation from the West and developed Asian neighbors, foreign investments in Vietnam largely came from the Soviet Union. With the collapse of the USSR, however, and subsequent stoppage of any economic assistance, the Vietnamese economy nearly collapsed. Faced with a desperate need to make some radical changes, the pragmatic Vietnamese government adopted an economic policy known as "Doi Moi" (economic renovation) in the early 1990s, which in essence moved the country toward a free market economy. Most of the world responded favorably to this change in economic policy, pouring millions of dollars into the Vietnamese economy in hopes of capturing a share of this untapped market.

Despite the obvious economic opportunities of early entry and possible threats to profit potential from the presence of other competitors, the United States still delayed full diplomatic and trade relations with Vietnam. A major stumbling block was the U.S. perception that the Vietnamese still were not co-operating enough in trying to account for the MIAs and POWs from the war. Finally, the Vietnamese government agreed to make an increased effort to help resolve the MIA/POW issue. Convinced that the Vietnamese government was moving in the right direction, President Clinton lifted the trade embargo on February 3, 1994. This allowed U.S. companies, including automakers, to set up offices in Vietnam and begin negotiations with the government and local businesses.

Market Potential for U.S. Automakers

As political tensions between the two countries were easing, U.S. automakers, along with all types of MNCs, have

Source: This case was prepared specially for this book by Alexander Stajkovic, Department of Management, University of Nebraska. Dan Thorsfeldt assisted in preparing and writing this case.

been carefully analyzing the potential of the Vietnamese market. For example, in this country of over 70 million people, only a very small percentage own vehicles, most of which traditionally are registered to the government or private corporations. Automobile production also is in its infant stages. There have been only two automakers in Vietnam: (1) Mekong Corporation, a Vietnamese-Japanese-South Korean joint venture, and (2) Vietnam Motor Corporation, a joint venture with the Philippines. The combined production of both plants is below 10,000 units per year. Imports of automobiles also have been low but are growing. For example, the number of imported automobiles expanded from 58 in 1988 to over 3000 in 1993. Nearly all these imports came from Japan.

While the United States was tied down in political negotiations, Japanese MNCs were aggressively drafting strategic plans to establish manufacturing operations and distribution channels in Vietnam. For example, in 1992, Mitsubishi Motor Corporation submitted a master plan to the Vietnamese government outlining how to set up vehicle assembly factories and auto-parts production for the next 20 years. Had it been implemented, this plan would have effectively given Japanese companies a dominant hold on automobile manufacturing for all of Vietnam. Rather than accepting Mitsubishi's plan, however, the Vietnamese government invited other automakers, such as General Motors, Chrysler, French Renault, and Italian Fiat, to offer their ideas for the future of the Vietnamese auto industry.

Given the opportunity after Vietnam was opened up, U.S. manufacturers increased their efforts to gain a foothold in this country's car market. The "Big Three" began finalizing business deals with Vietnamese partners that would enable them to start in-country operations. For example, Ford completed a feasibility study and signed a joint-venture agreement with Song Cong Diesel. Pending government approval of an assembly plant license, they plan to begin production in 1997. General Motors and Chrysler also are heavily engaged in negotiations with other Vietnamese car manufacturers. General Motors has signed a memorandum of understanding exploring the possible co-operation with Vietnam Motors, and Chrysler reportedly is close to an agreement to start a joint venture with Mekong.

Possible Risks of Entering the Vietnamese Market

Judging by previous experience, U.S. companies know that Vietnam might be a very risky place to invest. During the Vietnam War era, entire assets of U.S. companies were frozen or, even worse, confiscated by the Vietnamese communist government. Only recently (after almost 30 years) have the Vietnamese agreed to compensate ($208.5 million) the U.S. government and private companies for expropriated assets. Considering that the Vietnamese government still is run by the Communist Party, it is understandable that U.S. companies might be leery of entering any long-term agreements that would require substantial investments, such as in the automobile industry.

Another possible problem for foreign investment is the increasing corruption at the local-government level. As the central government wavers on decision making and law ratification, local governments are left on their own to enact laws and establish rules for foreign investors. An often-heard complaint by outside businesspeople is that investment projects usually are approved at random instead of on their merits and depending on pay-offs to local officials. Corruption at the local-government level is a main reason why about three-fourths of all foreign investments in Vietnam currently are in the form of joint ventures, either with provincial governments or local business partners.

Finally, for automakers (and other manufacturers) to succeed fully in the Vietnamese market, they must overcome the severe problems of Vietnam's infrastructure. The mobility of trade and passenger travel in Vietnam presently is at the mercy of crumbling two-lane roads and long ferry rides across rivers. Especially relevant to automakers, roads and traffic are so bad in Vietnam that, for example, a trip from Hanoi to Halong Bay, which should only require 2 hours, currently takes up to 6 hours. If the drastically needed improvements in Vietnam's infrastructure are not made immediately, the automobile industry might be stifled by a high demand for automobiles in a country with no place to drive them.

In conclusion, the long-awaited opportunity for U.S. MNCs such as automobile manufacturers to enter the Vietnamese market has arrived. Although the challenges and risks facing these MNCs are almost as great as the opportunities, there is little doubt that the U.S. MNCs, judging by current trends, will join the others from around the world in taking their chances and aggressively pursuing the emerging Vietnam market.

1. What are the reasons in favor of U.S. automakers' entry into the Vietnamese car market? Outline specific opportunities.
2. Why have U.S. automakers waited so long to enter the Vietnamese market? Have the conditions changed lately? What risks are involved if U.S. automakers choose to invest in Vietnam?
3. What do you think the future is for doing business in Vietnam? Would you recommend that MNCs vigorously pursue this market?

DOING BUSINESS IN CHINA

With a population of over 1.2 billion, China has exploded into a huge potential marketplace for the world's production of goods and services. U.S. policy makers and business executives alike have realized a powerful long-term trend in Southeast Asia: the rise of the great China economy. Paced by a rapid rate of investment and given the abundance of trained human capital, the Asian Rim, of which China is a leading nation, has become the fastest growing region of the world. Many observers expect this trend to continue for at least the rest of the decade—and most likely into the next century.

Background on China

Foreign trade in China is almost completely dominated by the state. In 1979, China relaxed certain trade restrictions, paving the way for increases in the relatively small foreign investment and trade activity. By the late 1980s, yearly exports totaled about $41.1 billion and imports $46.4 billion, and both have increased sharply since then. The principal Chinese exports include crude and refined petroleum, cotton fabric, silk, clothing, rice, pork, frozen shrimp, and tea. Among the major imports are machinery, steel products, automobiles, other metals, synthetics, agricultural chemicals, rubber, and wheat. Most of China's trade is with noncommunist countries, including Japan (its main trading partner), Hong Kong, Canada, and the United States. Other countries with which China has extensive trade relations are Germany, Taiwan, and Singapore.

China has been undergoing a dramatic transformation to a market economy. As a result, it currently is the world leader in terms of economic growth, industrial expansion, and exports. It contains an array of potential consumers that far exceeds the markets in Europe or the Western Hemisphere, and it is rapidly emerging as a new epicenter for industry, commerce, and finance. In addition, the so-called "Greater China" has substantial amounts of technology and manufacturing capability in Taiwan; outstanding entrepreneurial, marketing, and services acumen in Hong Kong; a fine communications network in Singapore; and a tremendous pool of financial capital in all three. When these resources are combined with the very large endowments of land, resources, and labor on the mainland, China already is a major superpower in the global economy.

The Chinese government is still very heavily involved in the ownership, if not the operation, of enterprises. In addition to the many private ventures (often in collaboration with foreign investors), the government owns a great variety of businesses, ranging from the central government's giant steel mills to local government factories. Trading companies that engage in a variety of commercial, banking, and manufacturing activities are owned by governmental units, ranging from the army to local counties.

Most foreign investments take the form of joint ventures with the government, for which there is a strong demand. These ventures usually leave the foreign investors as minority partners and Chinese officials in charge. These officials occupy strong bargaining positions, because they typically will demand that a certain fixed percentage of production be exported. Such investment is particularly risky, however, because government companies, being cogs in the central economy, do not operate to turn a profit or compete. The concept of bankruptcy and the consequences of poor performance are alien to state companies.

As a result, dealing with the Chinese government is no easy task. For example, there can be a great deal of uncertainty about when a contract is a contract. It is important that foreign firms investigate and anticipate as much as possible before spending any money. Amid the potential for future explosive growth, there also are great risks and uncertainty involved with doing business in China.

Political Risks in China

When Chairman Deng launched the economic revolution, deep splits emerged within the Communist Party over the pace and extent of these ambiguous reforms.

Source: This case was written specially for this book with the assistance of Hubert H. Barnes and Christopher B. Hill.

Deng had to overcome the resistance of Communist Party hardliners in provincial governments. The resulting dilution of central government control—and the mounting tension between Beijing and the provinces—has become a serious problem that requires tough discipline to keep the economy in check.

Moreover, the People's Republic now is making it clear that it wants to participate actively in determining the future direction of the economy of Hong Kong. However, to date, there is little clarity as to the nature of that participation or the desired direction of change. Likewise, at best, relations between Beijing and Taipei can be described as ambiguous and still potentially explosive.

Hong Kong often has been referred to as the gateway to China, and it is considered to be one of the most aggressive, pro-business economies in the world. On June 30, 1997, Hong Kong will revert from British to Chinese rule. The Chinese government has made pronouncements that have caused many companies currently doing business in Hong Kong to be very leery of the impending change. Beijing repeatedly has said that it will dismantle the newly elected legislature and also is causing fear among Hong Kong's Civil Service by demanding access to the confidential personnel files of senior officials.

One of the most serious actions taken by Beijing is its refusal to go ahead with plans to establish a court of final appeals for Hong Kong issues, which would be the equivalent of the U.S. Supreme Court. Beijing currently claims it has jurisdiction over all cases that have anything to do with the responsibilities of the central government; this could literally include anything that the Chinese government wants it to include. According to some experts, the Chinese government slowly is trying to break down some of the democratic practices instituted by the British through causing as much mischief as possible before 1997. Some foreign companies have complained that they are invited to take the risks of doing business only to be blocked from reaping the rewards. For example, one foreign oil company doing business in China has long been frustrated because every time the firm locates oil, the government buys the surrounding properties. Foreign companies also complain that contracts simply are reopened if the government sees that the foreign firm is doing too well. Sometimes, this is because the Chinese partner feels that the foreign side received too sweet a deal.

In addition to backing out of contracts, China also is making it clear that it will award contracts only to companies that are considered to be politically correct. At the same time, these companies cannot be sure that they will

hang on to their business. McDonald's, Northern Telecom, and Coca-Cola provide examples of the types of problems a business can encounter with the Chinese government.

McDonald's in Beijing   The confidence of foreign companies doing business in China recently was shaken after the Chinese government announced it no longer would allow McDonald's to continue operating at its Beijing location. This announcement came just 3 years after McDonald's signed a 20-year lease with the city. At the time McDonald's signed the lease, most investors were shying away from China because of the bloody crackdown on pro-democracy demonstrators in June 1989. The city now wants to give the McDonald's property to a Hong Kong tycoon who plans to build an office and commercial complex on the site. The Director-General of the Chinese Ministry of Foreign Trade and Economic Cooperation recently announced that the two sides had reached an agreement whereby the Chinese government would relocate the McDonald's restaurant temporarily while the Hong Kong–financed development is built on the site. He also said that the company would be compensated for the move. The Director-General made this statement just after the London-based Economist Intelligence Unit (EIU) country-risk group downgraded its rating for China and said it had "serious doubts" about the country's near-term prospects. This dispute with McDonald's has forced many potential investors to rethink their plans. If this could happen to a powerful, visible company such as McDonald's, they reasoned, it could easily happen to them.

Northern Telecom of Canada   In early 1993, Northern Telecom of Canada was awarded a contract for $9 million to take telephone service to the Chinese masses and provide state-of-the-art data communications equipment to meet the needs of sophisticated telecommunications users. Northern Telecom, which is the third-largest supplier of switching equipment in China, had been there since 1972 and recently intensified its focus. It is one of many companies that spent hundreds of millions of dollars to enter the Chinese market in this industry. In January 1994, however, Chinese officials abruptly announced that by July, they wanted to deal with only a handful of suppliers for network transmission equipment. This announcement spells doom to most companies within the industry. All, including Northern Telecom which has had a tremendous investment in China over the years, now are fighting to stay alive.

Coca-Cola   Another example of Chinese reluctance to fully establish free market principles is the position they have taken regarding Coca-Cola and other foreign soft-drink firms. Legislators of the National People's Congress (NPC), China's parliament, have raised protectionist cries over foreign domination of the local soft-drink market. Foreign brands, notably Coca-Cola, are proving too successful in a market that has a dearth of national brands. Thirty-two NPC deputies recently submitted a motion asking authorities to restrict the expansion of Coca-Cola in China. This proposal was presented on the premise that traditional beverages need to be protected from the onslaught of foreign competition.

As the beverage market in China increases, so does the need for production capacity. Foreign companies such as Coca-Cola, which have a great deal of money and know-how, are able to continually increase capacity and, consequently, sales—unlike the local players. Coke operates in China through ventures with Hong Kong–based Swire Beverages and Kerry Beverages groups. Its strategy is to take a 12.5 percent share in the ventures by supplying concentrates from its wholly owned plant in Shanghai. Coke forecasts that sales should continue to grow at a rate between 30 and 35 percent annually to the year 2000, but to satisfy this booming market, Coke needs to increase production capacity either by expansion of the present plant or construction of a second factory. Both of these expensive expansion strategies are threatened by NPC action.

Foreign Exchange Control Problems

Some foreign exporters now complain that the cash-depleted Chinese banks make them wait as long as 6 months for payments on goods delivered to Chinese customers. Under China's austerity program, the money supply has been tightened and interest rates raised to contain runaway economic growth and inflation. This program also has meant that banks have trouble getting foreign exchange to pay foreign companies.

Under the Chinese system, any foreign firm that is exporting goods to China must sell through a state-owned import-export company. Customers from retailers to factories must pay this middle person in renminbi. The import-export company's bank then remits the money to the foreign supplier in foreign exchange. One controller at a large Hong Kong chemical company has noted that because of the shortage in renminbi in China's banking system, they have to find the money somewhere, so they hold back on payments.

Potential Social Unrest, Anarchy, and Disorder

In June 1989, government troops fired on pro-democracy demonstrators who rallied in Tiananmen Square and killed some of them. As the Chinese economy continues to open up to businesses from the West, the infiltration of Western lifestyle and the Communist Party's penchant for keeping the populace under control are combining to create a potential time bomb for disorder in the country. The inflation rate, now approaching 25 percent, is especially dangerous, because it exaggerates the problem of acute regional disparity. There may be boom times in the country's special economic reform zones in the south (near Hong Kong) and developed coastal areas such as the relatively modern port city of Shanghai, but the rural interior provinces, with 70 percent of the population, increasingly are being left behind. Such regional disparity can create social and political instability.

Most-Favored-Nation Status and Human Rights Violations

U.S.–China trade relations were severely imperiled in 1993 when the United States threatened not to renew China's "most favored nation" (MFN) trading status unless human rights conditions improved. The United States eventually renewed China's MFN status even though the Chinese government has made little progress toward improving its human rights record.

The Clinton administration has been criticized with claims that it sacrificed its human rights agenda in China in favor of U.S. commercial interests. The Clinton administration, however, still is working with U.S. businesses to produce a set of ethical principles for conducting business in China. President Clinton is hoping that U.S. firms will draft a "statement of principles" that will cover the workplace rights of their employees in China.

One example is Reebok's "Human Rights Production Standards," which state that the company will only do business with firms that: (1) do not discriminate in hiring and employment on the grounds of race, color, national origin, gender, religion, political or other opinion; (2) do not require more than 60-hour work weeks on a regularly scheduled basis, except for appropriately compensated overtime in compliance with local laws; and (3) do not use forced labor, including labor that is required as a means of political coercion or punishment. In addition, the firm will not purchase materials that are produced by forced prison or other compulsory labor and will terminate its business relationships with any sources that are found to use such labor.

Human rights advocates argue that such a code must be an explicit legal requirement for doing business in China. They argue that laws are needed to maximize pressure on China to improve its human rights performance. The main worry among business leaders, however, is that company-by-company statements of principles on the treatment of their workers in China could be transformed by Congress into legally binding requirements that would get them tossed out of the country and invite direct challenges by Beijing.

The Future

China represents an alluring, huge market for companies that have been competing to survive in more mature, developed markets that have been flat and where competition for contracts is very intense. Economists estimate that mainland China's economy could exceed that of Japan by the turn of the century, and if the trend continues, China could become the world's largest economy, surpassing even that of the United States. China remains a communist country, however, and severe strains in mainland China are arising as an economically backward, communist-led nation attempts to move toward an advanced capitalist system. Adoption of a private enterprise system, however halting and incomplete, means broadening the society's power base and considerable decentralization of decision making. The existing political power structure is not likely to respond to these changes passively.

In the past, setbacks have occurred in the economic and political development of Southeast Asia, and future detours are likely. Some experts offer pessimistic assessments, believing that China can never truly prosper while the Community Party retains its monopoly on power. In their view, any gains resulting from piecemeal economic reforms will merely benefit the communists by pacifying the citizenry. Many informed outsiders report that their dominant impression of China's economic activities is one of official favoritism, inside deals, and outright bribery. Under such circumstances, it may take years for China to lay the groundwork for sustainable growth.

1. What should be the major concerns of international companies entering China?
2. What are some ways in which firms doing business in China can maintain their competitive strengths and handle potential conflicts with the government of China?
3. Is the potential for growth and market opportunities in China worth the risk?
4. What part does technology play in the risks faced by companies doing business in China?

CULTURAL DIFFERENCES DOOM A SEEMINGLY PERFECT ALLIANCE BETWEEN CORNING AND VITRO

Vitro is a Mexican glass manufacturer located in Monterrey, Mexico. Vitro's product line concentrates on drinkware but includes dozens of products, from automobile windshields to washing machines. Vitro has a long history of successful joint ventures and is globally oriented.

Corning, Inc., is most famous for its oven-ready glass wear; however, Corning has diversified into fiberoptics, environmental products, and laboratory services. Like Vitro, Corning has a long history of successful joint ventures and globalization. Vitro and Corning share similar corporate cultures and customer-oriented philosophies.

After realizing such similarities and looking to capitalize on NAFTA by accessing the Mexican market, Corning, Inc., entered into a joint venture with Vitro in the fall of 1992. The similarities in history, philosophy, culture, goals, and objectives of both companies would lead to the logical conclusion that this alliance should be an instant success. However, as Francisco Chevez, an analyst with Smith Barney Shearson in New York, said, "The cultures did not match … it was a marriage made in hell." As history reveals, Corning and Vitro dissolved the joint venture 25 months after the agreement. Both companies still have an interest in maintaining the relationship and continue to distribute each other's products.

A further look at the strategic history of Corning and the joint venture between Corning and Vitro will lead to a better understanding of the difficulties that are involved in creating and maintaining foreign alliances. A more in-depth investigation also will reveal the impact of culture on business transactions.

The Strategic History of Corning

Corning, Inc., has been an innovative leader in foreign alliances for over 73 years. One of the company's first successes was an alliance with St. Gobain, a French glass maker, to produce Pyrex cookware in Europe during the 1920s. Corning has formed approximately 50 ventures over the years. Only 9 have failed, which is a phenomenal number considering one recent study found that over one-half of foreign and national alliances do not succeed. Over the last 5 years, Corning's sales from joint ventures were over $3 billion, which contributed more than $500 million to its net income.

Corning enters into joint ventures for two primary reasons, which are best explained through examples of its past ventures. The first is to gain access to markets that it cannot penetrate quickly enough to obtain a competitive advantage. Corning currently has multiple ventures that exemplify market penetration. Samsung-Corning is an alliance in which Corning provided its distinctive competency of television tube production while Samsung provided expansion into the television market. Corning was able to achieve a strong market share in the Asian market, with sales in excess of $500 million.

The second reason is to bring its technology to market. For example, the strategic alliance of Corning with Mitsubishi led to the creation of Cometec, Inc. Corning produces the ceramic substrates in automotive catalytic converters. The venture employs coating technology

Source: This case was written specially for this book by Cara Okleshen, University of Nebraska.

developed by Mitsubishi that extends Corning's business into stationary pollution control. Corning reports that the venture is quite successful.

Corning's CEO, James R. Houghton, summarizes the major criteria for deciding whether an equity venture is likely to succeed as follows:

1. You need a solid business opportunity.
2. The two partners should make comparable contributions to the new enterprise.
3. The new enterprise should have a well-defined scope and no major conflicts with either parent company.
4. The management of each parent firm should have the vision and confidence to support the venture through its inevitable rough spots.
5. An autonomous operating team should be formed.
6. Responsibility cannot be delegated.

Houghton also emphasizes that the most important dimension of a successful joint venture is trust between the partners.

Corning's track record indicates that it has been able to establish and run a large number of joint ventures successfully. What went wrong with the recent Vitro venture? Vitro and Corning seemed to have similar operating procedures, and Vitro's product line complemented Corning's consumer business. Therefore, how could a seemingly perfect alliance fail so miserably? Probing deeper into the Corning–Vitro joint venture reveals the important role that culture may play in international alliances.

Background on the Corning–Vitro Joint Venture

The Corning–Vitro venture seemed to be ideal. However, a strong Mexican peso, increased overseas competition, and strong cultural differences spelled trouble for the alliance. The economic problems are understandable, but the cultural differences should have been given more attention before the alliance was entered.

Although both companies appeared so similar on the surface, they really were quite different. Cultural clashes erupted from the very beginning of the venture because of differing approaches to work. One example was in the marketing area. Vitro's sales approach was less aggressive than the Americans at Corning thought necessary; the slower, deliberate approach to sales in Mexico was a result of the previously highly controlled economy. Corning's sales approach, on the other hand, was more quick-action oriented and aggressive, which had developed from decades of competition.

Once in the venture, the Mexicans thought the Americans were too forward, and the Americans believed that their Mexican partners wasted time being too polite. The Americans perceived the Mexican characteristics to include an unwillingness to acknowledge problems and faults. With respect to speed, the Mexicans thought Corning moved too quickly, while the Americans thought Vitro moved too slowly.

Another obvious cultural difference was the conflicting styles and time allotment for decision making. Vitro is bureaucratic and hierarchical, and loyalty is to family members and patrons in the ranks of the company. Decisions often are left either to a member of the controlling family or to top executives, while middle-level managers seldom are asked to contribute their opinions, let alone to make important decisions. Mr. Loose (Corning's chief executive of the joint venture) observed, "If we were looking at a distribution decision, or a customer decision, we would have a group of people in a room, they would do an assessment, figure alternatives and make a decision, and I as chief executive would never know about it. My experience on the Mexican side is that someone in the organization would have a solution in mind, but then the decision had to be kicked up a few levels."

These examples indicate that culture was an especially sensitive issue between Corning and Vitro, and the alliance was not able to overcome these problems. Corning felt that the cross-cultural differences were depriving both companies of the flexibility to take the fast management action that is necessary in the dynamic business climate of both countries. Vitro basically agreed. Corning gave Vitro back its $130 million investment, and the joint venture was called off. The companies still recognize the opportunity to continue business with each other, however. They have changed their relationship into a mutual distribution of each other's products.

The Aftermath of the Breakup

Vitro and Corning each responded publicly to the dissolution of their alliance, and each indicated the strong differences in culture. Corning wanted to discuss the problems and learn from them, while Vitro was hesitant to criticize anyone, especially a visible U.S. partner like Corning. The Mexicans preferred to concentrate on continuation of the marketing arrangement between the companies. Houghton, the Corning CEO, openly spoke of the alliance as one that stopped making sense. He stated that cross-cultural differences inhibited the potential of the alliance. Corning's chief executive of the venture, Mr. Loose, openly acknowledged the different decision-making styles between the two cultures. Vitro executives were defensive and disappointed that Mr. Loose had expressed his views so frankly in public. "It is unfortunate that he made those comments," said an anonymous Vitro executive. The president of Vitro, Eduardo Martens, flatly denied that the cultural differences were any greater than in other alliances. In an interview with the *Harvard Business Review,* however, he admitted, "Business in Mexico is done on a consensus basis, very genteel and sometimes slow by U.S. standards."

Corning feels they learned a lesson in the failed Vitro alliance; both foreign and domestic alliances require additional skills and more management time. CEO Houghton says that alliances carry a lot of risk and misunderstandings, but they can be significantly beneficial to the operations of a company if they are done carefully and selectively. Corning continues to analyze why the cultural differences with Vitro were too strong to overcome.

1. Identify and discuss Corning's strategic predisposition toward a joint venture with Vitro.
2. Cultural clashes among partners in joint ventures are not a new issue. Discuss why an MNC, and specifically Corning, would be interested in fully understanding the culture of a potential partner before deciding on an alliance.
3. If Corning and Vitro had decided to remain in the alliance, how could they have overcome their differences to make the partnership a success?
4. Discuss why both companies would continue to distribute each other's products after the joint venture failed. What impact might the public statements about the failure have on this relationship?

THE ROAD TO HELL

John Baker, chief engineer of the Caribbean Bauxite Company of Barracania in the West Indies, was making his final preparations to leave the island. His promotion to production manager of Keso Mining Corporation near Winnipeg—one of Continental Ore's fast-expanding Canadian enterprises—had been announced a month before, and now everything had been tidied up except the last vital interview with his successor, the able young Barracanian, Matthew Rennalls. It was crucial that this interview be successful and that Rennalls leave his office uplifted and encouraged to face the challenge of a new job. A touch on the bell would have brought Rennalls walking into the room, but Baker delayed the moment and gazed thoughtfully through the window, considering just exactly what he was going to say and, more particularly, how he was going to say it.

John Baker, an English expatriate, was 45 years old and had served 23 years with Continental Ore in East Asia, several African countries, Europe, and for the last 2 years, the West Indies. He hadn't cared much for his previous assignment in Hamburg and was delighted when the West Indian appointment came through. Climate was not the only attraction. Baker had always preferred working overseas (in what were termed "the developing countries"), because he felt he had an innate knack—better than most other expatriates working for Continental Ore—of knowing just how to get along with the regional staff. After 24 hours in Barracania, however, he realized that he would need all this "innate knack" to deal effectively with the problems that awaited him in this field.

At his first interview with Hutchins, the production manager, the problem of Rennalls and his future was discussed. There and then it was made quite clear to Baker that one of his most important tasks would be "grooming" Rennalls as his successor. Hutchins had pointed out that not only was Rennalls one of the brightest Barracanian prospects on the staff of Caribbean Bauxite—at London University he had taken first-class honors in the BSc engineering degree—but being the son of the minister of finance and economic planning, he also had no small political pull.

The company had been particularly pleased when Rennalls decided to work for it rather than the government in which his father had such a prominent post. The company ascribed his action to the effect of its vigorous and liberal regionalization program, which since World War II had produced 18 Barracanians at midmanagement level and given Caribbean Bauxite a good lead in this respect over all other international concerns operating in Barracania. The success of this timely regionalization policy led to excellent relations with the government.

This relationship was given an added importance when Barracania, 3 years later, became independent—an occasion that encouraged a critical and challenging attitude toward the role that foreign interests would play in the new Barracania. Therefore, Hutchins had little difficulty in convincing Baker that the successful career development of Rennalls was of primary importance.

The interview with Hutchins was now 2 years old, and Baker, leaning back in his office chair, reviewed his success in grooming Rennalls. What aspects of the latter's character had helped and what had hindered? What about his own personality? How had that helped or hindered? The first item to go on the credit side would, without question, be the ability of Rennalls to master the technical aspects of the job. From the start, he had shown keenness and enthusiasm and often impressed Baker with his ability in tackling new assignments as well as the constructive comments he invariably made in departmental discussions. He was popular with all ranks of Barracanian staff and had an ease of manner that placed him in good stead when dealing with his expatriate seniors. These were all assets, but what about the debit side?

First and foremost, there was his racial consciousness. His 4 years at London University had accentuated this feeling and made him sensitive to any sign of condescension on the part of expatriates. It may have been to give expression to this sentiment that as soon as he

Source: This case was prepared by Gareth Evans and is used with permission.

returned from London, he threw himself into politics on behalf of the United Action Party, which later won the preindependence elections and provided the country with its first prime minister.

The ambitions of Rennalls—and he certainly was ambitious—did not lie in politics, because staunch nationalist that he was, he saw that he could serve himself and his country best—for bauxite was responsible for nearly half the value of Barracania's export trade—by putting his engineering talent to the best use possible. On this account, Hutchins found that he had an unexpectedly easy task in persuading Rennalls to give up his political work before entering the production department as an assistant engineer.

Baker knew that it was Rennalls' well-repressed sense of race consciousness that had prevented their relationship from being as close as it should have been. On the surface, nothing could have seemed more agreeable. Formality between the two men was at a minimum: Baker was delighted to find that his assistant shared his own peculiar "shaggy dog" sense of humor so that jokes were continually being exchanged; they entertained each other at their houses and often played tennis together—and yet the barrier remained invisible, indefinable, but ever present. The existence of this "screen" between them was a constant source of frustration to Baker, because it indicated a weakness that he was loath to accept. If he was successful with all other nationalities, why not with Rennalls?

At least he had managed to "break through" to Rennalls more successfully than any other expatriate. In fact, it was the young Barracanian's attitude—sometimes overbearing, sometimes cynical—toward other company expatriates that had been one of the subjects Baker had raised last year when he discussed Rennalls' staff report with him. He knew, too, that he would have to raise the same subject again in the forthcoming interview, because Jackson, the senior draftsperson, had complained only yesterday about the rudeness of Rennalls. With this thought in mind, Baker leaned forward and spoke into the intercom, "Would you come in, Matt, please? I'd like a word with you." As Rennalls entered the room, Baker said, "Do sit down," and offered a cigarette. He paused while he held out his lighter, then went on.

"As you know, Matt, I'll be off to Canada in a few days' time, and before I go, I thought it would be useful if we could have a final chat together. It is indeed with some deference that I suggest I can be of help. You will shortly be sitting in this chair doing the job I am now doing, but I, on the other hand, am 10 years older, so perhaps you can accept the idea that I may be able to give you the benefit of my longer experience."

Baker saw Rennalls stiffen slightly in his chair as he made this point. Consequently, he added in explanation,

"You and I have attended enough company courses to remember those repeated requests by the personnel manager to tell people how they are getting on as often as the convenient moment arises and not just the automatic 'once a year' when, by regulation, staff reports have to be discussed."

Rennalls nodded his agreement, and Baker went on. "I shall always remember the last job performance discussion I had with my previous boss back in Germany. He used what he called the 'plus and minus' technique. His firm belief was that when a senior, by discussion, seeks to improve the work performance of his staff, his prime objective should be to make sure that the latter leaves the interview encouraged and inspired to improve. Any criticism must, therefore, be constructive and helpful. He said that one very good way to encourage a person—and I fully agree with him—is to tell him about his good points—the plus factors—as well as his weak ones—the minus factors. I thought, Matt, it would be a good idea to run our discussion along these lines."

Rennalls offered no comment, so Baker continued. "Let me say, therefore, right away, that, as far as your own work performance is concerned, the plus far outweighs the minus. I have been most impressed, for instance, with the way you have adapted your considerable theoretic knowledge to master the practical techniques of your job—that ingenious method you used to get air down to the fifth-shaft level is a sufficient case in point—and at departmental meetings I have invariably found your comments well-taken and helpful. In fact, you will be interested to know that only last week I reported to Mr. Hutchins that, from the technical point of view, he could not wish for a more able man to succeed to the position of chief engineer."

"That's very good indeed of you, John," cut in Rennalls with a smile of thanks. "My only worry now is how to live up to such a high recommendation."

"Of that I am quite sure," returned Baker, "especially if you can overcome the minus factor which I would like now to discuss with you. It is one that I have talked about before, so I'll come straight to the point. I have noticed that you are more friendly and get on better with your fellow Barracanians than you do with Europeans. In point of fact, I had a complaint only yesterday from Mr. Jackson, who said you had been rude to him—and not for the first time either.

"There is, Matt, I am sure, no need for me to tell you how necessary it will be for you to get on well with expatriates, because until the company has trained sufficient people of your calibre, Europeans are bound to occupy senior positions here in Barracania. All this is vital to your future interests, so can I help you in any way?"

While Baker was speaking on this theme, Rennalls sat tensed in his chair, and it was some seconds before he replied. "It is quite extraordinary, isn't it, how one can convey an impression to others so at variance with what one intends? I can only assure you once again that my disputes with Jackson—and you may remember also, Godson—have had nothing at all to do with the color of their skins. I promise you that if a Barracanian had behaved in an equally peremptory manner I would have reacted in precisely the same way. And again, if I may say it within these four walls, I am sure I am not the only one who has found Jackson and Godson difficult. I could mention the names of several expatriates who have felt the same. However, I am really sorry to have created this impression of not being able to get along with Europeans—it is an entirely false one—and I quite realize that I must do all I can to correct it as quickly as possible. On your last point, regarding Europeans holding senior positions in the company for some time to come, I quite accept the situation. I know that Caribbean Bauxite—as it has been doing for many years now—will promote Barracanians as soon as their experience warrants it. And, finally, I would like to assure you, John—and my father thinks the same too—that I am very happy in my work here and hope to stay with the company for many years to come."

Rennalls had spoken earnestly. Although not convinced by what he heard, Baker did not think he could pursue the matter further except to say, "All right, Matt, my impression *may* be wrong, but I would like to remind you about the truth of that old saying, 'What is important is not what is true but what is believed.' Let it rest at that."

But suddenly Baker knew that he didn't want to "let it rest at that." He was disappointed once again at not being able to break through to Rennalls and having yet again to listen to his bland denial that there was any racial prejudice in his makeup. Baker, who had intended to end the interview at this point, decided to try another tactic.

"To return for a moment to the 'plus and minus technique' I was telling you about just now, there is another plus factor I forgot to mention. I would like to congratulate you not only on the calibre of your work but also on the ability you have shown in overcoming a challenge which I, as a European, have never had to meet. Continental Ore is, as you know, a typical commercial enterprise—admittedly a big one—which is a product of the economic and social environment of the United States and Western Europe. My ancestors have all been brought up in this environment for the past 200 or 300 years, and I have, therefore, been able to live in a world in which commerce (as we know it today) has been part and parcel of my being. It has not been something revolutionary and new that has suddenly entered my life." Baker went on, "In your case, the situation is different, because you

and your forebears have had only some 50 or 60 years in this commercial environment. You have had to face the challenge of bridging the gap between 50 and 200 or 300 years. Again, Matt, let me congratulate you—and people like you—once again on having so successfully overcome this particular hurdle. It is for this very reason that I think the outlook for Barracania—and particularly Caribbean Bauxite—is so bright."

Rennalls had listened intently and when Baker finished, replied, "Well, once again, John, I have to thank you for what you have said, and, for my part, I can only say that it is gratifying to know that my own personal effort has been so much appreciated. I hope that more people will soon come to think as you do."

There was a pause, and for a moment, Baker thought hopefully that he was about to achieve his long-awaited breakthrough, but Rennalls merely smiled back. The barrier remained unbreached. There remained some 5 minutes of cheerful conversation about the contrast between the Caribbean and Canadian climate and whether the West Indies had any hope of beating England in the Fifth Test before Baker drew the interview to a close. Although he was as far as ever from knowing the real Rennalls, he nevertheless was glad that the interview had run along in this friendly manner and, particularly, that it had ended on such a cheerful note.

This feeling, however, lasted only until the following morning. Baker had some farewells to make, so he arrived at the office considerably later than usual. He had no sooner sat down at his desk than his secretary walked into the room with a worried frown on her face. Her words came fast, "When I arrived this morning, I found Mr. Rennalls already waiting at my door. He seemed very angry and told me in quite a peremptory manner that he had a vital letter to dictate that must be sent off without any delay. He was so worked up that he couldn't keep still and kept pacing about the room, which is most unlike him. He wouldn't even wait to read what he had dictated. Just signed the page where he thought the letter would end. It has been distributed, and your copy is in your tray.

Puzzled and feeling vaguely uneasy, Baker opened the confidential envelope and read the following letter:

From: Assistant Engineer

To: Chief Engineer,
         Caribbean Bauxite Limited

                                14 August

Assessment of Interview between Baker and Rennalls

It has always been my practice to respect the advice given me by seniors, so after our interview, I decided to give careful thought once again to its main points and so make sure that I had understood all that had been said. As I promised you at the time, I had every intention of putting your advice to the best effect.

It was not, therefore, until I had sat down quietly in my home yesterday evening to consider the interview objectively that its main purport became clear. Only then did the full enormity of what you said dawn on me. The more I thought about it, the more convinced I was that I had hit upon the real truth—and the more furious I became. With a facility in the English language which I, a poor Barracanian, cannot hope to match, you had the audacity to insult me (and through me every Barracanian worth his salt) by claiming that our knowledge of modern living is only a paltry 50 years old whereas yours goes back 200 or 300 years. As if your materialistic commercial environment could possibly be compared with the spiritual values of our culture. I'll have you know that if much of what I saw in London is repre-sentative of your most boasted culture, I hope fervently that it will never come to Barracania. By what right do you have the effrontery to condescend to us? At heart, all you Europeans think us barbarians; as you say amongst yourselves, we are "just down from the trees."

Far into the night I discussed this matter with my father, and he is as disgusted as I. He agrees with me that any company whose senior staff think as you do is no place for any Barra-canian proud of his culture and race—so much for all the com-pany "clap-trap" and specious propaganda about regionaliza-tion and Barracania for the Barracanians.

I feel ashamed and betrayed. Please accept this letter as my resignation, which I wish to become effective immediately.

cc: Production Manager
      Managing Director

IS INFORMATION TECHNOLOGY JAPAN'S ACHILLES' HEEL?

Considerable attention has been given as to how the Japanese "miracle" emerged in the past 25 years. Cited reasons for this success come from a variety of perspectives, including a superior education system, cultural values that support a strong work ethic, effective management practices, government supports, and aggressive exporting into international markets such as the United States and China. Then, however, reality hit the Japanese economy. Since the early part of this decade, Japan has been in a recession.

At least part of the reason for Japan's fall from its "miracle" status can be attributed to how far behind the Japanese are in actually implementing and using information technologies in the workplace compared with other industrialized nations. The Japanese education system, culture, management approach, and government were well suited for the economic development that occurred during the 1970s and 1980s, when the economy primarily was based on manufacturing and exporting. Now that they are faced with a new global economy requiring speed, knowledge, and communication, the Japanese are beginning to pay the price for often outdated, or sometimes even absent, information technologies and applications. Has information technology become Japan's Achilles' heel? The future of the Japanese economy may well depend on how fast they can catch up in the "information age" with the rest of the world.

The Status of Japanese Information Technology

While Japan still has state-of-the-art factories with the most advanced manufacturing processes and technolo-

Source: This case was written specially for this book by Steve Farner, University of Nebraska.

gies (including computer-based robotics), the front office of some organizations lags far behind those of their international competitors. For example, it is estimated that at present, only a small minority of Japanese employees work with computers. Of the computers in the Japanese workplace, most are still not connected on a network, compared with the United States where the majority are. In addition, Japan is well behind the United States or Europe in developing or using an information superhighway or Internet.

There are several reasons why the Japanese have gotten so far behind in information technologies. The following sections identify some of the major barriers the Japanese must overcome to join fully and compete economically in the information age.

Government Overregulation

Although the Japanese government system of numerous rules, regulations, and licensing requirements protecting Japanese manufactures from foreign and domestic competition has worked quite well, it no longer works in the new information age. For example, according to Hiroshi Inose, the Director-General of the National Center for Science Information Systems, the Japanese use of on-line services is well behind that of the United States. Part of the reason is the obstructionist role that Japanese government ministries play. The different arms of the government are not co-operating to the degree necessary to make a nationwide computer system work. For example, several years ago, the government embarked on a $95 million dollar project designed to link supercomputers among various government laboratories. What is interesting to note is that this project was limited to government laboratories only. The universities currently are trying to network, but this necessary project is being supervised slowly by the Ministry of Education. In addition, the costs for leasing a direct phone line for high-speed data transfer can be up to 10 times that in the United States. This prohibitive phone cost mostly is because of the high fees imposed by the Ministry of Posts and Telecommunications (MPT).

Complexity of the Japanese Language

Perhaps the major reason for the limited use of certain information technologies involves the complexity of the written Japanese language. While the English language generally depends on combinations of 26 letters and 10 numbers, the Japanese system is a much more complex system of symbols. Japanese schoolchildren learn about 2000 of these symbols by the sixth grade; many thousands more must be learned to become proficient at communicating in the workplace. This complexity is a strong factor in determining which information technologies will be desired in the workplace. For example, e-mail using the Japanese language is not widely used partially because of the difficulty in typing. The many thousands of symbols that are necessary makes keyboarding in the Japanese language quite cumbersome. In fact, keyboards that were able to handle the 10,000 plus character language were not even available until after 1980. This makes facsimile machines a desirable technology for transmitting documents, although their use did not become widespread until recent years, again mostly because of cumbersome government regulations regarding the use of telephone lines.

Workplace Climate and Office Conditions

Another barrier inhibiting the development and use of information technology in Japan can be traced to the emphasis on blue-collar, manufacturing industries both in general and even within specific companies. As Japan's economy grew after World War II, a labor shortage developed. The focus tended to be on hiring enough front-line workers, not on making the front office and the support infrastructure run smoothly and efficiently. The efficient, high-quality products that were produced by Japanese manufacturers tended to mask and overshadow what could be considered very inefficient office and information systems.

A typical office may consist of a large, open room with desks facing each other in rows. This does eliminate problems associated with allocating the best office space. Also, supervisors can better monitor work when everybody is in sight. However, no thought was given to information flows or effective co-ordination and interaction. The Japanese may have teams and quality circles on the shop floor, but they often seem to run the front office as a strict bureaucracy.

Besides language complexities, a cultural problem in implementing information technology in the workplace is that older Japanese managers may not only be unfamiliar in the use of computers, as in most countries, but many older Japanese managers do not even like to be seen using a computer. The feeling is that this is work that should be done by the female clerical staff; and they feel it is beneath their status to be seen near computers.

Another cultural barrier is that the Japanese greatly prefer either face-to-face or telephone contact rather than written reports or computer e-mail. Although this of course is changing, having a textual message appear on a computer screen still seems to be considered a rude form of impersonal communication for many in the Japanese culture.

Decision-Making Structures

The Japanese system of management decision making is still largely based on participation and consensus. This is deeply imbedded within their collective cultural values, and the intricate working relationships of Japanese management can be described by the concept of *wa*. This can be translated as "peace, harmony, unity, and conformity." This application of *wa* involves much more than simply asking subordinates for input. All employees, regardless of level, are responsible for activities in their immediate work environment. In the United States, the tendency is to rely on more of a centralized, top-down approach to decision making. In addition, the Japanese approach is intentionally very ambiguous as to who is responsible for a decision, because groups reaching consensus are responsible for managerial decisions as opposed to individual managers.

Besides *wa*, another cultural concept driving Japanese management is *ringi*. This involves the individual with an idea gaining the informal support from his work group. Then, a written proposal is circulated from the group to those who would be responsible for implementing the decision. At this point, all the involved parties conduct meetings and bring in experts to formalize the proposal. After the proposal is formalized, it moves through the organization to get seals of approval from each level of management. This assures consensus throughout the organization.

The *ringi* method, of course, is quite time-consuming. An individual's idea literally can have 50 or 60 stamps of approval before it is implemented. Although one benefit of consensus is acceptance, the time-consuming aspect has had a negative impact on speed-based competition in the information age. Also, these approaches tend to inhibit creativity and innovation. Emphasis on consensus, conformity, and getting along tends to be more important than coming up with new ideas. Driven by *wa* and *ringi*, Japanese business decisions have a tendency to be low risk, which greatly inhibits competitiveness in today's global economy. This same decision-making pattern is common in the government as well. The deliberate, slow, low-risk approach that worked so well in a manufacturing-based economy is ill-suited to a rapid, technology-driven, information-based service economy.

The Japanese Education System

The Japanese form of education often has been cited as being superior to that of other countries around the world. The structure is similar to that of the United States. There are 6 years of elementary school, 3 years of junior high, and 3 years of high school. While the structure parallels that of the United States, the way this system operates is much different. Over 95 percent of students continue into high school, with over 35 percent going on to college. This college percentage probably would be much higher if the entrance requirements were not so strict. The entrance exams are very difficult and demanding, and students spend a significant amount of time preparing for them. In fact, this preparation begins at age 10. Cramming for these exams leaves little time for extracurricular school activities. While the West tends to value outside activities, whether music or sports, in the total development of youth, the Japanese tend to focus more on studying for these exams. While U.S. children are taught to be different, Japanese children are taught to be the same, and the system they have in place for education supports this conformity.

Like the cultural dimensions of *wa* and *ringi,* this educational system tends to suppress innovation and creativity. The typical Japanese employee is highly literate, knows the basics, but is not independent enough to be innovative and creative. Yet, the innovation and creativity of all human resources are recognized as the major competitive advantage in the information age.

Lifetime Employment

Traditionally, at least in the large MNCs, lifetime employment was a cornerstone of Japanese human resource management. In the West, the tendency has been to focus on a skill or set of skills (e.g., computer skills) as opposed to a specific company. In Japan, the main focus has been on the employer. Japanese employees may have a variety of jobs within one organization throughout a career; however, because of downsizing and re-engineering, which became popular in recent years to make organizations more efficient and reduce costs, lifetime employment became a huge obstacle. Information technology in particular goes hand-in-hand with downsizing and re-engineering; lifetime employment does not.

Conclusion

Japan has been a major economic player in the previous two decades, and this resulted primarily from production of quality products in state-of-the-art factories using dedicated, team-oriented, secure workers. However, the new information age is forcing organizations that wish to compete in the hypercompetitive global economy to restructure to capitalize on the benefits associated with the emerging information technologies. The challenge facing Japan is whether it can overcome serious barriers to join this new information-based way of doing business and, once again, join and sustain the "miracle" status it once enjoyed as an economic superpower.

1. How important do you think it is for Japanese organizations to embrace and use e-mail?
2. What economic implications does the "information superhighway" have for Japan? How will this affect the Japanese economy if they continue to lag in the development of such an information system?
3. The Japanese treat the white-collar, front-office portion of the organization much differently than Western organizations. What are some of the cultural reasons for this? What, if anything, can be done to change this?
4. Discuss how you see the global economy unfolding in the beginning of the twenty-first century. Do you think Japan will be a superpower? How do you think they will compete against the United States (or your own country)?

GLOBAL INTEGRATION VS. LOCAL DIFFERENTIATION: LESSONS TO BE LEARNED FROM SUCCESSFUL MNCs

Global integration means that if an MNC takes an internationalization or globalization strategy, it believes that their products or services will sell anywhere in the world. This assumes homogeneous consumer tastes and standardized foods and services. On the other hand, a national (or regional, local, or cultural) responsiveness strategy assumes there are different and unique consumer tastes that require a segmented marketing approach. Also, each country has different laws, regulations, and standards.

In their widely recognized book on *Managing across Borders,* Christopher Bartlett and Sumantra Ghoshal identified General Electric, Kao of Japan, and ITT as demonstrating three different but important dimensions of an integration versus differentiation strategy. Bartlett and Ghoshal provide important global strategy lessons from these successful MNCs.

GE's Failure in Consumer Electronics

For General Electric, a leading role in the global consumer electronics industry was once a very reasonable expectation. GE had more technological capabilities than anyone in the field, and its utter dominance in the electrical appliances industry provided a base from which to build. After years of investment and effort, however, GE withdrew from this industry.

This MNC's failure in consumer electronics illustrates a problem that would hurt many European and U.S. firms

in a variety of industries: the lack of global efficiency. Globalization has led to a unified world marketplace in which companies must capture economies of large-scale to remain competitive. One example would be the shift that occurred in the watch industry. The Swiss once dominated this industry with a labor-intensive, craftsperson approach; however, the introduction of quartz technology made watchmaking a scale-intensive global industry the Japanese now dominate.

Forces beyond economies of scale also drove companies to integrate their operations globally during the 1970s and 1980s. Consumer tastes and preferences began homogenizing. Customer demands once differed greatly from one national market to the next. Again, major external discontinuities largely facilitated this trend. A good example was the oil shortages of the 1970s, which started a demand for smaller, more fuel-efficient automobiles around the world. Bartlett and Ghoshal point out that the forces driving companies to integrate their operations worldwide spread from industries where external structural change or discontinuity dictated a global strategy to industries in which managers had to create the opportunity for global economies of scale. GE's consumer electronics division eventually was overwhelmed by these new challenges.

Kao's False Assumption

Kao, Japan's leading producer of soaps, detergents, and personal-care products, is recognized as one of the top Japanese companies. Similar to other large Japanese firms, Kao made a strategic commitment to globalization. At first, the firm moved aggressively into neighboring Asian countries such as Indonesia, Malaysia,

Source: This case was written specially for this book by Brett C. Luthans, Missouri Western State College.

Singapore, the Philippines, and Hong Kong. Kao then tried to enter the more advanced markets in the United States and Europe. However, despite enormous investments and an established reputation for supplying high-quality products at low prices, by the late 1980s Kao still was not a powerful global player in the soap, detergent, and personal-care industry.

Kao's fundamental problem was not inappropriate products or marketing strategies; it was the inability to understand differences between markets and adapt appropriately. Kao acquired industrial chemical operations in Mexico and Spain in the late 1970s and joined with Colgate in the United States and Beyersdorf in Europe to form joint ventures; however, these joint ventures failed to provide the local sensitivity and market understanding the company needed.

Kao's problems can be traced to the lack of national responsiveness; its failure to understand local needs. Kao mistakenly believed globalization meant that soap was soap throughout the world, that the world's consumers were homogeneous. The failure of firms such as Kao have forced the management of global companies to be more sensitive to cultural differences and local interests in the host countries where they wish to operate. Adapting to local differences became a high priority by the late 1970s, especially among Japanese MNCs. Increasingly, MNCs in a wide range of industries are becoming very sensitive to local markets and host-country expectations and pressures.

ITT Loses Out

By 1980, ITT, which based its worldwide expansion strategy on being in touch with local national interests and market needs, was one of the top suppliers of telecommunications equipment worldwide. Originally, it was set up with strong, independent local entities that were responsible for the development, manufacturing, marketing, installation, and service of its products. During the late 1950s, ITT's informal management was replaced by a strong emphasis on formal management control while continuing to develop and implement local strategies on an independent basis.

In the late 1970s, two developments altered the overall strategy of ITT. First was the development of digital switching technology. Several hundred million dollars were needed to design and manufacture a new switch, and no single-country unit could manage this colossal investment on its own. Second was a trend toward deregulation, which opened numerous national markets to international competitors, thus reducing the benefits of local differentiation. Consequently, integrating the technological capabilities of the national entities to de-

velop and build a standard global product became essential.

ITT, however, failed to integrate its substantial technical resources and knowledge. Its large systems houses refused to co-operate with each other and resisted accepting common standards. An even bigger problem came when the company decided to take "System 12" to the U.S. market and begin a huge R&D effort. The eventual failure of this led to the end of ITT's direct involvement with the global telecommunications market, and it illustrates the third important strategic dimension for competing in global markets: the need to develop and diffuse technologic innovations internationally.

Conclusions

The early failures of these three prominent MNCs provide some important lessons for developing an integration versus differentiation strategy. Bartlett and Ghoshal summarize these as follows:

1. In the past, all three MNCs were characterized by a single dominant strategic demand. Each could compete effectively as long as its capability fit the strategic demand of the business. By the mid-1980s, however, the forces of global integration (in the case of GE consumer electronics), local differentiation (in the case of Kao), and worldwide innovation (in the case of ITT) all had become important to success in the global marketplace. To compete effectively in this new situation, MNCs had to develop global integration, local flexibility, and worldwide innovation capability simultaneously.

2. Building multiple strategic competencies for global integration, local differentiation, and global diffusion of innovation requires new organization design and management thinking. Bartlett and Ghoshal call this new model a transnational approach for organizing and managing. This transnational model goes beyond the traditional international model not just by reacting to expanding markets, but by being able to accommodate and anticipate multiple strategic demands. This transnational model allowed MNCs such as P&G, NEC, and Unilever to respond successfully to the new and complex demands of their international business environments. By the same token, a major reason why GE, Kao, and ITT failed in this new international environment was because they were not able to handle the strategic complexity with a traditional model of organization and management.

3. Becoming a transnational firm is not easy. Going from a multinational, global, or international model to a transnational model of organization and management

requires time, top management attention, and effort. The transnational approach involves building a learning and self-adaptive organization that also is competitive and flexible.

What Bartlett and Ghoshal propose is a "transnational" solution to the integration versus differentiation dilemma. The essence of this solution is that both integration and differentiation should be the strategy of today's MNCs. Sony's famous CEO Akio Morita coined the term *glocalization* to refer to this combination of global integration and local responsiveness. In other words, what Bartlett and Ghoshal as well as Morita suggest for effective strategic management in today's complex international environment is integration or "globalization" combined with differentiation related to local

cultures. The lesson to be learned from GE, Kao, and ITT is that the move toward an overall global strategy is necessary to take the MNC's products or technological innovations to any or all parts of the international marketplace. In the rush toward such integration and diffusion, however, MNCs also must be careful to recognize cultural differences.

1. What lessons did GE, Kao, and ITT provide for international strategic management?
2. What do Bartlett and Ghoshal mean by transnational organization and management? How does it differ from the traditional international approach?
3. What are some specific ways that MNCs can become more transnational and actually implement a "glocalization" strategy?

THE COLA WAR IN BRAZIL

Brazil, the largest country in South America and the fifth-largest in the world, is located on the east coast of the continent and covers 3.3 million square miles of tropical rain forests, mountain ranges, and farmland. There are 165 million people in Brazil, and over 9 million live in São Paulo, the capital city. A wide range of living standards exist in Brazil. While the rich live lavishly in the cities, the poor live in mud huts in the country and in deplorable slums in the cities. This gap between rich and poor is a serious problem, but the middle class, which is made up of teachers, businesspeople, and government employees, is growing. During the 1960s and 1970s, Brazil not only was able to absorb its high population increase but also to raise the standard of living for its people. This occurred because Brazil's economy was growing by about 7 percent a year, one of the highest growth rates in the world. Industrialization, the mechanization of agriculture, and the building of highways, power plants, and cities all were taking place simultaneously. Brazil has had a history of intermittent military rule, political scandal, and instability. Two decades of military rule ended in 1985 when civilian rule was re-established once again.

Background on the War

In 1988, the cola war was underway in Brazil. While Coca-Cola had a foothold in the Brazilian market with Coca-Cola Classic, PepsiCo was devising a strategy to boost international sales by moving into developing countries with relatively youthful populations. Because more than 30 percent of Brazil's then 140 million population were in the prime cola consumption age range of 10 to 24, this soft-drink market was very attractive to both firms. Consuming 5 billion liters of soft drinks per year, Brazil was the world's third-largest soft-drink market, after the United States and Mexico. Thanks to the Brazilian Minister of Health Borges da Silveira, however, the

producers of Coke and Pepsi were enmeshed in a conflict quite different from the battle for market share they were accustomed to in other parts of the world. The Brazilian government had not yet opened the market to diet colas.

Since 1971, Brazil had officially prohibited artificial sweeteners and not allowed the importation of diet soft drinks. With their large plantations, the country's powerful sugar-cane growers had been very successful at keeping nonsugar drinks out of the soft-drink market, but Coke and Pepsi both now had ambitious plans for diet soft drinks in Brazil. Coke and Pepsi—and a number of domestic soft-drink manufacturers—eagerly anticipated the government's go-ahead for production and distribution of diet soda in Brazil's lucrative soft-drink market. As a whole, Brazil's soft-drink market had room to grow. Annual per-capita consumption was only 36 liters, compared with 204 liters in the United States and 92 liters in Mexico. Antonio Kriegel, marketing director of Pepsi's Brazilian subsidiary, said his company estimated that diet drinks eventually would represent 5 percent of the total Brazilian soft-drink market. This diet market was valued at $2 billion per year.

How Sweet It Is: Stevia

Although scrapping with market leader Coca-Cola would have been tough enough for Pepsi, new soldiers were emerging on the battlefront. Ready for war were the noncaloric sweeteners, aspartame, saccharin, and Brazil's home-country favorite, stevia. A proposal came from the health ministry that stevioside, a sweetener derived from the South American stevia plant, be included in any sugar-free soft drinks appearing in the Brazilian marketplace. If this proposal became a reality it would throw a hitch in the cola company's plans and halt all product introduction until a fight between the Brazilian Health Ministry and the Agricultural Ministry over who had regulatory jurisdiction was resolved.

One company that would benefit immediately from a ruling in favor of the proposal would be Inga Companhia Desenvolvimento Industrial de Maringa (Maringa), Brazil's only commercial manufacturer of stevioside. In fact, much of the initial research on the sweetener was

Source: This case was written specially for this book by Tammi Sufficool.

carried out in Maringa, in the state of Parana, which also is the home turf of Health Minister da Silveira. Industry observers believed that Brazil's Health Council would require that sweetener formulations for diet soft drinks contain a percentage of stevioside rather than a formulation exclusively of stevioside.

It may be time for Brazil's soft-drink makers to rethink their strategies. Coca-Cola's current diet-drink formula will have to go "back into a drawer" if use of stevioside is made mandatory, says Raymond De Lagrave, vice-president of Coke's Brazilian operation. Stevia derivatives are 200 to 400 times sweeter than sugar and significantly lower in calories. However, industry observers note that unlike other artificial sweeteners, the Brazilian sweetener alters the taste of foods and drinks.

As part of the Health Ministry's approval of diet drinks, the Brazilian Soft Drink Manufacturers' Association agreed to study stevia. Batavo yogurt is the only other Brazilian product in which stevia is used. In Japan, more than 50 companies use it in soft drinks, canned foods, ice cream, and candies. Pepsi's Pepsi Lite is among the products using stevia in Japan.

Pepsi's Kriegel noted that his company was already thinking ahead and testing four formulas for blends of sweeteners "so as to not be caught napping by any change in legislation." So far, however, he says that Pepsi's experiments "have shown that stevia leaves a very strong aftertaste compared with other products."

The Pepsi Challenge

In December 1994, or six years and four attempts later, PepsiCo initiated operations in Brazil in what the soft-drink giant called one of its largest production launches ever, including an investment of approximately $350 million. Having failed in four previous efforts to establish a strong presence in Brazil, Pepsi was determined to gain market share and thus opened three new plants and a vast distribution network. Running the operation was Pepsi's first so-called regional superbottler, Buenos Aires Embotelladora SA (Baesa) and its well-regarded chief executive officer, Charles Beach. Mr. Beach started in Latin America by turning around the Puerto Rican Pepsi franchise. He made his biggest mark in Argentina, however, when he obtained control of a floundering Buenos Aires bottler in 1989. Between 1990 and 1993, Charles Beach and the Baesa bottlers boosted PepsiCo's market share from a mere 3 to 41 percent. Will Pepsi be successful this time in Brazil? What makes this such a difficult market to penetrate? Does the political climate of Brazil affect Pepsi's entry?

MNCs like Pepsi are being faced with problems of ethnocentricity and political risk in all corners of the globe. Host countries like Brazil guard against outside exploitation by protecting their own interests through economic, financial, social, and labor policies, and through pending legislation, power networks, and key agencies and officials. Host countries also protect themselves through their attitudes toward the private sector. If MNCs want to enter these markets, they need to understand the culture, political risks, and rules of the game.

Will Pepsi break through this time? Perhaps, if the political and economic conditions are optimal. They have been operating successfully for over 6 months, and maybe for Pepsi, the "fifth time is a charm."

1. Describe the climate for doing business in Brazil. Comment on why Brazil has been a difficult market for Pepsi to penetrate.
2. Discuss how a macro and micro analysis of political risks might have provided Pepsi with valuable strategic information.
3. Suggest a rationale for Charles Beach's success in other South American countries. Discuss the likelihood of success with his Brazilian undertaking.

QUESTIONABLE STRATEGY AT THE PEBBLE BEACH GOLF LINKS: AN INTERNATIONAL INVESTOR GOES OFF COURSE

To dedicated golfers, the Pebble Beach Golf Links on California's beautiful Monterey Peninsula is "hallowed ground." The chance to play Pebble Beach is considered a once-in-a-lifetime thrill. Pebble Beach has attained its celebrated status for a variety of reasons. First, it truly is one of the most gorgeous, natural settings in golf. Second, several important golf tournaments are televised from Pebble Beach each year, and many members of the golfing public feel they personally "know" the course. Moreover, Pebble Beach has been the site of several memorable U.S. Open Golf Championships, most recently in 1992. Finally, Pebble Beach is distinctive in that average golfers *do* have the opportunity—albeit an expensive one, with the cost of a single round of golf ranging between $150 and $200—to play Pebble Beach. Although privately owned, Pebble Beach has been open to the general public for its entire history. Thus, while actually playing Pebble Beach likely will remain a distant dream for most golfers, a unique combination of circumstances has resulted in considerable public interest in its welfare.

Pebble Beach as a real estate commodity also has evoked a great deal of interest from a diverse group of investors. In fact, the history of investment in Pebble Beach mirrors the changing nature of the global economy over the past century. Initially purchased and developed by a group of U.S. railroad barons in 1880, Pebble Beach over the years has been owned by an early environmentalist, who managed to protect most of the area's natural beauty in the early years; a sand-mining firm, which ru-

Source: This case was written specially for this book by Rex Karsten, the University of Northern Iowa.

ined parts of the peninsula; a Hollywood film company; a cunning Denver oil billionaire; and most recently, and reflective of the evolution of international economic power, two dissimilar groups of Japanese investors.

A brief overview of the investment history of Pebble Beach provides a context for understanding the curious nature of transactions in a global economy and, specifically, the unique problems and opportunities faced by international investors.

Pebble Beach Yesterday and Today

The original owners (a group of railroad barons) purchased several thousand acres of undeveloped land on the Monterey Peninsula for approximately $35,000 in 1880. These developers built a resort and golf course (the first of four) to attract members of San Francisco's high society. In 1915, they hired Samuel F. B. Morse to manage the resort. Morse, who eventually would purchase the course in 1919, is credited with preventing the overcommercialization of the area, developing a second golf course—Pebble Beach—on the stretch of coastline originally earmarked for houses. Ironically, Morse was not much of a golfer, and perhaps not much of an environmentalist, because his main goal in developing the course was not to protect the coastline but primarily to enhance the value of the real estate. Morse ran the resort complex until his death in 1969. From 1969 to 1979, the complex was rather benignly owned by a sand-mining firm called Wedron Silica Company, which would later change its name to the Pebble Beach Corporation.

In 1979, flush with cash from its successful film *Star Wars,* 20th Century Fox purchased the Pebble Beach Corporation for $72 million and held it until 1981. Then,

Marvin Davis, a shrewd billionaire from Denver, Colorado, purchased 20th Century Fox and all its holdings for $722 million. The Pebble Beach property alone was valued at $150 million when purchased by Davis and would be worth approximately $300 million 4 years later. By that time, because of completion of a new inn and golf course, the Pebble Beach Corporation consisted of four golf courses, two hotels, a scenic $6-per-car toll road, and a 5300-acre forest potentially open to additional lucrative development.

The value of the property continued to grow and attracted considerable interest from a variety of investors from several countries. By 1988, Davis had set a price of $900 million for Pebble Beach, although neutral appraisers suggested its true value was closer to $550 million. The high price did discourage most potential investors, and Davis was without a buyer for 2 years. In September 1990, however, a Japanese businessman named Moritsu Isutani agreed to purchase Pebble Beach for approximately $841 million (the price has been estimated to be even $100 million higher by some sources). Although the purchase involved a U.S. landmark and a significant amount of money, Isutani's purchase was relatively small compared with many other overvalued real estate properties acquired by the Japanese during this time period. There was not the U.S. public uproar, for example, that accompanied the Mitsubishi Estate Corporation's purchase of Rockefeller Center in New York the previous year. Indeed, Isutani's purchase probably would have attracted little attention had his plan to recoup his purchase price been successful.

Unfortunately, Isutani's plan did encounter several major obstacles. In combination with a declining Japanese stock market, rising interest rates, a growing worldwide recession, and the developing crisis in the Persian Gulf, Isutani's apparently less-than-ideal strategy forced him to relinquish ownership of Pebble Beach. The current owners (also Japanese)—the Sumitomo Credit Service Corporation, and the Taiheyo Club, Inc.—purchased Pebble Beach from Isutani in January 1992 for $574 million. The saga of Moritsu Isutani provides an interesting glimpse into the complicated world of international management.

Isutani and the Pebble Beach Strategy

Moritsu Isutani was no stranger to high finance, golf courses, or international investment. Isutani, an avid and very competent golfer, was a secretive figure in both Japan and the United States. In fact, some business observers described him as a "stealth" investor. It was known that he owned at least 9 golf courses in Japan, however, and as many as 17 around the world. In addition, at the time of his purchase of Pebble Beach, he was involved in at least three other major golf course development efforts within the United States: a planned $30 million golf course (opposed by environmentalists) on a flood plain in the San Fernando Valley in California; a $200 million golf course–casino complex outside Las Vegas; and a $357 million golf and hotel complex along Hawaii's Kona Coast. In other words, Isutani was familiar with investment and development in the United States and should have been well prepared to garner a profit from a venture such as Pebble Beach in spite of its inflated purchase price. Indeed, Isutani attempted to implement a strategy that apparently had been successful in past—although lesser—development efforts.

Isutani's plan was to sell golf course memberships at very high prices to anyone who could afford them. This is a regular practice in Japan, where it is not unusual to pay more than $1 million to secure a "lifetime" of tee times. It was rumored that Isutani believed he could sell more than 700 memberships for over $700,000 apiece, potentially generating more than $500 million and defraying a considerable portion of Isutani's debt.

Importantly, however, was that to implement his membership plan, Isutani had to obtain the approval of the local county board of supervisors and the California Coastal Commission. Both groups regulate land use along California's coastline. This approval process also brought the plans of the mysterious new owner of Pebble Beach to the attention of the previously unconcerned local public.

Local Reaction

A local environmentalist first suggested that the expensive membership plan would effectively privatize the Pebble Beach golf course, limiting access to the course—and subsequently the coastline—to the very wealthy. The California Coastal Act of 1976, which requires that any new coastal development guarantee public access to the coastline, was employed to block, or at least slow, Isutani's development efforts. Because Isutani had borrowed almost the entire purchase price, he could ill afford to wait any length of time before beginning to pay off his enormous debt.

Noting, and eventually sharing, the environmentalist concern with privatization, local golfers also became incensed, envisioning wave after wave of rich Japanese golfers swarming over Pebble Beach, denying locals the opportunity to ever play "their" course again. Isutani's representatives insisted this would never be allowed to happen, but their pleas fell on disbelieving ears. This lack of trust may have been exacerbated by Isutani's secretive nature. During the entire time he owned the course, he seldom visited or made public appearances. He made no effort to get to know local politicians, civic leaders, the press, or even golfers. Because of his perceived secretive nature, local citizens were inclined to believe largely unsubstantiated rumors about Isutani's involvement in a variety of shady deals—for example, overselling memberships in his Japanese golf courses—and even his possible ties to the *yakuza*, Japan's mafia.

In November 1991, stating that their decision was based on a continuing concern with the impact of privatization, the Coastal Commission vetoed the last of a series of revised membership plans. Because he was unable to make payment on his debt, cash flow became a problem for Isutani. On December 12, Monterey County declared that the Pebble Beach Corporation was $3 million behind in property taxes.

Isutani finally granted a local interview in late December and portrayed himself as a victim of increasing interest rates and plunging property values in Japan, as misunderstood by the U.S. press and public, and as originally misled by Marvin Davis to believe that his private membership plan would be acceptable to local authorities. Not unaccustomed to disgruntled buyers, Davis, who incidentally once referred to Pebble Beach as a mere "pimple" on his total assets, denied the charge. In spite of these difficulties, by the end of 1991 Isutani still did not believe he would be required to sell Pebble Beach.

National and International Reaction

To compound Isutani's local problems, the U.S. Open—the premier annual golfing event in the United States—was scheduled to be played on the Pebble Beach Golf Links in June 1992, only 6 months away. U.S. Golf Association officials began to worry if a potentially bankrupt Pebble Beach would be able to host such an event. Contingency plans were made to shift the event to another site. Interestingly, while the fate of the Open was of considerable concern to U.S. golfers, the Japanese business establishment apparently was even more disturbed. Relations between the United States and Japan already were less than ideal, and Isutani's Pebble Beach–U.S. Open difficulties were seen by the Japanese business community as a potential source of great embarrassment in the eyes of the U.S. public. If disruptions in scheduling the U.S. Open on a classic U.S. golf course were attributed to a Japanese businessman, the image of Japanese investors in the United States could only suffer more damage.

Under considerable pressure from the Japanese business establishment, Isutani sold Pebble Beach to Japan's Sumitomo Credit Service Corporation and Taiheyo Club, Inc., for approximately $574 million. In other words, 18 months after purchasing Pebble Beach, Isutani sustained losses approaching $270 million. He later would be quoted as saying that he bought the property with 50 percent of his business mind and 50 percent of his golf mind because that was his dream, but he learned a very severe lesson from this transaction.

The New Owners

The new owners quickly moved to remove any lingering doubts about Japanese ownership of Pebble Beach. The famous public relations firm of Hill and Knowlton—known for its handling of controversial issues—was retained to improve public perception and acceptance of its new clients. The new owners were encouraged to be visible and available to the public and to assure locals that plans to privatize Pebble Beach were now a dead issue. The new owners explained that unlike Isutani, they were influenced by Japanese pride, as well as profit, in their acquisition. They wished to provide quality ownership, appreciating Pebble Beach as more than just a piece of real estate.

The Sumitomo Credit Service Corporation and Taiheyo Club, Inc., apparently have provided that type of ownership. The 1992 U.S. Open was played without difficulty, and the right of public golfers willing to pay $200 per round to play Pebble Beach has been safeguarded. The new owners also have been careful to avoid Isutani's mistakes. In addition to increasing their local visibility, they changed the name of the corporation (at the suggestion of Hill and Knowlton) to the very California-sounding Lone Cypress Corporation. Interest in a partnership with U.S. investors has been expressed, and a joint board of Americans and Japanese for Pebble Beach has been suggested by the Japanese multinational corporation. It appears a complicated and expensive lesson in international management has been learned, and a new course of action has put Pebble Beach back on course.

1. Identify and discuss Moritsu Isutani's strategic predisposition toward the purchase and management of Pebble Beach. Suggest and defend alternatives.
2. Identify and discuss strategy implementation issues pertinent to this case, particularly in regard to ownership, locale, and functional implementation.
3. Political risk is the likelihood that a business' foreign investment will be constrained by a host government's policies. Discuss how a macro and micro analysis of political risk might have provided Isutani valuable strategic information before his purchase.
4. The new Japanese owners of Pebble Beach have suggested several options regarding local participation in the management of Pebble Beach. Identify and discuss those options most likely to encourage managerial success in the current environment.

GILLETTE'S PRESCRIPTION FOR INTERNATIONAL BUSINESS SUCCESS: IN-HOUSE TRAINING AND EXPAT EXPERIENCE

Alfred Zeien, Chairperson and CEO of internationally prominent Gillette, recently was quoted as saying, "It takes at least 25 years to build an international management corps that possesses the skills, experience and abilities to take a global organization from one level of success to the next." With this philosophy as the foundation, Gillette is committed to following two key strategies for building its worldwide management corps. The first is the firm's in-house International Trainee Program; the second is development through expatriate experience, hiring and assigning foreign nationals to staff operations not only in their home countries but around the world.

Background on Gillette

Gillette has four main divisions and subsidiaries: the North Atlantic Group, the Diversified Group, the Stationery Products Group, and the International Group. The International Group makes and markets Gillette's personal-care, shaving, and stationery products and staffs operations throughout the world (excluding North America and Western Europe). The International Group is made up of three geographic groups: (1) Africa, Latin America, and the Middle East; (2) Eastern Europe; and (3) the Asian Pacific. The Latin American and International headquarters are in Boston; the Asian Pacific headquarters are in Singapore; and the headquarters for the Middle East, Africa, Russia, and Eastern Europe are in London. By 1993, Gillette had 57 manufacturing facilities in 28 countries. More than three-fourths of the company's employees work outside the United States. As indicated by this organizational structure, Gillette is a globally involved consumer-products company. The firm now has more than 90 years of experience in the international marketplace, and it competes in three major consumer businesses: personal grooming products for men and women, small electrical appliances, and stationery products. Widely recognized brand names such as Liquid Paper, Paper Mate, Oral-B, Braun, and Jafra are among this MNC's products, which are distributed through retailers, wholesalers, and agents in more than 200 countries and territories around the world.

A good example of Gillette's international efforts was the launch of the SensorExcel razor a few years ago. Using a global communications strategy, the SensorExcel was announced simultaneously in 19 countries. A comprehensive guidelines manual was developed and served as the "blueprint" for the public relations launch. This manual put forth a strategic framework for the

Source: This case was written specially for this book. The assistance of Jill Ormesher is acknowledged, as well as the following references: Jennifer J. Laabs, "Building a Global Management Team," *Personnel Journal*, August 1993, p. 75; Jennifer J. Laabs, "How Gillette Grooms Global Talent," *Personnel Journal*, August 1993, pp. 65–68, 71, 73, 76; and "Gillette: Cooperation Between Client and Firm Yields Successful 19-Country Product Launch," *Public Relations Journal*, August 1993, p. 24.

program, communicated Gillette's overall business goals, and provided country-by-country guidelines for the new product launch. The company combined a global integration and local differentiation strategy by ensuring consistency of the messages on product quality across the market area, but the nature of the message delivery was left to local discretion. This differentiation recognized that each culture and clientele was unique.

The International Trainee Program

Besides the strategic marketing emphasis, the Gillette Company made a significant recruitment and management-development decision during the mid-1980s. Already bringing in high-priced executives on a "just-in-time" basis to provide the needed talent for Gillette's global operations, the company also decided to develop managers internally. The International Trainee Program (ITP) was launched in 1983 by Gillette's international human resources department.

When the ITP began, students from countries outside the United States were hired by Gillette to come to Boston as interns. At that time, the company's reasons were purely philanthropic. A few years later, the vice-president of human resources for Gillette International realized that the internship program could be turned into an in-house management training program. In the words of top management, the objective was "to bring recent graduates to Boston specifically to groom them for Gillette jobs in their home countries." After a few years, responsibility for identifying foreign students was moved from an outside international student-exchange program to the human resources director and general manager for each of Gillette's worldwide operations. Each manager was responsible for identifying the top business students in prestigious universities internationally, who were to be recruited into the program.

The approach taken by the ITP is representative of Gillette's regiocentric approach to international management. In international operations, Gillette relies on managers from a particular geographic region to handle things in and around that location. The regiocentric approach also guides the manner in which training is set up. On entering Gillette's program, junior trainees typically work for 6 months at the Gillette subsidiary in their home country. Gillette corporate management then may choose to transfer them to one of the company's three international headquarters: Boston, London, or Singapore. These assignments usually last for 18 months and depend on which world region their subsidiaries fall into. The trainee program basically is the same in each location; however, Boston (where the program originated) has more trainees than either London or Singapore.

Gillette's international trainee program and on-site training programs both have personal and organizational objectives. At a personal level, Gillette provides the training and direct experience to improve the management trainee's ability to interact effectively with the local people at foreign operations and, in particular, with their own direct reports. Such training not only enhances the individual's competitiveness and marketability within Gillette but also with other companies. Gillette generally extends permanent job offers to nine of every ten trainees who go through the ITP. Eight of the nine usually accept, and six of these stay with the firm longer than a year after returning to their home countries. Although graduates often receive other job offers at higher salaries, Gillette has been successful in keeping its graduates. In the first 10 years, 113 trainees went through the program, and over one-half are still with the company.

Besides the personal benefits from the training, the company also clearly benefits. For example, trainees note that they are much more willing to communicate with headquarters and other operations, because they know people at the home office and understand how things work at other facilities around the world. The trainees also gain an appreciation for different ways of doing things during their training. Most enter the program having only limited experience with people and customs from cultures other than their own. After living and working for a year and a half with people from different cultures, the trainees naturally emerge as more open-minded managers and take this with them wherever they go on their permanent assignment.

The international-trainee program costs Gillette $20,000 to $25,000 per trainee per year. However, expatriates sent to overseas assignments can end up costing much more. In Boston alone, the total trainee-program budget is about $1 million per year; however, the firm estimates that only three expatriates could be hired for that amount. The head of international human resources feels that the cost of the ITP is worth it to Gillette even though it may take longer to develop managers this way. He states, "This is the core of our international recruiting. All of our efforts and resources are directed toward this program."

After completing their 18-month terms, trainees return to their home countries to take entry-level manager positions. If they show continued success, they usually will move on to assignments in other countries, ultimately returning to their home countries as general managers or senior operating managers. For example, many ITP graduates of several years ago now hold mid- to senior-level management positions. Gillette looks to ITP graduates beyond expatriate assignments; they are slated to be this MNC's future senior international leaders.

Development through Expatriate Experience

Besides the in-house ITP, Gillette also provides expatriate experience to its managers. For example, about 80 percent of the 40 top executives have had at least one foreign assignment, and more than 50 percent have worked in at least three countries. In 1993 alone, 269 Gillette employees were on expatriate assignments, representing 38 home countries and 47 host countries.

A very large majority of Gillette's expatriates come from one of the other 27 countries in which the company has operations. Most of the time, Gillette hires foreign nationals to staff management positions in countries other than the United States. Often, these individuals are first identified while studying at U.S. universities for their MBAs. On a training track similar to those in the company's international trainee program, these new hires typically work for a year at Gillette's Boston headquarters and then return to a Gillette subsidiary in their home country. Then, after working in their home countries for approximately 4 years, these managers usually are moved to other countries and assignments. A major side benefit of Gillette managers gaining such broad international experience is that as they do so, they teach and develop other potential managers within the organization.

Managers with international experience often are prime candidates for positions that open when Gillette enters joint ventures or new markets. A good example is the joint venture that Gillette undertook with a company in China. Gillette began planning this alliance more than 4 years before it solidified and actually occurred. Importantly, Gillette began identifying individual managers who would be right for assignments in the China business early in the process. Gillette knew that managers who had Chinese experience had to be pulled from other countries, such as Australia, England, and France, but also that others in the company with relevant experience would then have to move into the positions these people left behind.

Chairman and CEO Zeien recently told his shareholders: "I contend that the transferability of management is the glue that holds the various parts of the company together." And Dieu Eng Seng, area vice-president of Oral-B, Asia Pacific, echoed this philosophy and that of his Gillette management colleagues in saying, "One of my key objectives is to identify, recruit and develop competent managers. I'm confident that these good people will generate a flow of business growth and profits for the future."

1. How does Gillette's overall management philosophy and strategy influence its training and development program?
2. What are some benefits of training home-country nationals at one of Gillette's international headquarters?
3. What does Gillette feel that graduates of the international trainee program offer the company?

HUMAN RESOURCES MANAGEMENT IN JAPAN

In the 1980s, much of the success of Japanese MNCs was attributed to human resources management (HRM). As more and more companies do business in Japan, an overview of the major Japanese HRM functions of recruitment/selection, training, compensation/reward systems, and labor relations could prove to be valuable. Understanding Japanese HRM is important not only for MNCs doing business in Japan but also to gain some ideas and lessons for effective HRM in other parts of the world.

Recruitment and Selection

In general, recruitment of college graduates in Japan takes place only once a year. In a company's direct recruitment of graduates, their professors play a dominant role. Japanese firms develop relationships with professors, who then are asked to recommend students with special qualifications in certain fields. According to Puick's report in the *Human Resource Management Journal,* this reliance on intermediaries (e.g., college professors) for selection decisions serves a number of purposes. First, it eliminates the difficulty of evaluating a student's technical potential based on a short interview. Most interviews deal with little up-to-date technical background, but the technically competent professors interact with students over a long period of time. Second, because of the competition for top graduates, recruiters must develop good relations with college professors, who then recommend certain firms to the students. By doing this, the firms get their "fair share" of talent, and this prevents a self-defeating bidding war that would

raise starting salaries. It also prevents disrupting the carefully balanced compensation systems of Japanese internal labor markets. Finally, college grades are not seen as being the most important selection criterion. Specific seminars (courses taken with a professor's permission) are seen as more selective than others and thus develop an "elite" reputation for the students who take them. The educational reputation of the school from which the student is graduating is weighted heavily. Given the intense and very rigorous competition to enter first-tier schools, companies rely on the university entrance examination as an indicator of the potential of the employee's "latest ability."

An additional factor that should be considered when recruiting in Japan is the strong emphasis that is given to long-term relationships and trust. Therefore, it is not surprising to find that large MNCs in Japan usually recruit at junior levels, while senior positions are filled by internal promotion. Because of the tradition of lifetime employment and long-term relationships, the recruiter must be prepared to spend a great deal of time with a prospective Japanese recruit, and because of this long-term commitment, the potential employee will want to gather large amounts of information about the employer before making a decision. A critical factor in recruiting Japanese managers is convincing them that the company is growing and offers long-term opportunities.

Some practical recommendations for the recruitment function of Japanese HRM would be to recruit potential employees at the end of the Japanese school year. During the recruiting process, it would be important to establish personal contacts with college professors to select the best possible candidates. Finally, it would be important for the recruiter to develop a trusting relationship with a potential employee and to provide as much information as possible for the recruit to see a long-term relationship with the company.

Source: This case was written specially for this book by Kyle W. Luthans, University of Nebraska.

571

Training

The large majority of Japanese business enterprises conduct in-house job training. It generally is recognized that the Japanese give relatively more attention to training than any other country. Not only do the Japanese give more training to employees, they emphasize a different type of training. Instead of just the highly specialized, technical training that is typical in U.S. firms, Japanese tend to give all employees the big picture. A Japanese training program may include the organization's role in society, relationship to the competition, and marketing goals and objectives. In short, Japanese training seeks not only to develop the individual worker to see the whole picture but also to respond to it. Japanese HRM works on the assumption that focusing on this type of training will minimize turnover and absenteeism.

Besides providing more of the big picture in training, the Japanese also differ in the way that they train college graduates to become managers. As indicated in the discussion of recruitment, the Japanese feel that pre-employment education is important, then the initial managerial education on-the-job. This may take months, if not years, to learn the various functions and cultural values of the organization. In addition, because of their tendency toward collectivism and consensus decision making, the Japanese emphasize training that facilitates a spirit of harmony and teamwork among employees.

Practical guidelines for the Japanese HRM training function would start with the value placed on lifelong learning. Because of this, virtually every Japanese organization does some type of training. Second, training does not have to be limited to specific jobs; instead, it also can focus on making the Japanese employee more of a functioning member of the organization as a whole. Finally, training of managers is long-term and includes socializing the new member into the cultural values of the organization and becoming an effective team member in group decision making.

Compensation/Reward Systems

In his book *Human Resources,* Schuler pointed out that one of the main "pillars" to the Japanese employment system is the seniority system that determines wages and promotions. Under this system, an employee rarely works under someone with less seniority in service length, assuming that both have similar educational backgrounds. This system has its roots in the traditional *Oyabun-Kobun,* or parent–child relationship, which attaches great respect for the older or senior member of the family (company). Because of this seniority system, companies generally pay the same starting salary for new hires. After that, however, an employee's annual earn-

ings increase according to merit. In addition, earnings will increase annually based on seniority even if the employee's job responsibilities remain unchanged.

Because the Japanese have strong collectivist values, individually based pay for performance seldom is used, and it is not as effective here as group incentives. An example of a Japanese reward system would be a group-gainsharing bonus at the end of the year based on good organizational performance.

Reward systems in Japan also go beyond basic salary compensation. For the large Japanese firms, the typical compensation package includes things such as a form of housing allowance, daily living support (transportation, meals, uniforms), recreational benefits, and full medical and health care.

In summary, compensation/reward systems in Japanese HRM start with the seniority system. Second, it is important to realize that group incentives such as gainsharing are more important than individual incentives. A third factor to be considered is the importance of nonfinancial rewards in the form of benefits and services.

Labor Relations

Relative to North American and European countries, Japanese union–management relationships are extremely co-operative. Japanese culture dictates a nonconfrontational approach. Although labor agreements generally are fairly open-ended and vague, they tend to be settled in a peaceful and co-operative manner when disputes do arise regarding interpretations. Sometimes, it is necessary to bring in third-party mediators or arbitrators, but there are no prolonged disputes that result in the workplace being closed down because the two sides cannot work together. Typically, a strike is used merely to embarrass management and seldom lasts longer than a week. It is possible to resort to legal action when resolving strikes, but such a formal approach generally is looked down on by both management and labor. Both sides of a labor dispute try to stay away from using a strike as a means to resolve their problems.

Traditionally, Japanese unions are most active during the spring and end of the year, because this is when bonuses are negotiated. However, these negotiations usually do not result in a management–labor conflict. If there is a strike, it is more likely when a Japanese union is negotiating with management during industry-wide negotiations. Even here, however, the objective is to show that workers support the union and not to indicate a grievance with management per se. In overall terms, Japanese workers tend to subordinate their interests to those of the group (again, the strong collectivist nature of the Japanese). This cultural value helps to account for a great deal of the harmony and co-operation that exists between unions and management.

On the whole, Japanese management and unions tend to regard each other as trustworthy partners, and there is no hint of the assumption that so often characterizes such relationships in the West—that the interests of companies and unions in most respects are fundamentally opposed and combative. Over the years, the company union is one of the greatest strengths of the Japanese employment system, enabling Japanese management to concentrate its attention on competing with competitors rather than fighting with their own employees.

As for practical guidelines, outsiders must realize that unions in Japan are much different than in other countries. Instead of the typical adversarial relationship, Japanese unions are much more co-operative. This is based on the cultural values of the Japanese and more directly on the fact that instead of having nationwide trade unions, as are typical in the West, Japan has a system of within-company enterprise unions. In other words, Japanese unions have more of an identity and personal stake in the success of the company. Japanese unions re-

alize that pay and benefits directly relate to their companies' performance. In essence, it is necessary for Japanese unions to treat their companies as partners, not as enemies, and vice versa. Because of this co-operative relationship, it is important for both parties in Japanese labor relations to negotiate in good faith while building a long-lasting, trusting relationship.

1. Briefly summarize the major characteristics of Japanese HRM. How does this approach differ from that in the United States (or your country)?
2. In the 1980s, HRM was given as a major reason for the phenomenal success of Japanese MNCs. When Japanese MNCs have been experiencing some difficulties in recent years, the HRM system has been blamed. What are some specific HRM approaches that have helped Japanese MNCs become so successful but now may be putting them at a competitive disadvantage?
3. Using your answer to question 2 above as a point of departure, what would you recommend the Japanese do at this point? How would a new or revised Japanese HRM approach affect the way that outside MNCs do business with the Japanese?

DOING BUSINESS IN GERMANY: THE IMPACT OF LABOR RELATIONS

The economies of most Western nations were hampered by slow growth during the first half of the 1990s. In Germany, the additional economic burden from reunification resulted in a particularly acute and extended recessionary period marked by a significant decline in real personal income. At the same time, throughout the early to mid-1990s, a national drama began to unfold, casting Germany's industry leaders against labor unions and government social reformers.

Labor Unrest in Germany

Years of worker frustration in Germany climaxed in March 1995, when 11,000 workers abandoned their jobs at 22 metal and electronics companies. Members of the powerful labor union IG Metall were demanding a 6 percent wage increase, a 35-hour work week, and increased Christmas bonuses. Union leaders vowed that unless progress was made immediately in negotiations with management, as many as 20 additional German firms would be struck in the subsequent weeks.

With 3 million members nationwide, IG Metall represented more than 165,000 strikers in 628 Bavarian factories. Entering its first strike in 11 years, the union was determined to win higher wages for its members, who had made significant concessions during the earlier recession. Striking workers were equally determined to gain some relief from a substantial loss of buying power resulting from a recent tax increase levied to maintain social programs that had been overwhelmed in the wake of the costly reunification of East Germany.

While some labor leaders may have seemed overly combative to outside observers, and perhaps even to their own rank and file, they contended that the increases being sought were only to offset losses in real income incurred over the prior 3 years because of big social security and income tax hikes. Employers, however, countered that they felt the tax burden as well, and they would fight to hold on to double-digit gains in productivity. The battle lines were drawn, and the payoff from years of restructuring to compete in the world market was at stake.

On the surface, the union seemed to hold a slight edge in its negotiations with industry leaders, because Germany's economy was growing at a healthy 3 percent pace for the year. Moreover, German leaders at the time expressed strong fears that the economy could not withstand a long-term strike, and although German companies had been slow to respond to union demands, they did not want to jeopardize higher sales and profits with such a strike. Auto industry officials in particular expressed concern that the strike would endanger their still-fragile recovery. Their cost-cutting had increasingly led to adopting just-in-time production systems, in which suppliers deliver components almost directly to the production line. As a result, car companies were especially vulnerable to production disruptions in their vast network of suppliers.

The union was proceeding cautiously, however, which indicated to industry leaders that IG Metall was simply using the strike as a brinkmanship tactic. BMW and Audi were conspicuously absent from IG Metall's list of targeted companies, and analysts observed that in general, the union was being overly tentative.

From the perspective of German industry, there was no room for concession to the union's demands, which allowed almost no flexibility in labor terms. High global competition and an increased German mark (up 14 percent against the U.S. dollar since December 1993) was a severe price handicap to German producers. Until March, this understanding of the competitive

Source: This case was written specially for this book with the assistance of Dan McKendry and Alexander Saitta.

disadvantage of German firms had kept the labor union's demands in check, and their restraint had permitted German export firms to earn high profits. Many economists agreed with exporters that maintaining the status quo in labor terms was Germany's best hope for a competitive comeback.

While some companies were seeking separate, intraindustry settlements as opposed to union-negotiated, universal contracts, most German industry leaders saw the standoff with IG Metall as a crucial battle in which they could not afford to relinquish ground. They believed that the outcome of the strike would set the stage for future negotiations with other labor groups. As a tribute to its power, the IG Metall contract did, in fact, usually set the pattern for more than a dozen other major unions in Germany's equivalent of the AFL-CIO, the Dusseldorf-based Deutscher Gewerkschaftsbund (DGB).

The March strike was not the first incident in which IG Metall took a tough stand in German labor negotiations. Porsche had witnessed first-hand the union flexing its political muscle. The German automaker had fought hard for 3 years to slash large losses, using measures ranging from layoffs to lean production, so when sales rose by 23 percent in the first half of fiscal 1995, many believed that the breakeven point was within reach. Then, 3 days after the January 27 annual stockholder meeting, workers at the Porsche plants near Stuttgart walked off the job for half an hour.

The walkout at Porsche proved to be only a prelude to the March showdown in Germany's labor negotiations. At the time, however, industry leaders perceived the guerrilla-style "warning strike" against Porsche as merely an attempt to intimidate. IG Metall's leaders were just "talking tough," they believed, and the companies to be affected were well positioned to resist. It was expected that union workers eventually would concede to wage increases of about 3 percent—slightly above the inflation rate.

Industry leaders maintained the same firm position against IG Metall in March as they held in January with its members at Porsche. German economists sided with management, denouncing the union's demands as a threat to competitiveness and a possible harbinger of inflationary increases in other industries. Economists considered IG Metall's acceptance of a 3 percent increase as crucial for Germany's economic recovery, especially considering that contract negotiations for 7 million other workers would be patterned after the deal reached by this union. They predicted that hefty wage increases would prompt the Bundesbank to raise its 4.5 percent discount rate, thus placing the economic recovery in serious danger.

Members of IG Metall eventually ended their strike after only 10 days. The new agreement called for two raises before the end of 1995, but the combined increase fell well short of the 6 percent the union had desired. For now, the German economy appeared to be on course for solid growth, boosted by exports, in GDP. At best, the settlement was a shallow victory for German labor, but given the relentless strains on the nation's economy and federal budget, one could not expect this fragile accord to be maintained.

Averting a Crisis at IBM

Perhaps the most dramatic power struggle to emerge in this labor dispute occurred in the German subsidiary of International Business Machines, Inc. (IBM). Eager to revive sluggish earnings and rattled by the development in German labor relations, IBM Deutschland had not engaged in national collective bargaining with IG Metall since 1992, when the computer manufacturer effectively withdrew from annual wage negotiations conducted between the German Employers Association and the 3-million-member German union. In the long run, IBM felt it could not stay competitive in the computer service business under the union's conditions.

IBM's withdrawal from negotiations was a stunning move by one of the largest foreign MNCs operating in Germany, and it underlined how hard IBM was willing to push to cut costs. Most of the country's main exporters—electrical, engineering, and auto manufacturers—participated in negotiations with IG Metall. Germany had always placed a high premium on co-operation between labor and management, and it was rare for a major employer like IBM to risk the political heat of leaving the annual wage talks.

Pressure for action had been mounting at IBM, however. In 1994, the German unit's pretax earnings slipped 2.8 percent, to 958 million marks ($681 million), while profits fell 31 percent, to 473 million marks. As in other IBM units, the payroll had been trimmed by 1000 employees in 1994 and would shrink another 1500 by the end of 1995. In fact, IG Metall leaders suspected that IBM might phase out its German production completely if the economy and the company's sales did not improve.

A similar wave of cost-cutting measures was sweeping through other major electronics manufacturers in Germany, including AEG-AG, ANT Nachrichtentechnik GmbH, and Siemens AG. High labor costs, inflexible working hours, and the soaring strength of the German mark, coupled with a global recession, were forcing German-based manufacturers to make drastic cuts.

Even before the strike in March 1995, IBM executives recognized a growing threat from rising production costs resulting from expensive labor, and they responded with a strategy to shift work away from IG Metall as a cost-control measure. IBM's strategy, implemented by CEO Hans-Olaf Henkel, was to pull more than 70 percent of the workers out of the national labor contract with IG Metall. In this way, IBM management sought to leverage the union into submission to its demands for greater performance and higher gains in productivity. The strategy called for the creation of four separate operating companies, only one of which would remain under contract with IG Metall. Thus, most of IBM's German labor force, more than 15,000 workers, would be outside the labor union's contract.

IBM presented its restructuring strategy as an effort to appease the union while controlling costs. The company began applying a 36-hour work week, as stipulated in its 1993 contract with IG Metall; however, it applied the terms of the contract only to operations directly involving production, which affected just 7,000 workers. The remaining 15,000 workers in the service sectors were given a so-called "house contract," which had been agreed to previously with a separate, white-collar worker's union known as the DAG. That contract called for a 38-hour average work week.

In Hamburg, IBM management pursued its strategy of circumventing union contracts with such audacity that the local industry tribunal had to intervene. According to IG Metall, IBM tried to impose the terms of the DAG contract on its union members. Thus, workers were told by management in March 1994 that their work week would be increased from 36 to 38 hours for the same salary. However, the Hamburg tribunal decided that the longer working time was valid only for DAG members, not for IG Metall workers.

IBM's strategy of shifting operations to combat IG Metall and control costs was a classic example of an organization capitalizing on a strength in one area to ward off a threat in another. In this situation, IBM's strength was its size and well-established channels of distribution, particularly its ability to exert greater control over distribution outlets where vendors generally are willing to adhere to their terms. Strength in distribution afforded IBM the luxury of relative independence from German-based manufacturing operations. In retrospect, IBM's strategy may have even enhanced the company's market distribution, because the personal computers being built in its German facilities were targeted primarily toward the U.S. market anyway. (Germany's PC market largely is serviced with Chinese-made computers.)

IBM and other industry leaders no doubt realized that despite their show of defiance, Germany's unions had a lot to lose in a strike. They knew the unions were in a squeeze and needed to sound tough to recruit new work-ers. In reality, unions were experiencing shrinking membership as manufacturers downsized and moved production overseas. Since 1991, the 16 big unions forming the DGB had lost 17 percent of their total membership. Compounding this problem was a declining pool of potential recruits as better-educated, part-time, and women workers in burgeoning service industries were tending to shun unions.

Also, declining income had been forcing unions in Germany and throughout Europe to reduce their operations, thus hampering their clout. As a result, employers were becoming more inclined to negotiate deals on their own rather than to go along with the universal terms for all German industries that were set by employers' organizations. Moreover, union officials knew that over-blown wage demands would price more jobs out of existence, and the 9.9 percent unemployment rate was a powerful motive for labor moderation.

Recent German Economic Conditions

Since the crisis in March, a number of labor taboos have been dropping. DGB leaders, for instance, have offered a major concession by shortening the work week to 4 days at lower wages; however, employers still are reluctant to grant the job guarantees that unions want.

The mood of business in Germany now represents a 180-degree reversal from the gloom that had gripped the nation a few years ago when the problems of financing Eastern Germany seemed unsurmountable. One-half of the East's GDP—more than $100 billion—came straight from Bonn's coffers. Business bankruptcies ballooned to record levels, and 1 million jobs disappeared in a year—one-third of those created in the last decade. Debate raged over whether Standort Deutschland—that is, "Germany as a place to do business"—had any future.

Beginning early in 1994, however, Chancellor Helmut Kohl used the sense of crisis surrounding the labor dispute as a lever to restart a stalled reform program. Radical restructuring now was possible in Germany, because the 45-year-old social contract between industry, labor, and government was unanimously recognized as being null and void. Reunification had allowed business to challenge practices that once seemed carved in stone. In Eastern Germany, companies were refusing to join employers' federations that negotiated with labor unions. In this way, they escaped binding labor agreements covering the whole industry, and they could concentrate on individual company bargaining. In the west, IBM Deutschland effectively took all nonproduction workers out of the IG Metall contract for the same reason, leading the way for hundreds of other companies to follow.

Since reunification, German companies no longer react with their former knee-jerk generosity to labor's requests. As a prime example, the chemical workers union, known as IG Chemie, recently was pressured into an unprecedented concession by agreeing that employers could hire younger or long-term unemployed workers at 90 percent of union scale. Concessions similar to those yielded by IG Chemie and IG Metall may be in store for other German unions, especially when negotiating wage increases. The average cost per worker per hour in Germany is the highest among the G7 nations—$25, compared with $16.50 in Japan and $15.50 in the United States—and with items such as vacation pay and supplemental pensions factored in, fringe benefits add up to as much as gross wages. Increasingly, the high cost of labor is forcing German industry to move production of low-profit items with heavy labor content out of Germany, while keeping the high-tech products at home. Luxury car makers BMW and Mercedes-Benz both are building plants in the United States, where potential efficiency gains are enormous. BMW's new plant will be able to turn out 100,000 cars in a year with 2000 employees; in Germany, it takes 6000 workers to produce 150,000 cars. Some industries such as textiles and apparel are being exported on a massive scale as well.

Where Does Germany Go from Here?

Germany has all the ingredients for a world-class, competitive economy: a highly educated work force, impressive scientific centers, big research and development budgets, and a strong culture of export-driven companies. German industry needed a shakeup, however. The old ways created a deep aversion to risk-taking, and venture capital was virtually nonexistent. Everything from shopping hours to building permits and biotech research were regulated to protect the current way of doing business. Besides cutting labor costs, however, German business still must push for regulatory changes that allow more flexible working hours and more freedom to offer discounts.

The first steps toward dismantling the bureaucracy of government regulation already are being taken. Chancellor Kohl has lined up state-controlled airline Lufthansa and phone company Deutsche Telekom for privatization. Also, the government has trimmed welfare payments by 3 percent and made other long overdue changes, such as allowing private employment agencies to compete with the Federal Employment Office.

The trouble with deregulation is that these reforms require legislation, and German legislators are reluctant to push so many concurrent labor reforms as a priority over much-needed social reforms. German social programs represent one-third of the nation's GDP, and many are in serious need of reform, particularly the tax system and the social welfare net, which covers everything from child-care allowances to retirement benefits. As technology continues to break down the barriers of international trade, it appears that Germans eventually may be forced to choose between the interests of business and those of social programs.

1. With the changing labor environment in Germany, what strategy should IBM Deutschland pursue? Why?
2. What are the current trends in the computer industry, and how will they influence IBM's German subsidiary regarding labor relations in the future?
3. What role does the German government have in the current labor negotiations, and what effect will these negotiations have on MNCs operating in Germany?
4. Given that IG Metall is a competitor in the labor supply business, what competitive forces are acting on the union to affect its bargaining power? Explain.

COLGATE'S DISTASTEFUL TOOTHPASTE

Colgate is a well-known consumer products company based in New York. Its present products are in the areas of household and personal care, which include laundry detergents such as Ajax and Fab, health-care products manufactured for home health care, and specialty products such as Hill pet food. The household products segment represents approximately 75 percent of company revenues, while the specialty segment accounts for less than 7 percent. Colgate's value has been set in excess of $5.6 billion. Through both recessionary and recovery periods in the United States, Colgate has always been advocated by investment analysts as a good long-term stock.

Colgate's lagging domestic market share has been present for several years. In the 1970s, when diversification seemed to be the tool to hedge against risk and sustain profits, Colgate bought companies in various industries, including Kosher hot dogs, tennis and golf equipment, and jewelry. However, such extreme diversification diverted the company's attention away from its key money-making products: soap, laundry detergents, toothpaste, and other household products. The product diversification strategy ended in 1984 when Reuben Mark became CEO. At the young age of 45, he ordered the sale of parts of the organization that deviated too far from Colgate's core competency of personal and household products. He followed consultant Tom Peters's prescription for excellence of "stick to the knitting."

Colgate's International Presence

Colgate traditionally has had a strong presence overseas. The company has operations in Australia, Latin America, Canada, France, and Germany. International sales

Source: This case was written specially for this book by Alisa L. Mosley, University of Nebraska.

presently represent one-half of Colgate's total revenue. In the past, Colgate always made a detailed analysis of each international market for demand. For instance, its entry into South America required an analysis of the type of product that would be most successful based on the dental hygiene needs of South American consumers. Because of this commitment to local cultural differences, the company has the number-one brand of toothpaste worldwide, Total.

To create a strong share of the Asian market without having to build its own production plant, Colgate bought a 50 percent partnership in the Hawley and Hazel group in August 1985 for $50 million. One stipulation of this agreement was that Colgate had no management prerogatives; Hawley and Hazel maintained the right to make the major decisions in the organization. This partnership turned out to be very lucrative for Colgate, with double-digit millions in annual sales.

Enter the Distasteful Toothpaste

Hawley and Hazel is a chemical products company based in Hong Kong. The company was formed in the early part of the twentieth century, and its only product of note, believe it or not, was called "Darkie" toothpaste. Over the years, this had been one of the popular brands in Asia and had a dominant presence in markets such as Taiwan, Hong Kong, Singapore, Malaysia, and Thailand.

"Darkie" toothpaste goes back to the 1920s. The founder of this product, on a visit to the United States, loved Al Jolson, then a very popular black-faced entertainer (i.e., a white person with black make-up on his face). The founder decided to recreate the spirit of this character in the form of a trademark logo for his toothpaste because of the character's big smile and white teeth. When the founder returned to Asia, he copyrighted the name "Darkie" to go along with the logo. Since the 1920s, there has been strong brand loyalty among Asians for this product. One housewife in Taipei whose family used the product for years remarked, "The toothpaste featuring a Black man with a toothy smile is an excellent advertisement."

The Backlash against Colgate

"Darkie" toothpaste had been sold in Asia for about 65 years. After Colgate became partners with Hawley and Hazel and its distasteful product, however, there was a wave of dissatisfaction with the logo and name from U.S. minorities and civil rights groups. There really has been no definite source on how this issue was passed to U.S. action groups and the media; however, a book entitled *Soap Opera: The Inside Story of Procter and Gamble* places responsibility in the hands of Procter and Gamble in an effort to tarnish Colgate's image and lower its market share.

The Americans' irate response to "Darkie" was a surprise to the Hawley and Hazel group. They reasoned that the product had always been successful in their Asian markets, and there had been no complaints. In fact, the success of "Darkie" had led the firm to market a new product in Japan called "Mouth Jazz," which had a similar logo. A spokesperson for Hawley and Hazel remarked, "There had been no problem before, you can tell by the market share that it is quite well received in Asia."

ICCR, the Interfaith Center on Corporate Responsibility, started the fight against Colgate about 10 years ago when it received a package of "Darkie" toothpaste from a consumer in Thailand. ICCR is composed of institutional investors that influence corporations through stock ownership. At the time the movement against Colgate's racially offensive product started, three members of ICCR already owned a small amount of stock in the company, and they filed a shareholder petition against Colgate requesting a change in the logo and name.

In a letter to Colgate, the ICCR Executive Director summarized the position against the distasteful toothpaste as follows:

> "Darkie" toothpaste is a 60-year-old product sold widely in Hong Kong, Malaysia, Taiwan and other places in the Far East. Its packaging includes a top-hatted and gleaming-toothed smiling likeness of Al Jolson under the words "Darkie" toothpaste. As you know the term "Darkie" is deeply offensive. We would hope that in this new association with the Hawley and Hazel Chemical Company, that immediate action will be taken to stop this product's name so that a U.S. company will not be associated with promoting racial stereotypes in the Third World.

In response to this letter, R.G.S. Anderson, Colgate's director of corporate development, replied, "No plans exist or are being contemplated that would extend marketing and sales efforts for the product in Colgate subsidiaries elsewhere or beyond this Far East area." Anderson then went on to explain that Darkie's founder was imitating Al Jolson and that in the Chinese view, imitation was the "highest form of flattery." The ICCR then informed Colgate that if the logo was not changed, the organization would create a media frenzy and help various civil rights action groups in a possible boycott.

Because Colgate still refused to remove the logo, ICCR did form a coalition with civil rights groups such as the NAACP and National Urban League to start protest campaigns. The protest took all forms, including lobbying at both the state and local levels. At one point, after heavy lobbying by the ICCR, the House of Representatives in Pennsylvania passed a resolution urging Colgate to change the name and logo. Also, similar resolutions had been proposed in the U.S. Congress.

The pressures at home placed Colgate in a difficult position, especially as it had no management rights in its agreement with Hawley and Hazel. In the Asian market, neither Colgate nor Hawley and Hazel had any knowledge of consumer dissatisfaction because of racial offensiveness, despite the fact that the local Chinese name for "Darkie" (pronounced *hak ye nga goh*) can be translated as "The Black Man" toothpaste. The logo seemed to enhance brand loyalty. One Asian customer stated, "I buy it because of the Black man's white teeth."

The demographics of the Asian market may help to explain the product's apparent acceptance. There are a relatively small number of Africans, Indians, Pakistanis, and Bangladeshis in the region; therefore, the number of people who might be offended by the logo is low. Also, some people of color did not seem disturbed by the name. For example, when asked about the implications of "Darkie" toothpaste, the secretary of the Indian Chamber of Commerce noted, "It doesn't offend me, and I'm sort of dark-skinned."

Initially, Colgate had no intentions of forcing Hawley and Hazel to change the product. R.G.S. Anderson issued another formal statement to the ICCR as follows: "Our position ... would be different if the product were sold in the United States or in any Western English-speaking country; which, as I have stated several times, will not happen." Hawley and Hazel concurred with the stance. The alliance was very fearful of a loss of market share and did not believe that the complaints were issues relevant to Pacific Rim countries. A spokesperson for the alliance referred to the protest campaign as "a U.S. issue." The tradeoff for revamping a successful product was deemed to be too risky and costly.

Colgate's Change of Heart

The issue did not go away. As U.S. leaders in Congress began to learn about this very offensive logo and name, the pressure on Colgate mounted. Interestingly, however, the value of Colgate's stock increased throughout this period of controversy. Wall Street seemed oblivious to the charges against Colgate, and this was another reason why Colgate took no action. Colgate management believed that an issue about overseas products should not have a negative effect on the company's domestic image. However, pressures continued from groups such as the Congressional Black Caucus, a strong political force. Colgate finally began to waver, but because of its agreement with Hawley and Hazel, it felt helpless. As one Colgate executive remarked, "One hates to let exogenous things drive your business, but you sometimes have to be aware of them."

Colgate CEO Reuben Mark eventually became very distressed over the situation. He was adamantly against racism of any kind and had taken actions to exhibit his beliefs. For instance, he and his wife had received recognition for their involvement in a special program for disadvantaged teenagers. He commented publicly about the situation as follows: "It's just offensive. The morally right thing dictates that we must change. What we have to do is find a way to change that is least damaging to the economic interests of our partners." He also publicly stated that Colgate had been trying to change the package since 1985, when it bought into the partnership.

Colgate's Plan of Action to Repair the Damage

The protest campaign initiated by ICCR and carried further by others definitely caused Colgate's image to be tarnished badly in the eyes of not only African-Americans but of all Americans. To get action, some members of the Congressional Black Caucus (including Rep. John Conyers, D-Mich.) even bypassed Colgate and tried to negotiate directly with Hawley and Hazel. To try to repair the damage, Colgate, in co-operation with Hawley and Hazel, finally developed, although two years after ICCR's initial inquiry, a plan to change the product. In a letter to ICCR, CEO Mark stated, "I and Colgate share your concern that the caricature of a minstrel in black-face on the package and the name 'Darkie' itself could be considered racially offensive." Colgate and Hawley and Hazel then proposed some specific changes for the name and logo. Names considered included Darlie, Darbie, Hawley, and Dakkie. The logo options included a dark, nondescript silhouette and a well-dressed Black man. The alliances decided to test market the options among their Asian consumers; however, they refused to change the Chinese name ("Black Man Toothpaste"), which is more used by their customers.

They decided that changes would be implemented over the course of a year to maintain brand loyalty and avoid advertising confusion with their customers. There was the risk that loyal customers would not know if the modified name/logo was still the same toothpaste that had proven itself through the years. Altogether, the process would take approximately 3 years, test marketing included. Colgate also decided to pay for the entire change process, abandoning their initial suggestion that the change be paid for by Hawley and Hazel.

Colgate and Hawley and Hazel then made a worldwide apology to all insulted groups. Although Hawley and Hazel was slow to agree with the plan, a spokesperson for the group emphasized that racial stereotyping was against its policy. It also helped that Hawley and Hazel would pay no money to make the needed changes. They felt that the product was too strong to change quickly; thus, three years was not too long to implement the new logo and name fully into all Asian markets. Further, they insisted that as part of the marketing campaign, the product advertising use the following statement in Chinese, "Only the English name is being changed. Black Man Toothpaste is still Black Man Toothpaste."

Response Worldwide

Colgate and Hawley and Hazel still suffer from the effects of their racially offensive product. In 1992, while dealing with its own civil rights issues, the Chinese government placed a ban on Darlie toothpaste because of the product's violation of China's trademark laws. Although the English name change was implemented across all markets, the retained Chinese name and logo still were deemed derogatory by the Chinese, and the government banned the product. Also, Eric Molobi, an African National Congress representative, was outraged at the toothpaste's logo on a recent visit to the Pacific Rim. When asked if Darlie toothpaste would be marketed in his country, the South African representative replied, "If this company found itself in South Africa it would not be used. There would be a permanent boycott."

Today, the name of Colgate cannot be found anywhere on the packaging of what is now called Darlie toothpaste. In a strategic move, Colgate has distanced itself completely away from the controversial product. In the Thailand and Indonesia health-products markets, Colgate even competes against Darlie toothpaste with its own brand.

1. Identify the major strategic and ethical issues faced by Colgate in its partnership with Hawley and Hazel.
2. What do you think Colgate should have done to handle the situation?
3. Is it possible for Colgate and Hawley and Hazel to change the toothpaste's advertising without sacrificing consumer brand loyalty? Is that a possible reason for Colgate's not responding quickly to domestic complaints?
4. In the end, was a "no management rights" clause good for Colgate? What could have happened during the negotiations process to get around this problem?

LEVI'S TAKES ITS ETHICAL ASPIRATIONS INTERNATIONAL

In 1993, Levi's decided to terminate most of its business relations with Chinese contractors. (It had no foreign direct investment in China.) As a reason, it gave what it termed China's "pervasive violation of human rights." At the time, some commented that neither Levi's nor China would be much affected by the action—Levi's because it only had small contracts with Chinese sewing and laundry firms, and China because Levi's trade amounted to only about $50 million annually of some $13.5 billion in total U.S. purchases. Nevertheless, Levi's withdrawal from China was recognized as having serious implications for its ability to do business there in the future. On the one hand, its competitors would be well established in the China apparel market. Furthermore, the Chinese government would be expected to hold Levi's in permanent disfavor, thus making it difficult for the company to either open manufacturing facilities there or win a change to China's policy of stiff tariffs on imported clothing.

Background on Levi's

The history of Levi Strauss & Company is almost an archetype of the American dream, including twenty-first century updates. The company was founded in the 1850s by a European immigrant who found success by listening to the customer. Levi Strauss tailored the first jeans from tent canvas in response to California gold miners' complaints that trousers just could not take the abuse of panning nuggets and staking claims. Furthermore, Strauss accepted incremental improvement ideas from suppliers; the copper rivets at stress points were suggested by a tailor who was part of Levi's downstream

network. The company is private, having been taken through a leveraged buyout in the 1980s by its current chairman and CEO, Robert Haas, great-grandnephew of the founder.

Levi's enjoyed a stream of record sales and earnings from 1989 through 1993. Several milestones also were reached in 1993: a 36 percent increase in profits, to $492 million on sales of $5.9 billion. Its 1993 sales earned Levi's the number-90 position in the Fortune 500. The following year, however, the company dropped to number 193. Its 1994 revenues rose only 3.1 percent over 1993, to $6 billion, and its profits dropped by 34.8 percent to $321 million. Levi's profit margin of 5.3% ranked only 222nd within the Fortune 500, although its rankings were considerably better for profits as a percentage of assets (8.2 percent, rank 82) and for profits as a percentage of stockholder's equity (21.8 percent, rank 80). Within the apparel industry, Levi's sales ranked first of seven competitors; its revenues of $6074 million compared favorably to the $4972 million for VF and to the industry median of $2163 million. Levi's sales increase of 3 percent from 1993, however, was well below the industry median of 12 percent. The profit comparison is similar. Levi's $321 million profit compared with $270 million for VF and was well above the industry median of $79 million, but Levi's 35 percent loss in profits compared with 1993 was considerably below the industry median of 12 percent. Levi's profits as a percentage of revenue and of assets were both right on the industry median, at 5 percent and 8 percent, respectively.

Analysts explained Levi's slowdown in 1994 by the company's problems in new product development and distribution. For example, the company estimates it lost at least $200 million in sales by its delay in developing wrinkle-free slacks (the fastest-growing segment of the men's-pants business). Likewise, it may take Levi's two or three times as long to replenish its supply of pants for major retailers compared with the 10 days achieved by competitors.

Source: This case was written specially for this book by Jan Hansen, Bellevue University.

Levi's Reputation

Despite recent problems, Levi's remains a strong company with a reputation for high-quality clothes and an impressive brand name. The company also has other valuable assets that bring it recognition within its industry. In *Fortune* magazine's annual poll to determine the "most admired" corporations, Levi's repeatedly earns top place in the 10-company apparel group. Companies are rated on attributes such as quality of management, quality of products, innovativeness, long-term investment value, financial soundness, human resources practices, and responsibility to the community and environment. Levi's 1995 score of 7.82 compares with 7.30 for Berkshire Hathaway (second place in the apparel group) and 8.65 for the most admired company overall, Rubbermaid, Inc.

Part of Levi's reputation rests on its organizational culture, its mission and vision. As articulated by chairman and CEO Bob Haas, this involves "responsible commercial success." In other words, the company should not just be profitable but ethical; it should not only make a profit but make the world a better place in which to live. To guide this twofold endeavor, company executives crafted what they call an "Aspiration Statement" spelling out the kind of firm that Levi Strauss & Company intends to become together with the kind of leadership that will be needed to make these aspirations reality. Not just words on paper, management and employees together incorporate the mission and aspiration statement into daily decisions and actions. Applications range from open and direct communication, commitment to diversity, recognition and related compensation and reward systems, empowerment, and ethical management practices to expectations for ethical behavior by suppliers. In today's business environment, cynics might attribute such principles to a public relations ploy or a proactive defense against employee litigation, but Levi's chairman Haas insists, "We are doing this because we believe in the interconnection between liberating the talents of our people and business success"—in other words, responsible commercial success.

The Application of Levi's Ethical Values in the International Arena

Levi's aspiration statement has been applied specifically to international contracting. In the 1980s, Levi's management felt that it was lax in keeping informed about conditions for employees at its overseas factories. A little-publicized incident involving the working conditions of its Saipan contractor caused Levi's management to re-examine its monitoring, and a committee of top executives was named to review the company's dealings with its suppliers. In 1992, following 3 years of work, the committee's guidelines for contractors were adopted, covering employee working conditions, labor relations, environmental impact, and regular inspection for compliance—the first such code adopted by any MNC. Following its code, the company has terminated business relations with 30 businesses and demanded changes from 120 others around the world. Two outcomes made headlines. When it was found that a contractor in Malaysia employed underage children, Levi's and the contractor found a solution that allowed the children to continue to contribute to their families' support: The contractor pays the children to attend school, Levi's pays for the school (tuition, texts, uniforms), and the contractor will hire the children back at the legal age of 14. The second outcome was Levi's withdrawal from China in response to what it considered "systemic labor inequities." Conditions in China's garment industry are bleak. For example, a recent article by William Beaver in *Business Horizons* reports that in Shenzhen, the work schedule requires 12-hour days plus overtime, with only 2 days off each month, for pay below the legal minimum of 12 cents an hour. Poor safety conditions in China's apparel factories also have resulted in dozens of employee deaths.

Responsible commercial success applies not just to the ethical position of Levi's international operations but also to its profitability. The international division contributed significantly to Levi's strong profit picture throughout the late 1980s and into the 1990s. In 1992, sales outside the United States accounted for 38 percent of company revenues—but 53 percent of profits. In part, this reflects the connection that consumers make to Levi's as an icon of U.S. styles and attitudes; in part, it also reflects Levi's pricing strategy, which is leveraged on that brand position. Levi's sell for a higher price overseas than in the United States. Internationally, they are regarded as a premium product, in contrast to their commodity position domestically. Therefore, international profit margins are higher (e.g., for 501 jeans, 45 percent vs. 30 percent), and sales are strong.

Another element in the success of Levi's international division is its management practices. The president of Levi Strauss International, Lee C. Smith, says, "We seek out the best ideas [among our worldwide operations] and trade them." This internal benchmarking only is possible because local units are encouraged to innovate. By encouraging foreign managers to adapt to local tastes as they change, Levi's achieves responsiveness, and at the same time, headquarters has globally integrated the form of organization (subsidiaries rather than licensing to assure quality and brand identity) as well as information systems (e.g., the Levi Link system to track sales and manufacturing).

Conclusions

The international division has not always been successful. In 1984, it posted a loss, but by 1990, when Levi's U.S. sales were up only 6 percent over the previous year, foreign sales were booming: up 19 percent in Asia, up 27 percent in Latin America, and up 47 percent in Europe. Nearly 40 percent of the company's total revenues and 60 percent of its pretax profit before interest and corporate expenses came from abroad.

Plans for the future of Levi's international operations are truly global in scope. Corporate president Thomas Tusher recently indicated, "We're starting up in India. We're looking at Russia, South Africa, China, Southeast Asia. And there are places where we've just started: Hungary and Poland, Korea and Taiwan, Turkey. The Czech Republic is next." Therefore, although Levi's withdrew from doing business in 1993 for ethical rea-sons, it now is looking once again at China, among other sites, for global expansion. The questions are whether the company can ethically reopen operations in China or, practically speaking, will China's government allow the company back?

1. Conduct the two preliminary steps for strategic planning for the Levi's corporation, with specific focus on the China question. What are the significant issues in Levi's environment, and what features of its internal resources are significant? What implications does this have for Levi's China strategy?
2. What political risk factors exist for Levi's in China? How might Levi's respond?
3. What alternatives does Levi's have for organizing its international operations? What seems to be the best fit with Levi's strategy?

THE STATUS OF WOMEN MANAGERS IN CENTRAL AND EASTERN EUROPE

In the past decade, all parts of the world have experienced both an increase in the numbers of and a change in the role of women in the workplace. In particular, considerable attention has been given to women managers in the United States, Western Europe, and even Asia. The focus in the former communist countries of Central and Eastern Europe (CEE) has been on their struggle to transform to a market economy; the role of women managers in these countries has been largely overlooked. Even so, the past and present role of women managers in CEE countries in some ways is quite different and in others very similar to their counterparts in other areas of the world.

Background: Before the Fall of the Berlin Wall

In Russia in 1918, Lenin declared that women were equal to men, and this powerful decree gave women a jump start in Russia's traditionally male-dominated society. In the early years following the communist revolution, women throughout the CEE countries became aviators, factory managers, government officials, and diplomats—as well as construction workers and field hands. During World War II, a Russian women's bomber squadron served with distinction, and women throughout CEE fought as partisans behind the German lines.

Up to the fall of communism at the beginning of this decade, women played a dominant role in most professions. For example, a large majority of the CEE nations' doctors and a predominant proportion of secondary-school staffs were women. At the time of the demise of the Soviet Union, they had the largest number of women professionals and specialists in the world, and close to 90 percent of its women were in the work force.

Although the role of women appeared to be impressive in communist CEE, men still largely held the power. Women played little or no role inside the power establishment of the communist regimes. For example, in the U.S.S.R., men occupied every seat on the all-powerful, policy-making Politburo and the Central Committee's Secretariat; this contrasts starkly with the country that produced the first female ambassador and the first woman in space. Women indeed were employed in the public sector and the professions as a visible condition of equality. Also under communism, the official policy was to have the responsibility for housework and child-care shift from the individual household to the collective.

Because of the disruption of World War II and then because of large-scale unemployment or underemployment, rampant inflation, and conservative political policies, few resources were devoted to meaningful social programs to help women. Although opportunities for women in the workplace were present and state enterprises provided day care and schools for children, in most cases women were never really freed from running the household or being responsible for the children.

With the collapse of the communist system, many women in CEE today express a yearning for a traditional female role centered around the family and the home. They are frustrated and exhausted by decades of surface equality and the double burden of work and family responsibilities made more difficult by consumer shortages. (A recent survey from Russia shows that 275 billion hours, equal to 90 percent of the time devoted to paid work in the national economy as a whole, are spent on shopping, child care, and housework each year, most of this by women.) Although there is some sentiment for returning full-time to the home, recent national polls still

Source: This case was written specially for this book by Laura Riolli, University of Nebraska.

show that only a small percentage of Russian women would quit their jobs—even if they could afford to. And, of course, most CEE women, like their U.S. and Western European counterparts, still not only need to work full-time to make ends meet but seek equal opportunity in the workplace. They still seek a work climate that permits them not to be harassed or prevented from realizing their full potential to reach top management.

The Role of Women Managers in CEE

Although reliable figures still are hard to obtain, the general consensus is that the percentages of CEE women employed in the professions (e.g., university teaching, scientific research, medicine, law) and in the management of both public and private enterprises still are relatively high. Despite the so-called equality from the past, however, male managers still far outnumber female managers in most CEE countries. The same discriminatory factors that inhibit women's career progress in the West and Asia also seem to be present in CEE. For instance, there is considerable evidence of women's exclusion from top-level posts. Women managers in CEE appear to confront the same "glass ceiling" that is encountered in other parts of the world. As one Russian woman described, "The higher the post, the fewer the women."

A discussion of the primary factors affecting women's access to managerial jobs and their advancement into top management starts with gender-role stereotypes. These stereotypes are strong in CEE countries, and they hinder women's preparation for managerial roles as well as their opportunities for promotions once in the ranks of management. Cultural stereotypes that are transmitted through socialization influence not only the characteristics that women themselves embody but also the attitudes that others hold about them.

In CEE countries, negative attitudes and stereotypes about female leaders abound. Many men as well as women believe that female bosses are unfair, disorganized, narrow-minded, and unable to work with men. A recent survey in CEE of attitudes toward female managers revealed that "there remains much resistance to women leaders among the less educated." This resistance seems to be particularly true in rural areas, where it still is perceived as culturally inappropriate for women to hold leadership positions in relation to men.

A way in which stereotypes could be interpreted as helping women in the workplace was the perceived physiological differences between women and men that traditionally have been used in CEE countries to justify providing women with certain privileges. For example, women were entitled to rest periods during pregnancy and breast-feeding and were granted liberal maternity leaves. These supposed benefits actually worked as a double-edged sword, however, because employers interpret these privileges as costly and detracting from the productivity of women. Thus, although employers are not supposed to discriminate against women based on the benefits they receive, they often do.

The situation is changing, but CEE women also face the problem of restricted access to recruitment pools, which in the old days often required membership in the Communist Party. Typical job assignments for women also impede their chances of both becoming managers and advancing through the managerial ranks. Traditionally, the number of women was restricted in certain specialties (e.g., petroleum, navigation, geology, metallurgy). Women faced more difficulty than men in obtaining educational qualifications for management positions, and they were—and still are—limited in the types of jobs for which they can obtain training. To overcome the past formal education restrictions, many female managers currently are enrolled in business classes to raise their educational qualifications; however, there is evidence that female managers still may have less access than their male counterparts to such new training.

Workplace Practices that Inhibit Women in Management

Certain discriminatory workplace practices that often are found in CEE countries prevent women from reaching top-level management. One is the common requirement that women retire at an earlier age (55 years) than men (65 years). Although the justification usually given is biological (e.g., menopause), this practice actually serves some societal needs. Women who retire early free places in the highly unemployed or underemployed work force for those who are "waiting to work." Moreover, the retired women become available to do the domestic work and day care for grandchildren in their children's households. In effect, however, this early retirement prevents long-run career advancement, and it justifies not considering women for present or future senior-level positions.

Like their counterparts in the West and Asia, female managers in CEE countries generally are excluded from male networks. Such networks provide men, but not women, with the important and necessary connections and influence they need to get ahead in CEE countries. Not being a part of such networks also makes it difficult for women to start new ventures or effectively run entrepreneurial enterprises, except on a small scale, where they are not dependent on men to make the needed outside arrangements for supply procurement as well as marketing distribution and sales.

The Dual Burden

In CEE countries, almost all women face a dual burden: society as a whole and their own families in particular expect them to have children as well as to participate in work outside the home. Probably even more than in the West, CEE women managers are married and have children. Although this situation is beginning to change, it still is customary in most CEE countries for wives' positions to be lower in prestige than those of their husbands. For example, in a study done in Russia, all female managers were married to men with jobs equal to or higher in status than their own. By contrast, male managers for whom data were available were married to women with lower-status jobs than their own.

Although it is changing, a patriarchal division of labor in which household tasks are relegated to women still exists in CEE countries, with women's domestic roles viewed as being equal to or more important than their careers. Thus, working women have the dual responsibilities of engaging in paid work and maintaining the home. Although governments are encouraging men to be "model husbands," and most husbands do provide their wives with moral support, they rarely do an equal share of the housework.

Surprisingly, at least to date, CEE women do not appear to suffer as much as their counterparts in other countries from the work–family conflict. This may be because they are able to delegate many domestic responsibilities to others. Because of the traditionally close-knit, extended family structure, grandmothers who have retired at relatively early ages often assist with child care and domestic duties. In addition, the government traditionally has provided working women with some support services in child care. Day care is readily available and free or inexpensive. These factors help to ease the domestic burden and stress on CEE working women, thus allowing them more time to concentrate on their careers.

Conclusions

The recent turbulent political and economic changes in CEE countries making the transition to a democratic, free enterprise system probably will help *and* hinder the progress of women managers. Although these dramatic changes are opening up new economic opportunities for women and breaking some of the old stereotypes of the role that women play in society and the workplace, this new situation, at least in the short run, will not eliminate the discrimination that CEE women still encounter in the workplace. In fact, the increased emphasis on marketplace competitiveness and downsizing may result in women losing some of the special privileges they traditionally have had; for example, day-care centers and schools run by the enterprise may be seen as too costly and be eliminated.

As one woman manager recently noted, "Russia's economic changes impose new demands on managers, and women will have to improve themselves in order to be able to cope with these changes." Many women managers in CEE countries are responding to the new challenges by acquiring advanced management education and training. Governments must assure, however, that their access to such training is not limited, and that they receive the support they need to be able to take advantage of the opportunities afforded them. Moreover, as more women become educated and highly trained, it will be harder for both CEE government regulations (e.g., the low retirement age) and society as a whole to sustain negative attitudes about women's competence. Therefore, some of the detrimental gender-role stereotypes that are a carryover from the old days likely will erode. Similar to women in the other parts of the world, however, in the short term, the situation may not be easy for CEE women who are already competent and only need an equal opportunity. In the workplace, they still experience resistance from both men, and women, who believe that male leadership prerogatives should not be questioned. Likewise, within the family, marital conflicts may arise if both the wife and husband are career-minded and the woman strives for a higher-prestige position. Such conflicts are exacerbated when the government assigns spouses to work in different locations, as frequently is the case.

It probably will be many years before CEE women truly have the opportunity to "hold up half the sky" (i.e., achieve true equality in the workplace). In the meantime, CEE women join other women in the world in their "long march" toward full equality with men.

1. What are some similarities between the situation facing women managers in CEE countries and those in the United States (or your country)? What are the differences?
2. What specific recommendations would you make for both government regulations and employers in CEE countries to overcome the barriers currently facing women?
3. What concerns would a U.S. MNC face when assigning a woman manager to a subsidiary in a CEE country?

REFERENCES

CHAPTER 1

Privatization in Great Britain John Moore, "British Privatization—Taking Capitalism to the People," *Harvard Business Review,* January-February 1992, pp. 115–124; Paula Dwyer and Wendy Zellner, "This Splice Could be Golden," *BusinessWeek,* February 8, 1993, pp. 36–37; Robert Neff, "Japan Airlines Cinches Its Seat Belt," *BusinessWeek,* February 1, 1993, p. 42; and "A Great Train Crash," *Economist,* January 5, 1995, p. 20.

International Management in Action: Separating Myths from Reality Stanley J. Modic, "Myths about Japanese Management," *Industry Week,* October 5, 1987, pp. 49–53; Richard M. Hodgetts and Fred Luthans, "Japanese HR Management Practices: Separating Fact From Fiction," *Personnel,* April 1989, pp. 42–45; and Jon Wonoroff, *The Japanese Management Mystique* (Chicago: Probus Publishing, 1992).

In the International Spotlight: India Anthony Spaeth, "India Beckons—and Frustrates," *Wall Street Journal,* September 22, 1989, p. R23; Subrata N. Chakravarty, "Getting the Elephant to Dance," *Forbes,* July 20, 1992, pp. 130–139; Rahual Jacob, "India Is Now Open for Business," *Fortune,* November 16, 1992, pp. 128–130; John F. Burns, "India Now Winning U.S. Investment," *New York Times,* February 6, 1995, pp. C-1, C-5; "The Trouble With Democracy, Part 2," *Economist,* December 17, 1994, pp. 17–18; and Rahual Jacob, "India Gets Moving," *Fortune,* September 5, 1994, pp. 101–102.

CHAPTER 2

America Goes to the Mat Robert Neff, Brian Bremner, and Edith Updike, "The Japanese Have a New Thirst for Imports," *BusinessWeek,* June 5, 1995, pp. 52, 54; Gabriella Stern and Nichole M. Christian, "GM Plans to Sell Saturn Line in Japan in Network of Stand-Alone Dealerships," *Wall Street Journal,* June 2, 1995, p. A4; Keith Bradsher, "U.S. Called Ready to Compromise on Date for Japan Trade Talks," *New York Times,* June 1, 1995, pp. C1, C15; and Bhushan Bahree, "Auto Talks by U.S., Japan Seem Set for Geneva in June," *Wall Street Journal,* June 1, 1995, p. A11.

International Management in Action: A Global Rush Edith Updike et al., "Japan's Auto Shock," *Fortune,* May 29, 1995, pp. 44–47; Patricia Sellers, "Winning Ideas in Marketing," *Fortune,* May 15, 1995, pp. 201–206; and Carla Rapoport and Justin Martin, "Retailers Go Global," *Fortune,* February 20, 1995, pp. 102–108.

In the International Spotlight: Vietnam Mary Ann Von Glinow and Linda Clarke, "Vietnam: Tiger or Kitten?" *Academy of Management Executive,* November 1995, pp. 35–47; Amy Borrus and Michael Collins, "What's Keeping U.S. Companies out of Vietnam? The U.S.," *BusinessWeek,* April 17, 1995, p. 60; Pete Engardio and Bruce Einhorn, "Rising from the Ashes," *BusinessWeek,* May 23, 1994, pp. 44–48; and Joyce Barnathan et al., "Destination, Vietnam," *BusinessWeek,* February 14, 1994, pp. 26–27.

CHAPTER 3

International Management in Action: Where's the Quality Service in Deutschland? Greg Steinmetz, "Customer-Service Era Is Reaching Germany Late, Hurting Business," *Wall Street Journal,* June 1, 1995, pp. A1, A8; G. Pascal Zachary, "Service Productivity Is Rising Fast—and So Is the Fear of Lost Jobs," *Wall Street Journal,* June 8, 1995, pp. A1, A10; and Richard M. Hodgetts, *TQM in Small and Medium-Sized Organizations* (New York: Amacom, 1996), Chapters 2–3.

International Management in Action: Bit Players Bite The Dust Amy Borrus, Edith Hill, and Keith Naughton, "This Trade Gap Ain't What It Used to Be," *BusinessWeek,* March 18, 1996, p. 50; Brian Bemner and Steven Brull, "At Last—Sayonara to the Blahs," *BusinessWeek,* January 22, 1996; and Andrew Pollack, "Japan Inc.'s Dying Bit Players," *New York Times,* May 27, 1995, pp. 17–18.

In the International Spotlight: France Stewart Toy, Linda Bernier, and Bill Javetski, "Now, the Whirlwind," *BusinessWeek,* May 22, 1995, p. 59; Stewart Toy et al., "Can Anyone Fix This Country?" *BusinessWeek,* May 8, 1995, pp. 56–58; and Philip R. Harris and Robert T. Moran, *Managing Cultural Differences,* 3rd ed. (Houston: Gulf Publishing, 1991), pp. 464–471.

CHAPTER 4

Business Customs in Japan William Morrow, "Speaking the Japanese Business Language," *European Business,* Winter 1974, pp. 45–46; Ted Holden and Suzanne Wolley, "The Delicate Art of Doing Business in Japan," *BusinessWeek,* October 2, 1989, p. 120; and Roger E. Axtell, *Do's and Taboos around the World,* 2nd ed. (New York: Wiley, 1990), pp. 33, 90.

International Management in Action: Common Personal Values George W. England, "Managers and Their Value Systems: A Five-Country Comparative Study," *Columbia Journal of World Business,* Summer 1978, pp. 35–44; Geert Hofstede, *Culture's Consequences: International Differences in Work-Related Values* (Beverly Hills, CA: Sage Publishing, 1980); and Geert Hofstede, *Cultures and Organizations: Software of the Mind* (London: McGraw-Hill U.K., Ltd., 1991).

In the International Spotlight: Taiwan Dori Jones Yang, "Taiwan Isn't Just for Cloning Anymore," *BusinessWeek,* September 25, 1989, pp. 208–212; *The World Almanac* (New York: Pharos Books, 1993), p. 803; Michael J. Marquardt and Dean W. Engel, *Global Human Resource Development* (Englewood Cliffs, NJ: Prentice-Hall, 1993), pp. 183–186; and "China (Taiwan)," *Europa World Year Book 1995,* vol. 1 (London: Europa Publications, 1995), pp. 833–842.

CHAPTER 5

International Management in Action: Ten Key Factors for MNC Success James F. Bolt, "Global Competitors: Some Criteria for Success," *Business Horizons,* January-February 1988, pp. 34–41; Tom Peters, *Liberation Management* (New York: Knopf, 1992); and Alan S. Rugman and Richard M. Hodgetts, *International Business* (New York: McGraw-Hill, 1995), Chapter 1.

Managing in Hong Kong J. Stewart Black and Lyman W. Porter, "Managerial Behaviors and Job Performance: A Successful Manager in Los Angeles May Not Succeed in Hong Kong," *Journal of International Business Studies,* First Quarter 1991, pp. 99–112; Geert Hofstede, *Cultures and Organizations: Software of the Mind* (London: McGraw-Hill U.K., Ltd., 1991), Chapters 4–6; and Michael J. Marquardt and Dean W. Engel, *Global Human Resource Development* (Englewood Cliffs, NJ: Prentice-Hall, 1993), pp. 187–188.

In the International Spotlight: Mexico David Wessel, Paul B. Carroll, and Thomas T. Vogel Jr., "How Mexico's Crisis Ambushed Top Minds in Officialdom, Finance," *Wall Street Journal,* July 6, 1995, pp. A1, A4; Craig Torres and Paul B. Carroll, "Mexico's Mantra for Salvation: Export, Export, Export," *Wall Street Journal,* March 17, 1995, p. A6; and "Mexico," *Europa* (London: Europa Publications, 1995), pp. 429–444.

CHAPTER 6

International Management in Action: The Big Gamble Richard M. Hodgetts, *Modern Human Relations at Work,* 6th ed. (Fort Worth, TX: Dryden Press, 1996), pp. 424–445; Edith Updike, "Roadblocks, Roadblocks Everywhere," *BusinessWeek,* June 19, 1995, p. 58; and Fred Luthans, *Organizational Behavior* (New York: McGraw-Hill, 1995), pp. 496–511.

International Management in Action: Matsushita Goes International P. Christopher Earley and Harbir Singh, "International and Intercultural Management Research: What's Next," *Academy of Management Journal,* June 1995, pp. 327–340; Karen Lowry Miller, "Siemens Shapes Up," *BusinessWeek* May 1, 1995, pp. 52–53; Christine M. Riordan and Robert J. Vandenberg, "A Central Question in Cross-Cultural Research: Do Employees of Different Cultures Interpret Work-Related Measures in an Equivalent Manner?" *Journal of Management,* vol. 20, no. 3., 1994, pp. 643–671; and Brenton R. Schlender, "Matsushita Shows How To Go Global," *Fortune,* July 11, 1994, pp. 159–166.

CHAPTER 7

International Management in Action: Sometimes It's All Politics John Stackhouse, "India Sours on Foreign Investment," *Globe and Mail,* August 10, 1995, Sec. 2, pp. 1–2; Peter Galuszka and Susan Chandler, "A Plague of Disjointed Ventures," *BusinessWeek,* May 1, 1995, p. 55; and Marcus W. Brauchli, "Politics Threaten Power Project in India," *Wall Street Journal,* July 3, 1995, p. A14.

Negotiating with the Japanese Rosalie L. Tung, "How to Negotiate with the Japanese," *California Management Review,* Summer 1984, pp. 62–77; Carla Rapoport, "You Can Make Money in Japan," *Fortune,* February 12, 1990, pp. 85–92; Margaret A. Neale and Max. H. Bazerman, "Negotiating Rationally," *Academy of Management Executive,* August 1992, pp. 42–51.

CHAPTER 8

International Management in Action: Point/Counterpoint Wendy Bonds, "Fuji, Accused by Kodak of Hogging Markets, Spits Back: 'You Too,'" *Wall Street Journal,* July 31, 1995, pp. A1, A5; "Photo Wars: Shuttered," *Economist,* August 5, 1995, pp. 59–60; and

Mark Maremont, "Next a Flap Over Film," *Business-Week,* July 10, 1995, p. 34.

Joint Venturing in Russia Keith A. Rosten, "Soviet-U.S. Joint Ventures: Pioneers on a New Frontier," *California Management Review,* Winter 1991, pp. 88–108; Steven Greenhouse, "Chevron to Spend $10 Billion to Seek Oil in Kazakhstan," *New York Times,* May 19, 1992, pp. A1, C9; Louis Uchitelle, "Givebacks by Chevron in Oil Deal," *New York Times,* May 23, 1992, pp. 17, 29; and Craig Mellow, "Russia: Making Cash from Chaos," *Fortune,* April 17, 1995, pp. 145–151.

You Be the International Management Consultant: Go East, Young People, Go East Amy Borrus et al., "The Asians Are Bracing for a Trade Shoot-Out," *BusinessWeek,* May 1, 1989, pp. 40–41; John W. Verity, "If It Looks Like a Slump and Crawls Like a Slump . . . ," *BusinessWeek,* May 1, 1989, p. 27; and Geoff Lewis, "Is the Computer Business Maturing?" *BusinessWeek,* March 6, 1989, pp. 68–78.

CHAPTER 9

Organizing in Germany Hermann Simon, "Lessons from Germany's Midsize Giants," *Harvard Business Review,* March-April 1992, pp. 115–123; Carla Rapoport, "Europe's Slump Won't End Soon," *Fortune,* May 3, 1993, pp. 82–87; and Robert Neff and Douglas Harbrecht, "Germany's Mighty Unions Are Being Forced to Bend," *BusinessWeek,* March 1, 1993, pp. 52–56.

You Be the International Management Consultant: Getting In on the Ground Floor Some of the data in this case were reported in Thane Peterson and Mark Maremont, "Adding Hustle to Europe's Muscle," *BusinessWeek,* 1989 special edition, pp. 32–33.

CHAPTER 10

International Management in Action: Foreign Perceptions Mona Casady, "An International Perspective of the United States," *The Bulletin,* March 1992, pp. 20–25; Bill Powell and Bradley Martin, "What Japan Thinks of Us," *Newsweek,* April 2, 1990, pp. 18–24; and Philip R. Harris and Robert T. Moran, *Managing Cultural Differences: High-Performance Strategies for a New World of Business,* 4th ed. (Houston: Gulf Publishing, 1996).

Communicating in Europe Karen Matthes, "Mind Your Manners When Doing Business in Europe," *Personnel,* January 1992, p. 19; Philip R. Harris and Robert T. Moran, *Managing Cultural Differences: High-Performance Strategies for a New World of Business,*

3rd ed. (Houston: Gulf Publishing, 1991), Chapter 16; and Alan Rugman and Richard M. Hodgetts, *International Business* (New York: McGraw-Hill, 1995), chapter 16.

You Be the International Management Consultant: Foreign or Domestic? The auto sales data can be found in Doron P. Levin, "In Autos, U.S. Makes Strides," *New York Times,* March 24, 1989, pp. 23, 25.

CHAPTER 11

International Management in Action: Kodak Goes Digital Wendy Bonds, "Fuji, Accused by Kodak of Hogging Markets, Spits Back: 'You Too,'" *Wall Street Journal,* July 31, 1995, pp. A1, A5; Peter Nulty, "Digital Imaging Had Better Boom Before Kodak Film Busts," *Fortune,* May 1, 1995, pp. 80–83; and Mark Maremont, "Kodak's New Focus," *BusinessWeek,* January 30, 1995, p. 62.

How the Japanese Do Things Differently Ford S. Worthy, "Japan's Smart Secret Weapon," *Fortune,* August 12, 1991, pp. 72–75; Brenton R. Schlender, "Hard Times for High Tech," *Fortune,* March 22, 1993, p. 98; Ronald Henkoff, "Companies that Train Best," *Fortune,* March 22, 1993; and Jim Carlton, "Sega Leaps Ahead by Shipping New Player Early," *Wall Street Journal,* May 11, 1995, pp. B1, B3.

CHAPTER 12

International Management in Action: Up, Up, and Away Eamonn Fingleton, "Jobs for Life: Why Japan Won't Give Them Up," *Fortune,* March 20, 1995, p. 125; "Nice Work," *Economist,* December 10, 1994, p. 67; and "Mexico Mandates Benefits," *Personnel,* January 1992, p. 18.

***Karoshi,* or Stressed Out in Japan** William S. Brown, Rebecca E. Lubove, and James Kwalwasser, "*Karoshi:* Alternative Perspectives of Japanese Management Styles," *Business Horizons,* March-April 1994, pp. 58–60; Karen Lowry Miller, "Now, Japan Is Admitting It: Work Kills Executives," *BusinessWeek,* August 3, 1992, p. 35; and Philip R. Harris and Robert T. Moran, *Managing Cultural Differences: High-Performance Strategies for a New World of Business,* 3rd ed. (Houston: Gulf Publishing, 1991), pp. 393–408.

CHAPTER 13

International Management in Action: The Jury Is Still Out Jeremy Main, "B-Schools Get a Global Vision," *Fortune,* July 17, 1989, pp. 78–86; Lawrence E.

McKibbin, "Forward," in Sheila M. Puffer (ed.), *The Russian Management Revolution* (Armonk, NY: M.E. Sharpe, 1993), pp. xv–xvi; and Lester Thurow, *Head to Head* (New York: Morrow, 1992).

Global Teams Charlene Marmer Solomon, "Global Teams: The Ultimate Collaboration," *Personnel Journal*, September 1995, pp. 49–58; Andrew Kakabdse and Andrew Myers, "Qualities of Top Management: Comparison of European Manufacturers," *Journal of Management Development*, vol. 14, no. 1, 1995, pp. 5–15; and Noel M. Tichy, Michael I. Brimm, Ram Chran, and Hiroraka Takeuchi, "Leadership Development as a Lever for Global Transformation," in Vladimir Pucik, Noel M. Tichy, and Carole K. Barnett, (eds.), *Globalizing Management: Creating and Leading the Competitive Organization* (New York: John Wiley & Sons, 1993), pp. 47–60.

In the International Spotlight: Germany The statistics on unified Germany come from Bill Javetski and John Templeman, "One Germany," *BusinessWeek*, April 2, 1990, pp. 47–49; "Putting on Weight," *Time*, March 28, 1990, p. 36.

CHAPTER 14

International Management in Action: Important Tips on Working for Foreigners Faye Rice, "Should You Work for a Foreigner?" *Fortune*, August 1, 1988, pp. 123–124; John Holusha, "No Utopia, But to Workers It's a Job," *New York Times*, January 29, 1989, Sec. 3, pp. 1, 10; and Roger E. Axtell (ed.), *Do's and Taboos around the World* (New York: Wiley, 1990).

Recruiting Managers in Japan James C. Morgan and J. Jeffrey Morgan, *Cracking the Japanese Market* (New York: Free Press, 1991); Richard M. Hodgetts and Fred Luthans, "U.S. Multinationals' Expatriate Compensation Strategies," *Compensation & Benefits Review*, January-February 1993, p. 61; Philip R. Harris and Robert T. Moran, *Managing Cultural Differences: High-Performance Strategies for a New World of Business*, 3rd ed. (Houston: Gulf Publishing, 1991), p. 393; and Alan M. Rugman and Richard M. Hodgetts, *International Business* (New York: McGraw–Hill, 1995), pp. 498–499.

You Be the International Management Consultant: A Selection Decision William H. Davidson, "Creating and Managing Joint Ventures in China," *California Management Review*, Summer 1987, pp. 77–94; Denis Fred Simon, "After Tiananmen: What Is the Future for Foreign Business in China?" *California Management Review*, Winter 1990, p. 106; and S. Gordon Redding, *The Spirit of Chinese Capitalism* (New York: Walter de Gruyter, 1990).

CHAPTER 15

International Management in Action: The Cultural Integrator Robert C. Maddox and Douglas Short, "The Cultural Integrator," *Business Horizons*, November-December 1988, pp. 57–59; Peter J. Dowling and Randall S. Schuler, *International Dimensions of Human Resource Management* (Boston: PWS-Kent, 1990); and Michael J. Marquardt and Dean W. Engel, *Global Human Resource Development* (Englewood Cliffs, NJ: Prentice-Hall, 1993).

U.S. Style Training for Expats and Their Teenagers Dawn Anfuso, "HR Unites the World of Coca-Cola," *Personnel Journal*, November 1994, pp. 112–121; Karen Dawn Stuart, "Teens Play a Role in Moves Overseas," *Personnel Journal*, March 1992, pp. 72–78; Richard M. Hodgetts and Fred Luthans, "U.S. Multinationals' Expatriate Compensation Strategies," *Compensation & Benefits Review*, January-February 1993, p. 61; and Philip R. Harris and Robert T. Moran, *Managing Cultural Differences: High-Performance Strategies for a New World of Business*, 3rd ed. (Houston: Gulf Publishing, 1991), Chapter 9.

CHAPTER 16

International Management in Action: They're Leading the Pack Steven R. Weisman, "More Japanese Workers Demanding Shorter Hours and Less Hectic Work," *New York Times*, March 3, 1992, p. A6; "Germany's Mighty Unions Are Being Forced to Bend," *BusinessWeek*, March 1, 1993, p. 52; and Christopher Farrell and Michael J. Mandel, "Riding High," *BusinessWeek*, October 9, 1995, pp. 134–146.

Unions Do Well in Germany Terence Roth, "German Firms Bemoan Production Costs," *Wall Street Journal*, January 29, 1992, p. A8; Ferdinand Protzman, "German Companies Finding Low-Cost Locations in U.S.," *New York Times*, May 26, 1992, p. C3; Alfred L. Malabre, Jr., "Protectionist Calls Belie Competitiveness," *Wall Street Journal*, January 27, 1992, p. A1; Terence Roth, "German Employees Settle Strike after 11 Days as Wage Offer Rises," *Wall Street Journal*, May 8, 1992, p. A6; "A Very German Strike," *Economist*, March 4, 1995, pp. 50–52; John Templeman, "A Serious Blow to German Competitiveness," *BusinessWeek*, March 27, 1995, p. 60; Peter Gumbel, "VW Agrees to 2.5% Yearly Raises, Wins Concession on Work Hours," *Wall Street Journal*, September 13, 1995, p. A9; and Charles Goldsmith, "Daimler-Benz's Dasa to Cut 9,000 Jobs," *Wall Street Journal*, October 24, 1995, p. A17.

You Be the International Management Consultant: Helping Them Make a Comeback Doron P. Levin, "For VW, the Future Is Its Past," *New York Times*, August 8, 1989, pp. 25, 41; John Templeman, "A Hard U-Turn at VW," *Business Week*, March 15, 1993, p. 47; and "Kohl Prods the Giant," *Business Week*, January 25, 1993, p. 52.

CHAPTER 17

International Management in Action: Fighting Back Tim Holden and Jennifer Wiener, "Revenge of the 'Office Ladies,'" *Business Week*, July 13, 1992, pp. 42–43; Steven R. Weisman, "Landmark Harassment Case in Japan," *New York Times*, April 17, 1992, p. A3; and Urban Lehner and Kathryn Graven, "Japanese Women Rise in Their Workplaces, Challenging Traditions," *Wall Street Journal*, September 6, 1989, pp. A1, A10.

Getting Tough . . . Or Else Amy Borrus, Dexter Roberts, and Joyce Barnathan, "Counterfeit Disks, Suspect Enforcement," *Business Week*, September 18, 1995, p. 68; Pete Engardio and Joyce Barnathan, "China: Strife at the Top May Spark a War on Corruption," *Business Week*, March 6, 1995, p. 53; Seth Faison, "Razors, Soap, Cornflakes: Pirating in China Balloons," *New York Times*, February 17, 1995, pp. A1, C2; and "Copy to Come," *Economist*, January 7, 1995, pp. 51–52.

CHAPTER 18

Doing Business in India John F. Burns, "Indian Politics Derail a Big Power Project," *New York Times*, July 5, 1995, pp. C1, C4; Sharon Moshavi, "Get the Foreign Devils," *Business Week*, October 23, 1995, pp. 48, 50; Subrata N. Chakravarty, "Getting the Elephant to Dance," *Forbes*, July 20, 1992, pp. 130–139; Anthony Spaeth, "India Beckons—and Frustrates," *Wall Street Journal*, September 22, 1989, pp. 22–25; Suman Dubey, "India Relaxes Trade Policies for Five Years," *Wall Street Journal*, April 1, 1992, p. A11; and Joyce Barnathan, "Can India Compete on the Fast Track?" *Business Week*, April 12, 1993, pp. 46–47.

International Management in Action: It's the Little Things that Count Jane E. Lasky and Aaron Sugarman, "Getting Through Customs," *Inc.'s Guide to International Business*, 1988, pp. 46–50. The Japanese section is drawn from Ted Holden and Suzanne Woolley, "The Delicate Art of Doing Business in Japan," *Business Week*, October 2, 1989, p. 120; and Roger E. Axtell, *Do's and Taboos around the World* (New York: John Wiley, 1990).

GLOSSARY

Achievement culture   A culture in which people are accorded status based on how well they perform their functions.

Achievement motivation theory   A theory which holds that individuals can have a need to get ahead to attain success and to reach objectives.

Act of state doctrine   A jurisdictional principle of international law which holds that all acts of other governments are considered to be valid by U.S. courts, even if such acts are illegal or inappropriate under U.S. law.

Adaptability screening   The process of evaluating how well a family is likely to stand up to the stress of overseas life.

Adaptive organizations   Organizations that are characterized by reaction to required changes but failure to anticipate them and stay on or ahead of the cutting edge.

Administrative co-ordination   Strategic formulation and implementation in which the MNC makes strategic decisions based on the merits of the individual situation rather than using a predetermined economically or politically driven strategy.

Affective culture   A culture in which emotions are expressed openly and naturally.

Analytical manager   A manager who is systematic and logical and carefully weighs alternatives to problems.

Arbitrator   An individual who provides a solution to a grievance that both sides (union and management representatives) have been unable to resolve themselves and that both sides agree to accept.

Ascription culture   A culture in which status is attributed based on who or what a person is.

Assessment center   An evaluation tool used to identify individuals with potential to be selected or promoted to higher-level positions.

Authoritarian leadership   The use of work-centered behavior designed to ensure task accomplishment.

Balance sheet approach   An approach to developing an expatriate compensation package that is based on ensuring the expat is "made whole" and does not lose money by taking the assignment.

Benchmarking   The process of identifying what leading-edge competitors are doing and then using this information to produce improved products or services.

Bicultural group   A group in which two or more members represent each of two distinct cultures, such as four Mexicans and four Taiwanese who have formed a team to investigate the possibility of investing in a venture.

Cafeteria approach   An approach to developing an expatriate compensation package that entails giving the individual a series of options and letting the person decide how to spend the available funds.

Centralization   A management system under which important decisions are made at the top.

Chaebols   In South Korea, very large, family-held conglomerates, including internationally known firms, in which many key managers have attended school in the West and use this education to help formulate successful international strategies for their firms. *Chaebols* have considerable political and economic power in Korea.

Civil or code law   Law that is derived from Roman law and is found in the non-Islamic and nonsocialist countries.

Codetermination   A legal system that requires workers and their managers to discuss major decisions.

Collective bargaining   The process whereby formal labor agreements are reached by union and management representatives; it involves the negotiation of wages, hours, and conditions of employment and the administration of the labor contract.

Collectivism   A culture in which people tend to belong to groups or collectives and to look after each other in exchange for loyalty.

Common law   Law that derives from English law and is the foundation of legislation in the United States, Canada, and England, among other nations.

Communication   The process of transferring meanings from sender to receiver.

Confrontation meetings   The gathering and analysis of information related to intra- and intergroup conflict followed by the formulation of a plan of action by the participants for the purpose of resolving these problems.

Conglomerate investment   A type of high-risk investment in which goods or services produced are not similar to those produced at home.

Content theories   Theories that explain work motivation in terms of what arouses, energizes, or initiates employee behavior.

Controlling   The process of evaluating results in relation to plans or objectives and deciding what action, if any, to take.

Cross-cultural school of management thought   An approach to international management holding that effective managerial behavior is a function of the specific culture: a successful manager in one location may not be effective in another location around the world.

Cultural assimilator   A programmed learning technique designed to expose members of one culture to some of the basic concepts, attitudes, role perceptions, customs, and values of another culture.

Culture   The acquired knowledge that people use to interpret experience and to generate social behavior. This knowledge forms values, creates attitudes, and influences behavior.

Decentralization   Pushing decision making down the line and getting the lower-level personnel involved.

Decision making   The process of choosing a course of action among alternatives.

Delayed differentiation   A manufacturing strategy in which all products are manufactured in the same way for all countries or regions until as late in the assembly process as possible, with differentiation of features or components introduced in the final stages of production.

Diffuse culture   A culture in which both public and private space are similar in size and individuals guard their public space carefully, because entry into public space also affords entry into private space as well.

Direct controls   The use of face-to-face or personal meetings for the purpose of monitoring operations.

Doctrine of comity   A jurisdictional principle of international law which holds that there must be mutual respect for the laws, institutions, and government of other countries in the matter of jurisdiction over their own citizens.

Downward communication   The transmission of information from superior to subordinate.

Economic imperative   A worldwide strategy based on cost leadership, differentiation, and segmentation.

Eiffel Tower culture   A culture that is characterized by a strong emphasis on hierarchy and orientation to the task.

Empowerment   The process of giving employees the resources, information, and authority they need to effectively carry out their jobs.

Enterprise unions   Unions that represent both the hourly and salaried employees of a particular company.

Environmental scanning   The process of providing management with accurate forecasts of trends related to external changes in geographic areas where the firm currently is doing business and/or is considering setting up operations.

Esteem needs   The needs for power and status.

Ethics   The study of morality and standards of conduct.

Ethnocentric MNC   An MNC that stresses nationalism and often puts home office people in charge of key international management positions.

Ethnocentric predisposition   A nationalistic philosophy of management whereby the values and interests of the parent company guide the strategic decisions.

Ethnocentrism   The belief that one's own way of doing things is superior to that of others.

European Research Cooperation Agency (Eureka)   An agency that funds projects in the fields of energy, medical technology, biotechnology, communications, and the like, with the objective of making Europe more productive and competitive in the world market.

Expatriates   Those who live and work away from their home country. They are citizens of the country where the multinational corporation is headquartered.

Expropriation   The seizure of businesses by a host country with little, if any, compensation to the owners.

Factual manager   A manager who looks at the available information and makes decisions based on that data.

Family culture   A culture that is characterized by a strong emphasis on hierarchy and orientation to the person.

FDI cluster   A group of countries clustered by foreign direct investment, or FDI, that usually are located in the same geographic region and have some form of economic link to a member of the triad (United States, EU, or Japan).

Femininity   A situation in which the dominant values in society are caring for others and quality of life.

Foreign Corrupt Practices Act (FCPA)   Made into U.S. law in 1977 because of concerns over bribes in the international business arena, this act makes it illegal to influence foreign officials through personal payment or political contributions.

Formalization   The use of defined structures and systems in decision making, communicating, and controlling.

Franchise   A business arrangement under which one party (the franchisor) allows another (the franchisee) to operate an enterprise using its trademark, logo, product line, and methods of operation in return for a fee.

Fully owned subsidiary An overseas operation that is totally owned and controlled by an MNC.

Geocentric MNC An MNC that seeks to integrate diverse regions of the world through a global approach to decision making.

Geocentric predisposition A philosophy of management whereby the company tries to integrate a global systems approach to decision making.

Global area division A structure under which global operations are organized on a geographic rather than a product basis.

Global functional division A structure which organizes worldwide operations primarily based on function and secondarily on product.

Global international trade affiliations Trade relationships that cut across regional and industrial groups and are heavily concerned with political activities.

Globalization The production and distribution of products and services of a homogeneous type and quality on a worldwide basis.

Globalization imperative A belief that one worldwide approach to doing business is the key to both efficiency and effectiveness.

Global product division A structural arrangement in which domestic divisions are given worldwide responsibility for product groups.

Global sourcing The use of worldwide suppliers, regardless of where they are located geographically, who are best able to provide the needed output.

Grievance A complaint brought by an employee who feels that he or she has been treated improperly under the terms of the labor agreement.

Groupthink Social conformity and pressures on individual members of a group to conform and reach consensus.

Guided missile culture A culture that is characterized by a strong emphasis on equality in the workplace and orientation to the task.

Home-country nationals Expatriate managers who are citizens of the country where the multinational corporation is headquartered.

Homogeneous group A group that is characterized by members who share similar backgrounds and generally perceive, interpret, and evaluate events in similar ways.

Horizontal investment An MNC investment in foreign operations to produce the same goods or services as those produced at home.

Horizontal specialization The assignment of jobs so that individuals are given a particular function to perform and tend to stay within the confines of this area.

Host-country nationals Local managers who are hired by the MNC.

Hygiene factors In the two-factor motivation theory, job context variables that include salary, interpersonal relations, technical supervision, working conditions, and company policies and administration.

Incubator culture A culture that is characterized by a strong emphasis on equality and orientation to the person.

Indigenization laws Laws that require that nationals hold a majority interest in the operation.

Indirect controls The use of reports and other written forms of communication to control operations.

Industrial democracy The rights that employees have to participate in significant management decisions.

Industrial internationals Affiliates of the global international trade groups that focus on a particular industry.

Integrative techniques Techniques that help the overseas operation become a part of the host country's infrastructure.

International Confederation of Free Trade Unions (ICFTU) The most important global international trade union confederation.

International division structure A structural arrangement that handles all international operations out of a division created for this purpose.

International joint ventures (IJVs) Formal arrangements with foreign partners who typically, although not always, are located in the country where the business will be conducted.

International Labour Office (ILO) A United Nations affiliate, consisting of government, industry, and union representatives, that works to promote fair labor standards regarding health and safety, working conditions, and freedom of association for workers.

International management The process of applying management concepts and techniques in a multinational, multicultural environment.

International selection criteria Factors used to choose personnel for international assignments.

Intimate distance Distance between people that is used for very confidential communications.

Intuitive manager A manager who is imaginative, innovative, and able to jump from one idea to another.

Islamic law Law that is derived from interpretation of the *Qur'an* and the teachings of the Prophet Mohammed and is found in most Islamic countries.

Job content factors In work motivation, those factors internally controlled, such as responsibility, achievement, and the work itself.

Job context factors In work motivation, those factors controlled by the organization, such as conditions, hours, earnings, security, benefits, and promotions.

Job design A job's content, the methods that are used on the job, and the way the job relates to others in the organization.

Joint venture An agreement in which two or more partners own and control an overseas business.

Karoshi Overwork or job burnout, in Japanese.

Keiretsu In Japan, a newly emerging organizational arrangement in which a large, often vertically integrated group of companies co-operate and work closely with each other to provide goods and services to end users; core members may be bound together by cross-ownership, long-term business dealings, interlocking directorates, and social ties.

Key factor for success (KFS) A factor necessary for a firm to effectively compete in a market niche.

Kinesics The study of communication through body movement and facial expression.

Labor relations The process through which management and workers identify and determine the job relations that will be in effect at the workplace.

Leadership The process of influencing people to direct their efforts toward the achievement of some particular goal or goals.

Learning The acquisition of skills, knowledge, and abilities that results in a relatively permanent change in behavior.

Learning organizations Organizations that are able to transform themselves by anticipating change and discovering new ways of creating products and services; they have learned how to learn.

License An agreement that allows one party to use an industrial property right in exchange for payment to the other party.

Localization An approach to developing an expatriate compensation package that involves paying the expat a salary comparable to that of local nationals.

Lockout A company's refusal to allow workers to enter the facility during a labor dispute.

Lump sum method An approach to developing an expatriate compensation package that involves giving the expat a predetermined amount of money and letting the individual make his or her own decisions regarding how to spend it.

Macro political risk analysis Analysis that reviews major political decisions likely to affect all enterprises in the country.

Management by objectives (MBO) A management system for the joint setting of subordinate goals, coaching and counseling personnel, and providing feedback on their performance.

Maquiladora industry An arrangement created by the Mexican government that permits foreign manufacturers to send materials to their Mexican-based plants, process or assemble products, and ship them back out of Mexico with only the value added being taxed.

Masculinity A culture in which the dominant values are success, money, and things.

Mass customization Tailor-making mass-production products to meet the expectations of the customer.

Mediator A person who brings both sides (union and management representatives) together and helps them to reach a settlement that is mutually acceptable.

Micro political risk analysis Analysis directed toward government policies and actions that influence selected sectors of the economy or specific foreign businesses in the country.

Ministry of International Trade and Industry (MITI) A governmental agency in Japan that identifies and ranks national commercial pursuits and guides the distribution of national resources to meet these goals.

Mixed organization structure A structure that is a combination of a global product, area, or functional arrangement.

Motivation A psychologic process through which unsatisfied wants or needs lead to drives that are aimed at goals or incentives.

Motivators In the two-factor motivation theory, the job content factors which include achievement, recognition, responsibility, advancement, and the work itself.

Multicultural group A group in which there are individuals from three or more different ethnic backgrounds, such as three U.S., three German, three Uruguayan, and three Chinese managers who are looking into mining operations in South Africa.

Multidomestic A firm that operates production plants in different countries but makes no attempt to integrate overall operations.

National responsiveness The need to understand the different consumer tastes in segmented regional markets and respond to different national standards and regulations imposed by autonomous governments and agencies.

Nationality principle A jurisdictional principle of international law which holds that every country has jurisdiction over its citizens no matter where they are located.

Negotiation The process of bargaining with one or more parties for the purpose of arriving at a solution that is acceptable to all.

Neutral culture A culture in which emotions are held in check.

Nonreciprocal trade partners   Nations that sell (export) goods to other countries but do not buy (import) from them.

Nonverbal communication   The transfer of meaning through means such as body language and the use of physical space.

Normative manager   A manager who is idealistic and concerned with how things should be done.

North American Free Trade Agreement (NAFTA)   A free trade agreement, including the United States, Canada, and Mexico, that will effectively eliminate trade barriers between the three countries.

OD intervention   The structured activity in which targeted individuals, groups, or units engage in accomplishing task goals that are related to organization development.

Operational risks   Government policies and procedures that directly constrain management and performance of local operations.

Organization development (OD)   The deliberate and reasoned introduction, establishment, reinforcement, and spread of change for the purpose of improving an organization's effectiveness.

Organization for Economic Cooperation and Development (OECD)   A government, industry, and union group founded in 1976 that has established a voluntary set of guidelines for MNCs.

Organizational culture   A pattern of basic assumptions that are developed by a group as it learns to cope with problems of external adaptation and internal integration and that are taught to new members as the correct way to perceive, think, and feel in relation to these problems.

Ownership-control risks   Government policies or actions that inhibit ownership or control of local operations.

Paradox   A statement that appears to be contradictory but is not, such as "increases in product quality often result in a decline of the cost of producing the goods."

Parochialism   The tendency to view the world through one's own eyes and perspectives.

Participative leadership   The use of both a work- or task-centered and people-centered approach to leading subordinates.

Particularism   The belief that circumstances dictate how ideas and practices should be applied and something cannot be done the same everywhere.

Paternalistic leadership   The use of work-centered behavior coupled with a protective employee-centered concern.

Personal distance   In communicating, the physical distance used for talking with family and close friends.

Personal efficacy   A psychologic characteristic of confidence and the belief that one both can and should learn to influence significantly the world in which one lives.

Physiologic needs   Food, clothing, shelter, and other basic, physical needs.

Political imperative   Strategic formulation and implementation utilizing strategies that are country responsive and designed to protect local market niches.

Political risk   The likelihood that a business's foreign investment will be constrained by a host government's policies.

Polycentric MNC   An MNC that places local nationals in key positions and allows these managers to appoint and develop their own people.

Polycentric predisposition   A philosophy of management whereby strategic decisions are tailored to suit the cultures of the countries where the MNC operates.

Power distance   The extent to which less powerful members of institutions and organizations accept that power is distributed unequally.

Practical school of management thought   A traditional approach to international management, which holds that effective managerial behavior is universal: a successful manager in one location will be effective in any other location around the world.

Principle of sovereignty   An international principle of law which holds that governments have the right to rule themselves as they see fit.

Problem-solving teams   Employee groups that discuss ways of improving quality, efficiency, and the overall work environment.

Process theories   Theories that explain work motivation by how employee behavior is initiated, redirected, and halted.

Product proliferation   The creation of a wide array of products that the competition cannot copy quickly enough.

Profit   The amount remaining after all expenses are deducted from total revenues.

Protective and defensive techniques   Techniques that discourage the host government from interfering in operations.

Protective principle   A jurisdictional principle of international law which holds that every country has jurisdiction over behavior that adversely affects its national security, even if the conduct occurred outside that country.

Proxemics   The study of the way people use physical space to convey messages.

Public distance   In communicating, the distance used when calling across the room or giving a talk to a group.

Quality control circle (QCC) A group of workers who meet on a regular basis to discuss ways of improving the quality of work.

Quality imperative Strategic formulation and implementation utilizing strategies of total quality management to meet or exceed customers' expectations and continuously improve products and/or services.

Regiocentric MNC An MNC that relies on local managers from a particular geographic region to handle operations in and around that area.

Regiocentric predisposition A philosophy of management whereby the firm tries to blend its own interests with those of its subsidiaries on a regional basis.

Regional internationals Subdivisions of the global affiliation; regional applications of the global's activities.

Regional system An approach to developing an expatriate compensation package that involves setting a compensation system for all expats who are assigned to a particular region and paying everyone in accord with that system.

Repatriation The return to one's home country from an overseas management assignment.

Repatriation agreements Agreements whereby the firm tells the individual how long she or he will be posted overseas and promises to give the individual, on return, a job that is mutually acceptable.

Return on investment Return measured by dividing profit by assets.

Ringisei From Japan, decision making by consensus.

Safety needs In Maslow's hierarchy of needs, the desire for security, stability, and the absence of pain.

Self-actualization needs In Maslow's hierarchy of needs, the desire to reach one's full potential by becoming everything one is capable of becoming.

Self-managing teams Employee groups that take over supervisory duties and manage themselves; teams consist of individuals who learn all the tasks of all the group members, allowing team members to rotate jobs.

Simplification The process of exhibiting the same orientation toward different culture groups.

Smallest space analysis (SSA) A nonparametric multivariate analysis. This mathematic tool maps the relationship among the countries by showing the distance between each. By looking at this two-dimensional map, it is possible to see those countries that are similar to each other and those that are not.

Social distance In communicating, the distance used to handle most business transactions.

Social needs The need to interact and affiliate with others and the need to feel wanted by others.

Socialist law Law that comes from the Marxist socialist system and continues to influence regulations in countries formerly associated with the Soviet Union as well as China.

Sociotechnical designs Job designs that blend the personnel and the technology.

Specialization An organizational characteristic that assigns individuals to specific, well-defined tasks.

Specialized internationals Trade union associations that function as components of intergovernmental agencies and lobby within these agencies.

Specific culture A culture in which individuals have a large public space they readily share with others and a small private space they guard and share only with close friends and associates.

Strategic fit An approach to strategically managing an organization that involves aligning resources in such a way as to mesh with the environment.

Strategic planning The process of determining an organization's basic mission and long-term objectives, then implementing a plan of action for attaining these goals.

Strategic stretch The creative use of resources to achieve ever more challenging goals.

Strategy implementation The process of providing goods and services in accord with a plan of action.

Strike A collective refusal to work to pressure management to grant union demands.

Subsidiary board of directors A board that oversees and monitors the operations of a foreign subsidiary.

Survey feedback An OD intervention that involves the gathering and analysis of information related to group behavior and problems and the feeding back of this information to develop effective action plans.

Team building An extension of classic T-groups (training groups) and sensitivity training that is geared to enhancing organizational effectiveness through cooperation and a "team" effort of key personnel.

Technology paradox (Also see **Paradox**) That high-tech businesses can thrive at the very moment that their prices are falling the fastest.

Territoriality principle A jurisdictional principle of international law which holds that every nation has the right of jurisdiction within its legal territory.

Theory X manager A manager who believes that people are basically lazy and that coercion and threats of punishment often are necessary to get them to work.

Theory Y manager A manager who believes that under the right conditions people not only will work hard but will seek increased responsibility and challenge.

Third-country nationals Managers who are citizens of countries other than the one in which the MNC is headquartered or the one in which the managers are assigned to work by the MNC.

Third-party peacemaking The diagnosis of group conflict followed by the use of an outside party (usually the OD change agent) to facilitate a constructive resolution of a problem.

Token group A group in which all members but one have the same background, such as a group of Japanese retailers and a British attorney.

Total quality management (TQM) An organizational strategy and the accompanying techniques that result in the delivery of high-quality products and/or services to customers.

Training The process of altering employee behavior and attitudes in a way that increases the probability of goal attainment.

Transfer risks Government policies that limit the transfer of capital, payments, production, people, and technology in and out of the country.

Transition strategies Strategies used to help smooth the adjustment from an overseas to a stateside assignment.

Transnational corporations (TNCs) Multinational corporations that view the world as one giant market.

Two-factor theory of motivation A theory that holds there are two sets of factors that influence job satisfaction: hygiene factors and motivators.

Uncertainty avoidance The extent to which people feel threatened by ambiguous situations and have created beliefs and institutions that try to avoid these.

Union An organization that represents the workers and in collective bargaining has the legal authority to negotiate with the employer and administer the labor contract.

Universalism The belief that ideas and practices can be applied everywhere in the world without modification.

Upward communication The transfer of meaning from subordinate to superior.

Validity The quality of being effective, of producing the desired results. A valid test or selection technique measures what it is intended to measure.

Values Basic convictions that people have regarding what is right and wrong, good and bad, and important or unimportant.

Variety amplification The creation of uncertainty and the analysis of many alternatives regarding future action.

Variety reduction The limiting of uncertainty and the focusing of action on a limited number of alternatives.

Vertical investment The production of raw materials or intermediate goods that are to be processed into final products.

Vertical specialization The assignment of work to groups or departments where individuals are collectively responsible for performance.

Virtual corporation A network of companies that come together to exploit fast-changing opportunities and share costs, skills, and access to global markets.

Virtual organization An organization that is able to conduct business as if it were a very large enterprise when, in fact, it is much smaller, made up of core business competencies and the rest outsourced.

Work centrality The importance of work in an individual's life relative to other areas of interest.

World-class organizations (WCOs) Enterprises that are able to compete with anybody, anywhere, anytime, anyway.

World Trade Organization (WTO) Started in 1995 to replace GATT, the WTO has power to enforce rulings in trade disputes and monitor trade policies.

NAME AND COMPANY INDEX

INDEX OF GEOGRAPHIC LOCATIONS

SUBJECT INDEX